Brief/Update

The Psychology of Being Human

The Psychology of Being Human

Third Edition

Zick Rubin

BRANDEIS UNIVERSITY

Elton B. McNeil

LATE, UNIVERSITY OF MICHIGAN

1817

HARPER & ROW, PUBLISHERS, New York
Cambridge, Philadelphia, San Francisco,
London, Mexico City, São Paulo, Sydney

Sponsoring Editor: Kathy Robinson
Developmental Editor: Jackie Estrada
Project Editor: Karla Billups Philip
Cover and Text Designer: Gayle Jaeger
Production Manager: Jeanie Berke
Picture Editors: Betsy Wyckoff; Mira Schachne
Compositor: York Graphic Services, Inc.
Printer and Binder: The Murray Printing Company
Art Studio: J&R Technical Services, Inc.

THE PSYCHOLOGY OF BEING HUMAN, Third Edition: BRIEF/UPDATE
Copyright © 1983 by Zick Rubin

Library of Congress Cataloging in Publication Data

Rubin, Zick.
  The psychology of being human.

  Bibliography: p.
  Includes index.
  1. Psychology.   I. McNeil, Elton Burbank, 1924–1974.
II. Title.   [DNLM: 1. Psychology.   BF 121 R895p]
BF121.R75   1983   150   82-21254
ISBN 0-06-045649-3

Text and Illustration Credits

bottom, by Costa Manos, Magnum Photos. Photos, p. 280, courtesy of Dr. Albert Bandura, Stanford University. Photo, p. 282, courtesy of UPI. Photo, p. 283, courtesy of Dr. Philip Zimbardo, Stanford University.

Chapter 9 Photo, p. 285, by Erich Hartmann, Magnum Photos. Figure 9.1, p. 287, by Ken Heyman. Photo, p. 288, by Nina Leen, *Life Magazine* © 1965 Time Inc. Figure 9.2, p. 290, based on M. M. Shirley, *The First Two Years: A Study of Twenty-five Babies* (Minneapolis: University of Minnesota Press, 1931). Photo, p. 291, by Eric Schwab, World Health Organization. Photo, p. 292, by Erika Stone, Photo Researchers. Figure 9.3, p. 294, courtesy of Wisconsin Primate Laboratory, Madison. Photo, p. 295, by Ellan Young, Photo Researchers. Photo, p. 296, by Erika Stone, Photo Researchers. Photo, p. 299, by Myron Wood, Photo Researchers. Photo, p. 301, by Suzanne Szasz, Photo Researchers. Photo, p. 303, by Alice Kandell, Photo Researchers. Figure 9.5, p. 305, from J. M. Tanner, "Growth and Endocrinology of the Adolescent," in L. J. Gardner (ed.), *Endocrine and Genetic Diseases of Childhood*, 2d ed. (Philadelphia: Saunders, 1975), p. 28. Reprinted by permission. Photo, p. 306, by Eve Arnold, Magnum Photos. Photo, p. 308, courtesy of UPI. Photo, p. 309, by Ralph Norman, Brandeis University. Photo, p. 313, by Maureen Fennell, Photo Researchers. Figure 9.6, p. 313, after L. Belmont and F. A. Marolla, "Birth Order, Family Size, and Intelligence," *Science*, 1973, *182*, p. 1097. Copyright 1973 by the American Association for the Advancement of Science. Reprinted by permission. Figure 9.7, p. 314, based on Carol Tavris, "The Baby Boom: The End of the IQ Slump," *Psychology Today*, April 1976, p. 70. Photo, p. 316, by Alice Kandell, Photo Researchers.

Chapter 10 Photo, p. 319, by Costa Manos, Magnum. Photos, p. 320, courtesy of UPI. Photos, p. 322: left, by Bernard Wolff, Magnum Photos; right, by Bill Owens, Archive Pictures Inc. Quoted material in Box 1, pp. 322–323, from *The Social Psychology of Aging*, by V. L. Bengston. Copyright © 1973 by The Bobbs-Merrill Co., Inc. Reprinted with permission. Photo, p. 323, by Bill Owens, Archive Pictures Inc. Figure 10.1, p. 324, from *The Seasons of a Man's Life*, by Daniel J. Levinson et al. (p. 57). Copyright © 1978 by Daniel J. Levinson. Reprinted by permission of Alfred A. Knopf, Inc. Photos, p. 326: left, by Bruce Roberts, Photo Researchers; right, by Abigail Heyman, Archive Pictures Inc. Photo, p. 327, by Townsend P. Dickinson, Photo Researchers. Photo, p. 329, by Abigail Heyman, Archive Pictures Inc. Photos, p. 331, courtesy of UPI. Figure 10.2, p. 333, courtesy of N. W. Shock, Ph.D., Baltimore City Hospitals. Quoted material in Box 3, p. 334, from *The Seasons of a Man's Life*, by Daniel J. Levinson et al. Copyright © 1978 by Daniel J. Levinson. Reprinted by permission of Alfred A. Knopf, Inc. Photo, p. 335, by Burk Uzzle, Magnum Photos. Photo, p. 337, by Hella Hammid, Photo Researchers. Photo, p. 338, by Gene Daniels, Black Star. Figure 10.3, p. 340, from J. L. Horn, "The Rise and Fall of Human Abilities," *Journal of Research and*

Development in Education, Winter 1979, *12*, p. 76. Reprinted by permission. Photo, p. 341, courtesy of Donald Hebb. Photo, p. 342, by David Hurn, Magnum Photos. Photo, p. 344, by Ruth Silverman, BBM Associates. Photo, p. 345, by Abigail Heyman, Archive Pictures Inc. Photo, p. 350, by David Seymour, Magnum Photos. Photo, p. 352, by Chester Higgins, Photo Researchers.

Update 3 Photos, p. 354: top, courtesy of the author; bottom, by UPI. Photo, p. 355, by Wide World. Photo, p. 356, reprinted by permission of the Trustees of Amherst College. Photo, p. 357, by Granger.

Part Four Photo, p. 359, by Burk Uzzle, Magnum Photos.

Chapter 11 Photo, p. 361, by Leonard Freed, Magnum Photos. Photos, p. 364, courtesy of UPI. Photos, p. 366: left, by Burk Uzzle, Magnum Photos; right, by Abigail Heyman, Archive Pictures Inc. Photo, p. 369, by Paul Fusco, Magnum Photos. Photo, p. 372, by George Roger, Magnum Photos. Photo, p. 373, by Charles Harbutt, Archive Pictures Inc. Photo, p. 374, courtesy of UPI. Photo, p. 378, by Ken Heyman. Photo, p. 383, by Hide Shibata. Photo, p. 388, courtesy of UPI. Letter, p. 389, from E. S. Shneidman, "Content Analysis of Suicidal Logic," in E. S. Shneidman, N. L. Farberow, and R. E. Litman (eds.), *The Psychology of Suicide* (New York: Science House, 1970), p. 77. Reprinted by permission. Photo, p. 390, from *The New York Times*.

Chapter 12 Photo, p. 393, by Alex Webb, Magnum Photos. Quoted material in text, pp. 395 and 397, from G. C. Davison and J. M. Neale, *Abnormal Psychology: An Experimental and Clinical Approach*, 2d ed. (New York: Wiley, 1978), pp. 472, 479. Reprinted by permission. Photo, p. 396, by Jan Lukas, Photo Researchers. Photo, p. 398, by Deke Simon. Photo, p. 401, by Don Hogan Charles, *The New York Times*. Photo, p. 402, by Costa Manos, Magnum Photos. Photo, p. 403, by Alex Webb, Magnum Photos. Photo, p. 404, courtesy of Wide World Photos. Photo, p. 406, by Sepp Seitz, Magnum Photos. Quoted material in text, p. 407, from M. Clark, "Drugs and Psychiatry: A New Era," *Newsweek*, November 12, 1979, p. 99. Copyright 1979 by Newsweek, Inc. All rights reserved. Reprinted by permission. Figure 12.2, p. 408, from Ib Ohlsson, "The Brain's Drug-Receptor Sites," *Newsweek*, November 12, 1979, p. 99. Copyright 1979 by Newsweek, Inc. All rights reserved. Reprinted by permission. Quoted material in text, p. 408, from Maggie Scarf, "Shocking the Depressed Back to Life," *New York Times Magazine*, June 17, 1979. Photo, p. 410, by Paul Fusco, Magnum Photos. Photos, p. 418: top, by Hella Hammid, Photo Researchers; bottom, by Alex Webb, Magnum Photos. Photo, p. 419, courtesy of UPI.

Update 4 Photos, p. 422: top, courtesy of the author; bottom, by Burt Glinn, Magnum Photos. Photo, p. 423, by Skoogfors, 1978, Woodfin Camp. Photo, p. 424, courtesy of Wide World Photos. Photos, p. 425: left, by Leonard Woolf, Magnum Photos; right, by Skoogfors, 1978, Woodfin Camp.

Part Five Photo, p. 427, by John Veltri,

Photo Researchers.

Chapter 13 Photo, p. 429, by Roger Malloch, Magnum Photos. Photo, p. 430, by Bob Adelman, Magnum Photos. Photo, p. 434, by Wayne Miller, Magnum Photos. Figure 13.1, p. 436, from *Man and Woman, Boy and Girl*, by John Money and Anke A. Ehrhardt. Copyright © 1972 by the Johns Hopkins University Press. Reprinted by permission. Photo, p. 438, by Joanne Leonard, Woodfin Camp. Photo, p. 440, by Leonard Freed, Magnum Photos. Photos, p. 442, courtesy of UPI. Figure 13.2, p. 444, from *Human Sexual Response* by W. H. Masters and V. E. Johnson (Boston: Little, Brown, 1966), p. 5. Reprinted by permission. Photos, p. 446: left, courtesy of Culver Pictures; right, by Jeff Albertson, Stock, Boston. Photo, p. 447, courtesy of UPI. Photo, p. 449, by Susan Meiselas, Magnum Photos. Photo, p. 451, by Leonard Freed, Magnum Photos. Photo, p. 456, by Abigail Heyman, Archive Pictures Inc. Photo, p. 458, by Alex Webb, Magnum Photos.

Chapter 14 Photo, p. 461, by Richard Kalvar, Magnum Photos. Photo, p. 462, © Mitchell Payne/Jeroboam, Inc. Photos, p. 463: left, by Charles Harbutt, Archive Pictures Inc.; right, by Charles Gatewood, Magnum Photos. Photo, p. 464, © Roger Lubin/Jeroboam, Inc. Photo, p. 465, by Erich Hartmann, Magnum Photos. Photo, p. 467, by William Vandivert and *Scientific American*, November 1955. Figure 14.2, p. 470, courtesy of Dane Archer. Photo, p. 471, by Richard Kalvar, Magnum Photos. Photo, p. 472, by Charles Harbutt, Archive Pictures Inc. Quoted material in text, p. 473, from *Liking and Loving: An Invitation to Social Psychology* by Zick Rubin. Copyright © 1973 by Holt, Rinehart and Winston, Inc. Reprinted by permission of Holt, Rinehart and Winston, CBS Educational and Professional Publishing. Photo, p. 474, courtesy of UPI. Figure 14.3, p. 476, from *Liking and Loving: An Invitation to Social Psychology* by Zick Rubin. Copyright © 1973 by Holt, Rinehart and Winston, Inc. Reprinted by permission of Holt, Rinehart and Winston, CBS Educational and Professional Publishing. Photo, p. 477, © Werner Hiebel, Alpha Press/Jeroboam, Inc. Photo, p. 479, by Abigail Heyman, Magnum Photos. Quoted material in Box 4, p. 489, from L. A. Peplau, Z. Rubin, and C. T. Hill, "Sexual Intimacy in Dating Relationships," *Journal of Social Issues*, 1977, *33*, 97–99. Reprinted by permission. Figure 14.4, p. 482, from "Breakups before Marriage," from *Divorce and Separation*, edited by G. Levinger and O. Moles. Copyright © 1979 by The Society for the Psychological Study of Social Issues. Reprinted by permission of Basic Books, Inc., Publishers, New York. Photo, p. 485, by Leonard Freed, Magnum Photos. Photo, p. 487, by Burk Uzzle, Magnum Photos. Letter, p. 488, to *Boston Globe*, July 9, 1980. Photo, p. 489, by Marc and Evelyne Bernheim, Woodfin Camp.

Update 5 Photo, p. 490, courtesy of the author. Photo, p. 491, by Forsyth from Monkmeyer. Photos, p. 492: top, by Heron, 1981, Woodfin Camp; bottom, by Wolinsky, Stock, Boston. Photos, p. 493, by Daily Telegraph, 1978, Woodfin Camp.

About the Authors

ZICK RUBIN, who prepared the second and third editions of *The Psychology of Being Human,* received his B.A. from Yale University, where he was a psychology major and the managing editor of the *Yale Daily News,* and received his Ph.D. from the University of Michigan. He served on the faculty of Harvard University before assuming his present position as Louis and Frances Salvage Professor of Social Psychology at Brandeis University. Dr. Rubin is widely known both as a researcher and as a popular writer in psychology. His research has centered on social interaction and relationships among both children and adults. He has received the Socio-Psychological Prize of the American Association for the Advancement of Science for his research on romantic love, and the National Media Award of the American Psychological Foundation for his book *Children's Friendships.* He is the author of *Liking and Loving: An Invitation to Social Psychology* and a contributing editor of *Psychology Today* magazine.

ELTON B. MCNEIL, who wrote the first edition of *The Psychology of Being Human,* received his B.A. in psychology from Harvard University and his Ph.D. in clinical psychology from the University of Michigan. He remained at the University of Michigan for 22 years, teaching undergraduate and graduate courses in introductory psychology, clinical psychology, and psychotherapy. Before his death in 1974, Dr. McNeil wrote and edited many books, including *The Quiet Furies, The Nature of Human Conflict,* and *Human Socialization.* He was also director of the clinical training center for emotionally disturbed and delinquent boys at the University of Michigan Fresh Air Camp, and he served in the Peace Corps as a field selection officer.

Contents in Brief

Contents

— *Chapter 2* —

The Brain and Nervous System

38

— *Chapter 3* —

Consciousness

70

Chapter 8
Personality
248

Chapter 9
From Infancy
To Adolescence
284

Chapter 12

Therapy

392

Update

—————— PART FIVE ——————

Relating To One Another 426

Chapter 13

Female and Male

428

Chapter 14
Social Relationships
460

Update

THE SOCIAL PSYCHOLOGY OF APPEARANCE
by S. Michael Kalick 490

Preface

FROM THE PREFACE TO THE THIRD EDITION

Continuity and *change:* These themes are central to human development through the span of life. As we grow older, we retain many of the skills, traits, and values that we had when we were younger. In this sense, our lives are marked by continuity. But as we grow older we also face new challenges, have new experiences, and acquire new skills, traits, and values. Superimposed upon the continuity is change.

These themes of development through life are also relevant to the development of a textbook. At least they are for this textbook. Those readers who are familiar with the first and second editions of *The Psychology of Being Human* will see in this third edition both continuity and change.

First, the continuities: In writing the first edition of *The Psychology of Being Human*, Elton McNeil wanted to share with his readers his own fascination with the science of psychology. He wrote as a person with a full range of feelings about psychology—respect for its historical foundations, excitement about its research frontiers, bemused skepticism about its fads and foibles, apprehension about its possible misuses, and faith in its ability to better people's lives—and he let these feelings be known. Elton McNeil wrote about psychology in a personal way rather than hiding behind a cloak of anonymity. And although Dr. McNeil took his psychology seriously, he also found the whole enterprise to be fun—and he let you know it. His death in 1974, a week before the publication of the first edition, was a great loss to the field of psychology.

I am, of course, a different person from Elton McNeil, and my own special loves and pet peeves about psychology differ somewhat from his. But I wholeheartedly share Dr. McNeil's basic approach toward psychology—his fascination for the field, his desire to communicate his enthusiasm to others, and his feeling that a comprehensive introductory psychology textbook can be written in a way that is personal, relevant to students' own concerns, and fun to read. In revising *The Psychology of Being Human*, I've tried to follow Dr. McNeil's example and, by doing so, to help make the study of psychology come alive for you.

There are other, more specific continuities in the development of this textbook. Several features of the text that Elton McNeil introduced in the first edition are still present in this third edition.

Each chapter of the text contains three or four boxes. Each box is a brief, self-contained treatment of some extension, application, or sidelight of topics covered in the text. Some of the boxes deal with current research advances, such as "Frontiers of Pain Control" (in Chapter 4) and "Training Your Heart" (in Chapter 5). Others discuss topics of personal and social concern, such as "Menstruation and Moods" (in Chapter 7) and "Children of Divorce" (in Chapter 9).

Scattered throughout the margins of the text are paragraphs that Elton McNeil called "teasers." "For the most part," Dr. McNeil wrote in his preface to the first edition, "these are composed of information that professors (myself included) often use to 'spice up' their lectures, and I wanted to share in a textbook some of the material that my students have found fascinating over the years." Although a large proportion of the teasers you will encounter are new, I hope that they are as interesting as ever. Read and enjoy them when you're in the mood. Ignore them when you're not.

Each chapter is followed by a special section called a *Psychological Issue*. Most of these sections concern applications of psychology to personal and social issues. For example, there are Psychological Issues on "Behavior Control" (after Chapter 5), "Violence" (after Chapter 8), and "Suicide" (after Chapter 11). The Psychological Issues emphasize that psychology is not an academic discipline that remains distant from the events of today's world. On the contrary, psychology is directly relevant to our lives and to the society in which we live.

Now for the changes: Psychology is a rapidly advancing science, so there are many new developments to be reported. For example, Chapter 2, on "The Brain and Nervous System," describes new techniques being used to study the brain's function and new discoveries concerning the brain's chemistry. Chapter 3, on "Consciousness," has been almost entirely rewritten to reflect recent research, and Chapters 5 and 6 have been extensively revised to incorporate recent developments in cognitive psychology. Chapters 11 and 12, on psychological disorders, have been reworked to accord with *DSM-III*, the newly adopted system for the diagnosis of mental disorders. Chapter 13, "Female and Male," includes a new section on current perspectives on human sexuality. More generally, every chapter of the book has been carefully revised and updated. Close to 50 percent of the bibliographical references are new to the third edition.

Not only does the science of psychology change, but so do the problems and challenges facing society. These changes led, in turn, to many changes in this book. New boxes on such topics as "Learning to Save Energy," "Is Day Care Dangerous?" and "Homosexuality and Homophobia" all relate to current social concerns and events. In all, over 40 percent of the boxes are brand new and many of the others have been updated. New or extensively revised Psychological Issues on such topics as "The Therapy Marketplace," "Changing Sex Roles," and "Prejudice and Racism" all reflect the status of these social phenomena in the 1980s.

This edition also includes a completely new chapter on "Adulthood and Aging" (Chapter 10), reflecting the greatly increased attention that psychologists have given to this field in recent years. Until recently it was generally believed that a person's character was well established by the time he or she reached adulthood—"set like plaster," as one of psychology's pioneers, William James, put it. It is now recognized, however, that people continue to develop through the years of early, middle, and late adulthood. Just as with this textbook, there is both continuity and change throughout life.

In addition to the changes I have already mentioned, revisions have been made throughout the text to increase its comprehensiveness and clarity. The photographs and drawings have been redone for the third edition, and they are accompanied by captions that make explicit how each photograph or drawing illustrates material discussed in the text.

"The more things change," according to an often quoted statement, "the more they stay the same." In a way, this aphorism embodies my goal in preparing the third edition of *The Psychology of Being Human*. I made many changes in this edition, but the changes were made so that the book could stay the same—so that it could live up to the tradition of scientific currency and of personal and social relevance that was set for me by Elton McNeil.

THE BRIEF/UPDATE EDITION

This Brief/Update Edition is a shorter version of the third edition of *The Psychology of Being Human*. This edition has been reorganized into five parts with 14 chapters, making it especially appropriate for courses in which the full third edition is too lengthy. There are also five essays, called "Updates," written especially for the Brief/Update edition. Each Update, one for each of the five parts of the text, was written at my invitation by a leading researcher in a different area of psychology. The purpose of the Updates is to report in a highly readable way on some of the most exciting psychological research that is going on *right now* in areas ranging from the influence of our emotions and attitudes on our health to the psychological aftermath of the Vietnam war 10 years after the last American soldiers returned home. The five Updates and their authors are:

Dr. Joan Borysenko, Harvard Medical School: *Psychoimmunology: Mind, Body, and Health*

Dr. Stephen M. Kosslyn, Brandeis University: *Mental Images*

Dr. William McKinley Runyan, University of California, Berkeley: *Psychobiography*

Dr. Arthur Egendorf, Center for Policy Studies, City University of New York: *Veterans and the Legacy of Vietnam*

Dr. S. Michael Kalick, University of Massachusetts, Boston: *The Social Psychology of Appearance*

ACKNOWLEDGMENTS

In preparing the third edition of *The Psychology of Being Human*, I profited greatly from the reactions and suggestions of many students and professors who read the second edition. In particular, the following professors provided valuable critiques of the second edition or of plans for the revision: Louis Fusilli, Monroe Community College; Michael Hughmanick, West Valley College; Melvin Kimmel, St. Ambrose College; Richard McGlynn, Texas Tech University; Terry Maul, San Bernardino Valley College; Barbara Robinson, Portland Community College; Robert Smith, Orange Coast College; Harold Unterman, Montgomery College; and Georgia Witkin-Lanoil, Westchester College. Professors McGlynn, Maul, Robinson, Unterman, and Witkin-Lanoil also provided valuable reviews of the first drafts of many or all of the revised chapters. I am also grateful to Terry Maul for preparing the *Instructor's Manual* that accompanies this textbook and to Dick McGlynn for preparing the *Study Guide*.

Other psychologists provided valuable critiques of chapters of the second edition in their areas of specialization. These included five of my colleagues at Brandeis University: Teresa Amabile (social psychology, Psychological Issue on creativity); Susan Goldberg (development); James Lackner (the brain and nervous system, perception); Solomon Levin (psychological disorder); and Arthur Wingfield (learning, memory, language, thought, and intelligence). In addition, the following psychologists at other colleges and universities reviewed chapters of the second edition: Gordon Bower, Stanford University (learning and memory); Gerald Davison, University of Southern California (psychological disorder and therapy); Elliot Entin, Ohio University (motivation and emotion); John Kihlstrom, University of Wisconsin (consciousness); Carroll Izard, University of Delaware (motivation and emotion); Carol Nagy Jacklin, Stanford University (female and male); Alan Leshner, Bucknell University (the brain and nervous system, Psychological Issue on violence); James McGaugh, University of California, Irvine (the brain and nervous system); Michael Mahoney, Pennsylvania State University (Psychological Issue on behavior control); Letitia Anne Peplau, University of California, Los Angeles (female and male); Robert Sternberg, Yale University (language, thought, and intelligence); Brian Wandell, Stanford University (perception); Diana Woodruff, Temple University (development).

Several other people helped me immensely in preparing the third edition. Dr. Anne Sandoval, now at the University of New Hampshire, played a major role in the revision. She worked closely with me throughout the revision process and drafted material for many portions of the textbook. I am deeply grateful to her. Jone Sloman, a graduate student in developmental psychology at Brandeis, drafted material for the chapters on development through life, and Marilyn Geller, a recent Brandeis graduate concentrating in clinical psychology, drafted material for the chapters on psychological disorder and therapy. I could not have asked for a more talented and conscientious group of collaborators. Lisa Savery, another Brandeis student, provided research and secretarial assistance and worked with me on the box on "Children of Divorce." I am grateful to Richard Davidson of the State University of New York College at Purchase, who drafted material that was useful in preparing the revision of the chapter on consciousness, and to Stephanie Hoffman of The Clinical Campus of Upstate Medical Center, SUNY-Binghamton, New York, who drafted material that was useful in preparing the new chapter on adulthood and aging.

As developmental editor for the book, Jackie Estrada did an outstanding job of polishing the prose, preparing the chapter summaries and glossary, compiling the bibliography, and more generally, holding the entire project together. I also want to thank the many people at Harper & Row who contributed in vital ways to the book's preparation and production. These include, among others, Ted Ricks, John Miller, and Kathy Robinson (past and present psychology editors); Karla Billups Philip (supervisor of editing); Betsy Wyckoff and Mira Schachne (picture editors); Tom Mellers (copyeditor); and Gayle Jaeger (designer).

Finally, I would like to thank members of my family for their help of varying sorts. My father, the late Dr. Eli H. Rubin, provided me with a lifelong model that made textbook writing seem like a natural thing to do. My mother, Adena Rubin, helped to instill in me a love of reading and writing. My wife, Carol Moses Rubin, provided valuable reactions to various portions of the manuscript and helped to keep me going. Especially when a deadline-racing psychology textbook writer gets to the sections on psychological stress, the midlife crisis and depression, emotional support is definitely needed. As I was preparing the third edition, my four-year-old son Elihu provided me with insights and examples about early development and also helped by scribbling over offensive portions of the manuscript. My two-month-old son Noam also provided me with insights—starting even before he was born—about the beginnings of life and also helped by spitting up on portions of the final page proofs that needed further work.

To all of you, my sincere thanks.

Part One

Brain, Mind, and Behavior

Psychology is a science that links the tangible with the intangible. It asks how the biological structures of our brains give rise to our behavior and even to our states of mind.

In Chapter 1, What Is Psychology?, we will survey the scope of psychology and examine the methods that psychologists employ to study behavior and the workings of the mind objectively. In the Psychological Issue on Parascience, we will contrast psychology to some of the alternative approaches to human behavior that have been taken through the ages, from counting the bumps on people's heads to charting the movements of the planets.

In Chapter 2, we will explore the workings of The Brain and Nervous System, the biological structures that underlie all our thoughts and actions. The Psychological Issue examines Biological Rhythms, the daily, monthly, and annual rhythms that reflect the interplay of our biological nature and the environment in which we live.

In Chapter 3, on Consciousness, we will focus on our states of mind, paying special attention to states of consciousness that differ from our usual waking state, such as sleep and drug-induced states. In the Psychological Issue, we will look into the psychology of Meditation, a popular means of expanding our inner experience.

Finally, in the Update on "Psychoimmunology," Joan Borysenko presents some of the new breakthroughs in understanding how our emotions and attitudes may have a direct impact on physical illnesses ranging from colds to cancer.

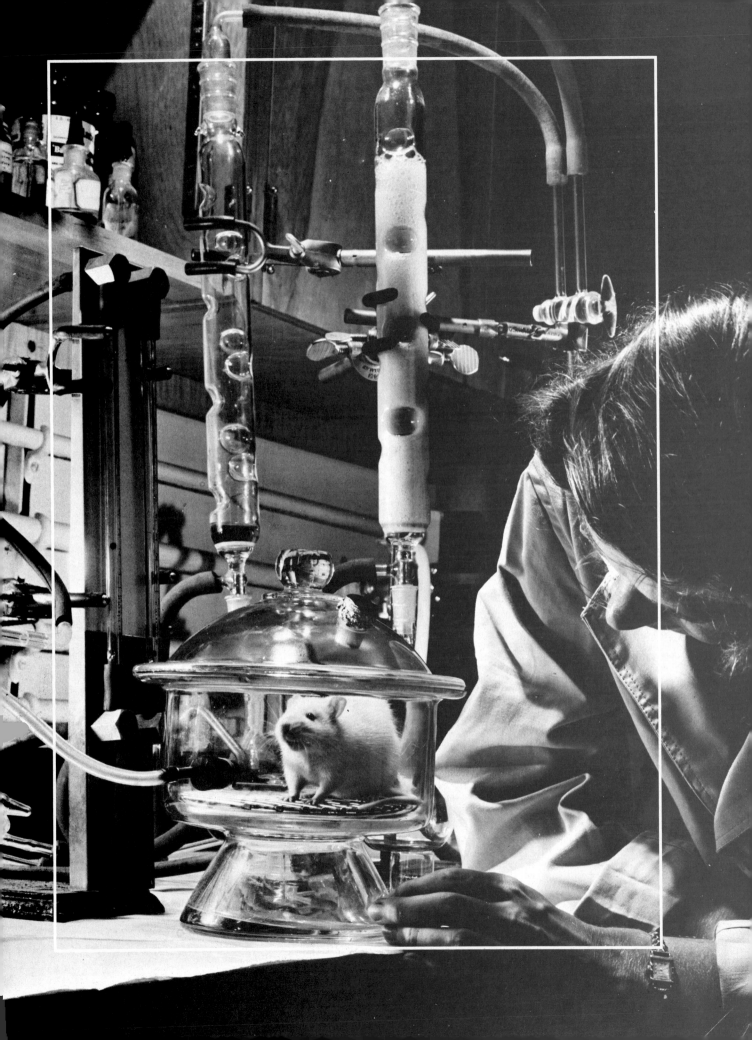

Chapter 1

What Is Psychology?

Even though this is probably your first course in psychology, you are a psychologist already. That's because the kinds of questions that psychologists ask and try to answer are very similar to the kinds of questions that all of us ask and try to answer in our everyday lives. The essential difference between you, as an "everyday psychologist," and the professional psychologist lies in the specific ways in which questions are posed and in the specific techniques that are used to answer them.

For example, here are a few questions that you might have asked yourself at one time or another:

Why is it that people who witness an emergency—say, a person who seems to be having a fainting spell—sometimes rush over to help but at other times walk right on by? (See pages 8–11.)

How does a person's birth order in a family affect her personality? Is it true, for example, that first-borns are more likely to become leaders than are later-borns, or that children without siblings are likely to be shy and lonely? (See the Psychological Issue for Chapter 9.)

Can our emotions and attitudes really affect our physical health? And if they can, how do they do so? (See the Update on "Psycho-immunology: Mind, Body, and Health".)

Why are some people so much better than others at developing creative solutions to problems or puzzles? Is it a matter of intelligence, or is some other process involved? (See the Psychological Issue for Chapter 6.)

4

SOUL, MIND, AND BEHAVIOR

The term "psychology" (actually *psychologia* in Latin) was apparently first used around 1530 by a German scholar, Phillip Melanchton, as a title for some lectures. Its original meaning—from the Greek *psyche* (or soul) and *logos* (or study)—was the "study of the soul." Later *psyche* became translated as "mind" rather than "soul." In this century, psychology was redefined as "the science of behavior and mental processes."

What leads two people to fall in love and two other people to feel nothing but disinterest in each other? And why do some love relationships last while others fall apart? (See Chapter 14.)

Why do some people need to sleep nine or ten hours every night, while others seem to get along on four or five hours? And why in the world do we all need to spend such a large portion of our lives sleeping anyway? (See Chapter 3.)

Is it essential for a preschool child's mother or father to devote full time to the child's care? Are children who spend weekdays in day-care centers likely to be any less well adjusted than children who are cared for by a parent at home? (See Chapter 9, Box 2.)

How can we possibly explain the many crimes of violence that we read about in the newspapers every day, such as John Lennon's murder in New York or the mass suicide at Jonestown? Were these the acts of deranged individuals, or do they reflect some fundamental characteristics of the human species? (See the Psychological Issue for Chapter 8.)

What leads some people to become afraid of everyday situations or to become extremely depressed? And what can be done to help people with such psychological difficulties? (See Chapters 11 and 12.)

These are the sorts of questions that people are likely to ask themselves at one time or another in their lives, even if they have never heard of the academic discipline called psychology. But they are also the sorts of questions that are the professional psychologist's bread and butter.

There is a simple explanation for the fact that most people ponder the same sorts of questions that psychologists do. *Psychology* is the science of behavior and mental processes, primarily among humans. And human behavior and mental processes are nothing less than the substance of our lives: our actions, our thoughts, our attitudes, our moods, even our hopes and dreams. It is no wonder, then, that psychology is a subject that all of us ask questions about. The purpose of psychology as a science and profession is twofold: first, to provide better answers to questions about behavior and mental processes than the "everyday psychologist" is likely to come up with; and, second, to help people make use of these answers in shaping their own lives.

Although questions about human mental life have been asked

— Box 1

Psychology's roots

Since ancient times people have been asking questions about why they behave the way they do. But the first people to formally speculate about the nature of human beings and their behavior were the early Greek and Roman philosophers. They were concerned with the question, "What is the mind?" and came up with some interesting answers. Aristotle, for example, thought that mental functions were located in the heart. Centuries passed before this

Aristotle

view was corrected and mental functions were assigned to the brain. Meanwhile, questions that today would be considered psychological were left to the realm of philosophy, and college courses concerned with the mind and behavior were confined to philosophy departments. It is only within the last century that psychology has become recognized as a distinct discipline.

Two streams of thought, one in philosophy and the other in the physical and biological sciences, eventually led to the early development of psychology as a separate area of study. The first stream was the concern in British philosophy of the nineteenth century with the nature of ideas and how ideas are associated in the mind. This approach had come out of the writings of John Locke (1632–1704), who attempted to answer questions about how we can obtain valid information about the physical world. Locke concluded that at birth a person's mind is a *tabula rasa*—Latin for a "blank slate"—on which sensory experience (vision, hearing, and so on) makes its marks. All knowledge, Locke believed, no matter how complex or abstract, derives from sensory encounters with the physical world.

John Locke

The second stream was in the biological and physical sciences of nineteenth-century Germany. In 1879 Wilhelm Wundt, a German physiologist and philosopher, opened a psychological laboratory in Leipzig. For this reason, many psychologists consider Wundt to be the "father of scientific psychology." (In fact, William James had established a laboratory a few years earlier at Harvard University, but his lab was used for class demonstrations rather than research.) Wundt's studies were aimed at discovering the nature of

throughout recorded history, psychology remains a very young science (see Box 1). There were virtually no psychology courses or psychologists before the twentieth century, and we psychologists are still a long way from having all the answers. Nevertheless, the approach that psychologists take in asking and trying to answer questions about human behavior is one that represents a significant advance from the approaches that have been taken by "everyday psychologists" throughout history. (For a glimpse at some other approaches to explaining and predicting human behavior, see the Psychological Issue on Parascience following this chapter.) Because the psychologist's methods of research are so central to understanding what psychology is all about, most of this chapter will be devoted to examining these methods.

Wilhelm Wundt

consciousness. Subjects were asked to describe sensations, images, and feelings as they were exposed to various experiences.

Wundt's psychology was thought by the German psychologists to be a "pure science," because there was no practical application of the findings. It was Wundt's students in America—James, Dewey, Cattell, and others—who became interested in finding ways for practical application of the study of conscious processes. Early American psychology became an applied discipline that developed into the

fields of child psychology, educational psychology, and mental testing, among others. Wundt and his followers were called *structuralists*, because they were interested in the anatomy or structure of conscious processes, whereas the practical Americans were called *functionalists*.

John B. Watson, a former functionalist, founded *behaviorism* as a reaction to the structuralists, who were then occupied with such undecidable questions—it seemed to Watson—as "Do all thoughts involve images?" Watson asserted that the only proper subject mat-

William James

ter for psychology was observable behavior. This assertion, coupled with the development of objective experimental methods, brought the study of conscious processes to a virtual end. The behaviorist approach, carried on by B. F. Skinner and others, has been the predominant one in American psychology for most of the past 50 years. We'll hear more about this approach in Chapter 5.

Quite recently—during the last 15 to 20 years—things have come full circle. Although behaviorism is still strong, many psychologists have returned to questions about consciousness, mental imagery, thought processes, and other aspects of "the mind." But now, such research is done with more sophisticated scientific tools than those employed by the early structuralists.

While structuralism, functionalism, and behaviorism were developing, mainly in the universities, another crucial development in psychology sprang from medicine and treatment of mental illness: Freud and his psychoanalytic theory. Freud emphasized unconscious motives and the importance of early life experiences in shaping personality. We'll have a lot to say about Freud and his theory in Chapter 8.

THE RESEARCH ADVENTURE

What does the word *research* mean to you? Perhaps it brings to mind a white-coated scientist scurrying around a laboratory with test tubes in hand. Or perhaps it evokes memories of sitting in the library, surrounded by a pile of almanacs, encyclopedias, and other reference works, trying to gather the information you need for a report or term paper. Psychologists do a good deal of work in the laboratory (where some of us even wear white coats) and in the library. But neither the laboratory nor the library is essential to psychological research. In fact, research can be done in a wide variety of locales—in board rooms and bars, airports and laundromats, nursery schools and retirement communities. And, regardless of where it is done, there is a sense in which psychological research is like a detective story. As researchers, we begin with a mystery that we want to solve, and then we gradually trace a series of clues that, we hope, will ultimately lead to a solution.

To help give you the flavor of this research adventure, we will trace two psychological detective stories in some detail. Each comes from a different area of psychology: the first deals with a troublesome aspect of people's behavior toward their fellow human beings; the second, with a remarkable aspect of human memory.

The Case of the Good Samaritan

Have you ever walked down the street and watched a person collapse on the sidewalk? Or seen a fight break out between two children, with one of them really seeming to hurt the other? In some such cases, a bystander will immediately come to the aid of the victim. If the incident seems too difficult for the one helper to handle, he might recruit other people or call the police for assistance. In other cases, however, incidents like these—or worse—occur in the presence of many bystanders, yet nobody does anything at all. Some years ago, for example, a young woman named Kitty Genovese was attacked by a male assailant one night as she returned to her home in New York City. Thirty-eight of her neighbors watched from their apartment windows without doing anything to intervene—even though it took her attacker over half an hour to murder her (Rosenthal, 1964). Since that time, many similar cases have been played up in the news, usually in urban locations.

What determines whether or not a person will come to the aid of a victim in an accident or emergency? It was the desire to answer this question that motivated two psychologists, John Darley and C. Daniel Batson (1973), to investigate the case of the Good Samaritan. In setting up their study of factors that affect helping, Darley and Batson got *their* help from an unexpected—well, perhaps not so unexpected—source: the Bible. "Fortunately," Dr. Batson later recounted, "Jesus showed us the way—with his parable of the Good Samaritan" (1976, page 207).

In the parable of the Good Samaritan, recounted in the Gospel of Luke, Jesus described the situation of a man who had been robbed, beaten, and left half dead along the road from Jerusalem to

Psychologists are interested in finding out why bystanders sometimes come to the aid of victims in an emergency but at other times fail to help.

Jericho. A priest came down the road but walked right on by without stopping. Later a Levite (a member of the group who assisted the priests in the temple) came down the road, but he did not stop to help either. Finally, a Samaritan—a member of a group of religious outcasts—stopped, took care of the man's wounds, and took him to an inn where he could recover. The message of the parable, of course, is that we should not be like the priest or the Levite, so-called "religious" people who did not stop to help; instead, we should emulate the Good Samaritan, an "irreligious" person who nevertheless had compassion for a fellow human being.

The parable of the Good Samaritan suggested to Darley and Batson two factors that might have an effect on whether a person would offer to help in an emergency: first, what the person happens to be thinking about when she notices the victim, and second, the person's time schedule. Darley and Batson speculated that the priest and Levite, as religious functionaries, were likely to have had their heads full of prayers, rituals, and Biblical passages; they may have been so preoccupied with "religious" thoughts that they could not pay attention to the plight of the victim. Darley and Batson also reasoned that the priest and Levite, as prominent public figures, might have been in more of a rush than the Samaritan and that this, too, might have decreased their willingness to help.

Finally, the parable of the Good Samaritan suggested to Darley and Batson a concrete way of setting up an experiment. They selected as their experimental site a narrow, usually deserted alley that ran between two campus buildings at Princeton University. The students who took part in the study were sent from one building to the other. As a student walked along the deserted alley, he encountered the victim—a young man slumped in a doorway, with head down and eyes closed. As the student went by, the victim coughed twice and groaned, keeping his head down. Darley and Batson's main interest was in whether or not the student offered to help the victim. The victim, of course, was an accomplice of the researchers; he went into his act on a signal from the experimenter. If the subject stopped and offered help, the victim assured him that he was all right and thanked the subject for stopping and offering help.

Because Darley and Batson's study had a religious theme, they decided to recruit divinity school students as their subjects. The students were told that they would be sent to the other building to tape-record a short talk. Half of the subjects were asked to give a talk on a nonreligious topic. The other half of the subjects were to give a talk that was not only religious but specifically relevant to the ideal of helping victims: they were to talk on the parable of the Good Samaritan. All of the students were given a chance to think about their talk briefly before being sent over to the other building. We can assume, therefore, that subjects in the two different experimental conditions had rather different thoughts on their minds as they walked along the narrow road.

The experiment had another variation, crosscutting the first one (see Figure 1.1). One-third of the subjects were told that the experiment was running late and that they would have to get over to the other building in a hurry. Another one-third of the students were simply told to go right over to the building. The remaining one-third were told that they could take their time, because it would be a few minutes before the assistant in the other building would be ready for them. Thus, some subjects were in a big hurry as they walked down the road, some were in a moderate hurry, and some were in no hurry at all.

What was the evidence in the case of the Good Samaritan? All told, 40 percent of the subjects helped the victim, either by stopping and offering help directly or at least by telling someone else about the

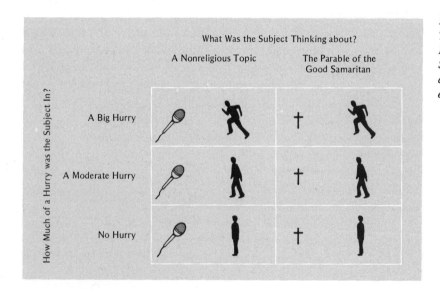

FIGURE 1.1
The experimental conditions in Darley and Batson's Good Samaritan study. There were approximately seven subjects in each of the six conditions.

emergency; 60 percent did not. But these rates were markedly affected by the experimental variations. How much of a rush the subjects were in clearly affected their behavior: 63 percent of the no-hurry subjects offered help, compared to 45 percent of the moderate-hurry subjects and only 10 percent of the big-hurry subjects. This factor probably has an effect on helping in other situations as well. For example, the fact that city-dwellers are often less likely than country-dwellers to help others (Milgram, 1970) does not imply that people who live in cities are a less compassionate breed of human beings than people who live in the country. Rather, it may be a consequence of the fact that city-dwellers are more likely to be in a rush, which in turn tends to narrow their focus of attention.

The subjects' thoughts as they walked along the road also had an effect on their helping behavior: 53 percent of those preparing to give a talk about the parable of the Good Samaritan offered aid to the victim, compared to 29 percent of those who were preparing to talk about a nonreligious topic. These results indicate that thinking about the religious ideal of compassion for victims can itself promote compassion. It should be stressed, however, that thinking helpful thoughts does not always lead to helpful action—indeed, almost half of the subjects in this condition did *not* offer any assistance to the victim. "On several occasions," Darley and Batson report, "a seminary student going to give his talk on the parable of the Good Samaritan literally stepped over the victim as he hurried on his way" (page 107).

The case of the Good Samaritan is by no means closed. Much more research needs to be done before we will have a full understanding of why people are sometimes Good Samaritans and sometimes not. A great deal of research is currently being conducted on the sorts of situations that are more or less likely to elicit helping. Other research focuses on the sorts of people who are especially likely to help others in emergency situations. More generally, psychologists interested in explaining social behavior must be concerned with the interplay of people's personality characteristics and the characteristics of specific situations in which people find themselves.

The Case of the Flashbulb Memory

Like the case of the Good Samaritan, our second research adventure also has its roots in personal experience. Practically everyone in the United States who was at least ten years old in 1963 can tell you, often in great detail, the exact circumstances under which she first heard of President John F. Kennedy's assassination—where she was and what she was doing, who told her about the assassination, and the first thing she did after hearing the news.

Psychologist James Kulik recalls, for example:

I was seated in a sixth-grade music class, and over the intercom I was told that the president had been shot. At first everyone just looked at each other. Then the class started yelling, and the music teacher tried to calm everyone down. About ten minutes later I heard over the intercom that Kennedy had died and that everyone should return to their homeroom. I remember that when I got to my homeroom my teacher was crying and everyone was standing in a state of shock. They told us to go home.

Psychologist Roger Brown, an older colleague of Kulik's, recalls:

I was on the telephone with Miss Johnson, the Dean's secretary, about some departmental business. Suddenly she broke in with: "Excuse me a moment; everyone is excited about something. What? Mr. Kennedy has been shot!" We hung up, I opened my door to hear further news as it came in, and then resumed my work on some forgotten business that "had to be finished" that day.

These are examples of memories so sharp and vivid that they seem to have been recorded in the sudden glare of a flashbulb. And so, Brown and Kulik (1977), who decided to investigate such memories systematically, have named them *flashbulb memories*. They are not memories for a historical event itself, but rather enduring memories of the setting and manner in which one heard of the event. Brown and Kulik suspected that the Kennedy assassination was not unique in prompting this special kind of memory and that people

Many people remember exactly where they were and what they were doing when they first heard the news of President Kennedy's assassination. Roger Brown and James Kulik called this phenomenon a flashbulb memory.

Another incident that triggered flashbulb memories in people around the world occurred on December 8, 1980. Millions of people—especially those who came of age in the 1960s—will always remember just what they were doing when they learned that John Lennon had been murdered.

might experience flashbulb memories several times in their lives. They proceeded to design a study that would shed light on the circumstances that give rise to such memories.

The two psychologists had certain hunches about the requirements for a flashbulb memory. First, they suspected that the event around which such a memory occurs must be very sudden. Second, they believed that the event had to be personally important—it had to be perceived as having a real impact on the rememberer's life. Indeed, the more consequential the event, Brown and Kulik believed, the more likely it would be to give rise to a full-blown flashbulb memory that would remain vivid for years to come—perhaps for one's entire life. This notion that the more personally important the event, the more likely it would be to set off a flashbulb memory is an example of a *hypothesis*—an educated guess about a cause-and-effect relationship. Brown and Kulik set out to test their hypotheses by administering a questionnaire to a sample of people about their flashbulb memories.

In the questionnaire, the researchers described what they meant by flashbulb memories and then asked their subjects—eighty Americans ranging in age from 20 to 60—to indicate whether they had such memories for each of nine events that had occurred during the previous 15 years. The events included the assassinations of President Kennedy in 1963 and of Martin Luther King and Robert F. Kennedy in 1968. In addition, the subjects were asked whether they had a flashbulb memory for any personal events in their lives, such as the death of a friend or relative. Those subjects who did have flashbulb memories were asked to recount those memories in detail. The subjects were also asked to indicate how important each of the events was for them personally—that is, how much of a difference they felt the event had made in their lives.

When Brown and Kulik analyzed the questionnaire responses, they found, first of all, that most people indeed had flashbulb memories. All but one of the eighty subjects reported flashbulb memories connected with President Kennedy's assassination, and seventy-three reported flashbulb memories connected with a personal shock—most often the unexpected death of a parent. Many of the accounts were extraordinarily vivid, including such details as "The weather was cloudy and gray," "We all had on our little blue uniforms," and "I was carrying a carton of Viceroy cigarettes, which I dropped."

Brown and Kulik also found clear evidence for the link they had hypothesized between the personal importance of an event and flashbulb memories. For example, the blacks in the sample rated the assassination of Martin Luther King, the great civil rights leader, as being of considerably greater personal importance to them than the whites did. And, in accord with the researchers' hypothesis, the blacks were considerably more likely than the whites to have flashbulb memories surrounding Dr. King's murder: thirty of the forty blacks in the study, but only ten of the forty whites, had such memories. Similarly, thirteen blacks and only one white remembered what they were doing when they first heard of the assassination of the black leader Malcolm X in 1965.

More generally, the researchers found a strong relationship between subjects' judgments of the personal importance of events and the fullness and sharpness of their memories. On the whole, the subjects judged their private shocks, such as the death of a parent, as having the greatest impact on their lives, and also reported the most detailed flashbulb memories related to those events. On the other hand, events that were of relatively little personal importance to the subjects, such as Edward Kennedy's incident at Chappaquiddick in 1969, gave rise to relatively few flashbulb memories, and those that were reported were not very detailed. It seems, then, that a sudden event is not enough to trip the flashbulb in our minds; the event must be important enough to prompt a strong emotional response, as well.

Just why we are likely to form flashbulb memories for sudden and impactful events remains an unanswered question. As Brown and Kulik point out, however, there is reason to think that the ability to record in memory the circumstances surrounding sudden and important events probably had great value to our ancestors in prehistoric times, as the human species was evolving. After all, the hunter who could remember the precise circumstances under which he first encountered a dangerous animal would be more likely to survive. Because of this survival value, Brown and Kulik speculate, our brain structures may have evolved in such a way as to make such flashbulb memories likely. There has also been some speculation about the specific brain structures that make flashbulb memories possible (Livingston, 1967), but so far it remains just that—speculation. Whatever the physiological basis for flashbulb memories, they are a unique kind of memory experience. We now understand this experience somewhat better than we did before Brown and Kulik's research adventure, and with further research we will surely come to understand it better still.

Where Do Psychologists Get Their Ideas?

As the two cases we have just examined suggest, psychologists get their ideas for research questions and ways of answering them from a wide variety of sources. Personal experience is one of the most important sources of research questions and hypotheses, whether it concerns one's tendencies to help others, one's memories, or one's emotions. As the examples in Box 2 illustrate, the events of psychologists' own lives often have an important impact on the research they choose to conduct.

Psychologists get their ideas from more than just personal experiences, however. Events in the news may suggest important research questions. The case of Kitty Genovese and her thirty-eight neighbors directly inspired many valuable studies of helping behavior. Similarly, the horrors of the Nazi era in Germany led psychologist Stanley Milgram to conduct important experiments on the causes of people's obedience to authority. And, as the case of the Good Samaritan indicates, psychologists can also get important insights from religious, philosophical, or literary writings. In addition, research is often prompted by the desire to find ways of solving pressing psychological

— *Box 2* —

The personal side of psychological research

Why do psychologists decide to do particular sorts of research? The reasons they usually give are scientific ones—the desire to test a theory or to continue the work of other researchers in a given area. Although underlying reasons are usually not stated in research reports, the decision to investigate particular topics has its personal roots, too. Frequently, something about a psychologist's own life and personal concerns motivates her to explore particular questions. The following first-hand accounts by four researchers provide good examples.

Daniel Levinson is a clinical and social psychologist at Yale University. Beginning in the late 1960s, Levinson embarked on a major study of men's development in the middle years of life—especially the years between 35 and 50. (We will be looking at this research in Chapter 10.) Levinson explains that he had an intellectual interest in the possibility of adult development. But he adds:

The choice of topic also reflected a personal concern. At 46, I wanted to study the transition into middle age in order to understand what I had been going through myself. Over the previous ten years my life had changed in crucial ways; I had "developed" in a sense that I could not articulate. The study would cast light on my own experience and, I hoped, contribute to an understanding of adult development in general. (Levinson, 1978, page x.)

Kelly Gersick is a social-clinical psychologist who wrote a dissertation (one of the requirements for a Ph.D.) about the characteristics of "fathers by choice"—men who seek custody of their children following divorce. In the preface to his dissertation, Gersick explains that he chose his research topic because of personal, as well as scientific, reasons:

This dissertation grows out of two closely related developments. One is my growing intellectual sense that something important is happening to the relationships between men and their children in our society, and as psychologists we know very little about it. The other development is my own new paternity. The pretesting and literature review for this thesis was done while my wife and I were expecting our first child, Andrew; the data gathering and analysis were completed during his early months, and the writing by his first birthday. (Gersick, 1975, page ii.)

Toni Falbo, a psychologist at the University of Texas, decided to undertake research on the personalities of only children—for reasons that came close to home. She frequently heard the view expressed by educators, psychologists, and physicians that a child without siblings is likely to become selfish, lonely, and maladjusted. As an only child herself, Falbo was not convinced. "I was getting a bit peeved by the stereotype," she later admitted, "[so] I decided to see whether the only child was really as unfortunate as reputed" (Falbo, 1976). We'll learn about what she discovered in the Psychological Issue for Chapter 9.

Dan Batson, one of the psychologists who conducted the Good Samaritan study, also had personal reasons for deciding to study helping behavior, stemming from his religious concerns and his prior training as a minister. When one of us asked him about this, Batson wrote back:

It's true that I had some designs on "tending the flocks" before being called by the Lord of Wundt, James, and Watson [see Box 1]. Actually, I carried through to the point of being ordained (still am—Presbyterian), getting a Ph.D. at Princeton Seminary, and teaching part-time while I completed my Ph.D. in psychology. Bizarre, perhaps, but really quite enjoyable and overall a solid educational experience. My difficulty with the Seminary was that I kept wanting to know what religion actually did in people's lives (quite apart from whether it was true or not). Did it, as advertised, encourage them to be more caring? Or the opposite? Both, neither, etc.? Pursuit of these questions led me across campus to psychology—and research on helping behavior.

So, as you see, psychologists' decisions to study particular aspects of other people's lives have a great deal to do with their own lives as human beings.

and social problems, whether it is to develop ways to help people conserve energy (see Chapter 5, Box 2), to study more effectively (see Chapter 5), or to reduce racial prejudice (see the Psychological Issue for Chapter 14).

In addition to all these sources of research ideas, most of psychologists' ideas and methods are closely related to previous research questions and answers. One of the hallmarks of scientific research is that it is a *cumulative* process, in which each researcher builds on the work that has already been done in a particular area. In this process, psychologists are often guided by *theories*. You have probably heard of some theories in other sciences, such as Darwin's theory of natural selection or Einstein's theory of relativity. Each theory, whether in biology, physics, or psychology, is a set of concepts and hypotheses that fit together to provide a perspective on some aspect of the world. In Chapter 8, for example, we will survey several different theories of personality, including psychoanalytic theory and social learning theory.

A psychologist's theoretical perspective affects the way he is likely to interpret events or findings. Thus, for example, a psychoanalytic theorist might explain a 5-year-old boy's attempts to do things the way his father does in terms of the notion of *identification* (see Chapter 8), while a social learning theorist might explain the same behavior in terms of the notions of *social reinforcement* and *modeling* (see Chapter 8). At the same time, theories point the way to new research. Beginning with the concepts and hypotheses of a particular theory, the researcher derives specific predictions about behavior that she can then design a study to test.

While psychoanalytic theory and social learning theory are both wide-ranging perspectives on behavior, other theories are more narrowly focused sets of concepts and hypotheses that concern a specific problem, such as the theories of emotion that we will consider in Chapter 7. A great deal of research is done in an effort to test and refine theories and, in the long run, to replace inadequate theories with better ones.

THE METHODS OF PSYCHOLOGY

To understand how psychologists go about the process of accumulating knowledge about human behavior, we need to look more closely at the methods they use. Although psychological researchers may derive important insights from their personal experience, such experiences are likely to be casual and sketchy and to be based on a rather small and unsystematic body of evidence. Our own experiences are also likely to be colored by our motives and moods, so that what one person sees in a particular situation may be quite different from what another person sees. Depending on how you feel about yourself and what sort of mood you are in, for example, you may interpret the expression on another person's face as either a friendly glance, a puzzled look, or a hostile stare. In contrast, psychologists strive to study behavior in ways that are *systematic* (based on a thorough and well-organized search for facts) and *objective* (based on

SERENDIPITY

Sometimes a psychologist's insights arise by accident, as an outgrowth of other work that the psychologist happened to be doing. For example, the Russian physiologist Ivan Pavlov was studying the process of salivation in dogs when they were fed. He noticed that after a while the dogs began to salivate even before they were fed, as soon as they saw the experimenter who was about to feed them. This unexpected observation led Pavlov to discover the type of learning known as classical conditioning (see Chapter 5). An incident such as this—finding something you're *not* looking for—is called *serendipity*.

careful observations that different observers can agree on, rather than on one person's intuitions).

In their efforts to gather systematic and objective information, psychologists may use a wide variety of methods. No single method, such as the laboratory experiment or the nationwide survey, is the best method for psychological research, any more than a hammer is the best tool for the carpenter or a putter is the best club for the golfer. The particular method a researcher chooses will depend on the nature of the problem, the methods that previous researchers have used, and the researcher's own personal tastes and preferences. Here we will consider some of the most commonly used methods of the psychological researcher.

Whom Do Psychologists Observe?

The psychologist's business is to make systematic observations of behavior. But no psychologist can study *everyone's* behavior. Instead, the researcher chooses a *sample* of people to study. Just as a geologist may attempt to determine the composition of the moon by analyzing a small sample of rocks, so the psychologist attempts to discover principles of human behavior by studying a small but representative sample of humans. In some cases, the nature of the psychologist's sample is dictated by the problem being studied. If the researcher is interested in alcoholism, he will study a sample of alcoholics—and, preferably, a sample that reflects as closely as possible the characteristics of alcoholics more generally. Similarly, a psychologist interested in child development will study children; one interested in mental illness will study people suffering from psychological disorders.

The psychologist's choice of a sample of subjects is also likely to be dictated by convenience. By one count, fully 80 percent of psychological research with humans has made use of college students as subjects (Schultz, 1969). This is not too surprising: Because most psychological researchers work in colleges and universities, students—especially those taking psychology courses—provide their most readily available supply of subjects. The heavy reliance on college students as subjects presents certain problems, however. Because most college students are young, white, and middle class, it may not always be possible to generalize from the behavior of college students to the behavior of people from other segments of society. For example, a large number of studies have shown that people often devote a great deal of effort to making sure that their behavior seems *consistent* to themselves and others. As a result of these studies, consistency has been viewed by many psychologists as a fundamental motive of human beings. But this conclusion needs to be taken with a grain or two of salt. In fact, the large majority of studies demonstrating the consistency motive were conducted with college students. It may well be the case that in the course of writing papers and giving class presentations students are taught that consistency is a virtue and inconsistency is a vice. As a result, college students may be especially likely to behave consistently in experiments. If the same experiments were done with people who are not college students, considerably

YOUR OBEDIENT SUBJECT

People—or other animals—who take part in psychological research are generally called *subjects*. However, some psychologists object to the connotations of the word subject. It suggests that people are subjected to the whims of the researcher, much in the way that a king's subjects are under the control of the king. The word subject may also perpetuate an impersonal attitude toward the people who take part in research. Instead of saying, "I interviewed two men and two women yesterday," psychologists sometimes catch themselves saying, "I ran four subjects yesterday." As a result, some psychologists would like to do away with the word subject—at least for humans—and to replace it with a less objectionable word, such as "participant."

less evidence for a "fundamental human motive" of consistency might be found.

In fact, the degree to which the results of research can be generalized from one group of people to another depends in large measure on the particular problem being studied. Whereas basic processes of learning and memory may work in much the same way for almost all human beings, patterns of social behavior are more likely to depend on people's social and cultural background. There is no easy answer to the problem of selecting subjects for psychological research. Being aware of this difficulty, you should ask yourself when reading about a psychological study: "Who were the subjects? Are their responses typical of what my own would be? Do their findings apply to me?"

In most cases, the psychologist includes a fairly large number of subjects in any given study. By observing the behavior of 30 or 50 or 100 people, the researcher can look for common patterns, as well as individual differences, in their behavior. Sometimes, when researchers are trying to describe the behavior or attitudes of a large group of people, they conduct surveys of hundreds or even thousands of subjects. At the other extreme, the psychologist can sometimes learn a great deal about human behavior by closely observing a single subject. For example, in his studies of memory, Hermann Ebbinghaus made use of only one subject—himself. Similarly, clinical psycholo-

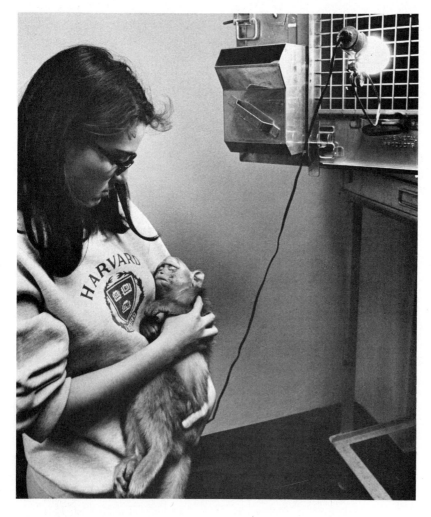

Primates such as this monkey are used in many kinds of psychological research. Although results of experiments on animals cannot be directly applied to human beings, they can provide clues to some fundamental bases of human behavior.

gists can often learn and communicate a great deal about personality from intensive *case studies* of individuals.

Since most psychologists are ultimately concerned with human behavior, it may seem surprising that much of our research is conducted with nonhumans. The best-known animal subjects are pigeons, monkeys, and most popular of all, white rats. But psychologists have also conducted research with many other species, including houseflies, worms, elephants, kangaroos, and cockroaches. Psychologists use nonhuman subjects for a variety of reasons. For one thing, animals can be kept captive in laboratories for long periods of time, so it is easier to observe their behavior. Animals are also less likely than humans to try to second-guess the experimenter or to be suspicious of the researcher's stated intentions. There are also certain techniques, such as brain surgery or severe electric shocks, that cannot ethically be used with humans but sometimes can be used with animals.

Some critics argue that human beings are a unique species and that research with nonhumans is not likely to be applicable to human behavior. It certainly is true that some human problems have no known parallels among other animals. As Robert Zajonc (1972) notes, "No amount of experimentation with animals would tell us whether the possession of handguns by private citizens enhances crime and violence, or what to do about industrial conflict or how to deal with poverty" (page 2). On the other hand, there are often striking continuities between animal and human behavior. Much of what we know about human learning, for example, is based on studies of parallel processes in pigeons, rats, and other animals (see Chapter 5). In addition, as Zajonc points out, studying other animals helps to keep us honest about our own behavior. Human beings are a unique species in many ways, but we must remember that we, too, are members of the animal kingdom, and we cannot be viewed in isolation from other animals.

What Do Psychologists Observe?

Psychologists cannot observe everything about a person's (or animal's) behavior at once. They must instead devise ways of observing and measuring those specific aspects of behavior that they are most interested in. In many instances, the researcher will record particular aspects of a subject's overt behavior—for example, the number of times a baby smiles or cries, the amount of food a person eats in a given situation, or the length of time it takes for a cat to figure out how to open the door to its cage. In the case of the Good Samaritan, there was a direct measure of helping behavior: whether or not the subject stopped to help the victim. In addition, researchers sometimes use special equipment to record a subject's physiological responses, such as heart rate, blood pressure, or sweat gland activity. Finally, researchers often record people's responses to questions put to them, whether in the form of personal interviews, questionnaires, or tests of personality, intelligence, or ability. For instance, the flashbulb memory study is an example of a *survey,* a study in which many people are asked for their *self-reports*—their own personal assess-

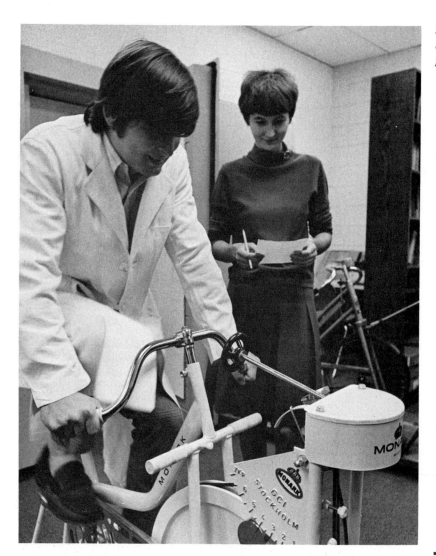

Some behaviors can be observed and measured directly in a psychologist's laboratory.

ments—about some topic, either on a questionnaire, over the telephone, or in person. The fact that it is possible to obtain self-reports from them is one way in which humans are clearly superior to other animals as research subjects. Whereas we can observe the overt behavior of both people and other animals, only humans can provide the researcher with their own assessments of their thoughts and feelings.

As with methods of research more generally, there is no single best measure for the psychologist. In many cases, the researcher will do best to use several different measures simultaneously, to find out how they compare with one another. For example, one of us once attempted to define and measure one of the more mysterious facets of human behavior, romantic love (Rubin, 1973). My primary approach was to obtain college students' self-reports of their attitudes and feelings toward their boyfriends or girlfriends. To do this, I asked the students to indicate how much they agreed or disagreed with statements like, "If I were lonely, my first thought would be to seek ＿＿out," or "I would do almost anything for ＿＿." In each case, the blank space denoted the student's boyfriend or girlfriend. In addition, I obtained a behavioral measure of love by recording the

UNOBTRUSIVE MEASURES

When people know that their behavior is being observed, they are likely to behave differently than they might otherwise. And when they are asked direct questions about their attitudes or actions, they do not always provide objective reports. To get around these problems, psychologists sometimes make use of *unobtrusive measures*—that is, measures that are unlikely to have any effect on the attitude or behavior being measured. For example, one investigator wanted to find out how much liquor was being consumed in a town that was officially dry. He didn't want to ask people directly about this illegal behavior, however. His solution: count empty bottles in trashcans. In a study of another delicate topic, researchers investigated cultural differences in sexual attitudes by comparing the inscriptions on toilet walls in the Philippines and the United States (Webb et al., 1966).

amount of time couples spent looking into each others' eyes while they were waiting for an experiment to begin. I found, as I had hoped, that the two measures related to each other: The more the students indicated that they loved each other on the attitude scale, the more eye contact they tended to make (see Chapter 14).

Where Do Psychologists Observe?

A large proportion of psychological research is conducted in laboratories. There are many different sorts of psychological laboratories. For example, an animal learning laboratory may have rooms full of cages in which the animals are kept and special boxes and mazes in which the animals are tested. A human group laboratory may have rooms in which groups of people can meet around a table and equipment for observing and videotaping group discussions. Laboratories are of great importance to psychologists, because they help us to study behavior under precise, well-regulated conditions. There are also certain problems with laboratory research, however. Because the laboratory is a rather artificial environment, it is sometimes difficult to generalize from the ways subjects behave in the laboratory to the ways they would behave in other situations. For example, studies of aggression in the laboratory can never give us a complete understanding of the determinants of violence in the streets. An additional problem is that, when people are studied in the laboratory, they are aware of the fact that they are being studied. This awareness may lead people to be on their best behavior or to respond in ways that are not typical of their usual behavior. To get around these problems, many psychologists conduct research in nonlaboratory settings. Although it may be difficult to do so, it is often worthwhile to study an animal's behavior in its natural habitat, whether jungle, marsh, or stream. Psychologists often study human behavior in natural settings as well, including dormitory rooms, parks, churches, subways, factories, and even elevators. The case of the Good Samaritan made use of *both* laboratory and natural settings. The subjects began the study in the laboratory but then were sent across campus, encountering the emergency in a narrow alley—a natural setting.

Description, Correlation, and Experimentation

In addition to decisions of where, what, and whom to observe, the psychologist must also decide on a research plan or strategy for addressing the questions she is particularly interested in. There are three major research strategies that we will consider here: description, correlation, and experimentation.

Description. When a researcher is engaged in *description*, she is primarily concerned with setting forth a clear account of the subject's behavior or self-reports. One approach to description is the *observational study*, in which the researcher observes behavior as it occurs in a particular setting. For example, a psychologist might observe the social behaviors of several children in a nursery-school classroom, either taking notes in narrative form or counting the occurrences of specific behaviors (such as "plays alone," "plays cooperatively," "fights," "calls for the teacher," and so on). Other descriptive studies make use of *interviews*, in which the researcher summarizes the subjects' own appraisals of themselves. In Chapter 14, for example, we will discuss research on loneliness that makes use of extensive interviews with people who have experienced separation or loss. Descriptive studies are a central part of the psychologist's effort to come to terms with human behavior. However, they do not in themselves permit the researcher to test specific hypotheses about cause-and-effect relationships. A good description of behavior can tell us what is happening, but it can't tell us with any certainty why it is happening.

Correlation. In a correlational study, the researcher tries to discover the relationship (or *correlation*) between two or more aspects of people's behavior, attitudes, or background. Brown and Kulik's flashbulb memory study is an example of a correlational study—subjects' ratings of the personal importance of events were related to their flashbulb memories of those events. To take another example of a correlational study, suppose that you were interested in determining the relationship between people's training in psychology and their sensitivity to other people's feelings. You might go about such a study by choosing a sample of students, asking each one how many psychology courses he has taken, and finally giving them a test of interpersonal sensitivity. You would then be able to chart the relationship between your two measures. Figure 1.2 presents one possible set of results from such a study, suggesting that the two measures (sometimes called *variables*) are in fact related to one another.

As far as we know, this particular study has never been done, but it would certainly be an interesting one to do. Such a correlational study has its limitations, however. Although our hypothetical study demonstrates that training in psychology and interpersonal sensitivity are related to each other, it does not provide a clear test of hypotheses about cause and effect. One hypothesis would be that training in

DOES SEX CAUSE HAPPINESS . . . OR DOES HAPPINESS CAUSE SEX?

According to one study, a married couple's frequency of sex minus their frequency of arguments is highly correlated with their marital happiness (Howard and Dawes, 1976). This correlation could mean that sex enhances marital happiness and that arguments detract from it. However, it could also mean that happy couples are predisposed to have sex more and argue less. Cause and effect remain uncertain and, unfortunately, manipulating any of the variables is probably out of the question!

FIGURE 1.2

The results of a hypothetical study relating training in psychology to scores on a test of interpersonal sensitivity. Each dot represents one subject. The results show a high correlation between two variables.

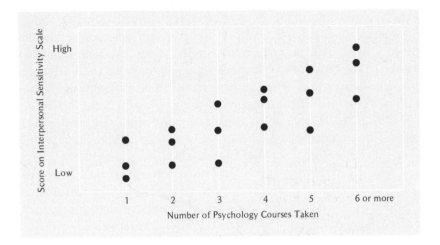

psychology increases people's sensitivity to others. But the causal link might go in the other direction: People who are sensitive to others may be especially interested in taking psychology classes. It is even possible that neither of the variables has any effect on the other and that both of them are caused by a third factor that we neglected to measure. For example, students who come from particular family backgrounds may be especially likely to be interpersonally sensitive and to take psychology, while people from other family backgrounds may tend to lack sensitivity and to avoid taking psychology. Similarly, in the flashbulb memory study, we can't be completely sure that the personal importance of events is what caused the flashbulb memories. Perhaps it worked the other way around, and the experiencing of flashbulb memories led the subjects to believe that the associated events must have been important. The moral of the story is that *correlation does not imply causation.* In other words, simply knowing that two variables are related does not in itself tell us what is causing what.

Experimentation. In order to test cause-and-effect hypotheses more definitely, psychologists also conduct experiments. An *experiment* is a study in which the researcher exerts direct control over some aspect of the subject's environment and then assesses the effects. The Good Samaritan study is an example of an experiment. Subjects were assigned to different conditions—what they were thinking about, how much of a hurry they were in—by the researchers, who then observed the effects of these conditions on the subjects' behavior.

Let's say you wanted to conduct an experiment to check out the hypothesis that training in psychology will increase people's sensitivity to others' feelings. You might do it in the following way: First, select a sample of incoming freshmen who have not yet taken psychology. Next, randomly divide your sample into two groups (you can do this by putting the subjects' names on slips of paper, mixing them up, and then dividing them into two piles). Give the students in both groups a test of interpersonal sensitivity. Now give the students in one group a weekly assignment from a psychology textbook. Give the students in the other group a weekly reading assignment of the same length but in some other field, such as history or economics.

Finally, at the end of the term, give all the students another test of interpersonal sensitivity. If the psychology training increased sensitivity to others' feelings, you should find that the average sensitivity scores of the first group increased significantly more than the average sensitivity scores of the second group. (A statistically significant difference is one that is highly unlikely to have come about by chance, and therefore can be attributed to the impact of your experimental treatments. For a discussion of statistical significance and how it is determined, see the Appendix.)

Because in this experiment you had direct control over your subjects' psychology training, it is now possible for you to find out whether it actually *caused* increases in social sensitivity. In experiments, the variable that the researcher has control over (in this case, training in psychology) is called the *independent variable,* and the variable that may be affected by the independent variable is the *dependent variable* (in this case, interpersonal sensitivity). The group of subjects who receive the special treatment (in this case, the training in psychology) is called the *experimental group,* and the group of subjects that one compares them with (in this case, those who were assigned reading in some other field) is called the *control group.*

The control group plays a vital function in an experiment by ruling out the effects of extraneous factors on the dependent variable. It is possible, for example, that college students generally tend to become more interpersonally sensitive over the course of a year as the result of their increasing maturity and their accumulating experiences with other people. If our experiment did not include a control group, we would not know whether changes in interpersonal sensitivity were caused by the independent variable (training in psychology) or by the increased maturity that would have taken place anyway. By including the control group, whose subjects also got older during the year but who did not get training in psychology, we can determine whether the psychology training in fact made the difference.

Some experiments compare more than one experimental group and one control group. In the Good Samaritan study, for example, there were six groups involved (see Figure 1.1). In that study, there were two independent variables: the topic of the talk to be given and the hurry in which the subjects had to cross the campus. The dependent variable—whether the subject stopped to help the victim— was compared across all six conditions of the experiment.

It is not always easy, or even possible, to conduct experimental studies of particular hypotheses. This is because it is often difficult or impossible to gain control over the independent variable. For example, you might be interested in assessing the impact of a person's sex on her aggressiveness, or the effects of physical appearance on marital happiness. But it would be difficult, to say the least, to conduct experimental studies along these lines. It is impossible to randomly assign subjects to "male" and "female" subgroups or to randomly decide that some subjects will henceforth be physically attractive and that others will be unattractive. In these instances, the researcher would be content to do a correlational study. Another difficulty in conducting experiments—the possible effects of the experimenter's expectations on the results he obtains—is discussed in Box 3.

— Box 3 —

Finding what you're looking for

One of the pitfalls of psychological research is the possibility that the researcher may sometimes inadvertently produce precisely the results he expects to find.

Robert Rosenthal (1966) has conducted many studies that demonstrate the existence of such *experimenter expectancy effects.* In one study, ten advanced undergraduate and graduate students were recruited to serve as experimenters. Each experimenter was assigned a group of twenty students to serve as subjects. The experimenters were to show the subjects a series of photographs of people's faces. The subjects

How much "success" is depicted in this face? Rosenthal found that subjects' answers to this question about similar photos depended on the results an experimenter expected.

were to guess the degree of "success" or "failure" expressed in each face, on a scale that went from −10 (extreme failure) to +10 (extreme success). The experimenters were all given the same set of instructions about how to conduct the experiment and were told not to deviate from them. Finally, the experimenters were given an idea of the average ratings they could expect to obtain in the study, on the basis of previous research. Half were told that most people tended to rate the faces in the photos as quite successful; the other half were told that people tended to rate the faces as quite unsuccessful. After this briefing, the experimenters began their research. The results of the Rosenthal study were clearcut: The experimenters who were led to expect "success" ratings in fact obtained much more "successful" ratings from their subjects than did the experimenters who were led to expect failure ratings.

How do experimenter expectancy effects work? The best guess is that experimenters do not intentionally set out to shape their subjects' responses. Nevertheless, subtle nonverbal cues such as facial expressions and tone of voice can provide signals to the subject as to what sort of response is expected. And once they have picked up on these cues, subjects may unconsciously shift their responses in the direction that the experimenter seems to expect.

You can probably demonstrate similar effects yourself. Go up to a friend with a smile on your face

and ask, in a bright tone of voice, "How often do you get depressed?" Go up to another friend and ask the same question, but this time wear a sorrowful expression and use a somber tone. There's a good chance that the way you ask the question will affect the response you get.

The fact that researchers may unintentionally affect the results of their research presents a problem for psychologists. It suggests that our results may not always be as objective and reliable as we would like them to be. As a result of the work of Rosenthal and others, however, psychologists have become aware of this problem, and they have taken measures to combat it.

One device is to present instructions to subjects in writing or on tape, so that the experimenter will not be able to behave differently toward different subjects. Another precaution is for the researchers to keep themselves in the dark about the experimental condition being run. The less the experimenters know about what to expect from subjects, the reasoning goes, the less likely they will be to unwittingly influence the results. In the Good Samaritan study, for example, the "victim," who had to record the subjects' helping responses, remained unaware of (or "blind" to) the experimental condition of the subjects who came down the road. By employing such safeguards, researchers can reduce the likelihood that they will find just what they are looking for.

RESEARCH AND APPLICATION

Psychological research has been applied to a wide variety of practical issues, from helping people make better career decisions to suggesting more effective policies of environmental control. The translation from research to application is not easy or automatic, however. Whereas some psychological research has obvious and immediate applications, other research has no apparent application at all. To understand more fully the links between research and application, it is useful to think of two sorts of psychological research: basic research and applied research.

The purpose of *basic research* is to advance our understanding of behavior without any immediate concern for the practical uses of this understanding. The flashbulb memory study is an example of basic research. It adds to our understanding of human memory and experience, but it does not have any direct applications to the solution of personal or social problems. Although basic research seldom has any direct application, in the long run it may prove to be of great practical importance. For example, basic research on helping behavior, such as the Good Samaritan study, may eventually lead to ways of encouraging people to be more responsive to the plight of others. The "Good Samaritan laws" enacted in some states, which provide that a person cannot be sued or held liable for attempting to help others in emergencies, or that compensate people for losses incurred in their attempt to help others, are one sort of encouragement; psychological research has also helped to evaluate the effectiveness of such laws (Geis and Huston, 1976).

Applied research is work that attempts, from the outset, to help solve a practical problem. For example, research into biofeedback techniques (use of equipment that monitors and reports such physiological processes as heart rate, blood pressure, and brain waves) may help people to improve their health (see Chapter 2, Box 3). Applied research also helps in such areas as designing equipment (such as airplane instrument panels) to suit human perceptual and motor abilities and preparing educational materials that motivate students. In other instances, psychologists have done research that has direct bearing on court cases or on decisions about government programs. For example, Sandra Bem and Daryl Bem (1973) conducted experiments that demonstrated that certain newspaper want ads were worded in such a way as to steer women into particular sorts of jobs and men into others. Their findings played an important role in the court decision that one of the largest American corporations had engaged in discriminatory hiring practices.

In addition to conducting basic and applied research, many psychologists are also involved in the *practice* of psychology—that is, in making direct applications of psychological knowledge. These activities include providing psychological help for individual clients, working with groups and organizations, and playing a role in the development of social policies and programs. In the next section we will take a closer look at the variety of activities, including both research and practice, that psychologists are involved in.

SUBFIELDS OF PSYCHOLOGY

Many people have a specific image of what psychologists do. One popular conception is that psychologists, like television's Bob Newhart, spend most of their time talking to people about their personal and emotional problems. Another is that psychologists can usually be

— Box 4 ——————————————————————————————

Some assorted facts about psychologists

HOW MANY PSYCHOLOGISTS ARE THERE?

There are currently well over 100,000 psychologists in the United States, and over 50,000 of them belong to the American Psychological Association (APA). Since its beginnings in this country around 1870, psychology has been expanding at a rapid rate, with the number of living psychologists doubling every dozen years. In 1951, E. G. Boring, a noted historian of psychology, calculated that if this rate of growth continued, by the end of the twenty-first century every man, woman, and child in the United States would be a psychologist (Lipsey and Brayfield, 1975).

WHERE DO THEY WORK?

Over half of the psychologists in America (51 percent) work primarily in colleges and universities; 15 percent work in hospitals and clinics, 8 percent in government or private agencies, 8 percent in schools, 8 percent in business or consulting firms. Seven percent work in independent or group practices (Boneau and Cuca, 1974).

PSYCHOLOGISTS AND PSYCHIATRISTS

Psychologists and psychiatrists differ in their training and in their professional activities. Psychologists are trained in graduate schools, where they receive M.A. or Ph.D. degrees. Psychiatrists go to medical schools and earn M.D. degrees, after which they go on to do additional work in psychiatry. Both psychiatrists and one group of psychologists—clinical psychologists—are concerned with the diagnosis and treatment of psychological problems and mental illness. Clinical psychologists more often use psychological tests as part of this work, and they are more likely to draw on theory and research from other areas of psychology. Psychiatrists, because they are M.D.s, are able to make use of drugs and other medical treatments.

---

found showing people inkblots and asking them what they see in them. Still another image is that of people with stopwatches and clipboards who tirelessly watch rats run mazes until, after a while, they begin to look a little like rats themselves. All these images have a grain of truth to them in that therapy, psychological testing, and research with laboratory animals are all among the activities of psychologists.

As you probably realize by now, however, each of these images provides an inaccurate picture of the psychologist. In fact, not all psychologists are alike. Rather, different psychologists specialize in different subfields of the discipline. Some conduct therapy, some give tests, some study laboratory animals, and some engage in a wide range of other activities. In this section we will provide a brief tour of the different psychology subfields (as categorized by Lipsey and Brayfield, 1975) in order to give you a fuller idea of what psychologists do. (Assorted facts about psychologists can be found in Box 4.)

Experimental Psychology. Although psychologists in several different subfields conduct experiments, the term *experimental psychology* is generally reserved for research on the most fundamental psychological processes, such as perception, learning, memory, motivation, and emotion. Experimental psychologists do much of their work in laboratories, using both animal and human subjects. Included in the general category of experimental psychologists are *comparative psychologists,* who compare the behavior patterns of different animal species, and *physiological psychologists,* who study the operation of the brain and nervous system. One experimental psychologist may be engaged in studying the physiological effects of meditation; another may be conducting research on how loud noises

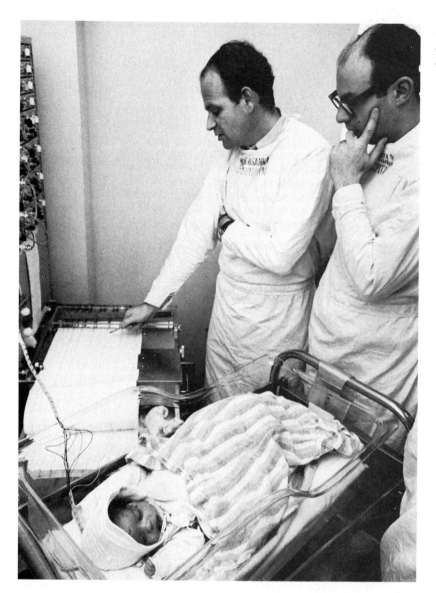

Experimental psychologists may find themselves studying sleep patterns in infants.

affect people's ability to solve problems; and a third may be concerned with explaining why lesions in particular areas of the brain cause rats to overeat.

Clinical, Counseling, School, and Community Psychology. These subfields of psychology are all concerned with helping people deal with problems and decisions in their lives. *Clinical psychologists* work in schools, hospitals, and mental health centers and in private practice; they diagnose psychological difficulties and provide therapy for those who need it. *Counseling psychologists* work with people who, for example, are trying to choose a career (vocational counseling), pondering decisions about marriage (marriage counseling), or trying to cope with a severe illness or injury (rehabilitation counseling). *School psychologists* work with children who are having difficulty in school, consult with teachers and parents, and help to design special school programs, such as those for retarded or gifted children. *Community psychologists* specialize in preventing and treating psychological problems at a community level—for example, by work-

WHAT'S IN A NAME?

A questionnaire administered to 376 college students on three campuses found consistent differences in student reaction to hearing the names *Counseling Center* and *Psychological Center*. The name *Counseling Center* was associated with the treatment of minor problems. *Psychological Center* was associated with the treatment of more serious problems. The *Psychological Center* was seen as more medical, expensive, professional, embarrassing to go to, and competent than the *Counseling Center* (Sieveking and Chappell, 1970).

Clinical psychologists may use tools such as inkblot tests to help identify people's underlying problems.

ing with organizations of elderly people or with youth groups. Psychologists in any of these fields may also do research—for example, on the causes of psychological disorders or the effectiveness of particular modes of therapy.

Personnel, Organizational, Engineering, and Consumer Psychology. Psychologists in these areas generally work in commercial or industrial settings. *Personnel psychologists* are concerned with selecting workers for particular jobs and with handling questions of morale and job satisfaction. *Organizational psychologists* are called upon to develop ways for businesses and other organizations to function more effectively. *Engineering psychologists* are concerned with making sure that the design of equipment, from telephone systems to space capsules, takes into account the abilities and limitations of the people using it. *Consumer psychologists* are concerned with the application of psychology to questions involving the purchase and consumption of goods and services, from packaging a new brand of shampoo to developing a campaign to encourage people to conserve gas and electricity.

Developmental and Educational Psychology. Developmental psychologists are concerned with the development of human capacities and behavior, from conception and birth through old age and death. A developmental psychologist might study the effects of day care on children's adjustment or the effects of retirement on older people's mental health. *Educational psychologists* are involved with the design of educational settings and techniques and with the training of teachers.

Personality and Social Psychology. Psychologists in these related fields are concerned with the nature and dynamics of human personality and with the ways in which people's behavior is affected by other people and by the social environment. A *personality psychologist* might study the function that religious or racial prejudice serves for some people, while a *social psychologist* might examine the processes that take place when groups—such as a jury in a court case—have to arrive at joint decisions.

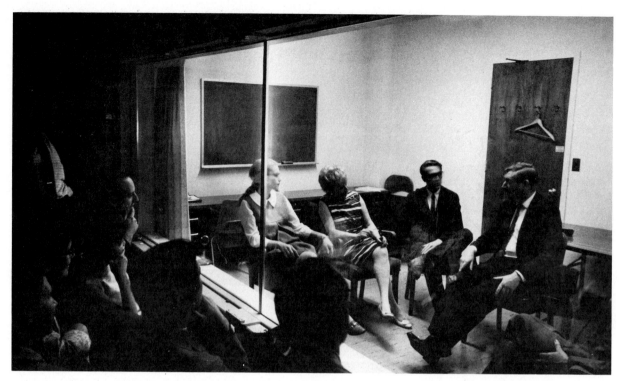

Social psychologists are interested in observing how people act in relation to each other.

It should be clear by now that even though psychology consists of a diverse set of specialties, these specialties are often closely related. An educational psychologist, for example, may call upon research generated in experimental psychology (on principles of learning), organizational psychology (as it relates to the workings of a school system), clinical psychology (on disorders that may affect the educational process), developmental psychology (on the development of intellectual abilities), and social psychology (as it relates to interracial attitudes among students in a recently integrated school).

Because of these many interconnections, there are in fact no absolute dividing lines between the various specialties. And the careers of individual psychologists often span several of the subfields. For example, Elton McNeil began as an experimental psychologist, was then trained to be a clinical psychologist, worked as an educational consultant to school systems and as a school psychologist, directed a training center for persons planning to work with emotionally disturbed and delinquent boys, worked on psychological aspects of disarmament proposals, and was a field selection officer for the Peace Corps.

Before we conclude this discussion, we should mention a final activity of psychologists: the role of *teaching* psychology. People who teach psychology often engage in other psychological work as well, such as research, counseling, or therapy. But teaching remains the primary activity of about one-fourth of all psychologists (Boneau and Cuca, 1974), including the authors of this book. For us, as for most teachers of psychology, teaching is another way of putting research into practice. By presenting psychological theory and research to our students, we hope to inspire them to think about how this work applies to their own lives.

SUMMARY

1. *Psychology* is the science of behavior and mental processes. Psychologists attempt to systematically ask and answer questions about why people act, think, and feel the way they do.

2. The science of psychology is relatively new; in the late nineteenth century the German Wilhelm Wundt founded the first psychological laboratory. His theory of *structuralism*, which focused on conscious processes, became an applied science for *functionalists* in America. As a reaction against structuralism, Watson developed *behaviorism*, in which mental processes were discounted. Now things seem to have gone full circle with renewed interest in the conscious mind.

3. Darley and Batson designed an experiment to see what factors affect helping behavior. In their Good Samaritan study, they learned that people's mental preoccupations and hurriedness can influence whether or not they will stop to help someone who is in trouble.

4. Brown and Kulik hypothesized that *flashbulb memories*—vivid memories of what one was doing when one heard of a certain event—are more likely to occur with events that are personally important. They used a questionnaire to examine people's experiences with flashbulb memories and found support for their hypothesis.

5. Psychologists get their research ideas from a variety of sources: personal experience, events in the news, philosophical and literary writings, a need to solve an urgent psychological or social problem, and previous research.

6. Psychological *theories*—sets of ideas that fit together to provide a perspective on some aspect of behavior—serve to organize knowledge and point the way to new research.

7. Psychologists use a wide variety of methods for systematically gathering objective and reliable information about human behavior. These methods range from laboratory experiments to nationwide surveys.

8. The subjects in a psychological study may be chosen on the basis of appropriateness, convenience (most subjects are college students), and the nature of the problem being studied. The *sample*, or group of subjects representing a larger population, may range from a single person to thousands. Animal subjects are widely used in psychological research, but the applicability of results to humans depends greatly on the aspect of behavior being studied.

9. Psychologists must narrow down the focus of their study; they may choose to measure overt behavior, to record physiological responses, or to gather self-reports in the form of interviews, questionnaires, or tests. Often more than one type of measure is used in examining a single phenomenon.

10. Research may take place in a variety of settings, from different types of laboratories to factories, parks, and subways. Because the laboratory is an artificial environment, it is often difficult to be sure that subjects are behaving "normally" there.

11. *Descriptive studies* are primarily concerned with observing and recording subjects' behavior or self-reports.

12. *Correlational studies* are those in which a researcher tries to discover a relationship between two factors by measuring each separately and comparing the results. A limitation of such studies is that a high correlation does not necessarily imply that one factor has caused the other.

13. In an *experiment,* the researcher exerts direct control over one factor (the *independent variable*) to see what effect, if any, it will have on another factor (the *dependent variable*). The group for whom the independent variable is being manipulated is called the *experimental group;* the results for the experimental group are then compared with those for a second group, called the *control group.*

14. One problem in psychological research is the influence of *experimenter expectancy effects.* It seems that if a researcher expects an experiment to turn out a certain way, that expectation can subtly influence the outcome of the experiment.

15. *Basic research* is work that aims to advance our understanding of behavior without any immediate concern for its practical implications. *Applied research* attempts, from the outset, to help solve a practical problem. The *practice* of psychology involves making direct applications of psychological knowledge.

16. Psychology contains numerous subfields, each devoted to research and practice of psychology in a specific area. However, a working psychologist is likely to draw from many of the subdisciplines in doing her own work. In addition, nearly one-fourth of all psychologists are principally teachers of the discipline.

17. Psychology is a growing field, with more and more professionals joining the ranks each year. The majority of psychologists work in educational institutions; most others work in government and business jobs. Psychologists generally have an M.A. or Ph.D. degree, whereas psychiatrists are M.D.s.

PARASCIENCE

Psychology is based on the traditional approaches and methods of science, including the systematic gathering of data, putting hypotheses to careful tests, and the cumulative building of knowledge. But there are alternative ways of looking at human behavior that are not based on such a scientific view of reality. The worlds of mysticism and the occult, for example, begin with a set of premises that differ sharply from those of the scientific world. Such alternative views are often referred to as being "pseudoscientific" or "parascientific." We prefer the term *parascience* (the prefix *para-* meaning "beside or apart from") to the traditional derogatory label *pseudoscience* (meaning "false science").

One reason we prefer the term *parascience* is that it is not always as easy as one might suppose to distinguish "real science" from "false science." After all, every

What is "accepted science" shifts over time.

accepted scientific principle started out as an unorthodox thought in the mind of some person. Scientists laughed at the germ theory of disease when it was first proposed in the nineteenth century, but now it is taken for granted. Astrono-

mers are now making serious attempts to listen for signals from intelligent beings in other galaxies, an idea that would have been ridiculed a dozen years ago. And there is currently debate among psychologists as to the possible existence of extrasensory perception, although it remains beyond the bounds of accepted science (see the Psychological Issue following Chapter 4). As James Trefil (1978) points out, what is "accepted science" shifts over time. Ideas that are on the outer fringes of science sometimes become the next decade's research frontiers, and some of this research, such as Einstein's work on relativity, moves on to a position of universal scientific acceptance.

The realm of parascience is often difficult for scientists to treat in an objective, impartial manner. The authors of this book, like other psychologists, have accumulated certain convictions over the years about the approaches that can legitimately be taken toward human behavior. We label these convictions "scholarly conclusions." But those who disagree with us might call them "personal biases." So as you read the rest of this Psychological Issue, subtract what you take to be the authors' personal bias, and keep your own mind open. And keep your skepticism about what you read, with the possibility in mind that those of us who have gone before you

have figured it out all wrong. After all, history teaches us with great certainty that the "facts" of the year 2000 or 2050 will not be the same as the "facts" of the early 1980s. What we would urge most, however, is that you retain a healthy respect for the search for the facts, as opposed to unsubstantiated claims.

In discussing some of the parasciences concerned with human behavior, we'll begin with one that has seen its day and is no longer in vogue: phrenology. Then we'll turn to three parasciences that currently enjoy a great deal of popularity: graphology, biorhythms, and astrology.

PHRENOLOGY
Phrenology is the study of personality characteristics through examination of the bumps and hollows of the skull. It is based on the idea that the shape and size of the various parts of the growing brain represent the overdevelopment or underdevelopment of specific personality traits.

The discipline of phrenology began in the early nineteenth century with Franz Joseph Gall (1758–1828). He was curious about a possible relationship between the physical characteristics and psychological traits of people. After examining the skulls of his friends and of imprisoned criminals, he came up with a list of 37 powers or propensities (from combativeness to marvelousness) that could be equated to specific areas of the brain, as reflected in bumps on the skull (see the Poster on page 34).

By 1840 phrenology had become a popular craze, offering a quick, "scientific," inexpensive way to get vocational guidance and assure happiness. There were phrenology parlors scattered across the country, and traveling phrenologists crisscrossed the nation on lecture tours. Phrenology had a reasonable

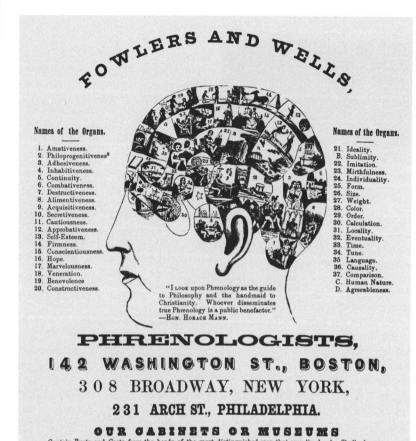

has suggested that graphology would be useful in hiring personnel, evaluating therapy patients, helping young people choose careers, and making medical diagnoses. In our view, however, these claims are vastly overstated. Graphology is more of an art than a science, and it is not an art that is likely to yield particularly accurate results.

This is not to say that people's handwriting is totally unrelated to their personalities and emotional styles. Recent studies have suggested, for example, that the size of people's signatures is positively related to their status and self-esteem. The more confident people feel about themselves, the larger their signatures tend to be (Zweigenhaft, 1977). John Hancock, whose signature on the Declaration of Independence was twice as big as anyone else's, certainly seemed to be a man with a mighty ego.

> **The size of people's signatures is related to their status and self-esteem.**

When research on handwriting is done systematically and objectively, it becomes a legitimate part of the science of psychology. But most of the practice of graphology is not based on systematic research. The reliance of graphologists and their clients on handwriting analysis seems to be based on faith, rather than on objective evidence. But although the evidence is weak, the faith remains strong. As Anthony puts it, "The 'easy art' of handwriting analysis has answered the needs of the drawing room psychologizers who seek a dramatic new path to personal popularity" (1967, page 76).

ring to it in that day and age, even though today's scientists reject the notion that the brain is like a muscle that becomes weak or strong depending on how much it is exercised.

GRAPHOLOGY

Graphology is another method that purports to provide insight into personality—this time by handwriting analysis. The possibility that people's personality is revealed in their handwriting is plausible enough to many people to encourage them to obtain—for a fee—a personal analysis from a graphologist. Some business organizations have also made use of such analyses. Indeed, the practitioners of graphology have made astonishing claims about its uses. One modern advocate, Daniel Anthony (1967),

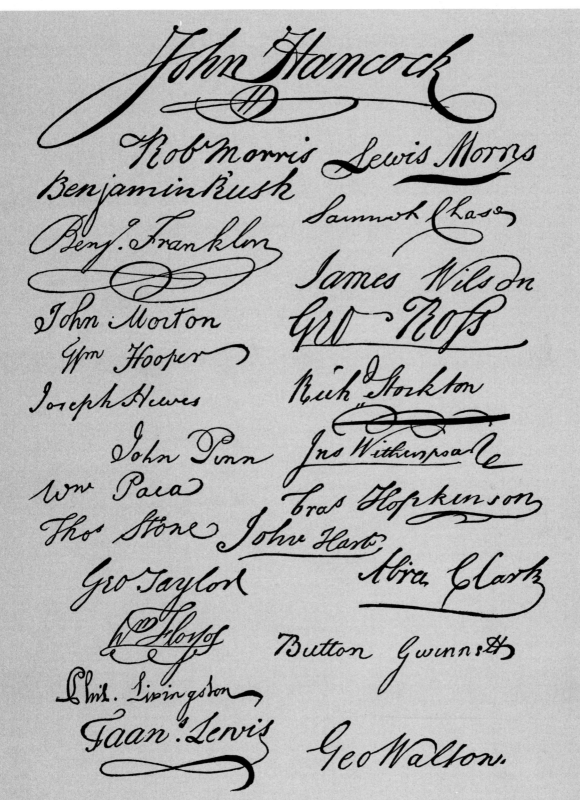

Each of us—including these signers of the Declaration of Independence—has a distinctive handwriting style that may reveal something about our personality.

BIORHYTHMS

Don't get *biorhythms* and *biological rhythms* confused with each other. *Biological rhythm* is a general term referring to a wide variety of cyclic variations in biological systems, such as the wake-sleep cycle and the menstrual cycle. Biological rhythms are real, and we'll discuss them in the Psychological Issue for Chapter 2. *Biorhythms,* on the other hand, is a popular fad that sometimes purports to be "scientific" but really is—and here go our personal biases again—a lot of malarkey.

Biorhythms theory was first developed in the late nineteenth century by Wilhelm Fliess, a nose-and-throat specialist and acquaintance of Sigmund Freud. This theory is based on the assumption that there are three important biological rhythms: a 23-day "male" or physical rhythm, a 28-day "female" or emotional rhythm, and a 33-day intellectual rhythm. Everyone is supposed to be influenced by all three of these rhythms, which are said to begin at birth and to continue uninterrupted until death. You can calculate whether you are at a high or low point on one or more of the rhythms simply by counting the number of days since your birth. As a result of the growth of the biorhythm fad in recent years, you can even buy a calculator that will compute your biorhythms for you.

Unfortunately, there is no scientific evidence for the whole idea. Yes, we *do* have mood cycles. For women, mood swings may sometimes correspond to the menstrual cycle, and there is some evidence for comparable sorts of emotional rhythms among men. But there is no good reason to believe that such cycles are as regular as the proponents of biorhythms would have it or that such cycles begin at the moment of birth.

"So," you ask, "what about all the research *proving* the importance of biorhythms?" You may have seen headlines reading something like "Japanese Bus Drivers Have Fewer Accidents When Warned of Critical Days." Unfortunately, this kind of study doesn't prove anything, except maybe that workers will be more careful when they are warned to be. Sure, accidents were reduced when workers were warned on critical days, but accidents would probably be reduced just as much if they were warned on *noncritical* days. There have been some systematic attempts to compare people's biorhythms with past events, including deaths, recuperative time after operations, professional golfers' scores (Holmes et al., 1980), performances in baseball and boxing (Louis, 1978), and aircraft accidents (Woolcott et al., 1977). The evidence from such studies is uniformly negative.

Still, biorhythms are touted as the key to health and riches. Nationwide best sellers have been written about them, and gamblers are supposed to bet by them. "My uncle went to Las Vegas on one of his 'up' days and won a bundle," says psychologist Joseph Dewhirst (1979). "But he went back on the next 'up' day and lost it all. It looks like the only way to make money using biorhythms theory is to write a book about it."

ASTROLOGY

The belief that the planets and stars exert an influence on human behavior and events has been entertained for at least as long as recorded history. And today many thousands of people look past their morning newspaper's headlines, even past the sports page, to first check their horoscopes for the day. Depending upon their "sign"—which, in turn, depends on their birthdate (Aquarians were

born between January 20 and February 18; Pisces between February 19 and March 20, and so on)—they will receive advice to guide them in their day's activities:

Take time for a long talk with associates.
Don't act in too forceful a manner with superiors.
Use tact in handling a personal matter.
Get in touch with a neglected friend in the evening.

Sound a little like Chinese fortune cookies? The basic principle is the same. Each of the twelve messages, one for each birth sign, contains advice that would be suitable for almost anyone in almost any circumstances. The horoscopes are sufficiently vague to be highly applicable to most people. Most of us, for example, have a neglected friend somewhere in our lives, a personal matter that requires tact, and a superior who doesn't take well to being pushed around.

Thousands of people begin their day by checking their horoscopes.

Most people who consult their horoscope every day don't take it too seriously and certainly don't think there is anything "scientific" about it. Many astrologers believe their work has a scientific basis, however, and they demand to be taken seriously. They point out that some rhythms on earth are clearly caused by forces emanating from the sun (our day-night rhythms) and from the moon (the rhythm of the tides). And they take that link to its "logical" conclusion: Heavenly bodies influence more than a few limited aspects of life on earth; in fact, they influence *all* of them (Gauquelin, 1969).

Horoscope

Millions of people begin their day by reading their horoscope in the morning newspaper.

There is, to be sure, little evidence for these claims. Systematic attempts by psychologists to check out astrological predictions have repeatedly yielded negative results. Nevertheless, there are at least a handful of psychologists who are unwilling to write off the claims of astrologers altogether. For example, one recent study—published in a respected British psychological journal—reported significant correlations between people's personalities (whether they were extroverted or introverted) and the positions of the planets at their birth (Gauquelin, Eysenck, and Eysenck, 1979). Most psychologists would probably regard this result as a fluke. But maybe, just maybe . . .

THE APPEAL OF PARASCIENCE

The appeal of parasciences such as biorhythms and astrology does not really seem to depend on their scientific credibility. Rather, the popularity of these parasciences seems to reflect needs that run deep in many of us. There have always been people who like to believe that control of their lives is out of their own hands, that the ultimate responsibility lies elsewhere—whether in our "rhythms" or in the stars. These people have consulted ouija boards, tarot cards, the I Ching, and horoscopes for clues about what these outside forces have planned. There are also people who want to believe that we are not alone in the universe, that there are forces beyond us that somehow impinge upon us. This need to believe that we are not alone may also help to explain the recent resurgence of interest in UFOs (as shown in the popularity of such films as *Close Encounters of the Third Kind*) and in the possibility of communicating with beings from distant planets.

The parasciences seem to reflect needs that run deep in many of us.

Part of the appeal of the parasciences may be the fact that they are *not* scientific—that their "predictions" cannot be accounted for in terms of accepted scientific principles. As Trefil (1978) writes, "Pseudoscience has been around at least as long as (and perhaps even longer than) conventional science. Perhaps it serves some deep need of human beings to believe that there is still some mystery—something unknown—left in life."

SUMMARY

1. The *parasciences* are alternative ways of looking at reality that are not based in science. It is difficult to examine the parasciences objectively.

2. *Phrenology*, the study of personality via examination of the bumps and hollows of a person's skull, was a popular fad in the 1800s.

3. *Graphology*, or handwriting analysis, is not typically based on systematic research and is more a matter of faith between graphologist and client.

4. According to *biorhythms* theory, our lives are influenced by three biological cycles. However, there is no scientific evidence to support this theory.

5. *Astrology*, the belief that our lives are influenced by the stars and planets under which we were born, has not been proved to have a scientific basis.

Chapter 2

The Brain and Nervous System

Compared to our animal neighbors, we human beings are creatures of modest physical endowment. We have a poor sense of smell, just average hearing, only passable vision, thin skin, weak jaws and teeth, unimpressive muscular strength, middling running speed, and so-so stamina. Our one saving grace, the one that distinguishes us from the rest of the animals and allows us to master our environment, is the human brain.

This remarkable organ allows human beings to do things unparalleled in the animal kingdom: create works of art, compose symphonies, build machines, communicate by means of highly abstract forms of language, wrestle with mathematical problems, contemplate the meaning of life, and, not least of all, explore the mysteries of the brain itself.

Most of us have not thought much at all about our brains, since we seldom think of any part of the body unless it malfunctions. A headache makes us acutely aware of the housing that holds our brain; the pain from touching a hot pan makes us well aware of the nerve endings in our fingertips. But the brain and the nervous system function at all times—not only at those moments that strike our awareness. Our thoughts, our emotions, our actions are all governed by processes occurring in the brain.

The brain is the central part of the nervous system, the complex apparatus that provides the mysterious links between the "mind," the body, and behavior. These links were once considered to be in the domain of religion or philosophy and not a proper subject for scientists to study. But now biologists and psychologists have gotten up the nerve (if you'll forgive the pun) to examine these links, and they

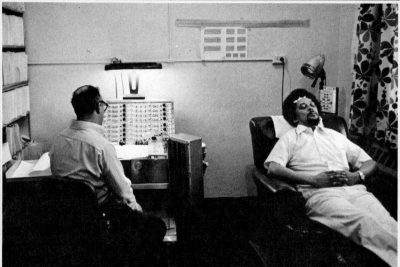

have already discovered a great deal about how brain functioning influences behavior and experience.

We will begin by surveying the structure of the entire nervous system, then we will narrow our focus to examine the smallest part of the nervous system, the individual nerve cell (*neuron*) and the way in which messages travel through the system from one neuron to another. Then we will turn our attention to the central switchboard, the brain itself.

THE NERVOUS SYSTEM

The human nervous system is a marvelously complicated network of pathways that allow us to receive information from the outside world; to learn, think, feel, and plan; and to speak, write, and act.

The Divisions of the Nervous System

The human nervous system consists of two main subdivisions: the central nervous system and the peripheral nervous system (see Figure 2.1). The *central nervous system* consists of the brain and spinal cord and is the place where information processing occurs. The *peripheral nervous system* supplies the inputs and outputs for the central nervous system. The peripheral nervous system consists primarily of two types of nerve cells: those that carry messages from the sense organs to the spinal cord and brain (called *afferent*, or sensory,

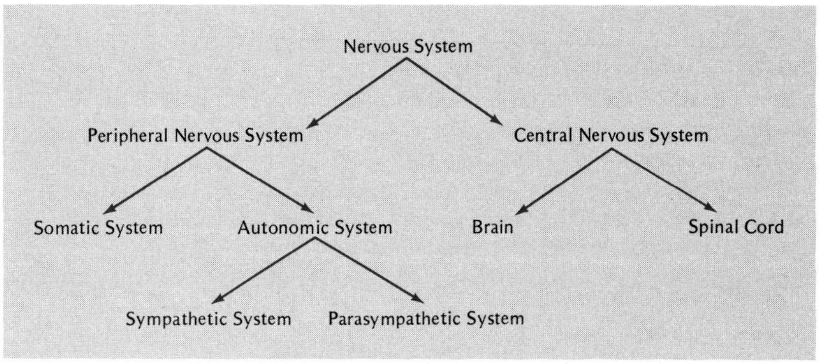

FIGURE 2.1
The divisions of the nervous system.

neurons) and those that carry messages from the brain and spinal cord to the muscles and glands (called *efferent,* or motor, *neurons*). In addition to afferent neurons and efferent neurons, there are neurons that make connections between incoming and outgoing messages. These are called *association neurons.* Most of the nerve cells in the brain are association neurons.

The functions of these three types of neurons can be seen in a typical reflex action, such as the knee-jerk response. A *reflex* is an automatic response that occurs without the involvement of higher centers in the brain. When your knee is hit with a heavy object, sensory neurons carry the message directly to the *spinal cord,* a large bundle of fibers running through the hollow center of the backbone. The spinal cord functions primarily as a pathway for nerve impulses traveling from the outlying portions of the body to the brain. But in a simple reflex, association neurons in the spinal cord receive the message from the sensory neurons and immediately initiate a response. Motor neurons carry the message to the muscles of body in which the reflex will occur—for example, the leg muscles that cause the knee to jerk (Figure 2.2). Because there is no brain involvement, the reflex response is quick and uncontrolled. But any more complex actions must involve the brain.

As Figure 2.1 shows, the peripheral nervous system can be divided into the *somatic nervous system,* which controls voluntary movements, and the *autonomic nervous system,* which governs glands and involuntary muscles. Of special interest to many psychologists is the autonomic nervous system, because it is intimately involved in many of our emotional reactions. The autonomic system has two parts: the *sympathetic* branch and the *parasympathetic* branch. Both branches are involved in controlling the glands and blood vessels in the body, but they have opposite actions (see Figure 2.3). The sympathetic division is most active whenever the body is under stress. It causes the heart to pound, the pupils to enlarge, digestion to stop, breathing to increase, and blood to rush to muscles. The parasympathetic division, on the other hand, sends messages that reduce the emergency reaction. It signals the heart to beat a little slower, the pupils to contract, the stomach muscles to relax and resume digestion, and breathing to slow down. Thus, the sympathetic system arouses the body, while the parasympathetic calms it down. Just before the start of a race, for example, a runner's sympathetic

FIGURE 2.2

An example of a reflex. Receptors in the knee send a message to the spinal cord that the knee has been struck. Association neurons in the spinal cord receive the signal and relay it to motor neurons, which in turn carry a message to the muscles of the leg, causing the knee to jerk.

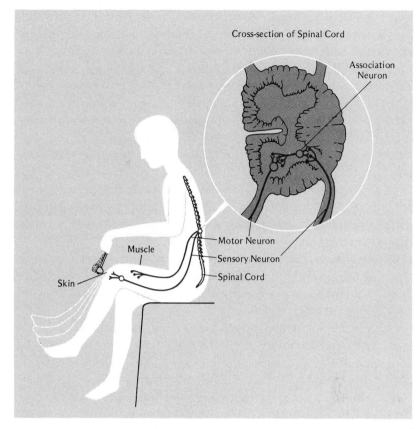

FIGURE 2.3

The sympathetic and parasympathetic divisions of the autonomic nervous system have opposing effects in many parts of the body.

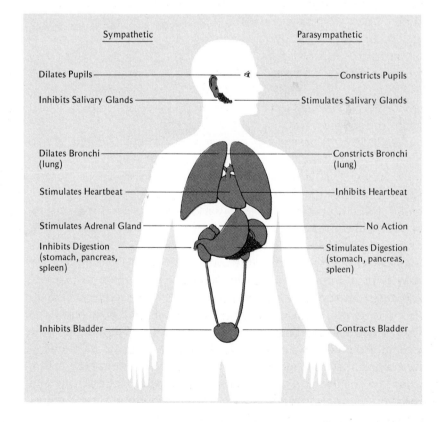

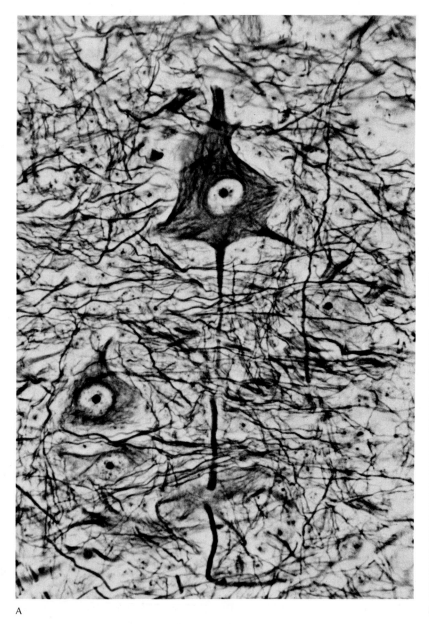

A

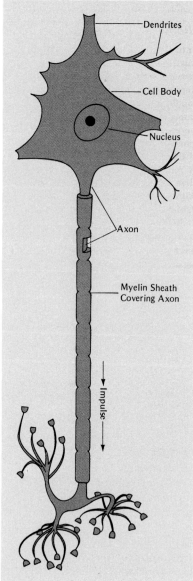

B

FIGURE 2.4

(A) A neuron as seen through a
powerful microscope. (B) Schematic
drawing of a neuron showing the
cell body, axon, and dendrites. The
myelin sheath is a fatty tissue that
covers the axon and enhances its
ability to carry electrical messages.

system will be especially active. After the race is over, the parasympathetic will come to the fore. How these systems relate to emotion is
discussed in Chapter 7.

One way in which the autonomic nervous system affects the
body is by stimulating organs in the *endocrine system* to produce
hormones. The endocrine glands are organs that secrete chemicals
directly into the bloodstream. These chemicals (the hormones) can
directly influence body functions and behaviors. For example, the
adrenal glands (located on top of the kidneys), release *adrenalin,* a
hormone that helps to activate the body in times of stress. The male's
testes and the female's ovaries produce hormones (testosterone and
estrogen) that play a vital role in sexual behavior and reproduction,
as well as contributing to the physical differences between men and
women. And hormones produced in the pituitary and thyroid glands
control body metabolism and growth.

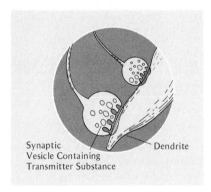

Synaptic
Vesicle Containing
Transmitter Substance

Dendrite

FIGURE 2.5

Schematic drawing of a synapse. Synaptic knobs at the end of the terminal branches of axons contain chemical transmitter substances. When a message travels along the axon, these knobs are stimulated to release their chemicals into the tiny gap between the knob and the cell membrane of another neuron. These chemicals make the receiving neuron either more or less likely to fire.

Nerves and Their Messages

When we talk about the various divisions of the nervous system we are actually talking about an immense network of interacting nerve fibers continuously carrying messages throughout the body. How do these messages get from one part of the body to another?

To understand this process of neural transmission, we must first look at an individual neuron. A neuron consists of three principal parts: the *cell body*, which contains the nucleus; the *dendrites*, which are short fibers that project from the cell body and that receive messages from nearby cells; and the *axon*, a longer fiber that extends away from one side of the cell body and transmits messages to other neurons or to muscles and glands (see Figure 2.4). While all neurons have these general features, they differ greatly in their dimensions. A neuron in the spinal cord may have an axon 2 or 3 feet long, whereas neurons in the brain may be as short as a few thousandths of an inch.

Nerve messages normally move in one direction—from the dendrites and the cell body along the axon to the dendrites or cell body of the next neuron or to a muscle or gland. Messages are transmitted in two ways: along the surface of a single neuron and from one neuron to another. Transmission along a neuron's surface is called *axonal transmission;* transmission between neurons is called *synaptic transmission.*

In axonal transmission, an electrical impulse is sent from one end of the neuron to the other, and the neuron is said to have *fired.* Each axon requires a certain minimum level of stimulation before it will fire. If the stimulus, whether from a sense organ or from other neurons, does not reach this minimum level, the neuron will not fire. But once a stimulus is strong enough to cause the neuron to fire, it will fire completely. This is called the *all-or-none principle.* In some ways it is like the firing of a gun. You must pull the trigger hard enough to fire, but pulling harder on the trigger will not cause the bullet to travel any faster or any farther.

Once a neuron has fired, synaptic transmission can occur. A microscopic gap separates the end of each axon from the dendrite or cell body of another neuron. This tiny space is called a *synapse* (see Figure 2.5). When an impulse reaches the tip of an axon, it causes a chemical *transmitter substance* to be released. This substance crosses the synapse and gives a message to the next neuron. This message may be *excitatory,* increasing the likelihood that the next neuron will fire, or *inhibitory,* decreasing the likelihood of such firing. In either case, the effect is that a message is communicated from one neuron to the next. Nerve cells are not usually hooked up in a single chain, however. Especially in the brain, it is common for one neuron to receive messages from hundreds of other neurons simultaneously (see Box 1). The rate at which any one nerve cell will fire depends on the sum total of all the excitatory and inhibitory signals reaching it at any point in time.

One of the current frontiers in brain research is the exploration of the chemical transmitter substances that carry messages between neurons. We will discuss some of this research after we have examined the basic structure and functions of the brain.

— Box 1 —

The brain and the computer

In our modern age, it is fashionable to liken the human brain to a computer—in the words of a recent advertisement for a book about the brain, "the most complex, sophisticated and powerful computer on earth." This analogy has a good deal of intuitive appeal. Both the brain and the computer receive information (or *input*), process this information rapidly, and produce responses (*output*). For many of us, thinking of the brain as a computer may make this mysterious organ seem just a bit more comprehensible.

But whereas the analogy between the brain and the computer has its appeal, it is also likely to be misleading. Recent brain research has made it clear that there are some fundamental differences between the operations of the brain and those of the computer. F. H. C. Crick (1979), a Nobel Prize-winning biologist who has recently turned to the study of the brain, has summarized some of these differences:

In a computer, information is processed at a staggeringly rapid rate, and the process is *serial*—that is, messages are sent one at a time from one point to another. In the brain, the rate of transmission is slower, but the information can be handled on millions of channels *in parallel*. That is, as part of any one mental act, millions of neurons may be sending messages in millions of directions, all at the same time.

The components of a modern computer are extremely reliable—they almost always work precisely as they are supposed to—but removing even one or two of them can ruin an entire calculation. The neurons of the brain are less reliable, but the deletion of quite a few of them

Can the human brain really be compared to a computer?

is unlikely to make much of a difference.

Whereas the computer makes use of a very strict and inflexible electronic code, the brain is much less precise and more flexible in its operations. The brain is apparently able to adjust the number and complexity of its own synapses in order to adapt its operations to its needs.

Because of fundamental differences such as these, the brain and the computer are best suited for

rather different sorts of functions. A computer can far surpass the brain in performing intricate mathematical computations. Computers can even be programmed to play chess at a higher level than any but the most skilled human chessplayers. But the brain can recognize faces and patterns in ways no existing computer can begin to approach. And the brain can make judgments, exercise imagination, and even reflect on itself in ways that will forever be beyond the computer's reach.

THE BRAIN

At first glance the brain may seem an unlikely candidate for its role as commander-in-chief of the entire nervous system. It has the consistency of soft cheese, and with its many convolutions and ridges it looks and feels something like a giant walnut. But in cellular terms the brain is impressive. The human brain is believed to contain about 100 billion nerve cells—about the same number as the stars in our galaxy (Stevens, 1979). It also contains perhaps ten times as many *glia*—cells that provide nourishment and support for the neurons. In proportion to body weight, the human brain is the largest of all brains, with the dolphin in second place. For the sake of comparison, a dog, a gorilla, and a human all of the same body size would have brains of one-half, one, and three pounds, respectively.

The human brain is made up of many structures, including the brain stem, the cerebellum, the limbic system, and the cerebral cortex. Before we describe the roles of these parts of the brain, however, we will examine some of the techniques scientists have used to find out about these roles.

Unlocking the Brain

The brain is a difficult organ to study. It is locked up inside a bony skull and is protected by several layers of membrane and cushioning fluid. In the early days of brain study, the brains of lower animals or of humans were removed after death and sliced into sections for examination. Such studies helped reveal the brain's basic anatomy. However, since then a variety of techniques have been developed to help us learn more about the functioning of the brain.

One important technique involves *electrical stimulation* of parts of the brain to discover their specific functions. Most of these studies have been done with animals (see Box 2). In the 1940s and 1950s, however, important work on mapping the human brain was con-

Remote control of the brain

Would you stand in a bullring without cape or sword while an enraged bull charged at you? You might if you were José Delgado and if you had a radio transmitter that could send a "stop" message to the bull through electrodes implanted in its brain. Although it may sound like science fiction, Delgado has demonstrated that *electrical stimulation of the brain (ESB)* can be done by remote control and can be used to direct an animal's behavior.

Delgado's method of ESB involves drilling a small hole in the skull of an animal, introducing tiny electrode wires into precise, preplanned locations of the brain, and connecting the wires to sockets anchored in the skull. Some of the chimpanzees Delgado first used as subjects have had up to 100 electrodes implanted for more than four years. Each wire is attached to a generator capable of transmitting minute electrical im-

José Delgado used his radio transmitter to stop the charge of a raging bull.

ducted by Wilder Penfield (1959) and his colleagues at the Montreal Neurological Institute. During brain surgery, specific parts of the cerebral cortex were stimulated with tiny electrodes while the patients—who remained conscious—reported what they felt. Depending upon which point was stimulated, a patient might report a tingling in his mouth, in his hand, or in his foot. Such studies using electrical stimulation with both animals and humans have taught us most of what we know about which locations in the brain are responsible for specific sensory and motor functions.

The study of people with *brain damage*—from injury, tumors, or strokes—has also provided important clues to brain function. Because these people usually suffer damage to only a limited area of the brain, the nature of the resulting impairment can help us to discover the function of the damaged area. Studies with animals have also

pulses to the brain. Depending on the placement of the electrodes, a chimp can be made to open or shut its eyes, turn its head, hop, yawn, sneeze, stick out its tongue, or flex its limbs, merely at the flick of a switch.

Delgado has developed what he calls the *stimoceiver*, a 1-ounce transmitter-receiver capable of stimulating the brain by remote radio command and recording the electrical activity of the brain. The stimoceiver is small enough to be carried on a monkey's collar or under a human patient's head bandage. And recently Delgado and his colleagues (1975) have developed a stimoceiver that can be implanted under an animal's skin and still receive and send back signals reliably.

The bullring escapade was the most dramatic of Delgado's remote-control demonstrations. In another experiment, one monkey in a colony learned to activate the radio stimulator to inhibit the aggressiveness of the mean-tempered boss-monkey of the group. However, neither of these experiments implies that there is actually an "aggression center" in the brain that can be controlled. Rather, as Eliot Valenstein (1978) makes clear, a behavior as complex as

aggression involves many parts of the brain, not just one location. What the stimulation *does* do is cause a repetitive turning or circling movement. The bull may not be any more or less "aggressive" than before, but as long as it keeps circling, it cannot charge at Delgado.

ESB may be good for more than entertaining demonstrations. For example, physicians are now using implanted electrodes to help control pain, epileptic seizures, and certain spastic muscle contractions. These treatments are new and controversial, but some success has been reported (Valenstein, 1978). One possibility being explored is computer-controlled feedback. A patient with epilepsy, for example, could have a stimoceiver installed in the brain that would send signals to a faraway computer. When brain activity of a preseizure sort begins to appear, the computer would react by sending radio signals to the brain that would counteract the seizure.

The development of such new techniques for ESB suggests exciting future possibilities. Delgado speculates that ESB might be used to restore the "vision" or "hearing" of blind or deaf patients

by sending information about the world directly to sensory areas of the brain (Delgado et al., 1975). Even more futuristically, Delgado conjures up the possibility that direct brain-to-brain communication between individuals might be established, through the use of stimoceivers implanted in each person's scalp. In such a future, two people speaking about being on "the same wavelength" might mean it literally.

For all its exciting prospects, ESB also makes many of us uneasy about the idea of some people controlling other people's minds. As ESB technology becomes more fully developed, we will need to have ethical and legal safeguards against exploitive use of these techniques. At the same time, we should keep in mind the limitations of ESB. As Delgado notes, electricity is only a monotonous, nonspecific stimulus; it cannot itself create ideas or emotions. "Language, beliefs, and culture in general are learned through the eyes and ears but cannot be introduced into the brain by wires and electronics. . . . Electrical stimulation may activate patterns of response already in the brain, but it cannot create them" (Delgado et al., 1975, page 272).

made use of *brain surgery*, in which specific areas of the brain are destroyed or removed. Brain surgery has occasionally been resorted to in humans as well, for treating people with severe neurological disorders, such as uncontrollable seizures. By observing people who have undergone such surgery, researchers have been able to determine some of the effects of tampering with particular parts of the brain.

Another method of studying the brain relies on its electrical activity. It has been known since 1875 that the brain has a small fluctuating electric field. But it wasn't until the 1920s that scientists learned to amplify the brain's electrical activity and record it on graph paper. When such brain recordings, or *electroencephalograms* (EEGs), are examined, they reveal regular fluctuations in patterns that change in a consistent manner, depending on what the person is doing or think-

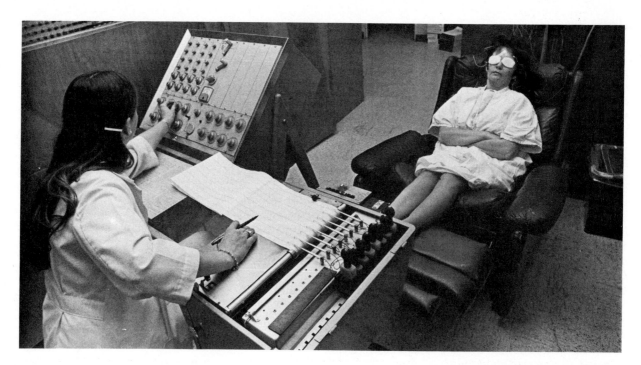

ing. We now call these rhythmic fluctuations of brain impulses *brain waves*. There are four basic brain waves—called alpha, beta, theta, and delta waves—each with a characteristic pattern that shows up on the EEG. Although none of these waves is ever emitted exclusively by the brain at any one time, one wave may be more pronounced than the others (see Box 3).

Brain waves can be detected by electrodes attached to a person's forehead or skull. Examination of the EEG patterns allows doctors to determine whether an individual's brain waves indicate brain tumors or epilepsy, and psychologists can use EEG readings to learn about dreams, sleep, and other states of consciousness (see Chapter 3).

Although brain waves provide us with reflections of the activity of the brain, they do not provide direct information about specific brain structures. In recent years researchers have been developing new techniques for monitoring the activity of specific brain areas. For example, microelectrodes can be implanted in an animal's brain to record the firing patterns of individual neurons as the animal engages in different behaviors. With humans, new techniques make it possible to monitor the activity of specific portions of the brain from outside the skull. In one such procedure a radioactive substance is injected into the brain's blood supply. The amount of blood flowing to different parts of the brain can be precisely measured as the subjects perform different activities (see the photograph on page 50). This *blood-flow measurement* provides a good indicator of the functioning of these parts of the brain, because the more activity in any part of the brain—that is, the more frequently its nerve cells are firing—the more blood it needs to provide oxygen to support the activity (Lassen, Ingvar, and Skinhøj, 1978). Another new technique, called *positron-emission tomography* (or *PET*), monitors the activity of the sugar glucose in different parts of the working brain; the more active a part of the brain, the more glucose is used in that area.

Brain waves are measured by an electroencephalograph (EEG) machine, which creates a printout that can be examined. Having an EEG made is a simple and painless process.

BRAIN WAVES ON MADISON AVENUE

As scientists learn more about how to assess the brain's activity, men and women in the advertising business have been interested in putting this research to use. The *evoked potential* is a computer-derived average of the brain waves produced in response to a particular stimulus. Advertising researchers have begun to make use of the evoked potential as an index of a person's interest in commercials that are being tested. For example, one airline recently used the test to measure people's reactions to film clips of twenty-five British actors and actresses. The one who stimulated the most brain arousal presumably had an inside track for a job in the airline's commercials (Goleman, 1979).

— *Box 3* ——————————————————

Biofeedback

There has been an enormous interest in recent years in the phenomenon of *biofeedback*—the use of electronic devices to amplify various physiological measures so that the individual can monitor and perhaps alter certain aspects of body functioning. For example, biofeedback is used in monitoring heart rate and blood pressure (see Chapter 5, Box 1).

Some of the most interesting studies with biofeedback have involved efforts to control brain waves. Electrodes are attached to the subject's skull, and changes in brain waves are indicated by signals in the instruments (such as a sound or a light) that can allow a person to identify internal changes and perhaps to learn to control them. Just as you learn to ride a bicycle by feeling your body move and correcting your movements to keep balance, so people in these experiments learn to relax and alter their brain waves by getting feedback from an EEG machine (Luce and Peper, 1971). Using EEG readings to guide them, biofeedback experimenters are trying to teach people to shift the brain from states of high alertness to states of rest.

To try to determine the emotional states associated with different brain waves, Barbara Brown (1970) devised an experiment in which she used lights of three colors to represent three different kinds of brain waves. Whenever a person was producing alpha waves, for example, a blue

light would shine. Brown then asked twenty-six subjects to write down their feelings as they observed each color. She found that most of the subjects described their experience during the alpha state as pleasant and tranquil, while in the beta state many of the subjects reported feelings of anger, fear, and excitement. In the rarer theta state, only a few of the people could identify definite feelings, although eight subjects indicated that their minds were involved in some sort of problem-solving process. (The fourth type of brain wave, delta, was not tested, because it is found only in deep sleep and the minds of infants.)

Over a decade ago, studies such as Brown's showed that people can be trained to produce either an increase or decrease in alpha waves. It has been claimed that these increases are associated

with a pleasant, relaxed state of consciousness, much like states of meditation (see the Psychological Issue for Chapter 3). However, more recent studies have shown that some people experience increased alpha waves as unpleasant, rather than pleasant, and that it is possible to feel anxious even when in a high alpha state (Orne and Wilson, 1978).

Brain wave biofeedback may have some beneficial uses. For example, it has been introduced as a treatment for epilepsy, a condition in which people are likely to have uncontrollable seizures. M. B. Sterman (1978) has found that epileptics have a deficiency in a certain pattern of brain waves called the "sensorimotor rhythm." Although the results of studies are not entirely consistent, it appears that training epileptics to produce these brain waves can in some cases control their seizures.

Our current understanding of the structure and function of the brain relies on a combination of all these techniques for unlocking the brain. Our understanding still remains incomplete and preliminary, however. Because of the current explosion in research on the brain, and especially the continued development of techniques to study the human brain as it does its work, we can expect to learn much more about the brain's functions in the 1980s.

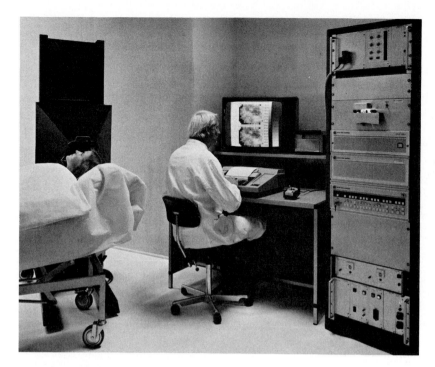

The equipment used for blood-flow measurement. A saline solution containing a harmless radioactive isotope is injected into the subject's carotid artery, which carries blood to the brain. Radiation detectors located in the box behind the subject's head record the arrival of the isotope in the cortex and its progress through the brain. A computer analyzes the recordings and displays the results on a color TV screen.

The Structure of the Brain

The human brain is composed of four basic sets of structures: the brain stem, cerebellum, limbic system, and cerebral cortex (see Figure 2.6). At the base of the brain lies the *brain stem*. From an evolutionary point of view, the brain stem is the "oldest" part of the brain. In lower animals, whose behaviors are largely automatic and instinctive, the brain stem structures make up virtually the entire brain. In humans, the brain stem also concerns itself with automatic functions, as well as with the "gut reaction" aspect of emotion. The brain stem comprises several connected structures. The *medulla*, for example, lies at the bottom of the brain stem. It controls such basic physical rhythms as heartbeat and breathing, and it contains the reflex centers for vomiting, sneezing, coughing, and swallowing. The *hypothalamus*, located higher in the brain stem, monitors the automatic aspects of such behaviors as eating, drinking, sexual activity, and sleeping, and it plays a role in such emotions as rage, terror, and pleasure.

The *cerebellum* is positioned behind the brain stem and is largely concerned with automatic control of body position and motion. For example, it monitors the tension of arm muscles and keeps track of where the arm is in relation to the rest of the body and its surroundings. When you make a conscious effort to move your arm, the cerebellum acts as an intermediary between command and execution, translating the order into a series of specific motor impulses that results in a coordinated and controlled movement. A patient with damage to the cerebellum will have a hard time getting a cup of coffee to his mouth without spilling it (Restak, 1979).

The *limbic system* is a set of structures attached to the bottom of the cerebral cortex. Only mammals have a limbic system. Although its functions are not well understood, it appears to be involved with

FIGURE 2.6

A cross-section of the brain showing some of its major structures: the brain stem, cerebellum, limbic system, and cerebral cortex.

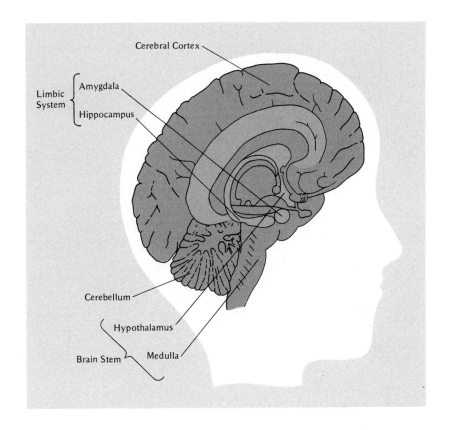

emotional expression. Electrical stimulation of one limbic structure, the *amygdala,* can cause "sham rage" in animals—frenzied displays of aggression without apparent cause. Removal of the amygdala can have the opposite effect. A naturally wild animal such as the lynx can become as gentle as a kitten after having the amygdala surgically destroyed. The amygdala seems to have similar functions in humans. In a few cases, brain disorders causing both seizures and violent behavior have been linked to abnormalities of the amygdala (Mark and Ervin, 1970). Another structure in the limbic system, the *hippocampus,* appears to play a critical role in short-term memory. In one famous patient, known as H. M., surgical removal of both right and left hippocampi produced an inability to form any new memories.

Perhaps the most distinctively human part of the brain is the *cerebral cortex.* As one comes up the evolutionary scale, from the simple to the complex animals, the cerebral cortex grows markedly in size (see Figure 2.7). In a shark, for example, the cerebral cortex is a very small portion of the brain. In contrast, a human brain is 80 percent cerebral cortex. As the cortex has grown larger, it has assumed many tasks originally performed by the brain stem. Thus, if you cut away the section of the cerebral cortex associated with vision in a rat, the rat can still see, although it will be unable to distinguish patterns. Do the same to a man, and he will become blind. The lower portions of the rat's brain perform basic visual functions, but in humans these functions have been passed on to the more developed cerebral cortex. As two prominent brain scientists have noted, "A man without a cortex is almost a vegetable, speechless, sightless, senseless" (Hubel and Wiesel, 1979, page 150).

THE HEAVY HEAD

There is a correlation between the brain size of various animal species and the ability of those species to solve problems. The correlation is not perfect and there are a number of crude exceptions, such as elephant brains that weigh 13 pounds and whale brains at 19 pounds. The principle of brain weight and ability holds true, however, if brain weight is figured as a proportion of body weight. Thus, an elephant's brain, compared to its size, is 1/1,000 of its weight. The ratio for the whale is 1/10,000. The ratio for humans is 1/60. Within the human species, however, there is no evidence that brain size and intelligence are correlated.

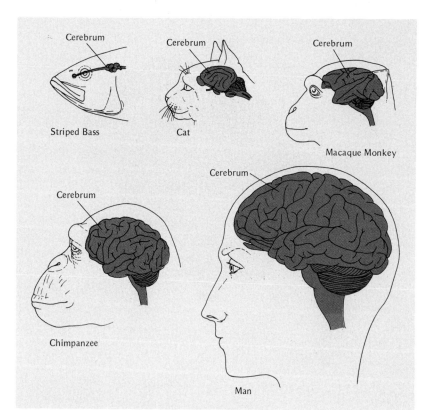

FIGURE 2.7

As we move up the evolutionary ladder, the cerebral cortex takes up a greater proportion of the brain.

In humans, the cerebral cortex is the place where sensory impulses concerning sight, sound, taste, smell, and touch are interpreted. It is the site of thought and intelligence. Portions of the cerebral cortex integrate the sensory and motor systems, acting as a sort of final switchboard between what comes in and what goes out.

Using as reference points two prominent grooves, or *fissures*, that run through the cerebral cortex, it can be divided into four regions, or *lobes*, on each side of the brain: the left and right frontal, temporal, parietal, and occipital lobes (see Figure 2.8). We still have only a preliminary understanding of the functions of the various parts of the cortex, but it seems clear that the lobes—and specific areas within each lobe—play distinctive roles in sensation, thought, and behavior. For example, the *frontal lobes* seem to contribute to our understanding of time and to be involved in emotional experience. The *parietal lobes* help to keep us physically oriented in our environment—literally, to know which end is up. The *occipital lobes* receive most of their input from the eyes and are largely concerned with vision. And the *temporal lobes* seem to be involved with hearing, language, and memory.

A narrow band of cortex at the top of the head controls the motor responses of the whole body. Just behind it is another strip of cortex that controls the sensory responses of the body. The amount of sensory and motor tissue devoted to a particular body part is not related to the size of that particular portion of the anatomy. What seems more relevant is the complexity of the functions that the body part must perform. Thus the hands and mouth make up only a small

FIGURE 2.8

The cerebral cortex is divided into four lobes on each side. In addition, a narrow band of cortex at the top of the head controls sensory and motor responses (see Figure 2.9).

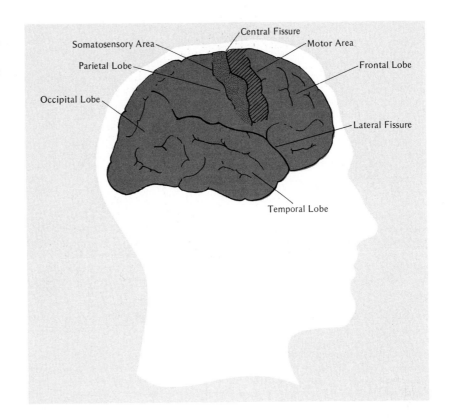

percentage of body volume but they merit almost half of the motor cortex (see Figure 2.9).

The entire cerebral cortex is divided into two halves, the right and left *cerebral hemispheres*. The two hemispheres are, for the most part, mirror images of each other. As we will see later in this chapter, however, there is reason to believe that in most people the two hemispheres perform rather different functions.

Specialization of Brain Function

Different regions of the brain perform different jobs. We have already seen that specific areas of the cerebral cortex control the sensations and the movements of specific parts of the body. Specialized brain areas seem to handle higher mental functions, as well. Much of our knowledge of such specialization comes from studies of brain-damaged patients. For example, damage to different sites in the cortex has been found to give rise to different forms of *aphasia*, or language breakdown. If there is damage to an area in the left frontal lobe known as *Broca's area*, patients have difficulty articulating words and their grammar is faulty. When asked about a dental appointment, for example, a patient with Broca's aphasia might say, in a hesitant and blurred voice, "Yes . . . Monday . . . Dad and Dick . . . Wednesday 9:00 . . . doctors . . . and . . . teeth." If there is damage to another area, known as *Wernicke's area*, located in the left temporal lobe, the patient's pronunciation and grammar are normal but the words chosen are often inappropriate or nonsensical. For example, a

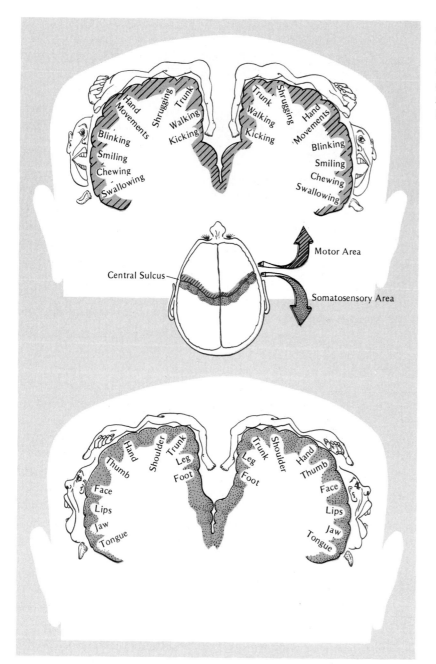

FIGURE 2.9
Specific portions of the motor area (top drawing) and somatosensory area (bottom) of the cerebral cortex are responsible for movement and sensation of different parts of the body.

patient with Wernicke's aphasia was asked to describe a picture that showed two boys stealing cookies behind their mother's back. He reported: "Mother is away here working her work to get her better, but when she's looking the two boys looking in the other part." These defects have enabled researchers to develop a general understanding of the ways in which brain centers must work together to produce normal language (Geschwind, 1979).

Another example of brain localization of a complex mental function comes from a condition called *prosopagnosia*—the inability to identify people from their faces. A patient with this disorder is unable to name a person she sees face to face or in a photograph. Such a patient may even fail to recognize her own spouse and children. The

Monoamines

Dopamine

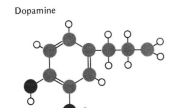

Norepinephrine

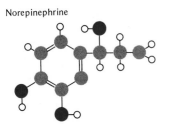

Serotonin

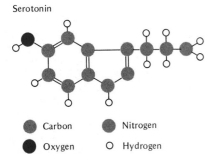

● Carbon   ● Nitrogen

● Oxygen   ○ Hydrogen

FIGURE 2.10

The chemical structures of three major transmitters in the brain: dopamine, norepinephrine, and serotonin.

identity of familiar people is not lost to the patient, for when the other person speaks the patient recognizes the voice and can say the name immediately. Moreover, the patient can perceive and describe facial features quite accurately. The deficiency seems to be confined to the specific mental function of forming associations between faces and identities. In prosopagnosia the damage is found in the underside of both occipital lobes. In normal people, these areas of the brain apparently are entrusted with the task of linking faces and identities (Geschwind, 1979).

Even though different portions of the brain perform highly specific functions, any complex human activity is likely to involve many areas of the brain working together. Recent studies of blood flow in the brain have indicated, for example, that when we read silently, at least four areas of the brain are activated, including the visual association area in the occipital lobe and Broca's area in the frontal lobe. When we read aloud, additional brain areas related to the mouth and hearing are also activated (Lassen, Ingvar, and Skinhøj, 1978). A current challenge for brain scientists is to map more precisely the neural messages that are being sent from one area to another during such activities.

In addition to the transmission of neural messages from one part of the brain to another, the brain's functioning seems to depend on the overall level of activation—or rate of neural firing—of the cerebral cortex. When people are given difficult mental tasks or are placed in stressful situations, neural activity increases in "diffuse pathways" throughout the cerebral cortex. These pathways fan out from a portion of the brain stem called the *reticular formation*. Such general activation of the brain is indicated both by patterns of brain waves and by blood-flow analysis. Such overall activation of the brain seems necessary to allow more specific neural messages to travel between widely separated parts of the brain.

The Chemistry of the Brain

As we've seen, the brain's operation depends on the ability of neurons to send messages to one another by means of chemical transmitter substances. Researchers have recently made major strides in identifying these transmitter substances and determining where in the brain they work and how they exert their effects. So far, about 30 types of proteinlike molecules are known or are suspected to be chemical transmitters in the brain (Iversen, 1979). Among the best known are *dopamine, norepinephrine,* and *serotonin* (Figure 2.10). Many more transmitter substances—perhaps as many as 200—remain to be discovered (Snyder, 1980).

It is now known that neurons in specific areas of the brain and spinal cord will send and receive only specific transmitter substances. When molecules of the "right" substance cross a synapse, they fit precisely into regions of the receptor neuron's surface, much as a key fits into a lock. Once the "key" is inserted, a chain of chemical events takes place that makes the receptor neuron more likely or less likely to fire, depending on whether the substance is excitatory or inhibitory.

The brain   **55**

Scientists are especially interested in the role that brain chemicals play in neurological and psychological disorders. For example, dopamine has the effect of exciting neurons in the *corpus stratium*, a portion near the center of the brain that regulates complex motor activity. A deficiency of dopamine in this area has been linked to the muscular rigidity and tremors found with Parkinson's disease. As a result of this discovery, forms of dopamine that can be manufactured in the laboratory are being used to treat the disease. Dopamine also transmits messages to portions of the limbic system that regulate emotional responses. An excess of dopamine in these areas is now believed to be a cause of the hallucinations and other disruptions of thought and emotion that characterize schizophrenia (see Chapter 11). As we will see in Chapter 12, drugs (such as Thorazine) that are used to treat schizophrenia work by attaching themselves to dopamine receptors, thus preventing the dopamine from reaching them. Other psychoactive drugs, such as amphetamines and LSD, work by influencing or mimicking the effects of the brain's own chemical transmitter substances (see Chapter 3).

The most recently discovered transmitter substances in the brain are a family of chemicals called the *neuropeptides*. Although these chemicals are found in only minute quantities, they have major effects on experience and behavior. In particular, the *enkephalins* and *endorphins* are similar chemically to the pain-killer morphine and have the same ability to reduce pain (see Chapter 4, Box 3). These chemicals are concentrated not only in the brain's pain centers but also in emotional centers, such as the amygdala, where they may serve to keep our moods under control. "Maybe we all carry our own dope within our heads, so we don't get uptight," a brain scientist speculates, "or at least to help us overcome our being uptight" (Edson, 1978).

Other neuropeptides have been found to have direct effects on drinking behavior, sexual behavior, and memory—at least in laboratory animals. The "neuropeptide revolution," as some scientists are calling it, has raised hopes that synthetic versions of neuropeptides can be developed as pain-killers, as relaxants, and even as ways of enhancing intellectual skills and creativity. "In the future," one psychologist predicts, "we may all go to a psychopharmacy to pick up brain pills that give us whatever mental or emotional traits we may want at a given time" (Edson, 1978). But, of course, not everyone views such future possibilities eagerly. David Leff (1978) asks some of the troubling questions: "What would be the impact of such a chemical keyboard of mind and mood control? Would such manipulation dehumanize people? Or would it lead them to a more joyful existence?" With the amazing results of some of the current research on the chemistry of the brain, it seems almost certain that these questions will become the focus of impassioned debate in the future.

OUR TWO BRAINS

Imagine what it would be like to have two brains, one controlling the left side of your body, the other controlling the right side. Each brain would control one hand and one leg, and each brain would have a separate consciousness. You could think with one brain, daydream with the other. Or you might write a paper with one brain while playing the harmonica with the other. Quite literally, your left hand might not know what your right hand was doing.

Actually, this description isn't too far from the truth. The brain— or more precisely, the cerebral cortex—is composed of two separate halves, or hemispheres. Each cerebral hemisphere is capable of functioning independently of the other, and each controls one side of the body. In fact, the right side of the brain controls the left side of the body, and the left side of the brain controls the right side of the body. This is because most sensory nerve fibers cross over when they reach the brain. As a result, everything touched with the right hand is registered in the left hemisphere, and everything touched with the left hand is registered in the right hemisphere.

But the two hemispheres are not identical twins. There are slight physical differences between the two. More important, during the course of evolution of the human species the two halves began to specialize in their functions. In right-handed people, the left hemisphere has primary control over linguistic abilities, such as speaking, reading, and writing, whereas the right hemisphere has primary control over certain nonverbal skills, including musical ability, recognition of complex visual patterns, and the expression and recognition of emotion. In left-handers these functions seem to be more evenly distributed between the hemispheres.

The evidence for this specialization between hemispheres comes from studies of patients with strokes or lesions that damage parts of the brain. For example, 95 percent of brain-related language disorders result from damage to the left hemisphere, which is in charge of our linguistic abilities. Patients with lesions to the left side typically feel depressed (quite understandably), whereas those with damage to the right hemisphere often seem unconcerned about their condition. This inappropriate lack of concern would seem to reflect impairment of these patients' emotional capacity, which is governed to a large extent by the right hemisphere. Moreover, patients with left hemisphere damage may not be able to understand what someone is saying but can still recognize the emotional tone being expressed. Patients with right hemisphere damage, on the other hand, usually understand a person's meaning but often don't realize that the person is speaking with an angry or humorous tone of voice (Geschwind, 1979).

For most of us, the division of labor between the two halves of the brain is difficult to detect. This is because the two hemispheres are connected by a body of nerve fibers called the *corpus callosum.* Messages are constantly being transferred through this cable from one hemisphere to the other, enabling them to work together on most tasks. In this way the two hemispheres let each other know what they are up to.

But there are a few human beings walking around today whose two hemispheres cannot communicate with each other, because their corpus callosum has been surgically cut. Brain surgeons have performed this operation on people afflicted with uncontrollable epilepsy in hopes of confining seizures to one side of the brain. The operation has proved to be remarkably successful, producing an almost total elimination of attacks. And the side effects are much less chaotic than you would expect, considering the fact that after this operation people in effect have two brains. The operation produces no noticeable change in the patients' temperaments, personalities, or general intelligence. Such *split-brain* patients appear to be so normal that special laboratory experiments were required to reveal the unusual effects of the operation.

Roger Sperry and Michael Gazzaniga devised several experiments to determine how cutting the corpus callosum had affected their patients (Gazzaniga, 1967). The experimenters set up situations in which information would be sent to only one side of the brain. For example, pictures would be flashed in only the right visual field (the area seen by the right half of each eye), or placed in the right hand, so that they would be "seen" or "felt" only by the left hemisphere. Whenever items were shown to the left hemisphere, the person could verbally describe the items because speech is located in the left hemisphere. But when objects were presented to the right hemisphere (such as by being placed in the left hand), the person was unable to identify them verbally. Instead, the person would guess at what had been shown or would deny that he had seen anything. However, if the person was asked to point to or pick up the object that had been shown, the right hemisphere had no problem picking the right one.

For example, some patients were shown the word "heart" with the "he" positioned in the left of the visual field and the "art" in the right (see Figure 2.11). When asked to pronounce the word they had seen, the patients would say "art," for that is what the speaking left hemisphere saw. But when patients were asked to point with their left hand to the word they had seen, they pointed to the word "he," for that is what the right hemisphere, which controls the left hand, saw.

In normal people, as we've noted, there is constant communication between the two hemispheres, through the corpus callosum. Nevertheless, there is evidence of the specialization of function of the two hemispheres in the normal brain, as well. For example, when the brain waves of people engaged in verbal tasks are recorded, the left hemisphere shows more activity than the right. But when spatial activities, such as recognizing patterns, are involved, the right hemisphere becomes more active (Ornstein, 1972).

Evidence for the idea that the right hemisphere plays a primary role in emotional recognition can be obtained by using the faces in Figure 2.12. Try showing the faces to ten friends, and ask each of them which face looks happier. Even though the two faces are mirror images, most people judge Face A as happier. This is apparently because people tend to pay more attention to the left side of the face than to the right, as that is the part of the face that goes more directly to the right brain, which is skilled in analyzing faces. Because in Face A the *left* side (from the viewer's standpoint) is "smiling," it is the face that generally seems happier (Schmeck, 1980).

Research on hemispheric specialization has received a great deal of attention from psychologists in the past decade—so much so that some scientists consider it a fad. It is important to keep in mind that

FIGURE 2.11
The left hemisphere of the brain "sees" material presented to the right visual field (ART), and the right hemisphere "sees" material presented to the left visual field (HE).

IT'S A RIGHT-HANDED WORLD

For the almost 94 percent of us who are right-handed, the left hemisphere is "dominant." Unfortunately for the left-handers among us, we seem to live in a right-handed world. Try playing the violin, cutting with scissors, or opening a refrigerator door with your left hand; you will learn just how right-handed our culture is. Pilots find that most of the aircraft controls are on the right. The same thing is true of TV sets. There are only a few settings, such as professional baseball, in which left-handers seem to get an even break.

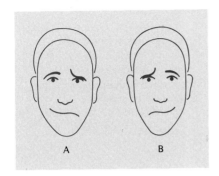

FIGURE 2.12
These two pictures are mirror images, yet most viewers consider the face on the left to be happier. (See the text for explanation.)

in normal people, almost everything we do involves the two hemispheres working together. Investigators of blood flow in the brain were recently surprised to discover, for example, that when people were engaged in activities that involved language, both hemispheres were activated in much the same manner (Lassen, Ingvar, and Skinhøj, 1978). It is believed that the right hemisphere does contribute to our linguistic ability, albeit not in as essential a way as the left. In some cases, if linguistic abilities are lost because of damage to areas in the left hemisphere, the right hemisphere even seems to be able to take over these functions. Such a takeover of function is more likely if the damage occurs early in life (before age 8) or if the person is left-handed, since specialization of hemispheres seems to be less extensive in left-handers. More generally, most human tasks, from reading a book to deciding what to have for supper, seem to involve the complex coordination of both hemispheres (Geschwind, 1979). It might be nice in a way to have "two brains," but we probably do even better with our single one.

EFFECTS OF EXPERIENCE ON THE BRAIN

Scientists have long thought that whatever we learn or remember must somehow be reflected in changes in the brain—perhaps physical changes, perhaps chemical changes. Until recently, however, they did not have the tools to detect such changes.

In the 1870s, for example, the French physician Paul Broca measured the heads of medical students and of male nurses and found that the medical students had larger heads. He concluded that the difference was the result of the extra training the medical students had received. Other scientists pointed out, however, that skull size bears no relation to brain size, and they found other problems with Broca's conclusions as well. Fifty years passed before scientists seriously addressed the question again.

In the early 1950s, David Krech, Mark Rosenzweig, and their coworkers conducted experiments with rats that demonstrated definite brain changes as a result of experience (Rosenzweig, Bennett, and Diamond, 1972). These researchers began by taking three males from each of about a dozen litters of rats. Of each group, one rat was placed in a standard laboratory cage with some other rats, the second rat was placed in an "enriched" environment, and the third rat was put in an "impoverished" environment (see Figure 2.13). The enriched environment consisted of a large cage in which several rats were able to interact with each other and to play with a variety of toys that were changed daily. In the impoverished condition a rat was confined alone in a cage. At the end of the experimental period (from a few days to several months), the researchers sacrificed the three littermates and examined their brains. They found several key changes in the brains of the rats that had lived in the enriched environment: greater weight and thickness of the cerebral cortex, greater total activity of certain chemical transmitters, more glial cells, and larger cell bodies and nuclei. The greatest differences were found in the occipital lobe of the cortex, which is primarily related to vision.

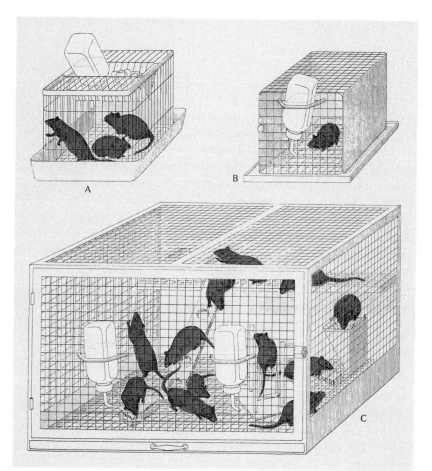

FIGURE 2.13
Krech and Rosenzweig's experiment relating environment to brain anatomy in rats. (A) Standard laboratory environment. (B) Impoverished environment. (C) Enriched environment.

The experimenters consistently found that the enriched rats had brains in which the weight of the cortex had increased in relation to the weight of the rest of the brain. This finding is particularly significant, since the cortex is essential for all the brain's higher functions: learning, memory, and thinking.

In addition, the enriched rats in at least one study showed an increase in the size of the synaptic junctions in the brain. As you will recall, the synapse is where messages pass from one neuron to another. Perhaps the larger such "message centers" are, the more information the brain can handle. What this experiment seems to imply is that experience with varied objects in the environment allows rats to handle even more information.

Does this experiment tell us anything about the human brain? Obviously, the same experiments cannot be done on humans, but the more we learn about brain development in animals, the more clues we will have about our own brains. Recent research has suggested that nutrition also effects brain development (see Box 4).

The experiments by Krech, Rosenzweig, and their associates raise some interesting questions. One such question is whether it would be possible to bring about greater development of a specific brain region by exposing it to a great deal of stimulation. For example, could listening to or playing a great deal of music enhance the development of the auditory cortex? Another question deals with the "critical peri-

— *Box 4*

Nutrition and the brain— you are what you eat

We all know that nutrition can affect physical development and resistance to disease, but few of us stop to consider its potential effects on psychological development and behavior: how we think, feel, and act. The brain and nervous system are parts of the body, just like the muscles and bones, and their demands for nutrition are stronger than those of any other part of the body.

Recent research illustrates the devastating effects of malnutrition on brain development (Lewin, 1975). One effect of malnutrition is to reduce the number of brain cells in the cerebellum, the portion of the brain responsible for fine motor control and coordination. Another effect is on the quality of nerve cells: Axons in malnourished animals shrink in diameter in many parts of the brain. Finally, malnutrition has an enormous impact on the synapses—the connection between nerves—in the brain. Researchers have found reductions of up to 40 percent in the number of synapses in the cerebral cortexes of undernourished animals. Malnutrition may well have similar effects on humans. It is not surprising that tests on undernourished children

Lack of adequate nutrition can be greatly detrimental to brain development, especially in the early years.

show them to be retarded in many physical and intellectual skills.

Researchers have pinpointed the mechanisms for some specific nutritional effects on brain activity. For example, foods rich in lecithin, such as soybeans, eggs, and liver, can increase the amount of *acetylcholine*, a transmitter substance in the brain. This chemical seems to be involved in memory, sleep disturbances, and motor coordination. Similarly, the consumption of carbohydrates may affect the levels of *serotonin*, a transmitter substance that apparently plays a role in temperature regulation and sensory perception.

As a result of such recent discoveries, there has been a burst of research activity on nutrition and the brain. Much of this research has focused on how diet can help patients with psychological disorders. Brain scientist Richard Wurtman predicts that this new research will uncover new ways to treat certain mental illnesses, as well as ways to combat the forgetfulness that often comes with aging. "It is conceivable," he writes, "that we will eventually know enough about how diet affects brain chemistry to lessen pain and control our moods . . . to be more alert by day or sleepy by night, and even to improve our memory and concentration" (Wurtman, 1978, page 140).

ods" of brain development (see Figure 2.14). How early in life must experience be obtained for it to have an effect on brain development?

The past two decades have seen tremendous advances in our knowledge of the brain. Scientists now have a reasonably good understanding of basic brain structure and of how nerves send messages. But for all this increase in knowledge, most of what is important about the brain's functioning still remains to be learned. As David Hubel (1979) writes, "Brain research is only at its beginning. The incredible complexity of the brain is a cliché, but it is a fact." For the time being, it is clear that we cannot address many of the most important questions about human behavior and experience in terms of the brain mechanisms that underlie them. Instead, we must con-

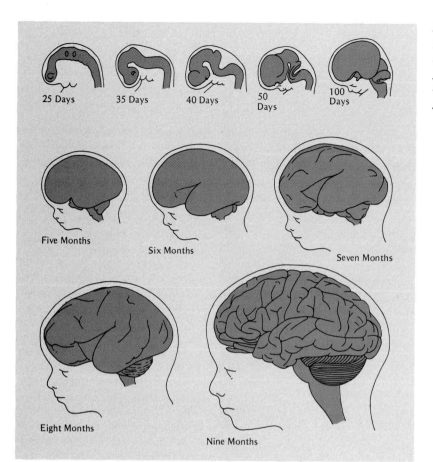

FIGURE 2.14
During the nine months of prenatal development, the human brain grows from a few undifferentiated cells, to a smooth organ, to a greatly convoluted structure.

25 Days 35 Days 40 Days 50 Days 100 Days

Five Months Six Months Seven Months

Eight Months Nine Months

tinue to explore behavior with the tools we have available. Nevertheless, as we do so, we must always keep the brain in mind. It is the remarkable organ that makes everything else about human behavior and experience possible.

SUMMARY

1. The human nervous system consists of two major subsystems: the *central nervous system* (brain and spinal cord) and the *peripheral nervous system*.
2. *Afferent neurons* collect messages and carry them *to* the brain or spinal cord; *efferent neurons* carry messages *away* from the brain and spinal cord to the muscles and glands. *Association neurons* make connections between incoming and outgoing messages.
3. The *spinal cord* serves as a pathway for nerve impulses to the brain and also handles simple reflex actions.
4. The peripheral nervous system is divided into the *somatic nervous system*, which controls voluntary movements, and the *autonomic nervous system*, which governs glands and involuntary muscles.
5. The autonomic nervous system has two parts: the *sympathetic*

branch, which prepares the body for action, and the *parasympathetic branch,* which has a calming effect.

6. Glands in the *endocrine system* produce *hormones* that can directly influence body functioning and behavior.

7. A neuron consists of a *cell body,* short *dendrites,* which receive messages, and a long *axon,* which transmits messages. Messages travel along the surface of the neuron from the dendrites, through the cell body, and along the axon. This electrical process is called *axonal transmission.*

8. Neural messages move from one neuron to the next through the chemical process of *synaptic transmission.* For such transmission to occur, the neuron must *fire.* The *all-or-none principle* refers to the fact that neurons will fire only if the impulse they pick up is above a certain minimum intensity. The firing of a neuron causes a chemical *transmitter substance* to cross the synapse between neurons, thereby exciting or inhibiting the firing of the next neuron.

9. Although comparing the brain to a computer is an interesting analogy, there are significant differences between the two.

10. The brain contains about 100 billion nerve cells and about 1000 billion *glia*—cells that provide nourishment and support for the neurons.

11. Our knowledge of the brain has come from the use of a variety of techniques, including *electrical stimulation of the brain* (ESB), study of brain-damaged people, use of brain surgery, analysis of *brain waves* as recorded on *electroencephalograms* (EEGs), *blood-flow measurement,* and *positron-emission tomography.*

12. The human brain comprises four basic sets of structures: the brain stem, cerebellum, limbic system, and cerebral cortex.

13. The *brain stem* is the most primitive part of the brain and is concerned with automatic functions. Among structures found in the brain stem are the *medulla,* which controls basic physical rhythms and reflexes, and the *hypothalamus,* which monitors such behaviors as eating, drinking, and sleeping.

14. The *cerebellum,* located behind the brain stem, is involved in balance and coordination.

15. The *limbic system,* including such structures as the *amygdala* and the *hippocampus,* is found only in mammals. It appears to be involved in emotional expression and short-term memory.

16. The *cerebral cortex* contains centers for sight, hearing, taste, smell, and touch. It is the site of thought, intelligence, and memory. Two major *fissures* serve to divide each side of the brain into four functionally separate lobes: the *frontal, parietal, occipital,* and *temporal.* Two narrow strips of cortex at the top of the head control the sensory and motor responses of the body.

17. Evidence of specialization of brain function often comes from studies of brain-damaged patients. Patients with damage to *Broca's area* in the frontal lobe have difficulty articulating

words and have faulty grammar. Patients with damage to *Wernicke's area* in the left temporal lobe often choose inappropriate words. Patients with damage to the underside of the occipital lobes may suffer from *prosopagnosia*—the inability to recognize faces.

18. *Biofeedback* techniques have been used to monitor and control brain waves, particularly the alpha rhythm.

19. The overall level of activity in the brain appears to be governed by a portion of the brain stem called the *reticular formation.*

20. About thirty chemical transmitter substances in the brain have been identified. Specific neurons in the brain and spinal cord will send and receive only specific transmitter substances. Among the most recently discovered transmitter substances are the *neuropeptides.*

21. The cerebral cortex is divided into two halves, the left and right *cerebral hemispheres.* The left hemisphere has primary control over verbal abilities, while the right hemisphere has primary control over such nonverbal skills as musical ability, recognition of complex visual patterns, and expression and recognition of emotion. The right side of the brain controls the left side of the body, and vice-versa.

22. The hemispheres are connected by a band of fibers called the *corpus callosum.* When this band is severed, the individual in effect has two separate brains.

23. In *split-brain patients*, the left hemisphere can communicate by speaking or writing, whereas the right hemisphere can communicate only by pointing, gesturing, or drawing.

24. Studies have shown that rats raised in "enriched" conditions experience key changes in their brains. These findings appear to indicate that experience produces definite changes in the brain.

25. Nutrition can influence the levels of various transmitter substances in the brain and can thus have an effect on behavior.

BIOLOGICAL RHYTHMS

The sun rises and sets. The moon passes regularly through its phases. Spring turns to summer, which gives way to autumn. This may sound more like the stuff of poetry than the domain of a psychologist. But there are daily, monthly, and annual rhythms—as well as other, quicker rhythms—in our lives that reflect the interplay of our biological nature with the rhythmic environment in which we live.

There are rhythms in our lives that reflect the interplay of our biological nature with the rhythmic environment in which we live.

"In adapting over evolutionary time to a periodic environment," writes psychiatrist Peter Whybrow (1979), "animals including man have developed within themselves many sophisticated clocklike mechanisms. . . . Partly innate and partly shaped by the individual's prevailing surroundings, the rhythms serve to keep us functioning at an optimal level in a predictable but ever-changing environment." We are not ordinarily aware of our own biological rhythms, or of the social and cultural rhythms that accompany

them. Recently, however, psychologists and other scientists have begun to explore these cycles of human behavior and experience.

CIRCADIAN RHYTHMS

Some of the best-known biological rhythms take place over a 24-hour period. Most of us regularly sleep about one-third of the 24-hour day and are active for the other two-thirds. This type of pattern—one that goes through a full cycle in about 24 hours—is called a *circadian rhythm*. The term *circadian* comes from the Latin meaning "about a day."

There are many circadian rhythms in our bodily functioning. Body temperature, blood pressure, heart rate, blood-sugar level, and secretion of certain hormones all reach a peak and drop to a low once in each 24-hour period (Luce, 1971). Blood sugar, for example, begins to drop slowly in the late afternoon. It reaches its low point by about 3 A.M. to 6 A.M. and then begins to rise again. Blood pressure is generally highest at about 6 P.M. Pulse rate and respiration also have daily rhythms, although they rise and fall at different times for different people. Although we are not usually aware of many of our circadian rhythms, we may notice some of their effects. If you have ever stayed up all night, you probably felt cold by about 4 A.M. despite a constant room temperature. That's because body temperature drops to its lowest point a few hours before dawn.

Sensory acuity also shows rhythmic variations. Even though our bodies use food most efficiently in the morning, many people eat their biggest meal in the evening. One reason for such a preference may be that our senses of smell and taste tend to be most sensitive in the evening hours. Such heightened sensitivity may be related to fluctuations in the production of adrenal hormones, which influence taste and smell (Luce, 1971).

Our bodies use food most efficiently in the morning. Our senses of smell and taste tend to be most sensitive in the evening.

Not everyone runs on the same biological clock. Although most people share basic patterns, there are also wide variations between individuals. "Morning people" awake refreshed and alert and are most productive in the early part of the day. "Night people" drag themselves out of bed, stay half asleep for an hour or two after rising, and prefer to work in the evening hours. Being a night or morning person may be related to rhythmic changes in the levels of certain hormones (Fitzgerald and Bundy, 1975). Two investigators interested in family interactions have found that most people can readily identify themselves as morning or night people (Adams and Cromwell, 1978). These researchers suggest that "mismatched" spouses—that is, a morning person married to a night person—may have to rely on creative compromise to overcome the lack of synchrony in their personal rhythms.

Jet lag can temporarily throw our biological rhythms out of sync.

Our biological clocks are normally synchronized with the day and night cycles of our environment—when it is daytime we are awake and alert; as night approaches our bodies prepare for sleep. But if you've ever traveled across a time zone, you know what it is like to have your biological rhythms "out of sync" with your surroundings. The discomfort travelers experience, commonly known as jet lag, results from the desynchronization of biological rhythms. For example, a traveler arriving in London at 9 A.M. from New York may be prepared intellectually to begin the day. But for her body it is only 4 A.M. and not yet time to get up. One problem is that some rhythms adjust to changes more quickly than do others. Sleep rhythms may become reestablished after a few days, while body temperature and hormonal fluctuations appear to take longer to adjust (Goldberg, 1977).

If you've ever traveled across a time zone, you know what it's like to have your biological rhythms "out of sync."

You can imagine what happens to the performance of an executive engaged in delicate negotiations when her body is on New York time and the negotiations are in London. When her counterparts are refreshed, relaxed, and ready for the day's business, her body is crying, "Help! I should be sleeping!" Many governments and corporations have attempted to reduce such problems by insisting that their representatives leave early for trips overseas so their bodies have time to adjust. Travelers may also try to remain on "home time" whenever possible, a trick long used by pilots. For example, a sales representative from Boston who lands in San Francisco might eat dinner at 3 P.M., retire to bed at 7 P.M., and rise for breakfast at 3 A.M.

ULTRADIAN RHYTHMS

The daily rhythms of sleeping and wakefulness are themselves composed of shorter cycles of biological activity. These shorter cycles are called *ultradian rhythms* (from the Latin for "more often than daily"). Our regular, rhythmic patterns of heartbeats and breathing are examples of ultradian rhythms. Another sort of ultradian rhythm occurs as we sleep. As we will see in Chapter 3, sleep is marked by four different stages, each characterized by a distinctive type of electrical activity in the brain. We pass through all four sleep stages several times each night; the complete cycle of all four stages takes about 90 minutes.

Human brain waves are marked by a peak in mental activity about every 90 minutes.

Scientists have suspected that a similar 90-minute cycle may recur through the waking hours, as well as during sleep. Sleep researcher Nathaniel Kleitman (1970) suggests that there is a "basic rest-and-activity cycle" built into our nervous systems that programs continuous alternations between activity and rest. For example, Michael Chase (1979) has found a pattern in human brain waves marked by a peak in mental activity about every 90 minutes; there is a trough in activity 45 minutes after each peak. Chase refers to the peaks as "brainstorms." Studies have also shown 90-minute cycles in people's susceptibility to visual illusions, in stomach contractions (Hiatt and Kripke, 1975), and in daydreaming (Kripke and Sonneschein, 1973).

Why do all of these changes occur at approximately 90-minute intervals? What sort of internal clock leads to patterns of neural firing in the brain at these intervals? So far, researchers simply don't know.

INFRADIAN RHYTHMS

Our bodies also show cycles of activity that take longer than a day to complete. These cycles are called *infradian rhythms* (from the Latin for "less often than daily"). One infradian rhythm is the female menstrual cycle, which lasts about 28 days. The menstrual cycle is defined by shifts in the levels of female sex hormones. The cycle begins when these hormones are at the lowest levels, at the time of menstrual bleeding. The hormone levels peak about two weeks later, at the time of ovulation, and then begin to drop again. Variations in these hormone levels have sometimes been associated with fluctuations in women's moods (see Chapter 7, Box 4).

One researcher found more cyclical mood changes in men than in a control group of women.

Is there a comparable cycle in men's hormones? When Charles Doering and his colleagues (1975) studied the levels of testosterone, the male hormone, in a group of men, they found cycles in hormone level that varied from 3 to 30 days from one peak to the next. They did not find that fluctuation in testosterone levels corresponded to mood reports, however. Nevertheless there do seem to be male mood cycles, ranging from 6 to 90 days. In fact, Mary Brown Parlee

(1978) found more cyclical mood changes in men than in a control group of women. Parlee did not measure hormone levels, so it wasn't possible to tell whether the men's mood changes were related to hormonal fluctuations. Parlee suggests that social conventions—for example, working Monday through Friday and relaxing on Saturday and Sunday—may also be important influences on infradian rhythms.

INTERNAL CLOCKS OR EXTERNAL FORCES?

Many scientists believe that our biological rhythms are set by an internal *biological clock*, a mechanism in the central nervous system that programs the timing of changes in biological functions. From this point of view, biological rhythms may become synchronized with external rhythms (such as the day-night cycle), but the rhythmicity itself is internally regulated. The specific biological source of these rhythms—the nature of the internal pendulum, as it were—is not yet understood. And one respected scientist, biologist Frank Brown, doubts that there is any such internal clock at all. Instead, he argues, all biological rhythms are directly produced by the external rhythms of our environment.

Many scientists believe that our biological rhythms are set by an internal biological clock.

It is well known, for example, that the rhythms of the ocean's tides are set by the shifting gravitational pull of the moon. Brown has demonstrated that the moon's force can affect biological rhythms, as well—although his study dealt with oysters rather than humans. Brown transported oysters from the New England coast to Evanston, Illinois. For a few weeks the oysters remained on New England time, opening their shells every 24.8 hours, corresponding to the high tide in New England. But then they began opening their shells on Evanston time, in synchrony with the position of the moon in Evanston. On the basis of this and other experiments, Brown has concluded that such environmental forces as light-dark cycles, gravity, radiation, and electromagnetic activity are the real determiners of biological rhythms (Brown, Hastings, and Palmer, 1970). Brown's research has been welcomed by astrologers, who have long argued for the influence of the stars and planets on human beings. His position remains highly controversial, however, especially as we shift our attention from oysters to humans.

To be sure, throughout recorded history people have speculated about the relationship between the moon's phases and human behavior. Murder and madness have been associated—at least in folklore—with the full moon. (In fact, the word *lunatic* comes from the Latin word for "moon.") Recently there have been suggestions that the association is not entirely mythical. One extended study of homicides in Ohio and Florida found that homicides were most common after the new and full moon phases (Lieber and Sherin, 1972). The researchers who conducted this study suggested that the moon might influence "biological tides"—including levels of hormones and brain chemicals—just as it influences ocean tides. However, other researchers have failed to obtain similar findings in different geographical areas. And examinations of the links between psychotic episodes, suicides, and the lunar phase have not shown any relationship (Campbell and Beets, 1978). If the moon does exert an influence on human affairs, it has not yet been conclusively documented.

SEASONAL RHYTHMS

In addition to all the other rhythms we have considered, our physical and psychological functioning is also affected in important ways by the annual cycle of the seasons. Greek and Roman scholars believed that each season was associated with a dominant humor, or bodily substance, that was accompanied by a corresponding temperament. For example, the "sanguine," or cheerful, humor (associated with blood) was thought to dominate in the spring, while the "melancholic," or depressed,

The sun rises and sets. The seasons pass through their annual cycle. And these rhythms affect our lives.

humor (associated with black bile) was thought to dominate in the fall.

Today's scientists have little use for the theory of the humors, but they are still faced with explaining the variations in health, mood, and behavior that occur over the course of the year. Birth rates, for example, are highest between March and June in Canada and between July and October in the United States. Deaths are most likely to occur in the winter, especially those caused by heart disease, stroke, and respiratory disease (Kevan, 1979). Do these variations mean that there is some sort of "biological calendar" inside us, causing annual cycles in our behavior? Probably not. But they do suggest that the changes that occur with the seasons—day length, weather, and social and cultural events—have important effects on our experience.

Perhaps not surprisingly, national surveys suggest that Americans tend to be the happiest in the spring and summer and gradually decline in mood throughout the fall and winter (Smith, 1979). One factor that may be associated with the upsurge of happiness in the spring and summer is increased day length and the increased likelihood of sunshine. In one recent study, Michael Cunningham (1979) found that the sunnier it was, the more positively people rated their moods and the more willing pedestrians were to stop and answer questions for an interviewer. These heart-warming effects of sunshine may be in part biological. For example, solar radiation can increase the concentration of negative ions (electrically charged particles) in the atmosphere, which may in turn be related to levels of the chemical transmitter serotonin in the brain and to relaxation (Krueger and Reed, 1976). But sunshine may also brighten our mood for aesthetic and symbolic reasons.

The sunlight brightens everything around us, recalls memories of happy times, and makes the world look shiny and pleasant.

Americans tend to be happiest in the spring and summer.

Among the best-documented seasonal effects on behavior is the rise in suicide rates and in mental hospital admissions during spring and early summer. It is possible that emotional disorder increases in spring as a result of increased glandular activity, triggered by increasing day length. For many people, such stirrings of the glands may contribute to the feelings of optimism and "thoughts of love" that are associated with springtime. But some vulnerable individuals may experience excessive glandular activity, precipitating emotional disorder and breakdown. Such biological effects of increasing day length clearly play a central role in the reproductive lives and migrations of many animals and birds. But their operation among human beings remains a topic of controversy.

A different sort of explanation of the springtime upturn in emotional distress involves the interplay of weather and people's self-perceptions. In the spring, as the weather warms, people spend more time out-of-doors and a general mood of optimism prevails; people who feel alone, unloved, and unsuccessful are likely to feel most acutely distressed by comparison. What's more, people in northern climates can blame their troubles during the winter on the cold, the ice, the frostbite, the stalled cars, the frozen pipes, the perpetually to-be-shoveled snow. When the spring

comes, there is nothing left to blame troubles on but oneself, one's fears, one's ruined relationships, one's unfulfilled dreams. In the spring, we must account to ourselves more honestly for our failings, which may push some troubled people over the edge of despair.

SUMMARY

1. *Circadian rhythms* occur on a 24-hour cycle. They include rhythmic peaks and drops in body temperature, blood pressure, heart rate, blood-sugar level, and secretions of certain hormones, as well as changes in sensory acuity. Biological rhythms can go "out of sync" with the environment when one travels across time zones.

2. *Ultradian rhythms* occur in cycles that are shorter than 24 hours. The most obvious example is the cycle of stages that occurs every 90 minutes during sleep.

3. *Infradian rhythms* occur in cycles that last longer than a day. The menstrual cycle, for example, occurs about every 28 days. There may be similar cycles of hormone changes in men.

4. Many scientists believe that biological rhythms are controlled by an internal *biological clock*, but others maintain that the rhythms are produced by external forces, such as light-dark cycles, gravity, and electromagnetic activity. There is little evidence, however, that the changing phases of the moon influence human biology or psychology.

5. Seasonal changes appear to have effects on people's moods and behavior. Both biological factors (such as glandular activity) and psychological factors (such as self-perceptions) may account for these variations.

Chapter 3

Consciousness

Cindy wakes up in the morning and lies in bed for a while, no longer asleep but not quite awake. Groggily she pulls herself from the bed, and before long she feels alert enough to get ready to face the day. She puts on her clothes, not really paying attention to what she's doing since she's done this so many times before. As she thinks about the test coming up, she absentmindedly squeezes a tube of hand-cream onto her toothbrush instead of toothpaste. At school she is "up" for the test and puts her total attention into answering the questions. But her after-lunch class is dull and she finds herself drowsing in the middle of the lecture, especially since she stayed up so late studying the night before. After class she heads to the track to run a few miles. She alternates between being absorbed in the running itself and letting her mind wander to wherever it wishes to go. That night she drops into bed and enjoys a deep sleep, punctuated by vivid dreams.

Sound familiar? In the activities of Cindy's typical day, she experiences many different states of consciousness, from full alertness to deep sleep. Similarly, we all go through our lives alternating between different modes of consciousness. *Consciousness* refers to our subjective awareness of our own actions and of the world around us. In this chapter we will explore what is still a largely uncharted area of psychology—human consciousness. After a preliminary survey of the nature of consciousness, we will focus on several specific states of consciousness, including the ordinary states of waking, sleeping, and dreaming and the altered states induced by drugs, hypnosis, and (in the Psychological Issue that follows this chapter) meditation.

THE NATURE OF CONSCIOUSNESS

Consciousness is a difficult concept to describe, because it is fundamental to everything we do. In fact, it is somewhat artificial to use *consciousness* as the title for a single chapter of this book, because it is involved in all forms of behavior, perception, thought, and emotion. Here we will discuss some central characteristics of consciousness and how consciousness has been studied by psychologists.

Characteristics of Consciousness

It seems easy to recognize consciousness when we experience it. Most of us feel quite conscious or aware of learning a new skill or of making a difficult choice. But consciousness is not essential for all behaviors, because most of our routine activities—tying shoes, descending stairs, speaking English—are performed quite automatically and unconsciously. For instance, we are seldom aware of the movements our legs and bodies make when we are walking. We may be talking with someone or looking at things around us. Because our attention is directed at other things, our walking occurs unconsciously. However, we can focus our attention on walking if we want to, thus making it a conscious behavior. If you've ever had to walk with a twisted ankle, you know what it's like to be very aware of your walking behavior. In some cases focusing attention on an automatic behavior can actually hinder it. Try running down a flight of stairs while thinking about what your feet are doing—but be sure to bring plenty of bandages.

Consciousness also plays a role in the choices we make. Many of our choices are deliberate—we speak of making a "conscious decision" about something, such as which course to register for or what movie to see. But other choices are less intentional and thus involve less conscious thought. For example, we go to the supermarket and select specific items from the shelves. Although there are many alternatives available, we often automatically and unconsciously choose particular items and brands out of habit.

We have referred here to *unconscious* behaviors and choices as being mental activities that are not part of our conscious awareness but that can become conscious if we want them to. Sigmund Freud had a different meaning for the term *unconscious*. He saw the unconscious part of the mind as a repository for sexual and aggressive thoughts and impulses that are too threatening to think about consciously. As we will see later in this chapter, Freud believed that one way to probe the unconscious mind is through dreams. (Freud's approach is described in detail in Chapter 8.)

Consciousness can also vary in its quality. Our subjective experiences can range from subdued and ordinary to exciting and intense. At some times we become totally absorbed in our environment, while at other times we focus most of our attention on ourselves, displaying a high degree of self-consciousness. Consciousness can also vary in the accuracy with which we perceive the environment. In our normal waking state we perceive our surroundings accurately, but when we dream or daydream we perceive things that are not really in our environment at all. And people in drug states experience a variety of distortions in their perceptions of the world.

The Study of Consciousness

The study of consciousness has had its ups and downs in psychology. In the early days of the field, in the late nineteenth century, the structuralists (see Chapter 1, Box 1) felt that psychology's central concern should be the study of consciousness. E. B. Titchener and other structuralists sought to learn about consciousness through *introspection*—the careful examination of their own conscious experience. For instance, Titchener was concerned with determining the number of "mental elements" and in 1896 had determined that there were more than 44,000 sensory elements that come together to form perceptions and ideas. For example, he considered each color that we can see and each tone we can hear to be a sensory element.

It soon became apparent, however, that the introspective method was unreliable, and structuralism gave way to a new school, behaviorism, which focused on the study of overt behavior, employing observations that everyone could agree on. Declared John Watson, the founder of behaviorism: "The time seems to have come when psychology must discard all reference to consciousness; when it need no longer delude itself into thinking that it is making mental states the object of observation" (1913, page 164).

Recently the tide has turned again, with psychologists returning to the study of such subjective states as sleeping, dreaming, hypnosis,

THE RIGHT HEMISPHERE AND THE UNCONSCIOUS

Is one-half of the brain more "conscious" than the other half? Recent studies suggest that for right-handed people, the left hemisphere may be more involved in highly conscious processes that involve intentional behavior and the focusing of attention. The right hemisphere, in contrast, may be more involved with automatic and unconscious actions and more sensitive to material outside the conscious focus of attention. For example, the Soviet neuropsychologist Simernitskaya (1974) found that people with damage to the left hemisphere had greater problems with consciously executed writing, while those with right-hemisphere damage had greater problems with writing that is less conscious and more automatic, such as signing one's name.

and drug-altered states of consciousness. One example of the new approach is current research on daydreaming, as presented in Box 1.

This burst of new research is closely connected with the revolution in brain research, with scientists trying to discover how states of consciousness are related to measurable brain activity. As we will see later in this chapter, for example, a particular kind of brain wave that occurs during sleep has provided insights into some of the age-old questions about how long dreams last and whether everyone dreams.

Studies of the physiological basis of consciousness raise the central philosophical question of mind and body: How do electrical and chemical events in the brain give rise to our experiencing the taste of a juicy apple or the sadness of a loved one's death? The idea that the mind (or consciousness) is separate from the brain is known as *dualism*, a philosophical approach popularized by René Descartes in the seventeenth century. According to the dualist approach, there must be something else besides brain function that allows us to think, make choices, and feel.

But most current researchers approach the mind-body problem by assuming that the brain and the mind are essentially identical. According to this view, all features of mental activity can eventually be described in physiological terms. Proceeding on this assumption, researchers are attempting to identify the physical and chemical processes within the brain that account for consciousness.

SLEEP

There are two major states of consciousness that each of us experiences every day: being awake and being asleep. Even within the waking state there are, as we have seen, variations in our conscious experience. Within the state of sleep, too, there are different states of consciousness. But the distinction between being awake and being asleep remains a fundamental one. When we are awake we are more physically active and responsive to the outside world. When we are asleep, our physical activity is greatly diminished, and our responsiveness to the environment is greatly decreased.

One-third of Our Lives

We spend about one-third of our lives in the state of consciousness called sleep. By age 60, you will have slept the same 20 years that Rip Van Winkle slept. Sleep appears to be an automatic behavior necessary for survival. Yet one of the biggest mysteries about sleep is just *why* it is necessary. Although different theories have proposed that sleep is needed to restore the body's energies or to reestablish chemical balances, no one has yet discovered just what it is that is being restored (Webb and Bonnet, 1979).

As far as we know, people in cultures all over the world generally sleep 5 to 9 hours in every 24 hours and usually do so at night. A study of college students (White, 1975) found that the average student slept 7.4 hours a night (8.5 hours on weekends). But the "aver-

WHO NEEDS AN ALARM CLOCK?

Some people claim they can wake up at a predetermined time just by setting the "alarm clock" in their heads. Believe it or not, it's true. In one experiment, subjects were sent to bed with a target time to wake up. The subjects were offered a pay bonus if they could hit the target (give or take 10 minutes). They found that they could do it, no matter what stage of sleep they were in before waking. They didn't do it by "sleeping with one eye open," either. They slept as deeply as they usually did (Zung and Wilson, 1971).

— **Box 1** —

Daydreaming

Frank is driving to a job interview. He wants the job very badly, and as he weaves in and out of the busy early morning traffic, he considers the upcoming conversation. In the midst of organizing his presentation, he has an image of the interviewer making fun of him and virtually laughing him out of the office. The image is gone as quickly as it came, and if you were to ask Frank about it later he would probably say he has no memory of it.

Janet has received a C+ on her sociology paper. She had worked hard on the paper and really thought she'd get an A. As she rereads the paper and goes over her professor's comments, Janet imagines herself storming into the teacher's office, hurling the paper on the teacher's desk, and telling the woman just what she thinks of her. This fantasy passes in a moment.

Lou is in Janet's sociology class and got an A− on his paper. He's quite excited. As he walks to his car, he starts to think about graduate school for the first time and wonders what it's like to be a professor. He imagines himself sitting in a cluttered office, surrounded by adoring students who are taking notes as he outlines his latest research project.

Frank, Janet, and Lou are daydreamers. Like most of the rest of us, their days are made up of more than looking, touching, re-

age" amount is not necessarily the right or best amount for you. In fact there are wide variations in what makes a "normal" night's sleep (see Box 2).

   The amount people sleep varies with age. A 3-day-old infant may sleep anywhere from 12 to 22 hours per day (with an average of 16), spread over five or six periods during the day and night. As the infant matures, the amount of sleep during the day slowly decreases, while the length of night sleep stays at about 10 hours. The mature adult

sponding. As they move through their varied activities, their behavior is accompanied by a private stream of consciousness. The total stream of consciousness includes the information they process, the events they remember, the plans they make. But a part of that stream is daydreaming, and it is as much a part of most people's lives as eating.

For most of this century, psychology has been committed to studying only observable behavior. This situation has left the realm of daydreaming—like other aspects of consciousnesss—largely neglected. But in recent years Jerome L. Singer of Yale University has addressed himself to the phenomenon of daydreaming, examining such questions as: Does everyone daydream? What types of daydreams are most common? And why do we daydream at all?

After questioning hundreds of people about their daydreams, Singer (1975) has concluded that virtually everyone daydreams, and he has identified three different types of daydreamers. The first type, like Frank, typically has rather anxious daydreams, often centered on fears of failure. These daydreams are unorganized, fleeting, and vague. The second type of daydreamer, like Janet, is given to self-criticism and self-doubt and is most likely to have hostile fantasies. The third type, whom Singer calls the "happy daydreamer," has positive fantasies, like Lou's. These daydreams usually include clear visual images and reflect

self-acceptance. Not surprisingly, people in the third group enjoy daydreaming the most.

Women and men daydream equally often and in similar ways. However, women are slightly more likely to have personal, passive, and body-oriented fantasies, while men more frequently fantasize about athletic or heroic achievement (Singer, 1976a). People seem to daydream less and less as they get older. Those who were "happy daydreamers" in their youth are the most likely to continue fantasizing in old age (Giambra, 1974).

Our daydreams and night dreams are probably related to each other. Anxious or hostile daydreamers tend to have anxious or hostile night dreams; happier daydreamers have correspondingly positive night dreams (Starker, 1974). Daydreaming appears to peak every 90 minutes or so (similar to night dreaming), and this peak is associated with reduced eye movement and a particular type of brain wave (Kripke and Sonneschein, 1973). Thus it is possible that some of the same brain mechanisms are involved in both daydreaming and night dreaming.

But there are important differences between daydreaming and night dreaming. As we will see later in this chapter, night dreaming is associated with rapid eye movements—our eyes move during dreams as if we were watching a movie behind our closed lids. While we daydream, however, we tend to move our eyes much less

than usual, as if we were staring at some far off point in space (Singer and Antrobus, 1965).

Why do we daydream? Singer speculates that daydreaming is necessary for optimum intellectual functioning, self-control, and a peaceful inner life. Our fantasies can keep us from going bananas when performing boring tasks and can provide periodic relaxation when doing demanding intellectual work (Singer, 1976b).

Daydreaming can also provide us with the rewards we need when the world around us fails to do so. Singer suggests that for people with limited internal lives the external world becomes especially compelling. "For them, the social and physical environment seems to say, 'Eat me! Drink me! Touch me! Kiss me!' and they simply can't resist these appeals" (Singer, 1976b, page 32). In the absence of an inner world, rich in images and interest, nondaydreamers may respond to the demands of the external world in nonadaptive ways, such as crime, overeating, or drug abuse. Singer found, for example, that delinquent adolescent boys daydreamed very little.

Of course, the absence of daydreaming does not necessarily produce delinquents or drug addicts. But daydreaming does appear to be important to psychological well-being. The thread of daydreaming woven through our fabric of thought may serve an important function in tying the rest of consciousness together.

sleeps 7 to 8 hours a day on the average. Those in middle and old age tend to sleep less and to wake up more frequently during the night.

Sleep patterns can also vary from day to day. Physical exercise in the afternoon is likely to lead to longer sleep that night. People also tend to sleep less soundly during their first night in a new place, such as when they are on a vacation or during their first night in a sleep laboratory, where volunteers take part in systematic studies of sleep (Webb and Bonnet, 1979).

We spend a third of our lives asleep, yet we know very little about why we sleep.

When we want to go to sleep, we ordinarily seek a quiet room, turn the lights off, lie down, and close our eyes. These actions have important effects on our nervous system. The quiet environment and closing of our eyes reduces external sensory input. By lying down, we cut off a significant portion of the feedback from muscles that keep the brain aroused when we are sitting or standing. All these changes decrease the general level of activation in the brain, thereby helping us to move from waking to sleeping.

We usually think of "falling asleep" as being a slow, gradual process. In fact, however, it happens in an instant. As William Dement (1972), a leading sleep researcher, put it, "One second the organism is aware—the next second it is not. Awareness stops abruptly, as if 10 billion furiously communicating brain cells were suddenly placed on 'stand-by' status."

Although sleep occupies a large portion of our lives, researchers are still in the early stages of studying it. Dement believes that scientists have been much too slow in focusing their attention on sleep. He was recently observed waving a huge medical text in the air and shouting to his students, "This book represents three hundred years' study of the human body—but only in the waking state! What we need is three hundred years' study of the human body during sleep!" (Galvin, 1979, page 53). So far we have had only about 30 years of intensive study on sleep. But this work has already led to a greatly increased understanding of this mysterious third of our lives.

Stages of Sleep

A major discovery made by sleep researchers is that sleep is not a single state. Rather, during a single night's sleep we move through a sleep cycle that consists of several different stages of sleep, each associated with its own distinctive pattern of brain waves (see Figure 3.1).

FIGURE 3.1

The stages of sleep, as indicated by specific patterns of brain waves.

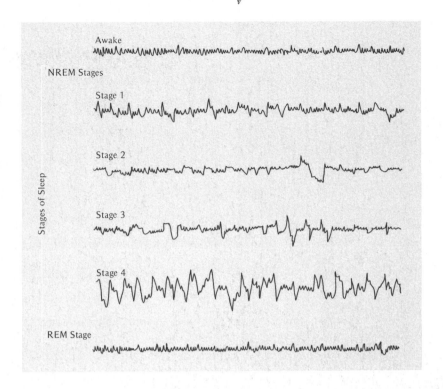

DALI'S NAP

What is the shortest nap a person can take? The story goes that Salvador Dali, the surrealist painter, used to put a tin plate on the floor and then sit on a chair beside it, holding a spoon over the plate. He would then go into a doze. The moment that he fell asleep the spoon would slip from his fingers and clang onto the plate, immediately awakening him. Dali claimed that he was completely refreshed by the sleep that took place between the time the spoon left his hand and the time it hit the plate (Dement, 1972).

Stage 1 is falling asleep, the stage that usually occurs a few minutes after climbing into bed. Brain waves are irregular, and they lack the pattern of alpha waves that characterize the relaxed waking state. The heart rate begins to slow, and muscles relax. The person in stage 1 is easy to waken and may not realize that he has fallen asleep.

In *stage 2*, brain waves show bursts of activity called "spindles," so named because their tracings on an EEG chart resemble thread wrapped around an old-fashioned spindle. Stage 2 is a deeper stage of sleep than stage 1.

In *stage 3*, even deeper sleep, the spindles disappear and long, slow (about one wave per second) brain waves called delta waves appear. At this stage the sleeper is difficult to waken and unresponsive to external stimuli. Heart rate, blood pressure, and temperature continue to drop.

Stage 4 is the deepest stage. It is called *delta sleep* because it is characterized by the slow delta waves. In young adults delta sleep occurs in 15- or 30-minute segments interspersed with lighter stages, during the first half of the night. As one grows older, delta sleep lessens.

After a sleeper has gone through stages 1 through 4, he then starts back up through the stages, through a period of 3 and 2. But when the brain waves again reach stage 1, the sleeper does not waken. Instead, his eyes start darting and rolling around under his closed eyelids. This is the start of a stage of sleep called *REM (rapid eye movement) sleep*. As we will soon see, it is during REM sleep that we dream. The REM periods are easily visible to anyone who looks closely at the sleeper's eyelids. An hour or so after the person has gone to sleep, the first REM period of the night usually starts and lasts about 5 to 10 minutes. Later in the night REM periods last as

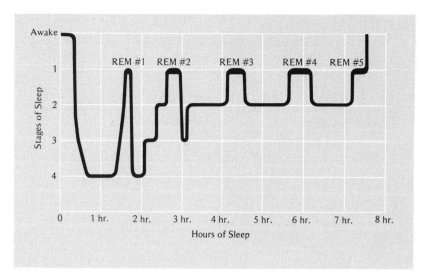

FIGURE 3.2

A typical night's sleep. Sleep stages occur in cycles during the night, with the deepest sleep appearing primarily in the first few hours and REM periods, during which we dream, lengthening in the later hours.

long as 25 minutes. Such eye movements do not occur in stages 1 through 4, so they are referred to as non-REM (NREM) sleep.

During a typical night's sleep, a person goes up and down through the stages, but with each cycle the REM period becomes longer and the slow-wave stages become shorter. In later cycles it is common for the sleeper to go only to stage 2 and then back to REM. These cycles are about 90 minutes long (see Figure 3.2).

REM and NREM sleep differ greatly in their mental activity. Almost every time people are awakened during a REM period they report that they have been dreaming. But people who are awakened during NREM sleep rarely report that they have been dreaming. And the mental content they do report usually seems more like random thoughts than real dreams with vivid images. Many researchers have therefore concluded that REM sleep and dreaming are almost synonymous. When the sleeper's eyes dart around during REM sleep, she may well be looking at the various people and events of the dream. (We'll have more to say about dreaming a little later in this chapter.)

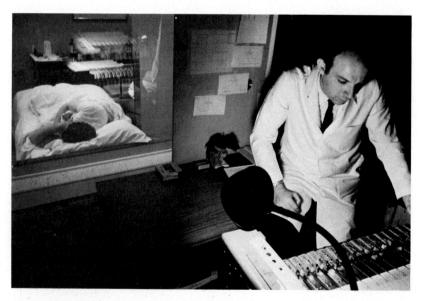

In a typical sleep laboratory, subjects are made comfortable for the night and are hooked up to EEG monitoring equipment. Researchers can observe them through one-way windows in order to record any movements or behaviors in addition to the brain wave tracings.

REM sleep is often referred to as "paradoxical sleep" because the brain seems to be highly activated, even though the person is clearly asleep. During REM sleep, pulse rate and respiration are a bit faster than during NREM sleep, blood pressure is higher, and all three processes are less regular. There is also a major decrease in muscle tone during REM sleep.

— Box 2

Long-sleepers and short-sleepers

Napoleon Bonaparte apparently flourished on only 4 to 6 hours of sleep each night. Albert Einstein, on the other hand, was a very long sleeper. Recent evidence suggests that the contrasting sleep preferences of eminent and ordinary people alike may be related to differences in both personality and brain function.

Napoleon Bonaparte, a short-sleeper.

Of course, most of us are not extremely long- or short-sleepers. Furthermore, it is difficult for us to tell which we are, because many aspects of our environments interfere with the expression of our natural sleep preferences. However, Ernest L. Hartmann (1973) was able to study groups of short- and long-sleepers under carefully controlled conditions, in which late-night movies and early-morning classes could not get in the way. Free to sleep as little or as much as they pleased, the short-sleeping subjects averaged only 5½ hours of sleep each night. They usually fell asleep within about 15 minutes and spent little time awake in bed. The long-sleepers, in contrast, averaged about 8½ hours of sleep each night, took over 30 minutes to fall asleep, and spent at least another 30 minutes awake each night in bed. Long-sleepers seemed to regard sleep as a luxury, while short-sleepers considered it almost a chore.

Albert Einstein, a long-sleeper.

Hartmann carefully monitored the sleep patterns of both groups. The two groups showed approximately equal durations of the four stages of non-REM sleep. However, long-sleepers spent almost twice as much time each night (2 hours as compared to only 1 hour for short-sleepers) in REM sleep, suggesting that long-sleepers also dream much more than short-sleepers.

Some studies have failed to find any personality differences between long- and short-sleepers (e.g., Webb and Friel, 1971). But Hartmann's research suggested that, on the average, short-sleepers are more extroverted, carefree, and confident than long-sleepers, while long-sleepers tend to be more introverted, anxious, and unsettled. Short-sleepers may be more productive, but long-sleepers appear to be more creative. To Hartmann, eminent short-sleepers seemed to be extremely efficient and practical persons—leaders in business and government, administrators, and applied scientists. Famous long-sleepers, on the other hand, resembled the "tortured genius."

Hartmann believes that REM sleep may help restore the effectiveness of certain brain pathways in which norepinephrine is a transmitter substance. For some unknown reason, some people may have more norepinephrine—or may restore it more quickly—than others. Other people may need more REM sleep to replenish their norepinephrine. Since brain levels of norepinephrine appear to be related to motor behavior, memory, attention, and mood, suggestions of an association between sleeping patterns and personality may be reasonable.

Sleep Disorders

A surprisingly large number of people have trouble falling or staying asleep, a problem called *insomnia*. Some people toss and turn restlessly until they get to sleep but then sleep well the rest of the night. Others wake up repeatedly throughout the night. In a recent survey in Los Angeles, over 40 percent of adults reported having a current or past problem with insomnia, and it was most prevalent among older people (Bixler et al., 1979). Insomniac clubs have been formed in some cities and, as you might expect, meetings are held late at night when no one can fall asleep.

There are several causes of insomnia. Some people take all their daytime worries to bed with them, which prevents them from relaxing enough to sleep. Others are actually afraid of falling asleep, for fear of nightmares or of emergencies that might arise. In addition, people with irregular schedules often have difficulty dropping off. Sleep is one of the body's natural rhythms (see the Psychological Issue for Chapter 2), and changing schedules can throw the rhythm off balance. Paradoxically, both sleeping pills and alcohol can produce insomnia. Although these drugs are sometimes helpful in small doses, they require ever-increasing amounts to be effective, and they disrupt the natural sequence of sleep stages. On the other hand, methods of relaxing the mind and muscles have proven to be effective in beating sleeplessness.

Insomnia is the most common sleep disorder, but it is not the only one. Most of us have had the embarrassing experience of falling asleep in an inappropriate situation, such as in a class or at a movie with friends. Fatigue and boredom are usually the culprits. A small number of people have a much more serious problem with "sleep

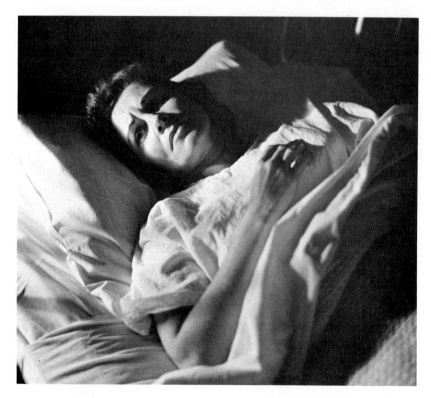

Worries and tensions from the day are among the factors that can prevent us from falling asleep at night.

attacks," a disorder called *narcolepsy*. At any time of the day they may suddenly drop into a deep sleep for up to 15 minutes. In attacks of narcolepsy, the person is plunged directly in REM sleep, unlike the normal sleep pattern in which REMs appear after 90 minutes or so. Although the precise causes of narcolepsy are not known, it may involve a disorder in the brain mechanisms that control REM sleep (Webb and Bonnet, 1979).

Sleepwalking is another sleep disorder, most common among children. Sleepwalkers are not acting out dreams, as has sometimes been assumed. Sleepwalking occurs during stage 4 sleep when there is very little, if any, dreaming. People awakened while sleepwalking generally don't report any dreams. Sleepwalking is usually outgrown, but some adults continue to walk in their sleep.

Some people experience attacks called *night terrors* that waken them directly from a deep stage of sleep. Night terrors are different from nightmares, which are scary dreams that occur during REM sleep. Nightmares raise the heartbeat only slightly and may be forgotten with the morning light. But night terrors involve sudden awakening from deep sleep (stage 4). The person awakes in a panic, may scream or cower in fear, has an elevated heart rate, and may break out in a cold sweat. Night terrors are most common in children. They peak between the ages of 3 and 5, but are occasionally seen in adults.

DREAMING

I have a key that opens a closed drugstore. I go in as if I'm looking for something. I am a sweet, young, responsible girl, like Teresa Wright in Shadow of a Doubt. *I also have a key to the beauty parlor next door. I go in in order to leave something (a comb and mirror?) in the window. I come back to the drugstore when it is open and decide to have a dessert. I inquire about a letter I sent to myself at this address but it hasn't arrived. I finally find it on a counter—this is what I have been looking for in the drugstore—and I leave. Next I am playing hopscotch with some little girls as it grows dark. Police come and arrest me. They ask me why I killed the little girl (some days earlier, I assume). I say it was because she was very unhappy. They take me away.*

This account, taken from one woman's "dream diary," emphasizes the fact that in dreams we do things that we cannot do in real life. We fly, we change identities, we even kill people. Through most of the world's history, humans have regarded dreams as magical states, as ways of exchanging one's worldly identity and limitations for new selves and new capacities, and as messengers of divine instructions and prophecies. In many cultures people who were thought to have the ability to interpret dreams were likely to be highly respected leaders. Today we are still fascinated by dreams and their meanings. One approach, the interpretation of dreams and their symbols, was given new impetus by Sigmund Freud, who saw dreams as the "royal road to the unconscious." More recently, systematic studies are exploring the physiological bases of dreaming, as well as its contribution to our emotional well-being.

The Interpretation of Dreams

Sigmund Freud came into prominence with the publication of *The Interpretation of Dreams* in 1900. In this work, Freud stated dreams represent the fulfillment of unconscious impulses, unacceptable on a conscious level. He also thought that dreams function to preserve sleep by disguising these wishes and impulses through the use of symbolism, condensation, and displacement.

By *symbolism* Freud meant that unacceptable ideas are presented in a more acceptable—symbolic—form in dreams. Freud focused primarily on sexual symbols, suggesting that sharp, elongated objects (umbrellas, swords, sticks) were symbols of the penis and that containers (cups, boxes, houses) were symbols of the vagina. By *condensation* Freud meant that one image in a dream could represent several elements in a person's life. For example, a dream about scoring a touchdown in a football game may bring together a man's feelings about competition, fame, and sexual accomplishment. By *displacement* Freud meant that events in a dream could focus unacceptable wishes on an object or thing different from the real object of the wishes. For instance, dreaming of hitting a tiger with a baseball bat might represent a displaced wish to harm an authority figure in one's life.

While we sleep, Freud believed, our repressed wishes—especially sexual desires—thrust to the surface and are fulfilled. Disguising these impulses is necessary so that the guilt associated with the disturbing impulse will not perturb the sleeper. If the meaning of the dream were to become known to the dreamer—if a woman actually dreamed of having sexual relations with her father, for instance—she might awaken in order to get rid of such unacceptable thoughts.

Freud distinguished two types of content in dreams: the latent content and the manifest content. The *latent* content is the underlying meaning of the dream. The *manifest* content is the disguised form

The surrealistic world of our dreams lends itself to many interpretations that can provide insights into our waking lives.

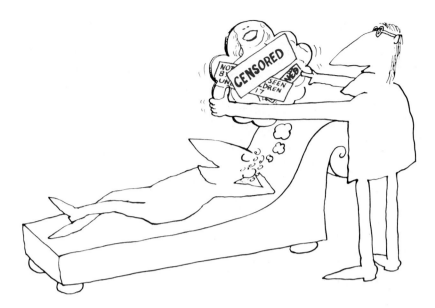

of the dream that we remember when we wake up. For example, a woman may dream that she is playing a carnival game where she tosses a ring onto a bottle and wins a giant teddy bear. That is the manifest content of the dream. The latent content may be that she wishes she could conceive and have a baby.

Freud's specific approach to the interpretation of dreams can be—and has been—criticized. Because sexual impulses play a central role in Freud's theory of personality, Freud almost always found sexual desires in the latent content of dreams. Other dream theorists do not give sex such important status in their interpretations. In addition, Freud's approach was based on analyzing the dreams of his patients, and he concentrated on those dreams that could be interpreted meaningfully in his framework. Today, most dream analysts feel that dreams can have a much wider range of meanings and functions than Freud believed. Calvin Hall (1966), a leading dream researcher, suggests that we view a dream as "a personal document, a letter to oneself." Hall has also pointed out that gathering and interpreting a series of dreams—looking at the common themes that run through them—can be more helpful than focusing on a single dream.

Where Do Dreams Come From?

People in some cultures have believed that dreams come from the travel of the soul outside the body. Freud believed that dreams originate in unconscious wishes. But recent research provides a different perspective: the idea that dreams originate in the activity of different portions of the brain during REM sleep. According to the *activation-synthesis model* of dreams recently put forth by Allan Hobson and Robert McCarley (1977), the dream process begins with the periodic firing of nerve cells known as *giant cells* in the brain stem. This firing leads to the rapid eye movements and brain waves characteristic of REM sleep, and it also leads to high levels of *activation* in other areas of the brain, including those areas concerned with sensation (especially vision), motor activity, and emotion. At the same time, this neu-

A WELL-EXECUTED DREAM

We often incorporate external stimuli into our dreams, sometimes in highly creative ways. If water is squirted on a dreamer, he may dream of being caught in a thunderstorm. Or a pinprick may become an injection in a doctor's office. In a book written in 1861, André Maury reported a dream set during the French Revolution. The dream included his trial, conviction, and travel to the place of execution. Maury climbed onto the scaffold, was bound, and felt the guillotine fall. He awoke to find that the top of his bed had fallen and had struck him in the back of the neck. The bedtop hitting his neck had been worked into the dream as his execution (Webb and Bonnet, 1979).

ral firing greatly reduces the tone of the major muscles of the body, such as in the arms and legs, producing a kind of paralysis.

During a dream, of course, the activation of sensory areas of the brain does not correspond to actual events, as it does when we are awake. And the inhibition of muscles during REM sleep prevents the actual acting out of motor impulses. Instead, we *synthesize* a dream mentally, coming up with content that corresponds to the pattern of brain activation. For example, stimulation of brain centers for vision, as well as feedback from rapid eye movements, may lead to the rapidly shifting scenes that are characteristic of dreams; stimulation of the brain centers of the vestibular senses (sense of balance) may lead to sensations of spinning or floating. According to the activation-synthesis model, it is the unusual intensity and rapidity of the brain stimulation, often activating simultaneously areas of the brain that are unlikely to be activated simultaneously when we are awake, that accounts for the highly changeable and sometimes bizarre content of our dreams.

Although the Hobson-McCarley model helps to link physiological events with the events of dreams, it raises more questions than it answers about the content of dreams. What leads a person to synthesize a dream that includes specific persons and incidents? Our memories, emotions, and personality styles, as well as the previous day's events are all likely to play a prominent role. In the dream quoted at the beginning of this section, for instance, the woman might have seen Hitchcock's *Shadow of a Doubt* on the day before she had the dream or she may have gone to the drugstore. Dreams may still serve as wish-fulfillments, as Freud believed, even as they correspond to patterns of physiological activation.

The Functions of Dreaming

The need to dream appears to be as basic as the need to sleep. Young adults dream about two hours a night on the average—whether or not the dreams are remembered. In one experiment, people were awakened for five consecutive nights just as the periods of REM sleep began (Dement, 1960), so they were prevented from dreaming. These dream-deprived individuals became anxious, irritable, and angry; they had difficulty concentrating, and some began to hallucinate. Moreover, as subjects were deprived of REM sleep their need for it seemed to build. When they went back to sleep, they entered REM sleep more often. And for as many as five nights following REM deprivation, the subjects spent more time in REM sleep than usual— sometimes as much as double the normal amount.

Why do we have such a strong need to dream? Freud believed, as we have seen, that dreams provide for the expression of repressed impulses, albeit in disguised form. Carl Jung (1964) took another view of the function of dreams. He argued that dreams compensate for things that we lack when we are awake and thus serve to restore our overall psychological balance. Wish-fulfillment may sometimes be a part of this balancing mechanism. If a woman has a strong desire to punch her boss in the nose but can't actually do it in her waking life, she can do it in her dreams. In other cases, Jung believed, dreams can bring us messages from our unconscious minds, including warnings of personal weakness.

Recent research has begun to document the ways dreams can help people deal with problems in their waking lives. Rosalind Cartwright (1978) has found that people seem to handle emotional situations more realistically after dreaming. In one study, she presented students with incomplete "problem stories" before bedtime in a sleep laboratory. The stories dealt with common concerns of young adults, such as separation from home. The subjects then went to sleep. Some were allowed to dream (they were awakened only during NREM sleep), while others were not (they were awakened only during REM sleep or were not allowed to sleep at all). In the morning, when asked about possible solutions to the problem posed in a story, the subjects who had been allowed to dream were better able to acknowledge the realistic dimensions of the problem. The results of this and other studies have led Cartwright to propose that dreams provide "a kind of workshop for the repair of self-esteem and competence."

In a book called *Creative Dreaming* (1974), Patricia Garfield suggests that we can train ourselves to dream about specific issues that are troubling us. Such methods have apparently been used for generations by the Temiar, a Malaysian people who teach their children to report their dreams each morning, to control the frightening ones, and to take their dreams into account in their waking lives. There is no solid evidence to date that people in the Western world can, in fact, control their dreams, at least in experimental situations in a sleep laboratory. Nevertheless, if further research bears out current speculation about the functions of dreams, such attempts to "take our dreams in hand" may benefit many people.

DRUGS

Throughout history people have taken various chemical substances to change their mood, perception, and thought processes. Today is no exception, with a wide variety of drugs available to lift one up, bring one down, expand one's consciousness, or shake up one's senses. Such chemicals that have a noticeable impact on mood, behavior, or perception are called *psychoactive drugs*. In this chapter we will focus on several of these psychoactive drugs—LSD, marijuana, amphetamines, and cocaine—and explore their effects on consciousness. Other common drugs are discussed in Box 3.

Even though different psychoactive drugs have different effects, they all work by altering chemical events in the brain, although the exact mechanisms are just now being uncovered. As we noted in Chapter 2, communication between nerve cells (neurons) is primarily through chemical messengers called transmitter substances. Many psychoactive drugs are chemically similar to certain of the brain's transmitter substances. In some instances, these drugs can attach themselves to receptor neurons and exert effects that mimic those of the brain's own transmitters. In other cases, psychoactive drugs produce chemical reactions that either stimulate or inhibit the production of the brain's transmitter substances.

Why Do People Take Drugs?

There is a long list of reasons why some people choose to try drugs and others abstain. The possibilities listed by Lipinski and Lipinski (1970) are:

Curiosity.

The feeling of missing something, or not being "with it."

A need to prove one's intellectual depth and emotional maturity (particularly for shy people who don't relate easily to others).

A search for meaning. Failing to find a clear answer in the outside world, the quest turns inward.

Escape from feelings of inadequacy. Hoping for a magical cure for emotional problems without the embarrassment of revealing "weakness" to others.

An end to isolation. Drugs may give the feeling of greater closeness with others.

In addition to these motivations, drug use also depends on people's social environment and on the examples set by others. For example, Smart and Fejer (1972) found a positive association between the drug use patterns (including alcohol and tobacco) of 8865 Toronto students and the patterns of their parents. Their data suggested that young people may often use their parents as models in deciding whether or not to try drugs.

LSD and the Psychedelic Drugs

LSD–25 (*lysergic acid diethylamide*) is a *psychedelic drug*—that is, a drug that causes a profound alteration of sensory, perceptual, cognitive, and emotional experiences. It takes only a tiny speck of this substance to produce intense hallucinations and distortions of vision, sound, time, and feelings. Sensations merge into each other, and the person may say he can taste color or see sounds. The effects of the drug depend to a great extent on the personal characteristics of the user, on the setting in which the drug is taken, and on the purity of the substance being used.

LSD was originally used in research on social problems. It was tried with alcoholics to help them stop drinking and with autistic children to increase their contact with people in the real world (Ungerleider and Fisher, 1970). In an effort to produce greater pain tolerance and a calmer acceptance of death, LSD has also been used by persons dying of cancer.

There are several other psychedelic drugs that produce psychological effects similar to those of LSD. *Peyote* (a Mexican cactus), is made up of alkaloids (one of which is mescaline) that produce intense color awareness and hallucinations. Reflexes seem heightened, hearing and sight seem intensified, and ideas flow rapidly (Nabokov, 1969). Some Indian tribes have used mescal buttons (from the peyote cactus) for centuries in religious ceremonies. Another drug, *psilocybin,* is derived from mushrooms that have been used in Indian religious rites since ancient times. Psilocybin is not nearly as potent as LSD, but it produces similar hallucinogenic effects.

The manner in which LSD and the other psychedelics operate is still far from clear. However, one prominent theory holds that LSD may work by blocking the effects of serotonin, a transmitter substance. Serotonin usually acts to inhibit thought processes and emotions. LSD, which is chemically similar to serotonin, may attach itself to serotonin receptors in the brain. This may prevent the normal functioning of serotonin, causing the consciousness to become flooded with remote associations and feelings (Siegel and Jarvik, 1975).

Marijuana

Marijuana is made from the flowering tops of the hemp plant, *Cannabis sativa*, and except for alcohol it is probably humanity's oldest drug. It was used in ancient China and eventually found its way to India, North Africa, and Europe. In fact, it may have been brought to Europe by Napoleon's troops returning from Egypt. Marijuana has been used for centuries in Central and South America but became important in the United States only after 1920.

During the 1930s and 1940s an aggressive law enforcement and publicity campaign condemning marijuana as "the assassin of youth" helped restrict its use to the poor and eccentric. But during the 1960s marijuana had an explosion of popularity. As of 1979, an estimated 43 million Americans had smoked marijuana at least once. At least half of those people were regular users, despite the fact that the drug was illegal (Schmeck, 1980). More and more adolescents are

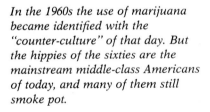

In the 1960s the use of marijuana became identified with the "counter-culture" of that day. But the hippies of the sixties are the mainstream middle-class Americans of today, and many of them still smoke pot.

smoking marijuana, and they are doing so at earlier ages. A 1978 survey showed that 28 percent of high-school seniors had smoked marijuana before they reached the tenth grade; over 10 percent were daily users (Gelman et al., 1980). The ready availability of the drug, along with peer pressure to use it, has made marijuana a staple in many young people's lives.

For many users, marijuana provides a "high"—a sense of elation or well-being. Some people say it enhances enjoyment of food and sex and that it heightens all sensory perceptions. Marijuana has two easily observable physiological effects: it increases heart rate and enhances appetite. It also affects brain function, producing detectable changes in brain waves. But researchers are not yet sure just how it works. While many researchers believe that marijuana operates on transmitter substances in the brain (Maugh, 1974), it has also been suggested that the drug has a direct effect on nerve fibers (Byck and Ritchie, 1973).

Partly because of the growing wave of use and the debate about its legalization, researchers have been concentrating on the long-term effects of marijuana use. The results are conflicting, however. Emotions tend to run high on this issue, and even "objective" scientists are prone to show some personal bias for or against marijuana use. Nevertheless, it is possible to draw some general conclusions regarding the effects of marijuana on behavior. Some of the most serious charges leveled against the drug—such as that it causes permanent brain damage—are probably not justified (Zinberg, 1976). Some of marijuana's opponents have contended that its extended use decreases male sex hormone levels. These hormone levels have been found to drop slightly in male smokers, but they still stay within normal limits (Clark, Hager, and Shapiro, 1980). Nor does it appear that marijuana is addictive, as some people have charged. Smokers do develop a tolerance for marijuana, needing greater and greater amounts to achieve the same effects. But addiction does not occur in the same sense that it does with alcohol and other drugs; stopping smoking produces no withdrawal symptoms (Zinberg, 1976).

These findings may make marijuana sound as benign as aspirin. But that isn't quite the case. Marijuana elevates heart rate, and it is probably dangerous for people with a heart condition to use it. And because marijuana reduces perceptual acuity and motor coordination, driving or operating machinery while high can be dangerous (Clark, Hager, and Shapiro, 1980). Smoking any substance can cause lung damage. Because of its unpredictable effects on judgment and emotions, use of marijuana—like other intoxicants—can be risky for the young or the emotionally troubled.

On the other hand, marijuana may actually have some medically beneficial effects for certain groups of people. It has been found to be helpful for some patients suffering from glaucoma, a painful eye disease that can cause blindness (Schmeck, 1980). Research continues on the use of marijuana in treating cancer patients who are receiving chemotherapy or radiation therapy. These treatments cause serious nausea and lack of appetite, which marijuana sometimes appears to alleviate. Experiments are also continuing in the use of marijuana to treat asthma, epilepsy, and pain (Cohen, 1978).

Amphetamines

Amphetamines are a group of drugs that act as central nervous system stimulants. In 1887 a German pharmacologist synthesized the first amphetamine (Benzedrine) but he was not interested in exploring the pharmacological properties of the drug and put the project aside. In 1932, the Benzedrine inhaler was made available to the public in drugstores across the country. It was taken as a medicine for hay fever, asthma, and other disorders involving nasal congestion. The American Medical Association gave this new drug the generic name *amphetamine*, from *a*lpha-*m*ethyl-*phet*hyl-*amine*. The only caution for the drug at the time was that "continued overdose" might cause "restlessness and sleeplessness." Physicians were assured that no serious reactions had been observed. By the end of World War II, at least seven different inhalers containing large amounts of amphetamine were on the market and all could be purchased without a prescription.

In recent years, amphetamines as prescription drugs have been produced in the billions of tablets per year. They have been prescribed as "pep pills" and have been used by countless students staying up all night cramming for exams and by long-distance truck drivers trying to stay alert on all-night hauls. Amphetamines can also suppress the appetite, and they were widely prescribed as diet pills until the Food and Drug Administration recently banned them for this purpose, judging them to be ineffective and dangerous.

Although amphetamine has its uses, it is a dangerous drug on which people can become dependent. People who abuse amphetamines ("speed freaks") take the pills in large doses or even inject amphetamine in liquid form. They may spend several days on a "run," keeping a continuous high by injecting the drug every few hours. When the amphetamine high is over, the physical and psychological effects can be terribly uncomfortable. The user may suffer extreme lethargy, anxiety, headaches, muscle cramps, terrifying nightmares, severe depression, and disorientation; he may also become extremely irritable and demanding.

Amphetamine use can also lead to *amphetamine psychosis*, a group of symptoms remarkably similar to those of the psychological disorder called paranoid schizophrenia (see Chapter 11). In fact, without prior knowledge of a patient's history of drug abuse, a psychiatrist or psychologist may misdiagnose amphetamine psychosis as

The effects of amphetamine on the web spinning of an adult female spider.

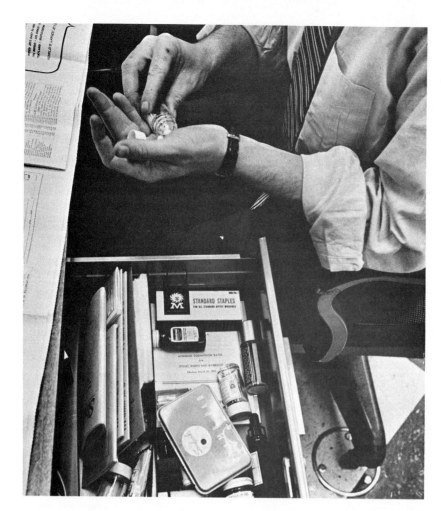

People from all walks of life have come to depend on certain kinds of drugs to help them deal with their problems.

schizophrenia. Solomon Snyder has described the state of amphetamine psychosis: "The harbinger is vague fear and suspicion—*What was that? I heard something. Is somebody trying to get me?* Soon the paranoia centers around a specific delusion. . . . Acting on his delusions the speed freak may become violent—*to get them before they get me*" (1972, page 44). The person caught in amphetamine psychosis may also spend hours in a compulsive stereotyped behavior, such as counting grains of sand, without seeming to be fatigued or bored.

Because of the similarity of amphetamine effects to schizophrenia, researchers believe that if we could understand how amphetamines affect the brain we might get important clues about the biological bases of schizophrenia. As with the psychedelic drugs, amphetamines produce their psychological effects by influencing neural transmission. Specifically, amphetamines seem to trigger the release of dopamine from neurons in the brain. Dopamine is an excitatory transmitter associated with the arousal and emotional functions of the brain (Iversen, 1979).

Cocaine

Cocaine, like amphetamine, is a stimulant. It is a chemical compound extracted from the leaves of the coca plant. This plant has been grown for thousands of years in South America, where peasant workers regularly chew its leaves. In the eighteenth century European explorers noted that the leaves seemed to help the workers tolerate hunger, cold, and fatigue. Considered a boon to good health, the drug was gradually introduced to Western Europe and, from there, to North America. By the late nineteenth century cocaine was a featured ingredient in dozens of patent medicines. Its benefits were extolled in the treatment of disorders ranging from colds to loss of sexual desire.

Cocaine's most famous fictional user was Sherlock Holmes. But the exasperated disapproval of Dr. Watson reflected changing public attitudes. By the 1920s cocaine use was becoming associated with the "fringe" of society: performing artists, casual laborers, and minority racial groups. The *New York Times* called for a ban on the drug, and the Coca-Cola company eliminated cocaine from their product, substituting caffeine. In 1922 Congress prohibited import of the plant and drug (Grinspoon and Bakalar, 1977).

What was the threat posed by cocaine? This is a difficult question to answer, because little research has been done on the drug. But a few general effects are known. Whether it is chewed, drunk as tea, inhaled in powder form, smoked, or injected, cocaine typically produces a feeling of alertness, mastery, and self-confidence, often accompanied by talkativeness. It may also produce nervousness, irritability, restlessness, and exhaustion from lack of sleep. Users may experience mild depression when "coming down," but this aftereffect is regarded by cocaine users in much the same way as the hangover is treated by social drinkers: a small price to pay for the pleasure of indulgence.

Cocaine acts by stimulating the central nervous system. Like other stimulants, cocaine increases heart rate and breathing rate, raises body temperature and blood-sugar levels, increases muscle tension, and dilates pupils. The drug does not appear to cause physiological dependence or addiction, although people may become dependent on it psychologically (Grinspoon and Bakalar, 1977).

Cocaine use is on the rise today. It is estimated by the National Institute on Drug Abuse that about 14 percent of males between the ages of 20 and 30 have tried cocaine at least once. Because the drug is difficult to import and refine, it is extremely expensive. Pharmaceutical companies can purchase the drug legally for a little over $30 an ounce; the street price is close to $3000 an ounce. This price effectively restricts the drug's use to high-income groups. Cocaine appears to be as much a part of the rock industry as rehearsals. What is new is that people in more traditional professions are beginning to use the drug as casually as alcohol and nicotine. Because of its apparently limited physical effects, there have been calls for the legalization of cocaine. But until we know more about its short- and long-term effects, cocaine use remains a risk.

In addition to the psychoactive drugs that we have discussed, there are other drugs that large numbers of people ingest every day, beginning with their breakfast cup of coffee. We discuss these common drugs in Box 3.

— Box 3 —

The common drugs

A nation of drug addicts? Well, not quite, but most of us do use drugs a great deal more than we are aware.

Cigarettes, for example, are a common source of nicotine, a drug that acts by blocking transmission in the sympathetic nervous system. Nicotine causes constriction in the peripheral blood vessels, elevates heart rate and blood pressure, and increases stomach activity. Perhaps for this reason smokers often find cigarettes after meals quite pleasurable.

Caffeine, in coffee, tea, and cola drinks, acts as a central nervous system stimulant. People who consume too much caffeine may experience tremors, rapid heartbeat, overactivity, restlessness, and nausea. Strangely enough, caffeine is the "extra ingredient" in many common pain relievers, though its effects on pain are not clear.

Caffeine—like nicotine—is mildly addictive, a fact that has been discovered by millions of people who feel they can't function without beginning the day with a cup of coffee (or, for some people, a can of cola). Indeed, it has been suggested that if caffeine were a newly introduced drug, it would not be made available without a prescription (Timson, 1978).

Ethyl alcohol is consumed in huge quantities in beer, wine, and liquor. Alcohol abuse is the biggest drug problem in America today, in all age groups. Small doses cause dilation of the pupils, slight increases in blood pressure, and temporary elevation of blood sugar level. Larger doses interfere with fine discrimination, motor control, and self-restraint. Excessive doses can cause coma and death.

Finally, there are a large number of drugs that are not quite as popular but are by no means uncommon. Codeine, a narcotic, is used for pain relief and for remedy of coughs. Sedatives and tranquilizers are used by thousands of people to promote relaxation, reduce anxiety, and induce sleep. Large numbers of people trap themselves in a vicious cycle, taking one pill for pep in the morning, various other stimulants and anxiety-reducers during the day, and a sleeping pill at night.

Nicotine, contained in tobacco, is a mildly addictive drug.

HYPNOSIS

Don't look up while you're reading this. There may be someone nearby whose piercing eyes are waiting to catch your attention, hypnotize you, destroy your willpower, and make you a slave. At least, that's what you might believe if you watch too many old movies. The mystery surrounding hypnosis was inevitable, because it can produce so many unusual phenomena. Although there is still some controversy about it, hypnosis can be considered an altered state of consciousness, in which the hypnotized subject can be influenced to behave and to experience things differently than she would in the ordinary waking state. Whereas drugs can induce changes in consciousness chemically, hypnosis is a non-chemically-induced altered state. Naturally you have some questions about this unusual state of consciousness, and we will try to answer a few of them for you.

A subject in a hypnotic trance becomes highly receptive to the suggestions of the hypnotist.

What Is Hypnosis?

Hypnosis is a state of increased suggestibility (or willingness to comply with another person's directions) that is brought about through the use of certain procedures by another person, the hypnotist. The hypnotist usually begins by asking the person to focus on an object or by telling the person that she is getting sleepy. The point is to get the subject to relax, to use her imagination, to attend closely to what is said, and to stop fighting it. The rest is up to the subject and her willingness to go along with the hypnotist's suggestions.

The hypnotist might then suggest that the subject perform certain behaviors, such as hopping on one foot or singing a song in the style of Elvis Presley. Or the suggestion might be to hallucinate or imagine something that isn't really there, such as a fly buzzing around the subject's head. A subject may be told to forget specific material, such as her boyfriend's name; this type of suggestion, when it works, creates *hypnotic amnesia*. Or the subject may be instructed to perform certain behaviors on a signal after she is back in the waking state; this is termed *posthypnotic suggestion*. For example, the suggestion might be for the subject to stand up whenever the hypnotist says the word *day*. After the subject comes out of the trance she is not aware of this posthypnotic suggestion and is baffled by the fact that she stands up when the hypnotist says, "This sure is a beautiful day."

Who Can Be Hypnotized?

Most people are susceptible to hypnosis to some degree, but some people are much more susceptible than others. Ernest Hilgard (1965) and his colleagues developed the Stanford Hypnotic Susceptibility Scale to measure how easily a person can be hypnotized. After a short attempted hypnotic induction, the subject is given a series of suggestions—to sway, to close his eyes, to imagine a buzzing fly, and so on. The more items that the subject "passes"—for example, by swaying when asked to or by grimacing to acknowledge the buzzing fly—the higher his susceptibility score. This score provides a good indication of how susceptible subjects will be to full-fledged hypnotic inductions.

In general, men and women are equally hypnotizable. People who have vivid imaginations and who feel comfortable accepting the commands of others tend to be hypnotized more easily. Susceptibility to hypnosis rises during childhood to a maximum at age 8 to 10, then declines slowly after that (Morgan and Hilgard, 1971). Josephine Hilgard (1970) has also found a clear link between children's involvement in imaginative activities such as reading and fantasy play and their later hypnotizability as adults.

Can Hypnosis Reduce Pain?

There is no question that some people can free themselves from even severe pain through hypnosis. Dental patients, burn victims, women in childbirth, and terminal cancer patients have all been relieved of pain through hypnosis (Hilgard and Hilgard, 1975). One method of studying pain in the laboratory uses the *cold pressor response,* which is the pain experienced when the hand and forearm are placed in circulating ice water. The pain is quite severe for most people and increases very rapidly over 30 to 45 seconds. But hypnotized subjects placed in this situation and given suggestions to the effect that the experience is not painful report very little pain. Instead they may describe what they feel as "a slight tingle" or "like a cold wind blowing on my arm."

While subjects in this situation report very little pain, physiological measures such as heart rate and blood pressure are extremely high. Ernest Hilgard (1977) views this phenomenon as a *dissociation,* or separation between different aspects of consciousness. Hilgard considers pain to be a complex state with at least two separable components: the sensory aspect (such as the sensation of extreme cold) and the emotional aspect (the feeling of suffering that commonly accompanies the sensation). Hilgard concludes that the hypnotic suggestion primarily affects the emotional component and not the sensory component. This type of dissociation is very different from the mechanism of pain reduction found with certain pain-reducing drugs (see Chapter 4, Box 3). The drugs appear to act by blocking the transmission of pain signals to the brain, especially to the areas that control thought and emotion. Hypnosis apparently does not cause this sort of blocking. Instead, the pain information does reach the brain but the emotions that are produced are kept from conscious awareness.

How Does Hypnosis Work?

No one really knows how the hypnotic state is produced. As noted above, hypnosis has not yet been clearly related to physiological or chemical events. This vagueness has led some researchers to doubt whether a unique condition called the "hypnotic trance" even exists. Theodore X. Barber (1970) is the leading advocate of the viewpoint that it does not. For instance, hypnotized subjects do not exhibit an

EEG pattern different from that found in the ordinary waking state. Barber believes that the "hypnotized" person is simply someone who is highly motivated to cooperate with the hypnotist's suggestions and who is good at "playing the role" of hypnotized subject, much as a good stage actor can display a wide range of emotions and behavior when the director calls for it. Barber's research suggests that anything you can do while "hypnotized" you can do in a wide-awake state.

Although hypnosis does rely heavily on cooperativeness and role playing, other researchers believe that such hypnotic phenomena as the reduction of severe pain indicate that hypnosis is a special state of consciousness. To help establish this point, Martin Orne (1972) has conducted experiments to show that hypnotized subjects are likely to behave quite differently from subjects who are pretending to be hypnotized. In a typical experiment, two hypnotists are involved. The first one hypnotizes one group of subjects and instructs another group of subjects to "simulate" hypnosis—to act as if they have been hypnotized. A second hypnotist, who does not know which subjects are hypnotized and which are simulators, then gives them various suggestions.

Can we tell the difference between the two groups of subjects? In fact, subjects in the two groups behave quite similarly, but there are also intriguing differences. For example, in one experiment the subjects were told that a helium balloon was tied to a finger on their right hand and that the balloon was pulling their arm up. All the subjects complied by raising their right arms. Suddenly the lights went out in a fake power failure. Infrared videotapes later revealed that in the dark most of the simulators had put their arms down, while the real subjects continued to hold their arms up. These results suggest that being hypnotized is more than simply trying to be a "good subject."

As with the nature of consciousness in general, the nature of hypnosis remains largely uncharted. But there has been a great deal of recent research on hypnosis, and it seems certain that our understanding of this mysterious phenomenon will continue to expand. The same can be said for our understanding of consciousness generally—of attention and fantasy, sleep and dreams, and drug-induced states. From a domain that was not long ago viewed as inappropriate for psychological study, consciousness has become perhaps the most exciting frontier of current psychological research.

SUMMARY

1. *Consciousness* refers to our subjective awareness of our own actions and of the world around us.
2. Our actions and choices may be conscious or unconscious (that is, automatic). Conscious mental processes can vary in quality, from subdued to intense. Consciousness can also vary from accurate perception of one's surroundings to major distortions (as in dreaming or drug-induced states).
3. In the late nineteenth century the structuralists used *intro-*

spection to study consciousness. But the behaviorists declared that consciousness was not a proper subject for psychology. In recent times psychology has returned to the study of consciousness, using technology to examine such things as the relation of brain activity to conscious states. Such research has raised the issue of mind-body dualism—can all mental functions be reduced to the firing of neurons?

4. *Daydreaming* is a state of consciousness that differs from night dreaming in that daydreaming has minimal eye movement and more sensory interference from the environment. Singer suggests that daydreaming is necessary for our mental well-being.

5. We spend about one-third of our lives in sleep. The human propensity to sleep at night appears to be universal. The amount of time people spend sleeping varies with age, with infants sleeping more than 12 hours a day and old people sleeping less than 8 hours.

6. Some people sleep longer or shorter than the average night's sleep. Hartmann found that short-sleepers tend to be extroverted, carefree, confident, and productive, while long-sleepers tend to be introverted, anxious, unsettled, and creative.

7. When deprived of sleep, people will suffer impairment of performance on certain tasks, may have tremors in their hands, and will fall asleep more quickly than usual when they finally go to bed.

8. The process of falling asleep seems to be triggered by the reduction of sensory input afforded by a quiet, dark environment and a reclining position.

9. While sleeping we pass through *sleep cycles*, each running about 90 minutes and consisting of four distinct stages. As we pass from stage 1 to stage 4 and back to stage 1 again, we go into progressively deeper, then lighter levels of sleep. Brainwave patterns are different for each stage.

10. Returning to stage 1, we enter a new stage—*REM (rapid eye movement) sleep*—during which we dream. Dreamless stages 1 through 4 are called the *non-REM*, or *NREM*, stages.

11. Among the sleep disorders that plague certain individuals are *insomnia* (inability to sleep), *narcolepsy* (attacks of REM sleep), *sleepwalking*, and *night terrors* (anxiety attacks suffered primarily by children).

12. Sigmund Freud thought that dreams provide wish fulfillment and in so doing reduce the tension created by unacceptable desires. He also thought that dreams preserve sleep by disguising unacceptable impulses in the form of *symbolism, condensation,* and *displacement*. He referred to the underlying meanings of dreams as their *latent content* and to the outer description of dreams as their *manifest content*.

13. Freud's approach has been criticized for its emphasis on sexual interpretations and for its basis in the dreams of selected disturbed patients. Other dream theorists give a wider range of meanings and functions to dreams.

14. According to the *activation-synthesis model* of dreaming, dreams begin with the firing of giant cells in the brain stem. This firing leads to the activation of certain areas of the brain. The dreams we then synthesize depend on which areas of the brain were stimulated. Stimulation of the brain center for our sense of balance, for example, might lead to a dream that involves spinning around.

15. Dreaming appears to be a basic need. People deprived of REM sleep become anxious, irritable, and confused. Sometimes they hallucinate. Such REM-deprived individuals seem to need to "catch up" on their REM sleep once they are allowed to return to it.

16. Many theorists, including Freud and Jung, believe that dreams serve important functions in helping us to deal with problems in our waking lives. Dreams may help us handle emotional situations better, and analyzing dreams may give us insights into our problems.

17. *Psychoactive drugs* are those that have a noticeable impact on consciousness and behavior. Users of psychoactive drugs experience alterations in thinking, in their sense of time, in emotional expression, in perception, and in their sense of control. Drugs generally work by affecting the action of transmitter substances in the brain.

18. People take drugs for a variety of reasons—to satisfy their curiosity, to escape, to fit in, to find meaning, to prove maturity. There appears to be a strong relationship between patterns of drug use by parents and by their children.

19. *LSD* is a *psychedelic drug* that produces profound alterations of sensory, perceptual, cognitive, and emotional experiences. Other psychedelics include *peyote* (mescaline), and *psilocybin*. LSD appears to work by blocking the action of the transmitter substance serotonin.

20. *Marijuana* is a drug, made from the hemp plant, that generally creates a feeling of well-being when smoked. The drug is highly controversial, although the most serious charges against it are probably not justified. Marijuana may be dangerous for some people, but it may also have useful medical applications.

21. *Amphetamines* are drugs that stimulate the central nervous system. People who use amphetamines for dieting or staying awake usually take pills, whereas true "speed freaks" inject the drug while on a several-day "run." Excessive use of amphetamines can lead to *amphetamine psychosis*, in which the user has delusions and paranoia similar to those of paranoid schizophrenia. Amphetamines appear to exert their effects by stimulating production of the transmitter dopamine.

22. *Cocaine* is a stimulant extracted from coca leaves. Because there has been little research on this drug, not much is known about its short-term and long-term physiological effects. It is an expensive drug, so its use occurs primarily among higher-income people.

23. Among drugs commonly used in America are nicotine (in cigarettes), caffeine, alcohol, sedatives, and tranquilizers.

24. *Hypnosis* is a state of increased suggestibility that is brought about through certain relaxation procedures. The hypnotist may suggest that the subject perform certain behaviors, forget specific material (*hypnotic amnesia*), or perform some act on a signal after coming out of the trance (*posthypnotic suggestion*).

25. People vary in their susceptibility to hypnosis. Those with well-developed imaginations tend to be more susceptible.

26. Hypnosis has been used to reduce pain in dental patients, burn victims, and terminal cancer patients, among others. Hilgard suggests that the hypnotized person *dissociates* the physical sensation of pain from its emotional components.

27. Some researchers, such as Barber, believe that hypnosis is nothing more than a form of role playing and cooperation, rather than a distinct state of consciousness. But hypnotized people do seem to behave differently from people who are pretending to be hypnotized.

MEDITATION

The search for the meaning of life and for some way to cope with life's pressures is as ancient as mankind itself. Recently, this quest has led to a widespread interest in meditation as a possible answer.

What is meditation? According to Claudio Naranjo and Robert Ornstein (1971):

Meditation has been described as a process of calming the ripples on a lake; when calm, the bottom, usually invisible, can be seen. In another metaphor meditation is likened to the night: stars cannot be seen during the day, their faint points of light overwhelmed by the brilliance of the sun. In this image, meditation is the process of "turning off" the overwhelming competing activity that is the light of the sun, until . . . the stars can be seen quite clearly. (page 214)

Meditation leads to a deep passivity combined with awareness.

As these metaphors suggest, meditation leads to a deep passivity combined with awareness—a suspension of the usual rat race of mental and physical activity in order to *experience* things rather than just *do* them. Usually, our mind bounces from one idea to another, reacting to every sensation, thought, or stimulus. In order

to reach new and unusual experiences, we must learn how to ignore the usual, familiar stimuli; we must learn to meditate.

LEARNING TO MEDITATE

The position used in meditation is important. It should let you relax, yet not allow you to fall asleep. The cross-legged "lotus" positions used by some meditators are very difficult and uncomfortable for most beginners. These positions are not essential to the meditative state. You can meditate while sitting up straight but relaxed in a regular chair. In that position you can practice concentrating and

eliminating distractions. You don't fight to prevent them. You just bring your attention back again to the object of your meditation every time your attention wanders. If you try too hard to prevent distractions, you can get distracted by the very task.

Most meditators sit alone or with a small group in a special room set aside for meditation. Some meditators burn incense to give a consistent odor to the place of meditation and to mask other odors that might break concentration. Typically, meditation is practiced for 20 minutes twice a day.

In psychological terms there are two general kinds of meditation. One kind involves restriction of awareness by focusing attention on an object or repeated word. The second type involves opening up awareness to experience everything in greater depth.

These two approaches to meditation appear to result in different physiological effects. The type that involves restriction of awareness results in reduced responsiveness to external stimuli. Practitioners of this method seem not to register strong sensory stimuli (such as

loud noises) in their brains. In the opening-up type of meditation a different pattern is seen: practitioners show a consistent and persistent response to external stimuli. Instead of showing the usual decline in responsiveness (or *habituation*) associated with prolonged exposure to a stimulus, these individuals continue to respond at a high level.

Both forms of meditation place a critical emphasis on the self-regulation of attention. One goal of all meditation practices is to train attention so that all actions will be performed with total awareness. To achieve this goal, meditators practice various exercises. They may decide to concentrate on one part of their body, to focus on their breathing, or to stare at an object without blinking. One form of meditative practice uses the *mantra*, a series of words used as the focus of awareness. The mantra is repeated over and over, aloud or silently, while all other thoughts and stimuli are excluded. "Mantras are sonorous, mellifluous words, which repeat easily. An example is OM. This mantra is chanted aloud in groups, or used individually in silent or voiced meditation. Another is OM - MANI - PADME - HUM" (Naranjo and Ornstein, 1971, page 150).

The simpler forms of meditation can be learned quickly. In one study (Maupin, 1965) college students learned to concentrate on the natural process of breathing. Those who did best at the task of focusing attention on their breathing and the movements of their belly reported that they were able to reach a deeply satisfying state of consciousness. They described this state as one of extreme detachment from the outside world and pleasant bodily sensations.

Another method that has been explored as a possible means of achieving a meditative state is alpha wave biofeedback (see Chap-

ter 2, Box 3). However, the general outcome of explorations into this area has been disappointing (Orne and Wilson, 1978). It has been found that the presence of alpha waves is not necessarily associated with meditative experiences. In fact, meditation appears to involve a complex pattern of physiological changes, so training just one function in isolation does not reliably produce the state.

TRANSCENDENTAL MEDITATION

Transcendental meditation (TM) is a system developed by an Indian guru (or holy man) named Maharishi Mahesh Yogi. TM advocates have included quarterback Joe Namath, singer Stevie Wonder, and perhaps as many as 600,000 other Americans. TM includes a number of exotic elements, including an initiation ceremony in which the initiate brings an "offering" of a white handkerchief, several pieces of fruit, and a bunch of flowers, symbolizing, respectively, the cleansing of the spirit, the seed of life, and the flowers of life. In a private room, the initiate's guru or teacher places the offering on an altar under a picture of Guru Dev (the Maharishi's teacher). The teacher then introduces the medi-

Maharishi Mahesh Yogi

tator to his own personal mantra, on which he is to meditate for the rest of his life.

Transcendental meditation advocates have included as many as 600,000 Americans.

The Maharishi Mahesh Yogi is the only one in the TM movement who is not expected to meditate on a regular basis. "He doesn't have to," one of his secretaries explained. "He long ago achieved a perpetual fourth state of consciousness. The clarity of his mind is awesome." *Time* magazine reports that the Maharishi believes that if only 1 percent of the population of any community or country is meditating, the other 99 percent of the population will feel the good effects and crime will be reduced. If 5 percent meditates, great things will begin to happen, says the Maharishi. "A good time for the world is coming. I see the dawn of the Age of Enlightenment. I am only giving expression to the phenomenon that is taking place" (*Time*, October 13, 1975).

Transcendental meditation is, of course, only one meditative technique. Other methods are possible and, throughout history, have produced similar effects. In addition, some nonmeditative techniques, such as progressive relaxation (used in systematic desensitization, described in Chapter 12) and hypnosis (described in Chapter 3) appear capable of yielding many of these effects. Herbert Benson (1975) has proposed that there is an integrated physiological pattern, which he labels the "relaxation response," that results from TM, progressive relaxation, hypnosis, and several other procedures.

Benson suggests that four elements are necessary to elicit the relaxation response: (1) A quiet environment; loud noises should be absent and the eyes should be closed. (2) Decreased muscle tone; the posture should be comfortable and the muscles relaxed. (3) A passive attitude; distracting thoughts should be eliminated. (4) A "mental device"; attention should be shifted from logical thought to an object or sound (such as a mantra).

Transcendental meditation and other techniques would appear to be successful because they incorporate these four elements. The mystical and religious overtones of these methods may be icing on the cake.

MEDITATION AND BODY CONTROL

For a great many years psychologists dismissed the claims made in behalf of meditation as unscientific and mystical. In recent years, however, research has shown that meditators can alter their bodily metabolism and even the patterns of their brain waves.

Meditators can alter their bodily metabolism and even the pattern of their brain waves.

For example, Wallace and Benson (1972) found that striking physiological changes were produced during transcendental meditation. These changes were different from those produced by either hypnosis or sleep. In meditation, less oxygen was consumed, the heartbeat was slowed, respiration was retarded, and brain waves changed. Various bodily measures indicated that the meditators were extremely relaxed, but wide awake.

Other investigators have learned that experienced meditators show improved cardiovascular efficiency, faster reaction times, lower blood pressure, decreased anxiety and irritability, and increased self-assurance and emotional stability. Wallace and Benson suggest meditation might prove to be a valuable tool for maintaining psychological health—especially for those caught up in the bustle of industrial society.

Practicing yogis have made much more fantastic claims of body control. It is said that they can be buried alive or walk on hot coals. Until recently, such actions were considered impossible, since the yogi would have to control parts of the nervous system traditionally thought to work only on an autonomic basis. We have known for some time, however, that the mind can produce profound changes in the body. The fact is now evident that yogi masters, with years of practice, can accomplish astonishing control over what happens to their bodies.

In addition to its other benefits, meditation appears to reduce interest in drug use. A study of nearly 2000 practitioners of TM found dramatic decreases in the use of marijuana, LSD, amphetamines, barbiturates, narcotics, cigarettes, and other nonprescribed drugs after they began their meditation program. Perhaps meditation makes drugs unnecessary; it

---

Meditation appears to reduce interest in drug use.

---

may be a cheaper, more reliable, and more direct route to altered consciousness (Benson and Wallace, 1972).

We can only guess at the final effect that meditative experience will have on the study of consciousness.

We don't really know the true limits of meditation. We can only guess at the final effect that meditative experience will have on psychology and on the study of consciousness.

SUMMARY

1. In meditation one experiences a detachment from the outside world and very intense concentration. Meditators try to create an atmosphere in which they will not be subject to distractions.
2. Meditation may involve a restriction of awareness to one subject or word (such as a mantra) or it may mean opening up awareness to experience the world in greater depth.
3. Transcendental meditation (TM) is practiced by the followers of Maharishi Mahesh Yogi. Techniques such as progressive relaxation and hypnosis seem to produce results similar to those of TM.
4. Efforts to achieve meditative states through the use of biofeedback of alpha waves have failed. It seems that many complex physiological changes are involved in meditative states.
5. Some skilled meditators are able to alter many of their physiological mechanisms, including heart rate, breathing, and brain waves. Meditators have shown that many processes previously thought to be beyond voluntary control may actually be within conscious direction.

PSYCHOIMMUNOLOGY: MIND, BODY, AND HEALTH
Joan Borysenko

Joan Borysenko

Most of us are aware that psychological factors can be involved in certain physical ailments: work pressures may produce a splitting headache; anxieties may give rise to an upset stomach. But recent research points to more dramatic and surprising links between our state of mind and our state of health. Work in the new field of psychoimmunology shows that states of mind can affect illnesses ranging from colds to cancer, and suggests that changing an ill person's beliefs may sometimes be an effective treatment. Dr. Joan Borysenko of the Harvard Medical School, the author of this Update, is both a cell biologist and a clinical psychologist. She is one of those researchers at the vanguard of the new explorations into the links between mind, body, and health.

Mary Peters and Arlene Delano both had breast cancer. The disease had been discovered at the same stage of progression in the two women, and both received identical treatment: a mastectomy (breast removal) followed by intensive drug treatment. Mary died within two years. Arlene has lived for five years without a reappearance of cancer and may well live a normal life-span. What made the difference?

Although the cases of Mary Peters and Arlene Delano are fictional, they illustrate a real phenomenon: Diseases often take very different courses in individuals for reasons that cannot readily be explained by preexisting physical differences. An increasing body of research suggests that psychological factors, including differences in the person's mental attitude, can have a major impact on the course of physical diseases. It is possible, for example, that Arlene was a "fighter," who vowed that she would prevail over her cancer, while Mary was resigned to letting the disease take its course. In a well-designed study of women who underwent mastectomy for early-stage breast cancer, Steven Greer and his coworkers in England found that women who reacted to their diagnosis with either a fighting spirit or strong denial were significantly more likely to be free of disease five years later than were women who reacted

with stoic acceptance or with feelings of helplessness (Greer, Morris, and Pettingale, 1979).

More generally, recent research has documented that people's attitudes, personalities, and styles of coping with stress can have a major impact on their susceptibility to a wide range of diseases, from colds to cancer, as well as on their ability to recover from such diseases. And, for the first time, psychologists and medical researchers are beginning to pin down the mechanisms through which such effects take place. In many cases, psychological factors

appear to influence disease and health by means of their effects on the body's immune system, a collection of billions of cells that travel through the bloodstream and move in and out of tissues and organs, defending the body against invasion by foreign agents, such as bacteria, viruses, and cells that become cancerous. Because of its focus on the impact of psychological factors on the immune system, this exploding new field of research is known as *psychoimmunology*.

The notion that states of mind can influence health is far from a

A healing dance of the !Kung San of the Kalahari Desert in southern Africa. People in many cultures believe that such rituals can cure disease.

new idea. Throughout history, people have thought that faith and belief can modify the course of illness. Anthropologists who have studied the healing rituals of primitive cultures sometimes report remarkable cures resulting from faith-healing rituals, although in such cases it is hard to document the true nature of the diseases that are healed. In the Western world, as well, the history of medicine is replete with remedies that seem outlandish in light of modern science. Moss scraped from the skull of a hanged criminal, powdered reindeer horns, and various "bitters" have all had their day as wonder drugs. The real wonder of such treatments is that in many cases they actually seemed to work. It is now clear that these nostrums could not have exerted their effects through specific biological action. Rather, some innate physiological reaction of the patient was apparently put into gear by her faith in the healer or in the treatment.

Until recently, however, medical researchers have not taken seriously the possibility that "attitude" or "faith" could have major effects on such diseases as cancer. To be sure, people in ancient cultures believed that people's thoughts and actions were primary determinants of health. As medical knowledge increased, however, the direct causes of many diseases were traced to such external agents as bacteria and viruses. These discoveries helped to extricate science from superstition, but they also led to the premature conclusion that mind and body were entirely separate. It is only in the past decade that new research in health psychology and behavioral medicine, including research in psychoimmunology, has begun to bridge the gap between mental and physical events, revealing that the mind is indeed a two-edged sword that can both wound and heal.

As Figure 1 indicates, there are three main causes of disease. Two of these are biological: hereditary

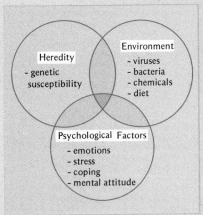

FIGURE 1. *Hereditary predispositions, environmental factors, and psychological factors may interact with one another in producing disease.*

predispositions and environmental factors; the third cause is psychological. The hereditary predispositions include inherited weaknesses in certain body tissues or organs that increase susceptibility to disease. The environmental factors include bacteria and viruses that cause disease, chemical pollutants in the air or water, and even some natural ingredients of the food we eat, such as saturated fats (which may contribute to heart disease). Some diseases are caused by hereditary or environmental factors alone, while others occur only when there is both a hereditary predisposition and subsequent exposure to an environmental agent. But psychological factors can also contribute to the disease process. Psychological reactions are sometimes the primary determinants of disease, as in certain types of headache, hypertension, or stomach ulcer (see the discussion of "Stress and Disease" in Chapter 7). In other cases, psychological factors interact with biological factors in producing disease: That is, states of mind can determine whether processes that are initiated by hereditary or environmental factors will in fact cause disease or will be fought off.

Some of the clearest examples of such mind-body interactions involve the effects of stress on the body's immune system and, as a result, its ability to ward off certain diseases. *Stress* can be defined as pressure from the environment that makes physical or emotional demands on us (see Chapter 7). Stress can lead to bodily reactions that impair the functioning of our immune system. Many people have noticed, for example, that they tend to catch cold right after a stressful period such as final examinations. Viruses are the direct biological cause of colds. We are all exposed to cold viruses continually, but our body's immune system usually succeeds in fighting them off. When we are stressed, however, the function of the immune system is temporarily suppressed, increasing the chances of infection. Working in our laboratory, John Jemmott recently showed that the stress of exam periods caused a significant decrease in students' immune function, as measured by the levels of virus-fighting antibodies in their saliva. Students with a hard-driving personality style (as measured by

Psychological stress, such as the stress of taking final examinations, can impair the functioning of our immune system and make us more susceptible to colds.

personality tests) were the most stressed by their exams, had the lowest antibody levels, and caught more colds than other students (Jemmott et al., 1981).

One of the most powerful stresses is the death of a close relative. We often read or hear accounts of people who die within weeks or even minutes after the death of a spouse or a child, and these occurrences may well be more than coincidences. Indeed, studies have shown that in the 18 months following such a loss, people have a greater risk of death from a variety of illnesses, including heart attacks and cancer, than do others of the same age and sex (Kraus and Lilienfeld, 1959; Engel, 1971). Some of these deaths involve changes in the autonomic nervous system that can lead to heart attack and stroke. Others, such as infectious disease and cancer, are more directly associated with impairment of the immune function. Recent studies have definitively shown that bereaved people have reduced immunity to disease (Bartrop et al., 1977; Schleifer et al., 1980).

Recent research in psychoimmunology has begun to show just how stress exerts such effects on the immune system. Emotional arousal, such as that produced by stress, activates the sympathetic branch of the autonomic nervous system (see Chapter 2). This sympathetic arousal causes the secretion of hormones which, in turn, produces various bodily changes. Anyone who has ever been badly frightened remembers how quickly the heart starts beating, the mouth dries out, and the palms become sweaty. These changes demonstrate the bodily effects of a coordinated release of adrenalin, corticosteroids, and a host of other hormones that prepare the body for a fast reaction when the mind senses danger. In prehistoric times, this well-orchestrated symphony of events was called into action by real threats, such as attacking animals, that necessitated either fighting or running away if the person was to survive. But in twentieth-century society this hormonal surge is usually brought on by circumstances in which neither "fight" nor "flight" is appropriate—bad drivers, news reports, job pressures, family problems, and other frustrations of modern life. Such inappropriate calls to action of a powerful fast-reaction system can have undesirable effects on bodily function. Adrenalin has been found to inhibit the ability of certain lymphocytes to release chemicals that kill invading germs or cells (including cancer cells) that the body recognizes as foreign. The corticosteroids not only inhibit the release of such disease-fighting chemicals, but also prevent immature lymphocytes from developing into mature lymphocytes that properly perform their disease-fighting function.

We can get a fuller sense of the mechanisms linking stress with disease susceptibility by focusing on experiments with animals in which the key factors can be systematically manipulated in ways that would be impossible with human subjects. Animals who are stressed—for example, by the administration of electric shocks—

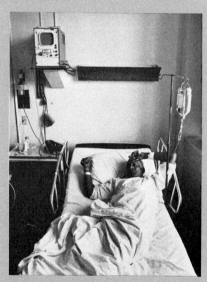

The patient's attitude toward his disease—whether he feels resigned to it or decides to "fight back"—may affect his chances of recovery.

have generally been found to be more susceptible to infection by viruses, bacteria, and parasites than are unstressed controls. Stress has also been found to increase mice's susceptibility to cancer, and to increase the cancer's rate of growth once it is established. Vernon Riley (1981) found that stressed mice who were injected with a standard number of cancer cells developed tumors that grew faster and led to earlier death than did mice who were injected with the same number of cancer cells but were not stressed. The stress quickly increased the mice's levels of corticosteroid hormones, reducing their immune systems' ability to destroy the cancer cells. Riley (1975) has also explored the interaction between heredity, environmental factors, and psychological factors in causing cancer. When mice with a hereditary predisposition to breast cancer were infected with a cancer-causing virus, stress caused the cancer to form in middle age rather than in old age. In old age, the immune system naturally declines, allowing cancers to grow. In Riley's study, then, stress hastened the appearance of cancer by raising corticosteroid levels and depressing immune function at a time of life when it is normally high.

Additional experiments with animals have shown that the ability to control one's environment can minimize stress and help to maintain the body's defenses against disease. In one study, Lawrence Sklar and Hymie Anisman (1979) first injected three groups of mice with the same number of cancer cells. One group was then exposed to an electric shock that they could learn to escape by jumping over a barrier to safety. A second group was exposed to the same duration of shock as the first group, but they had no means of actively coping with the stress themselves. Instead, their shock was turned off only when a mouse from the _first_ group jumped over the barrier. The third group was never shocked. Cancers grew fastest and led to earliest death among the animals that had no means of coping with their stress. In contrast, the animals in the first group who received the same amount of shock, but who could mount an adaptive escape response, did not differ significantly in tumor growth from those who had never been shocked at all. Martin Seligman (1975) believes that the inability to exert control in such situations produces a sense of *helplessness* that often predisposes organisms—including people—to disease.

It is believed that small cancers form frequently in everyone, but that our immune systems usually reject them. Helplessness and depression, however, may lead to elevated levels of corticosteroids, as well as lower levels of the neurotransmitter norepinephrine in the brain. These changes, as well as other changes that are not yet as well understood, apparently make it harder for the immune system to reject cancer cells. There is evidence that this may be true in humans, as well as in other animals. In one dramatic study, Shekelle and his coworkers (1981) studied over 2000 men who had taken a psychological test that assessed depression and other emotional states. Seventeen years later, the researchers found that men who had been highly depressed at the time of the testing had twice the odds of dying of cancer than men who had not been depressed. Since depressed people might drink more alcohol or smoke more cigarettes which could lead to cancer, Shekelle took this into account when he analyzed the data. The association between depression and greater likelihood of death from cancer still held, regardless of drinking or smoking rates.

In another study, Steven Locke (1982) made use of psychological tests to assess students' coping abilities. "Good copers" are people who are able to deal effectively with the shocks and challenges of

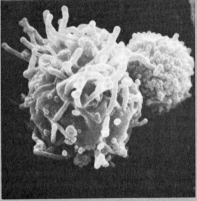

This electron micrograph shows a large cancer cell (magnified about 8000 times) in the foreground. The smaller cell in the background is a type of white blood cell called a "natural killer cell." The killer cell produces chemical changes that cause the cancer cell to swell up and burst like a balloon. But when people are under stress, the ability of their natural killer cells to destroy cancer cells may be impaired.

life, while "poor copers" are people who easily fall prey to depression, anxiety, and helplessness when they are challenged. Locke found that "poor copers" who were also experiencing major life changes showed diminished function of a type of white blood cell (called the "natural killer cell") that fights viruses and cancer cells. But "good copers," even when they were experiencing major life changes, had normal white cell function.

These findings may help us to understand how the mental attitude of cancer patients, such as the two women who were introduced at the start of this Update, may affect their chances of recovery. Patients like Mary Peters, who resign themselves to their disease, may experience the sort of helplessness that continues to impair the function of their immune system. If the patients themselves are not "fighting back," neither are their immune systems. On the other hand, patients like Arlene Delano, who *believe* that they will be cured and refuse to give up, may as a result enhance the ability of their im-

mune systems to fight their cancers. A number of studies support the possibility of such effects among both men and women with many different types of cancer (Derogatis et al., 1979; Greer et al., 1979). As more people come to understand how the mind can help the healing process, however, a new danger is emerging. Some people give up medical treatments that could cure them in favor of alternatives such as nutritional programs, unproven drugs, or faith healing. As a result, people who could have been saved die unnecessarily. Keeping a positive attitude and maximizing faith can supplement medical treatments, but should not replace them.

The fact that states of mind can influence our susceptibility to disease, as well as our ability to get well again, leads to a vital challenge for psychologists and medical researchers. As more and more is discovered about the types of personality and emotional states that resist disease, we should become better able to design psychological treatments that maximize the body's defenses against disease. Meditation, for example, produces a set of bodily changes, including slower heart and respiratory rate, lower blood pressure, and increased alpha brain waves, collectively known as "the relaxation response" (Benson, 1975). (See the Psychological Issue after Chapter 3.) These bodily changes are precisely opposite to those typically caused by stress. Future studies will reveal whether the relaxation response, which people can be trained to produce, can prevent the suppression of the immune response that would otherwise be caused by stress. Similarly, if the will to fight can be instilled in cancer patients, and their helplessness and depression alleviated, perhaps these patients can be helped to live longer. These explorations are part of a new phase of growth for psychology, in which wellness of body will be as central a concern as wellness of mind.

Part Two

Perceiving, Learning, and Thinking

Human beings are information processors. We take in information about the world, we learn and remember things, and we think about the things we know and do.

Chapter 4, Perception, deals with the ways in which we experience the world through our senses, and the ways in which we make sense out of this experience. In the Psychological Issue on Extrasensory Perception we will consider the possibility that there are other ways of experiencing the world—ways that do not depend on our senses.

Chapter 5 examines the central processes of Learning and Memory. The Psychological Issue that follows will explore the possibility— frightening to some—that our knowledge of the principles of learning can lead to Behavior Control.

Chapter 6 is devoted to the interrelated topics of Language, Thought, and Intelligence. It is followed by a Psychological Issue on Creativity that explores the potential of human beings to think things that have never been thought before.

In the Update on "Mental Images," Stephen Kosslyn describes exciting new research on another aspect of human information processing: the ways in which we construct and make use of mental images of physical objects and places.

Chapter 4
Perception

So here we are, each of us with our own brain and nervous system, in a world filled with a dazzling array of objects—houses and sidewalks, plants and dogs, hamburgers and roses, ballpoint pens and computers, not to mention billions of other people. Or at least that's where we think we are. But how do we really know? How does the complex and diverse set of things "out there" get inside our brains so clearly and vividly? Philosophers have grappled with such questions throughout the history of civilization. Now, within the past century, these issues have become central ones for psychologists.

Perception refers to the processes by which people come to experience the stimuli in their environment. Our study of these processes will begin with a discussion of the human *senses*, the organs and neural pathways through which information about our environment is received. Our senses include vision, hearing, the skin senses, smell, and taste. When we say we "sense" something, we are actually experiencing activity in our brain and nervous system. Physical energy (such as light, sound waves, heat) emanating from objects must be transformed by the sense organs into a code that can be transferred to and interpreted by the brain. The first step in this process is the work of the *receptor cells,* which respond to particular forms of energy. These receptors include cells in the retina of the eye that are particularly sensitive to light and structures in the ear that are sensitive to sound waves. The energy is next converted into electrical impulses, which travel from the sense organs along nerve fibers to the central nervous system and eventually to the appropriate area of the cerebral cortex (see Chapter 2). Here in the brain, the information is collated, processed, and interpreted to yield our experienced percep-

tions. How we put isolated lights, colors, shapes, and sounds together to form an integrated picture of our physical surroundings is a central problem in the study of perception.

VISION

A large portion of all we know about the outside world comes to us through our eyes. Indeed, vision dominates our life. Vision has played a dominant role for researchers as well. Scientists have studied sight more than any of the other senses. For these reasons, our discussion of the senses will focus primarily on vision.

The Eye

The human eye is the "camera" that we always carry with us. Like a camera, the eye admits light through a small hole and passes it through a lens that focuses an image on a photosensitive surface. In the eye, light first passes through the *cornea*, a transparent protective coating over the front part of the eye (see Figure 4.1). Light next passes through the *pupil*, an opening that can be enlarged or reduced to let more or less light in by contractions in the muscles of the *iris*, the colored part of the eye. Light passes through the pupil to the *lens*, which can be adjusted to bring near or far objects into focus. The light is focused through the lens onto the inner lining of the back of the eyeball, the *retina*, analogous to the film in a camera. The light stimulates chemical processes in receptor cells in the retina called *rods* and *cones*.

Vision   **109**

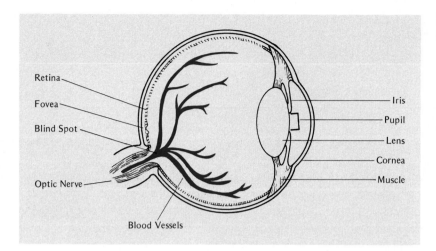

FIGURE 4.1
Cross-section of the eye.

More than 6 million cones and 100 million rods are distributed on the retina. Rods are slim nerve cells that contain a light-sensitive chemical called *rhodopsin* (visual purple). Cones are thicker than rods, with a cone-shaped tip at one end, and contain other photosensitive chemicals. When light waves strike the retina, they break down the chemicals in the rods and cones, which in turn generate an action potential in sensory neurons connected to the rods and cones. These sensory neurons are connected to other neurons that converge to form the *optic nerve*. The optic nerve then carries this activity to the brain.

The rods are not sensitive to color and are located mainly at the edges of the retina. The cones are color receptors and are packed together in the center of the eye. The *fovea*, a depressed spot on the retina directly behind the lens, has a high concentration of cones, but no rods. A few cones are mixed with rods all the way to the outer edges of the retina, but the center of the eye is the most color-sensitive portion.

When you first go into a dark movie theater, you stumble

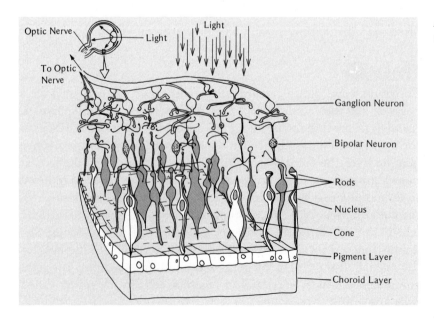

An illustration of the retina as seen through a powerful microscope.

THE WING OF A BEE

A sensory threshold is the smallest amount of stimulation that can be detected by one's sense organs. Here are some approximate human thresholds (Galanter, 1962):

Vision A candle flame seen at 30 miles on a dark clear night.

Hearing The tick of a watch under quiet conditions at 20 feet.

Taste One teaspoon of sugar in two gallons of water.

Smell One drop of perfume diffused into a three-room apartment.

Touch The wing of a bee falling on your cheek.

around, barely able to make out the shapes of the people or the seats. After you have been in the theater for a while, however, you are able to see quite well. As you go from bright to dim light, the rods and the cones adapt to the change in illumination. In dim light the chemicals in the rods and cones are built up faster than they are broken down by light stimulation. The greater the concentration of these chemicals, the lower the *visual threshold*—the smallest amount of stimulation the rods and cones will respond to. Thus, adaptation to darkness is in part a matter of building up a surplus of rhodopsin in the rods and of other chemicals in the cones.

The cones adapt quickly in the dark (10 minutes or so), but the rods adapt slowly and continue to adapt even after 30 minutes or more of darkness. When completely adapted, the rods are much more sensitive to light than the cones. Thus, if you want to see a dim light in pitch darkness, do not look directly at it, since the center of the eye contains only the less sensitive cones. If you look away from the object, the image will fall on the edge of the retina, where the rods are. You will be much more likely to see the dim light in this manner.

Visual Acuity

Visual acuity is the ability to discriminate the details in the field of vision. One way this ability can be measured is by using the familiar eye chart. Standard perfect vision is often called 20/20 vision. If you stand 20 feet from a standard eye chart and see the material on a certain line of the chart clearly, you are seeing normally. If you do not see normally, some or all of the material will be blurred. If you are standing 20 feet away but see what a person with normal vision could see at 50 feet, you have 20/50 vision. If you have 20/10 vision, you see things 20 feet away as sharply as the person with normal vision sees them at 10 feet.

Part of the retina, the *blind spot*, has no visual acuity. This spot is the point at which the nerves of the eye converge to form the optic nerve. The optic nerve exits through the back wall of the eyeball and connects the eye to the brain. People are usually unaware of the blind spot—they compensate for this blank spot in their vision by making use of the other eye and by mentally filling in uniform patterns (see Figure 4.2).

Visual acuity is greatly affected by the shape of a person's eyeball. If the eyeball is too long, the lens focuses the image *in front of* the retina rather than directly on it. Under these circumstances, one sees near objects rather clearly, but far objects appear fuzzy and blurred. This condition is known as *nearsightedness*. If the eyeball is too short, the lens focuses the image *behind* the retina, making close objects indistinct even though far objects are in sharp focus. This condition is known as *farsightedness*.

Color Vision

We cannot see ultraviolet rays, x-rays, radio and television waves, or radar waves. But we can see the *spectrum* of color that occurs when

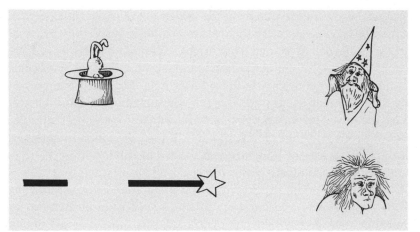

FIGURE 4.2
A test to help you find your blind spot. Close your right eye and look at the magician. Move the page closer or further away until the rabbit disappears and the wand appears unbroken. It's not really magic—the images of the rabbit and of the break in the wand are now falling on your blind spot, where the optic nerve connects to the eye.

we pass sunlight through a prism, where light is converted into bands of red, green, yellow, and blue.

Any color can be created by combining three different colored lights in different proportions. A similar process apparently underlies color vision, although it is not yet fully understood. According to one theory, initially proposed in 1845, our retinas contain three types of cones—one sensitive to red, one to green, and one to blue. Each cone contains a single type of photosensitive pigment and, in combination, their stimulation gives us the experience of color. Just how the messages from the three types of cones combine in the brain remains a subject of some controversy. It does *not* appear that the three messages simply add together to produce a new color sensation as in the case of light mixtures.

About 7 percent of the people in the world cannot see one or more colors. Most of these partially color-blind people are men, since color blindness is an inherited, sex-linked characteristic. The most common type of color blindness is *dichromatic:* Color vision is normal in two of the three primary colors but deficient in the third, perhaps because one of the three types of cones is deficient or missing. In one type of dichromatic color blindness—red-green deficiency—the person sees the world almost entirely in blues and yellows. A red fire engine appears dull yellow, and grass is blue. The person with yellow-blue color blindness, in contrast, sees a world of reds and greens. Red-green color blindness is by far the most common, and blue-yellow is the least common. People with *monochromatic* color blindness see nothing but black, white, and shades of gray, because they have no cone cells.

Although color-blind people may miss out on one sort of experience that other people have, they can still function quite well without color cues—so much so that some people don't even know they're color-blind. For example, it's not hard for a red-green color-blind person to know whether a traffic light is green or red, since the red light is always at the top and the green light is at the bottom. Color-blind people can also discriminate between different colors because there is usually a perceivable difference in brightness. Special tests have been devised to eliminate such cues when determining whether a person is color-blind. Most commonly these tests consist of buried figures composed of dots of different colors but of equal brightness to surrounding dots. A person who is red-green color-blind, for example, won't be able to distinguish the red dots from the green ones and won't be able to see the figure.

Depth Perception

How do we know how close or how far away objects are? How can we tell that objects are three-dimensional just by looking at them, when all that is recorded on the retina is a two-dimensional image? Seeing depth or distance depends on the positioning of the two eyes. The right and left eye each get a slightly different image of the object being looked at. If you cover your right eye and then your left, you will see the object you are focusing on jump from left to right. When both eyes look at an object they see a unified three-dimensional image. Humans are among the many animals who have the benefit of *binocular vision*, in which the two eyes cooperate to give solidity and distance to objects. If you close one eye and survey a scene, you will perceive depth less clearly. And if you squint that one open eye, the scene may begin to look like a two-dimensional canvas rather than a three-dimensional world. But there are ways in which we can see depth with only one eye. For one thing, objects overlap, which gives us a clue that one is in front of another. Another clue to depth is the size of objects—if one tree is larger than another, we assume that the larger one is closer. And all art students know about perspective—the fact that lines converge when stretched into the distance, such as the lines that form railroad tracks. The patterns of shadowing on and around an object also tell us about its three-dimensionality. All these clues—overlap, relative size, perspective, and shadows—are called *monocular cues* because they work even when we use only one eye.

Some of the cues for depth perception, such as the evaluation of the relative sizes of objects, seem to result from experience. Many psychologists used to believe, in fact, that learning is necessary for depth perception to occur at all. But studies with the *visual cliff* have provided convincing evidence that much of depth perception is innate. James Gibson and Richard Walk (1960) devised the original visual cliff apparatus, consisting of a large tabletop with a wide wooden board down the center. On one side of the board was a glass-covered checkerboard pattern. On the other side was a clear sheet of glass, and the same checkerboard pattern was painted on the floor three-and-a-half feet below the table. When viewed from above, the entire tabletop appeared to contain the checkerboard pattern. Infants from 6 to 14 months old were then placed on the tabletop and allowed to crawl about. Very few babies would venture onto the "deep" side, even when urged to do so (see page 114).

The fact that 6-month-old babies have depth perception does not in itself prove that this ability is innate—a good deal of learning might have taken place during the first 6 months of life. But other experiments, using animals such as lambs and chickens that can walk within a day after birth, demonstrated that newborn animals also avoid the deep side of the cliff, suggesting that the reaction is in fact innate. As a result of millions of years of evolution, we seem to be

The visual cliff. Infants as young as six months old will not crawl beyond the perceptual "edge" of the cliff, indicating that even at this young age they have depth perception.

born "prewired" with whatever connections in the nervous system are needed to perceive depth when we receive the appropriate stimulation (Hochberg, 1978). Nevertheless, depth perception continues to improve as we gain greater experience in dealing with our three-dimensional world.

HEARING

To understand hearing, imagine throwing a stone into a pool of water. What happens? Wave after wave of ripples circles out from the center. The waves strike the edge of the pool and bounce back. Similarly, whenever any object is struck, it tends to vibrate. As it does so, the molecules of air around it are pushed away—just as a stone thrown in the water pushes water molecules away from it. These movements of air molecules are called *sound waves*. When these waves reach your ear, they set in motion a series of mechanical processes in the outer, middle, and inner ears (see Figure 4.3). The *outer ear* is composed of an inch-long canal and the *tympanic membrane* (the eardrum). Changes in air pressure cause vibrations in this flexi-

FIGURE 4.3

A cross-section of the ear and its basic structures.

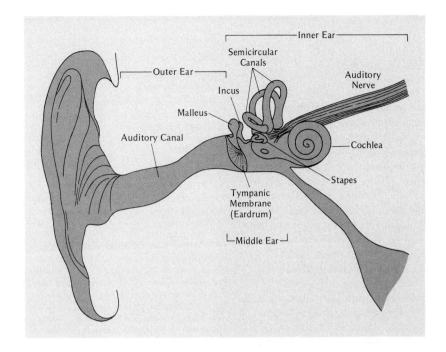

ble membrane. The *middle ear* is composed of three bones, the *malleus*, the *incus*, and the *stapes*. (These terms are Latin for "hammer," "anvil," and "stirrup," and are derived from the shapes of the three bones.) These bones make up a system that conducts sound waves to the *inner ear*. In the inner ear the vibrations are transmitted to the fluid inside the snail-shaped *cochlea*. There the sound waves reach the receptor cells for hearing and are translated into nerve impulses, which travel to the brain via the *auditory nerve*.

The sounds we actually perceive are related to different characteristics of the sound waves. *Loudness* is related primarily to the amplitude of the sound wave—the amount of expansion and contraction of the pressure changes that form a sound wave. When you turn up the volume of a radio, you increase the amplitude of the vibrations and therefore the sound is louder. When sounds get *very* loud, they can be bad for our health (see Box 1). *Pitch* refers to the high or low quality of a sound. It is primarily determined by the frequency of wave vibrations—the faster the vibration, the higher the pitch. Another property of sound is *timbre*, the richness or quality of a sound that comes from a particular sound source. Each sound source actually produces a distinctive combination of sound waves, and it is this combination that determines the sound's timbre. Thus, a note played on a violin will not sound exactly like the same note played on a trumpet or a piano.

The ears are far enough apart to allow people to locate the position of a sound source. If a noise is two or three feet away from your left ear, it will reach that ear a tiny fraction of a second before it reaches your right ear. The sound will also be louder in your left ear than in your right ear. The time lag and difference in loudness allow you to localize the sound as being on your left. Thus, to properly locate a sound, both ears are necessary.

THE SOUND OF BORSCHT

Most of us see with our eyes, hear with our ears, and taste with our tongue. But there are people who report occasional mixups in links—when, for example, sounds may be experienced as colors or tastes. This experience of sensory blending is called *synesthesia*. The Russian psychologist Alexander Luria gave an account of a person for whom a pure tone of 1,000 cycles per second produced "a brown stripe against a dark background that had red, tonguelike edges [and] the taste . . . of sweet-and-sour borscht." Many psychologists are skeptical of such reports, but others believe that synesthesia may result from a mechanism in the nervous system that connects the senses with each other (Marks, 1975).

— **Box 1** —

Noise pollution

American cities, with their screeching cars, thundering trucks, roaring subways, wailing sirens, blaring horns, and bellowing factories, are tremendously noisy places, and they are getting noisier. Because of the devastating effects that sustained high levels of noise can have on human functioning, noise pollution has become one of modern society's greatest environmental hazards.

For one thing, high levels of noise can literally be deafening. The Environmental Protection Agency estimates that more than 16 million people in the United States suffer from hearing loss caused by noise. When the cells of the inner ear are bombarded with loud sounds, they can be damaged, leading to hearing loss. Even a relatively mild noise level of 70 decibels (see table), about the level of a cocktail party, can damage hearing if one is subjected to it year in and year out. And higher levels of noise can have much worse effects. In one study, guinea pigs were played blaring rock music (at about 110 decibels) for prolonged periods. They suffered severe hearing loss, and it was later found that their

Approximate Intensity of Some Common Sounds

Rustling leaves	12
Human whisper	30
Normal conversation	50
City traffic	80
Subway train	95
Motorcycle	110
Rock band (amplified)	110
Snowmobile	115
Pain threshold	*130*
Sonic boom	130

The column on the right shows the decibel intensity of some common sounds (Dempsey, 1975). A decibel is the smallest difference in intensity of sound that the human ear can detect. The scale is a mathematical power function. At around the middle of the scale, every increase of 10 decibels represents approximately doubling of sound intensity.

inner ear's sensory cells "had collapsed and shriveled up like peas." One disco owner reacted to the experiment with the comment, "Should a major increase in guinea-pig attendance occur at my place, we'll certainly bear their comfort in mind." Unfortunately, analogous effects can take place in humans as well.

In addition to its effects on hearing, noise can have harmful psychological effects. In one series of studies, students heard tape-recorded bursts of either extremely loud (110 decibels) or soft (56 decibels) noise over a period of 20 minutes (Glass and Singer, 1973). After a short while, the subjects adapted to the noise, and they were able to perform clerical tasks successfully. But the loud noise had unwelcome aftereffects. Immediately after the noisy period, subjects who had heard the loud noise were impaired in their ability to work efficiently on problem-solving and proofreading tasks.

In this and other studies, David Glass and Jerome E. Singer found that the predictability and controllability of the noise made a big difference in subjects' reactions to it. When subjects knew when the loud noise was coming, its harmful aftereffects were greatly reduced. And when subjects knew they could stop the noise if they wanted to, the effects were also reduced—even though they didn't actually make use of their "stop" button. You are probably much less bothered by the clatter of your own typewriter than you are by that of your roommate's, since in the former case you have direct control over the noise. Unfortunately, most of the noise that pervades our cities is of the worst kind—it comes in unpredictable

THE SKIN SENSES

The sense of touch is actually a combination of at least three sensations: pressure, temperature, and pain. If you unbend a paper clip and probe an area of your skin lightly, you will feel pressure at certain points where the wire contacts your skin, but not at every point. If you do the same thing with a cold wire, you will feel cold at other specific points. If you probe your skin with a warm wire, you will feel warmth at still other points. A pin point will produce spots of pain. Thus, different points on the skin are serviced by receptors that are sensitive to different kinds of stimuli.

The experience you have when you are touched lightly with a single hair is called *pressure* or *touch*. The amount of pressure required to produce this experience varies for different parts of the

bursts, and it comes from sources over which we have no control.

When noise continues over a period of years, it can have adverse effects on intellectual abilities. In four New York City apartment buildings spanning a noisy highway, elementary school children who lived on the lower floors (where noises were loudest) were found to have less ability to discriminate between sounds than children who lived on higher floors (Cohen, Glass, and Singer, 1973). Children on the lower floors also had poorer reading skills than those on the higher floors.

Glass and Singer suggest that in

tuning out a noisy environment, children may fail to distinguish between speech-relevant sounds and speech-irrelevant sounds. The unhappy result is that the longer children must endure noise, the more likely they are to ignore all sounds, and this, in turn, may make reading more difficult.

Another study compared children who attended school near an airport, where they were subjected to the noise of aircraft landings and takeoffs at unpredictable times during the day, with children who attended an otherwise similar school in a quiet neighborhood (Cohen et al., 1980). At both

schools, the children were tested in a soundproof trailer. Children from the noisy school were somewhat more likely to fail on a cognitive task (a puzzle) and they were more likely to give up before the time to complete the task had elapsed. It appears that continued exposure to uncontrollable noise may induce a feeling of helplessness that can impair intellectual performance. If children know that disturbing noise may be coming at any moment, it may be hard for them to persevere in their work.

The sound of all this is not very encouraging. And the noise levels of our cities—and, increasingly, of the countryside as well—are getting worse and worse. By one extreme estimate, the urban sound level is increasing at the rate of 10 percent a year, enough to make us all deaf by the year 2000 (Dempsey, 1975). It is possible to combat this trend. One way is by encouraging the production of quieter jets, trucks, cars, and appliances. As things stand, however, people don't necessarily want quieter machines. One manufacturer found that people would not buy his newly designed, quieter vacuum cleaner—since it didn't make a lot of noise, consumers assumed that it couldn't be doing a good job!

body. The tip of the tongue, the lips, the fingers, and the hands are the most sensitive areas. The arms, legs, and body trunk are less sensitive. People experience pressure not only when an object touches the skin, but also when the hairs on the body are slightly moved.

In addition to pressure receptors, the skin contains receptors for both *heat* and *cold*. There are about six times as many cold receptors as heat receptors in the skin. These temperature receptors are more concentrated along the trunk of the body, which is why the hands and feet can withstand greater temperature extremes than can the bare back. Hot and cold are relative terms: Anything that you touch that is colder than your skin will be perceived as cool; anything you touch that is hotter than your skin will seem warm. Interestingly, a really hot stimulus excites both cold and heat receptors.

Here's an experiment you can try. Place one hand in a bucket of cold water and the other hand in a bucket of warm water. In a little while you will be aware that the feeling of warmth or cold comes only from the area where the hand meets both water and air. Now, put both hands in a third bucket filled with lukewarm water. This water will feel warm to the hand that was in cold water and cold to the

— *Box 2* —

Frontiers of pain control

One of the greatest human miseries is chronic pain—continuing, often severe pain caused by such maladies as lower-back problems (slipped or ruptured disks), arthritis, and cancer. The pain is sometimes so great that it is incapacitating, and physicians are often at a loss in treating it effectively. In recent years, however, researchers have been developing some revolutionary treatments for chronic pain. Although most of these treatments are still in experimental stages, they hold great promise for success.

ACUPUNCTURE
Really an old rather than a new treatment, *acupuncture* was developed centuries ago in China. In this method, needles are inserted at specific points on the body's surface in order to relieve pain in other parts of the body. Indeed, Chinese physicians regularly use acupuncture as the only form of anesthesia (pain-killer) in major operations. As noted in the text, Melzack (1973) believes that acupuncture works by closing off the "gates" that allow pain signals to pass from the afflicted area of the body to the brain. Recent studies have suggested that acupuncture may also stimulate the production of enkephalins or endorphins, newly discovered chemicals that are thought to be transmitter substances in the brain and spinal

Acupuncture is one method being used to relieve pain.

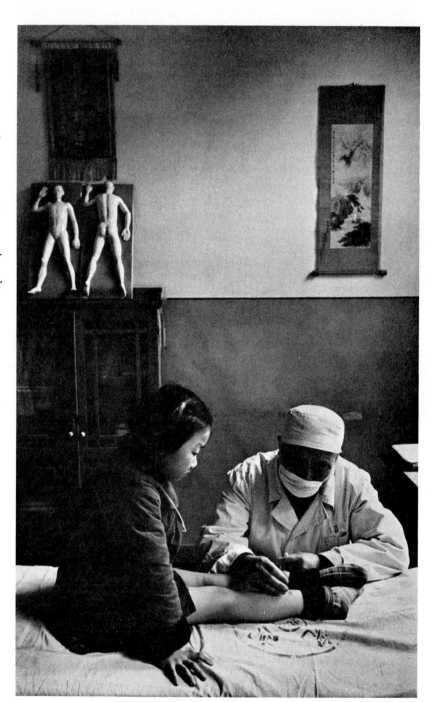

hand that was in warm water. The sensation from the hand depends on the temperature to which the skin was previously adapted.

A third type of receptor in the skin is the *pain* receptor. Psychologists are still debating whether pain is a separate sense with its own nerve structures or whether it results from a pattern of intense stimulation to any of a number of receptors. Pain seems to be received by a

cord (see Chapter 2). It is now believed that several other pain-killing techniques, such as electrical stimulation, may also work by causing the release of these chemicals in the brain and spinal cord (Iversen, 1979).

ELECTRICAL STIMULATION
Another approach to the control of chronic pain is the implantation of an electrical stimulator in the patient's back, just above the point at which nerves from the body part experiencing pain enter the spinal column. When the patient feels a stab of pain, he holds a tiny antenna over the stimulator. This produces a volley of electrical signals that can counteract the pain signals (Wang, 1977). In an even more dramatic procedure, a stimulator is implanted in a portion of the patient's brain stem, and he can then use self-stimulation for pain relief. In recent studies, this technique has relieved pain in the majority of patients being tested (Arehart-Treichel, 1978).

HYPNOSIS
Not everyone can be hypnotized, but for those who can be, hypnosis can sometimes provide dramatic pain relief (see Chapter 3). Major surgery, including leg amputations, has even been done under hypnosis. More commonly, hypnosis has been used in childbirth and in dentistry, both cases in which the patient's fear and anxiety concerning the procedure can be a major contributor to the pain she suffers. Even severe chronic pain will sometimes respond to hypnosis (Goleman, 1977).

DRUGS
Narcotic drugs, such as morphine, have long been used as pain-killers. But patients develop increasing tolerance for these drugs, which means that larger and larger doses are needed to be effective. In addition, narcotics are highly addictive and in rare instances can be lethal. Scientists have continually been trying to develop drugs that will relieve pain more safely. So far these efforts have not been notably successful. For example, heroin was introduced by a German drug company in the 1890s as a "non-addictive" form of morphine. But it soon proved to be even more addictive than the drug it was designed to replace. More recently developed drugs, such as methadone, have also given rise to disappointment.

Pharmacologists are now testing several new synthetic drugs of a class called antagonist-analgesic opiates. (Two of them, butorphanol and nalbuphine, have been approved by the Food and Drug Administration and are available to physicians in injectable form.) These drugs have as much pain-killing power as morphine but are safer and much less addictive. Nevertheless, large doses have been found to cause psychological disturbances in some patients, and researchers are keeping their fingers crossed (Tucker, 1979). Other researchers are trying to develop synthetic forms of enkephalins and endorphins that could be administered to patients. Because these chemicals occur naturally in the brain—in fact, *endorphin*

means "the brain's own morphine"—they should not be dangerous or addictive. For most everyday purposes, the most effective pain-killer remains aspirin, which has one of the best ratios of benefits to harmful effects. Unfortunately, for severe pain aspirin isn't enough.

PLACEBOS
Sometimes patients suffering from severe pain can be helped by "drugs" that aren't really drugs at all but rather sugar pills that contain no active chemical agents. The surprising effectiveness of placebos testifies to the psychological aspects of pain: if the person *believes* the treatment will work, it just might. But recent research suggests that placebos, too, may work by altering brain chemistry. In one study, volunteer dental patients—mostly college students—were given only placebos to relieve pain following tooth extractions. For some patients, the placebos worked. But for these individuals, the administration of naloxone, a chemical that is known to block the effects of enkephalins and endorphins, worsened the pain. This result clearly suggests that the placebo worked by stimulating release of the brain's own pain-killers (Fields, 1978).

A question of tremendous interest to scientists and pain-sufferers alike is whether people can learn to activate the brain's pain-suppressing systems voluntarily, thereby bringing the powers of the mind to bear on the sometimes painful workings of the brain.

variety of nerve endings—not only in the skin but in other organs as well; very bright lights, loud noises, high or low temperatures, or great pressures all yield pain sensations. Pain serves to warn us of tissue destruction. However, most internal organs of the body do not have sense receptors for pain and are unable to inform us when they are in trouble.

How do we experience pain? According to the *specificity theory* there are specific pain receptors that relay signals of pain to the spinal cord, and from there to the brain. A person should therefore feel pain exactly where the stimulation occurs, and the amount of pain felt should depend on the amount of stimulation at the pain site. But this theory does not account for the phenomenon of *acupuncture,* in which the insertion of needles into various sites on the body surface sometimes relieves pain in body regions quite distant from the needle site (see Box 2). Ronald Melzack and Patrick Wall came up with a new theory of pain that would account for the effects of acupuncture (Melzack, 1973). They propose that the transmission of pain signals depends on *gate-control mechanisms,* which permit or block the transmission of pain signals to the central nervous system. Stimulation of certain areas will open the gate to allow pain signals to pass; stimulation of other areas will close the gate, so that pain signals from any part of the body cannot reach the pain reception areas of the brain. In the case of acupuncture, Melzack and Wall believe, the needles themselves are inserted at the sites that activate the reticular formation of the brain stem—one of the gate-control areas of the nervous system. As a result, pain signals are blocked before they reach the brain, and no pain is perceived.

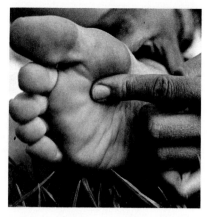

Pressure-sensitive receptors for touch are scattered all over the body but are most highly concentrated in the fingertips.

KINESTHESIS AND EQUILIBRIUM

Close your eyes and raise your hand. You still know where your hand is. Now touch your nose with your finger. You know where both parts are. The sense that tells you the positions and movements of your muscles and joints is called *kinesthesis.* Some kinesthetic receptors are embedded in the muscles and send information to the brain about the load on the muscle and its state of contraction. Other receptors are in tendons and joints. With these sensors you can detect a movement as slight as one-third of a degree in the shoulder and wrist. In the ankle more than a full degree of movement is needed for detection.

The kinesthetic senses provide information about active body movement. Thus, you can tell the relative weights of objects by lifting them. You can walk along the street without watching what your legs are doing. And you can talk without thinking about moving your tongue and jaw.

Kinesthesis is extremely important to daily life. When kinesthetic sensitivity is destroyed somewhere along the spinal cord, impulses coming into the spinal cord below the point of damage cannot find a path to the brain. If this were to happen to you, you would sway and have trouble keeping your balance with your eyes closed. You might

A PAINFUL MEMORY

Ronald Melzack, one of the world's leading pain researchers, reports the case of a patient who broke her jaw in an automobile accident and suffered excruciating pain. Ten years later, she experienced the same pain for no apparent reason. Melzack believes that the original painful stimulus may have produced some permanent changes in the nerves of the patient's brain, creating a "pain memory." Ten years later, something activated these nerves, bringing back a vivid memory of the pain. But there is no solid proof for the existence of such pain memories (Arehart-Treichel, 1978).

We all have a basic sense of balance but some individuals are able to refine this sense into a specialized ability.

KNOWING WHAT'S UP

Even when we close our eyes, we can tell that we are right-side-up, rather than upside down, by feeling the pressure of the ground against our feet or the pressure of a chair against our buttocks. But in zero gravity conditions, such as those encountered by astronauts once they have left the earth's atmosphere, knowing whether one is right-side-up or upside down becomes a difficult matter. In such a weightless condition, if someone applies pressure to the bottoms of your feet, you're likely to feel that you are standing upright, and if someone applies pressure to the top of your head, you'll feel as though you are upside down (Lackner, 1979).

not be able to lift your foot onto a curb without first looking at the foot, and you would walk with a peculiar gait.

The sense of balance, or *equilibrium*, works in conjunction with kinesthesis. Together, these senses keep track of body motion and body position in relation to gravity. The sense organs for equilibrium are in the inner ear. The *semicircular canals*, which are oriented in different directions, are filled with a fluid that moves when the head rotates. The fluid movement allows perception of the body's movement. If movement is extreme, the individual gets dizzy.

SMELL AND TASTE

The sense of *smell* results from stimulation of receptor cells in the nose. Most of what we smell comes from gaseous chemical molecules that are heavier than air. These molecules tend to collect on the floor or ground. When you stand erect, your nose misses most smells. Human beings often have to sniff when they want to smell things.

Breathing through the nose increases the number of molecules that hit the olfactory membrane, where smells are detected.

According to one theory, there are four basic odors—acid, fragrant, burnt, and caprylic (like limburger cheese)—and all of the odors we experience represent some combination of these four (Amoore, 1967). Most often we describe smells as being "like" some familiar odor. We say "it smells like burning rubber" or "it smells like a locker room." Some smells are distinctly unpleasant, but fortunately we *adapt* to those smells that we are exposed to for an extended period of time, so that after a while we are no longer aware of them. Zick Rubin's dentist, who spends much of his time in close contact with people's mouths, reports that he is virtually never aware of the powerful odors he often encounters.

Your *taste* buds are scattered across the upper surface and side of the tongue. They respond to four basic taste qualities: sweet, sour, bitter, and salty, and your taste experiences are mixtures of these four basic qualities. All in all, the sense of taste is a quite restricted sensory experience. Foods take on their distinctive flavors because of the combination of taste with smell. If you could not smell your food, you could not tell what you were eating. If you find this hard to believe, try closing your eyes and holding your nose the next time you eat some steak.

Perception was once thought to be a passive and more or less automatic process. All you had to do was keep your eyes and ears open, and the world would magically represent itself in your head. We now know that this view was mistaken. In fact, the achievement of meaningful perceptions is an active process, with the individual perceiver playing a major role in determining his or her own experiences. This role goes far beyond simply deciding where to look or what to touch. We rarely experience just one sensation at a time. Instead, we are constantly being bombarded with a multitude of messages that must be sorted out, identified, and interpreted. We must select certain messages from the incoming array, identify them, and figure out how they relate to one another, in order to construct a meaningful picture of reality. As we will see, this process depends not only on the impinging sensations themselves but also on our past experiences, our needs, and our values. (On the other hand, there are special circumstances in which our sensory stimulation is severely limited—see Box 3).

Principles of Perceptual Organization

One illustration of the active nature of perception comes from the fact that objects can often be perceived in more than one way and it is the perceiver who actively gives structure to these objects by employing various principles of perceptual organization. These structural principles were first identified by the *Gestalt psychologists,* a group of German psychologists who did much of their work in the 1920s. (Many of them later came to America.) The word *Gestalt* means "whole," or "configuration," reflecting the emphasis these psychologists gave to our perception of figures and forms as a whole.

The Gestalt psychologists concentrated on the ways in which we interpret images in two-dimensional space, such as the images that appear on the pages of a book. One basic feature of perceptual organization that they identified is our tendency to differentiate between *figure*—the part of an image that seems to be an object—and *ground*—the background against which the object stands. In many drawings it is possible to see one portion as being either figure *or* ground, depending on how we look at it. In Figure 4.4, for example, we can see either a vase or two faces, depending on which part of the drawing we perceive as the figure and which part we perceive as ground.

Another central aspect of perceptual organization is the principle of *closure:* when we see a figure that is disconnected or incomplete, as in Figure 4.5, we are primed to mentally fill in the gaps and to see it

FIGURE 4.4

As you keep looking at this drawing, what is figure and what is ground is likely to shift back and forth.

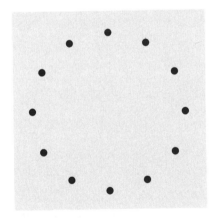

FIGURE 4.5

The principle of closure. Although parts of the letters are missing in the word, we tend to fill in these gaps and to perceive the whole letters and, therefore, the whole word. Similarly, we tend to fill in the gaps between the dots and see the figure as a circle.

— Box 3 —

Sensory deprivation

During practically all of our waking lives, we are constantly bombarded with stimulation to our senses. What would happen if we were deprived of this sensory stimulation?

Psychologists became interested in studying the effects of sensory deprivation in the early 1950s. Researchers enlisted volunteers to spend days at a time in environments that permitted virtually no sensory stimulation. In one well-known study, Woodburn Heron (1957) paid male college students $20 a day to lie on a bed in a lighted cubicle, around the clock, for as many days as they could. The subjects wore translucent plastic visors, permitting them to see only constant, diffuse light, but no objects or patterns. They wore gloves and cardboard cuffs to restrict skin sensation. Hearing was limited by a U-shaped foam rubber pillow and by the unchanging hum of air-conditioning equip-

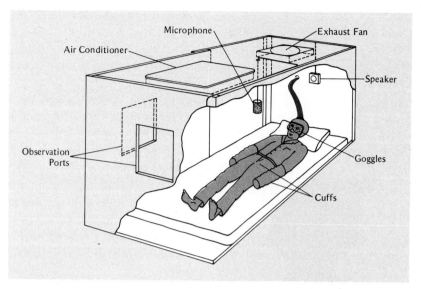

A sensory deprivation chamber, such as the one used in Woodburn Heron's experiment.

ment. There were only brief time-outs for meals and for going to the toilet.

After one or more days in this setting, subjects' performance on a variety of intellectual tasks was markedly impaired. In addition,

they were found to be highly persuadable: When a tape recording arguing for the reality of ghosts was played, the subjects found it to be much more believable after the period of sensory deprivation than before it. Some

as a complete figure. The Gestalt psychologists also noted that we tend to organize our perceptions in terms of the *proximity* of their elements. In Figure 4.6A, we can see the dots as either horizontal rows or vertical columns. As the dots get closer together horizontally, as in Figure 4.6B, we are more likely to view them as rows; as they get closer together vertically (Figure 4.6C), we are more likely to view them as columns. This tendency to view objects in terms of the proximity of their elements is relied on in printed photographs, comic

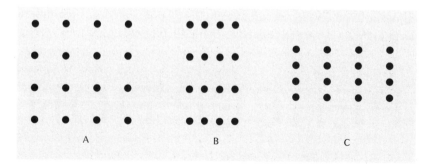

FIGURE 4.6
The principle of proximity. We tend to see things that are near each other as going together. The same set of dots can be arranged so that they can be perceived as either columns or rows (A), as rows (B), or as columns (C), depending on the proximity of the dots to each other.

students reported that they were afraid of seeing ghosts for several days after the experiment.

The most dramatic results of Heron's experiment were the hallucinations subjects experienced while in the chamber. At first, they "saw" dots of light, lines, or geometrical patterns. Later, they began to see more complex images, such as marching squirrels with sacks over their shoulders or processions of eyeglasses walking down the street. Initially, these cartoonlike visions were entertaining, but as they continued, they became more frightening. One subject reported, "My mind seemed to be a ball of cotton wool floating above my body." After emerging from several days of sensory deprivation, subjects experienced perceptual distortions—straight lines seemed curved, and stationary rooms seemed to be in motion.

Heron concluded: "A changing sensory environment seems essential for human beings. Without it the brain ceases to function in an adequate way." It has been speculated that the brain structure called the reticular activating system (see Chapter 2) sends advance warnings of incoming stimulation to the higher brain centers. These warnings are needed if the brain is to function efficiently. When we are deprived of sensory stimulation, however, the reticular activating system slows down. As a result, brain functioning is disturbed.

These effects of sensory deprivation point to real dangers. Many crucial jobs are typically done in highly monotonous, unchanging settings. If radar operators scanning screens for enemy missiles were to begin to see nonexistent blips—or if they were to miss real ones—the consequences could be disastrous. Truckers on long hauls sometimes report seeing nonexistent animals running across the road. It may be in part to reduce the monotony of these hauls that truckers make such extensive use of their Citizens Band radios.

But the effects of sensory deprivation are not all negative. Peter Suedfeld (1975) notes that severe emotional reactions to sensory deprivation experiments are in fact extremely rare. One of the reasons that negative reactions have been reported in some studies may be that the subjects were swayed by their expectations. As long as researchers assumed that sensory deprivation was harmful—an image that was fostered by psychology textbooks and brainwashing film scenarios—subjects may have approached the situation apprehensively and may have proceeded to react negatively. When sensory deprivation is administered in calm surroundings, there seem to be few such negative effects.

Suedfeld suggests that sensory deprivation may also have some unexpected benefits. In some cases, sensory deprivation may sharpen subjects' visual and auditory acuity. It can also lead to greater openness to new experiences, and thus may help to foster artistic creativity.

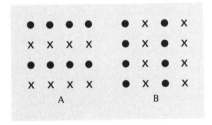

FIGURE 4.7

The principle of similarity. We tend to perceptually group things that are alike. Thus, in (A) we see rows and in (B) we see columns.

book panels, and television pictures, which are all actually arrays of dots or lines that we perceive as shapes and objects.

Still another Gestalt principle of organization is *similarity*. In Figure 4.7A, we are likely to see horizontal rows, while in Figure 4.7 B, we see vertical columns. In each case, we are predisposed to organize the elements in terms of their similarity to one another. All of these Gestalt principles emphasize the strong tendency we all have to give our perceptions a total structure.

Paying Attention

As you sit reading this page, stop and look around the room for a minute. The room you are in is full of objects, surfaces, colors, shapes. The room is probably full of sounds as well: distant voices, footsteps, perhaps music from a radio or traffic sounds from outside. If the room has a window, there is even more for your eye to see and your ears to hear. Feel the soft pressure of your clothes against your body and of your feet against the floor. Sense the rhythm of your breathing and your heartbeat. Notice any little itches, twinges, or aches in your body. All of these stimuli have been present as long as you have been reading, but you have selected only the printed page (perhaps with greater or lesser success) for concentration. The process of focusing on one or two stimuli while ignoring others is called *attention.* We never attend to all the stimuli around us at once. Our nervous systems would be hopelessly overloaded if we did. Instead, we select the item we want to attend to—a book, a conversation, a TV show, even our own thoughts—and the surrounding events seem to fade into the background of consciousness.

Some psychologists have described attention as a pool of resources or energy (Norman and Bobrow, 1975). The more energy we give to processing one stimulus, the less is left over for coping with other stimuli. If the stimulus you have selected for concentration is a difficult one, you'll have that much less attention to pay to surrounding events; you have to devote more "attention energy" to difficult stimuli. So, as you read a textbook, you may be less aware of the surrounding sights and sounds than if you were doing something that requires less attention, such as washing dishes.

How do we manage to focus attention in this way? Some stimuli capture attention almost automatically, without any effort on our part. A brightly lit neon sign on an otherwise dark street will capture attention because it stands in such a sharp contrast to its surroundings. And although the red and blue mailbox that you pass each day may go unnoticed, a purple mailbox would probably catch your eye because it is unexpected. Both *contrast* and *novelty* are characteristics that consistently grab attention (Berlyne, 1970).

But even when we are not confronted with striking stimuli we manage to keep our attention focused. Consider, for example, a crowded, noisy party. You are surrounded by voices, as dozens of people engage in loud conversation. Yet you are able to keep track of your own conversation and to ignore others. One way you accomplish this is by relying on physical cues, such as the sound pattern of particular voices and the direction they are coming from (Broadbent, 1958). Perhaps even more important, you can follow a single conversation despite surrounding noise by "tuning in" to the meaning of what is being said. If one person standing near you is talking about

**WAIT A MINUTE—
ARE YOUR SHOES ON?**

Our senses are better suited to informing us about changes in stimulation than about stimulation that remains constant. Our visual system is designed to give special attention to contrast and movement, and our skin receptors generally respond better at the beginning or end of a stimulus (such as pressure on the skin) than they do to constant stimulation. This makes sense in terms of what we need to know about the outside world. As David Hubel (1979) writes, "We need to know about changes; no one wants or needs to be reminded 16 hours a day that his shoes are on" (page 51).

When we are in a group of people we are bombarded with a wide variety of sensory stimuli. In order to function in such a situation, we must be able to focus our attention on a few stimuli and push the rest into the background.

existential philosophy and another is talking about football, you will probably be able to keep track of what one speaker is saying without being derailed by the other.

In a series of experiments, Anne Treisman (1964) showed that people listening to pairs of tape-recorded messages simultaneously could follow one meaningful message, even when the voice of the speaker changed or the message switched from one ear to the other. Thus, physical cues are important for helping us pick out a target for concentration, but the target's meaning is more important as we hold and follow it.

But what becomes of the material that is filtered out? We probably do take note of most of what is going on around us at some level of awareness (Lewis, 1970). You may have had an experience like that of one of the authors. On a recent rainy day, I was sitting by myself at a table at McDonald's, totally absorbed in making corrections on one of the boxes for this book. There was music coming through the piped-in system and conversations at nearby tables. I was not consciously aware of any of this—it was all a blur in the background. But all of a sudden I was aware of three words that had just been said by a man at one table to a man at another table. The words were "Buick . . . lights on." I looked up with a start, thought for a moment, and then said to the man, "Did you say that there's an old Buick with its lights on?" The man confirmed that he had indeed said so. I immediately ran out into the rain to turn out the lights on my car, just in time to save the draining battery.

Although I was absorbed in my work, at some level I was obviously monitoring the conversations around me. It is as though we can set our levels of attention for different kinds of stimuli. We might set the attention level at high for a particular stimulus—a person talking, a television screen, a book—while keeping a low setting for the remaining environmental activity. While the background events may not reach full awareness, neither are they completely blocked out. When something happens that is unusual or important enough, it will arouse sufficient attention to spring to our conscious awareness.

Seeing What You're Looking For: Perceptual Set

In interpreting the messages that bombard our senses, we tend to see (or hear, feel, smell, or taste) what we're looking for—that is, what we expect to see. This phenomenon is called *perceptual set*. E. M. Siipola (1935) demonstrated this phenomenon in his studies of individuals' responses to words. He told one group of people they would be shown words that referred to animals. He then showed them, for brief time intervals, combinations of letters that did not really spell anything (*sael, dack,* or *wharl*). Most of the group perceived the letters as the words *seal, duck,* and *whale*. He told a second group he was going to show them words pertaining to boats. He showed this group the same combinations that the first group saw. People in this group reported seeing the words *sail, deck,* and *wharf*. Each group saw what they expected to see.

You can demonstrate the phenomenon of perceptual set using Figure 4.8. Show a friend Picture A and ask what he sees. Then pre-

A
B
C

FIGURE 4.8
An illustration of perceptual set.
(See the text for explanation.)

sent Picture C and ask what he sees. Most likely the friend will say that A shows an old woman and that C is another picture of the same woman. Now show another friend Picture B and then Picture C. Most likely, she will report that B is the picture of a young girl and that so is C. Thus, each friend will see something different in Picture C—and, of course, each will be right, since C includes both an old woman and a young girl, depending on how you look at the picture (Leeper, 1935). But the particular image that each friend sees depends on what he expects, based on previous experience. Researchers have shown that once a person is primed to see a picture in a particular way, it is very hard to change that set and see things differently. (You can try this with your friends: Ask them whether they see anything *else* in the picture, and find out how long it takes for them to come up with another possibility.)

Motivation can also affect perceptual set. If you need to mail a letter, you will suddenly be aware of that red and blue mailbox that you normally ignore each day. If you are hungry, you are especially likely to notice signs saying "restaurant" or "food" and you may even misread signs so that "claims" becomes "clams."

Jerome Bruner (1957) has suggested that the phenomenon of perceptual set reflects people's need to predict their environment and to get what they want. As a result, people tend to pay attention to stimuli that conform to their expectations, needs, and values. We find in our environment things we are looking for, and we overlook or avoid things that do not fit our interests. Sometimes this process leads to misperceptions or to ignoring information of great importance. But selectivity is unavoidable, and we are usually selective in an efficient way that reflects our best bets about what will happen and what is important.

Experiencing a Stable World: Perceptual Constancy

You are sitting in the cafeteria, at some distance from the food lines. You look up as a woman carries a tray from the food line, walks past

FIGURE 4.9

As you move closer to or farther away from an object, the size of the image on your retina gets larger or smaller. Yet you still perceive the object as being the same size. This phenomeonon is known as size constancy.

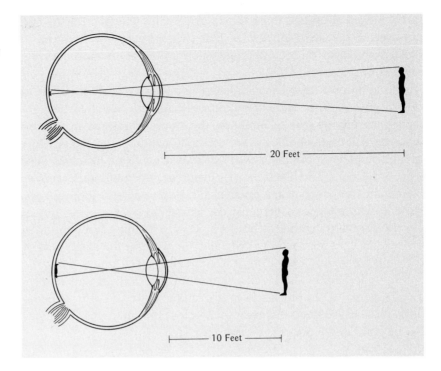

your table, and finally sits down at a table by the window. What are the successive patterns of visual stimulation that register on your retina as you watch this scene?

Every time the woman moves closer to you, the image on your retina gets larger (see Figure 4.9). As she moves from 20 feet away to 10 feet away, the height of the image on your retina doubles. The opposite occurs if the person moves away from you. In addition, as the woman moves nearer the window, more light is available, and her image on your retina gets brighter. When the woman moves away from the window, the image gets darker. That is what your retina senses. But what do you actually perceive? A changeable chameleon of a person who constantly gets larger and smaller, lighter and darker? Not at all. Instead, you see the same woman, who remains more or less the same size and brightness, regardless of the games her retinal image may be playing. We make adjustments in our perception of objects that take into account changes in the distance and lighting. By so doing, we manage to convert what would otherwise be a bewildering pattern of stimulation into a stable and meaningful world.

The process by which we take into account changing distances and other cues in order to perceive objects as staying the same size is known as *size constancy*. Some aspects of this process are apparently innate, but it also seems to depend on experience. Size constancy may be especially difficult to achieve when distance cues are not available or when we are dealing with unfamiliar objects. Colin Turnbull (1961) tells of the Bambuti Pygmies who live in the forests of the Congo and are not familiar with wide-open spaces. Turnbull took a Pygmy to a vast plain, and when the Pygmy looked at a herd of buffalo several hundred yards away, he asked what type of insects they were. He refused to believe they were buffalo. Because he

THE BETTER, THE BIGGER

People sometimes perceive objects they value highly as being larger than objects they value less highly. In one study, poor children—for whom the value of money must be particularly great—perceived coins as being larger than rich children did (Bruner and Goodman, 1947). Similarly, voters have been found to view their preferred candidates as taller than they really are (Kassarjian, 1963). There is a common assumption in our culture that bigger is better. As a result, we may be predisposed to view objects—or people—that are "better" as "bigger," too, even when they really aren't.

rarely looked at objects more than a few yards away, the Pygmy had not learned to take distance as well as retinal image into account. In most cases, however, people make such adjustments automatically and unconsciously.

In addition to size constancy, we also see the world in terms of *brightness constancy* and *color constancy*. As was noted earlier, objects generally appear to maintain the same brightness no matter what the lighting conditions. For example, white paper looks white and black paper looks black whether they are viewed in strong sunlight or indoors. The black paper outside may actually reflect more light than the white paper does inside, yet it will still look darker. How do we manage to perceive the actual brightness of an object despite changing lighting conditions? It is certainly not a conscious process. But we seem to have the ability to evaluate the brightness of the object by comparing it to other objects viewed under the same lighting conditions. The black paper in bright sunlight still reflects less light than other objects in bright sunlight, so we see it as being dark. Similarly, objects maintain their color no matter what the lighting or what other colors they are near.

Perceptual Illusions

Magicians are sometimes called masters of illusion, because they can make us "see" things (rabbits coming out of hats, cut ropes joining back together) that are not really there. Psychologists have a special interest in *perceptual illusions*—instances in which perception and reality do not agree—not only because of their intrinsic fascination but also because such illusions can help us to understand the process of perception.

One of the best known illusions is the Müller-Lyer illusion, named after the person who devised it in 1889 (see Figure 4.10). The illusion is an extremely powerful one. Even after you measure the two lines and prove to yourself that they are equal, you will still perceive the line with the reversed arrowheads (B) as being longer than the line with the standard arrowheads (A). What causes this

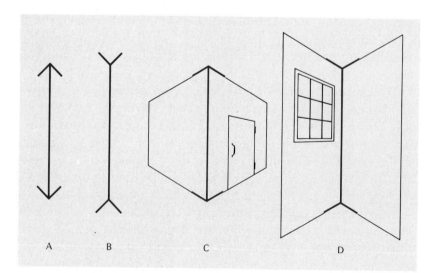

FIGURE 4.10

The Müller-Lyer illusion. Line B *appears to be longer than line* A, *yet they are both the same length. This illusion may be explained by the fact that our knowledge of perspective may lead us to see line* A *as if it were the outside corner of a building* (C) *and line* B *as if it were the inside corner of a room* (D). *(See the text for explanation.)*

illusion? Many hypotheses have been offered, but the most likely explanation has to do with the phenomenon of size constancy (Gregory, 1968). The arrangement of lines in A looks like the lines in a drawing of the outside corner of a building (such as C), whereas the lines in B resemble those of an inside corner of a building (such as D). This resemblance leads us to operate as if the line in A is closer to us than the line in B. To maintain size constancy, we reason that the vertical line in B must be longer than in A, because it seems to be more distant from the viewer. Because we know that more distant objects produce smaller retinal images, we compensate and see the "distant" object as *larger* than the retinal image. Normally, this correction enables us to see a world that corresponds to reality. But when three-dimensional objects are represented on a two-dimensional surface, as in drawings and photographs, these corrections can in fact lead us astray. These correction processes are not conscious ones. Indeed, they are so deeply ingrained that we keep using them even when we know them to be inappropriate.

Other perceptual illusions can similarly be understood as special cases in which the corrections that usually insure accurate perception are inappropriately applied. One of these is the Ponzo illusion (also known as the railway lines illusion), in which the top line (the one that would ordinarily be seen as more distant) appears larger than the bottom line (see Figure 4.11). Another famous illusion is the

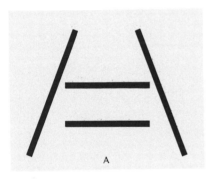

FIGURE 4.11
The Ponzo illusion. The two horizontal lines in A *are the same length, yet the top one appears to be longer than the bottom one. This illusion may be explained by the fact that our knowledge of perspective leads us to see the vertical lines as if they were railroad tracks receding in the distance (*B*). (See text.)*

Necker cube, devised in 1832 by a Swiss scientist named L. S. Necker. He noticed that a cube drawn in two dimensions (as in Figure 4.12) will spontaneously reverse its direction. The tinted area can appear as either an outer surface or an inner surface of a transparent box. When such three-dimensional figures are drawn in two dimensions, they become ambiguous. Our perception reflects this ambiguity, alternating back and forth between one interpretation and another.

The perceptual illusions we have discussed here have all been devised by scientists. Our senses and our perceptual processes function so well in ordinary circumstances that it took a great deal of ingenuity to come up with ways to trick our perceptions. So don't let magicians and psychologists make you begin to doubt your senses—they're amazingly trustworthy.

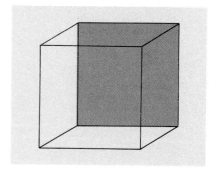

FIGURE 4.12
The Necker cube, an ambiguous figure.

SUMMARY

1. *Perception* is the active process of integrating and organizing information collected by the sense organs. The first step in the process of perception is for *receptor cells* in the sense organs to respond to energy in the environment. The energy is then converted to electrical impulses that can be transmitted to and interpreted by the brain.

2. *Vision* is the dominant human sense. The eye admits light (through the *pupil*) and focuses it (via the *lens*) onto the light-sensitive cells of the *retina*. These cells, the *rods* and *cones*, contain chemicals that break down when struck by light. The breakdown of chemicals triggers the sending of messages to the brain along the *optic nerve*.

3. The cones, which are packed together in the center of the retina, are the color receptors. The rods, which spread to the outer edges of the retina, are not sensitive to color. Adaptation to dim light occurs because chemicals in the rods and cones build up faster than they are broken down when there is little light stimulation. With more chemicals, the *visual threshold* is lowered, and less light is needed to stimulate the cells.

4. *Visual acuity* is the ability to discriminate the details in the field of vision. Poor visual acuity may be the result of *nearsightedness* (in which the eyeball is too long and the lens focuses the image in front of the retina) or of *farsightedness* (in which the eyeball is too short and images fall behind the retina). The *blind spot* is an empty spot in one's vision corresponding to the place on the back of the eye where the optic nerve exits to the brain.

5. According to one theory, color vision results from the "mixing" of stimulation of three types of cones, each sensitive to a different primary color. Defects in cones result in *color blindness*, which may be *dichromatic* (in which only two of the three types of cones are functioning) or *monochromatic* (in which none of the cones are functioning).

6. Depth perception is produced by *binocular vision*, in which the images received by the two eyes combine to give objects three-dimensionality. *Monocular cues* to depth perception include overlapping of objects, size differences, perspective, and shading. Experiments with the *visual cliff* indicate that depth perception is innate, although it improves with learning.

7. *Hearing* occurs when a *sound wave* causes the eardrum to vibrate, which in turn sets the three bones of the middle ear into motion. These bones transmit the vibrations to fluids in the *cochlea* in the inner ear, where receptor cells are stimulated, causing messages to be sent along the *auditory nerve* to the brain.

8. Among the qualities of a sound are *loudness* (determined primarily by the amplitude of the sound wave), *pitch* (determined primarily by the frequency of wave vibrations), and *timbre* (determined by the distinctive pattern of sound waves produced by the sound source).

9. Locating the source of a sound generally requires two ears: Sounds reach one ear a fraction of a second before the other, and they are also louder for the first (and closer) ear they reach.

10. *Noise pollution* can be harmful both physically and psychologically. Noise has been shown to impair performance on intellectual tasks, although the ability to predict and control the noise reduces the impairment. Prolonged noise over a period of years may also have adverse effects on the intellectual abilities of children.

11. The *skin senses* include receptors for pressure, heat, cold, and pain. The experiencing of warmth and cold is relative, depending on the temperature of the skin. Psychologists are uncertain whether pain is a sense in itself or a result of the intense stimulation of any of a number of receptors. According to the *specificity theory*, pain receptors send signals directly to the brain. According to the *gate-control theory*, there are areas in the nervous system that control whether or not a pain sensation will reach the brain.

12. Among methods of pain control currently being explored are acupuncture, electrical stimulation, hypnosis, and new drugs.

13. *Kinesthesis* is the sense of body movement and position. Receptors for this sense are located in the muscles, tendons, and joints. The sense of balance, or *equilibrium* (based in the *semicircular canals* in the inner ear), works in conjunction with kinesthesis to make one aware of body position in relation to gravity.

14. The sense of *smell* involves the reception of chemical molecules by cells on the olfactory membrane of the nose. According to one theory, there are four basic odors. There appear to be four basic *taste* qualities: sweet, sour, salty, and bitter.

15. Among the principles of perceptual organization identified by *Gestalt psychologists* are *figure-ground* distinctions, *closure*, *proximity* of elements, and *similarity* of elements.

16. Perception is *selective*—people pay *attention* to only a small percentage of the stimuli in their environment. According to one theory, we have a limited pool of energy to use for attending to things; the more difficult the task, the more energy we use for it and the less we use to notice other stimuli. Focusing attention is aided by the contrast, novelty, physical cues, and the meaning of the stimulus.

17. Studies of *sensory deprivation* in the 1950s showed that students who were placed in a room without sensory stimulation experienced hallucinations, were impaired in performance of intellectual tasks, and were more susceptible to persuasion. More recent research suggests that sensory deprivation is not as harmful as originally thought and can even have benefits, such as enhancing creativity.

18. People tend to perceive what they expect to perceive; this phenomenon is called *perceptual set*. Perception is also influenced by a person's needs and values.

19. People view objects as stable and unchanging despite changes in the pattern of stimulation received. The process of perceiving objects as staying the same size no matter what the distance is called *size constancy*, and perceiving them as maintaining the same brightness despite changing lighting conditions is called *brightness constancy*.

20. Perceptual *illusions* are instances in which perception and reality do not agree. Famous illusions include the Müller-Lyer illusion, the Ponzo illusion, and the Necker cube.

EXTRASENSORY PERCEPTION

A little after 11:00 on a Thursday night in 1976, Mrs. G. put down her book, switched off her radio, and turned over to go to sleep. At 11:30 she was startled out of her drowsing state by a tapping noise. Wide awake, Mrs. G. sat up and realized that the tapping sound was coming from her radio. She picked it up and stared at it. The tapping was clearly an SOS signal—a call for help in an emergency. After a few minutes it stopped. Mrs. G. was disturbed by the episode and slept badly that night. The next morning she told her brother about the strange occurrence and tried to put it out of her mind. The following day Mrs. G. was informed of her granddaughter's hospitalization: the young woman had been mugged on Thursday night at 11:30 (Nisbet, 1977).

> **In practically every culture the belief in extrasensory phenomena is common.**

This episode, and others like it, might be considered a dream, a coincidence, or a fantasy. But many people regard it as an example of *extrasensory perception*, commonly known as ESP. Many people believe that they can receive impressions of distant realities that do not reach them through sight, hearing, or any of the other "ordinary senses"—hence,

they are called extrasensory. In practically every culture of the world, the belief in such extrasensory phenomena is common (Sheils, 1978).

ESP takes several forms. *Clairvoyance* allows one to know about an object or event without employing the usual senses. *Telepathy* involves knowing another's thoughts without any sensory intervention. *Precognition* is foreknowledge of future events. The study of ESP is part of the enterprise of *parapsychology*—the study of mental phenomena that are beyond the usual bonds of psychology. Researchers in parapsychology cannot offer a satisfactory explanation of how this special form of perception operates, yet they are convinced of the reality of ESP and claim that most people have this ability to at least some degree. Most psychologists and other "conventional" scientists are not convinced that such abilities exist at all. Before we consider their objections, though, let us look at some of the research performed by parapsychologists.

RESEARCH ON ESP

Some of the earliest ESP experiments were performed by J. B. Rhine (1934) at Duke University, and his methods became widely used by others. Rhine used a special deck of 25 cards that included five different symbols—a cross, a circle, a star, a square, and a set of wavy lines. Subjects had to guess the order of the cards in the shuffled deck when the order was known to no one (clairvoyance) or when the experimenter or another

subject looked at the cards first (telepathy). Rhine's work was designed to determine whether ESP existed at all. More recent research assumes that it does exist and investigates such questions as which sorts of people are more sensitive than others and what circumstances are most conducive to ESP. ESP seems most likely to be demonstrated when subjects are concentrating highly and are emotionally aroused. To help create these special conditions, parapsychologists sometimes use hypnosis. One researcher found that instructing a hypnotized subject that "ESP is a proven fact" and that the subject is "very sensitive" was enough to improve the subject's performance on a subsequent card-guessing task (Casler, 1976).

Another team of researchers made use of both hypnosis and emotionally suggestive stimuli in an experiment on telepathy (McBain et al., 1970). Two-person teams were asked to send and receive five emotional concepts (such as home, sorrow, peace). The subjects were hypnotized in order to enhance their ability to express and sense the emotional content. On the average, over a series of 125 trials, the eleven teams scored about 27 correct guesses. By chance alone, teams would be expected to be correct one out of five times, so the teams did better than chance—but just barely. Same-sex teams produced about 29 correct guesses ("hits"), while opposite-sex teams scored only 24 hits. Furthermore, senders who were more susceptible to hypnosis tended to produce higher scores, although there was no comparable effect for receivers. In general, the results of "successful" ESP studies are similar to this one—subjects never hit on every trial, but they do hit at rates that are slightly better than might be expected by chance.

PROBLEMS WITH ESP RESEARCH

The problems parapsychologists face in their research are even greater than those of other psychologists. In any kind of study, an experimenter may subtly suggest the desired response to a subject without realizing it (see Chapter 1, Box 3). The rigorous controls set up in the experimental procedure help reduce this possibility. For example, in some experiments the experimenter does not know which condition of the experiment the subject is in. The experimenter cannot bias the research because she doesn't know what the desired responses are for that particular participant. Sometimes instructions are tape-recorded to insure that each subject hears the directions in exactly the same way. But establishing such controlled circumstances tends to weaken the findings in ESP experiments: the more rigorous the procedure, the harder it seems to be to obtain statistically significant results.

> **Believers perform better in ESP experiments than skeptics.**

Further, it is almost a truism in the field that believers perform better in ESP experiments than skeptics. Gertrude Schmeidler and R. A. McConnell (1958) separated research subjects into two categories: "sheep" (believers in ESP) and "goats" (nonbelievers). They found that the sheep regularly scored beyond chance in ESP experiments. The goats, however, consistently scored at chance or a little below. ESP researchers themselves cannot explain why only "sheep" are more likely to demonstrate a capacity we are all supposed to have. Most ESP experiments are performed with "sheep." When they are repeated with "goats," negative results are almost always obtained. The fact that ESP studies are conducted by believing researchers with believing subjects has the effect of making conventional psychologists suspicious of their validity.

> **The results of ESP experiments often fail to be confirmed.**

The results of ESP experiments often fail to be confirmed, even when they are repeated by the same researchers (Crumbaugh, 1969). For example, Bruce Layton and Bill Turnbull (1975) submitted the results of their research to a prestigious psychological journal. They had apparently discovered certain complex effects of people's own belief in ESP on their performance on a clairvoyance task. The editors of the journal agreed to publish the findings on the condition that the researchers attempt an exact *replication*—that is, that they repeat the procedures to see whether the same results would be obtained. They did, but this time there was no ESP of any kind. The most reasonable explanation seems to be that the first set of findings was a fluke—that is, a pattern that occurred by sheer chance.

SKEPTICAL ATTITUDES

Perhaps the greatest problem ESP researchers face is the skepticism of conventional scientists. The attitude of most American psychologists toward ESP is profoundly doubtful. It often seems that with ESP one either believes it or one doesn't. It depends on what one is willing to accept as proof. Correctly or incorrectly, this form of "perception" has thus far failed to be accepted as legitimate by most American psychologists. The physiologist Hermann von Helmholtz (1821–1894) expressed a sentiment that still seems evident among present-day psychologists. When asked what evidence would convince him of the reality of extrasensory phenomena, he said that not even what his own eyes recorded would convince him. He held that ESP was manifestly impossible. In 1951 a similar view was expressed by Donald O. Hebb,

a former president of the American Psychological Association, who stated, "Personally, I do not accept ESP for a moment, because it does not make sense. . . . My own rejection of ESP is—in the literal sense—a prejudice" (Hebb, 1951, page 45). More recently, Zick Rubin asked one of the nation's leading researchers on "ordinary" perception how scientists in this area view the continuing research on extrasensory perception these days. His answer: "We look the other way."

> *A scientist's answer: "We look the other way."*

Parapsychologists' toughest critics are other psychologists. Mahlon Wagner and Mary Monnet (1979) polled over a thousand professors at 120 colleges and universities on their attitudes toward ESP. The professors were from a wide range of academic areas: natural science, social science, humanities, arts, and education. While two-thirds of the total sample thought ESP was at least a likely possibility, only one-third of psychologists thought so. More than half of the psychologists said that ESP is impossible.

The skepticism of American psychologists reflects a cultural bias against scientific investigation of paranormal events. ESP seems to be considered a legitimate area of inquiry in the Soviet Union (Ebon, 1978). But in the United States, parapsychologists continue to be considered cranks by most of the scientific community. One reason for this is that fact that some "psychic" performers have in fact been proved fraudulent. The discovery of such frauds is enough to make many scientists (and lay-

persons) wary of any other demonstration of ESP.

A second reason for the scientific community's skepticism of ESP comes from the research problems discussed above. Science has certain rules and methods for exploring the universe. A phenomenon that doesn't yield to those rules and methods has, most researchers believe, no place in science. And for many women and men trained in the scientific method, whatever does not exist in science does not exist at all.

> *ESP may well exist, but it has yet to be demonstrated conclusively according to the rules of established science.*

Finally, psychologists have their own special reasons for rejecting parapsychology. The scientific method has been used with great success in psychology to explore

the mysteries of human perception. Many researchers have devoted their lives to the study of vision, hearing, and the other senses. The suggestion that all of this research gets at only a portion of our ways of knowing the world—that we have other modes of receiving information that are beyond the senses—may be threatening to such psychologists. Thus, psychologists are among the first to reject ESP.

ESP may well exist, but it has yet to be demonstrated conclusively according to the rules of established science. If ESP does exist, it will eventually enter the halls of science, despite strong resistance by the scientific establishment. And then we will be faced with the mind-boggling task of explaining how it works.

SUMMARY

1. *Extrasensory perception* is the ability to perceive objects and events by means different from the usual senses. ESP includes clairvoyance, telepathy, and precognition. The study of ESP is a branch of *parapsychology*—the study of mental phenomena that are beyond the usual bounds of psychology.

2. ESP research has taken the form of experiments in which subjects are asked to try to receive certain pictures or messages. Success of an experiment is judged by the statistical significance of the number of correct "hits."

3. The more scientific the setting and procedure, the less likely an ESP experiment is to produce significant results. Furthermore, people who believe in ESP perform better in ESP experiments than do skeptics. ESP experiments are also often difficult to *replicate*.

4. Most psychologists are highly skeptical of ESP research.

Chapter 5

Learning and Memory

Is this something like your typical day? You walk or ride or drive to school. You go to the correct rooms for your classes, and you make your way to the library almost without thinking. There, you read a book effortlessly. On your way to the student union you see someone you know and say, "Hi, Sue!" When you get home, you prepare yourself a snack and do some studying. Later, you play cards with some friends.

How is it that you can do all these things? When you were much younger, you couldn't do any of them. Gradually, over time, you've come to be able to do more and more. The basic process underlying all of these changes (from not being able to do something to being able to) is called *learning*. Learning is defined in psychology as a relatively permanent change in behavior as the result of experience or practice. Because so much of our behavior is learned—and because this simple fact has so many implications—learning has long been the cornerstone of American psychology.

Closely related to learning is the process of *memory*. To be able to say "Hi, Sue!" you must have learned Sue's name in the first place and you must have been able to remember it over some period of time. To be able to play cards, you must remember the rules of the card game and keep track of the cards play by play. And to do well in classes you need to learn and remember course material. The processes of learning and memory are thus closely connected.

Before getting into our discussion of learning and memory, we should point out that not *all* of our behavior is learned. Some animal and human behaviors are inborn rather than learned. As we saw in Chapter 2, *reflexes* are automatic responses to stimuli (such as blink-

138

ing at a flashing light) that do not have to be learned at all. And *instincts* are more complex, inborn, fixed patterns of behavior that are exhibited by all members of a species (of the appropriate age and sex). In addition, what an animal or person can learn depends in large measure on inherited capacities. No matter how much they practice, birds will not learn to speak (although some birds can imitate sounds), and people will not learn to fly. (We will focus on the interplay of heredity and learning in Chapter 9, when we consider the nature of human development.)

We will begin this chapter by discussing two basic forms of learning: *classical conditioning* and *operant conditioning*. These processes both involve learning to make new responses to particular stimuli. We will then turn to *cognitive learning*, an approach that emphasizes the fact that people learn not only behavioral responses but also information about their environment. From there, we will go on to consider two basic types of memory, short-term and long-term, and the way they work together to register, store, and retrieve information. Finally, we will draw from psychological research on memory to provide some tips on how you can study more effectively.

CLASSICAL CONDITIONING

We have defined learning as a relatively permanent change in behavior as the result of experience or practice. In other words, we assume that someone has "learned" something when his behavior changes in a certain way. The term *conditioning* is used for the basic learning processes of classical and operant conditioning, because in each case we focus on the conditions under which particular responses are made. In both types of conditioning particular *stimuli* (objects or events in the world) set up the conditions for the occurrence of our *responses* (the behaviors we perform). *Classical conditioning* focuses on the way in which involuntary responses (such as heart rate, blood pressure, or aspects of emotion that we have no direct control over) may be linked to particular objects or events. *Operant conditioning* focuses on the way in which voluntary responses (such as walking, writing, or talking) may be linked to the rewards and punishments we receive for making them. And, as we will see, there are other basic differences between these two kinds of conditioning. We will consider classical conditioning in this section and operant conditioning in the section that follows.

Pavlov's Discovery

The story of conditioning begins with the work of the Russian physiologist Ivan Pavlov (1849–1936). A Nobel Prize winner in physiology, Pavlov was experimenting on the salivary and digestive glands of animals—primarily dogs—to learn how digestion works. He found that animals would begin to salivate when food was presented to them; this is an automatic reflexive response that does not have to be learned. But Pavlov also discovered, to his surprise, that animals would begin to salivate as soon as the experimenter who had previously fed them entered the room. The same thing happens when you pick up your dog's feeding dish; it starts to respond as if it were time to eat. That is, stimuli that are merely *associated* with food produce the same response that the food does. Pavlov's curiosity was aroused by this phenomenon, and he began a long series of experiments on it because he thought it could serve as a basis for a theory of brain functioning. His theory has long since passed into obscurity, but his experiments demonstrated the basic principles of what is now called classical conditioning.

IVAN PETROWITOH PAWLOW.
Professor i fysiologi vid militär-medicinska akademien i St Petersborg. Född 1849.
Af Karolinska Mediko-Kirurgiska Institutet tilldelad Nobelpriset i medicin år 1904.

Ivan Pavlov, discoverer of classical conditioning.

We will use a typical experiment in Pavlov's laboratory to analyze classical conditioning. The animals were prepared so that their saliva flowed into a small glass funnel outside the cheek, allowing their salivation to be measured (see Figure 5.1). During the experiment the dog was placed in a harness while the experimenter sat on the other side of a partition, presenting stimuli to the dog and recording its responses. At this point in the experiment, before conditioning, two things could be observed:

1. Food presented to the animal elicited salivation. This is a reflex; it occurs automatically. Since no conditioning had yet taken place, Pavlov called food the *unconditioned stimulus* and salivation the *unconditioned response*.
2. Other stimuli that were irrelevant to salivation would evoke other responses from the dog. A bell, for example, would cause the dog to prick up its ears and turn toward the sound but would not cause saliva to flow. At this point, the bell would be called a *neutral stimulus*.

FIGURE 5.1

The laboratory apparatus used by Pavlov. The tube, connected to the salivary gland, collects any saliva secreted, and the number of drops is recorded on a revolving drum outside the chamber. An attendant can watch through a one-way mirror and deliver food by remote control. Thus, there is nothing to distract the dog except food and any other signals the attendant wishes to introduce.

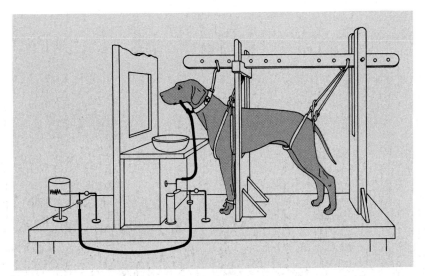

LEARNING WHAT MAKES YOU SICK

Animals seem to have biologically built-in predispositions to learn some associations more easily than others. Garcia and Koelling (1966) gave rats water with a distinctive taste, and while they were drinking they were exposed to flashing lights and clicking sounds. Then the animals were exposed to x-rays that made them sick to their stomachs about eight hours later. Despite the fact that their novel multimedia experience had occurred many hours before the sickness began, the rats almost totally avoided that distinctive taste from then on. They had "learned" that anything with that taste would make them sick. But they showed no aversion to the flashing lights or clicking sounds. It seems that the animals were predisposed to make associations that make sense biologically. After all, an animal is more likely to get sick from something it drinks or eats than from something it sees or hears.

The next part of the experiment was the conditioning phase, which took place over a period of several days. During conditioning, a bell was rung and a few seconds later a small amount of food was placed near the dog's mouth causing it to salivate. A dog would never, under normal circumstances, salivate at the sound of a bell. Yet, after about thirty such presentations of the bell and food together, the bell alone was sufficient to elicit a strong flow of saliva. The bell was now called the *conditioned stimulus*, and the salivation was called the *conditioned response*. This is the essence of classical conditioning: The subject learns to attach an existing response (such as salivation) to a new stimulus (such as the bell). For a summary of the classical conditioning process, see Figure 5.2.

One way of looking at classical conditioning is to observe that the animal has learned an *association* between two events in the environment—that they "go together"—in this case, the bell and the food. Once this association has been made, the animal reacts to the bell in the same way it would react to the food. It is as if the animal hearing the bell anticipates that the food will soon arrive and therefore responds accordingly. Yet this is all accomplished at a physiological level, with apparently no thought involved.

Classical Conditioning in Humans

In humans, classical conditioning plays an important role in learning emotional responses, such as fears, attitudes, or feelings toward particular objects. For example, suppose Bob and Fred are acquaintances. Bob is insulted by Fred one day, and he gets angry, causing his blood pressure to rise alarmingly. This is an involuntary, physiological response that occurs with many strong emotions (see Chapter 7). The next time Bob sees Fred, his blood pressure may automatically begin to rise. Fred becomes a conditioned stimulus for Bob; he is linked in Bob's mind to the insult, and as a result he can have effects on Bob's physiology without even doing anything.

Advertisers often make use of classical conditioning techniques in their attempts to produce positive attitudes toward their products.

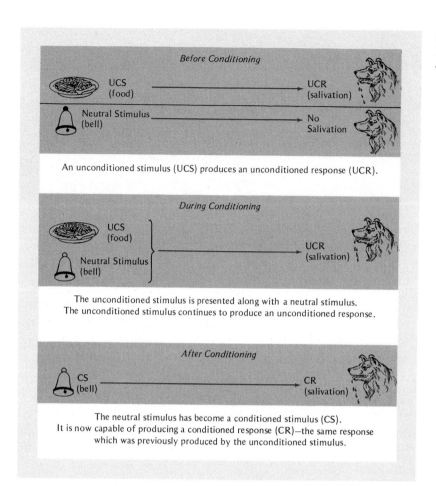

FIGURE 5.2
The process of classical
conditioning.

Before Conditioning

UCS
(food) ———————————→ UCR
(salivation)

Neutral Stimulus ———————————→ No
(bell) Salivation

An unconditioned stimulus (UCS) produces an unconditioned response (UCR).

During Conditioning

UCS
(food) ⎫
⎬ ———————————→ UCR
Neutral Stimulus ⎭ (salivation)
(bell)

The unconditioned stimulus is presented along with a neutral stimulus.
The unconditioned stimulus continues to produce an unconditioned response.

After Conditioning

CS ———————————→ CR
(bell) (salivation)

The neutral stimulus has become a conditioned stimulus (CS).
It is now capable of producing a conditioned response (CR)—the same response
which was previously produced by the unconditioned stimulus.

By repeatedly pairing a product (for example, a Coke) with images
and ideals that we are likely to feel good about, the advertiser attempts to make people have those same good feelings toward the
product itself. If the technique works, simply drinking a Coke can
make you feel good, even when the commercial is not playing in the
background.

Principles of Classical Conditioning

For a classically conditioned response to continue, there need to be
repeated pairings of the unconditioned stimulus and the conditioned
stimulus. If the conditioned stimulus is repeatedly presented *without* the unconditioned stimulus, however, the response becomes
weaker—less vigorous and less likely to occur. Thus, when Pavlov
would ring his bell (the conditioned stimulus) over and over without
giving his dogs food (the unconditioned stimulus), the dogs salivated
less and less. Such weakening of a learned response is called *extinction.* In our example of the acquaintances Fred and Bob, suppose
that over a period of time Fred is cordial to Bob every time they
encounter each other. Eventually Bob's automatic anger response
will die down and seem to disappear—it will be *extinguished.*

Although extinction involves a gradual decrease in the strength
of a response, it is important to keep in mind that the response does

FIGURE 5.3

Over a series of trials, learned responses may gain strength when they are reinforced (acquisition), lose strength when they are not reinforced (extinction), or regain strength after a rest period (spontaneous recovery).

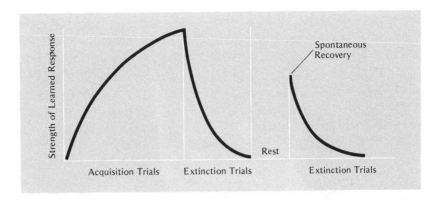

not just fade away. Rather, there is an active "unlearning" of the conditioned response as the animal or person discovers that a given consequence (such as food) no longer follows the conditioned stimulus. Many responses are never completely extinguished, as Pavlov observed with his dogs. Sometimes after a conditioned response had been extinguished it would suddenly reappear later. Pavlov called this phenomenon *spontaneous recovery* (see Figure 5.3). If the man in our example, Bob, doesn't run into Fred for a year and then suddenly encounters him, he may feel traces of the anger and high blood pressure that occurred with the original conditioning.

The phenomenon of spontaneous recovery indicates that even though a learned response may have been suppressed, it is not totally gone. Traces remain in some form in the nervous system. The more strongly a response is learned, the more resistant it will be to total extinction.

Two other principles that are involved in classically conditioned responses are generalization and discrimination. Pavlov found that a dog that was conditioned to salivate at the sound of a bell would also salivate—although to a lesser extent—at the sound of a tuning fork, a buzzer, or a metronome. The fact that stimuli similar to the conditioned stimulus can produce a similar conditioned response is called *generalization*. Pavlov also found that he could teach his dogs to make distinctions between stimuli. Using classical conditioning methods, he taught a dog not to salivate at the sight of a piece of dyed bread, which it was never allowed to eat. However, the dog continued to salivate to the stimulus of undyed bread—it had learned to *discriminate* between the two similar stimuli. One way to think of discrimination is that it involves conditioning of a response to one stimulus while extinguishing the response to a similar stimulus.

OPERANT CONDITIONING

A classically conditioned response is an involuntary one—Pavlov's dogs had no control over their salivation, and we typically have no control over sweaty palms or blushing cheeks. But most human behavior is voluntary. We do some things because we feel they will benefit us, and we do other things so that we can avoid having a bad experience. And we can change our behavior if we stop receiving the benefits or if we get punished. It is this capacity to change or shape

A psychologist records the responses of a pigeon in a Skinner box.

behavior on the basis of its consequences that is explained by the principles of operant conditioning.

The central principle of operant conditioning is that animals will produce particular behaviors if they learn that those behaviors will be followed by *reinforcement* (some event that is rewarding to them) and that they will stop producing behaviors that they learn will be followed by *punishment* (some unpleasant event or consequence). If a baby discovers that by bringing a bottle to his mouth he will be rewarded by the pleasant taste of milk, he will proceed to bring the bottle to his mouth repeatedly. Or if a woman discovers that by turning the radio dial to a particular station she will hear the kind of music she likes, she will learn to turn to that station in the future. Thus, the baby or the woman "operates" on the environment in order to get a reward or to avoid a punishment—hence the term *operant conditioning*.

Most of the research on operant conditioning has been conducted with animals such as rats and pigeons. In his pioneering studies of operant conditioning, psychologist B. F. Skinner designed a chamber—popularly known as a *Skinner box*—with enough room to allow an animal to move about somewhat and with devices to deliver food and water. The animal must perform specific responses in order to trip the mechanism that delivers reinforcement. For example, the box may contain a small bar or lever for a rat to press or a circular

GUIDED MISSILES—FOR THE BIRDS?

During World War II, B. F. Skinner came up with the idea of using pigeons to control guided missiles. Using operant conditioning techniques, the pigeons were taught to peck continuously for four or five minutes at the image of a target on a screen. The birds were then placed in the nose of a missile, harnessed in front of a similar screen. The idea was that when the missile was in flight, the pigeons would peck the moving image on the screen, which would produce corrective signals that would keep the missile on course. The missile was never used in actual warfare, however. A basic problem, Skinner later said, was that no one would take the idea seriously.

B. F. Skinner and friends.

key for a pigeon to peck, in order to receive a food pellet. The animal's rate of responding (such as number of bar presses per minute) can then be recorded automatically. The Skinner box makes it possible to experiment with different types of reinforcement under highly controlled conditions, and rats and pigeons can be taught specific responses using operant conditioning principles.

Shaping Behavior

The basic idea of operant conditioning is well known to animal trainers, who teach animals from pigeons to whales to obey by selectively rewarding their behaviors. They can teach an animal a complex behavior through the process of *behavior shaping.* That is, at first they reward any response that is roughly similar to the desired behavior. Then, one step at a time, they reward responses that are progressively more like the desired response. For example, if you want to teach your dog to roll over, you reward her at first when she lies down and then you only reward her for rolling movements while lying down. When she finally rolls over, you reward her only for that behavior from then on. Through this method of *successive approximation,* partial behaviors are eventually shaped into a sequence that produces the desired behavior.

Although most of the research on operant conditioning has involved other animals, the principles have been used to develop techniques of altering human behavior. The alteration of behavior through the systematic application of principles of learning is called *behavior modification.* In one experiment, for example, nursery-school teachers used a powerful reinforcement—their attention and praise—to increase the amount of time that 4-year-old children played with children of the opposite sex (Serbin, Tonick, and Sternglanz, 1977). When they saw a mixed-sex pair or group of children playing together cooperatively, the teachers commented approvingly, indicating the children's names and what they were doing. They would say, for example, "I like the tower John and Kathy are building." Such reinforcement was administered approximately every five minutes during a two-week experimental period. During this period, the rate of cross-sex cooperative play increased dramatically in each of the two classes in which the experiment was performed—from about 5 percent to 25 percent of the children's time.

After the experimental period the teachers discontinued their reinforcement to see whether the new behaviors would be maintained without reward. They weren't. The amount of cross-sex play declined to the same low level it had been at initially. In the absence of reinforcement, the new behavior was *extinguished*. In other cases, however, new responses may continue even after reinforcement is discontinued. In such instances, the person has discovered that the new behavior is rewarding in its own right. We will return to the topic of behavior modification, including the ethical issues that it poses about the control of human behavior, in the Psychological Issue that follows this chapter.

The ideas of generalization and discrimination between stimuli that we encountered in the case of classical conditioning are involved in operant conditioning as well. If you've learned to perform a response in one situation, in which it has led to reward, then you may generalize the response to similar situations. If you have learned, for example, that kicking a soft drink machine in a certain way often gets you a free drink, you may generalize the response and start kicking other food-dispensing machines.

Discrimination plays an especially important role in operant conditioning. Imagine the operant response of asking your father for money. In such a situation you want to be able to tell whether or not your father is in a good mood: A good mood signals reinforcement (money), while a bad mood signals nonreinforcement. In this example, your father's mood would be called a discriminative stimulus. A *discriminative stimulus* is one that becomes associated with the delivery of reinforcement because reinforcement is forthcoming in its presence if the appropriate response is made. In a Skinner box an animal can learn that bar pressing leads to reinforcement only when a light is turned on. Under these conditions, the animal does very little bar pressing when the light is off but is quite active when the light is on. When a behavior such as bar pressing occurs consistently in the presence of a discriminative stimulus such as light (but not in its absence), the behavior is said to be under *stimulus control*. Thus, if you were to ask your father for money only when he shows signs of being in a good mood, your behavior would be under stimulus control.

Reinforcement

A *reinforcement* is any event following a response that strengthens the response—that is, that increases the likelihood of that response occurring again. One of the most important challenges for anyone trying to teach something to an animal or a person is to figure out just what things are reinforcing to that individual. Some reinforcers seem to be naturally reinforcing, such as food, water, and affection; these are called *primary reinforcers*. Other events become reinforcing as a result of their association with primary reinforcers; these are called

Animal trainers can make use of operant conditioning to get animals to do
remarkable things. Pierrel and Sherman (1963) taught their rat Barnabus
to climb a spiral staircase, cross a narrow drawbridge, go up a ladder, pull a
toy car over by a chain, get into the
car and pedal it to a second ladder,
climb this ladder, crawl through a
tube, board an elevator, pull a chain to
raise a flag, and lower himself back to
the starting platform, where he would
press a lever to get a food pellet. After
the pellet was eaten, the remarkable
sequence of behavior began all over
again. In such a sequence, each behavior that is performed serves as the
stimulus for the next one, with the delivery of food serving as the ultimate
reward for the entire sequence.

secondary reinforcers. Secondary reinforcers play a big part in shaping our behavior: Think of all the behaviors we engage in to earn
awards, pats on the back, and grades. We have learned that the
awards, pats, and grades are rewarding, because they tend to go
along with other more basic rewards like affection and esteem.

One of the most important secondary reinforcers for human beings is money. Consider a dollar bill. To a child or to a person from a
culture that does not use paper money, a dollar does not seem to be
much of a reinforcement. It doesn't taste particularly good, it's not
much fun to rub against, and the expression on George Washington's
face looks, if anything, rather forbidding. But dollar bills become
reinforcers once we have learned that they can be exchanged for
food, clothing, and other items that are primary reinforcers. Similarly, poker chips, which in themselves have little value, are highly
reinforcing to gamblers, who know that they can cash in the chips for
money—and that they can later exchange the money for whatever it
is that they really find rewarding. Even monkeys can be taught new
behaviors using poker chips as a reward, as long as the monkeys have
previously learned that the chips can later be exchanged for food
(Wolfe, 1936).

Words—such as *yes* or *right*—can serve as reinforcers because of
their association with other rewards, such as a parent's affection or a
teacher's approval. As we saw in the experiment with preschoolers, a
teacher's comment was enough to reinforce cross-sex play.

Reinforcement can also be either positive or negative. In *positive
reinforcement,* a rewarding stimulus is presented after a response in

*Operant conditioning techniques are
used to train animals to do things
they might never do in their natural
environment.*

order to strengthen the response. In *negative reinforcement,* a response is strengthened by the *removal* or avoidance of an unpleasant stimulus. The use of positive reinforcement can be seen in the case of a group of psychology students who decided to turn the tables on their instructor (Sanford, 1965). On alternate days they either laughed at anything remotely funny in the instructor's lecture or did not crack a smile throughout an entire period. As a result, on days when humor was rewarded the instructor made many attempts to produce it, but on the laughless days the lectures became dedicatedly serious. In this case the students' laughter was positive reinforcement for the instructor's joke-telling behavior. Now imagine that the students had whispered to each other whenever the lecture was serious but stopped whispering for a while whenever the instructor told a joke. In this case, the removal of the unpleasant stimulus of whispering would have served as a negative reinforcement and would have tended to increase the instructor's attempts at humor.

Psychologists use both positive and negative reinforcement in studying learning in animals. A dog can learn to jump over a barrier in order to get food (positive reinforcement) or to avoid or escape an electric shock (negative reinforcement). In either case, the response of jumping over the barrier is strengthened.

Positive and negative reinforcers play a vital part in our daily lives. We buy food that tastes good and that fills us. We read books by authors who have pleased us in the past. We avoid parking in places where we previously received tickets. In each instance, we behave in a way that will produce rewards and avoid unpleasantness. Of course, people differ in what reinforces them. Some people enjoy horror movies; others are repelled by horror movies and much prefer comedies. Some people love spinach but would never touch an artichoke; others have exactly the opposite reaction. As they say, "Different strokes for different folks."

For reinforcement to be effective, it must be also well timed. *Delayed reinforcement,* administered some time after the response, is less likely to be effective than more immediate reinforcement. If an animal receives food a long time after it has pressed a bar, it may never make a clear connection between the behavior and the consequence, so the behavior is not as likely to be repeated. In addition, it is often frustrating, rather than rewarding, to have to wait for a reward that we think we have earned. Thus, if you tell me a joke and I laugh a minute later, your joke-telling behavior will probably not be reinforced at all.

As we have seen, operant conditioning can be applied to responses that are under our voluntary control. Recent research has suggested, however, that even involuntary responses—such as our heartbeat—may be altered by operant conditioning. This research is discussed in Box 1.

Schedules of Reinforcement

Total removal of reinforcement results in *extinction* of the learned response. In a Skinner box, if a rat is no longer reinforced with food for pressing a bar, the bar pressing will eventually cease. And as we

— Box 1

Training your heart

The research on operant conditioning makes it pretty clear that, given an adequate reward, animals and humans can be trained to perform new behaviors. These behaviors can range from lever pressing to changing eating habits, but all have one thing in common: they are voluntary actions. Thus, you might think that "involuntary" behaviors, such as one's heartbeat, have no place in the operant conditioning domain. How could someone ever learn to change her own heart rate, regardless of how much she was rewarded for doing so? But think again.

In recent years psychologists have gathered increasing evidence that people can in fact learn to control such involuntary responses as heart rate and blood pressure. Such control has been achieved through operant conditioning coupled with biofeedback techniques (see Chapter 2, Box 3), in which people are wired to monitoring devices that give them information about their heart rate or blood pressure. In a typical experiment, a subject might be directed to raise her heart rate. A light set in front of the subject flashes whenever her heart rate exceeds or drops below a given value. Or the subject watches a needle registering her blood pressure on a meter as she tries to raise or lower the pressure. The subjects are rewarded by success: the flash of the light or the movement of the needle indicates they have succeeded in their efforts.

By using such techniques, Neal Miller (1978), a pioneering researcher on learning and biofeedback, has trained subjects to alter the rhythm of their heart and to lower their blood pressure. Other investigators have confirmed his findings. Some subjects can even learn patterns of responses, such as changing blood pressure and

A subject attempts to lower his heart rate. The device on the table picks up the subject's pulse from his finger, measures the time between heartbeats, and displays these values in beats per minute. The device also flashes a light and sounds a tone each time the heart beats. The subject looks at the beat by beat values and, by relaxing, is able to slow his heart rate.

heart rate simultaneously in either the same or opposite directions (Schwartz, 1975). This is as clear an example of operant conditioning as rewarding a rat with food for learning to push a lever, even though it involves responses that were thought to be involuntary.

How do these subjects learn to regulate internal responses that most of us aren't even aware of? No one knows for sure, not even the subjects themselves. Some subjects report that they rely on visual images or thoughts to effect the physiological changes. Sexual images, an imaginary horse race, and running to catch a bus are some of the "pictures" subjects have used to elevate heart rate, while more serene images, such as lying on a beach, have helped some subjects to reduce heart rate or blood pressure. Other subjects, however, say they "just did it"; they thought about the response being studied and concentrated on producing the requested change. It will take more research to determine just what subjects who "just did it" really did to produce their results.

Psychologists who study learning know that the effects of operant conditioning can be maximized by scheduling reinforcement efficiently. Miller suggests that this factor may not be so important in operant conditioning of physiological responses. Instead, subjects' ability to discriminate internal physical stimuli—to really pay attention to their heartbeat or blood pressure—may be especially critical.

Most of the experiments on training heart rate have been done with healthy subjects. But physicians and psychologists are actively investigating the use of operant conditioning and biofeedback to treat cardiac problems and high blood pressure. The results so far have been mixed. Patients who have improved the most have been involved in programs that include relaxation training and other techniques along with biofeedback training (Katkin, Fitzgerald, and Shapiro, 1978). In such programs, patients may in fact be taught to control their hearts successfully, with great benefit to their health.

saw earlier, when nursery school teachers stopped reinforcing the children for cross-sex play, the children went back to their previous behavior. Similarly, you will stop shopping at a store that gives you bad service, and you will stop putting your money into a slot machine that never pays off.

The ease with which a response can be extinguished often depends on its original *schedule of reinforcement*, or the frequency or rate at which reinforcement occurs. Some of our behaviors are reinforced every time we produce them. When you press the elevator button, the elevator stops at your floor. When you go to a cafeteria for lunch, you get food. This is called *continuous reinforcement*. But it is much more common for responses to be rewarded on some occasions and not on others. If you are familiar with a soft drink machine that works only intermittently, you will understand the concept of *partial reinforcement*.

An interesting aspect of partial reinforcement schedules is that they tend to make a response more resistant to extinction. When responses are first acquired, continuous reinforcement is most effective in producing a strong response. However, such responses are easily extinguished. But if a response is reinforced on an intermittent schedule, it takes much longer for the response to extinguish when reinforcement is withdrawn. Why is this the case? With partial reinforcement, the person or animal comes to learn that not every response will be reinforced. As a result, the individual may keep trying even when reinforcement is withheld, in the hope that sooner or later reinforcement will be forthcoming. For example, suppose you have a very reliable car. It has always started without trouble, and you've never had a problem with it. Then one morning it simply won't start. You try to start it several times, but nothing happens. In this case, you will probably give up and call for a mechanic. But suppose you have an old clunker that starts right up some days and is sluggish on others. Again, one morning you try to start it and nothing happens. Because you know that this car is erratic, you will probably spend a much longer time trying to start this car. With the reliable car your starting response is likely to extinguish rather quickly, but with the clunker extinction may take hours. In fact, you may keep returning to the car at various points during the day to see if "just this time" it won't start.

Schedules of partial reinforcement can be set up in various ways. For example, if you use partial reinforcement to train an animal, you could decide to schedule reinforcement so that it is delivered after every third response the animal makes, after every fifth response, or whatever. In other words, a certain number of responses must occur before each reinforcement. This is called a *ratio* schedule of reinforcement. On the other hand, you could schedule the reinforcement according to the clock, so that a certain amount of time must pass before a response is reinforced. When time is the main factor, the schedule is called an *interval* schedule.

For both ratio and interval schedules another distinction can be made. If either the ratio or the interval is constant, the schedule is referred to as *fixed;* if the ratio or interval is not constant and varies somewhat each time, the schedule is called *variable*. Thus, there are

LEARNING TO PERSEVERE

In his novel *Walden Two*, B. F. Skinner (1948) envisioned the widespread use of operant conditioning techniques, which he called "cultural engineering." Partial reinforcement was used in Skinner's fictional community to develop frustration tolerance in children. Beginning at about age six months, babies were given certain toys designed to build perseverance. In order for the toy to be rewarding—for a music box to play a song or for a pattern of flashing lights to go off—the child had to give a certain response, such as pulling a ring. At first every pull of the ring was rewarded, but then the reward came every second response, every third, or even every tenth response, on a variable-ratio schedule. As Skinner pointed out, this method could be used to build up great perseverance "without encountering frustration or rage."

FIGURE 5.4
Schedules of reinforcement. Interval schedules are based on the time intervals between reinforcements; ratio schedules are based on the number of responses produced.

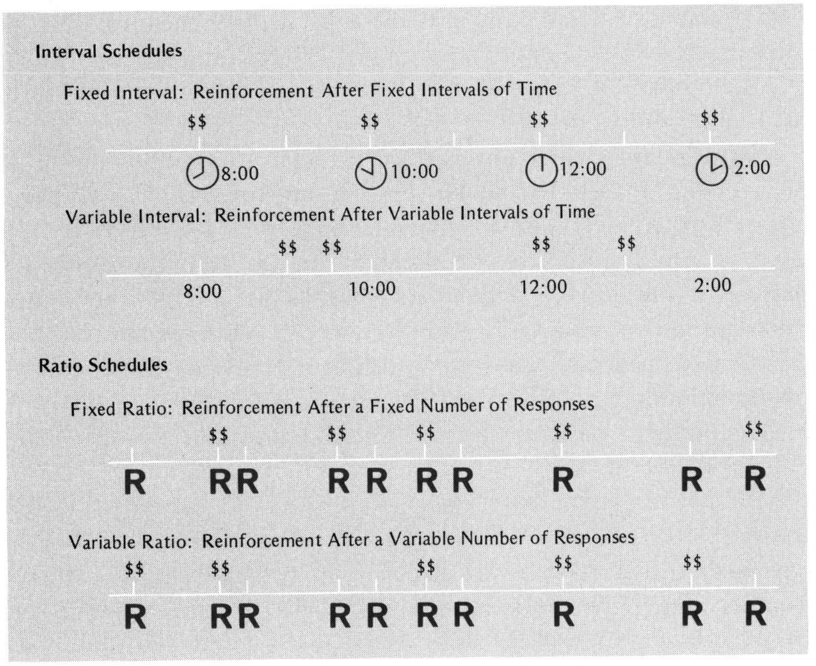

four basic schedules of reinforcement based on these two distinctions (see Figure 5.4).

Different schedules of reinforcement have different effects on behavior. With a fixed-interval schedule, the rate of responding is likely to fluctuate greatly, with the rate dropping off between reinforcements and picking up again at the end of the interval—for example, students who cram just before regularly scheduled exams. A variable-interval schedule, on the other hand, produces a steadier rate of responding—a student has to study regularly to be prepared for pop quizzes. On the whole, both kinds of interval schedules result in lower response rates than those produced with ratio schedules. Both kinds of ratio schedules tend to produce high rates of responding. Pigeons in a Skinner box will peck the response key up to several hundred times a minute on ratio schedules. And why not? The more pecking, the more food; if the pigeon slows down, so does the reinforcement.

In real life it is difficult to find pure examples of these four basic schedules, since the schedules of partial reinforcement that most often occur are *mixed* schedules that are combinations of ratio and interval, fixed and variable. You may be paid on the first and fifteenth of every month (fixed interval), but pay raises are more likely to be determined by the number of responses, or how hard you work (more like a variable ratio schedule).

Punishment

So far we have had a lot to say about rewarding behavior that we wish to encourage and very little to say about the other side of things: punishing behavior that we wish to eliminate. With *punishment*, the undesired response is followed by an unpleasant event or consequence. Punishment can be physical, such as a spanking, or psychological, such as a harsh word or a frown. Sometimes the most painful punishments involve depriving someone of expected rewards, such as sending a child to bed without his dinner or depriving him of a favorite television show.

Punishment clearly has a place in operant conditioning, as a means of decreasing the likelihood of responses. Suppose we have taught a rat in a Skinner box to press a bar in order to receive food. If we now administer an electric shock to the rat each time it presses the bar, it will quickly learn to decrease its bar-pressing behavior. Punishment is *not* the same thing as negative reinforcement, which we discussed earlier. Whereas punishment is the application of a painful stimulus, negative reinforcement involves the *removal* of a painful stimulus—a rat may learn to press a bar in order to turn off an electric shock.

Punishments are often extremely effective in suppressing responses. Dogs and cats will starve to death rather than eat if they have been subjected to severe electric shock when eating. And, on a cheerier note, people who have been criticized by their friends for smoking in class are likely to avoid this behavior in the future—at least while their friends are watching.

But although punished responses are temporarily suppressed, they are not actually "unlearned." Once the punishment is discontinued, these behaviors—assuming they were rewarding to the person in the first place—are likely to reappear. Thus, once the friends stop mentioning smoking, the smokers may resume their annoying habit.

A basic problem with the use of punishment in teaching and learning is that a punishment only tells people or animals what they should *not* do, and not what they should do. Thus, someone who is trying to connect an electrical appliance and who gets shocked in the process may learn that he's doing it wrong, but it won't teach him how to connect the appliance correctly. Similarly, a child who tries to get attention by telling wild stories may be punished by people who don't believe him, but that does not help her find other, more acceptable ways of getting attention. The person must still figure out what the correct or appropriate response is—or better yet, have someone else demonstrate it to him. Punishments can be effective, however, in compelling someone to switch from one response to a clearly available alternative response, which is then rewarded. For example, shocking a rat for taking a particular route in a maze may be a quick way of teaching him to take a different route instead. Animal trainers may also use punishment as a way of signaling an animal to discontinue one response and to replace it with another one, which is then rewarded.

The use of punishment carries with it some other common problems. One problem is that in some instances a "punishment" actually turns out to be rewarding and, as a result, strengthens the response that it was intended to eliminate. If little Morris is ignored whenever he is being a good boy but is yelled at (supposedly a punishment) whenever he does something wrong, he may find that doing "bad" things is an effective way of getting the attention he craves. Another problem is that the person may come to associate the punishment not so much with the behavior that was punished as with the person

THE EXTINCTION OF A PRESIDENT

When other people react to your statements approvingly, you are likely to make more of the same sorts of statements. Your conversational behavior has been reinforced. When others react with silence, on the other hand, you are likely to react quite differently. An example of this comes from one of the tapes from the Watergate trials, in which President Nixon had phoned his aide H. R. Haldeman at home. On the tape, Haldeman "sounds as if he has more important things to do than to talk to the President of the United States. His answers are monosyllabic, and there are long pauses when Nixon runs out of gas and Haldeman says nothing. Finally, Nixon hangs up" (Totenberg, 1975). As Nancy Henley (1977) explains, "Nixon is, in psychological terms, being *extinguished*. That is, his speaking behavior, in the absence of positive reinforcement in the form of interest or even minimal response, is dying out like a flame in the absence of oxygen" (page 70).

administering the punishment. A worker may do her best to avoid a supervisor who frequently criticizes her, which in turn makes it harder for the supervisor to have opportunities to employ positive reinforcement. Still another problem is that punishment often gives rise to stress and anxiety, states that do not usually make for efficient learning (Kahneman, 1973).

Because of all these problems with punishment, psychologists much prefer to use reinforcement in altering behavior. They often recommend, for example, that parents make a point of rewarding a child's good behavior and simply ignoring the child's misbehavior.

COGNITIVE LEARNING

Classical and operant conditioning involve simple stimulus-response processes of learning—people or animals come to associate a particular behavioral response with a particular set of stimuli. When a hungry pigeon in a Skinner box sees a bar, it presses. When a student is asked to spell a word, he responds with the right spelling. These stimulus-response associations are believed to be made as a direct result of rewards and punishments. For a long time, most psychologists viewed learning in such stimulus-response terms. They gave relatively little attention to the ways in which people learn not only specific responses to specific stimuli but also more complex stores of information about the world. One reason for the emphasis on stimulus-response learning is that most of the research on learning was conducted with animals such as rats and pigeons, whose capacity to think is far less developed than people's. Another reason for this emphasis was the insistence of psychologists of the behaviorist school (see Chapter 1), such as John B. Watson and B. F. Skinner, that only observable responses could be studied scientifically. Because we can't observe the knowledge that may be inside people's heads, these psychologists felt, it could not be seriously considered.

More recently, however, many psychologists have taken a more *cognitive* approach to learning, emphasizing the acquisition of information and of ways of dealing with information. Both classical and operant conditioning can be looked at from a cognitive viewpoint. In classical conditioning, we may view the animal as learning not so much an automatic response as an expectation: "That bell is a signal; it means that some food will be coming soon." Of course, a dog wouldn't put it quite that way, but some unspoken expectation may still be part of the process. In operant conditioning, the animal may be acquiring information about what leads to what in its environment. A rat may learn (once again putting words into an animal's mouth): "If I turn right, then left, then left again, I'll get to the end of the maze, where the food usually is." Or a student may learn: "When I approach Professor Plum at the end of class, rather than before, when he's a bit nervous, I'm more likely to get his full attention." From this point of view, what behaviorists view as the learning of stimulus-response associations is reformulated as the acquisition of information about the world and making use of it. Box 2 shows how

— Box 2 —

Learning to save energy

To learn many sorts of behaviors, it is often important to receive adequate *feedback*—information about how well one is doing—which may then be used to direct further efforts. For example, someone who is trying to lose weight will weigh himself daily on a bathroom scale to gauge his progress and to see whether his efforts to change his eating and exercise habits are proving successful. If the scale shows some loss, the person sees that he is on the right track, and is encouraged to continue his efforts. If it shows no loss or—heaven forbid—a gain, the person is informed that greater efforts or new strategies are needed. Many studies have shown that when people are given feedback their performance generally improves, on tasks ranging from solving simple arithmetic prob-

lems to loading trucks. (Biofeedback, which we discussed in Box 2, is a special case of feedback—information about one's own physiological responses.) Psychologists have recently applied similar feedback techniques to the pressing problem of teaching people to conserve energy.

As oil, gas, and electricity costs rise to new heights, most people are motivated to save energy. One of the obstacles to doing so, however, is that we typically do not really know how much energy we are using at any given time. Even if we turn down the heat in the winter or the air conditioner in the summer, we never learn just how much energy we have saved. Clive Seligman and John Darley (1977) set out to remove this obstacle by providing daily feedback to homeowners about their energy consumption.

Seligman and Darley conducted their experiment in 29 physically

such acquisition of information, through feedback on one's own performance, can help in the practical task of conserving energy.

Research on cognitive learning goes beyond classical and operant conditioning to look at a wider range of ways in which people acquire and organize information about their environment. The word *cognitive* comes from the Latin word meaning "to know," and that is what cognitive learning is about—how people come to know about their world. In fact, people acquire, store, and organize information even when they are not rewarded while they are doing so. For example, people—and, indeed, even animals—form *cognitive maps* of their physical environments (Siegel, Kirasic, and Kail, 1978). A cognitive map is a mental representation of the relationships between locations, just as a real map provides a visual representation of these relationships. If you are driving to school in the morning and encounter a road block, you can probably find a new route to campus, even if you have never traveled the alternative route before. This is because you have formed a cognitive map of the area in which your school is situated.

We also learn a great deal without any direct reward or punishment simply by observing the behavior of other people. For example, a child who is beginning nursery school may learn how to finger paint by watching the older children in the class. A college student

identical three-bedroom townhouses in the community of Twin Rivers, New Jersey. About half of the houses were randomly assigned to the feedback group. For three weeks during the hot summer, these families' electric meters were read every day. The researchers were able to compute how much the family's energy use the previous day was above or below their previous usage, and this figure was then displayed with plastic numerals that were dropped into a lucite holder attached to the kitchen window, where they could be seen from the kitchen and family area. For example, the number 80 indicated that the family's energy use on the previous day was only 80 percent of what would have been predicted on the basis of their previous usage. The number 120 indicated that they exceeded predicted usage by 20 percent. (These figures took into account fluctuations in weather that affected household energy use.)

The other half of the townhouses were assigned to the control group. These families agreed to take part in the study, and their meters were also read every day, but no feedback was provided. Both the feedback and control groups were also given information about how they could best conserve energy by raising the settings on their thermostats to reduce air-conditioning use. The researchers found that the feedback was indeed effective in reducing energy use: families in the feedback group used 10.5 percent less energy than families in the control group. Other recent studies have also found feedback to be effective in reducing both electricity consumption in the summer and heating costs in the winter (Becker, Seligman, and Darley, 1979).

Feedback seems to work for several reasons. It keeps people interested in and focused on the learning task at hand, and it provides information about the consequences of particular behaviors. When the feedback is positive, it serves as a reinforcement, motivating people to keep up the good work. And when it is negative, it serves as a punishment, impelling people to change their behavior. As one woman in the study told the researchers, "I felt I could see what I was doing. When the numbers went over 100 I really tried. I kept the shades down to keep the sun out."

Other attempts to help people conserve energy through feedback are now under way. In one such project, computerized meters are being installed in people's homes that will tell them immediately how much energy they are using—and, what is more, will automatically convert this information into the most meaningful form of all, dollars and cents.

who is beginning a part-time job at an ice cream parlor will learn how to make sundaes and milk shakes by following the example of her more experienced coworkers. This important process of learning is called *learning by observation*, or *modeling*.

SHORT-TERM AND LONG-TERM MEMORY

Almost a century ago, the pioneering American psychologist William James noted that there seem to be two distinct types of memory, one sort that is fleeting and another sort that appears to be permanent and indestructible. James wrote:

The stream of thought flows on, but most of its elements fall into the bottomless pit of oblivion. Of some, no element survives the instant of their passage. Of others, it is confined to a few moments, hours, or days. Others, again, leave vestiges which are indestructible, and by means of which they may be recalled as long as life endures. Can we explain these differences? (James, 1890)

James's remarks agree with everyday experience. Some thoughts—such as a telephone number we've just looked up—seem to be immediately present in our consciousness but do not stay there for very long. Other thoughts—such as the capital of Iowa—may be somewhere in our memory stores but we can't bring them to consciousness without an active search; such memories seem to be quite enduring, however.

Research on verbal learning and memory over the past several decades has suggested that James was in fact right about the existence of two distinct sorts of memory—short term and long term. *Short-term memory* appears to hold a small amount of material at a time, and to lose it quickly. *Long-term memory* holds a huge amount of material and loses it much more slowly—if at all. A model of memory that includes these two types has been proposed by Richard Atkinson and Richard Shiffrin (1968). If the model of memory that we are about to describe reminds you of a computer program, it is no accident (see Figure 5.5). In fact, this model was developed as a direct analogy to the ways in which computers register, store, and retrieve information.

Short-term Memory

Isaac Asimov (1967) estimates that the brain, in a lifetime, probably absorbs as many as one quadrillion—1,000,000,000,000,000—separate bits of information. At any moment, thousands of pieces of information impinge on our eyes, ears, and other sense organs. Very little of this information actually reaches our consciousness, however. From all of the incoming sensory stimulation, most is held in a stage of *sensory storage*, lasts but a fraction of a second, and then is lost (Sperling, 1960). Sensory storage holds information in "raw" form—the colors, shapes, flashes of lights, tones, and other stimuli that impinge on our sense organs but that have not yet been sufficiently analyzed in our brains to have any meaning. Only a small fraction of the material in sensory storage goes into our short-term memory, and it does so in

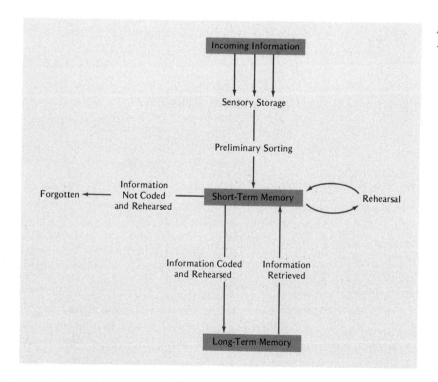

FIGURE 5.5
A model of memory.

Short-term memory is important in many of our daily activities, such as making phone calls to unfamiliar numbers.

a form that has some meaning, such as words, numbers, or images.

Short-term memory lasts much longer than sensory storage. But it, too, can hold only a limited amount of information. For example, if you recite a list of unrelated letters or numbers to someone and ask that person to repeat the list, she can usually handle lists of up to seven (or sometimes eight or nine) items, but not much more. Thus, short-term memory appears to have a limited capacity of about seven items (Miller, 1956). Maybe that's one reason why telephone numbers have seven digits.

Although short-term memory is limited, its span can be increased by organizing inputs into larger "chunks." Short-term memory is not limited to seven letters or numbers but rather to about seven pieces of information, which could be seven numbers, seven words, or even seven sentences. If we can manage to code a set of letters or numbers into a single piece of information (such as a word or phrase), the amount of information we can hold in short-term memory will be increased.

Even though short-term memory can be expanded in this way, its capacity remains limited, and the information is kept in mind for only a short time. Sometimes the information doesn't stay in mind for as long as we need it. You've surely had the experience of looking up a phone number, then being distracted before dialing and forgetting the number by the time you turn to dial. Or, when you are introduced to a lot of people, you may forget their names at almost the same rate that new names are introduced. In this instance, new information is arriving in short-term memory at a time when the storehouse is already full. In such a case the new information may bump the older information out of short-term memory before it can be readied for long-term storage.

In general, short-term memory can hold items fairly well for the first few seconds. After about 12 seconds, however, recall is poor, and after 20 seconds the information has disappeared entirely, unless we have kept repeating the material to ourselves (Peterson and Peterson, 1959). A phone number that we look up and dial is often forgotten by the time the call is answered. But a certain relatively small proportion of the material that enters short-term memory is not lost along the way. Instead, we manage to transfer this material to long-term memory for later reference. Thus, there are some telephone numbers that we once had to look up but that now we know without looking. These are the numbers that are important enough for us to have taken pains to record in our long-term memory store.

Long-term Memory

Sherlock Holmes, the fictional detective who was, among other things, a master of memory, once gave Dr. Watson the following advice:

I consider that a man's brain originally is like a little empty attic and you have to stock it with such functions as you choose. A fool takes in all the lumber of every sort that he comes across. . . . Now the skilled workman is very careful indeed as to what he takes into his brain-attic. He will have nothing but the tools which may help him in doing his work, but of these he has a large assortment, and all in the most perfect order. It is a mistake to think that that little room has elastic walls and can distend to any extent. Depend upon it that there comes a time when for every addition of knowledge you forget something that you knew before. (Doyle, 1937, page 21)

Long-term memory has been likened to a library card catalog system. Access to our memories depends on how well we have set up our filing system.

What Holmes referred to as the "brain attic" is what today's psychologists call long-term memory, the process by which we can retain information for days, years, or even a lifetime. Holmes's model of memory does not agree in all respects with that suggested by recent psychological research. In fact, the "attic" of long-term memory does seem to have elastic walls, in that its capacity seems to be unlimited. But Holmes was quite correct in emphasizing the importance of stocking the attic carefully. Unless information is carefully coded and filed, it will become impossible for us to retrieve the information when we need it—the task would be like trying to find a book in a large library where the books are arranged randomly and the card catalog is disorganized.

How do we get information from short-term memory into long-term storage? There are two basic processes: *rehearsal* of the information (repeating it to yourself or keeping a picture of it in your mind) and *encoding* it (linking it to concepts and categories that you have already learned). Of these two processes, psychologists now believe that encoding the material in a meaningful way is the more important. In fact, rehearsal may be important only insofar as it provides a better opportunity for meaningful encoding. Encoding is like filing things in a complicated, cross-referenced file system. The encoding process may either simplify or elaborate on the information to be stored or change it into a different form for storage (Bower, 1972). The process is analogous to labeling books, cross-listing them on cards, and storing the material in specified places in a library.

As Atkinson and Shiffrin (1968) emphasize, memory storage is not a passive process. Rather, we must decide for ourselves what information we would like to store in long-term memory by selecting the items to rehearse and encode. *How* we encode material is particularly important because, as we will see, our success at retrieving material from long-term memory depends in large measure on the efficiency with which it is stored.

As part of our attempt to stock our brain attics carefully, we have all learned to package the material in meaningful clusters. To demonstrate this process, you can do the following simple experiment, using a friend as your subject. Read the adjacent list of words to your friend, telling him to remember as many of the words as possible. After you've read the list of words, ask your friend to start with the number 42 and count backward by threes to zero. The purpose of this counting task is to provide some mental interference so that the memory task won't be too easy. Now ask your friend to tell you as many of the words as possible, in whatever order he likes. If your friend is like most subjects in this sort of experiment, he will remember a large proportion of the words—but he will report them in a different order from the order that you read them. Your friend will probably report them in clusters or categories—for example, first vegetables, then office furniture, then metals. It is, in fact, much easier to learn and remember a list of words that includes meaningful clusters than it is to learn a list of words that bear no relation to one another.

In establishing material in long-term memory, we try to provide meaning to the material by linking it to concepts and knowledge we already have. In one experiment (Hyde and Jenkins, 1969), college

SILVER
LETTUCE
TYPEWRITER
TOMATO
DESK
COPPER
CELERY
FILE CABINET
BRONZE
ZINC
BOOKCASE
CARROT

students were presented with a list of words. Some subjects were asked to rate each word as "pleasant" or "unpleasant," which forced them to notice the meanings of the words. A second group of subjects were asked to count the number of *e*'s in each word, and a third group were asked to count the number of letters in each word. In the second and third groups the subjects' attention was diverted from the words' meanings to the physical characteristics of the written words. On concluding their tasks, the subjects were asked to report back as many words as they remembered. The first group recalled significantly more words than did the other two groups. Thus, subjects remembered the material best when they had encoded it for meaning than when they had not encoded it for meaning.

While most material needs to be encoded in order to get into long-term storage, there may be exceptions. Some psychologists (such as Haber, 1970) believe that certain visual images, such as faces, go directly into long-term storage. This may explain why we are often able to recognize the faces of people we have seen only briefly when we encounter them again.

Whatever method is used to get material into long-term memory, the next problem is being able to *retrieve* the information at the moment that we need it—to get it out of the crowded attic and back into consciousness. What *is* the capital of Iowa? It's likely that you know the answer—that it's somewhere in your long-term memory—but that you can't get it out at the moment. Or can you remember the name of your third-grade teacher or what she looked like? That information, too, is in your long-term memory. The question is,

— *Box 3* ——————————————————

"It's on the tip of my tongue"

Not long ago, Zick Rubin was watching a news reporter on television. I had seen him before, and I knew that I knew his name, but I couldn't quite remember it. I struggled to get the name off the tip of my tongue and into my consciousness. Was it John Calhoun? That was close, it seemed, but it wasn't quite right. Was it John Coltrane? That seemed even closer, but it wasn't the name I was groping for. When I finally managed to get the right name in my mind, I felt tremendous relief. (It was John Cochran.)

This *tip-of-the-tongue (TOT) phenomenon*—the feeling of being almost but not quite able to recall a word—is something that most people are familiar with but have a difficult time explaining. The phenomenon involves an essential puzzle: How can you know that you know something without actually knowing what that something is? This puzzle also intrigued two psychologists, Roger Brown and David McNeill. They conducted an important study of the tip-of-the-tongue phenomenon that helps to explain aspects of the way we store names and other words in long-term memory.

To study the TOT phenomenon, Brown and McNeill (1966) read the definitions of obscure words to their subjects and recorded the words that came to mind for subjects who said they knew the correct word but could not quite re-call it. For example, they gave their subjects the definition: "A navigational instrument . . . stars at sea." The correct answer, or target word, was *sextant*. This definition put some subjects in the TOT state—they said they knew what the word was but couldn't bring it to mind. When asked which words *did* come to mind, the subjects generally listed words that were similar to the target word either in meaning or in sound. The words of similar meaning included *astrolabe, compass, dividers,* and *protractor.* The words of similar sound included *secant, sextet,* and *sexton.* The similar-sounding words were of particular interest to Brown and McNeill. The fact that these words came to mind made it clear that

can you retrieve it? One type of retrieval problem—the tip-of-the-tongue phenomenon—is described in Box 3.

As we have noted, one way to improve information retrieval is to store and encode things carefully in the first place. The more completely we inspect the incoming material and mentally connect it with things we already know, the more likely we are to remember it later (Craik and Lockhart, 1972). You probably know from your own experience that it is difficult to remember the contents of a textbook chapter that you didn't really understand when you first read it. But as your understanding of the material improved, the better you remembered it.

In addition to meaningful storage of information, retrieval is best when you have reminders, or *cues*, available that you can associate with the material to be retrieved. In the exercise with the word list, for example, if you ask your friend to remember the words the next day, he may be unable to recall more than a few of them. But if you remind him that the words were metals, vegetables, and office furniture, he may then be able to retrieve many more of them. As we will see shortly, forgetting is often due to the fact that we lack sufficient cues to retrieve a piece of information.

WHY DO WE FORGET?

Given the impressive capacities of human memory, we can ask a different sort of basic question: Why do we forget things at all? Several different reasons for forgetting have been identified. As we noted

What is this object called?

the subjects knew a great deal about the target word even though they could not quite remember it. As further evidence of this knowledge, subjects in the TOT state were remarkably accurate in identifying the first letter and the number of syllables in a target word.

On the basis of their results, Brown and McNeill proposed that our verbal storage is like a complex filing system, cross-referenced by both meaning and sound. One part of the filing system is arranged something like a thesaurus, indexed in terms of word meanings. The definition of a navigational instrument calls forth the mental file drawer for that category, including words like astrolabe and compass, as well as sextant. The other part of the filing system is organized something like a conventional dictionary, but with a difference: it is organized not only according to the way words are spelled but also according to the way they sound. The meaning-filing system helps us to recall the right word when speaking or writing: we retrieve the appropriate file from the appropriate file drawer and then search through it for the word we want. The sound-filing system is especially helpful in enabling us to recognize and understand words—if someone says something remotely like *sextant*, we can usually figure out what she means.

earlier, some information is forgotten almost as soon as it is learned. This is information, such as a telephone number, that is held for a brief period in short-term memory but is never transferred to long-term memory. Most researchers believe that once such information drops out of short-term memory, it is lost to us forever. When we talk about forgetting things, however, we are usually talking about information that we once knew—that was once part of our long-term memory store—but that we can no longer bring to mind. This type of forgetting is referred to as *retrieval failure*.

Retrieval Failure

Psychologists once believed that information in long-term memory would "decay" over time if it were never used or that it would fade as the result of interference from new material—which would correspond to Sherlock Holmes's idea that "for every addition of knowledge you forget something that you knew before." But recent research suggests that this is not the case. In fact, long-term memories seem to remain in indefinitely long—and perhaps permanent—storage, embedded in physical-chemical codes that scientists are just beginning to understand. In fact, with the right sort of cues, people can remember many things they thought they had forgotten.

Endel Tulving (1974) has concluded that much of what we call forgetting is actually a failure to locate information that is in one's memory. In his experiments, subjects memorized lists of words. When they were asked to recall these words later, many items seemed to be forgotten. But when subjects were then given cues to jog their memories—for example, the category to which the word belonged ("four-footed animal") or words that rhymed with the word to be recalled—much of the forgotten material was remembered.

You have probably had your own memory prompted by cues on many occasions. Suppose a friend mentions a day several months past on which you joined a group of people in the cafeteria for a cup of coffee. You have no recollection of the event. She reminds you that it was raining, it was the day that Joel showed up with his arm in a cast, and the group was discussing a particular movie. The incident suddenly comes back to you—an event you had forgotten.

In Tulving's view, forgetting is simply a matter of lacking the cues needed to retrieve a piece of information. With the right sort of prompting even long-lost information can eventually be dredged from our memories. One way to provide such cues may be to return to the situation in which we initially stored some material (it would be like remembering the day we first put something in the attic and trying to figure out where we might have put it). This return can be done mentally (by thinking back) or physically (as when police take witnesses to the scene of a crime). You have probably used this method in trying to find something you've misplaced, such as your car keys. You mentally retrace your movements after you got out of your car, and may even physically go over the route, until you eventually reach the spot ("Ah, the kitchen counter!") where you left the keys.

Motivated Forgetting

We sometimes forget material that is in our long-term memory not because we *can't* retrieve it but because we don't really want to. That is, we may sometimes forget things because remembering them would be embarrassing or painful. This process is called *motivated forgetting.* The existence of this type of forgetting often comes out in family discussions in which members reminisce about days gone by. Someone will bring up an incident in which another family member appears in a bad light, and the second person will say, "I never did that!" and will profess to no memory of the event.

Sigmund Freud's concept of *repression* deals with motivated forgetting on a deeper level. According to Freud, we are unable to retrieve some memories because they are related to emotional conflicts. If we remembered certain feelings and events, such as our early sexual and aggressive feelings, we would experience severe anxiety. To avoid this anxiety, we manage to repress this material and keep it from coming to the surface. In this way, "forgetting" serves to protect one's self-concept. On the other hand, if the anxiety can be allayed—as through psychoanalytic therapy (see Chapter 12)—the repressed material might return to consciousness.

Could we recall *everything* we ever knew, if only we had adequate retrieval cues and were highly enough motivated to do so? Some researchers believe we could; others remain doubtful. The question about the ultimate limits of our memories is one that psychologists cannot yet answer.

RECONSTRUCTIVE MEMORY

Until now, we have been talking about memories as if they were fixed entities, unchanged by the passage of time. But many psychologists have come to doubt this notion. Instead, they view memory retrieval as a *reconstructive* process, in which our wider knowledge of the world affects the way we remember a specific event. Remembering may actually be a process of mentally "rebuilding" an event rather than simply finding a permanent record of it in our long-term memory. For example, your memory of the first time you rode on a bicycle may be influenced not only by that event but also by your more general knowledge of how a bicycle works, your general picture of what you were like at that age, and stories your parents have told you about yourself as a child. In recalling such an event you may tie it into the context of your life at the time, rather than actually remembering every detail as it was.

To illustrate the ways in which our more general knowledge may influence specific memories, college students in one experiment were asked to read a brief biographical passage, such as the one in the margin (Sulin and Dooling, 1974). For half of the subjects the blanks were filled in with the name of Adolf Hitler; for the other half they were filled in with the name of a fictitious person, Gerald Martin. After reading the passage, the subjects were given a list of sentences and were asked which ones had appeared in the story. All of the sentences but one had actually appeared in the story; in place of the

_____ _____'S SEIZURE OF POWER

_____ _____ strove to undermine the existing government to satisfy his political ambitions. Many of the people of his country supported his efforts. Current political problems made it relatively easy for _____ to take over. Certain groups remained loyal to the old government and caused _____ trouble. He confronted these groups directly and silenced them. He became a ruthless, uncontrollable dictator. The ultimate effect of his rule was the downfall of his country.

actual sentence, the experimenters included, "He hated the Jews particularly and so he persecuted them." Significantly more subjects who read the description of "Adolf Hitler" thought they had seen this sentence than did subjects who read the description of "Gerald Martin." The subjects' prior knowledge of Adolf Hitler's life affected the way they remembered the passage, allowing them to "recognize" a sentence they had never seen before.

STUDY STRATEGIES

As we have seen, the ways in which we learn or encode information in the first place are of prime importance in memory. Research on memory and learning suggests a number of practical strategies to use in studying for your classes: spacing study periods, active recitation, reviewing the material, and giving the material meaning.

1. *Spacing study periods* is more efficient than learning material all at once, because your attention tends to wander after long periods of time and fatigue is more likely to set in. In addition, when you are trying to learn too much in a single session, it is likely to be harder for you to encode the material in a meaningful way. Instead, new material is likely to bump old material out of short-term memory before it can be transferred to long-term storage. The best length for study periods varies with the nature of the material being learned and with different people. For most students, four 1-hour intervals of study would result in better recall of the material in this chapter than would one 4-hour session.

2. *Active recitation* involves stopping every so often as you read and repeating to yourself what you have just learned. This procedure focuses your attention on the material at hand and gives you repeated practice in retrieving information that has been stored. Perhaps even more important, such recitation can provide more opportunity for you to think about what the material really means—and, thus, to encode it in an efficient way. As a result, active recitation

Taking notes about what you read helps make the material you are studying become more meaningful to you.

helps to ensure that you will be able to recall (not merely recognize) the material when it is needed.

3. *Reviewing* material follows the principle that it is easier to relearn material that has been learned previously. Therefore, if you know you will be tested on information learned early in the term, it pays to review the material every so often to refresh your memory about the parts you know and to learn those parts you had trouble with the first time. The more you review during the term, the less time you will need to spend going over old material for the final examination.

4. *Giving meaning* to the material is probably the most important of all study strategies. Rote learning is not nearly so efficient as learning accompanied by an understanding of how the material fits together with other materials and ideas that you already know. For example, instead of just memorizing these four study strategies, you could think about whether each one has been useful to you in the past, and you could think about how each of them relates to principles of memory introduced earlier in this chapter.

One way to help give meaning to what you read is to take notes, putting the central ideas in your own words, or to make an outline of the important points. Such note taking serves two purposes. First, it may be useful to refer back to the notes later to refresh your memory of the material. Second, in the process of taking the notes you will be mentally organizing the material in a way that is meaningful to you and, hence, easier to remember.

More generally, whenever we talk about "improving memory" we are not really talking about the *ability* to remember. That ability is a given, and it seems to be the same for all normal humans. What we *are* talking about is improving our methods of putting information into long-term memory in the first place so that we can ensure that it's there and that we can retrieve it easily. And the key to doing this is meaning—making things fit together in coherent ways.

SUMMARY

1. *Learning* is a relatively permanent change in behavior as a result of experience or practice. Some behaviors are inborn rather than learned, and what we can learn depends on our inherited capacities.
2. In *classical conditioning,* a neutral stimulus is paired with an *unconditioned stimulus* that elicits an *unconditioned response.* After repeated pairings, the neutral stimulus alone comes to elicit the response, and it is then called a *conditioned stimulus* and the response is called a *conditioned response.*
3. Classical conditioning involves making an association between two events in the environment and tying them to an involuntary response. In humans, classical conditioning is often involved in learning emotional responses and attitudes.
4. *Extinction* is the weakening of a learned response. In classical conditioning, extinction is accomplished by repeatedly presenting the conditioned stimulus without the unconditioned

stimulus. Sometimes an extinguished response suddenly reappears; this is called *spontaneous recovery.*

5. *Generalization* is responding in the same way to more than one stimulus with similar characteristics. *Discrimination* involves responding to one stimulus while not responding to a very similar stimulus.

6. In *operant conditioning,* an operant response (one that operates on the environment to produce some effect) that is rewarded is more likely to be repeated; a response that is not rewarded or that is punished is not likely to be repeated.

7. *Shaping behavior* involves rewarding responses that are closer and closer to the desired behavior until the desired behavior is produced.

8. A *discriminative stimulus* is one that becomes associated with the delivery of reinforcement because reinforcement occurs in its presence. When a behavior consistently occurs only in the presence of a discriminative stimulus, the behavior is said to be under *stimulus control.*

9. A *reinforcement* is any event following a response that increases the likelihood of that response occurring again. Naturally reinforcing rewards are called *primary reinforcers;* events that become reinforcing as a result of their association with primary reinforcers are called *secondary reinforcers.*

10. In *positive reinforcement,* a reward is used to increase the frequency of a response. In *negative reinforcement,* an unpleasant stimulus is removed in order to increase the frequency of a response.

11. Using operant conditioning techniques and *biofeedback,* people can learn to alter such involuntary responses as heart rate and blood pressure.

12. For reinforcement to be most effective, it must come immediately after the response. In *continuous reinforcement* every response is rewarded. In *partial reinforcement,* responses are rewarded after a certain number have been emitted (*ratio schedule*) or after a certain amount of time has elapsed (*interval schedule*).

13. The *schedule of reinforcement* influences the rate of responding and resistance to extinction. Responses are more resistant to extinction when reinforced in a partial schedule. Ratio schedules produce higher and steadier rates of responding than interval schedules.

14. *Punishment* is the following of an undesired behavior with an unpleasant event or consequence. Punishment can be effective in suppressing responses but it does not really eliminate them. Problems with using punishment include lack of direction toward a "correct" response, the possibility that the punishment may actually be rewarding, association of the punishment with the person doing the punishing, and creation of stress and anxiety.

15. *Feedback* is providing information about how well one is doing at a task. It can consist of both rewards and punish-

ments. Feedback about energy use in households can help people alter their energy-consuming behavior.

16. Not all learning is of a stimulus-response, conditioned nature. *Cognitive* aspects of learning involve acquiring and organizing information about one's environment—making sense out of things rather than just responding. Cognitive learning can be seen in the formation of *cognitive maps* of our surroundings and learning by observing the behavior of others (or *modeling*).

17. There appear to be two distinct sorts of memory—short term and long term. Information from the environment is first held in *sensory storage* for a fraction of a second and is then either discarded or passed on to short-term memory.

18. *Short-term memory* appears to have a limited capacity of about seven items. The amount of information held in short-term memory can be increased by organizing inputs into "chunks." Short-term memory lasts about 20 seconds at most without rehearsal. Information is either then forgotten or is passed on to *long-term memory*.

19. Information can be transferred from short-term memory to long-term memory by rehearsal or by encoding. The way material is encoded is a major factor in its later accessibility for retrieval. One useful coding method is to package information in meaningful clusters.

20. Retrieval of information from long-term storage is facilitated by using a meaningful process for storing the material in the first place and by using reminders, or cues.

21. One interesting retrieval problem—the tip-of-the-tongue phenomenon—seems to indicate that our verbal storage system is coded according to both meaning and sound.

22. There seem to be two kinds of forgetting of information in long-term storage. *Retrieval failure* is an inability to locate information in memory; it may be, however, that appropriate cues can trigger the memory. *Motivated forgetting* is the inability to recall information because it would be embarrassing or painful to do so. Freud called such purposeful forgetting of unacceptable memories *repression*.

23. Remembering may be a process of mentally reconstructing the event rather than simply finding a permanent record of it in long-term storage.

24. Among methods of improving memory that are particularly helpful in studying are spacing study periods, active recitation, reviewing, and giving meaning to the material.

BEHAVIOR CONTROL

It's 1984, or sometime thereafter, and you're getting ready for work. You smile into the bathroom mirror and soothing strains of Brahms' "Eternal Love" fill the air. When the smiling stops, so does the music.

You greet your fellow workers with a cheerful "good morning," and they respond with warm handshakes and grins. Any other greeting, and they would ignore you.

Those are the rules.

The rest of the day, and month, and year, are governed by similar "rewards" and "non-rewards." Your behavior becomes nearly automatic. You are "happy." (Greenberg, 1976)

As we learn more about the conditions that shape people's behavior, we become more capable—at least potentially—of controlling their behavior.

As we learn more and more about the conditions that shape people's behavior, we also become more capable—at least potentially—of *controlling* their behavior. In particular, the principles of operant conditioning have been espoused by B. F. Skinner (1971) and others as ways of changing people's behavior in positive ways, thereby making our society more produc-tive, just, and humane. Many other psychologists are frightened by this vision of utopia, as carica-

Behavior modification raises serious issues about possible threats to individual freedom and autonomy.

tured in the above description of 1984. Scientific behavior control—or *behavior modification* as it is generally called—can in fact have great practical benefits. By chang-ing people's behavior—and helping them to change their *own* behav-ior—in desired ways, psychologists can do a great deal to alleviate human misery. And yet, such be-havior modification also raises se-rious issues about possible threats to individual freedom and auton-omy. (We should point out here that behavior modification refers only to techniques based on prin-ciples of learning; it does *not*, for example, include electrical stimula-tion of the brain, brain surgery, or the use of drugs.)

BEHAVIOR MODIFICATION: FROM THE LABORATORY TO SOCIETY
Behavioral psychologists—espe-cially those who focus on the prin-ciples of operant conditioning—

began to move out of campus lab-oratories and into the larger world some 30 years ago. The first attempts to make practical use of learning principles were in the context of psychotherapy. As we will see in Chapter 12, many thera-pists make effective use of proce-dures based on principles of learn-ing when they deal with problems ranging from shyness to alcohol-ism. More recently, behavioral psy-chologists have moved further out into society—to such locales as classrooms, community centers, mental hospitals, rehabilitation wards, business organizations, fac-tories, and even movie theaters.

One popular innovation has been the *token economy*, which was first established as a way to encourage socially constructive activities among chronic psychotic patients in mental hospitals (Ayllon and Azrin, 1968). The token econ-omy relies on the fact that people will often behave in ways that they know will lead to future rewards. Mental patients can be given to-kens (such as poker chips) when-ever they engage in desired activi-ties, such as keeping clean, performing assigned tasks, and conversing with one another. The patients can later exchange the tokens for things they want, such as cigarettes, a walk outside, or a chance to watch television. This technique has led to striking im-provement in many patients, in-cluding some who were previously totally withdrawn. Similar token economies have been established with apparent success in schools and in homes for juvenile delin-quents (Goodall, 1972).

In a quite different application of behavior control, littering in a movie theater (measured by the amount of trash not deposited in trash cans) declined from 81 per-cent to 6 percent when patrons were given litter bags and were offered a dime for each bag of litter turned in after the show (Burgess, Clark, and Hendee, 1971). Other behavior modifiers have made effective use of learning principles to encourage such activities as interracial interaction in schools (Hauserman, Waylen, and Behling, 1973), riding the bus rather than driving one's car to work (Everett, Hayward, and Meyers, 1974), and refraining from smoking in public places (Jason, 1979).

Littering declined sharply when patrons were given a dime for each bag of litter turned in.

"What's new about all this?" you might ask. Certainly, public officials, business executives, merchandisers, teachers, and parents have always known that they could influence people's behavior by selectively rewarding them. That's what tax incentives, merit raises, give-away offers, and gold stars are all about. What *is* new about the approach of behavior modifiers, however, is that their efforts are more careful and systematic and are patterned specifically after techniques developed in laboratory research. In particular, psychologists who specialize in behavior modification place a heavy emphasis on careful measurement and evaluation of their programs. The result, they believe, is a technology of behavior change that will be more effective than those techniques used in the past. And this possibility that behavior control techniques will in fact become more and more effective is exactly what scares many other psychologists.

A corporation in Illinois found that sponsoring a weight loss competition was successful in producing weight loss among employees. Here the company president pays off the winning "losers" in Intermatic, Inc.'s fat loss derby. This is an example of how rewards can be used to shape people's behavior in desired ways.

THE HUMANISTS VERSUS THE BEHAVIORISTS

Few people would doubt that techniques of behavior modification can be used for laudable purposes, whether to help a severely retarded person learn language or to help a phobic person conquer incapacitating fears. But as behavior modification programs spread to "healthy" populations—schools, businesses, towns—some doubts begin to be raised. Among the most vocal doubters are the *humanistic psychologists*, who emphasize people's potential for self-determined growth and development.

The debate between the behaviorists and the humanists revolves around a central philosophical issue. The behaviorists emphasize control of our behavior by external forces—we act in ways that are

dictated by the reinforcements and punishments of our environment. The humanists, in contrast, emphasize our internal control of our lives, our ability to make choices and judgments on our own. The behaviorists stress determinism—we are a product of the conditions that shape us—whereas the humanists stress free will we set our own terms, our own conditions in life.

Behaviorists emphasize control of our behavior by external forces. Humanists emphasize internal control.

From the standpoint of B. F. Skinner, the idea of "freedom" is actually a myth. In his book *Beyond Freedom and Dignity* (1971) Skinner argues that even without scientific behavior control, our behavior is entirely controlled by external forces. Whether we are stopping at a red light, buying a certain brand of toothpaste, studying for an exam, dressing for work, or even kissing our spouse or feeding the cat, we are behaving in ways designed to gain rewards and avoid punishments. Behavioral techniques simply enable us to make use of such control more efficiently, and for socially desirable ends. Thus, Skinner talks of "designing a social environment in which people treat each other well, keep the population size within reasonable bounds, learn to work productively, preserve and enhance the beauty of the world, and limit the use of energy and other resources." Now, who can argue with that?

Some of the humanistic psychologists can—and do. The fatal flaw of Skinner's approach, argues Carmi Harari, is that ultimately one person or group must decide what is desirable for other people. And that smacks of totalitarianism. "You either view people as innately good," Harari says, "or as wild, antisocial beings that need control. The aim of control is to suppress the human spirit" (Greenberg, 1976).

WHO DOES THE CONTROLLING?
As we've already noted, the control of people's behavior seems to be a basic aspect of life in society. The basic moral issue, then, is not *whether* people's behavior will be controlled but rather by whom, by what specific means, and for what purposes. As Skinner himself writes, the techniques of behavior modification "can be used by a villain or a saint. There is nothing in methodology which determines the values governing its use" (1971, page 150).

Critics of behavior control sometimes maintain that it constitutes a set of tools used by powerful people to keep the powerless down. In token economies and other uses of behavior modification in mental hospitals and prisons, the controllers are the powerful authorities and the controlled are the powerless patients and inmates. Even though the authorities may have

The basic moral issue is not whether people's behavior will be controlled but rather by whom, by what means, and for what purposes.

the best intentions, one may wonder whether their exercise of behavior control is justified. Recent court decisions have addressed this issue. In the case of *Wyatt* v. *Stickney*, for example, the court ruled that certain items that had been used as reinforcers in token economies were in fact basic rights of the patients and therefore could not be withheld from them for not having enough tokens to "buy" them. In this and many other instances, including those involving the control of children by adults, we must ask the question: Who controls the controllers?

Another concern is that the techniques of behavior control will be in the hands of a scientific elite who will in effect become the decision makers for all of society. Be-

We must ask: Who controls the controllers?

havioral psychologists stress, however, that they have not been keeping the techniques secret. To the contrary, they have been active in teaching behavior modification techniques to others who might be able to use them productively, including teachers and parents.

In one study, a group of seven "incorrigible" junior high school students were taught to use rewards such as smiles, praise, eye contact, and shows of interest to

shape their *teachers'* behavior. During a five-week conditioning period, positive teacher-student contacts increased 400 percent while negative contacts dropped to zero. In the end, the teachers were happy because the students were learning, and the students were happy because they could control their relationship with the teachers (Gray, Graubard, and Rosenberg, 1974). As this example makes clear, techniques of behavior control can be used effectively by relatively powerless, as well as powerful, people.

In behavioral approaches to psychotherapy, patients are themselves deciding to be "controlled."

Critics of behavior modification also protest that it turns people into machines whose behavior can be manipulated without their even realizing it. But, as Albert Bandura (1974) points out, this fear is largely unfounded. In general, people will not behave in a certain way just because they have been reinforced for this behavior in the past. Rather, a key element in behavior modification is that people *recognize* that a particular behavior will produce a desired reward and they change the way they act accordingly. In behavioral approaches to psychotherapy, patients are themselves making the decision to be "controlled." The patient says to the therapist, in effect, "You teach me to stop smoking, or to stop eating so much, or to not be afraid of flying, and I'll not only go along with you, I'll pay you for it." Indeed, the patient is reinforcing the therapist for using behavior modification. In cases like these, one can argue that behavior modification is *increasing* people's freedom by helping to liberate them from confining habits or behaviors.

Proponents of behavior modification also point out that they almost always use rewards rather than punishments and that these rewards—whether material or social—are typically open, sincere, and genuine.

CONTROLLING YOUR OWN BEHAVIOR

The debate between free will and determinism may finally be resolved when we realize that people can also make use of behavioral techniques to control *themselves*. Indeed, helping people to change themselves in ways that they desire is now a major emphasis of work in the area of behavior modification.

Behavioral psychologists have had considerable success in teaching people techniques of self-modification. Such procedures are especially valuable in cases in which a particular behavior, such as buying and eating candy, may lead to immediate reinforcements (it tastes

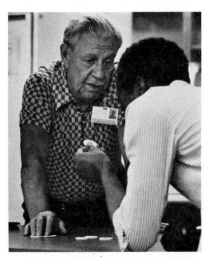
Volunteer accepting token in payment for food at a store for retarded adults.

good) but brings long-term punishments (being overweight). In such cases, people can be taught to use *stimulus control* techniques. For example, an overweight person who knows that passing a candy store is likely to result in buying candy can control his behavior by avoiding candy stores or by passing them only after eating a big meal (Kazdin, 1975).

When people want to motivate themselves to perform tasks that are not immediately reinforcing, they can be taught to make use of *self-reinforcement*. For example, someone who is trying to learn to play a musical instrument but who finds it difficult to keep practicing might specify a reinforcement of 5 minutes of free time following each 15 minutes of continuous practice. After a while, she might increase the practice time required for reinforcement. In other cases, a person might promise himself a reward, such as a small present or a phone call to an old friend, after completing a specified activity.

The trick with such self-reinforcement procedures is, of course, that the reward must really be contingent on the desired behavior. If you decide to give yourself the reward *before* you've done the activity (or if you secretly decide to have the reward anyway), the technique won't work. Psychologists have developed procedures to help train people to use self-reinforcement. In some cases, an external agent, such as a therapist or teacher, may at first reward a client or student for using self-reinforcement effectively. Once the basic technique is learned, the external reinforcements may no longer be necessary (Kazdin, 1975).

In still other current applications, self-control techniques have been used to help teach people how to behave more skillfully and assertively in social situations (Twentyman and Zimring, 1979)

and to change their eating patterns (Leon, 1976). Use of such techniques is thus giving new meaning to the idea of "exercising self-control."

Carl Rogers, one of the most eminent of the humanistic psychologists, once put his doubts about external behavior control in the following terms: "The human being is a trustworthy organism, and has vast abilities to improve himself if exposed to the right attitudinal climate. The individual modifies his own behavior, rather than having someone else in control" (quoted by Greenberg, 1976). And this principle would be endorsed by many behavioral psychologists, especially those who have been working on procedures for self-modification. By enabling people to select their own goals and helping them to achieve them, self-control techniques can actually increase people's individual freedom.

SUMMARY

1. Behavior modification refers to the use of learning techniques to alter people's behavior. One popular method of behavior modification is the token economy.
2. Behaviorists, who emphasize control of behavior by external forces, are in favor of careful and systematic behavior control. Humanistic psychologists, who emphasize internal control of one's life, find behavioral techniques to be dehumanizing and possibly totalitarian.
3. Behavior modification implies that someone will be controlling someone else's behavior. *Who* does the controlling is a major issue.
4. Behavioral techniques can be used by individuals who want to change themselves in some way, and thus may in fact increase individual freedom.

Chapter 6
Language, Thought, and Intelligence

Two police officers stood behind a large billboard to wait for speeding violators. One of them looked up the highway, the other looked down it, so as to cover all six lanes. "Mike," said one without turning his head, "What the heck are you smiling at?" How could he tell that Mike was smiling?

In order to answer this question (from Raudsepp, 1980), you must first understand what the words mean. You need to know what "police officer," "highway," and "smiling" are, for example. You also need to be able to manipulate these ideas mentally in order to come up with a solution to the problem. Have you figured it out yet? If not, the answer is at the bottom of page 174.

The mental manipulation of ideas—thinking—is inseparable from the set of symbols we use for communicating ideas—language. In this chapter we will first discuss language and its development and explore the possibility of language use in other animals. Then we will turn to two major aspects of thought: the use of concepts and the ability to solve problems. Finally, we will examine the nature of intelligence, which is a way of distinguishing individual differences in the ways individuals think and reason.

LANGUAGE

Language is the primary means by which we communicate with other people—the way we give and receive instructions, learn and teach, share and socialize. In addition, we use language as a means of formulating our thoughts and views of the world. Clearly, language is

172

much more than a set of sounds. Whether English, Hungarian, or Vietnamese, a language is a system of symbols that can be used to represent our activities, our thoughts, and our worlds. How this system works, and especially how each of us comes to acquire it, is one of the most fascinating questions one can ask about the human mind.

Theories of Language Development

A ruler of Egypt in the seventh century B.C. wanted to discover the original, universal language of humankind. To find out, he conducted the first controlled psychological experiment in recorded history—an experiment in psycholinguistics, reported by Herodotus. The ruler took two infants and gave them to a shepherd. They were to be brought up with his flock, and the shepherd was to make sure that no one uttered a word in their presence. The king wanted to learn whether isolated children would speak Egyptian words first and thereby "prove" that the Egyptians were the original race of humankind. The king apparently assumed that language is innate, ready to emerge full-blown in the child without any exposure or instruction. We don't know for sure how the experiment turned out, but it would be astonishing if the infants had developed any language at all.

A perspective quite different from the Egyptian king's has been advocated by the learning theorists (Mowrer, 1958; Skinner, 1957), who believe that language, whether Egyptian or any other, is not "built into" the developing child. Instead, they contend, language is learned behavior and follows the principles of operant conditioning discussed in Chapter 5. According to this theory, the infant acquires

Language   **173**

language skills largely by reinforced imitation of models. That is, every time the child copies an adult word or group of words, she is given a reward, such as attention, an immediate response, or a smile. Short language units are combined into larger units, which are also reinforced if they are correct. But there are problems with this theory. Infants who are given attention and who are smiled at when they babble may come to babble *more* (Rheingold, Gewirtz, and Ross, 1959). But there is little evidence that the *content* of infants' babblings—or of older children's use of words and sentences—is strongly affected by direct reinforcement. Just as a completely innate, or "built-in," theory, such as that of the Egyptian king, cannot explain language acquisition, neither can a completely environmental theory, such as that of the learning theorists.

A middle position is advocated by linguist Noam Chomsky (1968). Chomsky acknowledges that the particular language you learn is determined by your environment—put an American baby in China and she will learn to speak flawless Chinese. But Chomsky argues that people's *capacity* for language is innate. Most psychologists agree that the acquisition of a language, accomplished so effortlessly by virtually all children within the first four or five years of life, is a feat that cannot be explained solely in terms of imitation and reinforcement. Even small children can create novel sentences—sentences they have never before uttered or even heard. To explain this feat, Chomsky argues that the human brain is organized in such a way as to enable us to "soak up" within the first few years of life the basic rules of whatever language we are exposed to.

One sort of evidence for Chomsky's contention that language learning is not just a matter of imitation and reinforcement comes from the kinds of mistakes children make in learning to speak. The usual rule for forming the past tense in English is to add "-d" or "-ed" to the end of a verb. Thus, a child may learn to say, "I play*ed* in the park this morning" or "I bak*ed* a mudpie yesterday." The fact that young children actually learn this rule is revealed by their tendency to *overregularize* it—to apply it even in cases in which it happens to be incorrect. Thus the child will say, "I *goed* to the zoo with Mommy" or "I *maked* my bed all by myself." Similarly, children commonly form plurals such as "mans" and "foots" by overregularizing the rule that plurals are formed by adding an *s*. Because children are unlikely to have heard sentences or words like these from others, imitation is probably not involved. Even though the children are doing some violence to the language, their mistakes prove that they are learning basic rules.

But even though language learning does not seem to be primarily a matter of imitation and reinforcement, it does rely on the fact that children throughout the world are exposed to language in particular ways, involving a continual give and take between parents (or other speakers of the language) and children, beginning in infancy. As Box 1 suggests, parents speak to babies in special ways, and these ways may play a large role in the language-learning process.

Answer: The two police officers were facing each other.

CAN YOU LEARN LANGUAGE FROM TV?

What would happen to a child if his only exposure to language were through television? Psychologists recently reported the unique case of Jim, a normal-hearing child of deaf parents. Jim's parents could not speak and rarely directed sign language toward him, and he had little contact with other adults. However, Jim watched TV frequently. His language developed slowly, and in unusual ways. His first words, at age $2\frac{1}{2}$, came from jingles (like "Kool-Aid"). When he first came to the attention of researchers at age 4, he produced such sentences as "Going house a firetruck" and "Not broke that." Fortunately, therapy sessions led to rapid improvement in speech. Within five months, Jim had mastered grammar at a level appropriate for his age (Bard and Sachs, 1977).

In the babbling stage—starting at about 6 months old—infants can produce all of the sounds of all the world's languages.

I LOVE TO LISTEN TO YOUR VOICE

From birth, infants are highly responsive to speech. Newborns will learn to suck on an artificial nipple that is connected to a switch that turns on a brief recording of a person talking or singing. They won't suck as readily to hear instrumental music or other sounds (Butterfield and Siperstein, 1974). The ability to discriminate speech from nonspeech, as well as the preference for speech, is biologically built into the human organism and helps pave the way for the learning of language.

The Course of Language Acquisition

If Chomsky is right and the capacity for language is innate, then all languages should be learned in the same general way, even though specific rules may differ. And this in fact seems to be the case. Although there is a good deal of individual variation, most children begin to babble at about 6 months of age. They say their first word at about 1 year and begin to combine words when they are about 1½ or 2. By the age of about 4½, the basic grammar of adult speech is in use.

Vocalization is very limited during the first months of life, but by about 6 months infants are producing a great variety of sounds and putting them together in various combinations. During this babbling phase, infants can produce all the sounds that form the basis of any language. At this stage you can't tell the babbling of an American baby from that of any infant the world over (Atkinson, MacWhinney, and Stoel, 1970). The sounds in the infant's environment seem to have little bearing on the infant at this stage. Eric Lenneberg (1969) found that infants who had two deaf parents and who had few other sounds in their homes (from TV, radio, or voices) produced the same sorts of vocalizations as babies with "noisier" environments.

At around 9 months, the range of babbled sounds starts to narrow. The child now begins to distinguish the basic sounds that make a difference in her particular language. The recognizable sound units of a language—or *phonemes*—differ from one language to another. In Japanese, for example, the distinction between the "r" and "l" sounds is not made; and whereas there is a single "n" sound in English, there are five different "n" sounds in Spanish. Toward the end of the first year, then, babies in different parts of the world begin to sound different. These initial sound distinctions prepare the baby to combine the sounds into her first syllables and words, beginning at about 1 year old.

The baby's first words are typically the names of the people and

Talking to babies

All of the world's languages, from English to Urdu, share one special kind of speech: baby talk. Recent research has confirmed that in spite of the great differences among cultures and languages, the general properties of speech used with babies who are learning to talk remain the same.

Baby talk sounds different from adult speech. When talking to 1- and 2-year-olds, adults usually raise the pitch of their voices and adopt a "sing-song" intonation, in which the voice rises and drops dramatically, often ending a sentence at a high point. (Imagine the way you would say to a baby, "Hi, Johnny. You're playing with your teddy, aren't you?")

What is the point of these peculiarities? Research has shown that babies prefer sounds in higher pitch ranges (Kearsley, 1973). Adults may quickly learn that they

are more likely to get a smile or a satisfied gurgle from a baby when they raise their voices a bit. And the melodious rise and fall of the speech signal may hold the baby's attention—something that isn't easy to do. For the toddler who has begun to utter a few words, the rising voice at the end of the sentence serves as a signal: "Your turn." It marks the end of the adult's verbal offering and invites the child to make a response.

Adult speech to toddlers is also characterized by short sentences, limited vocabulary, and straightforward grammar. There are lots of questions and there is plenty of repetition (Snow, 1972). Furthermore, speech to beginning talkers tends to be tied to the here and now, with few references to the past or future. A father is much more likely to say, "See the birdie, Franny?" than "Do you remember the bird we saw yesterday?"

The grammatical simplicity and concreteness of baby talk help

make the structure and rules of language clearer to someone just starting to learn it, and they help ease communication with a small person who cannot yet understand much speech.

Adults seem to catch on to baby talk quite naturally. Catherine Snow (1972) found that non-mothers (who had almost no experience with babies) made the same speech changes when they talked to babies that mothers did. And Marilyn Shatz and Rochel Gelman (1973) found that even 4-year-old children will make similar speech modifications when talking to 2-year-olds. Babies themselves help to shape baby talk, through their reactions to adult utterances. When mothers were asked to talk to an imaginary baby, they did not simplify their speech as much as when they spoke to a real one (Snow, 1972). The child's presence—giving evidence of comprehension, boredom, or pleasure—was necessary to elicit "true" baby talk from the mothers. True baby talk, with its particular grammatical simplifications, does not appear in parents until the baby is about 18 months old and begins to demonstrate some understanding of what is being said (Phillips, 1973).

Roger Brown (1977) suggests that there is something else baby talk can do besides helping babies learn to talk: It can express affection in ways that normal speech can't. He points out that sometimes baby talk occurs between adults, but that such behavior is usually limited to lovers. And this may be as important a function as language learning and communication. Children need to learn to talk. They need to understand "Stay away from the stove" and "Don't eat the Swedish ivy." But they also need to hear "I love you" and to feel the meaning of these words even before the words themselves are actually understood.

In the course of a few short years children learn the basic vocabulary and grammar of their language.

objects that matter most in his world—words like "Mommy," "Daddy," "cookie," and "teddy." The first words also include those that achieve effects important to the child, such as "more" and "no." At first, children are likely to pronounce their words in simplified ways, and they may *overextend* words, using them in ways broader than the ways they are used by adults. When Zick Rubin's son Elihu was a little over a year old, "da" meant both "Daddy" and "Mommy," and "duh" meant not only "duck" but most other small animals and birds. Babies usually understand the differences between words even before they themselves can produce them (deVilliers and deVilliers, 1979). For example, Elihu could point to pictures of ducks, dogs, pigs and cats when he was asked to, even when he was still calling all of them "duhs."

At about age 2 (although there is a great deal of variation from child to child), children form their first sentences, combining two words in a meaningful way. Among the earliest sentences are those that indicate possession ("Adam ball," "Jill cup") or that link a subject with an action ("Adam fall," "Jill run") (Brown, 1973). Many linguists and psychologists consider to combine words into meaningful sentences—including sentences the child has never heard before—to be the distinctive characteristic of language. Thus, a child's first two-word sentence is a significant landmark in her development. "At this particular point, as far as I am concerned," the noted psychologist Jerome Bruner says, "she enters the human race as a speaker" (quoted in Pines, 1979).

From this point on, there is rapid development both in the child's vocabulary and in his ability to understand and produce longer and more complex sentences. By age 6, most children understand 8000 words (starting at 18 months old, this works out to an average of five new words a day). These linguistic developments go hand in hand with the child's cognitive development—his ability to understand the world in fuller and more sophisticated terms. Before the child can start using the past tense, for example, he must understand what it means for something to have already occurred. Before the child can understand adjectives such as "big," "tall," and "fat," he must acquire some initial concepts about size and space. We will return to the topic of children's cognitive development in Chapter 9.

It is possible that there are biologically based *critical periods* for language learning—periods of time during which language must be learned if the learning is to be complete and effective (see Chapter 9). If one puts a young child into a new language environment, she soon picks up the language and speaks it like a native. But for adolescents and adults, language learning is much more difficult. Eric Lenneberg (1967) suggests that the critical period for language development begins at about age 2 and ends at about age 14. The changes in the brain that occur by the time of puberty seem to alter the "prewiring" that makes learning so marvelously easy for young children. As we noted in Chapter 2, certain areas of the cerebral cortex seem to play specialized roles in language production and comprehension. But the specific ways in which the brain is organized to acquire language are still only dimly understood.

If I Could Talk Like the Humans

Language has traditionally been regarded as an exclusively human ability, something that separates us from all other members of the animal kingdom. But is it really? As one approach to answering this question, a number of investigators have attempted to do what others said couldn't be done—to teach language to chimpanzees, our closest animal relatives. In the 1930s and 1940s several researchers raised chimpanzees at home and were successful in teaching them to understand a large number of words, but not to speak them. It is unfair, though, to expect a chimpanzee to speak, since its vocal apparatus is not as well developed as ours. More recently, another approach has been attempted—to teach chimpanzees sign language.

The best known of these attempts was conducted by Allen and Beatrice Gardner (1969), who began their study of a female chimpanzee named Washoe in 1966, when she was about 1 year old. Washoe would spend much of each day interacting with humans speaking to her in American Sign Language (Ameslan), a language used by deaf people in America. At first, Washoe learned signs slowly; after six months of training, she used only a few. By age 4, however, she had a vocabulary of 85 signs, and by age 5 it had nearly doubled, to 165. Washoe's use of Ameslan remained crude, but the Gardners believe that she used it as a real language. She produced sequences of signs in ways that resembled sentences, and she sometimes seemed to create expressions of her own that she had never seen her trainers use. On one occasion, for example, she signaled "Open food drink"

Allen and Beatrice Gardner reported that Washoe (right) could use language. More recently, Herbert Terrace reported that Nim (below) couldn't. Was Washoe just imitating language rather than producing it, as Terrace suggests? Or is Nim just a "dumb chimp"?

while pointing at the refrigerator. On another occasion, when she saw a swan for the first time, she created her own name for it, making the two signs "water bird." During the past decade, other apes—more than a dozen chimps, two gorillas, and an orangutan—have been taught extensive sign-language vocabularies.

There is little doubt about the ability of apes to learn to understand and use individual signs that represent specific objects and events. But there is considerable controversy about whether the apes' accomplishments qualify them for the distinction of being "language users." For example, chimp language researchers have pointed out that some chimps can produce sequences of three or four signs in order to get something they want (Premack and Premack, 1972). But in such instances, the skeptics claim that the animals have merely memorized specific sequences and are not applying general rules. Even pigeons can be trained to peck at four keys in a specific sequence in order to obtain food, but no one would argue that they are using "language" when they do so.

One psychologist who has recently come to a negative conclusion about ape use of language is Herbert Terrace (1979). Terrace and his colleagues raised a chimpanzee named "Nim Chimpsky" in New York City apartments, beginning in 1973 when he was 1 month old. He was treated much like a young child and was toilet trained at 2½. Like the sign-learning chimps before him, Nim developed an extensive vocabulary in Ameslan. During the 44 months of the project, he learned 125 signs. Terrace initially concluded that Nim had really learned to use language, noting, for example, that Nim used signs in their proper order and sometimes created new sentences, such as "Me hug cat" and "You tickle me."

After an extensive analysis of the videotape record, however, Terrace changed his mind. Nim's course of "language" learning was very different from that of human children in several important ways. Whereas children's sentences become longer and longer as they acquire language, Nim's always stayed the same length—an average of between one and two words per "sentence." And whereas children come to imitate their parents' exact utterances less and less, Nim imitated more and more. In fact, over half of his sentences were exact imitations of what his trainers had just signed to him. Looking more closely at the videotapes, Terrace concluded that all of Nim's language could be accounted for in terms of prompting and imitation of his trainers, rather than by any capacity of Nim's to produce language on his own. After looking back at some films that had been made of Washoe's interactions with her trainers, Terrace suggested that a similar explanation probably accounts for Washoe's signing, as well.

Terrace's conclusion, then, is that whereas chimpanzees can certainly learn to use signs (usually to get things they want) they cannot use *language*, a rule-governed system of symbols in which new sentences can be generated. Many other scientists agree with Terrace's conclusion. But other researchers remain convinced that Washoe and her successors have in fact acquired language and that Terrace misinterpreted the films he used. Indeed, Washoe herself has reportedly been successful in teaching sign language to a baby chimp. And, as one psychologist pointed out, "Terrace can't say that no chimp could use grammar just because Nim didn't. Maybe Terrace got a dumb chimp" (Duncan, 1979). At present there is no clear consensus that nonhumans can or can't use language. Thus, the great ape debate goes on.

CONCEPTS

You are strolling through the park with a friend. Suddenly an object flashes through the air, startling you both. Then your friend says, in relief, "Oh, it's only a bird." In those few seconds between the initial perception and the ultimate labeling of the "bird," some complex mental events have occurred. In order to use the label, your friend has had to recognize important attributes of the flying object and then to categorize it among other similar objects while distinguishing it from still other objects. You are categorizing objects when you call apples, peaches, and plums "fruits" or when you call Barbra Streisand, Paul Simon, and Ray Charles "singers." Categories such as these are called *concepts*. A *concept* is a mental grouping of a set of objects or events on the basis of important common features. Concepts are basic to our use of language, our thought processes, and our experiencing of life.

How Concepts Are Learned

People are not born with ready-made concepts. Concepts have to be learned. Some concepts are communicated through explicit definitions, as when your physics instructor defines "gravity" or your psychology instructor defines "neuron." But most concepts are learned from examples. When a boy is told, "Go feed the birdie," he learns that the particular object hopping around on the ground is an instance of the concept "bird." And when the boy is later scolded for throwing crumbs to a cat, he learns that not all objects hopping around on the ground are birdies. Psychologists call examples that fit within a concept *positive instances;* robins, sparrows, eagles, and chickens are all positive instances of the concept "bird." Cats, dogs, rocks, and trees would be *negative instances*. Given enough encounters with both positive and negative instances, the person develops a refined picture of the attributes that characterize a bird. In other words, the person learns the concept. Concept learning is vitally linked to language since it involves developing a vocabulary—we depend on words as labels for categories of objects, actions, and attributes (see Box 2).

As we learn concepts, whether as children or as adults, our attention is not drawn equally to all attributes of the objects in question. Rather, we focus on the particular attributes that tend to be most common and that distinguish this object most clearly from other kinds of objects. As the child learns the concept "bird," for example, he is likely to focus on the bird's small size, its feathers, and its ability to fly. As a result, robins and sparrows, which have these characteristics, are considered to be better, or more *prototypical*, examples of the bird concept than are ducks and ostriches (Rosch, 1973). Similarly, most people consider apples and oranges to be more "prototypical" fruits than avocados or figs, because their size, shape, and texture correspond more closely to our general concept of fruit.

How Concepts Affect Our Lives

Once concepts are learned, they affect the way we interpret the world. As a result, they have a large impact on our everyday lives. In particular, concepts help us to predict and control events. For example, until we learn to incorporate "sharp teeth" into our concept of

THE "BEST" DISEASE YOU CAN FIND

What is the first thing that comes to mind when you think of a disease? of a crime? of a sport? If you are like the subjects studied by Eleanor Rosch (1973), certain instances of these concepts are more likely to come to your mind than others. For Rosch's subjects, cancer and measles are better examples of a disease than is rheumatism; murder is a better example of a crime than blackmail; and hockey is a better example of a sport than archery. In each case, the "better" examples, or prototypes, contain the attributes of the concept that are most central and important to most people.

— Box 2

What's in a label?

In order to determine the influence of language on our perceptions, Carmichael, Hogan, and Walter (1932) showed two groups of subjects stimulus figures similar to the ones in the middle column of this illustration. Each group was given a different set of labels as the figures were presented, and later the subjects were asked to redraw the figures from memory. Consistently, the redrawn figures looked more like the words associated with them than like the original figures.

This study shows us that the label we give to an object (the category we put it in) primes us to see a picture of that object, which in turn affects the way the picture is stored and recalled. The study also suggests that we may sometimes distort reality when we attempt to place new experiences in pre-existing categories.

Reproduced Figures	Word List One	Stimulus Figure	World List Two	Reproduced Figures
	Curtains in a Window		Diamond in a Rectangle	
	Bottle		Stirrup	
	Crescent Moon		Letter "C"	
	Beehive		Hat	
	Eyeglasses		Dumbbells	
	Seven		Four	
	Ship's Wheel		Sun	
	Hourglass		Table	
	Kidney Bean		Canoe	
	Pine Tree		Trowel	
	Gun		Broom	
	Two		Eight	

"dog," we risk being bitten. But concepts help us only if they *appropriately* organize our experience. The child who thinks that a rat is a "kitty" or that orange-flavored aspirins are "candy" is clearly in danger.

Eleanor Rosch and her colleagues have found that the more prototypical an object is as a member of a category, the more quickly we will recognize that it belongs to that category and the more likely we will be to treat it as such (Rosch, Simpson, and Miller, 1976). Thus, if someone asks us to buy some "fruit," we're more likely to bring home apples and oranges than figs or prunes. Or when we enter a living room, we're more likely to sit down on a piece of furniture with a back and four legs (a prototypical "chair") than on a modernistic chair that looks like a piece of sculpture.

We also come to categorize objects at different *levels of generality*—as instances of either broader, more inclusive categories or narrower, more specific categories. For example, is a particular object a "piece of furniture," a "chair," or a "Chippendale"? Is another object a "book," a "textbook," or "the fourth edition of Ledger's *Introduction to Accounting*"? The level of generality that we employ depends

Which looks most like a "bird" to you? Some birds are more "birdlike" than others. Thus, a robin is a better prototype of the concept of a "bird" than is an ostrich or a penguin.

on our experiences and on our needs. Thus, a particular object may be a "book" to someone who needs a convenient flat object to prop up a slide projector, a "textbook" to someone who is thinking of selling some possessions, and "Ledger's *Introduction to Accounting*" to someone studying for final examinations.

Roger Brown (1958) has noted that children learn to use different levels of generality as they grow older. For example, most children first learn to call all coins "money." Money is what Mommy and Daddy buy things with, and it is something you do not swallow or throw away. When the child is old enough to go to the store herself, it becomes important for her to distinguish the different coins; she must be able to tell nickels from dimes and pennies. At this point parents will begin using the new words "nickel" and "dime" and "penny." Hearing the new words and having the opportunity to use the coins, the child begins to differentiate her simple concept of "money" into a more refined one.

Concepts and Culture

As the above examples suggest, there is no single, objectively correct way to classify most of the objects in our experience. Classifications are determined to a great extent by social and cultural factors. Thus, we who speak English have only one word for snow, while the Eskimos have separate words for falling snow, fallen snow, packed snow, slushy snow, wind-driven snow, and still other varieties. Such distinctions make good sense for a people to whom snow of all types is an everyday occurrence and for whom survival may depend on knowing snow conditions. In contrast, the Aztecs reportedly used variations of a single word to communicate the concepts "snow," "cold," and "ice." In their hot climate, more extensive categorization was unnecessary (Whorf, 1956).

COLORFUL CONCEPTS

Different cultures have different color concepts, as revealed in the ways in which people categorize and describe different portions of the color spectrum. In English, for example, we identify six basic color ranges: purple, blue, green, yellow, orange, and red. Shona, an African language, uses one word for the range of colors between purple and red, a second for blue and green, and a third for orange and yellow. As Roger Brown (1965) notes, many color names derive from specific objects. The English color word *orange* is one example. Many coastal cultures that combine green and blue derive that color name from their word for sea. An object that is sea-color can, after all, be blue, green, or any shade in between.

Culture has a particularly important effect on our concepts of other people. Concepts about entire groups of people are called *stereotypes*. When you have a stereotype of blacks as being musical or of women as being emotional, it means that being musical or emotional is part of your concept of a black person or of a woman, in much the same way that having feathers may be part of your concept of a bird. As we have already pointed out, concepts are not necessarily correct. And, because stereotypes are so often based on small numbers of observed instances (and sometimes on no observed instances at all), they are particularly prone to error. We will come back to stereotypes and their effects in Chapter 13 when we discuss sex roles, and in the Psychological Issue following Chapter 14, when we look at racial prejudice.

PROBLEM SOLVING

As we go through life, we are constantly faced with problems, from small ones like arithmetic problems to large ones like planning a family budget or deciding how to patch up an argument with a close friend. Problems themselves can be categorized, just like birds and fruits and persons. In fact, categorizing a problem is often the first step toward its solution.

Trial and Error Versus Insight

We sometimes solve problems by a process of *trial and error*, trying out many possible solutions one by one, until the correct solution appears—we hope. The trial-and-error method can be useful in solving simple problems such as finding the right key to open a door. But for many other problems we must employ *insight*. Insight is a process by which we "see into" the basic nature of a problem and thereby discover its solution. Such discoveries sometimes come suddenly, which is why we speak of a "flash of insight." Often the problem solver has set aside the problem for a while when the answer finally strikes her, seemingly out of nowhere. During the period when the problem is set aside, the thinker may be unconsciously reshuffling her past experiences and searching for the solution. This sort of reshuffling is a central part of scientific creativity (see the Psychological Issue at the end of this chapter).

Wolfgang Köhler (1925) conducted a famous series of experiments with apes to demonstrate insight in problem solving. The task was for the apes to get food that had been placed on the floor out of reach. The ape was given a small stick, and on the floor between the ape and the food were two larger sticks (see Figure 6.1). In order to get the food, the ape had to use the first stick to get the second stick, then use the second stick to get the third stick, which was long enough to reach the food. Köhler's apes appeared to solve the problem suddenly rather than to stumble onto the solution while making random trial-and-error responses. And once they had the solution, they used it every time thereafter.

EUREKA!

Archimedes, the Greek physicist, provided one of the most famous examples of insight. He had been wrestling with a difficult problem: The king, suspecting that a golden crown contained more silver than it was supposed to, had asked Archimedes to devise a method for determining the crown's purity. While sitting in the bathtub, Archimedes noted that the bath water was overflowing. All of a sudden he came up with an ingenious method for solving the problem, involving the amount of water that would be displaced by a pure gold crown. According to legend, Archimedes was so excited by his discovery that he rushed naked out into the streets of Syracuse shouting, "Eureka!" ("I've found it!").

Functional Fixedness

Sometimes our use of particular concepts has the effect of blinding us to other concepts that might in fact be more useful to us. We keep trying solutions that worked for old problems instead of discovering solutions appropriate for the new one. One such rut we often get into is known as *functional fixedness*. That is, we think of an object in terms of its normal use and then remain "fixed" to that expectation and have trouble thinking of it in a different way. Consider the problem given in Figure 6.2. Given the materials presented in the picture, your task is to mount the candle vertically on the wall. Before reading on, see whether you can come up with a solution to this problem. Start now, and see how long it takes you.

FIGURE 6.2
A test of functional fixedness. How can you mount the candle vertically on the wall, using the equipment provided? The solution appears on page 186.

The correct solution, as you may have figured out by yourself, is to empty the tack box, then tack the box to the wall and place the candle in the box (Figure 6.3). Simple, isn't it? Yet most people take a long time to solve this problem—if they solve it at all. The major hindrance to working it out is functional fixedness. Because people see the tack box as a container for tacks, they fail to recognize its other possible uses. This functional fixedness can be broken or reduced. For example, subjects who are presented with the tacks loose on the table and an empty box solve the problem much more quickly (Glucksberg, 1962). Separating the container from its usual function helps the subjects to come up with new uses for it.

Functional fixedness affects scientists as much as it affects other problem solvers. Often scientists spend years trying to solve new problems with old methods, only to see those important breakthroughs made by young scientists who are more flexible in their approach. For example, Pascal's theorem, a great mathematical discovery, was published when Pascal was only 17 years old. And Einstein's most revolutionary work appeared when he was still in his twenties.

INTELLIGENCE

Although we all make use of concepts and solve problems every day of our lives, some of us seem to be capable of thinking and reasoning at a higher level than others. We refer to such differences in mental abilities as being differences in intelligence. But what exactly is intelligence? Although psychologists differ in their definitions of the term, most would agree with the general notion that *intelligence* is the capacity to acquire and use knowledge. A key feature of this definition

ARTIFICIAL INTELLIGENCE

Artificial intelligence is the name of a new science whose major goal is to program computers to do "intelligent" things—to converse with human beings, play chess and backgammon, prove mathematical theorems, and even draw analogies among Shakespearean plays. The goal of this research is to see how close a computer can come to simulating the human mind. So far the computers are not threatening to displace human beings. Even the most "intelligent" machine cannot understand English nearly as well as a 4-year-old child can. Furthermore, computers remain incapable of any real creativity (Begley, 1980).

is that intelligence is a *capacity* rather than the possession of particular information or skills. It is possible for someone to have a great deal of information drummed into him without knowing what to do with it—and, therefore, without being particularly intelligent. On the other hand, it is possible for someone to have little knowledge, perhaps because of limited experience, and still be highly intelligent.

Measuring Intelligence

Our definition of intelligence does raise one problem. How do we go about measuring a "capacity"? In practice, most of what psychologists know about intelligence is based on the scores people obtain on intelligence tests—their *intelligence quotients,* or *IQs.* As we will see, IQs are based on people's performance on particular measures of their skills, mainly those involving the ability to manipulate words and numbers. Whereas IQ scores tend to be highly related to school grades, there is a raging controversy about their relevance to people's capacity to acquire and apply knowledge in other areas of life. This debate is discussed in Box 3.

The first IQ tests were devised in the early 1900s by a group of French educators led by Alfred Binet and his colleague Theodore Simon. Their goal was to produce a method for determining which students required special instruction and which should go to a regular school. Binet assumed that intelligence changes with age and therefore decided that test items should be graded by both age and difficulty. So he introduced the concept of *mental age.* If a child can successfully answer the test items that the average 9-year-old child gets right, she is said to have a mental age of 9 years, regardless of her chronological age.

A child's intelligence quotient (IQ) is computed by dividing mental age by chronological age and multiplying by 100. Thus, a 9-year-old with a mental age of 9 would have an IQ of 100 ($\frac{9}{9} \times 100$), which is average intelligence. A 10-year-old with a mental age of 9 would have an IQ of 90 ($\frac{9}{10} \times 100$), which is below average, and an 8-year-old with a mental age of 9 would have an IQ of 112 ($\frac{9}{8} \times 100$), which is above average. For adults, however, this formula is not used—we certainly would not want to say that a 20-year-old woman has twice the IQ of a 40-year-old woman who answers the same number of questions correctly. For adults, an IQ of 100 is equal to the average score of a large sample of adults of all ages, and higher or lower scores mean that one did better or worse than this average.

In 1916 Lewis Terman of Stanford University revised Binet's tests, producing what is now called the *Stanford-Binet test.* This revised test, which was further revised in 1937, 1960, and 1972, emphasizes the scholastic aspects of intelligence: reading, writing, and arithmetic (Terman and Merrill, 1937). For example, 8-year-olds were asked to give the similarities and differences between two words, such as "orange" and "baseball." In adult tests, more difficult items were included. For example, the person would be asked to distinguish words that differ in subtle ways, such as "laziness" and "idleness."

In the 1930s David Wechsler observed that the Stanford-Binet

— Box 3

The IQ testing debate

The first intelligence tests in this country were greeted with tremendous enthusiasm. The expansion of public education made it seem vital to identify children's abilities so they could be given appropriate attention, whether this meant developing their special gifts or providing extra help where it was needed. As a result, the tests were eagerly snatched up by the school systems and colleges as a basis for student classification and guidance and for college admissions. As Lee Cronbach (1975) notes, "The momentum of the tests overrode all criticism."

Today, however, criticism of IQ tests is intense. For example, California, New York City, and Washington, D.C., have all banned standardized group intelligence tests from their schools because of doubts about their validity. More states and cities are likely to do so before long. The National Education Association, with its membership of 1.8 million teachers, has called for the abolition of all standardized tests on the grounds that they are "at best wasteful, and, at worst, destructive." And many maintain that the tests have done great harm by introducing irrelevant and unfair considerations into the way people are treated and by putting the students into "fast" or "slow" classes or categories that can influence their self-concepts and the attitudes of others toward them.

The most important use of IQ tests remains their ability to predict success in school. In fact, IQ tests are the single best predictor of scholastic success in the United States (McCall, 1975). On the other hand, it has been pointed out that extensive use of IQ tests may discriminate against blacks, Mexican-Americans and other minorities, and poor people. On the average, people from these groups score lower than whites, Anglos, and more affluent people. But this difference may not reflect fundamental intellectual differences so much as cultural differences. The tests are aimed primarily at traditional academic skills that are emphasized in white, middle-class culture. Critics contend that to use such "culture-specific" measures as a basis for making educational decisions about members of other cultural groups, such as blacks and the poor, is inappropriate and discriminatory (Garcia, 1972).

It must also be kept in mind that although IQ tests are rather good predictors of success in school, they do not necessarily predict success in other areas of life. IQ scores and school grades have been found to relate to how well people do their jobs in some occupations (such as being a stockbroker, which requires verbal and mathematical skills), but not in others (such as being a factory worker or an air traffic controller).

Because of the undeniable limitations and misuses of IQ tests, some psychologists want to do away with them. "Psychologists should be ashamed of themselves," David McClelland (1973) scolds, for promoting the use of intelligence tests to select people for certain jobs, such as police officers, even when there is no evidence that job performance is related to the test scores. McClelland suggests that educational testers stop talking about "intelligence" altogether and instead test for skills that are relevant to effective performance in particular areas, such as communication skills, patience, and the ability to set reasonable goals for oneself.

Other psychologists believe, however, that IQ tests do have important uses, especially in diagnosing learning problems and in helping provide the best possible education for all children. The important thing, they feel, is to make sure that the tests are used for appropriate purposes.

test relied very heavily on verbal skills, so he decided to develop a test that would include both verbal abilities (such as vocabulary and distinguishing word similarities) and performance skills (such as picture completion, object assembly, and picture arrangement). The tests he developed are the Wechsler Adult Intelligence Scale (WAIS) and the Wechsler Intelligence Scale for Children (WISC). Wechsler thought that including performance tests would provide a fairer assessment of an individual's intellect, especially for those whose social backgrounds did not promote verbal skills. A person's overall IQ score on the WAIS is derived by combining the scores from all the subtests (vocabulary, picture completion, and so on), but it is also possible to look at individual subtest scores to see which areas the person does particularly well or poorly in. Sample items similar to those on the WAIS are shown in Figure 6.4.

FIGURE 6.4
Items such as those used on the Wechsler Adult Intelligence Scale.

Both the Wechsler and Stanford-Binet tests are individually administered, but schools, industry, and government require tests that can be administered to large groups of people simultaneously. Thus, various tests have been developed to be given to large groups, as you probably know from having taken many such tests in your school career.

It should be noted that the score you achieve on an IQ test is a relative matter—it is an expression of your standing in comparison to those who were used to standardize the test. The *standardization* of intelligence tests consists of administering it to large representative samples of people and calculating their scores. The construction of intelligence tests is done so that the distribution of scores obtained by a large group of people is usually *normal* in shape. That is, a bell-shaped curve is produced in which the majority of the test takers achieve scores in the middle range, while increasingly fewer achieve

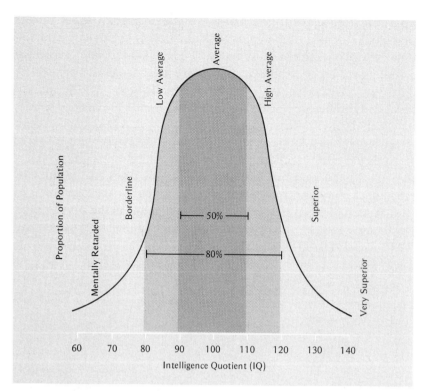

FIGURE 6.5

When we plot the distribution of IQs listed in Table 6.1, we come up with a normal curve. *Note that 80 percent of the population falls within the range described as "average."*

TABLE 6.1
Normal Distribution of IQ Scores

IQ	Classification	Approximate percentage in standardization sample
140 and above	Very superior	1
120–139	Superior	10
110–119	High average	18
90–109	Average	47
80–89	Low average	15
70–79	Borderline	6
69 and below	Mentally retarded	3

Source: From L. M. Terman and M. A. Merrill, *Measuring Intelligence: A Guide to the Administration of the New Revised Standford-Binet Tests of Intelligence* (Boston: Houghton-Mifflin). Copyright © 1960, 1937. Reprinted by permission of Riverside Publishing Company, Coralville, Iowa.

scores toward the higher and lower ends of the range (see Figure 6.5 and Table 6.1).

If the distribution of IQs follows a normal curve, then the odds of having a given IQ score may be determined. The average score on most IQ tests is around 100, and about half of the people taking a test will fall within 10 points of the average (between 90 and 109), and about 80 percent will fall within 20 points of the average (between 80 and 119).

The Nature of Intelligence

Just what is the capacity called intelligence? Is it a single, unitary entity, or is it a mixed bag of abilities that are not closely related to one another? Charles Spearman (1904), a British psychologist, took the view that intelligence is a single entity. He proposed that a single general-intelligence factor (which he labeled *g*) accounted for the correlations that are regularly found between different measures of mental ability. He described *g* as a wellspring of mental energy that flows into everything an individual does.

In contrast, L. L. Thurstone (1938) proposed that intelligence consists of eight primary abilities that are relatively independent of one another. He identified these eight abilities as verbal comprehension, perceptual speed, numerical ability, rote memory, word fluency, spatial visualization, inductive reasoning, and deductive reasoning. Excelling in any one of these, Thurstone believed, has little to do with excelling in any other.

Most of the evidence suggests that a compromise between these two positions is probably closer to the truth. That is, intelligence—at least as it is measured on intelligence tests—seems to include a general ability that underlies scores on a wide variety of subtests (such as those of the WAIS). The higher a person scores on any one subtest, the higher she will probably score on any of the other subtests. But there also seem to be clusters of intellectual abilities that are somewhat independent of one another; thus, some people are better at visual tasks, others at verbal ones. For example, a psychology professor we know is good at crossword puzzles (a verbal skill) but has a miserable sense of direction and often finds himself driving around in circles.

More recently, some researchers have shifted their attention from "abilities," whether general or specific, to look more closely at the step-by-step processes people use when they tackle intellectual problems. In such an *information-processing* approach to intelligence, researchers attempt to analyze what happens to the information in an intelligence test problem, from the time the test-taker perceives it until he provides a response. Consider, for example, the following analogy problem, similar to those found on intelligence tests:

> **LAWYER is to CLIENT as DOCTOR is to**
> **(a) Patient   (b) Medicine**

It took subjects an average of 2.4 seconds to solve a form of this problem used by Robert Sternberg (1979). These subjects were timed from the moment the choices were displayed on a screen until the moment they pressed a button to signal their response.

But, of course, some people can solve such problems more quickly and more easily than can others. Sternberg notes that solving such an analogy problem involves several different steps, or *components*. First, the subject must *encode* the terms of the analogy—she must identify what each of the words means, together with their various connotations. For example, a subject might retrieve from her memory the facts that lawyers provide legal services to their clients in offices and courtrooms and that doctors provide services to their patients in offices and hospitals. Subsequently, the subject must *infer* the relationship between the first two terms of the analogy (lawyers serve clients) and then *apply* this relationship to the second half of the analogy (doctors serve patients). At this point, the subject is ready to respond with the right answer.

Sternberg has devised ways to estimate the time taken by subjects to perform each of the problem-solving components. He finds that people who have high IQs and who are most successful at solving problems such as these actually take longer than people with lower IQs to perform the first step in the process, encoding. They are then able to perform the remaining steps more quickly and efficiently. Sternberg likens this finding to the operation of a library: more careful cataloging of books takes longer, but the time investment is more than repaid later by the quicker and more efficient access that correct cataloging permits.

From Sternberg's point of view, *g*—the general factor in intelligence that Spearman described—may refer most fundamentally to people's ability to decide ahead of time what sort of problem they are faced with and what sorts of strategies are needed to solve it. Thus, when faced with an analogy problem, the most "intelligent" people are those who realize that this is the sort of problem for which careful encoding of terms will be necessary. Once the terms are encoded correctly, the solution, as in the above example, is often simple and straightforward.

Heredity and Environment

One extreme view of intelligence is that it is a part of one's inheritance, transmitted from one's parents through the genes, much like eye color or blood type. Another extreme view is that heredity has nothing to do with one's intelligence—that it is totally a function of one's environment and experience. Of course, neither of these extreme views is correct. In fact, intelligence is a product of both heredity and environment. But although virtually all psychologists would agree with this statement, there is still a great deal of controversy—and some confusion—about the relative importance of each of these factors in determining intelligence.

The *heritability* of a trait is an estimate of how much of the variation between individuals in that trait is due to genetic factors. Heritability is calculated on the basis of the similarities between the traits of individuals who stand in different degrees of kinship to one another. Most scientists conclude that IQ has a substantial heritability. One revealing comparison is between similarities of IQ scores for pairs of identical twins and for pairs of fraternal twins. If IQ is highly heritable, then we would expect the IQs of identical twins (who are genetically identical) to be more highly correlated than the IQs of fraternal twins (who are no more similar genetically than ordinary siblings). This turns out to be the case. On the basis of data such as these, it is estimated that heredity accounts for about 40 to 60 percent of the variation in people's IQ scores within the populations that have been studied (see, for example, Loehlin, Lindzey, and Spuhler, 1975). It is important to note, however, that estimates of heritability of a trait refer only to the genetic influence on variations within the group that has been studied. These estimates do not shed any direct light on differences between groups—for example, different races—in the general population.

The fact that IQ has a substantial heritability does not imply that

WHEN BIGGER IS SMARTER

Even though identical twins tend to have very similar IQs, one twin typically scores slightly higher than the other. Churchill (1965) discovered that the twin who weighs more at birth usually has a higher IQ. His explanation is that both body size and brain maturation may be influenced before birth by the unequal sharing of nutrients in the womb.

The IQs of identical twins tend to be very similar, suggesting that IQ is a trait with high heritability.

environment has little impact on IQ or that one's IQ cannot be changed. One dramatic example was reported by psychologist H. M. Skeels (1966) in the 1930s. Skeels was working at an orphanage in Iowa, a bleak place where children lived in cramped quarters and ate, slept, and played according to a rigid schedule. Skeels noted in particular two baby girls who were undersized, sad, and inactive. Some time later he was greatly surprised to find the same two girls running about, alert, smiling, and healthy. He learned that each of the girls had been "adopted" by an older retarded woman in the institution who devoted many hours each day to caring for the child.

Inspired by this example, Skeels decided to try an experiment with ten more orphans who had been rated as retarded. Each child was lodged with retarded adults who could provide love, attention, and stimulation. Not only were these children healthier and happier, but later intelligence testing showed IQ increases of from 7 to 58 points, with an average increase of 28 IQ points. All but one of the children in Skeels's control group (who stayed in the orphanage) showed an IQ loss of from 8 to 45 points. Skeels was not able to assign children to the two conditions randomly, thus raising some doubts about the interpretation of his results (Longstreth, 1981). Nevertheless, his and other studies clearly suggest that environment is important in the development and improvement of IQ.

Many studies have shown that there are social-class differences in IQ. James Coleman and his colleagues (1966), for example, reported that children of lower socioeconomic status scored below the national averages on both verbal and nonverbal tests at all grades tested. It has also been shown that there are racial differences in IQ scores. Many researchers have observed that on the average the tested IQ of blacks is about 15 points lower than that of whites. Both blacks and whites score at all points along the IQ continuum, but there are proportionately more blacks at the lower end of the scale and more whites at the higher end of the scale (Loehlin, Lindzey, and Spuhler, 1975).

How do we account for these relationships between IQ and social class, and between IQ and race? Although hereditary influences can't be entirely discounted, most researchers have emphasized the role of the environment, including the nutritional, educational, and cultural factors that may determine the extent to which intellectual skills flourish. A decade ago Arthur Jensen (1969) caused a major controversy when he presented a detailed argument for the idea that black-white differences in IQ are accounted for primarily by heredity. Many other scientists argued that Jensen's analysis was flawed and that he overemphasized heredity and underemphasized environment. One recent study helps to document the enormous role that environment can play in black-white IQ differences. Sandra Scarr and Richard Weinberg (1976) measured the IQs of black children who were adopted and raised by white families in Minneapolis. In all cases, the children were reared in a more affluent environment than the one they were born in. The researchers found that the children's IQs were considerably higher than would have been expected if they had remained in an impoverished environment. Moreover, the earlier in life the children were adopted, the higher their IQs tended to be, pointing to the influence of experiences in early life.

Jensen himself recently conducted a study that attests to the impact of environmental factors on intelligence (Jensen, 1977). He analyzed the IQ scores of black and white schoolchildren in a rural area of Georgia, a section in which blacks are greatly disadvantaged, both economically and educationally. Jensen found that as the black children grew older, from age 5 to 16, their IQ scores tended to decrease, whereas no such decline was found for whites. As Jensen points out, it is difficult to account for this pattern (which he calls a *cumulative deficit*) in terms of any genetic differences between the races. Rather, it seems to reflect the impact of an environment that limits the opportunities for disadvantaged people to develop their intellectual skills.

EXTREMES OF INTELLIGENCE

Most people have intelligence that is in the "normal" range, with IQs between 70 and 135 (see Figure 6.5). But there is also a significant minority of people whose intelligence is higher or lower than this range. Although the specific IQ cutoff points are rather arbitrary, those people with IQs lower than 70 are regarded as *mentally retarded* and those with IQs higher than 135 are regarded as *intellectually gifted*. Each of these groups of people presents special challenges for society.

The Mentally Retarded

About 3 out of every 100 children born in the United States are diagnosed as mentally retarded at some time in their lives. The range of intellectual abilities included under this label is extremely broad. Some mentally retarded individuals are so profoundly handicapped that they have no speech and must be cared for as if they were infants. Others may have no noticeable intellectual impairment until confronted with mathematical problems or reading. Some mentally retarded individuals have physical handicaps as well, but many others are physically normal. Some retarded persons suffer from emotional problems, while others are well adjusted. Thus, no one description can encompass all persons with the label of mental retardation (Edgerton, 1979).

Most diagnoses of mental retardation are based primarily on IQ scores. The classification of retarded persons commonly employed includes four categories: *mild retardation* (IQ of 55–69), *moderate retardation* (IQ of 40–54), *severe retardation* (IQ of 25–39), and *profound retardation* (IQ below 25). Whereas the profoundly retarded require constant medical supervision (only about 1.5 percent of the retarded are in this category), mildly retarded persons can be educated, can hold jobs, and in many respects can lead normal lives.

The most important distinction among retarded persons is between the *clinically retarded* and the *socioculturally retarded*. Clinical retardation is a condition that is usually diagnosed at birth or in the first few years, and the retardation ranges from moderate to profound (IQ of less than 55). Clinical retardation usually has a specific neurological, metabolic, or genetic cause that can be determined. The most common cause of clinical retardation is a genetic disorder called Down's syndrome (formerly known as "mongolism"), which accounts for 25 percent of cases. Most Down's syndrome children have IQs between 35 and 54 (moderately retarded), although some have IQs near 70 and a few have normal intelligence.

Retarded adults can lead fairly normal lives if they are given the training and opportunities needed to work and to live independently. These two individuals are enrolled in a program designed especially for people who might not otherwise be able to maintain jobs.

Clinical retardation accounts for 20 to 25 percent of all retarded individuals; the remaining 75 to 80 percent are said to be socioculturally retarded. They have IQs in the 55 to 69 range. This type of retardation is usually not diagnosed until the child reaches school age and encounters problems with schoolwork. Whereas clinically retarded children can be found in families from all walks of life, socioculturally retarded children tend to be from families that are economically, socially, and educationally disadvantaged. It is difficult to determine the exact causes of sociocultural retardation, although disease, malnutrition, environmental hazards such as lead-paint poisoning, and lack of intellectual stimulation at home or encouragement to succeed in school are likely factors (Edgerton, 1979).

Whereas clinical retardation is usually easy to identify, diagnosing sociocultural retardation is controversial. Critics say that sociocultural retardation is no more than a discriminatory label, applied to those who are deficient in certain intellectual skills that are valued by middle-class society. The critics also note that a disproportionate number of minority children are labeled as retarded, at least in part because of bias in IQ testing.

Until recently, children diagnosed as retarded were generally placed in special classes of their own. Recently, however, there has been a trend toward *mainstreaming*—allowing retarded students to attend regular classes for most or all of the school day. Preliminary studies seem to indicate that students put in mainstream programs do better academically than those who remain in special classes.

Once socioculturally retarded individuals have completed their schooling and have reached adulthood, their options in society are limited. They can live in institutions for the mentally retarded, or they can remain at home and be cared for by their families. However, there is now a concerted effort in America toward *normalization* of the lives of retarded individuals. That is, they are given the opportunity of independent living arrangements, regular employment, and conditions of everyday life that are as nearly normal as possible. They are taught how to manage money, how to use public transportation, and how to cope with other normal problems of everyday life. Many retarded adults have benefited from such programs and now live normal lives in their communities, without noticeably being "retarded." Almost all retarded adults, however, have difficulty dealing with major stresses or unexpected events. In order for socioculturally retarded individuals to live relatively normal lives, it seems, they must be treated as human beings capable of controlling their own lives, but they must also be given access to assistance when it is needed; for example, a hotline to call in emergencies (Edgerton, 1979).

The Intellectually Gifted

At the other end of the range of intellectual capacity are those people who have extremely high intellectual potential—the *intellectually gifted*. As we noted earlier in this chapter, people's measured intelligence may have relatively little to do with their success in nonscholastic aspects of life. It remains true, however, that people who achieve eminence in science, law, politics, literature, the arts, and other fields are likely to have unusually high intelligence.

The most famous study of gifted children was begun by Lewis M. Terman in 1921. He located 1528 children with IQs of 135 or higher to use in his study. The purpose of the research, in his words, was "first of all, to find what traits characterize children of high IQ, and secondly, to follow them for as many years as possible to see what kind of adults they might become" (Terman, 1954).

In fulfilling the first purpose of his study, Terman found that the gifted children were, in general, healthier, better adjusted, superior in moral attitudes (as measured by certain tests of character), and far more advanced in mastery of school subjects than a control group of normal-IQ children.

The second part of Terman's study is still continuing (even though Terman died in 1956). The gifted individuals in the study have been subject to follow-up interviews and questionnaires several times since the 1920s, most recently in 1977. Three out of four of the surviving members of the sample (by this time most of them were well into their sixties) returned questionnaires. The follow-up research is being conducted by Pauline Sears and Robert Sears, who, it turns out, was himself one of Terman's "little geniuses." The latest follow-up found that the gifted individuals had encountered a wide range of outcomes in life. The most successful members of the sample not only had great intelligence but also had a special drive to succeed that had been with them from grade school on. The least successful people often said they felt guilty about not living up to their potential (Goleman, 1980).

Terman's "geniuses" attended ordinary classes and took part in no special programs. But today many educators and psychologists believe that gifted children need to have their talents nurtured—otherwise they are likely to get bored, "tune out" (some gifted children get labeled "learning disabled" for this reason), and fail to live up to their potential. This viewpoint has led to an upsurge in special programs to identify and nurture gifted children, such as programs to train grade-school children in the creative use of computers and to teach college math to junior-high students (Rice, 1980). The "elitist" idea of special programs for the gifted rubs some people the wrong way. But most educators believe that we have an obligation to make our educational system responsive to the special needs and potentials of the intellectually gifted, as well as to the special needs of the mentally retarded.

SUMMARY

1. *Language* is the system of symbols that we use to communicate with each other. Learning theorists believe that children learn language by being reinforced for imitating adult speech. Other theorists, such as Chomsky, contend that humans have an innate capacity to acquire language, as evidenced by children's tendency to *overregularize* grammatical rules.

AND NOW WE MEASURE FAMOUS MEN

Cox (1926) made use of extensive biographical information to estimate the IQs in early life of 300 famous people. The average of the estimated IQs was 155. The following are some of her estimates:

Sir Francis Galton	200
John Stuart Mill	190
Johann Wolfgang von Goethe	185
Samuel Taylor Coleridge	175
Voltaire	170
Alfred, Lord Tennyson	155
Sir Walter Scott	150
Wolfgang Amadeus Mozart	150
Henry Wadsworth Longfellow	150
Thomas Jefferson	145
John Milton	145
Benjamin Franklin	145
Napoleon Bonaparte	135
Charles Darwin	135

2. Baby talk is a special form of speech adults use with babies who are learning to talk. Besides helping the baby learn language, it is a method of expressing affection.

3. Children all over the world develop speech in a predictable sequence. They start with babbling, which at around 9 months starts to narrow to the basic sounds (or *phonemes*) of their culture, and then they begin making single-word utterances. By the age of 2 they are combining words into two- and three-word sentences. By the age of 4½, they have learned the basic grammar of adult speech.

4. There may be a biologically based *critical period* for language development—the years of childhood when the brain is primed to learn a language.

5. Many attempts have been made to teach chimpanzees to use language. The Gardners taught Washoe, a chimpanzee, American Sign Language, and she has been able to create a few novel sentences. Terrace has suggested that such apes have not really learned to use language but rather have simply learned to make signs through imitation and reinforcement.

6. *Concepts* are categories that we use to group a variety of objects or ideas according to their similar characteristics. A concept is learned by discovering both *positive instances* and *negative instances* in which the concept applies.

7. The more *prototypical* an object is as a member of a category, the more quickly we will recognize it as belonging to that category. We also come to categorize objects more broadly or more narrowly—that is, at different *levels of generality*—depending on our experiences and needs.

8. Concepts are to a great extent socially and culturally determined. Once learned, concepts can influence our perceptions and our behavior. For example, concepts about groups of people—*stereotypes*—can influence the way we behave toward people in these groups.

9. One simple method of solving problems is *trial and error*—trying every possible solution until one finally works. For many other problems we must employ *insight*—the process by which we see into the basic nature of the problem and thereby discover its solution.

10. The ability to solve problems is sometimes hampered by *functional fixedness*, in which the individual gets stuck on old uses for an object and ignores new uses that may be more appropriate to a new situation.

11. *Intelligence* may be defined as the capacity to acquire and use knowledge.

12. Among the tests developed for assessing intelligence are the Stanford-Binet and the Wechsler. A child's *intelligence quotient (IQ)* is computed by dividing *mental age* (as measured by an intelligence test) by chronological age and multiplying by 100. An adult's IQ score is determined by comparing his results with those of a *standardized* sample. Scores on a standardized IQ test are distributed on a *normal,* or bell-shaped, curve.

13. IQ tests are under criticism for unfairly placing people into categories. It has been suggested that use of IQ tests for such things as job placement is discriminatory against minorities and the poor because IQ tests are aimed at skills emphasized in white, middle-class culture.

14. Spearman considered intelligence to be a single factor (which he called *g*), while Thurstone thought intelligence comprised eight primary abilities.

15. Researchers using the *information-processing approach* to intelligence have studied the step-by-step processes people use to solve problems. The first step is *encoding* the problem. People with higher IQs appear to take a longer time encoding but are then able to perform the rest of the steps more quickly and efficiently.

16. The *heritability* of a trait is a measure of how much of the variation between individuals in that trait is due to genetic factors. Most scientists conclude that IQ has a substantial heritability, although environment also has a major influence.

17. Children of lower socioeconomic status and black children tend to score below whites on IQ tests. Jensen created a controversy by suggesting that these differences are primarily genetic, whereas other researchers have pointed out that nutritional, educational, and cultural factors can greatly influence IQ scores.

18. Mental retardation is usually divided into four categories: mild, moderate, severe, and profound. The most important distinction is between the *clinically retarded*, who have IQs lower than 55 and physical causes for their problems, and the *socioculturally retarded*, who have IQs in the 55 to 69 range, and who are not diagnosed until they reach school age.

19. Although clinical retardation is an obvious problem, the diagnosis of sociocultural retardation is more controversial. *Mainstreaming* of retarded students in regular classes seems to improve their academic performance.

20. Socioculturally retarded adults can be taught to live relatively normal and independent lives in their communities, although they may have special difficulty dealing with stresses or crises.

21. Terman found that *intellectually gifted* children—those who score above 135 on IQ tests—grew up to be healthier, better adjusted, and more successful than people from similar backgrounds with lower IQ scores.

CREATIVITY

We are often astonished by past examples of extremes in human creativity. The list of musical prodigies, for example, is long. Handel played the clavichord "when but an infant" and was composing by the age of 11. Haydn played and composed at the age of 6. Mozart played the harpsichord at age 3, composed at 4, and went on concert tours at 6. Mendelssohn was playing and composing at the age of 9, Debussy, at 11, Dvorak, at 12, and Berlioz, at 14.

Creative people seem able to enjoy the bizarre aspects of reality.

As if this information were not oppressive enough, John Stuart Mill began the study of Greek at the age of 3, and by the age of 8 had read Xenophon, Herodotus, and Plato and had begun to study geometry and algebra. At 12 he began logic, reading Aristotle in the original Greek. The next year he began the study of political economy, and at 16 was publishing controversial articles in the field (Pressey, 1955).

It's true that some creative geniuses have been regarded as "mentally disturbed"—among them the great artist Vincent van Gogh, who cut off his ear and later took his life. It's also true that highly

Mozart was a child prodigy who was touring as a musician by the age of 6.

creative people sometimes lean toward the abnormal on personality tests. But few truly creative people are seriously disturbed. The occasional appearance of "abnormality" may be part of the tendency to be different from others, but this is not necessarily a sign of mental problems. Creative people seem to be able to enjoy the bizarre aspects of reality (Barron, 1972).

THE CREATIVE PROCESS

The stages in the creative process have been described as: (1) preparation, (2) incubation, (3) illumination, and (4) verification or revision. Preparing for creative thinking may involve making a great many false starts. Preparation is a process of "sorting out" and organizing in order to arrive at a clear statement of what the problem is.

Preparing for creative thinking may involve making false starts.

In the stage of incubation, the creative person may stop working on the problem or stop consciously thinking about it. Some creative thinkers deliberately put the problem out of mind and simply let the issue sit for a while as they relax, play, read, or go to sleep. While their attention is thus diverted, some part of their mental apparatus is probably still examining the problem. Dreams may reflect this process. For example, inventor James Watt got the idea for manufacturing lead shot when he had a dream about walking through a storm of tiny lead pellets (Krippner and Hughes, 1970).

The sudden appearance of an idea after the period of incubation is the "illumination" regularly reported by creative thinkers. These periods of incubation and illumination are identical to the process of insight, which we described when we discussed problem solving. Insight is an essential part of the creative process.

After the illumination, intensive work is still necessary to carry out the idea or invention. As Thomas Edison once said, "Genius is 1 percent inspiration and 99 percent perspiration." The verification and revision process may then stimulate new ideas that allow the basic invention to be modified or improved.

Insight is an essential part of the creative process.

Highly creative people are not always in a good position to evaluate the quality of their work, however. To put it another way, their appraisals of their work may differ from the appraisals offered by the rest of the world. This is especially

true in the creative arts. For example, Handel thought that his own best works were operas that are seldom heard today. And Beethoven's own favorites among his symphonies, sonatas, and quartets are not those that are now considered his greatest works (Simonton, 1977).

THE CONDITIONS FOR CREATIVITY

So far we have been talking about creative geniuses—the van Goghs, the Edisons, the Beethovens. But all of us have the potential for creativity. The question of greatest interest then becomes not what sort of people are most creative, but what conditions are most likely to foster creativity in all of us. Teresa Amabile (1979) has proposed that we are *least* likely to be creative when we expect our work to be evaluated and when we are working to gain financial rewards, high grades, or the approval of others. When we are working for such external goals, we are most likely to stick to safe and uninspired approaches. Our creative potential is most likely to blossom when such external rewards are not important to us and when, instead, we are *intrinsically motivated* by the activity itself—that is, when we engage in an activity primarily for its own sake. In such cases we are more likely to be playful with ideas and materials, to take risks, and to explore new pathways. In fact, the activity will seem more like play than work.

In one recent experiment, Amabile asked 95 college students to make collages with colored paper and glue. Half of the subjects were told that their work was not going to be evaluated—they were told that the researcher was interested only in how the paper-pasting would affect their mood. The other subjects were told that their work would be evaluated by a group of graduate students in art and that the evaluations would be mailed back to them. Later, Amabile did obtain art students' evaluations of the "creativity" of all the collages. She found that the students who did not expect their work to be evaluated did more creative work than those who did

---

We seem least likely to be creative when we expect our work to be evaluated.

---

expect evaluation. And the subjects who did not expect their work to be judged were more interested in the collage-making activity itself. Thus, the specific external goal seemed to undermine subjects' intrinsic interest in what they were doing and, in the process, to reduce their creativity. (Intrinsic motivation is discussed further in the Psychological Issue for Chapter 7.)

There are, to be sure, exceptions to the rule that external goals will dampen creativity. When people are already highly motivated to

pursue some creative activity for its own sake, the prospect of external rewards may simply move them to work even faster. Thus, the biochemist James B. Watson (1968) admits that his brilliant discovery of the chemical basis of the DNA molecule was motivated in part by a race among scientists to

be the first to solve the problem and to win the Nobel Prize. And in a study of great composers, Dean Simonton (1977) found that honors, fame, and money did nothing to dampen the enthusiasm of these composers for their work. In many other cases, however, an overemphasis on external goals is likely to

---

Measuring Creativity

There is no single, agreed-upon measure of creativity, but psychologists have tried various methods of getting at people's ability to relate ideas and objects that would otherwise be unrelated. We can see how this might aid creativity—people might be able to find new uses for old tools, for example. One measure of this ability is Mednick's Remote Association Test (Mednick, 1962). Subjects are given a group of three words and are asked to give a fourth word that can be meaningfully linked to the first three. Sample items are: rat, blue, cottage; surprise, line, birthday; out, dog, cat; wheel, electric, high (answers are at the end of the box).

Another method of assessing this ability is to ask for new uses for common objects. For example, Guilford (1954) asked subjects to name as many uses as they could for such common objects as a brick, a toothpick, or a paper clip.

To get at a person's ingenuity, researchers have also asked for solutions to problems or completions of stories. Flanagan (1963) tried to measure ingenuity in response to stories such as the following:

A very rare wind storm destroyed the transmission tower of a televi-

sion station in a small town. The station was located in a town in a flat prairie with no tall buildings. Its former 300-foot tower enabled it to serve a large farming community, and the management wanted to restore service while a new tower was being erected. The problem was temporarily solved by using a _____.

Along similar lines, Getzels and Jackson (1962) had subjects write endings for fables such as "The Mischievous Dog":

A rascally dog used to run quietly to the heels of every passerby and bite them without warning. So his master was obliged to tie a bell around the cur's neck so that he might give notice wherever he went. This the dog thought very fine indeed, and he went about tinkling it in pride all over town. But an old hound said _____.

There are, of course, no *right* answers or stories. Rather, the solutions are rated according to how novel—yet appropriate—they are.

Answers for the Mednick Remote Association Test items: cheese; party; house; chair.

have such a stifling effect. When teachers begin to grade children's creativity, we can expect their efforts to backfire.

INTELLIGENCE AND CREATIVITY

Although many outstanding creative people have also been quite intelligent, creativity and intelli-

Creativity and intelligence may be viewed as independent aspects of thought.

gence may be viewed as independent aspects of thought. To determine the relationship between these two dimensions, Michael Wallach and Nathan Kogan (1967) did an extensive study of 151 fifth-grade, middle-class children. They used measures of creativity that were distinctly different from measures of intelligence so that children could score high on one and low on the other, or high on

both, or low on both. Their descriptive accounts of children with various combinations of intelligence and creativity make interesting reading:

High creativity—high intelligence. In the classroom, these children tend to have particularly long attention spans; they concentrate well on academic work. They also are the most socially "healthy" of the four groups.

Children with high creativity and high intelligence tend to be socially "healthy."

Low creativity—high intelligence. These children are least likely to engage in disruptive activities in the classroom. They tend to hesitate about expressing opinions and seem rather unwilling to take chances. They are characterized by a coolness or reserve in relations with their peers.

High creativity—low intelligence. Such young people tend to exhibit disruptive behavior in the classroom. They are least able to concentrate and pay attention in class, the lowest in self-confidence, and the most likely to express the conviction that their case is a hopeless one. They are relatively isolated socially.

Low creativity—low intelligence. Despite this combination of apparent handicaps, these children seem to make up for it to some degree in the social sphere. They are more extraverted socially, less hesitant, and more self-confident than the children of low intelligence but high creativity.

Richard Farson (1967) insists that if we seek creativity, education must not be limited to activities that seem to involve thinking. We must develop the other dimensions of humanness—the senses, feelings and emotions, taste and judgment, and an understanding of how humans relate to one another. We seem to want creativity in the young—but only if it follows all the rules, isn't too noisy, pleases the adults, and doesn't rock the social boat—conditions sure to kill all creativity in children.

SUMMARY

1. There appear to be four stages in the creative process: (1) preparation, (2) incubation, (3) illumination, and (4) verification or revision.
2. People are least likely to be creative when they expect their work to be evaluated or when they are working to gain a reward. People are most likely to be creative when they are *intrinsically motivated* by the activity itself.
3. Studies have shown that intelligence and creativity do not necessarily go together.

MENTAL IMAGES
Stephen M. Kosslyn

Stephen M. Kosslyn

How are the handles on your dresser drawers shaped? Does your psychology professor wear glasses during lectures? What buildings do you pass when you walk from the cafeteria to the library? You probably can answer questions like these by forming a mental image—a picture in your mind of the drawer handles, the professor, or the campus buildings. Until recently such mental images seemed to be private occurrences that psychologists had no way of studying systematically. But the research of an intrepid band of cognitive psychologists has changed that belief. These researchers have used ingenious experimental methods to stalk the mental image and have begun to find out just how we produce and manipulate these "pictures inside our heads." Dr. Stephen M. Kosslyn of Brandeis University, who wrote this Update, is the author of Image and Mind _and is one of the leading investigators of mental imagery._

Have you ever had the experience of "seeing" something when your eyes are closed? Although this experience is often associated with altered states of consciousness, such as dreams or drug-induced states, it also is an integral part of most people's everyday waking lives. For example, suppose you needed to buy window shades and discovered yourself in a store that had them, but you had not counted the number of windows in your living room. In this case you could have closed your eyes and mentally _pictured_ the room and _scanned_ along, _looking_ at each window. (How many windows are there in _your_ living room? Notice how you arrive at the answer.) Suppose you could choose between two different handles on the shade —brass or silver—and you wanted the handle to match the kind of latch on the window. Now you might _zoom in_ on an image of a window, and look at it in detail. You might do your imaging with your eyes either closed or open, depending on which way seems to work best for you.

Imaging is not just a way to remember things, but also a way to reason about visual properties. What was it like the last time you tried to fit a large amount of luggage into the trunk of a car? You might have mentally imaged each piece, and _rotated_ the images this

way and that, trying to get the best overall fit before actually loading the suitcases into the trunk. In short, imagery can be used to help you remember and reason about visual properties.

But what, exactly, are mental images? In order to answer this question we must first have some way of studying phenomena which occur in the ultimate privacy of a person's mind. How would you study imagery? The obvious way is simply to ask people about their images. A century ago, scien-

Drafting involves not only paper and pencil but also mental imagery. The draftsperson must turn the object over in his mind, visualizing how it will look from different angles.

tific psychology began with just this methodology. Wilhelm Wundt, the founder of modern scientific psychology (see Chapter 1, Box 1) trained his assistants to _introspect_ (literally, to "look within"), painstakingly noting and recording all the details of their imagery. Wundt thought that psychology was the study of experience, and that experiences are built up from sets of "elementary images." For example, a Wundtian psychologist studying imagery might report in detail about the shape, hue, intensity, and other basic aspects of his image of a wolf.

But this introspectionist approach was forcefully challenged in the early twentieth century by the behaviorists, spearheaded by the American John B. Watson, (see Chapter 1, Box 1). Let Watson speak for himself:
What then becomes of images? Why, they remain unproven—mythological, the figment of the psychologist's terminology. If our everyday vocabulary and the whole of literature had not become so enmeshed in this terminology we should hear nothing of imagery. What have we in their place? What does a person mean when he closes his eyes or ears (figuratively speaking) and says, "I see the house where I was born, the trundle bed in my mother's room where I used to sleep—I can even

see my mother as she comes to tuck me in and I can even hear her voice as she softly says goodnight"? Touching, of course, but sheer bunk. We are merely dramatizing. The behaviorist finds no proof of imagery in all this. We have put all these things in words long, long ago and we constantly rehearse those scenes verbally whenever the occasion arises. . . . What we mean by being conscious of events which happened in our past is that we can carry on a conversation about them either to ourselves (thought) or with someone else (talk). (Watson, 1928, pp. 76–77)

Because images are hidden mental events, Watson considered them mythical. And nobody could argue otherwise, except by introspection—which was not regarded as scientific because it could not be proven or disproven objectively.

This deadlock lasted until the middle 1960s, at which point there was a methodological breakthrough. You can track a bear by finding its tracks, even if you don't see the bear itself. And so too with mental images: The next best thing to seeing them directly is to discover observable properties of a person's behavior that reveal properties of the image. Consider the example of counting the windows on an image of your room. You may claim to scan around the image, looking at each window as you count. But how can we tell for sure if this is what you are doing? One way is to measure the time it takes you to scan from one window to the next and to see if this time increases when you claim to have scanned across a greater distance. If you are in fact scanning across a pictorial image, then more time should be taken to scan across greater distances.

My coworkers and I actually did this experiment, but in a modified way: College students first memorized the map illustrated in Figure 1. They were then given the name of one location (for example, "tree") and were asked to

FIGURE 1. Subjects first memorized this map, and then were asked to scan their mental image of it.

focus on that object in their mental image of the map. Shortly thereafter, they heard the name of a second object. Half the time this object was on the map (for example, "rock") and half the time it was not (for example, "bench"). If the second object was on the map—and therefore should have been in the mental image—the subject was to scan to it and push the right-hand button on a console in front of her as soon as the ob-

ject was in focus. In this way, it was possible to measure precisely the time taken by the subject to scan her mental image from the first object to the second. Over a series of trials, every object was focused on and scanned to from every other object. The results: As the distance between objects increased, so did the time (Kosslyn, Ball, and Reiser, 1978).

Thus, measuring the *time* it takes people to do things to their mental images has proven to be a useful way of "objectifying" their introspections. You say you seem to scan around an image of a room. We measure the time taken to scan and back up the introspection with objective measurements.

The use of objective measurements can even tell us things about imagery that are not evident in introspection. Roger Shepard and Jackie Metzler (1971) showed students pairs of blocklike figures like those illustrated in Figure 2. These subjects were asked to decide as quickly as possible whether or not the two objects had the same shape, regardless of their orientation. That is, can one be rotated so it fits directly over the other? The figures differed in

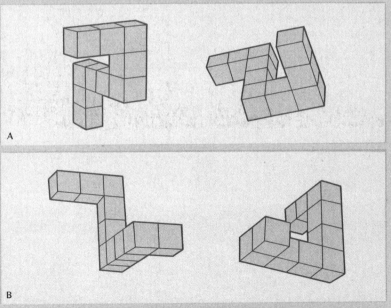

FIGURE 2. Problems in mental rotation: Within each pair of figures, can the left-hand figure be rotated so that it fits directly over the right-hand figure?

how much rotation would be necessary to bring them into congruence, and by whether rotation would be done clockwise or counterclockwise (as in Figure 2A) or in depth (as in Figure 2B). When people perform this task, more time is taken for orientations that are increasingly more disparate—just as expected if people really do "mentally rotate" the images, and greater rotations require more time. In addition, Shepard and Metzler found that it was just as easy to rotate images in *depth* as it was to rotate them clockwise or counterclockwise. This is not clear if you just try the task, which is not surprising given the small variations of time involved. Thus, the reaction times can reveal information that is not apparent to introspection.

We have been talking as if images occur on a kind of "mental screen," along which people may scan or rotate images. If so, then we can ask how *big* the screen is. Try this: Imagine an elephant far away, facing to the side. Now imagine that you are walking toward the elephant, so it seems to loom larger in the image. Is there a point where you get so "close" to the animal that the image seems to "overflow" the screen, not being visible all at once? Now try this with an image of a rabbit, moving toward it until it seems to overflow. Was the rabbit "closer" at the point when it began to overflow? When most people do this, the larger the object, the further away it seems when it begins to overflow. This is just what we would expect if images occur on a "screen" with a fixed size.

If images do appear on something like a mental screen of a fixed size, we can make a straightforward prediction about the sizes of objects in our images. Please image a rabbit standing next to an elephant, keeping both animals at the correct relative sizes (as in Figure 3A). Now wipe your mental screen clean and image a fly next to a rabbit, again keeping the correct sizes (as in Figure 3B). If

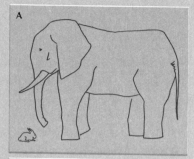

FIGURE 3. People can "see" more details in their mental image of a rabbit when it is standing next to a fly (as in 3B) than when it is standing next to an elephant (as in 3A).

images occur on a fixed-size screen, then the elephant should leave little room for the rabbit, so the image of the rabbit will be small. The fly, however, should allow you to form a bigger image of a rabbit. How could we tell for sure? We asked people to look for parts of the rabbit, such as the nose or tail, in the two conditions. And lo and behold: More time was taken to zoom in and "see" the rabbit's nose or tail when the rabbit was next to the elephant than when it was next to the fly. Thus, our images seem to be pictorial, we can scan them, rotate them, and they occur on a kind of "mental screen" that has a fixed size (see Kosslyn, 1980).

It is no accident that images seem like inner visions. We now know that visual imagery and visual perception (*actually* seeing things) involve some of the same mechanisms of the brain. To demonstrate this, try the following experiment invented by Lee Brooks (1967). The corners of the letters of Figure 4 can be categorized by saying "yes" if a corner is at the extreme top or bottom, and "no" if it is somewhere in the

middle. For example, starting at the lower left corner and working clockwise, the letter *I* would be categorized yes, no, no, no, no, yes, yes, no, no, no, no, yes. To the right of the letter is a column of pairs of *Y*'s and *N*'s. Now, memorize the *F*, and then categorize its corners (starting from the lower left) by *pointing* to a *Y* or *N* in each pair for each corner, working your way down the column. Don't look back at the *F* after beginning; cover it up and do it from memory. Now do it again—once again from memory—but simply *say* "yes" or "no" aloud for each corner. Compare how hard it is to respond by looking for a *Y* or *N* and pointing with your hand to how hard it is to respond by saying "yes" or "no" aloud. It should be much easier to say the words.

What is going on here? When you look for and point to the *Y*'s and *N*'s, you use mechanisms of the brain that are involved in vision. The same brain mechanisms are used to image and scan the letter. Because you are using the same brain mechanisms to do two different things simultaneously—imaging and looking for *Y*'s and *N*'s—the resulting interference makes the task difficult. But different brain mechanisms are used when you image and when you talk, so the interference is less—and the task easier—when you image the letter and say the responses.

Perhaps more striking evidence that visual imagery and visual

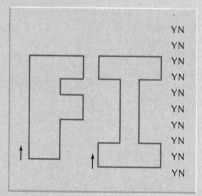

FIGURE 4. See the text for instructions to this task.

perception share common brain mechanisms comes from studying the effects of brain damage. Edoardo Bisiach and his colleagues in Milan, Italy, studied patients who had a startling syndrome, known as "unilateral visual neglect." This syndrome often results when there is damage to the right parietal lobe, as sometimes occurs when one has a stroke. Patients so afflicted literally ignore the *left* half of their visual field (the right hemisphere of the brain processes the left half of the body). Such patients sometimes forget to shave the left half of their faces or to dress the left half of their bodies.

Bisiach found that people suffering from this syndrome in vision have the same problems with their visual mental imagery. He asked a patient to imagine standing at a particular place in a familiar plaza, and to describe what he saw in his image. The man ignored everything on the left side of the plaza, naming only things on the right side. Then he was asked to imagine standing on the opposite side of the plaza, facing toward the first location, and to describe what he saw. Now he named everything he had just neglected, and ignored everything he had just described! Clearly, the parts of the brain responsible for seeing things to your left are also involved in "seeing" things on the left side of your mental images (Bisiach and Luzzatti, 1978).

Some people have much clearer mental images than others. In fact, the first studies of individual differences in mental abilities focused on differences in imagery. Back in 1883, Sir Francis Galton inadvertently began the systematic study of individual differences in mental imagery. He asked a group of his friends to describe the contents of their breakfast tables, and then to tell him about various properties of their images of the table—for example, the colors present and the vividness of the image. To Galton's surprise, many of these informants had no idea of

what he was talking about. They had no awareness of "mental images." These friends of Galton were professional men, such as doctors and lawyers. When he examined a broader range of people, however, he found that about nine out of ten people did report having clear mental images. The fact that his highly educated friends did not use imagery, presumably making use of words and abstract ideas rather than mental images, suggested to Galton that imagery was a relatively primitive form of thought.

It is of some interest, then, that by 1965, 97 percent of Mensa members reported having some form of imagery (see McKellar, 1965). Mensa is a club that requires a high IQ score for admission, and thus presumably includes those sorts of people who in Galton's day reported having no imagery. During the intervening period, Albert Einstein, acknowledged as one of history's great geniuses, reported using imagery in much of his thinking. But why, then, did Galton's initial subjects fail to report having images? I don't think they actually *lied*, but certainly one's willingness to describe experiences one way or another depends in part on how acceptable those experiences are. It seems likely that over the past century visual imagery has become a more acceptable—and even desirable—thing for a highly educated person to have.

In recent years, objective criteria have been used to study individual differences in mental imagery. Tests have been designed in which high levels of performance reflect good imagery ability. In one test, subjects must decide which of five shapes can be rotated and fit together to form a certain overall pattern. The results of these tests indicate that people do not differ simply in overall imagery ability. Rather, there are a number of relatively distinct abilities that are involved in mental imagery. These include the vividness of a person's images, the

number of objects or shapes that a person can image at the same time, and the ability to rotate or transform one's images. A person who is good (or poor) at one of these abilities will not necessarily be good (or poor) at the others.

Imagery abilities differ not only from person to person, but from types of people to types of people. Perhaps most notably, children seem to use mental imagery in their thinking more than adults do. To see one reason why children use imagery frequently, try this: What shape are a cat's ears? (Please answer.) Again, what shape are a cat's ears? (Please think about it and answer again.) Think some more and answer the question a third time. The first time you probably formed an image of the cat's head and saw that the ears are triangular. By the third time, however, you probably "just knew" the shape—without having to "look" at an image. The more you recall or use a fact, the more likely you will be to remember it verbally, rather than visually. Children, because they are less familiar with most physical objects than adults are, may often find themselves in the first situation, having to use imagery. But as children grow up and become more familiar with objects and their properties, they may use imagery less and less and verbal memory more and more.

To those readers who have trouble with imagery, a word of encouragement: When I began studying imagery, some dozen years ago, I was only middling good at it. After working on the topic, however, I noticed a marked improvement in my ability to hold and manipulate vivid images. And this observation is regularly repeated in the kind of experiments described above: People get better even in the space of an hour's worth of practice. Thus, although we can't fit glasses over myopic mind's eyes, we are getting to the point of being able to prescribe mind's eye exercises for improving one's "inner vision."

Part Three

Facing Life's Challenges

Life is full of challenges for each of us—goals to be strived for, obstacles to be overcome, milestones to be reached. The four chapters in this part all touch on the ways in which people meet these challenges of life.

Chapter 7 deals with Motivation, Emotion, and Stress—the inner motives that direct our behavior, the emotions that provide our greatest highs and lows, and the stress that is produced when we encounter pressures. The Psychological Issue focuses on one of the central arenas in which life's challenges are encountered, that of Work and Achievement.

The study of Personality, our topic in Chapter 8, concerns the unique ways in which people adapt to the situations of life. The Psychological Issue on Violence deals with a destructive challenge that both individuals and societies must face.

In Chapter 9, From Infancy to Adolescence, we discuss the tasks and the milestones of the first two decades of life. The Psychological Issue on Birth Order concerns one of the many factors that may influence the way a person approaches these tasks.

Chapter 10, on Adulthood and Aging, begins where the previous chapter leaves off, exploring the changes and challenges of early, middle, and late adulthood. This part concludes with a Psychological Issue about the final challenge for each of us, Facing Death.

In the Update on "Psychobiography," William McKinley Runyan discusses the potentials and the pitfalls of using psychological tools to analyze the lives of famous people.

Chapter 7

Motivation, Emotion, and Stress

In trying to solve a murder case, one of the detective's first questions is, "What was the *motive?*" Was the crime committed for money, for revenge, for sexual satisfaction, or for the "thrill" of it? The detective is not unique in wanting to know why people do things. In fact, we are always asking questions about the underlying *why's* of human behavior—in other words, about *motivation*.

In a sense, the entire study of psychology concerns the underlying causes of human behavior. But *motives* are certain kinds of causes—the internal factors that energize, direct, and sustain a person's behavior. These include such forces as hunger, thirst, sex, and curiosity. These and other forces all *move* a person to act in certain ways; in fact, the word *motive* comes from the Latin word for "move." To be sure, no one has ever seen a motive with the naked eye, or even under the microscope. Rather, motives are hypothetical concepts that psychologists employ to help understand the immediate causes of behavior.

Even without the help of psychologists, most people come up with the idea of motives on their own. If you think about it for a minute, you will discover that you already know a great deal about human motivation. For example, you watch the enthusiastic way Harvey is eating lunch one day, and you say to yourself, "Harvey is really hungry today!" You might also speculate about the reason for Harvey's unusual hunger: perhaps he missed breakfast that morning or had an especially active workout on the basketball court. Or you listen to Polly ask a foreign student a series of questions about his country, and you decide that she has a strong motive of curiosity. Perhaps that goes along with the fact that she reads so much about unusual places and peoples.

210

Emotions are closely related to motives. Like motives, emotions are internal factors that can energize, direct, and sustain our behavior. When we are happy, we are likely to walk with a spring in our step, to speak with a lilt in our voice, and to do nice things for other people. When we are angry, we are likely to rant and rave, and to strike back at the people or things that have made us angry. Most of us understand intuitively what the word *emotion* means, whether it be joy, pain, fear, or grief. But psychologists have not found it easy to measure or even to define emotions. Emotion has been characterized as the reflection of *physiological changes* in our bodies, as the *subjective feelings* we experience, and as the *expressive behavior* that we exhibit. It is probably most accurate to say that emotion is a combination of all three of these definitions. Consider, for example, the emotion of grief. It is likely to be associated with physiological changes such as a pounding heart or heaving chest; it brings with it a subjective feeling of sadness and loss; and it manifests itself in such expressions as crying. How these components relate to one another is one of the central questions addressed by psychologists who study emotion.

In this chapter, we will begin by surveying the range of human motives and the ways in which they operate. Then we will examine several prominent theories of emotion and explore the ways in which emotions develop in early life. Finally, we will look at the close association of emotion with the stresses of life and our reactions to those stresses. Whereas our emotions are usually seen as positive forces in our lives, they can sometimes overwhelm and even kill us. In the concluding section of this chapter, we will focus on stress and its links to disease and life crises.

Motivation, Emotion, and Stress **211**

— *Box 1* —

A hierarchy of human needs

Many psychologists have come up with lists of basic human "needs" and with ways of classifying those needs. One of the most famous is the "pyramid of human needs" developed by the late Abraham Maslow, a psychologist at Brandeis University and a founder of the humanistic movement in psychology (see Chapter 8). Maslow (1970) felt there are certain basic needs humans must meet before they can be concerned with satisfying other needs. Maslow's theoretical pyramid of human needs included (from the bottom going up): the basic physiological needs of food, water, and sex; safety and security needs; love and belonging needs; self-esteem needs; and the need for self-actualization.

Maslow said we must first satisfy one set of needs before we can become involved with satisfying the next set. He felt that some people may live their entire lives stuck on just one set of needs. There are millions of people who live out their lives at the bottom of the pyramid, barely able to keep themselves and their families alive. Some people move beyond safety and security needs only to fashion a life-style that is devoted entirely to the search for love from others. These people never

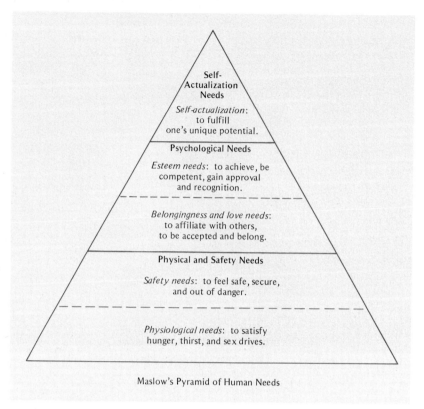

Maslow's Pyramid of Human Needs

have enough time or energy left to actualize the full potentials they were born with.

The ultimate need on Maslow's pyramid is the need for *self-actualization*—the need to realize one's innate capacities and talents. According to Maslow, self-actualized people are those who have been able to satisfy all their other needs in order to fulfill themselves

as human beings. Very few people qualify for this category—they are rare individuals indeed. We will return to Maslow's view of self-actualization in Chapter 8.

Although there has been little research that specifically supports Maslow's approach, his theory remains an interesting and valuable way to view the entire range of human motives.

THE RANGE OF MOTIVES

Psychologists have studied many different motives, from the need to eat to the need to fulfill one's potential. One famous psychologist, Henry Murray (1938), listed 20 different human motives (although he called them "needs"), including the needs for dominance, for achievement, and for autonomy. There are also many typologies or schemes for dividing up these motives. In this chapter we will organize them in terms of two major categories: *survival motives*, such as hunger and thirst, which must be satisfied if the organism—whether human or animal—is to survive, and the more distinctively human *competence motives*, such as the needs to understand, explore, and control our environment. There is a third category, *social motives*, which concerns our orientation toward other people. We will consider one such social motive, the need to affiliate with others, in Chapter 14, when we explore social relationships.

Both the survival motives and the competence motives that we will discuss can be viewed as part of a more extensive hierarchy of human motives. Such a hierarchy, Abraham Maslow's "pyramid of human needs," is presented in Box 1.

THE SURVIVAL MOTIVES

The most important survival motives are hunger, thirst, sex, and pain avoidance. The survival motives are needs that we share with other organisms. All organisms must eat, drink, and be able to avoid pain if they are to survive. And sex, although not necessary for the survival of the individual organism, is necessary for the survival of the species. All these motives have a clear physiological basis. They are regulated, at least in part, by the "lower" portions of the brain—in the brain stem and limbic system (see Chapter 2).

Drive Reduction Theory

One way of understanding the survival motives is in terms of the *drive reduction theory* of motivation. According to this theory, motivation begins with a physiological *need*, such as for nutrients (hunger) or for water (thirst). Through different biochemical mechanisms, this need becomes experienced as a psychological *drive*. The drive is an internal tension or pressure that becomes increasingly uncomfortable. It leads the organism to act in a certain way—for example, to find and eat some food or drink some water. The food or water is the *goal* toward which the drive is directed. When the goal is obtained, the physiological deficit is corrected and the unpleasant drive is reduced.

Hunger

Hunger comes from the body's need for nutrients used in growth, bodily repair, maintenance of health, and manufacture of energy. One way that we know we are hungry is through hunger pangs, which are caused by contraction of the stomach muscles when the stomach is empty. In fact, an early theory of hunger, put forth by Walter Cannon (1911), held that the stomach and its contractions were primarily responsible for the experience of hunger and for motivating us to eat. He theorized that the hunger drive was associated with the stomach pangs and that food reduced the drive by stopping the pangs. But, as Cannon himself realized, there are problems with trying to explain hunger and eating solely in terms of stomach activity. For one thing, people in affluent cultures like our own rarely experience hunger pangs. We fill ourselves up too often for such feelings to occur more than once in a while. So hunger pangs themselves can't explain why we eat when we do. In addition, there is evidence that humans whose stomachs have been surgically removed (for medical reasons) still feel hungry and that rats whose stomachs have been removed still behave like hungry rats.

A MOST STIMULATING EXPERIENCE

James Olds (1958) has provided some leads into what might be the brain mechanisms that underlie motivation. Olds found that rats that normally press a bar 25 times an hour for food will press it more than 100 times a *minute* to receive electrical stimulation to locations in the lateral hypothalamus in the brain. Rats and even monkeys will forego food, sometimes to the point of starvation, in order to obtain such brain stimulation. More recent studies have shown that areas of the frontal lobe in the cerebral cortex are also involved in the brain's reward system (Routtenberg, 1978). These studies suggest that there are "pleasure centers" in the brain and that rewards in everyday life (whether food, drink, sex, or whatever) may have effects on these brain centers.

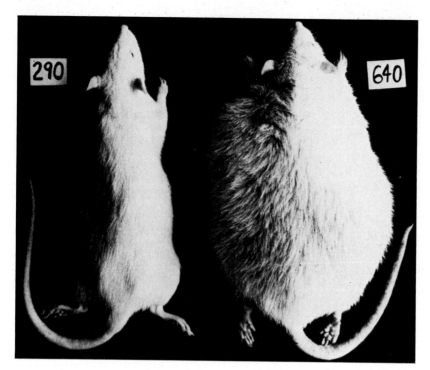

FIGURE 7.1
When portions of the hypothalamus in the brain are destroyed, a rat (such as the one on the right) may become hyperphagic and overeat so much that it grows to two or three times its normal body weight.

Although the stomach plays a role in regulating our eating patterns, other mechanisms, involving the hypothalamus in the brain, seem to play a more important role. First, the hypothalamus monitors the level of sugar in the blood. When blood sugar is low, the hypothalamus causes one to feel hungry and to eat more. Conversely, when the blood-sugar level is high, the hypothalamus inhibits eating. Second, the hypothalamus keeps track of the fat content of the body and apparently inhibits us from eating when the fat content goes above a certain "set point" (Nisbett, 1972). This regulatory mechanism enables humans and other mammals to maintain a remarkably stable weight. If you were to eat slightly more every day than you usually eat, your weight would rise quite rapidly, and if you were to eat a little less every day your weight would soon begin to plunge. But the hypothalamus's regulatory activity helps to keep most people's weight within a fairly narrow range.

When the functioning of the hypothalamus is impaired, an animal can no longer monitor blood-sugar levels or fat content, and weight no longer remains stable. This was demonstrated dramatically in an experiment in which portions of the hypothalamus were destroyed in laboratory animals (Teitelbaum, 1967). This operation had startling effects: The animals began to eat compulsively over an extended period of time, ultimately assuming monstrous proportions—often two to three times their normal body weight. Such effects have been obtained in rats, dogs, cats, monkeys, and chickens, among others. These animals are called *hyperphagic*, from the Greek words for "overeating" (see Figure 7.1).

The taste of food seems to play an unusually large role in regulating the eating behavior of hyperphagic rats. Whereas most animals will eat even bad-tasting food if they are hungry enough, the hyperphagic rat won't. If such rats are given only distasteful food (their regular chow with quinine added), they go on a hunger strike and become underweight (Teitelbaum, 1955). It has been speculated that the hypothalamic lesions reduce the rats' sensitivity to internal cues of satiation (such as blood-sugar level and body fat level) and instead they are at the mercy of external cues (such as taste). Stanley Schachter (1971) has pointed to some interesting similarities between the eating behavior of obese or overweight humans and that of hyperphagic rats. Like the hyperphagic animals, overweight humans seem to pay little attention to internal cues (such as hunger pangs) and base their eating habits more on external cues (such as the food's availability and taste). There is no evidence of impaired functioning in the hypothalamus of overweight humans, but since the hypothalamus apparently plays a major role in regulating eating behavior, it is possible that some of the differences between "thin eaters" (people who eat in a way that keeps their weight at normal levels) and "fat eaters" will be eventually traced to differences in the functioning of this part of the brain.

For most animals, the mechanisms of hunger and eating are fairly automatic. The animal responds to physiological drives without giving a great deal of thought to the matter. Humans are animals, too, and the same physiological mechanisms of hunger seem to operate in humans as in rats. But among humans there's more to it than that. Why do some people eat a great deal and others very little? Why do some people love ice cream while others go crazy for potato chips? Why is it that some days you can go without food for long periods of time without feeling deprived, while other days you can't seem to keep yourself from snacking constantly? Why do some people love to eat meat and others refuse to eat it at all? It is clear that among humans, cognitive factors—thoughts, attitudes, and values—also have a great deal to do with eating behavior.

Thirst

We can go without food substantially longer than we can go without water. People who have been deprived of both food and water for

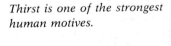

Thirst is one of the strongest human motives.

long periods of time report that the sensations of thirst soon become maddening, while the pangs of hunger tend to disappear after a few days. Experiments reveal that thirsty rats will learn to find a reward of water more quickly than hungry ones will learn to find food. Thus, thirst seems to be an even stronger motive than hunger.

It is obvious when we are thirsty: a dry throat and mouth tells us we need water. But easing this dryness is only one factor in alleviating the thirst drive. Dogs deprived of water will later drink amounts directly proportional to what their body needs (Adolph, 1941). Such precise estimation of the need for water cannot be explained solely in terms of dryness in the mouth and throat. The thirst drive is controlled by delicate biochemical balances within the body. A lack of water in the body cells leads to an increase in the level of salt in the bloodstream. According to one prominent theory, when the salt in the blood reaches a certain level, a particular location in the hypothalamus is stimulated and activates the thirst drive. Drinking returns the system to normal. In one demonstration of this mechanism, injection of a small amount of salt solution into the hypothalamus of a goat caused the animal to drink several gallons of water (Andersson, 1971).

Sex

Sex is a more complex motive than hunger or thirst. Including it among the survival motives may even be misleading. Clearly, sexual intercourse is necessary for animals or humans if the species is to survive. On the individual level, however, sexual activity is not necessary for survival. There is no good evidence that abstinence from sexual activity is detrimental to a person's health (Katchadourian and Lunde, 1975). It is also debatable whether sex in humans can be considered a "drive" analogous to hunger and thirst.

It may be useful to compare human sexual motivation with that of lower animals. In both cases, sex is often quite pleasurable, and the anticipation of this physical pleasure may strongly impel the animal to engage in sexual activity. For example, when male rats are deprived of food for up to six days and are then given a choice between food and a receptive female, they commonly choose the female (Sachs and Marsan, 1972). You can probably think of similar cases among humans, in which other rewards are given up for the sake of sexual pleasure.

But sexual motivation is less closely related to physiological needs in humans than it is in lower animals. Among lower mammals, such as rats, sexual behavior is strongly controlled by the sex hormones—*testosterone* produced by the male testes, and *estrogen* produced by the female ovaries. If the ovaries or testes of rats are removed, sexual activity decreases or stops. In humans, on the other hand, there is no clear relation between hormone level and sexual desire. Men and women whose testes or ovaries have been removed for medical reasons do not necessarily show changes in their sexual desires or behavior.

In humans, psychological and social motives play a large role in regulating sexual behavior. Sex may be engaged in as an expression

NEVER EAT IN PUBLIC!

Our sexual motivation is influenced by our society's attitudes and values about sex. Robert Baron and Donn Byrne (1977) make this point by describing a hypothetical society in which attitudes about sex and about food are reversed. People engage in public sex acts in sexaurants, and fast-sex stores dot the highways. But people *never* eat in public, and children are not taught the proper words for "knife" and "fork." Taking this idea a little further, one might guess that in such a society all eating is done "behind closed doors," although there may be movie houses that feature "food flicks" that appeal to "perverts" who often hide food items under their raincoats and sneak them into the theater. Well, you get the idea.

of love, a means of gaining popularity, or even an economic transaction. Some people engage in sexual behavior to calm their nerves; others use it as a form of self-expression. Moreover, the motives that encourage sex, as well as the forces that inhibit it, take different forms in different cultures. We will examine some of the factors influencing sexual attitudes and behavior in Chapter 13.

THE COMPETENCE MOTIVES

Whereas the survival motives are shared by humans and other animals, the *competence motives* are more distinctively human. Robert White (1959) suggests that the "master reinforcer" that keeps most of us motivated over long periods of time is the need to confirm our sense of personal competence. White defines competence as a person's capacity to interact effectively with the environment. Being able to master our environment is rewarding, whether it involves learning to ride a bike, bringing up a child successfully, or keeping one's head when everyone else panics. It is rewarding or reinforcing to feel that we are capable human beings. In this section we will consider two sorts of competence motives: the curiosity motive and the need for control over the environment. Both concern our desire to understand, predict, and control the world we live in. Another related motive, the need to achieve, is discussed in the Psychological Issue that follows this chapter.

These competence motives have sometimes been viewed in terms of the drive reduction theory that we discussed earlier. For example, some psychologists have postulated the existence of a "curiosity drive," which can build up over time and which we must reduce by exploring our surroundings. But the notion of drive doesn't really seem to be the most useful way of viewing the competence motives. For one thing, they are not the sort of needs that we can satisfy and then do without for a while. To the contrary, acquiring knowledge about our environment often motivates us to seek still more knowledge, not less. For another thing, these motives are not rooted in specific physiological needs, as in the cases of hunger and thirst. Competence seems to be a continuing, expanding motive, rather than one like hunger that comes and goes.

Curiosity and Exploration

What do Christopher Columbus, Albert Einstein, and an infant beginning to crawl have in common? Give up? The answer is that they all have a strong motive to explore their environment. To put it another way, they are all curious.

Some of us seem to have a stronger urge to explore the environment than others. Scientists, for example, choose their line of work because they want to know more about the inner workings of the atom or the outer reaches of the universe. But even infants in the first few months of life show curiosity about objects around them. They like to look at things that move, manipulate objects, and play peek-a-boo. In fact, much of what we call "play" in infants and children is

Humans seem to have a basic need to explore—to discover the unknown. In our time, this exploration is taking us into outer space.

part of the enterprise of exploring the environment (Piaget, 1952). Humans are not alone in their need to explore, as anyone who has spent time with a playful puppy or kitten knows. Monkeys, too, will explore their surroundings and manipulate objects, apparently just for the fun of it. Robert Butler (1954) found that monkeys given mechanical puzzles would learn how to solve them and then rework them over and over again for hours with no reward but the joy of solving the puzzle. (Perhaps this is where the expression "monkey around" came from.)

There are, of course, limits to curiosity. We sometimes get bored with places and experiences that are highly familiar to us and are motivated to explore new places and try new things. However, we tend to avoid trying things that are *too* different from what we are accustomed to. Most of us would be willing to try a luscious-looking European dessert, for example, but few of us have a strong desire to munch on french-fried grasshoppers or raw squid. At some point, in other words, the curiosity motive gives way to fear of the unknown. Our desire to explore new horizons also depends on our state of mind at the time. Daniel Berlyne (1967) has proposed that exploring the unfamiliar tends to increase our degree of arousal. If we experience too little arousal, we feel bored; if we experience too much arousal, we feel overly tense and excited. Thus, when we are feeling relaxed we are more likely to welcome novel and challenging experiences—to increase our arousal—whereas when we are already tense or preoccupied we would rather face things that are more familiar and easier to deal with.

The Need for Control

One of the most important of all human motives is the desire to be in control of one's own fate rather than to remain at the mercy of external forces. Although we enter the world in a helpless state, one of the central themes in growing up is the attempt to gain more control over our environment and our lives. As we will see later in this chapter, people who do not have control over their environment may find it difficult to cope with stress. Such people may also fall victim to depression (see Chapter 11). When we do feel "in control," on the other hand, we are more likely to feel secure, competent, and effective.

The need for control is very closely associated with the need for freedom—that is, to be free from the controls and injunctions of other people. As Jack Brehm (1966) writes, an individual is motivated to feel "that he can do what he wants, that he does not have to do what he doesn't want, and that . . . he is the sole director of his own behavior" (page 9). When our freedom to behave the way we want is threatened, we are likely to react by reasserting the freedom in question. Brehm calls the motive to restore or reassert a threatened freedom *psychological reactance*. If a parent tells a child that he can't play with a particular toy, for example, the child may make even more of a fuss about the toy than he would have otherwise. The same principle was illustrated in an experiment on people's reactions to censorship. Subjects were told that they would be able to choose whether or not to listen to a certain speech. They were later informed that the speech had been censored and that they would not be able to listen to it. As Brehm's theory of reactance would predict, these subjects now wanted to hear the speech more than they did before they learned about the censorship (Worchel and Arnold, 1973).

Although we are often motivated to reassert our freedom when it is threatened, we may also give up rather than fight back. In such cases, we decide that we simply don't have control over our own outcomes in life—that we are helpless. Martin Seligman (1975) has suggested that such *learned helplessness* is a likely result of experiences in which we repeatedly find ourselves unable to control the outcome. Seligman originally demonstrated this phenomenon with dogs. The dogs were placed in a harness and were given a shock from which they could not escape. Later the same dogs were placed in a box with two compartments and were shocked again, but this time they could escape the shock by jumping over a barrier to the other compartment. Untrained dogs had no trouble learning the escape route, but the dogs that had been given the inescapable shock treat-

REVERSE PSYCHOLOGY

If you want someone to do something, it is sometimes quite effective to tell him that he *must* do the opposite. The person may be so eager to reassert his freedom and control that he will defy you and, as a result, do exactly what you really want. Parents have been known to use this somewhat sneaky tactic as a means of child control. In the musical play *The Fantastiks*, two fathers want to get their children—a young man and a young woman—interested in each other. They forbid the two to see each other and, sure enough, they quickly fall in love.

— *Box 2* —

Ideological motivation

The competence motives that we have considered—curiosity and exploration and the need for control—may also be categorized as *cognitive* motives. They are based in people's higher mental processes—their thoughts and attitudes—rather than in their physical needs. As we go up the evolutionary ladder, from lower animals to humans, thoughts and ideas play a progressively more important role in motivation. The strongest form of such cognitive motivation is that provided by *ideologies*, systems of belief to which people may become strongly committed.

William Dember (1974) reminds us of several striking examples of such ideological motivation:

Diana Oughton, daughter of a wealthy midwestern family, described as sensitive and warm-hearted, was killed with two Weatherman companions when bombs they were constructing in a Greenwich Village apartment exploded.

Our behavior is often motivated by our values and ideals.

An assistant pastor and a layman of the Holiness Church of God in Jesus Name of Carson Spring, Tennessee, died in agony after drinking a mixture of strychnine and water. They were testing their faith in the Bible, where it is said of those who believe, "if they drink any deadly thing, it shall not hurt them" (Mark 16:16–18).

Countless religious martyrs and political prisoners have undergone torture and death in the service of their faith, their party, their country.

Ideology is sometimes so potent that our commitments to it can override all our other motives and emotions.

---

ment howled at first and then sat passively, taking the shock. These dogs had learned that they were helpless, and so they remained passive and suffered even when they could have done something to relieve their pain.

Similar results have been obtained in experiments with humans. In such experiments people are given various problem-solving tasks, but the experiment is set up so that the subjects are bound to fail. Once subjects find that they keep failing no matter what they do, they are likely to stop trying on subsequent tasks. Their need for control has been at least temporarily burned out.

Thus, people whose sense of control is threatened may display either psychological reactance (trying to reassert control) or learned helplessness (giving up). Camille Wortman and Jack Brehm (1975) propose that when people initially expect to have control over the outcomes of their actions, an experience of failure leads to reactance—to renewed efforts to gain control. But with further experiences of failure, people may finally become convinced that they cannot control the outcome and will stop trying. People who, because of past experience, *don't* expect to control their outcomes are less likely to experience reactance and will give up more quickly (Roth and Kubal, 1975). People particularly subject to repeated experiences of lack of control, and thus to learned helplessness, are the poor and the old.

UNCONSCIOUS MOTIVES

We are quite conscious of many of our motives. We usually know when we are hungry, when we are curious about something, or when we are trying to achieve a good grade in a course. Often, however, we are unaware of our own motives. We seek goals that, for one reason or another, we don't consciously know we are seeking. For example, a politician may seek public office without fully realizing that he has a strong power motive that impels him to have an impact on other people's lives (Winter, 1973). He may instead say or believe that his motivation is altruistic or directed toward some specific cause.

The psychologist who first gave major emphasis to unconscious motives was Sigmund Freud (see Chapter 8). Freud believed that certain of our emotions are *repressed*, or banished from consciousness, because they are too anxiety-arousing for us to deal with. But these motives still have clear effects on our behavior. As we will see later, for example, Freud believed that small children have a desire to have sexual relations with their opposite-sex parent. Throughout the world, however, such incestuous behavior is regarded as repulsive and, indeed, unthinkable. So this desire that arises in childhood must become repressed, pushed into the unconscious. Freud argued that the strength of the prohibition (known as the *incest taboo*) is itself evidence of the strong desire for such sexual relationships—otherwise there would be no need for such a strong taboo. But although the actual desire to make love with one's father or mother is repressed, this motive may continue to operate in a subtle or disguised form. For example, a man may fall in love with a woman who reminds him of his mother—although he himself would be quick to deny any such connection. This type of unconscious motivation may seem a bit far-fetched, but there are more obvious ways in which people repress their motives. An accident-prone woman may complain that fate has been unkind to her, while those around her may see that her accidents are unconscious ways of expressing a desire to hurt herself. Or an obese person may claim that he eats because he has "too many fat cells" or has no will power, when his unconscious motive for eating may be that he uses food as a substitute for love.

Freud paid special attention to people's slips of the tongue as one reflection of unconscious motivation. In his honor, these are commonly referred to as "Freudian slips." Although these slips are often passed off as accidental, sometimes they are not accidental at all. One of Freud's colleagues, a Dr. Brill, provided the following example:

While writing a prescription for a woman who was especially weighted down by the financial burden of the treatment, I was interested in her saying, "Please do not give me any big bills because

---

WHY MEN GIVE BLOOD

Ernest Dichter (1964), a noted motivational researcher, once lent his talents to a Red Cross blood drive. He concluded that many men were reluctant to give blood because of unconscious anxieties about the loss of strength and virility. He recommended, therefore, that the campaign focus on masculinity, implying that each man in the audience had so much virility that he could afford to give away a little. Dichter also suggested that the Red Cross try to make the men proud of any suffering. Each donor should be given a pin in the shape of a drop of blood—the equivalent of a wounded soldier's Purple Heart. Dichter reported that these techniques produced a sharp increase in men's blood donations.

I cannot swallow them." Of course she meant to say pills. (*Freud, 1915, page 103*)

It seems that this patient was not fully aware of her concern about spending too much money, but the idea slipped out "accidentally."

THEORIES OF EMOTION

Emotions seem to involve physiological arousal (a racing pulse, a shortness of breath), a subjective feeling ("I am thrilled," or "I am down in the dumps"), and expressive behaviors (a smile, a laugh, a grimace). But how do these three elements relate to one another? Does the physiological arousal lead to the subjective feeling, or is it the other way around? Does the overt expression of emotion come after the emotion is experienced subjectively, or do the feeling and the expression occur simultaneously? Over the past century several theories of emotion have been put forth that take different positions on these questions. As a backdrop to these theories, we will first examine the physiological changes that are associated with emotion. We will then review two theories formulated in the late nineteenth and early twentieth centuries, the James-Lange theory and the Cannon-Bard theory. Although neither theory is accepted today, each influenced the way that today's psychologists view emotion. Then we will examine a more recent theory of emotion, cognitive labeling theory.

The Physiology of Emotion

The experience of emotion is often accompanied by striking changes in our body's functioning. When we are emotionally aroused, our hearts may accelerate from their normal rate of about 72 beats per minute to as much as 180 beats per minute. Our breathing is likely to become rapid and uneven, and our blood pressure may rise alarmingly.

Some of the most interesting research on the physiology of emotion focuses on two powerful emotions: fear and anger. In most respects, the physiological responses associated with fear and anger are quite similar. Both fear and anger are controlled by the sympathetic branch of the autonomic nervous system (see Chapter 2). As a result, when you are afraid or angry, movements of your stomach and intestines usually stop, interfering with the digestion and absorption of food. Your body's metabolism speeds up and sugar in the bloodstream and fats from the body's tissues are burned off at a faster rate. (Yes, if you were in a rage or a panic all the time, you'd probably lose a lot of weight, but there are safer and saner ways to diet.) In addition, your salivary glands stop working, causing the feeling of dryness in the mouth that often accompanies fear and anger. Your sweat glands may overreact, producing a dripping forehead, clammy hands, and "cold sweat." Finally, the pupils of your eyes may enlarge, producing the wide-eyed look that is characteristic of both terror and rage.

In spite of these similarities, there seem to be some physiological

STAGE FRIGHT

The pianist Vladimir Horowitz reportedly suffers terrible stage fright whenever he performs, and Arthur Rubinstein calls stage fright "the price I have to pay for my wonderful life." Stage fright can involve heart rates of up to 200 beats per minute—almost three times the normal rate—and a very dry mouth. In one case a promising French horn player got dry in the mouth at every audition. "You can't play the French horn if you haven't got spit," a music school official pointed out. Fortunately, the player conquered his fear with the help of psychological counseling and landed a job with a symphony orchestra (Sobel, 1979).

differences between fear and anger. Albert Ax (1953) studied the physiological response of subjects experiencing fear or anger. Ax's laboratory assistants produced anger in subjects by making insulting remarks in the course of the experiment. They provoked fear by acting uncertain about how to operate some dangerous-looking electrical equipment. Ax then recorded the subjects' pulse rate, heartbeat, respiration, galvanic skin response (which reflects sweat gland activity), and other physiological responses. He found that while both fear and anger tend to produce increases in blood pressure, the increases are greater during anger. On the other hand, heart rate, respiration, muscle tension, and sweat gland activity all tend to increase more during fear than during anger. For the most part, however, the physiological changes produced by fear and by anger remain quite similar.

The physiological changes that take place when we experience fear or anger are part of our body's preparation to act in a threatening situation, whether by escaping (as in the case of fear) or fighting back (as in the case of anger). Our increased heart rate, breathing, and metabolism provide us with the additional energy we need for quick action. Such bodily reactions can be very helpful in coping with an emergency, whether it is perceived as terrifying or as infuriating. If we were to remain angry or fearful for long periods of time, however, these reactions could take a severe toll. We will consider the ways in which emotions can damage physical health later in the chapter, when we focus on the effects of prolonged stress.

The James-Lange Theory

The common-sense notion about the links between subjective experience, physiological arousal, and behavior is that some event causes a person to feel a particular emotion (the subjective experience) and this emotion then causes certain physiological changes as well as certain behaviors (crying, striking back, running away). But William James, the great American psychologist, was not satisfied with this common-sense explanation. He proposed that in fact the sequence is quite the reverse: An event or stimulus causes bodily changes (both internal responses, such as increased heart rate, and overt actions, such as crying or running) and these bodily effects in turn produce the experienced emotion. The experience of emotion, according to James, is a direct result of a person's perception of his own bodily changes and behaviors: "We feel sorry because we cry, angry because we strike, afraid because we tremble" (James, 1890).

In developing his theory, James drew on the related ideas of a Danish psychologist named Carl Lange. As a result, the theory that the experience of emotion results from the perceptions of one's bodily changes has become known as the *James-Lange theory*. For reasons that we will outline below, the James-Lange theory does not seem today to provide an adequate explanation of emotion. Nevertheless, there is evidence that one of the theory's implications may well be correct—that we can often gain control over our emotions by consciously altering our behavior. This idea will be discussed in the section on facial feedback theory.

The Cannon-Bard Theory

Even though we may sometimes infer our feelings from our own behavior, it is now clear that the James-Lange theory does not provide an adequate account of the origins of emotion. The theory is on weak ground in its attempts to link physiological changes with the experience of emotion. According to James and Lange, a person might confront a particular stimulus (say, a beautiful sunset), experience a particular pattern of physiological change as a result (such as tingles down one's spine), and then perceive this physiological change and experience a particular emotion (such as awe or reverence). But this theory assumes that each emotion has its own characteristic pattern of physiological change. And, as physiologist Walter Cannon pointed out in 1929, this does not seem to be the case. The same "tingles" that are associated with a beautiful sunset might also be experienced when one is watching a horror film. How, then, is one to tell what emotion one is supposed to be experiencing—awe or terror? As we noted earlier, researchers have found some distinctions between the physiological aspects of fear and anger, but there is no evidence that each of the many emotions that we are capable of feeling has its own characteristic pattern of internal bodily changes.

Cannon (1929) criticized James's theory on this and other grounds and proceeded to offer his own explanation of the links between physiological arousal and the subjective experience of emotion. His theory was later modified by Philip Bard, and it became known as the *Cannon-Bard theory*. Cannon and Bard postulated that when one encounters an emotion-arousing stimulus, nerve impulses first pass through the region of the brain called the thalamus. At that

"I MADE MYSELF FEEL THAT WAY"

Do men and women experience emotion in the same ways? For the most part they do, but there may also be some differences. Arlie Hochschild (1975) asked students to provide descriptions of their emotional experiences. She found that women were more likely than men to report that they actively managed or manipulated their own feelings. Women were more likely to use such phrases as "I made myself feel that way," "I snapped myself out of it," or "I tucked my feelings in." Men, in contrast, were more likely to take a passive attitude toward their emotions, as something beyond their control. If this difference really exists, how can we explain it?

point, they suggested, the nerve impulse splits: one portion goes to the cerebral cortex causing the subjective experience of emotion (fear, disgust, happiness); the other portion goes to the hypothalamus, which gives the body its physiological marching orders. According to this model, then, neither the subjective nor the physiological reaction to a stimulus causes the other; instead, they are produced simultaneously. Although recent physiological research has not supported the details of the Cannon-Bard theory, it, too, has had an important impact on subsequent theory and research.

Cognitive Labeling Theory

Stanley Schachter (1967) put forth a *cognitive labeling theory* of emotion that has enjoyed considerable popularity among psychologists. Schachter's theory can be viewed as a refinement of the James-Lange theory in that it holds that bodily changes precede the experience of emotion. But instead of assuming that each emotion has its own characteristic pattern of physiological changes, Schachter made the more plausible assumption that the patterns of physiological change associated with different emotions are quite similar. A person who feels physiologically aroused must, in fact, *decide* which particular emotion she is feeling. These interpretations, or labels, Schachter went on to postulate, depend on the situation in which the arousal occurs. If you feel a racing pulse and a shortness of breath at a party, where everyone is making merry, you may interpret the emotion as elation. If you experience the same arousal after someone has insulted you, you may interpret it as anger. The same form of physiological arousal, therefore, might lead to two different emotions, depending on the surrounding circumstances.

Schachter's theory has been called the "jukebox theory of emotion" (Mandler, 1962). According to this analogy, the state of physiological arousal is like the state of a jukebox after a coin has been inserted. It is all set to go, ready to play its tune. But just which tune it will play—a love song, a lament, an exultant march—will depend on which button is pushed. And which button is pushed, in Schachter's view, depends on the way in which the individual interprets his environment.

To demonstrate the validity of this theory, Schachter and Jerome E. Singer (1962) had a physician inject subjects with epinephrine. Epinephrine is a chemical that produces physiological reactions usually associated with strong emotions: pounding heart, rapid breathing, sweating palms. Some subjects were told what the effects of the injection would be. These subjects were in the "epinephrine-informed" group. Other subjects were not told about these effects; they were in the "epinephrine-uninformed" group. Schachter and Singer predicted that subjects who knew that epinephrine caused their arousal would not experience any strong emotion. They would say to themselves, in effect, "I'm aroused; I guess it's because of the epinephrine." On the other hand, subjects who were not informed about the effects of the drug would attribute their arousal to an emotion relevant to the social situation. For example, if the

I FEEL GOOD—
SO I'LL HELP YOU OUT

People's emotions can have a direct impact on their behavior toward others. In several studies, some subjects were put in a good mood when they unexpectedly found a dime in the coin return of a pay telephone. These "happy" people were then found to be much more likely than people who had not found a dime to help a passerby pick up a folder full of papers that she had dropped (Isen and Levin, 1972) or to mail a lost letter (Levin and Isen, 1975). When we're feeling good ourselves, we're often motivated to spread the goodwill to others.

experimenter were to show them a tarantula, they might say to themselves, "I'm aroused; it must be because I'm afraid." In other words, Schachter and Singer were proposing that when people experienced physiological arousal that was otherwise unexplained, they would search for an explanation, and, as a result, would come to experience an emotion.

To facilitate this labeling process, Schachter and Singer created two social situations. In one condition, the subjects watched another student (actually a confederate of the researchers) act in a wild and silly way, playing with a hula hoop and shooting wads of paper at a wastebasket. In the other situation, the confederate objected strenuously to a questionnaire that he and the real subject were filling out. The confederate escalated his protest until he finally tore up the questionnaire and left the room. Schachter and Singer expected their subjects to use the confederate's behavior as a cue in identifying their own emotions. They predicted, therefore, that when—and only when—the subjects were not informed about the effects of the epinephrine they would report feeling the same as the confederate; that is, they would be happy or angry, depending on how the confederate had behaved.

In general, the results supported the hypothesis. The epinephrine-uninformed subjects tended to attribute their physiological arousal to elation or anger, depending on the social context

THERE GOES THE THUMP OF MY HEART

Stuart Valins (1966) played recorded thumping sounds to male college students while they were watching slides of nude women taken from *Playboy* centerfolds. Some of the subjects were given false information that the thumps were in fact the amplified sounds of their own heartbeats. The thumping sounds speeded up or slowed down while the subjects were viewing particular slides. Afterward, the subjects were asked how attracted they were to each of the women. They rated those women who had apparently caused their hearts to speed up—or to slow down—as most attractive. How can this result be explained in terms of the cognitive labeling approach to emotion?

FIGURE 7.2
Two subjects in Schachter and Singer's experiment. When subjects were not informed about the drug's arousing effects, they tended to "catch" the emotion displayed by the confederate.

they were in (Figure 7.2). And once they had interpreted their physiological state as an emotion, they then proceeded to behave in a way appropriate to that particular emotion, acting either giddy or irritated themselves. It should be noted, however, that Schachter and Singer's results were not really clear-cut, and more recent studies have not obtained similar results (Maslach, 1979; Marshall and Zimbardo, 1979). Consequently, the validity of Schachter's cognitive labeling model is currently a topic of debate among psychologists. Nevertheless, the cognitive labeling model often does seem quite applicable to aspects of our emotional experience. Even that most mysterious of emotions, romantic love, sometimes seems to require us to make sense of our own internal experience by giving it a label (see Box 3).

It should be noted that the three theories that have been presented here are not necessarily mutually exclusive. Each of them may in fact provide part of the explanation of emotional experience. Recent theories of emotion have, in fact, attempted to combine all these—and still other—elements into a more complex and comprehensive model (for example, Izard, 1977).

THE DEVELOPMENT OF EMOTION

As adults we express a wide variety of emotions, from mild annoyance to intense jealousy. Newborn babies do not express such a wide range of emotions, nor are they able to distinguish between such emotions in the adults around them. How does an individual develop the ability to display and to differentiate between various emotional states as she grows from infancy to adulthood?

The Differentiation of Emotions

It used to be thought that at birth the only clearly recognizable display of emotional expression is one of unfocused excitement. According to this view, babies wriggle, jerk, and thrash about, not as a specific response to specific stimuli, but as a general reaction to changes in the external environment. Similarly, a baby's crying was viewed as an all-purpose response to a wide range of physical needs or discomforts. Katharine Banham Bridges (1932) proposed that emotions develop in a treelike pattern, from the infant's state of general excitement toward more specific emotional states, such as fear, jealousy, and affection.

Although it seems likely that infants and toddlers learn to differentiate among emotional states, as Bridges suggested, some researchers now believe that a range of distinctive emotional expressions—for surprise, happiness, disgust, distress, and interest—is present at birth (Izard, 1978). By the time infants are 8 or 9 months old, they seem to be capable of displaying—under what seem to be appropriate circumstances—distinctive expressions of joy, surprise, sadness, anger, disgust, contempt, and fear (see Figure 7.3) (Izard et al., 1980). According to Carroll Izard, the three expressions that are most difficult to distinguish from one another in infants are anger, disgust, and contempt—and, indeed, these emotions are often difficult to distinguish in adults, as well.

As children grow older, they not only come to experience a fuller and more complex range of emotions, they also come to realize that the emotions they experience internally need not always be expressed in their behavior. Carolyn Saarni (1979) showed children of different ages sequences of photos in which a central character could be expected to be feeling a particular emotion. In one sequence, for example, a boy brags about his skating ability and then falls down. In the last photo the boy is looking away from the camera, so his expression cannot be seen. The children were then asked to select (from a set of photos) the facial expression they felt the boy would show in the final frame and why. Older children used more sophisticated reasoning about the display of emotions than younger children. For ex-

— Box 3

The label of love

Recent studies of falling in love have indicated that love is like a Brooks Brothers suit or a Saks Fifth Avenue dress. For one's feelings toward another to be experienced as "love," they must not only feel good and fit well, they must also have the appropriate label. Sometimes a sexual experience contributes to such labeling. One college student told an interviewer that she was surprised to discover that she enjoyed having sex with her boyfriend, because until that time she had not been sure that she loved him. The pleasant experience helped to convince her that she was actually "in love" (Peplau, Rubin, and Hill, 1977).

Paradoxically, however, people sometimes label as "love" experiences that seem to be negative rather than positive (Berscheid and Walster, 1974). Consider the rather interesting case of fear. Ovid noted in *The Art of Love*, written in first century Rome, that

an excellent time for a man to arouse passion in a woman was while watching gladiators disembowel one another in the arena. Presumably the emotions of fear and repulsion stirred up by the grisly scene would somehow be converted to romantic interest.

Ovid himself did not conduct any controlled experiments to check the validity of the fear-breeds-love principle, but two psychologists at the University of British Columbia have done so (Dutton and Aron, 1974). They conducted their experiment on two footbridges that cross the Capilano River in North Vancouver. One of the bridges is a narrow, rickety structure that sways in the wind 230 feet above the rocky canyon; the other is a solid structure upriver, only 10 feet above a shallow stream. An attractive female experimenter approached men who were crossing one or the other bridge and asked if they would take part in her study on "the effects of exposure to scenic attractions on creative expression." All they had to do was write down

their associations to a picture she showed them. The researchers found that the men accosted on the fear-arousing bridge were more sexually aroused than the men on the solid bridge, as measured by the amount of sexual imagery in the stories they wrote. The men on the high-fear bridge were also much more likely to telephone the young woman afterward, ostensibly to get more information about the study.

The best available explanation of these results comes from Schachter's cognitive labeling theory of emotion. Schachter's experiments suggested that the experience of emotion has two necessary elements. The first is physiological arousal—a racing heart, heightened breathing, sweating, and the like. These symptoms tend to be more or less identical for any intense emotion, whether it be anger, fear, or love. The second necessary element, therefore, is the person's subjective labeling of her arousal. In order to determine which emotion she is experiencing, the person must look around and decide

ample, older children discussed differences between what the child was "really feeling" and the emotion he displayed. They pointed out that the boy who fell down would not try to show his pain because, as one child said, "He'd be pretty stupid to show he's hurt after he's been bragging how good he is." As we grow older, then, we learn to regulate our expressive behavior in ways that are appropriate to particular situations, regardless of how we may be "feeling inside."

How Fears Develop

To look further into the development of emotions, let us examine the specific case of fear. In general, we are not born with our fears; we *learn* to be fearful of specific things as a result of both cultural precepts and our own experience. Human beings may also be biologically predisposed to learn to fear some things more than others. For example, we seem to learn especially quickly to be afraid of fire, insects, and other naturally occurring phenomena (Scarf, 1974).

Nevertheless, it seems that we can learn to fear just about any-

According to cognitive labeling theory, the emotions we feel in a physiologically arousing situation may be labeled as "love" if we are in the presence of a person to whom we are attracted.

what external stimulus is causing the inner upheaval.

This labeling is a complicated process, and (as Ovid apparently knew some 2000 years ago) mistakes can happen. In the Capilano Canyon study, subjects apparently relabeled their inner stirrings of fear, at least in part, as sexual arousal and romantic attraction. This sort of relabeling is undoubtedly encouraged by the fact that the popular stereotype of falling in love—a pounding heart, shortness of breath, trembling hands—bears an uncanny resemblance to the physical symptoms of fear. With such traumatic expectations of what love should feel like, it is no wonder that it is sometimes confused with other emotions. As the Supremes put it in a song of the 1960s, "Love is like an itching in my heart."

There is, of course, much more to love than cognitive labeling. Indeed, love cannot be regarded as only an emotion. As we will see in Chapter 14, it is also a particular sort of social relationship that takes time to grow and develop.

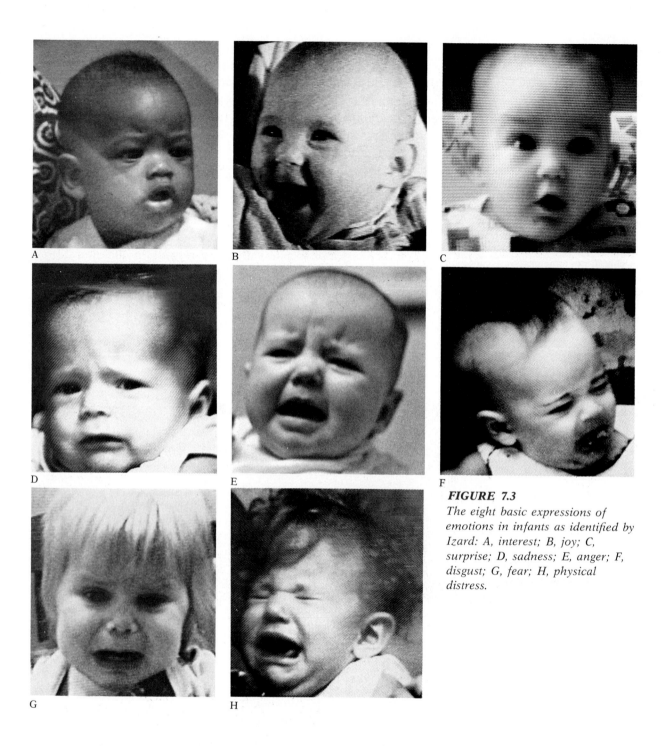

FIGURE 7.3
The eight basic expressions of emotions in infants as identified by Izard: A, interest; B, joy; C, surprise; D, sadness; E, anger; F, disgust; G, fear; H, physical distress.

thing if our experiences with it are unpleasant enough. In addition, we can learn to fear things that are not in themselves harmful but that we have come to associate with experiences or objects that *are* harmful or fear arousing. This sort of learning by association follows the basic principles of classical conditioning discussed in Chapter 5. In one of the nastier experiments in the psychological literature, John B. Watson and Rosalie Rayner (1920) demonstrated this possibility by classically conditioning an 11-month-old boy named Albert to fear a variety of furry things. They began by putting a white rat in Albert's room. At first Albert was not afraid of the rat at all. But as he reached

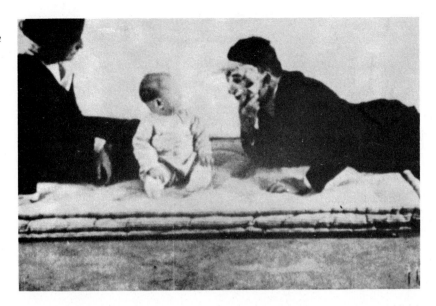

A rare photograph of Little Albert and John Watson taken from a film made in 1919 of this famous classical conditioning experiment.

to touch it, the researchers struck a steel bar near Albert's head, creating a terrifyingly loud noise. They continued to do this six more times, until Albert showed a strong fear of the rat, crying and shrinking away whenever the rat was placed near him. What's more, Albert showed fearful reactions to a variety of other furry objects, including a rabbit, a Santa Claus mask, and even Dr. Watson's hair. A process of stimulus generalization (see Chapter 5) seemed to be operating, with the original fear of the rat "spreading" to other stimuli that resembled it. Watson and Rayner speculated—although they didn't study Albert long enough to know for sure (see Harris, 1979)—that such *conditioned fears* are likely to persist indefinitely.

We don't know whether Watson and Rayner's subject, enshrined in the psychological literature as "Little Albert," is still alive today. Indeed, some psychologists now suspect that Albert was not really conditioned as effectively as Watson claimed he was (Samelson, 1980). Still, if you should happen to see a man in his sixties who turns pale and quickly crosses the street whenever he sees someone wearing a fur coat, shout "Albert!" and see whether he answers.

Although Albert's case is unique, the conditioning of fear to objects that are not harmful themselves is a common phenomenon. If you are the sort of person who feels shivers whenever you pass the street where your dentist's office is located, you will know what we mean. Most such conditioned fears, although "irrational," are harmless enough. But when a person has strong irrational fears that interfere with his functioning, such as an intense fear of venturing out-of-doors, he is said to have a *phobia* (see Chapter 11).

People also acquire fears from the attitudes of their family and culture. Some children learn to fear animals, others to fear flying, and still others to fear academic failure by observing and adopting the attitudes of their parents. In addition, different societies have their own traditions about what is fearful and what is not. In some cultures ghosts and demons are seen as playing a major role in

human affairs, while in other cultures they are seen as figments of the imagination. Cultural influences can affect our feelings about everything from meat eating to menstruation (see Box 4). Such cultural influences play a major role in determining what an individual within a culture is likely to be afraid of.

WHEN EMOTIONS DESTROY: THE CASE OF STRESS

Experiencing emotions has both advantages and drawbacks. Our emotions can spur us on to significant accomplishments. But our emotions can also destroy us, through the impact of *stress:* pressure from our environment that makes physical and emotional demands on us.

When we talk about the "stress and strain" of modern life, we are referring to a variety of pressures, such as those caused by competition in school or at work, deadlines, or worries about financial security. Such pressures can have damaging effects on our state of mind and on our physical well-being. Because of its potential destructiveness, psychologists have devoted a great deal of attention to the causes and effects of stress.

How does the body respond to stress? According to Hans Selye (1956), the response occurs in several stages. The first stage is the *alarm reaction,* which is similar to the physiological aspects of fear and anger that we discussed earlier. As the body prepares to cope with the stress, there is increased activity in the sympathetic nervous system, digestion stops, the level of blood sugar rises, heart rate and

blood pressure increase, and blood flow to the muscles increases. Then comes the stage of *resistance*. Now the body's resources are mobilized to overcome the stress or escape it. If these efforts are successful, the body returns to normal. If not, as may be the case with long-term stress, the stage of *exhaustion* is reached. Failure to cope with stress can result in physical and psychological breakdown and sometimes even death.

Stress and Disease

Some scientists have come to believe that virtually all diseases are related to emotional stress. For example, it has been demonstrated that people who work under conditions of great urgency are especially likely to have high blood pressure and eventually to suffer

Air traffic controllers are subject to a great deal of stress that can lead them to develop physiological problems, such as peptic ulcers.

— *Box 4* —

"That time of month": menstruation and moods

Menstrual syndrome is a label for the physical and emotional experiences women are thought to have each month at the time of menstruation. The symptoms that reportedly occur include weight gain, abdominal cramps, backache, headache, intestinal problems, depression, irritability, and a generally negative mood. These symptoms are described as being most severe during the few days preceding the menstrual period and during the first few days of the period. "I bloat up, feel fat and clutzy"; "My temper is short; I am near tears; I am depressed"; "My most tense time is just prior to my period when physical and emotional states are at their worst" (Weideger, 1976). And a disproportionately high percentage of the crimes committed by women, suicides attempted by women, and women's accidents and hospital admissions occur during the premenstrual and menstrual phases of the monthly cycle (Dalton, 1964).

Until recently, such periodic changes in mood and physical symptoms were believed to result from hormonal changes that occur in all healthy females throughout their reproductive lives. The pituitary gland and the hypothalamus in the brain control the process. During menstruation, levels of the female hormones estrogen and progesterone are extremely low. After the first day of the period, these hormone levels gradually increase until they peak, roughly in the middle of the monthly cycle. For a few days the estrogen and progesterone levels remain high; this is the point in the cycle when an egg is released from the ovaries. The hormonal levels then begin to drop until the next menstrual period, when the whole process starts all over again (unless the woman becomes pregnant).

There is no doubt that the physical processes underlying reproduction occur cyclically in women. But researchers have begun to suspect that such physiological changes cannot explain women's emotional and physical responses to menstruation. There are several reasons for these suspicions. First, the actual relationship between hormones and behavior remains

Women often come to expect that their menstrual periods will be times of emotional distress.

very unclear to scientists, although much research is now being done in this area. Second, although hormonal shifts occur in all women—from the first menstrual period until menopause—reports on how many women experience negative menstrual symptoms vary widely, ranging from 15 percent to 95 percent of women in different populations (Paige, 1973). If hormones are the basis of such

---

heart attacks (Friedman and Rosenman, 1974). Similarly, those factory workers who feel the greatest degree of job pressure have been found to be most likely to suffer from high blood pressure, angina, and ulcers (House et al., 1979). Other diseases that frequently result from stress include arthritis, asthma, and migraine headaches. And stress may also increase a person's susceptibility to infectious diseases, by lowering the body's resistance to bacteria and viruses.

Physical diseases that are caused at least in part by stress or other psychological factors are called *psychosomatic* diseases. Needless to say, the fact that diseases may often have psychological origins does not mean that they are any less real. Such diseases can incapacitate or kill just as easily as diseases that seem to have solely physical causes.

Let's take the example of stomach ulcers (or peptic ulcers). Stomach ulcers afflict one out of every twenty people at some point in their life, and each year they cause more than 10,000 deaths in the United States. Ulcers are a common disorder among people in many different occupational groups, from factory workers to physicians.

symptoms, why aren't all women similarly affected?

Finally, in recent studies in which women were asked to keep daily diaries of their experiences, it was found that their negative moods and symptoms were actually spread out fairly evenly over the month, rather than being concentrated in the days of low hormone levels (Ruble and Brooks-Gunn, 1979). It may be, then, that women are not objectively worse off when they are menstruating than at other times. But because of cultural beliefs about menstruation, women are more likely to attribute many discomforts to their menstrual cycle.

Indeed, no known culture has viewed menstruation positively (Weideger, 1976). In our society menstruating women are generally believed to be at less than their best—difficult, edgy, and unreliable. In more primitive societies, menstruating women are sometimes seen as dangerous and are isolated from their social group. The origins of menstrual prejudice are ancient. Blood and bleeding are often viewed as distasteful or even repulsive. Every language has its euphemisms for menstruation; in the U.S. they have included "riding the rag," "Bloody Mary," "red-letter day," and, of course, "the curse." Some of these are neutral, but none is positive.

It doesn't take little girls long to figure out that no one likes menstruation. Many children receive inadequate explanations of menstruation from their parents, and menarche (the first period) is often shrouded in secrecy. Even advertisements for menstrual protection products such as sanitary napkins and tampons suggest that menstruating is a negative experience. Ads for these products stress secrecy (no one must ever know that a woman is menstruating) and freedom from the debilitating restrictions of menstruating. It is therefore not surprising that Anne Clarke and Diane Ruble (1978) found that 12-year-old girls who had not yet started menstruating anticipated physical pain, disruption of social activities, and negative moods.

These negative expectations can lead to negative experiences when girls start to menstruate. If a woman *expects* to be upset and distressed at "that time of the month," the chances become greater that she will be. The woman's expectations make her more likely to associate any negative physical or psychological symptoms with her menstrual cycle, whether or not the association is real. Women may also "adopt" symptoms so that they can fit into the cultural stereotype of normal women (Parlee, 1973). When women in a recent study were informed that the research concerned menstruation, they reported more cyclical symptoms than women who were not told the purpose of the study (Englander-Golden, Whitmore, and Dienstbier, 1978).

Women may in fact experience cyclical changes that are both psychological and physical. But it seems clear that social learning shapes their perceptions of those changes. Menstruation can be viewed as a cleansing process (it rinses dead cells from the vagina), and as an affirmation of life, health, and femininity. But until these values become part of our culture, little girls will continue to learn that menstruation is a "curse" and will continue to attribute a variety of negative experiences to "that time of the month."

One group of workers with a particularly high frequency of ulcers is air traffic controllers. At least one-third of the traffic controllers in America reportedly suffer from ulcers, a higher incidence than in any other profession or group.

Why do air traffic controllers develop ulcers so frequently? Stress appears to be the culprit. For these people, stress results from the combination of constant vigilance and uncertainty. The controllers must remain alert and watchful at all times; they cannot afford to let their guard down for even a moment. In addition, there is the constant fear and uncertainty. There is always the possibility of an accident, no matter how careful the controller may be. Stress of this sort leads the body to increase the secretion of hydrochloric acid in the stomach. Hydrochloric acid normally helps to break down foods during digestion, but its presence in excess amounts can produce small lesions (ulcers) in the stomach wall. Further examples of how stress can contribute to disease—including even cancer—are provided in the Update on "Psychoimmunology: Mind, Body, and Health" on pages 102–105.

Stress is less likely to harm people if they have adequate *social support*—that is, friends, family members, and colleagues who can serve as confidants and who can provide help when it is needed. When you know there is someone you can count on, even if only to listen to your problems, a stressful situation is likely to seem a bit less threatening than it otherwise would be. Even if the stress itself is unavoidable, the social support can reduce its damaging effects on physical and mental health. For example, a supportive spouse can help an overloaded worker to realize that her job is not the only important thing in life and may encourage her to get the exercise, nutrition, and rest needed to resist stress (House and Wells, 1978). It has also been speculated that social support can have a "tranquilizing effect" on the endocrine system, thereby softening people's reactions to stress (Cassel, 1976).

Stress and the Executive

Like air traffic controllers, business executives often suffer from ulcers, and this condition is usually attributed to the demands and pressures of their job. Among these pressures are the need to react quickly in rapidly changing situations, with one's own success—and that of others—depending on these reactions. Joseph Brady (1958) demonstrated that such pressures can indeed cause ulcers, and he did so in a unique way—by making executives out of monkeys.

Brady set up a controlled experiment using pairs of monkeys. In each pair, two monkeys were joined (or yoked) by an apparatus that generated electric shocks. Whenever one monkey received a shock, so did the other. Both monkeys were given shocks at 20-second intervals, but only one monkey—called the "executive monkey"—could prevent the shocks by pressing a lever. The other monkey had a lever too, but pressing it had no effect on the shocks. This experimental procedure was a good way to distinguish the effects of physical and psychological stress. Both animals were subjected to the same physical conditions, including the same number of shocks, but only the executive monkey faced the stress of constant vigilance. For the duration of the study, the monkeys were placed on a continuous schedule: 6 hours of shock avoidance followed by 6 hours of rest.

In four pairs of monkeys, the "executives" developed severe ulcers and eventually died. In contrast, the yoked animals survived, with no apparent ill effects. The stress of constant vigilance, during several weeks of the hours-on, hours-off schedule, apparently had devastating physical effects on the executive monkeys. (It should be noted, though, that Brady's study has been criticized because the monkeys were not assigned randomly to the executive and control group positions.)

You shouldn't get the impression that having control over one's outcomes is always stressful. For Brady's executive monkeys, control over one's own and one's partner's outcomes was not, in itself, the key stress-producing factor. To the contrary, the ability to exert control over one's outcomes usually tends to reduce rather than increase stress. Jay Weiss (1972) demonstrated this with rats, in a series of experiments whose results at first glance seemed to contradict those

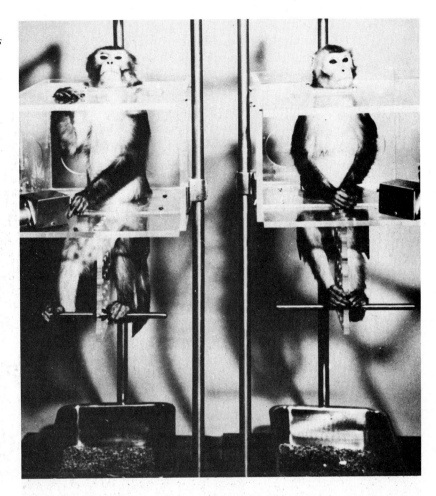

Brady's executive monkey experiment. Although both monkeys were equipped with control levers, only the one on the left (the "executive") could prevent both of them from being shocked.

of Brady. Weiss yoked pairs of rats so that each rat received the same number of shocks as its partner, as in Brady's study. In one study, the shocks were scheduled to be administered about once a minute. But each scheduled shock was preceded by a signal beep, and the "executive rat" could avoid and escape shock for itself and its compatriot by reaching through a hole in its cage to touch a panel just outside. After a continuous 21-hour session, both animals were sacrificed and their stomachs were examined for ulcers. Weiss found that the rats who could avoid and escape shock had much less ulceration than their helpless partners.

Why did the executive monkeys suffer increased effects of stress, while the executive rats suffered decreased effects? Weiss (1972) believes that the key difference lies in how certain the animal is that its efforts will be successful. In Brady's study, there was no warning signal preceding the shocks, so the monkey had to be on guard at all times. It could never be sure whether it had been successful in avoiding the next shock. In Weiss's study, however, there was a warning signal, and the executive rat knew that its efforts would be successful. The executive rat could safely relax until the next beep.

There is every reason to believe that control reduces stress in people as well as in monkeys and rats. For example, loud music coming from your stereo probably is not stressful—it's usually very enjoyable. But the same loud music coming from the place next door may be quite irritating. The ability to control events can be stress-reducing even when the control isn't exercised. As we noted in Chapter 3, David Glass and Jerome Singer (1973) found that merely knowing that one can control a noise seems to make it less bothersome. That's probably one reason why your blaring stereo doesn't bother you—you know you can always turn it off.

Unfortunately, control does not always have such stress-reducing effects. And that seems to be because many "controlling" situations for humans turn out to be more like the situation of Brady's monkeys than of Weiss's rats—the "executive" doesn't know for sure whether her efforts will be successful. Without such feedback, the ability to control can be more of a liability than an asset. Air traffic controllers may get their ulcers for this reason—they can never be sure that they are in complete control. Imagine how different the job of air traffic controller would be if there were more certainty. Imagine a computer announcing, "O.K., Jack, everything is cool. Take a breather." The job might even be enjoyable!

Stressful life crises can include both negative events, such as the death of a loved one, and positive events, such as marriage. In both cases, major adjustments of one's life are necessary.

Stress and Life Crises

The physical effects of prolonged stress can be quite dramatic. For example, when Thomas Holmes and his colleagues interviewed 5000 patients about life events that preceded physical illness, they uncovered an exceptional range of prior stresses and strains, from major calamities like the loss of one's job to such minor ordeals as a visit from one's in-laws.

Holmes and Richard Rahe (1967) assembled a list of life events that most frequently preceded illness and attempted to determine which of these events had the greatest impact and which had the least physical effect. In order to establish a scale that would predict the onset of disease, such as tuberculosis or heart disease, they asked 394 persons to rate the degree of social readjustment required by each of 43 major life events or *crises*—turning points in a person's life. The ratings indicated that the single most traumatic event in terms of necessary social readjustment was the death of a spouse. The top ten life crises were as follows: (1) death of a spouse, (2) divorce, (3) marital separation, (4) jail term, (5) death of a close family member, (6) personal injury or illness, (7) marriage, (8) loss of a job, (9) marital reconciliation, and (10) retirement. Further research confirmed that the more serious a crisis, the more likely it is to be followed by physical illness. Notice that these crises include events that are generally considered to be positive, such as marriage. But even a positive event such as marriage may require extensive readjustment of one's life patterns and hence can be stressful.

From studies such as these, showing that stress may contribute to a wide range of illnesses, it becomes obvious that our emotions can have dramatic negative effects on our lives. And we all know that such emotions as anger, jealousy, and fear can lead to psychological harm to ourselves and others. Yet few of us would choose to become unemotional creatures. Without the experience of emotion, we would miss the highs as well as the lows of human experience—the joys and the sorrows, the pride and the passion. Surely emotions can be distressing as well as gratifying, but they are an essential part of what it means to be human.

SUMMARY

1. *Motives* are internal forces that organize, direct, and sustain a person's behavior. Two major categories of motives are *survival* motives, such as hunger and thirst, and *competence* motives, such as the needs to explore, understand, and control one's environment.
2. Maslow developed a pyramid of human needs, with physiological needs at the bottom and self-actualizing needs at the top. He suggested that needs at each level must be satisfied before one can begin to satisfy needs at the next higher level.
3. According to *drive reduction theory*, motivation begins with a physiological *need* that is experienced as a psychological *drive*. The drive leads the individual to satisfy the need and is thereby reduced.
4. *Hunger* is a basic physiological motive. Although stomach

emptiness and hunger pangs play some role in regulating eating patterns, the major role is played by the hypothalamus in the brain. It monitors blood-sugar level and body fat content and stimulates or inhibits the hunger drive in order to keep these levels in the normal range.

5. Animals who have had portions of their hypothalamus destroyed become compulsive eaters and double or triple in weight. These *hyperphagic* animals no longer seem to be able to respond to *internal cues* for eating so instead depend on such *external cues* as the presence and taste of food. Schachter has suggested that, like hyperphagic rats, overweight humans base their eating habits on external cues, such as food taste and availability, rather than on internal cues, such as hunger pangs. However, other factors are also involved in human weight regulation.

6. *Thirst* seems to be an even stronger motive than hunger. The thirst drive is regulated by centers in the hypothalamus that monitor the level of salt in the bloodstream.

7. In lower animals the *sex drive* is strongly controlled by sex hormones, and it may be even stronger than the hunger and thirst drives. Psychological and social factors play a greater role than hormones in regulating human sexual behavior.

8. The drive reduction theory does not seem to apply to the competence motives. White sees competence as effective functioning in one's environment, which is reinforced by the feeling that one is a worthy human being. Competence seems to be a continuing, expanding motive rather than one like hunger, which comes and goes.

9. The desire to explore and master one's environment is seen in the play of human infants. Humans are motivated to explore new places and try new things. At some point, however, the curiosity motive gives way to fear of the unknown.

10. The desire to control one's own life is seen in the phenomenon of *psychological reactance*—the motive to reassert a threatened freedom. However, if one repeatedly finds that one has little influence on one's own life, *learned helplessness*—a resigned acceptance of one's own situation—may result.

11. The competence motives may also be categorized as *cognitive* motives, because they are based in people's higher mental processes. The strongest form of such cognitive motivation is that provided by *ideologies*, or systems of belief to which one has a strong commitment.

12. Some motives are unconscious. Freud felt that such *repressed* motives are sometimes revealed through slips of the tongue ("Freudian slips") or by other "accidental" means.

13. *Emotions* appear to have three elements: physiological changes, subjective feelings, and expressive behavior.

14. Physiological aspects of emotion are regulated by the autonomic nervous system. In both fear and anger, for example, sympathetic nerves shut down digestive functioning, metabolism speeds up, salivary glands stop working, sweat glands may overreact, and pupils may enlarge.

15. According to the *James-Lange theory*, an event or stimulus causes bodily changes, which in turn produce the subjective experience of emotion. One problem with this theory is that it falsely assumes that each emotion has its own characteristic pattern of physiological changes. According to the *Cannon-Bard theory*, the physiological changes occur simultaneously with the subjective experience.

16. Schachter has suggested that the experience of an emotion depends on what label a person puts on his physical arousal, and the label in turn depends on the particular situation in which the arousal occurs. Schachter's approach is called *cognitive labeling theory*.

17. The emotion of love can, in some situations, be explained in terms of the cognitive labeling approach. When people experience physiological arousal in the presence of a potential love object, they may label their arousal as love for this person.

18. According to Izard, infants are born with a range of distinctive emotional expressions. As children grow older, they come to experience a more complex range of emotions.

19. In their experiment with "Little Albert," Watson and Rayner demonstrated that through classical conditioning, people can learn to fear things that are not initially frightening.

20. People's particular emotions can also be influenced by their family and their culture, as illustrated by women's reactions to menstruation.

21. The case of *stress*, or pressures from one's environment, shows how emotions can be damaging to both physical and psychological health. Selye identified three stages in an organism's response to stress: the *alarm reaction*, the stage of *resistance*, and the stage of *exhaustion*.

22. Stress has been implicated in both chronic and infectious diseases. Diseases that are caused by stress or emotional problems are often called *psychosomatic*. For example, peptic ulcers are common among people in stressful occupations, such as air traffic controllers. The effects of stress can be reduced to some extent through adequate *social support*.

23. Brady's experiments showed that the stress of constant vigilance caused ulcers in "executive" monkeys who could prevent painful shocks only by pressing a lever in time. Weiss showed that "executive" rats in a similar experiment did not develop ulcers if they were given sufficient warning before being shocked.

24. For humans, the stressfulness of an event can be reduced if people feel they have some control over the event. In some situations, however, being in control may actually add to the stress.

25. Major life crises, such as death of a loved one, divorce, and retirement, can be highly stressful. Even positive events, such as marriage, can be stressful because they require people to readjust their life patterns.

WORK AND ACHIEVEMENT

thirds of these workers mentioned positive satisfactions with work, while about one-third felt that joblessness would make them feel lost, useless, and unable to decide what to do with their time. It seems that work is vital for many people; the job often becomes the organizing center of one's life. And

> *Eighty percent of workers said they would continue to work even if they didn't need to.*

unemployment can be a tragedy not only because of the loss of income but also because of the loss of a sense of purpose. As one unemployed woman told an interviewer:

Working on the job gave my time value. It gave my body value. It gave me value. (Maurer, 1979, page 290)

Most adult Americans spend at least one of every three waking hours working. We are part of a culture that weans us on fierce individualism, independence, the rags-to-riches myth, and a deep-rooted belief in achievement through imagination, energy, self-denial, and stick-to-itiveness. At the heart of our culture is the assumption that people can find pleasure in work. Thomas Carlyle declared in 1843, "Older than all preached Gospels was this unpreached, inarticulate, but ineradicable, forever-enduring Gospel: Work, and therein have well-being."

WHY WORK?

How does work provide this sense of well-being? If you can answer this question, you understand a lot about human motivation. To start with, a person who works can pur-

chase adequate food, shelter, and clothing and can contribute to the support of a family. So work helps people to satisfy their basic physical needs.

But work can contribute to psychological well-being, as well. Work is the prime arena in which many adults develop skills and show competence—and this, in turn, may lead to increased self-esteem. There are many other motives that may underlie a person's desire to work, including the inherent interest of the work, the opportunity to learn or use new ideas, and the opportunity to socialize with others.

In one study, researchers asked a sample of workers what they would do if they inherited enough money to let them stop working (Morse and Weiss, 1968). About 80 percent answered that they would continue to work anyway. Two-

INTRINSIC AND EXTRINSIC MOTIVATION

When you engage in an activity solely for the pleasure of it, psychologists say you are *intrinsically motivated*, since the activity is its own reward. If you do something for an outside reward, such as money or avoidance of punishment, you would be described as *extrinsically motivated*. People often receive both intrinsic and extrinsic rewards for doing a job; for example, they are paid for it, but they also enjoy the work itself. Sometimes, however, the promise of extrinsic rewards can reduce or undermine one's intrinsic motivation. For example, who do you think is likely to enjoy playing basketball more—a person who plays on an amateur team without pay, or a superstar who has just

signed a five-year, $3 million contract with a professional team? If you guessed that it is the amateur, there is evidence from laboratory studies that you are probably right.

Edward Deci (1975) used a three-dimensional puzzle to explore intrinsic and extrinsic motivation. He gave each subject four puzzle problems to solve. Half of the subjects were told they would get a dollar for each correct solution to a puzzle, while the other half were not paid for getting the right answers. After completing the four puzzles, each subject was left alone to do whatever he wished: read magazines, solve more puzzles, or do whatever interested him. Deci discovered that the money made a big difference. Subjects who had been paid spent significantly less time with the puzzles when they were alone and no more rewards were offered than did subjects who had worked the same puzzles for free. In other words, intrinsic motivation decreased when subjects had been given an external reward.

Why does external reward decrease intrinsic motivation? One explanation focuses on people's interpretations of their own behavior. Imagine asking one of Deci's subjects why he was working on the puzzle. The subjects who were not being paid would probably say, "Because I like to." The subjects who *were* being paid might say both "Because I like to" and "Because I earn money." In the later sessions when no reward was present, the unrewarded subjects would continue to play with the puzzle—after all, they "like to." But the rewarded subjects might not— after all, this time they wouldn't be rewarded. For similar reasons, a highly paid professional athlete may be less likely than an amateur to play "just for fun" during the off-season.

This *overjustification* explanation suggests that the presence of *any* extrinsic motivation or pressure should weaken existing intrinsic motivations. For example, if a little boy's behavior is closely observed by an adult, he may become less

A highly paid professional athlete may be unlikely to play "just for fun" during the off-season.

interested in what he is doing, since he can say to himself, "I'm only doing it because the teacher's watching" (Lepper and Greene, 1975). As we saw in the Psychological Issue following Chapter 6, knowing that one's work will be evaluated by others—leading to an extrinsic motivation to do well—

can also decrease people's creativity.

How do we resolve the problem of extrinsic pressures? Deci offers two solutions: (1) Create more activities that are inherently interesting and gratifying so that individuals may derive more satisfaction from their work and play, and (2) avoid using extrinsic rewards in ways that will lower people's interest in activities that are intrinsically motivating.

THE ACHIEVEMENT MOTIVE: DO A JOB RIGHT!

The *achievement motive* is the need to maintain or increase one's competence in activities in which a standard of excellence is thought to apply. One can either succeed or fail in such activities. The person who is highly motivated to achieve is one who will keep trying to succeed, by matching or exceeding her existing standard.

Who has the greater degree of intrinsic motivation—the high-paid professional (such as Reggie Jackson) or the unpaid amateur (such as Angela Lansbury in this softball game)?

People's achievement motivation has been measured by asking them to make up stories about a series of pictures. Some of these pictures come from a personality test called the Thematic Apperception Test, which we will discuss in Chapter 8. The four pictures originally used by David McClelland and colleagues (1953) depicted a work situation (a man at a machine), an academic situation (a boy at a desk), a father and son, and a boy who appeared to be daydreaming. Subjects are shown these pictures and are asked to tell what is happening at the moment, what led up to the situation, what is being thought, and what the outcome will be. Then the subjects' responses are scored for the number of achievement-related ideas or themes that their stories contain. For example, if a subject were to write the following as part

of his story about the boy who appears to be daydreaming, it would be coded as an achievement-related theme: "He is thinking about his ambition to become an astronaut and become the first person to visit Mars." In contrast, the following story would not be judged as achievement-related: "He is thinking about how much fun he had when he went to the beach with his family."

There is some controversy about this method of measuring achievement motivation. It turns out that when subjects are asked directly about their desire for achievement, their answers do not agree very closely with the themes that emerge in the stories they make up. People may not always be aware of the extent of their own achievement needs—and, if they are, they may not always want to admit them. McClelland believes

that the assessment of people's fantasies about achievement provides a less direct, but more useful measure of the strength of their achievement motives.

Why are some people high in the need for achievement, while others are low? Culture is clearly an influence. Some cultures put a greater emphasis than others on performance and excellence. In fact, McClelland (1961) discovered that the amount of achievement imagery in children's storybooks of thirty countries in the 1920s was related to the economic development in those countries 20 years later. The more achievement imagery in the stories, the greater the economic development. The cultural emphasis on achievement apparently led to harder work, which, in turn, led to greater economic progress.

There also seems to be a relation

between the achievement motive and childhood training. Marian Winterbottom (1953) found that the mothers of 8- to 10-year-old boys who were high in the need

Mothers of achievement-motivated boys had expected them to do things for themselves at an early age.

for achievement expected their children to have mastered at an early age such independent behaviors as obeying traffic signals, entertaining themselves, earning their own spending money, and choosing their own clothes. In contrast, mothers of boys low in need for achievement reported that they expected the same level of independence at a significantly later age.

In general, the higher a person's achievement motivation, the more likely he is to enter fields of work that involve risk and challenge, such as starting a small business, and to do better at such work (McClelland, 1971). In the light of this link between achievement motivation and business success, McClelland and David Winter (1969) set up a program to train small businessmen in India to be more achievement oriented, in an attempt to promote that country's economic growth. They reported that the program succeeded. The businessmen who were trained to think more about their personal standards of excellence started more new businesses, employed more workers, and increased the standard of living in their town, as compared with businessmen in another town who did not receive motivational training. Achieve-

ment-motivation training has also been used to improve small business performance and to increase employment among minorities in the United States (McClelland, 1978).

Are high achievers also the most competitive people? Recent research suggests that they are not. Janet Spence and Robert Helmreich have developed their own self-report measures of achievement motives, distinguishing among three separate motives:

1. *Work orientation*—the desire to work hard and do a good job.
2. *Mastery*—the preference for difficult and challenging tasks.
3. *Competitiveness*—the desire to win over others.

Spence and Helmreich have consistently found that the highest achievers are those people who are high in the work and mastery motives but *low* in competitiveness. This pattern of motives was found among college students who made the highest grades, business executives who made the highest salaries, and scientists who made the greatest scientific contributions (Spence, 1979). Spence speculates that competitiveness can interfere with achievement because it is mixed up with extrinsic motives,

The highest achievers may be high in work and mastery motives, but low in competitiveness.

such as outdoing one's peers in salary and prestige. As we saw earlier, such extrinsic motives can dampen one's interest in the task itself and, as a result, can diminish one's success.

WOMEN AND SUCCESS

Almost all of the initial research on the achievement motive was done with male subjects. After all, men are the ones who have traditionally been taught to achieve and get ahead in our society, while women have traditionally been taught to emphasize other motives and traits, such as nurturance and sociability. Matina Horner (1972) has suggested that many women have actually learned to *fear* success as being somehow unfeminine and, as a result, threatening.

In Horner's research, male and female college students were asked to complete a story about a man or a woman who was apparently meeting with great success. The story for a woman began:

After first-term finals, Anne finds herself at the top of her medical school class.

For men, the name "John" was substituted for "Anne." In her initial study, conducted in 1965, Horner found that 65 percent of the women but only 9 percent of the men told stories that reflected negative attitudes or conflict about the person's success. Many of the stories revealed a fear of social rejection, such as:

Anne will deliberately lower her academic standing the next term, while she does all she subtly can to help [her boyfriend] Carl. (Horner, 1968, page 60)

Other women's story completions reflected the fear that a successful woman in a traditionally male sphere is somehow abnormal. For example:

Anne is completely ecstatic but at the same time feels guilty. . . . She will finally have a nervous breakdown and quit med school. (Horner, 1968, page 61)

Horner found that those women

In the past decade, women have made great strides toward equal opportunity in the business and professional worlds.

who scored highest in fear of success, as measured by their story completions, performed poorly on tests of verbal ability (such as listing as many smaller words as you can that can be made out of the letters in the word *university*) when the tests were administered under competitive conditions. When you fear success, it appears, the possibility that you will outdo someone else is threatening enough to depress your performance.

There is no doubt that women have sometimes avoided achievements in traditional male spheres for fear that achieving too much would cost them popularity. Judith Bardwick, who is now a prominent psychologist, recalls her furious reaction as a college student when her name appeared in a college newspaper on a list of students who had earned an *A* average: "I was enraged, told the newspaper office 'they had some nerve,' and in general carried on outrageously. And the reason, which I was fully aware of, was my fear that now the girls would dislike me and the boys would be afraid of me. In other words, my academic success

would shoot my social life down" (1971, page 179).

In the past decade, however, things seem to have changed. Fewer college women exhibited fear of success in their story completions during the 1970s than during the 1960s—and, at the same time, fear of success seems to have increased among men (Hoffman, 1977). As we will see in Chapter 13, moreover, during the 1970s women

> *In the past decade, fear of success has decreased in women and increased in men.*

made great advances in the occupational world, with many more women entering such previously "male" occupations as medicine, law, and business. Whereas "Anne" would have been one of the few women in her medical school class in 1965, thus adding to her anxieties, she would have many more female classmates in the 1980s. Rather than being a

deeply ingrained aspect of women's personalities, the fear of success seems to reflect a society's expectations for achievement—or nonachievement—in certain spheres.

Whether or not a person will fear success in any domain will depend on her cultural values and on the way these values are communicated to her. "In 1972," P. S. Wood (1980) reports in the *New York Times Magazine*, "a lone girl entrant flashed across the finish line first in a local soapbox derby. Presented with her prize, she burst into tears, 'I didn't want to win,' she apologized. Five years later, another competitor, Janet Guthrie, became the first woman driver to qualify for the Indianapolis 500, and publicly thanked her parents 'for not bringing me up thinking I couldn't do something because I was a woman.'"

SUMMARY

1. The motivation to work comes from the desire to fulfill both physical and psychological needs.

2. Motivation may be intrinsic (the activity is rewarding in itself), extrinsic (an outside reward is required), or both. In some cases an extrinsic reward may decrease intrinsic motivation.

3. The level of one's achievement motive appears to be influenced by one's culture and by one's childhood training. High achievers tend to be high in the motives of work orientation and mastery but low in competitiveness.

4. Horner found that in the 1960s women exhibited a fear of success, perhaps because success was not considered feminine. In the past decade, however, women's fear of success has been reduced as they have made greater advances in the work world.

Chapter 8

Personality

Imagine you are in a restaurant, looking around at some of the people ordering, eating, and drinking. You notice that one woman sits right down, calls the waiter, and places her order without even looking at the menu. When the food arrives, she puts salt and ketchup on it without tasting it first. Then a man comes in. He spends a long time looking around trying to decide where to sit—he almost sits at one table, then tries another, and finally sits (without much assurance) at a third. Before ordering, he seems to consider every item on the menu, and after placing his order he proceeds to call back the waiter and change the order two different times. Some of the other diners exhibit still other patterns of behavior. When the waiter says that one of the items on the menu is not available, one patron gets furious while another smiles understandingly and orders something else. Some seem to savor every bit of food, letting it slowly roll around in their mouths; others seem to gulp the food down without tasting it. Some are sociable and talkative, others sit by themselves in silence.

In a restaurant, as in many other situations, each of us seems to have a distinctive temperament and style of behaving. We each have our own concerns, priorities, likes and dislikes, and ways of dealing with conflict and frustration. These differences between people are a central focus of the study of personality.

Personality refers to the distinctive patterns of behavior, thoughts, and emotions that characterize the individual's adaptation to the situations of his or her life (Mischel, 1976). In studying personality, we want to know how any given person is unique. But we are also interested in the ways in which people resemble one another and

in understanding how both the differences and the similarities come about.

Many psychologists have attempted to answer these questions about personality, and they have come up with a variety of theories and approaches. Each of the theories that we will discuss in this chapter reflects a particular conception of personality. In addition, different theorists use different methods for studying personality. Some make primary use of detailed individual case studies. They may interview the person intensively, give the person a series of personality tests, and try to understand the person's unique pattern of traits as fully as possible. This focus on the detailed study of individuals is called the *idiographic* approach to personality. A leading advocate of the idiographic approach was Gordon Allport (1962), who also suggested that psychologists study the individual personality through personal documents such as diaries, calendar books, personal letters.

Other personality researchers take a different approach. Instead of probing deeply into the personality of a single individual, they conduct experiments or administer tests to large numbers of people. By analyzing the relations between test scores and behaviors within such large samples of people, they hope to learn more about the similarities and differences between people. Such attempts to discover general patterns of personality reflect a *nomothetic* approach to personality. In practice, however, elements of the idiographic and nomothetic approaches can be combined in order to achieve an understanding of both individual uniqueness and more general patterns of similarities and differences between people.

FREUD'S PSYCHOANALYTIC THEORY

Sigmund Freud devised the best-known and most widely studied of all the personality theories, *psychoanalytic theory*. Freud believed that instinctual biological urges furnish the psychic energy that motivates every aspect of a person's behavior. Because these impulses, primarily sexual and aggressive, are strongly disapproved of by society, they are *repressed*—banished from conscious awareness. Yet these unconscious forces continue to dominate our personality and behavior.

From Freud's viewpoint, people begin life as biological organisms but become fully civilized and human by taming their biology. But the need to subdue biological impulses inevitably leads to emotional conflicts. Freud's model of personality depicts people as creatures who are perpetually at war with themselves.

Sigmund Freud in 1922.

— Box 1 —

Sigmund Freud

Born in Moravia (now Czechoslovakia) in 1856, Sigmund Freud was the son of middle-class Jewish parents. Freud's family emigrated to Vienna, Austria, when he was three, and he spent most of his life there. Although the Freuds were quite poor during Sigmund's childhood, he managed to obtain funds from a Jewish philanthropic society in order to begin medical study at the University of Vienna in 1873.

After receiving his medical degree, Freud opened a practice as a neurologist. But his interests soon came to center on the psychological rather than the physical aspects of mental disturbance. As a young physician, Freud treated many cases of hysteria, an emotional disorder in which patients suffered physical symptoms such as twitches, paralyses, and even blindness without any discernible physical basis. At first Freud treated these patients by hypnotizing them and suggesting that the symptoms would disappear. Hypnosis seemed to work, but the cures were only partial or temporary.

Freud then began to use the "cathartic" method developed by his friend Josef Breuer. In this method, the patient was asked—usually while under hypnosis—to recall the first time she experienced a symptom. This often led to a report of a highly emotional, anxiety-arousing experience earlier in life that the patient had forgotten. Once the patient could recapture the experience and "relive" the emotion felt at the time, the symptoms were likely to disappear. (Such expression of a bottled-up emotion is called *catharsis*.) Later Freud replaced the use

Sigmund Freud and his fiancée.

of hypnosis in his treatment with the method of *free association*, in which the patient is encouraged to say whatever comes to mind, without holding anything back. (Freud's approach to therapy is discussed in further detail in Chapter 12.)

Freud's continuing work with his patients gradually led him to his theory that repressed memories and wishes lie at the base of emotional disorder, and that personality involves a perpetual conflict between different mental forces. Between 1895 and 1900 Freud published several major works, spelling out his ideas about anxiety and the defense mechanisms that we use to control it and touching on the ideas of infantile sexuality and hostility against one's parents. In his book *The Interpretation of Dreams*, published in 1900, he developed these ideas further, making use of patients' dreams to probe their unconscious motives.

Most of Freud's work was ignored by scientists until 1905, when he proceeded to publish a much more explicit account of his theory of sexuality in infants and children. *Three Essays on the Theory of Sexuality* shocked the intel-

Freud grew up in the sexually repressed Victorian climate of nineteenth-century Austria (see Box 1). Perhaps that's why his initial theories of human psychology emphasized people's sexual urges. Later on, after he had lived through the horrors of World War I, Freud was so struck by the spectacle of millions of young men marching to their deaths that he modified his theory to include aggressive urges, as well. In Freud's later work, the "death" instincts (including aggression) held a place of prominence equal to that of the "life" instincts (including sex).

In addition to his emphasis on unconscious instincts and motives, Freud placed a major emphasis on the shaping of personality in the early years of life. He believed that the personality is almost fully formed by the time a child enters school, and that personality development after this time consists of elaborating and refining the basic structure.

Freud and his family. The 22-year-old Freud is standing behind his mother.

lectuals of nineteenth-century Vienna, and Freud quickly became the most unpopular scientist of his day. At the same time, Freud attracted a band of brilliant disciples, some of whom (such as Carl Jung and Alfred Adler) went on to develop major psychological theories of their own. Freud continued to expand and modify his theories throughout life. His model of the three mental forces of id, ego, and superego, representing a significant revision of some of his earlier work, was published in 1923, when Freud was 67.

Most of Freud's books were severely criticized by other scientists primarily because his speculations attacked many previously unquestioned beliefs. Toward the end of his life, however, Freud began to receive the recognition he deserved for his courageous exploration of the human mind. He was initiated into several scientific societies, received the Goethe Award for his writing, and was made a corresponding member of the prestigious Royal Society on his 80th birthday.

During this period of recognition, the Nazi persecutions had caused many of Freud's supporters to flee Germany, and Freud's books were confiscated and burned in Berlin. When the Nazis invaded Austria in 1938, Freud was persuaded to emigrate to England. One year later, a recurring cancer of the mouth from which Freud had suffered since 1923 terminated his life.

Freud is now universally viewed as one of the great thinkers of modern times. His psychoanalytic theory profoundly influenced psychologists of all theoretical persuasions, has been a dominant force in therapy, and has had a major impact on other disciplines, such as sociology, anthropology, and history. Many ideas that Freud developed have become part of our everyday vocabulary—repression, superego, Oedipus complex, death wish, and many others. In short, Freud has been one of the few people in history to exert a major impact on the way people think about themselves.

The Structure of Personality

For Freud, each person's personality consists of three elements that he labeled the id, the ego, and the superego—three distinct but interrelated systems of psychological functioning. The *id*, according to Freud, is the reservoir of basic biological urges that motivate the individual. The id is hunger, thirst, sexual impulses, and other needs that assure survival or bring pleasure or relief from pain and discomfort. The id remains an unchanging, powerful, active force throughout life, but its insistent demands are tempered and controlled by the ego. The actions of the id usually remain unconscious and out of our awareness.

The *ego* moderates and controls the id by requiring it to seek gratification within realistic and socially acceptable bounds. If the id wants to destroy another human being who is frustrating the id's quest for gratification, the ego decides whether or not this can be done easily and safely. Unlike the id, most of the ego's actions are conscious. The ego thus acts like an executive who sees to it that the gratification of impulses will not be painful, dangerous, or destructive to the organism.

The *superego* is that force within the self that acquires the values and ideals of parents and society. The superego is the moral part of the self. It looks to the ideal rather than the real, to what ought to be rather than what is. Further, the superego limits the sexual or aggressive impulses of the id. It pressures the ego to respond to socially approved moral goals rather than impulse-gratifying ones.

In this three-part structure, the ego mediates between the impulses of the id and the controls of the superego. The id powers the human vehicle, the ego steers it on a safe course, and the superego insists that the ego obey the traffic laws. As we will see, the conflict of id, ego, and superego causes anxiety, which, in turn, creates defense mechanisms.

GUILT

Guilt, in Freud's view, is the way our superego punishes us for violating its standards. We can feel guilty for a wide range of "transgressions," from actually harming another person to just thinking unacceptable thoughts. Some people feel guilty when they act assertive, or if they survive a plane crash in which others perished, or if they fail to realize their potential. Some therapists regard guilt as a destructive force and seem bent on erasing it from their patients' minds. But most psychologists distinguish between the "neurotic guilt" that one would best be rid of and the "normal guilt" that is a valuable part of our personalities because it helps us to enforce our positive values (Adams, 1979).

In Freud's theory, the superego is the part of the personality that pressures the ego to behave in socially approved and moral ways.

Psychosexual Development

To the staid Victorians of Freud's time, his theory seemed outrageous, because it emphasized the importance of sexual drives not only in adults but also in infants and children. Freud's concept of the sexual urge was very broad, however. In fact, his theory deals with not one but three separate pleasure-giving areas of the body. These areas, known as the *erogenous zones*, include the oral zone (mouth, lips, tongue), the anal zone, and the genital zone (penis or vagina). In each case, physical stimulation of the zone can be highly pleasurable, and it is such pleasure that Freud equated with sexuality.

As the child goes through successive stages of development, the different erogenous zones become prominent—first the oral, then the anal, then the genital. And the way in which a child goes through these *psychosexual stages* is a major determinant of personality in later life. For example, if a child receives too much gratification (is overindulged) or too little gratification (is deprived or frustrated) at the earlier stages, he may become *fixated* at that stage—his sexual impulses may stay focused on that stage, and his character structure may reflect the unresolved difficulties of that period. This idea will become clearer as we discuss each of Freud's developmental stages: the oral, anal, phallic, latency, and genital stages.

The Oral Stage. The oral stage, in the first year of life, is the first stage in the child's psychosexual development. According to Freud, during the oral stage the child's sexual energies are focused on the mouth area, in such activities as feeding, sucking, chewing, and biting. Psychologically, the child at the oral stage has to deal with issues of oral gratification, personal dependence, and trust, because he must depend on and trust adults for his sustenance. Freud believed an infant who passes successfully through the oral stage will develop into an adult who is able to enjoy oral gratification but is not obsessed with it. Such a person will be basically trusting of other people but not overly dependent on them. But Freud also believed that infants can become fixated in the oral stage if they find being fed *too* pleasurable or if nursing is painful or frustrating. Overgratification at the sucking stage can lead to an unreasonably self-assured adult, whereas a painful sucking period can produce excessive dependency in the adult. Frustration during the oral stage might also lead to aggressive oral habits, such as sarcasm or verbal hostility in later life.

The Anal Stage. During the anal stage, in the second year of life, the child's sexual energies focus around the anus and the act of defecation. This is the period of toilet training. When children are toilet trained, they acquire for the first time the power to resist their parents' demands. They can decide for themselves whether or not to defecate and whether or not to satisfy their parents' desires. The central psychological issues of the anal stage involve giving and holding back, cleanliness and messiness, and dominance and subservience. An infant who passes successfully through the anal stage should, according to Freud, develop into an adult who is flexible rather than obstinate or submissive, generous rather than stingy or a spendthrift, and tidy rather than fastidious or messy.

If too much anxiety is present at toilet training, the child may

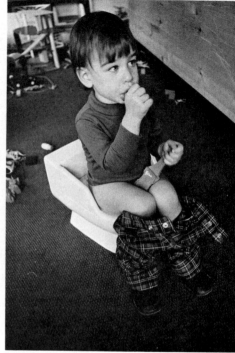

A   B

grow up to be compulsively clean and orderly and may become intolerant of those who fail to be the same. To ensure that everything is tidy in his life, a man may dictate to others and enforce severe and arbitrary rules much like those his parents imposed upon him. If the parents lose in the toilet-training contest and the child learns he can always get his way, he may develop a lifelong pattern of self-assertion, negativism, personal untidiness, and dominance over others.

The Phallic Stage. In the phallic stage of development (about ages 3 to 5), the sex organs become the focus of attention. The key event in this stage, Freud believed, is the child's feeling of sexual attraction toward the opposite-sex parent, together with envy of the same-sex parent. Freud labeled this situation, and the psychological conflicts it produces, the *Oedipus complex*, alluding to the Greek myth about Oedipus, who killed his father and married his mother, unaware of their true identity. Of course, falling in love with one's mother and killing one's father represents an extreme pathological resolution to the Oedipus conflict. But Freud believed that all children have to resolve such a conflict in one way or another and that the way one goes about doing so has a large impact on subsequent personality development.

According to Freud, the boy at this stage fears that his father will find out about his desire to replace him and will punish him by castrating him; this fear is called *castration anxiety*. If the Oedipus conflict is adequately managed, the boy learns to control his envy, fear, and hostility toward his father. He identifies with his father's power and masculinity and converts them into motivation for accomplishment in life. Now the boy wants to be like his father—to be an active, assertive male. This identification also leads to the development of

In Freud's oral stage (A), pleasure is focused on the mouth area. In the anal stage (B), the child develops control over a basic bodily function, thereby developing control over other things in his life as well. During the phallic stage (C), the child feels attraction toward his opposite-sex parent, while during the latency period (D), sexual energy is focused away from erogenous zones and the child's attention is turned to school and play. Sexuality resurfaces in the genital stage (E), when the adolescent becomes interested in heterosexual relationships.

C

D

E

Freud's psychoanalytic theory **255**

the superego—the boy incorporates parental ideals and values into his own personality. Failure to resolve the Oedipus conflict means growing up with an intense fear that a powerful and jealous father might punish the boy for his feelings toward his mother. The boy who fails to resolve the conflict will, Freud believed, become a man who is timid, passive, and effeminate.

What about girls? Well, to be honest, Freud hardly thought about the problem of female psychosexual development until after he had worked out the Oedipus cycle for boys. As a result, his theory of the Oedipus complex, expanded to include girls (for them called the *Electra complex*), seems rather strained. According to Freud, girls start, as boys do, loving their mother and resenting their father—because the father is a rival for the mother's attention. During the phallic stage, however, girls realize that they are lacking the more desirable sexual organ: the penis. As a result of "penis envy," the girl then becomes attracted to her father as a love object. But eventually the girl must renounce her attraction to her father and, if the Electra conflict is successfully resolved, decide to identify with her mother and find another man to replace her father as a sex object.

Freud's notion of the Oedipus complex and its resolution, even though it may sound a bit far-fetched, provides an explanation for the learning of sex roles (to be discussed in Chapter 13). Adherents of Freud's theory add that the reason that this sequence of early life events seems far-fetched is that, because the conflict is so full of threat and anxiety, we adults have had to banish it from consciousness.

The Latency Period. At the end of the phallic stage (at about age 5), the child enters a period of psychosexual latency. During this period, Freud believed, the child's attention is turned away from particular erogenous zones, previous sexual feelings are forgotten, and sexual urges lie dormant.

The Genital Stage. At puberty, when sexual interest is reawakened, the child enters the genital stage. During this stage, sexual energies are again focused on the genital organs—the penis and the vagina. This is the stage of adult heterosexual relationships. Freud didn't have very much to say about the genital stage; it's as if he thought that if you made it through the oral, anal, and phallic periods, you would be O.K. Freud's analysis of "adult" problems almost always involved presumed fixations at the earlier oral, anal, and phallic stages.

Anxiety and Defense Mechanisms

Anxiety is an exceptionally uncomfortable experience that is hard to cope with because it has no easily identifiable source. Freud believed that anxiety stems from people's unconscious fear that their instincts will cause them to do something they will be punished for. When the pressure of anxiety is excessive and cannot be relieved by practical, problem-solving methods, the ego must use maneuvers called *defense mechanisms*. Defense mechanisms have two primary characteristics. First, they deny, falsify, or distort reality. Second, they operate unconsciously, so that the person is not aware of them. Complex

THE PATH TO CIVILIZATION

Freud suggested that the development of civilization became possible when the energy of human beings was freed from basic survival needs. Converting primitive impulses to civilized ends is not always completely satisfying, however, and the tensions of being civilized periodically produce explosive behavior such as war. Imperfect as it may be, the ability to "sublimate" our impulses makes possible the ideas, values, attitudes, and activity that characterize the civilized adult human being (Freud, 1930).

defensive maneuverings begin in the early years of childhood as we deal with the many threats, conflicts, and frustrations that are a part of growing up. The outcome of the way we handle hundreds and thousands of little contests with anxiety and frustration sets the pattern of adult behavior we call personality. It will help us to understand Freud's developmental theory if we look briefly at how some of the defense mechanisms work.

Repression. Repression, the most basic and probably the most widely used defense mechanism, is the exclusion of unacceptable unconscious impulses from consciousness. For instance, you might repress agressive impulses toward your spouse, or sexual urges toward somebody else's spouse, because of the anxiety such urges would produce if allowed into consciousness.

Projection. Projection is the unconscious attribution of one's own thoughts and feelings to other people. These thoughts, feelings, and impulses are projected onto someone else because they would create anxiety if attributed to oneself. Thus, the censor who thinks modern movies are filthy may be concealing his own strong interest in such sexual activity—an interest that would produce anxiety if allowed into consciousness.

Reaction Formation. Reaction formation is the development of behavior patterns that are the opposite of those that might create anxiety. For instance, a person with strong unconscious aggressive urges might become a pacifist; an individual with a taste for whiskey might join a temperance movement. Through reaction formation, the individual is able to avoid the anxiety that would be produced if unacceptable impulses like these were actually brought into consciousness.

Displacement. Sometimes the object that will gratify an instinctual urge is not accessible. In such a situation, the urge may be displaced or redirected toward a substitute object. If a young man unconsciously desires to sleep with his mother, he will look for a woman who resembles his mother instead. If an executive is angry at her superior, she may displace her aggressive urge by yelling at her secretary. Substitute objects are rarely as satisfying as the original objects, but they are also less anxiety arousing.

Rationalization. Rationalization, one of the most common defense mechanisms, can be described as the attempt to substitute "good" reasons for our real reasons. We use rationalization to conceal from ourselves the fact that we have acted from motives that conflict with our standards. The man who mistreats his wife may rationalize his behavior by claiming that she needs a strong, dominant male as a mate. Or, if we fail at something we set out to do, we may insist that we didn't really try or that we didn't really want to do it in the first place.

Intellectualization. Through intellectualization, anxiety is dismissed by analyzing emotional issues intellectually and converting them to theory rather than action. By intellectualizing, problems become detached from the self and removed from unpleasant emotional consequences. Discussions in college dorms and coffee shops over questions of love and sex may be examples of such intellectualization.

Defense mechanisms are designed to help us escape the pain of anxiety. Most of us would not survive very well without occasionally resorting to such defenses. The trouble is that after sufficient practice they may become habitual, characteristic patterns of reacting to conflict; indeed, they may become permanent character traits. As a result, the use of defense mechanisms to deal with anxiety and conflict can sometimes be costly. We will return to the psychic costs of defense mechanisms in Chapter 11, when we discuss anxiety disorders.

Evaluating Freud's Theory

When Freud's ideas began to sweep the Western world in the 1930s, there was virtually no proof of their validity. Nevertheless, "the unexpected insight and scope of Freud's ideas armored them with an almost self-evident power of truth" (Greenberg and Fisher, 1978). But Freud had not really been in a good position to present scientifically convincing evidence. His theory was based on his observations of a limited number of patients and, like all personal observations, they were highly susceptible to bias and distortion.

It is not easy to evaluate psychoanalytic theory scientifically, because it typically does not make specific predictions about personality that can be tested. Consider, for example, Freud's suggestion that if a nursing baby is afraid her mother will reject or leave her, she will develop a fixation at the oral stage that will lead to an adult with an *oral-dependent* character structure. Such an adult takes a passive, dependent attitude toward the world. She expects to have things given to her when she is good and taken from her when she is bad, instead of learning to satisfy her needs through her own efforts. But does everyone who experiences oral anxiety in infancy develop such a character structure? Well, no. Because dependency of this sort is likely to arouse anxiety, such a person may also develop a character structure that defends against dependency. One person may make use of reaction formation, leading her to resist being dependent on anyone; she can't ask for anything, because that would call forth the anxiety. Another person may use the defense of projection and see *other* people as dependent and feel obligated to help them; such a person may enter a helping profession such as nursing or public service law (Hall, 1954).

Because of the abundance of possibilities, psychoanalytic theory cannot predict the outcome of a particular set of early childhood experiences. Freud himself recognized this limitation: "We never know beforehand which of the determining factors will prove the weaker or the stronger. We only say at the end that those which succeeded must have been the stronger" (1933, page 227). This state of affairs creates a problem for Freud's theory; almost anything can be neatly explained after the fact, while almost nothing can be predicted ahead of time.

Despite the difficulty of testing psychoanalytic theory, there is considerable evidence for the validity of some of Freud's central ideas, including unconscious motives and conflicts, the impact of early life events on later personality, and the role of defense mechanisms in handling anxiety. Most psychologists now believe, however, that Freud overemphasized sexual and aggressive instincts as the sole source of motivation and that he underestimated the potential for continuing personality development and change after the childhood years. As we will see, his ideas have been adapted and revised by later theorists, as Freud himself surely would have done as additional evidence became available.

Roger Greenberg and Seymour Fisher (1977) recently reviewed thousands of studies that have attempted to evaluate aspects of Freud's theory. The evidence, in a word, is mixed. On the topic of the Oedipus complex, for example, studies indicate that children generally do have to cope with erotic feelings toward the opposite-sex parent and hostility toward the same-sex parent, as Freud suggested. But there is little proof that Oedipal problems come to the fore at ages 4 to 5. And boys don't seem to develop a conscience primarily out of fear of castration or other punishment, as Freud theorized. Parental nurturance and warmth seem to be at least as important in moral development. On the basis of their overall review, Greenberg and Fisher concluded: "Psychoanalysis is not an entity that must be totally accepted or rejected as a package. It is a complex structure consisting of many parts, some of which should be accepted, others rejected, and the rest at least partially reshaped" (page 28).

THE PSYCHOANALYTIC DISSENTERS

Freud attracted an inner circle of followers interested in establishing the discipline of psychoanalysis. In 1902, Alfred Adler and a few other Viennese physicians gathered on Wednesday nights at Freud's home, beginning the first Psychoanalytic Society. In 1907, Carl Jung, a Swiss psychiatrist, joined the exclusive group. Before long, a series of theoretical conflicts occurred, and Adler and Jung each left the group to go his own theoretical way.

Carl Jung

Jung applied the psychological insights gained from Freud to the material that fascinated him when he was young—myths, fables, and ancient legends. These interests then flavored his interpretation of human nature. Once considered Freud's "crown prince," Jung became a dissident renegade whose views struck a more responsive chord among philosophers and poets than among psychiatrists.

Personality, for Jung, is a product of the balance achieved between conscious and unconscious forces. Jung's conception of the unconscious, however, differed from that of Freud. Jung distinguished two levels of the unconscious: (1) the *personal unconscious*, which encompasses repressed or forgotten material, and (2) the *collective unconscious*, a part of the human psyche that is filled with "primordial images," or "archetypes." The collective unconscious is common to all humans, having developed in the course of our evolution as a species. It includes representations of such universal human experiences as mothers, the earth, and even the caves in which we once lived. Jung believed that these unconscious forces and images are a central part of the healthy personality. Jung also put forth a

Carl Jung.

theory of personality types that we will discuss in the next section of this chapter.

Alfred Adler

Adler developed an *ego psychology* that focused on real or imagined feelings of inferiority. In fact, he was the inventor of the term *inferiority complex*. Adler had overcome a series of handicaps early in his own life. Because of rickets, he did not walk until age 4; he then developed pneumonia, which was followed by a series of accidents. These experiences suggested to him that people rely heavily on their brains as a means of compensating for felt inferiority. In the Adlerian system of psychology, security is accomplished by denying one's feelings of inferiority through the attainment of some master goal in life. Because much of human achievement is accomplished through our social interactions, Adler gives the social community a key position in healthy psychic life.

Alfred Adler.

The Neo-Freudians

Several other psychoanalytic theorists, referred to as *neo-Freudians*, were strongly influenced by Freud's theory but gave less priority to the role of instinctual drives and to fixed stages of development. Rather than viewing all human motives as derived from the biological urges of the id, they emphasized people's strivings to form satisfying social relationships and to fulfill their unique potentials. The neo-Freudians also gave greater attention than Freud did to the influence of society and culture in shaping human personality. One of the most widely known neo-Freudians, Erich Fromm (1900–1980), insisted that ideals like truth, justice, and freedom were genuine human strivings, not just rationalizations of baser motives. In his book *Escape from Freedom* (1941), Fromm noted that in modern society people often obtain personal freedom at the cost of a feeling of separateness and aloneness.

Among the other neo-Freudians, Karen Horney focused on people's needs for acceptance and for independence in their social relationships. Harry Stack Sullivan also emphasized the importance of social relationships, including those with friends as well as within the family, in shaping personality. And Erik Erikson, whose views will be discussed in Chapter 9, reformulated Freud's theory of psychosexual stages to encompass the entire life span. In addition to the influence of their work in its own right, the neo-Freudians provided an important bridge between Freudian theory and the more recent humanistic theories, to be discussed later in this chapter.

TYPE THEORIES

Long before Freud and his followers came along—in fact, long before there were *any* professional psychologists—physicians, philosophers, and ordinary people were sorting the people they encountered into *types.* Some people were considered pessimists or cynics, others were worrywarts or ne'er-do-wells. Each type of person presumably possessed one central characteristic that influenced a broad range of her behaviors. Classifying a person as a particular type made that person's behavior easier to predict and explain.

In one of the most time-honored type theories the ancient Greek physician Hippocrates proposed that there were four basic temperaments: choleric (irritable), melancholic (depressed), sanguine (optimistic), and phlegmatic (listless). Everyone supposedly fit into one of these four types. Hippocrates believed that each type was related to a predominance of one of the four bodily "humors," or fluids. The choleric type had too much yellow bile, the melancholic type too much black bile, the sanguine type too much blood, and the phlegmatic type too much phlegm.

Hippocrates' theory may seem primitive to us, but the notion that people's personality and their physical make-up are related persists even today. We often guess that fat people are jolly and that thin people are nervous and shy. Men who are powerful and muscular seem bold, extraverted, and confident. Many early personality theories were rooted in observations of a relationship between physical and psychological types.

Physique and Personality

William H. Sheldon (1940, 1954) classified human body types along three basic dimensions: ectomorphy, mesomorphy, and endomorphy. In his system of rating body build, the *ectomorph* is thin, long-boned, poorly muscled, and delicate; the *mesomorph* is well muscled and athletically built; and the *endomorph* is heavy and fat (Figure 8.1). A person's *somatotype* (or body type) reflects the contribution of each of these three dimensions to an overall description of physical structure. In assigning somatotype ratings Sheldon took into account many types of measurements that don't vary with diet or exercise, such as the length and width of major bones.

After developing his method for rating body types, Sheldon spent years interviewing and observing a group of young male sub-

FIGURE 8.1

The human body types identified by Sheldon. He believed that each body type was associated with a particular pattern of personality.

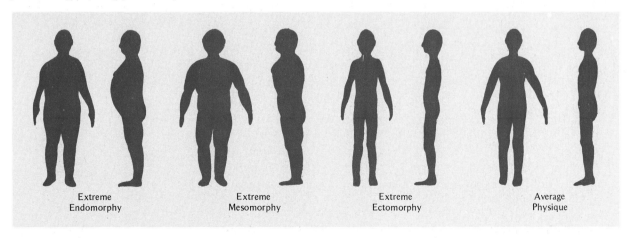

| Extreme Endomorphy | Extreme Mesomorphy | Extreme Ectomorphy | Average Physique |

jects. In the end, he reported an association between somatotype and personality. According to Sheldon the delicate ectomorphs are sensitive, solitary and cerebral; the muscular mesomorphs are assertive, daring, and independent; and the heavy endomorphs are relaxed, self-indulgent, and approval seeking. Many psychologists today are quite skeptical of Sheldon's specific conclusions. Nevertheless, the notion that there are links between physique and personality remains a plausible one.

Jung's Types

Unlike Hippocrates or Sheldon, Jung (1921) developed a theory of psychological types that avoids making connections between personality and physique. Jung developed the concepts of introvert and extravert as types. The *introvert* prefers to be alone and avoids people. He reacts to stress by crawling into his shell. The *extravert* is sociable and outgoing. He resorts to stress by seeking out others. Jung argued that every individual possesses innate mechanisms for both introversion and extraversion. In some circumstances, the mechanism for extraversion dominates and the individual behaves as an extravert; in other circumstances, the mechanism for introversion dominates and the individual behaves as an introvert. However, for some reason the dominance of one mechanism sometimes becomes chronic in some people. These people become types, either introverts or extraverts. Instead of displaying the normal variations in behavior that most people exhibit, these types behave in pretty much the same way in most situations.

Jung's approach to psychological types is quite flexible compared, for example, to that of Hippocrates. According to Jung, people don't necessarily fit into one type or another. The mechanisms of introversion and extraversion are within us all, complementing and usually counterbalancing each other. A person becomes a "type" only when one of the mechanisms wins permanent dominance.

Critique of Type Theories

Type theories have been of relatively little use in the study of human personality. A theory of types is useful only if it can be applied to a broad range of people. Hippocrates thought he could classify *everybody* as choleric, melancholic, sanguine, or phlegmatic. But people are too complex to be forced into such simple boxes. People are not always irritable, depressed, optimistic, or listless. There are innumerable other ways they can behave, and they can behave in more than one way at once. Furthermore, the same person may behave differently in different situations. So, the only reasonable use of types is as labels for extremes. Jung's introverts and extraverts, for example, are the extreme exceptions rather than the rule. But a theory of types that applies only to extremes doesn't take us far enough in predicting or explaining the endless variety in human personality, both within individuals and between them.

TRAIT THEORIES

In contrast to type theories, in which people are assigned to one category *or* another, trait theories of personality view people in many dimensions simultaneously. Each trait is a quality or characteristic that some people have more of than others. Some of the numerous traits that psychologists have postulated are dependency, emotionality, aggressiveness, and anxiety. Trait theorists are concerned with identifying the most important traits on which people can be compared and with developing reliable ways to measure them. These measurement techniques include self-ratings (in which you might be asked directly how "aggressive" or how "dependent" you think you are), peer ratings (in which you might be asked to answer the same questions regarding your roommate), and a variety of other psychological tests (see Box 2).

Gordon Allport (1961) was a leading trait theorist. Allport distinguished between what he called common and individual traits in the structure of personality. *Common traits* appear in different amounts in all people. *Individual traits* are characteristics that appear in only a small number of individuals. Dependency, for example, might be a common trait on which people can be compared. Various tests and ratings might reveal that some people are extremely dependent, some are moderately dependent, and others are not dependent at all. In contrast, the characteristic of being able to receive satisfaction from continually refining one's written prose may be an individual trait—one that is highly important to some people but on which large numbers of people cannot be meaningfully compared.

In addition to common and individual traits, Allport also emphasized that each individual has her own unique combination of traits. Thus, one person might be both highly dependent and highly aggressive, a second might be highly dependent and only moderately aggressive, and a third might be highly dependent and not aggressive at all. Allport believed it is important, therefore, to conduct intensive studies of individuals (the idiographic method) in order to understand the ways in which particular combinations of traits fit together.

While concentrating on description and measurement, trait theorists have paid relatively little attention to the origins of a person's traits—for example, in early life experiences. Some trait theorists have been interested, however, in assessing the stability of people's traits through the course of life. In one well-known longitudinal study (Thomas, Chess, and Birch, 1970), researchers found some degree of consistency between babies' temperamental styles ("easy," "slow to warm up," and "difficult") and their temperaments in childhood and adolescence. These researchers believe that the differences in the babies' dispositions are biological and that they may be hereditary. Other researchers have explored the hereditary aspects of personality by administering personality tests to pairs of relatives—for example, to pairs of identical and fraternal twins. Such studies have demonstrated that some personality traits, such as anxiety and dependency, as measured by tests such as the MMPI (see Box 2), have at least some genetic basis (Dworkin et al., 1976).

IDENTICAL PERSONALITIES?

In an effort to disentangle the effects of environment and heredity on personality, a group of scientists at the University of Minnesota are locating adult twins who have been separated since birth and are bringing them together for extensive testing. One pair of identical twin men, 47 years old, had diverse backgrounds: one had been raised as a Catholic in Nazi Germany and the other as a Jew in the Caribbean. Upon being reunited, the brothers discovered that they both wore mustaches, liked spicy food, thought it funny to sneeze in a crowd of strangers, flushed the toilet before using it, and read magazines from back to front. Other pairs of long-separated twins shared equally striking resemblances. Does this mean that certain aspects of our personalities are genetically determined? (Broad, 1980)

— Box 2 —

Personality assessment

Many tests have been developed to try to determine people's personality traits and characteristics. Among the most widely used tests are personality inventories and various types of interpretive tests.

A *personality inventory* is a collection of statements or questions to be answered in categories such as agree-disagree or like-dislike. Such inventories attempt to measure a great variety of traits, interests, emotional styles, and values. Answers to several items taken together make up a scale by which a particular characteristic can be measured.

The Minnesota Multiphasic Personality Inventory (MMPI), for example, was originally constructed from 550 items based on the cues usually used by clinical interviewers to describe personality. It includes questions to which the subject answers "true," "false," or "cannot say." The MMPI includes questions such as the following:

I get mad easily and then get over it soon.

I wish I could be as happy as others seem to be.

When I get bored I like to stir up some excitement.

Personality testing often is done on a one-to-one basis.

The test originators hoped that the MMPI would be helpful in

diagnosing psychological disorders. Although it did serve this

THE ISSUE OF CROSS-SITUATIONAL CONSISTENCY

Whereas psychoanalytic, type, and trait theories of personality have received a great deal of attention from psychologists, recent research has called into question a basic assumption that underlies all these theories. These approaches all assume that people have the same personalities at all times and in all situations. From a psychoanalytic viewpoint, for example, an "oral dependent" man would be expected to act in oral and dependent ways whether with his wife, his bridge partners, or his coworkers. A type theorist would expect an extravert to be sociable, talkative, and active whether at a party, in a classroom, or in the cafeteria. And a trait theorist would expect a highly aggressive person to behave aggressively in a wide range of situa-

purpose, before long its primary use became that of a general personality inventory.

Personality inventories rely on people's awareness of—and willingness to disclose—their own thoughts, feelings, and preferences. But people may also have attitudes and impulses which they are either unaware of or are unwilling to disclose. One approach to assessing such attitudes and impulses is through *projective tests,* so called because the individual is thought to "project" his inner concerns into his interpreta-

tions of various materials. One such projective test is the Thematic Apperception Test (TAT) designed by Henry Murray in 1938 (Figure 8.2). Murray employed a series of drawings portraying people in various situations. The person being tested is asked to indicate what he thinks is happening in the picture. The pictures were designed to elicit themes, conflicts, or moods common to most of us.

Another projective test, the Rorschach (1942), consists of ten inkblots printed on cards. These inkblots were originally produced by placing ink on a folded sheet of paper and pressing the halves of the sheet together. Since they were not designed to resemble actual objects, they can be interpreted to be whatever the person wants them to be (Figure 8.3).

Analysis of people's Rorschach responses seeks answers to such questions as: How much of the blot was used in the response? What features of the blot produced the response? What was the content of the responses? How did the person behave toward the examiner and the testing material? In the hands of a skilled clinical psychologist, what a person "sees in the blots" can provide valuable information about her personality and thought processes. There is,

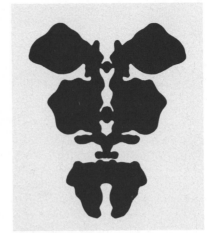

FIGURE 8.3
An inkblot similar to those used in the Rorschach test. What do you see in the blot?

however, a reliability problem with projective tests such as the Rorschach, because different clinical psychologists are likely to interpret the same test responses in different ways (Goldberg and Werts, 1966).

No personality test provides an unfailing pipeline to people's private thoughts and feelings. But these inventories and projective tests, especially when used in conjunction with biographical information and personal interviews, can provide valuable insights into people's personalities.

FIGURE 8.2
A drawing similar to those used in the Thematic Apperception Test. The person being tested is asked to indicate what he thinks is happening in the picture.

tions. These expectations are known as the assumption of *cross-situational consistency.*

This assumption is evident in the way most of us think and talk about people we meet every day. Most of us tend to be trait theorists. We say things like, "Oh, he's such an aggressive person!" or "But she's so domineering!" When we make such statements, we are implicitly assuming that these people are likely to behave aggressively or domineeringly in a wide range of situations.

But the assumption of cross-situational consistency has been challenged in a number of studies. In one of the earliest of these studies Hugh Hartshorne and Mark May (1928) provided children with opportunities to commit a range of "immoral" acts, including lying, cheating, and stealing. In addition, they gave each child the

opportunity to commit these acts in a number of different settings, including in the home, at a party, and in athletic contests.

At the time of Hartshorne and May's study, most psychologists would have predicted that the children would be consistently honest or dishonest in their behavior. According to the psychoanalytic theories that were popular then, a child with a well-developed conscience (superego) would avoid lying, cheating, and stealing in nearly all situations, whereas a child with a poorly developed conscience would succumb to these vices regularly. But these expectations were not supported by Hartshorne and May's study. They found only a minimal amount of consistency. A child who cheated or lied in one situation was not especially likely to cheat or lie in another. In fact, it was almost impossible to predict from a child's behavior in one setting what she would do in another setting.

The Hartshorne and May study is, by itself, hardly sufficient proof that cross-situational consistency in behavior is not great. But many other more recent studies have come to the same conclusion. After reviewing hundreds of correlational studies of such traits as dependency, masculinity-femininity, and self-control, Walter Mischel (1968) concluded that in fact our behavior is not very consistent across situations. Rather than being determined by underlying traits, our behavior is more often determined by the demands or requirements of the particular situation we happen to be in.

After a little reflection, this inconsistency across situations may not seem so surprising. Consider your own behavior. Are you talkative and sociable when out with friends? Well, then maybe you are extraverted. But aren't you sometimes shy and anxious with stran-

gers? Oh, then perhaps you are actually introverted. You are stubborn sometimes, right? Yet at other times you are flexible. You are easygoing but sometimes irritable; you are cheerful but sometimes grumpy. In fact, you are all of these things because your behavior depends not only on *you* but also on your situation—whom you are with, where, and when.

One reason for the common tendency to overestimate the degree of other people's consistency is that we usually see other people in only a small range of situations. Perhaps when your friend Joe is with you in the places where you usually go together he is likely to be jovial and overbearing. But it may well be that Joe is also sad and timid much of the time when you are not around.

This is not to say that there is *no* consistency in our behavior across situations. Most of us believe that we are consistent in some respects, and although we may be biased judges, we are probably right. Daryl Bem and Andrea Allen (1975) obtained extensive reports of students' friendliness and conscientiousness in a wide variety of situations. The data came not only from students' self-reports but also from reports by their parents and friends and from observations made by psychologists in several laboratory situations. In general, there was only a small degree of consistency in a person's friendliness or conscientiousness across situations. But there was much greater consistency for those students who themselves stated that they did not vary much from situation to situation on a particular trait. Some students felt that they were consistently conscientious or unconscientious, but not consistently friendly or unfriendly; others felt that they were consistently friendly or unfriendly but not consistently conscientious or unconscientious. In both cases, the students'

self-assessments generally seemed to be correct. We are presumably more consistent in those matters that are central aspects of our personality and that relate to our basic values. In other respects we are more likely to remain flexible and to behave in accordance with the situation.

Have you seen this young woman before? In fact, she also appears on pages 266 and 267. But she appears very different in the three situations. As discussed in the text, there is often little consistency between people's behavior in different contexts.

SOCIAL LEARNING THEORY

Psychoanalytic, type, and trait theories have had a hard time dealing with the evidence that suggests that there is relatively little cross-situational consistency in people's behavior. *Social learning theory*, in contrast, finds such lack of consistency to be quite understandable. The social learning approach tries to explain both consistency and inconsistency by focusing on the mechanisms by which patterns of behavior are learned and on the situations in which the learning takes place.

Social learning theory focuses directly on people's behavior and is not concerned with underlying motives or traits. The emphasis is on what people *do* rather than on the attributes they *have* (Mischel, 1976). In this respect, social learning theory is heavily influenced by B. F. Skinner's behavioristic approach to learning (see Chapter 5). According to this approach, people are most likely to behave in ways that have been reinforced in the past. If Johnny hits his younger brother and thus gets to eat his brother's candy bar—and if he successfully avoids punishment for this behavior—he is likely to do it again. What's more, he may learn from his experience that it is profitable to hit younger children in a variety of circumstances, such as when he wants to ride someone else's bicycle or play with someone else's toys. This is an example of behavioral *generalization*, because Johnny will be generalizing the behavior (hitting) to a variety of situations in which it will be rewarding. Similarly, Sally may learn that it is rewarding to cling to her mother's skirt in a variety of situations.

But social learning theory does not predict that Johnny will be aggressive all the time or that Sally will be consistently dependent. If Johnny is encouraged by his success and tries to hit his *older* brother, he may end up with a bloody nose. Or if he tries hitting his younger brother while his parents are around, he may end up sitting in his room without dinner. Because these new behaviors are punished rather than rewarded, he is unlikely to try them again. Similarly, Sally may discover that clinging to her mother's skirt is rewarded when her mother is in a good mood but that it is disapproved when her mother is tense or worried. As a result, Sally will learn to assess her mother's mood before she begins to cling. This learning process, as we saw in Chapter 5, is known as *discrimination*—Johnny and Sally learn to discriminate between situations in which a particular sort of behavior is likely to be rewarded and situations in which it is not.

From the standpoint of the social learning theorist, these processes of generalization and discrimination explain why there is typically only a small degree of cross-situational consistency in people's behaviors. As Walter Mischel points out, social learning theory suggests that people will behave consistently across situations only to the extent to which similar behavior is expected to have positive consequences. Because most social behaviors (such as aggression) are not reinforced in the same ways in different situations, a high degree of consistency cannot be expected.

Mischel gives the example of a woman who seems hostile and independent some of the time and passive and dependent at other times. Is she really an aggressive woman who puts on a facade of passivity, or is she basically a warm, passive person who uses aggression as a defense mechanism? Social learning theory allows for the fact that this woman can have all these characteristics—passivity, warmth, dependence, aggressiveness, hostility. Which she displays at any particular time depends on where she is, whom she is with, and what she is doing. "But each of these aspects of her self may be a quite genuine and real aspect of her total being" (Mischel, 1976, page 86).

Rather than considering such a woman to be inconsistent or fickle, social learning theorists would emphasize her adaptability. This ability to discriminate between situations is viewed as a sign of maturity, whereas extreme consistency may be more characteristic of disturbed people.

Although social learning theory is heavily indebted to Skinner's behavioristic theory, social learning theory extends Skinner's formulation by emphasizing the role of *modeling* and of other sorts of learning that do not depend on direct rewards and reinforcements. According to this viewpoint, behavior is shaped by people's *expectations* of reward or punishment in a particular situation. We form

THE NAZI PERSONALITY

It is easy to assume that the leaders of Nazi Germany, who were responsible for the annihilation of millions of people, were madmen. What else but warped personalities could account for their atrocities? Molly Harrower (1976) had the Rorschach responses of leading Nazi officials (obtained when they were awaiting trial at Nuremberg) scored by a panel of 15 authorities who didn't know whom they were evaluating. They did not identify the Nazis (including such infamous men as Adolf Eichmann and Herman Goering) as being mentally disordered. Nor did they discover any particular commonalities between these men. Harrower doubts that the Nazi leaders were insane, suggesting instead that they may have been normal people, caught in the grip of strong social forces.

these expectations not only from our own experience but also by watching other people, reading, and listening to other people's explanations. Thus, if Annie saw another girl steal an apple and get away with it, Annie might be tempted to try the same thing herself. On the other hand, if Annie saw the other girl get caught and punished, or if she had been convinced by her parents that "crime does not pay," she would not expect this behavior to lead to positive consequences and she would refrain from trying it herself. As we will see in the Psychological Issue that follows this chapter, observing violence can have a large impact on people's readiness to be violent themselves. People may also form more generalized expectations of what will bring rewards, as discussed in Box 3.

In recent years, social learning theory has become a popular and influential approach to the study of personality. Like most popular and influential approaches, however, it also has severe critics. Some of these critics contend that by concerning themselves only with people's behavior and not with their attributes, social learning theorists have ended up with a theory of personality that ignores the *person* (Bowers, 1973). In response to such criticisms, Mischel (1976) suggests that social learning theorists have not lost sight of the person. Instead, they have been moving toward an image of the person that stresses the ability to learn from experience and to respond flexibly in a variety of situations.

HUMANISTIC THEORIES

Humanistic theories of personality have been so named because they focus on what their proponents consider to be the unique characteristics of the human species. Rather than seeing behavior as deter-

— Box 3 ————————————————————

Internal and external control

Would you say that your grades are the result of your own efforts, or do you sometimes feel that you have little to do with the grades you get?

Is making a varsity team usually the result of hard work and persistence, or is it largely a matter of getting the right breaks?

Are you the master of your fate, or is most of what happens to you a matter of chance?

People answer these questions differently: Some people think they can easily control their success in school, in sports, or in life in general, while others feel that their outcomes are controlled by fate, luck, chance, or God's will. These differences are a topic of active current research, showing one application of social learning theory to the study of personality.

Julian Rotter (1966) has argued that people form generalized expectancies about their own behavior. The people who come to believe that they themselves control what happens to them are said to have an *internal locus of control*. The people who come to believe that their outcomes depend on external forces (fate, God, the government) are said to have an *external locus of control*. The questions listed at the beginning of this box are adapted from a scale Rotter designed to measure locus of control.

How does the behavior of internals differ from that of externals? As you might expect, people who believe that they can control their outcomes are more likely to try to actually exert that control. One way they can do so is by gathering information about their life situations. Among hospitalized tuberculosis patients, for example, not only did the internals (as measured by Rotter's scale) know more about their condition upon arriving at the hospital, but they

also asked doctors and nurses more questions once they had arrived (Seeman and Evans, 1962).

Internal people have also been found to play a more active role in planning their families. Several studies have shown that external people are less likely to use effective contraceptives, apparently believing that the decision of whether or not to have children is not really in their own hands (Chilman, 1979).

Internals may also try to control their outcomes by making active, concerted efforts to influence social policy and world events. In line with this hypothesis, a study conducted in the 1960s found that internal college students were more likely than externals to become actively involved in the civil rights movement (Gore and Rotter, 1963). Whereas internals believe that they can make a difference, externals are more likely to assume that their actions don't really matter.

Where does an internal or external locus of control come from? Rotter believes that these differences result from expectancies generalized from everyday experiences. If you repeatedly discover that your efforts are rewarded, you will come to expect to be able to exert such control over your reinforcements in the future. If you discover that your efforts are of no avail, you will become resigned to lack of control.

This formulation suggests that an external orientation will develop most often among people who actually have little control over what happens to them—people without money, power, or influence. In keeping with these predictions, it has been found that children from lower socioeconomic classes are more external than children from more privileged backgrounds (Battle and Rotter, 1963). Similarly, unionized workers have been found to be more internal than nonunionized workers, perhaps because the

Unionized workers have been found to have more of an internal locus of control than nonunionized workers.

unionized workers learned that they had greater control over what happens to them (Seeman, 1966).

As we saw in Chapter 7, we have a need to be in control of our environment and our outcomes. And people who believe they have such control may often derive both psychological and physical benefits. For example, smokers who successfully quit smoking have been found to be more internal than those who are unsuccessful (James, Woodruff, and Werner, 1965). The internal smokers are apparently better able to take themselves in hand and say, "I'm going to kick this habit," whereas externals are more likely to say, "Well, it's too late now—I'm hooked and there's nothing I can do about it." Similarly, in a recent study of executives who faced stressful events, those with an internal locus of control handled their problems more directly and were less likely to suffer from stress-related illness (Kobasa, 1979). It seems, then, that an internal locus of control can be good for your health.

mined by primitive instincts or learned habits, humanistic psychologists see people as rational, free to make their own choices about how to live, and motivated to maximize this freedom and to achieve personal growth. At the same time, humanistic theories focus on the individual—on how each person views and interprets his or her experience. These theories also emphasize the individual's subjective experience. What is important is not "objective" reality but the way reality is experienced by the individual. Most important is each person's image of himself or herself, especially the person's self-esteem (see Box 4). Among the humanistic theorists, Carl Rogers stresses the importance of the self-concept in determining behavior and Abraham Maslow stresses the person's striving to perfect the self.

Carl Rogers

Carl Rogers has practiced psychotherapy since 1927. Like Freud's theory of personality, Rogers's theory evolved from what he saw in his patients; but here the similarity ends. From the beginning, Rogers rejected most of the assumptions of psychoanalysis and focused on each person's unique, conscious, and immediate experiences and his need to fulfill the self. "At bottom," Rogers believes, "each person is asking, 'Who am I, *really?* How can I get in touch with this real self, underlying all my surface behavior? How can I become myself?'" (Rogers, 1961, page 108).

Carl Rogers.

According to Rogers, we each try to maintain an organized, consistent image of ourselves, and it is this *self-concept* that directs our behavior and determines how we see reality. The image of the self— as "strong" or "weak," for example—may or may not correspond to the way others see us. Each person develops her own view of events in the world, such that no one else can precisely understand an individual's unique reality. But we are by no means unconcerned about other people's views of us. To maintain a positive view of ourselves, Rogers believes, we all need *unconditional positive regard*—a general acceptance of who we are—from those most important to us.

Almost inevitably, conflicts arise between the values we have incorporated into our self-concept and our actual experiences. For example, Chris may view himself as a "good student" (the self-concept) and yet discover that he does not enjoy his courses (the experience). Or there may be a conflict between the person's *real self* (for example, Mary's view of herself as a gregarious and popular person) and her *ideal self* (she would like to see herself as making a greater contribution to humanity). Such discrepancies—or *incongruences*, in Rogers's terms—may propel people to alter either their behavior or their self-concept, in the service of personal growth. The person comes to recognize that "it rests within himself to choose; that the only question which matters is, 'Am I living in a way which is deeply satisfying to me, and which truly expresses me?'" (Rogers, 1961, page 119).

If the discrepancy between one's experience and self-concept becomes great, according to Rogers, reality becomes distorted and one uses defenses to try to maintain the self-concept. Roger's method of therapy for such instances is described in Chapter 12.

— Box 4 —

Self-esteem

Humanistic psychology emphasizes our feelings about ourselves as playing a crucial role in human happiness and effectiveness. We all feel more positive or negative about ourselves at certain times, for example after getting an A or a D on an examination. But, there are also relatively stable differences between people in how highly they regard themselves. An overall positive evaluation of oneself, or positive *self-esteem*, has been found to be related to many other positive attributes, such as being open to relationships, being less conforming, and setting high goals for oneself.

Stanley Coopersmith (1968) conducted a well-known study of self-esteem and its development. Coopersmith and his colleagues classified a sample of 10- to 12-year-old boys into three groups—high, medium, and low self-esteem—on the basis of the boys' own statements about themselves, teachers' reports of the boys' self-assurance, and psychological tests such as the TAT (see Box 2). A great deal of additional information was then gathered about the boys, including data from personality and ability tests and from interviews with their parents.

Coopersmith found that the boys with high self-esteem were active and expressive individuals who tended to do well both academically and socially. They were eager to express opinions, did not avoid disagreement, and were not overly sensitive to criticism. These boys were optimistic about their abilities, set high goals for themselves, and generally achieved those goals. In contrast, boys with low self-esteem presented a picture of discouragement, depression, and anxiety. In social situations they did not express or defend themselves. They avoided exposing themselves to attention and shrank from contact with others. The boys had little faith in their abilities and indeed rarely met with success.

When Coopersmith interviewed the boys' parents about their child's upbringing, he found that the parents of boys with high self-esteem were likely to have positive self-concepts themselves. In addition, he found very different attitudes about child-rearing between the three groups. Boys high in self-esteem had parents who showed a great deal of interest in them. They knew all of their son's friends and spent time with him discussing problems and engaging in joint activities. They set

Those with high self-esteem tend to set reasonable goals and to accomplish them.

high standards for their son's behavior and were consistent in enforcing the rules. They relied on rewards rather than physical punishment as a means of discipline. These parents clearly indicated that they regarded their son as a significant person, worthy of their interest. As a result, the boys came to regard themselves in a favorable light.

Parents of boys low in self-esteem, on the other hand, demonstrated less interest in the boy's welfare, were less likely to spend time with him, were less likely to know his friends or activities, and rarely considered his opinion in family decisions. These parents tended to be permissive, having no clear-cut rules for the boy's behavior yet dealing out harsh punishment when he gave them trouble. The low self-esteem boys thus had neither daily feedback about their importance as a person nor a consistent set of standards for their behavior. As a result, they came to have doubts about their own value and effectiveness.

On the basis of his findings, Coopersmith points out the fallacy of a number of notions about what contributes to self-esteem. A positive self-image did not seem to be related to physical attractiveness, height, social class, or an outstanding ability in a particular area. Thus, a good opinion of oneself does not require external signs of success such as appearance or material possessions. Instead, Coopersmith concludes, it derives from our day-to-day personal relationships with parents, teachers, and peers.

Self-esteem is not immutable. New learning experiences can raise or lower it. One of the central tasks of life, from the standpoint of humanistic psychologists, is to value and accept ourselves, even as we try to improve ourselves, and thus to keep self-esteem high.

Abraham Maslow

Abraham Maslow began his career in 1934 as a behaviorist, persuaded by the view that behavior can be understood in terms of rewards and punishments, without regard to conscious experience. He broke with this tradition, however, following the birth of his first child. Watching a child grow and change, he felt, made behaviorism look "foolish." Maslow spent the next decade in dialogues with prominent psychologists and thinkers from diverse perspectives and began to gather ideas for a new theory that explained the positive strivings of human beings. The events of World War II gave him added impetus to try to identify what was good in humankind. Until his death in 1970, he devoted his career to that task.

Maslow accepted the assumption that we have basic biological and social needs that direct our actions, but he felt that these needs were not sufficient to explain all human behavior. As we saw in Chapter 7, he believed each person progresses through a hierarchy of needs. Once the more basic needs (such as for food, safety, and acceptance) are met, the individual pursues the need for *self-actualization,* or the fulfillment of one's total potential:

Abraham H. Maslow.

Even if all these [more basic] needs are satisfied, we may still often (if not always) expect that a new discontent and restlessness will soon develop unless the individual is doing what he individually is fitted for. A musician must make music, an artist must paint, a poet must write, if he is ultimately to be at peace with himself. What a man can be he must be. He must be true to his own nature. This we may call self-actualization. (Maslow, 1954, page 46)

Maslow felt that too much of psychological theory had been derived from the study of neurotic patients; he sought instead to characterize the healthy, or self-actualized, person. He examined the lives of people who seemed to have lived up to their potential most fully, including Albert Einstein and Eleanor Roosevelt. Maslow found that self-actualized individuals shared certain attributes: They were accepting of themselves and others, deeply committed to their work, spontaneous in the expression of emotion and the appreciation of beauty, and relatively unconcerned about the opinions of others. In addition, these people all had a notable lack of guilt, shame, or anxiety.

Some critics have disagreed with Maslow's description of these particular people as "self-actualized." Furthermore, his criteria for self-actualization have been criticized as being too subjective and vague. Nevertheless, Maslow made an important contribution by discussing self-actualization as a central human motive. Although few of us can attain this ideal, most of us experience at least a glimpse of self-actualization in moments that Maslow called *peak experiences.* Such experiences of fulfillment may occur in scholarly insight or athletic achievement, in sexual experiences or childbirth, in moments of intense appreciation of music or art, or even in mundane activities when one suddenly feels total appreciation of that moment in time. According to Maslow, such moments play a role in making each of us continue to strive for self-actualization.

WHO ARE THE SELF-ACTUALIZERS?

On the basis of his study of people's lives, Abraham Maslow listed several public and historic figures as self-actualizers. *Definite* cases were Abraham Lincoln (in his last years) and Thomas Jefferson. *Probable* cases included Albert Einstein, Eleanor Roosevelt, Jane Addams, William James, Albert Schweitzer, Aldous Huxley, and Spinoza. *Possible* cases (suggested or studied by others) included George Washington Carver, Goethe, Pablo Casals, Martin Buber, John Keats, Adlai Stevenson, Sholom Aleichem, Robert Browning, Ralph Waldo Emerson, Frederick Douglass, Harriet Tubman, George Washington, Edward Bibring, Pierre Renoir, Henry Wadsworth Longfellow, Thomas More, Benjamin Franklin, John Muir, and Walt Whitman. But Maslow also found self-actualizing people among those who were not famous, including students at Brandeis University, where he taught for many years.

SUMMARY

1. *Personality* is the pattern of characteristic behaviors, thoughts, and emotions we use to deal with our environment. Personality theorists who focus on the detailed study of the unique characteristics of individuals follow an *idiographic* approach. Theorists who try to discover general patterns of personality between people reflect a *nomothetic* approach to personality.

2. *Psychoanalytic theory*, as formulated by Sigmund Freud, views personality formation in terms of an inner struggle between our basic biological urges and our need to subdue them.

3. In the psychoanalytic view, personality consists of three parts: the *id*, which seeks to gratify instinctual needs; the *ego*, which controls gratification for the id; and the *superego*, which embodies the standards and ideals of parents and society.

4. Freud identified five stages of psychosexual development, the first three of which centered around a particular *erogenous zone*. Failure to resolve conflicts at any of the earlier stages can result in *fixation* at that stage, as reflected in lifelong personality traits.

5. In infancy one goes through the *oral* and *anal* stages. At about age 3 the child enters the *phallic* stage. During this period the boy must resolve the *Oedipus conflict* and overcome castration anxiety, while the girl must deal with the corresponding *Electra complex*. The childhood years are called the *latency period*, while puberty brings on the *genital* stage.

6. Freud thought that individuals use *defense mechanisms* to unconsciously distort or deny reality so that *anxiety* will be reduced. Common defense mechanisms include repression, projection, reaction formation, displacement, rationalization, and intellectualization.

7. Freud's theory is difficult to evaluate scientifically, because his ideas can be used to explain things after the fact but not to predict behavior ahead of time. Nevertheless, some of his central ideas appear to be valid, while others have been discounted.

8. Carl Jung postulated that personality is the outcome of the balance between conscious and unconscious forces. In Jung's view, the unconscious consists of two parts: the *personal unconscious* of the individual and the *collective unconscious* that is common to all human beings.

9. Alfred Adler believed that personality development is a result of people's need to overcome inferiority by striving to master a major goal in life.

10. The *neo-Freudians*, such as Horney, Fromm, and Erikson, accepted many of Freud's basic ideas but emphasized the role of society and culture in influencing personality.

11. *Type theories* attempt to classify individuals according to the central characteristic they display. Sheldon related personality to three main body types: *ectomorph*, *mesomorph*, and *endomorph*. Jung suggested that types appear only as extremes, in the form of introverts and extraverts.

12. *Trait theories* attempt to describe individuals in terms of the identifiable qualities or characteristics they possess. Allport distinguished between common traits (found to some degree in everyone) and individual traits (found in a small number of individuals). Certain personality traits, such as anxiety and dependency, appear to have at least some genetic basis.

13. Many tests have been developed to assess personality traits. *Personality inventories*, such as the Minnesota Multiphasic Personality Inventory (MMPI), require individuals to respond to a series of statements on a printed test form. *Projective tests*, such as the Rorschach inkblot test, require individuals to invent stories about materials they are shown.

14. Most theories of personality assume the existence of *cross-situational consistency* in personality. However, several studies have found a minimal amount of consistency in people's behavior from situation to situation. For example, a person may be outgoing in some settings and shy in others. Nevertheless, characteristics that are central to one's personality and that relate to one's values tend to be reasonably consistent.

15. The *social learning theory* approach to personality focuses on the person's behavior rather than on underlying motives or traits. It was influenced by Skinner's behaviorist approach.

16. Children develop ways of behaving on the basis of rewards and punishments, generalization and discrimination. For example, a child may learn that aggression is rewarded in some situations and punished in others. Children can also learn from observing *models* and by developing *expectations* about what kinds of rewards and punishments will be connected with a particular situation.

17. People who learn that they can control their outcomes through their own actions have a *locus of control* that is *internal*. People who come to believe that their behaviors have no effect generally may come to expect failure; their locus of control is *external*. People with an internal locus of control seem better able to take themselves in hand and cope with difficulties.

18. *Humanistic theories* of personality focus on the individual—on how each human being makes choices of how to live and tries to maximize his or her potential. These theories also focus on how each person views and interprets his or her own experiences.

19. Coopersmith found that boys with high self-esteem tend to do well both academically and socially and to set high goals and achieve them. Boys low in self-esteem tend to be discouraged, depressed, anxious, and unsuccessful. Parents of boys with

high and low self-esteem seem to have distinctively different child-rearing styles.

20. According to Carl Rogers, one's *self-concept* directs one's behavior and determines how one sees reality. All of us need *unconditional positive regard* from others who are important to us, in order to develop a positive self-view. Conflict may arise between values incorporated into one's self-concept and situations one experiences in reality.

21. According to Abraham Maslow, individuals who have satisfied their basic needs are then motivated to pursue *self-actualization*. Self-actualized people are accepting of themselves and others and spontaneous in the expression of emotion. Most people get at least a glimpse of self-actualization through moments called *peak experiences*.

VIOLENCE

Man Shot in Market Holdup

Woman Found Strangled in Hotel Room

RACIAL BEATING VICTIM 'STABLE'

MURDER BY ARSON SUSPECTED

Shooting Blamed on Loan Fight

These headlines all appeared in the Boston *Globe* during a one-week period in March 1980. The newspaper is a respectable one, and the week was not particularly violent or eventful, as weeks go nowadays. The unfortunate fact of the matter is that violence has become an expected part of American life. Violence has always been a part of the American tradition, and in recent years the situation has gotten worse than ever. Between 1960 and 1978, the murder rate in the United States almost doubled and the overall violent crime rate tripled. In 1977 there were almost 20,000 murders and over a million violent crimes of all sorts. The homicide rate in the

United States is one of the highest in the world—about four times the rate in Canada, eight times the rate in England, and thirteen times the rate in Denmark, Norway, and Greece (U.S. Department of Commerce, 1979).

ARE PEOPLE NATURALLY VIOLENT?

Although homicide rates are higher in the United States than almost anywhere else, violence is not an exclusively American commodity. In fact, some theorists have suggested that, in the face of the prevalence of human aggression throughout the world, violence may be an inherent part of human nature. For instance, Konrad Lorenz (1966), a world-famous

ethologist (student of animal behavior), has argued that humans are naturally aggressive, just like baboons or wolves. Lorenz and other writers claim that through the course of evolution people—especially men—developed the capacity for violence, because violence was useful for survival. The aggressive man, they assert, controls territory, women, food, and other "resources."

Violence has become an expected part of American life.

But the "human nature" assumption does not account for the fact that there are some human cultures in which there is very little violence. Although we all share the same "human nature," some of us are more aggressive than others, and some situations are more likely than others to elicit aggressive responses. As a result, "human nature" falls short as an

innocent bystander (such as a passenger in your car).

Although there is a great deal of evidence for this *frustration-aggression hypothesis*, it also needs to be carefully qualified. Frustration often leads to aggression, but not always. For instance, John Whiting (1941) noticed that among the Kwoma of New Guinea, frustration leads at different times to submission, dependence, avoidance, and

---

Frustration often leads to aggression, but not always.

---

explanation for violence and aggression. We need to go beyond the assumption of human nature to a consideration of when and where aggression is most likely to occur.

FRUSTRATION AND AGGRESSION

Did you ever sit down, intending to watch your favorite TV show, only to have someone else barge in and change the channel? Have you ever searched for a parking space on a crowded city street only to have another driver sneak into the last available spot? Did you ever settle down for a good night's sleep only to be blasted out of bed by a neighbor's stereo? If so, then you've experienced what psychologists call *frustration*—the blocking of efforts to attain some desired goal. At times like these, you probably became angry and perhaps even violent. You may have felt a strong urge to punch someone in the nose.

Some years ago, John Dollard and his associates (1939) at Yale

University suggested that frustration is likely to lead to some sort of aggression. The aggression may be physical, such as a punch in the nose, or it may be verbal, such as a hostile joke or an insult. It may be directed toward the person who caused the frustration (the guy who stole your parking spot), or it may be *displaced* toward an

aggression. Alternative responses to frustration are also well known in our own culture. Imagine how different people would respond to losing a quarter in a Coke machine. One person might kick the machine and curse at it. Another might jot down the name and address of the company and write a letter demanding his quarter back.

Driving on America's clogged city streets is a frustrating experience that leads many to verbal if not physical aggression.

A third person might treat the loss as a fluke and insert another quarter. And a fourth person might become painfully depressed, wondering, "Why does this sort of thing always happen to me?" So, while aggression is one possible response to frustration, it is by no means the only possible response. And although frustration seems to be one common cause of aggression, it's certainly not the only cause.

GETTING IT OUT OF YOUR SYSTEM: CATHARSIS

The movie *Rollerball* portrayed a future age in which the passive members of a world society get rid of their violent and rebellious urges by watching a bloody hybrid of football and roller derby. The idea is that when frustrations mount up, we can reduce our aggressive drives by engaging in—or even just watching—violent activity. Presumably, we can make the world a more peaceful place by taking time each day to watch a bloody movie, scream at a wall, or pound a pillow. Psychologists refer to this method for releasing emotional tension as *catharsis*.

Konrad Lorenz has endorsed the theory of catharsis, arguing that we should all engage in violent, competitive sports in order to reduce aggression, both within countries and between them. Of course, Lorenz is only repeating an age-old folk wisdom. For centuries, people have been telling each other to go "blow off steam" whenever they feel angry or tense.

Unfortunately, aggressive catharsis probably doesn't work the way its proponents say it should. If you are angry at someone, striking out at that person may make you feel better, at least temporarily. There is even some evidence that such aggression can reduce an angry person's soaring blood pressure (Hokanson, 1970). But there is no evidence that harming anyone

other than the person you are angry at will have a cathartic effect. Nor is there any evidence that watching someone else behave aggressively, whether in a violent movie or on the football field, will help you to get rid of hostile feelings. In fact, quite the opposite result is more likely. As we will see shortly, aggression tends to breed aggression: the more we observe other people doing it, the more likely we are to continue to behave aggressively in the future (Berkowitz, 1973). And competitive sports do not seem to have a pacifying effect on societies. Those cultures having the most aggressive games and sports also tend to be the ones most often involved in wars (Sipes, 1973).

OBSERVING VIOLENCE

In recent years, there has been a continuing, heated debate over violence in movies and on television. Apologists for televised violence contend that it probably doesn't make viewers more aggressive. Referring to the catharsis hypothesis, they suggest that it may even help reduce aggressive drives. To opponents of televised violence, this seems absurd—it's like arguing that you will dissipate all of your sex drive by watching pornographic films. They suggest, instead, in accord with social-learning theory, that observing televised violence increases the likelihood that viewers will behave aggressively.

There is a good deal of evidence in support of this suggestion. In one well-known experiment, three groups of nursery-school children observed either a live adult, a filmed adult, or an animated cartoon cat attack an inflated plastic figure known as a "Bobo doll" (Bandura, Ross, and Ross, 1963). These adults, and the cat, served as "models" for the children. The models exhibited a num-

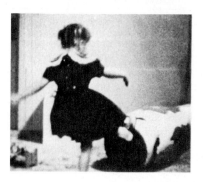

Frames taken from movies of Bandura's studies of the imitation of aggression. Children who saw a model punching and kicking a "Bobo doll" were likely to exhibit similar aggressive behavior themselves, as these frames show.

ber of distinctive aggressive acts, such as hitting the Bobo doll with a rubber mallet. Two other groups of children watched a non-aggressive adult model or no model at all. Later on, each of the children was observed at play in a room containing a Bobo doll. The researchers carefully recorded every aggressive act of the children.

Sometimes a child would attack the Bobo doll in a manner strikingly similar to that of the observed model (hitting the doll with a rubber mallet, for instance). This is known as *imitative aggression*, because the child seems to be imitating the model. At other times a child would attack the Bobo doll in ways different from those of the model. For example, the child might hit the doll with a baseball bat. This is called *nonimitative aggression*, because no direct imitation is involved. It turned out that children who had observed an aggressive model engaged in more of both types of aggression during the play period than did children who hadn't observed an aggressive model.

The children's imitative aggression is not too surprising. We've all seen children imitating adults in all sorts of ways. The adults demonstrate some action that is new to the child, like reading a newspaper or eating with a fork, and the child wants to try it out. The children's nonimitative aggression suggests that observing violence can have even more far-reaching effects. The aggressive model seems to have made a wide range of aggressive behaviors more acceptable to the children. Whereas children are often taught not to hurt others, the aggressive models let them know that these teachings do not necessarily apply. One can imagine violence on television having a similar effect. "Why can't I punch somebody I don't like?" the child might wonder. "Popeye does it all the time!" Thus, observing vio-

lence can actually produce violence in two ways: It teaches new ways to be violent and it makes violence seem acceptable.

Unfortunately, these effects of modeled aggression are not limited to children or to the laboratory. For example, Ross Parke and his fellow researchers (1975) arranged to have adolescent boys in an institution for juvenile delinquents see either violent movies (such as *Bonnie and Clyde* and *The Dirty Dozen*) or nonviolent movies (such as *Lili* and *Daddy's Fiancée*) every night for a week. Aggressive behavior was noted before, during, and after the movie week. The boys who had seen the violent movies exhibited a greater increase in aggressive behavior than the boys who had seen the nonviolent movies. And a recent British study found that prolonged exposure to television increased the degree to which London teenagers engaged in serious acts of violence (Muson, 1978).

Our recent history is chock full of specific instances of modeled aggression. For example, airline skyjacking was once very rare. Then, in the late 1960s, a handful of skyjackers received massive media coverage. Soon the incidence of skyjacking reached epidemic proportions (Bandura, 1973). Many of the later skyjackings were obviously suggested by earlier ones.

For another example: In 1975, Lynette ("Squeaky") Fromme attempted to assassinate President Gerald Ford. While among a crowd of well-wishers, she pointed a pistol at the President, and failed only because she had forgotten to push a cartridge into proper firing position. Scarcely two weeks later, Sara Jane Moore also attempted to assassinate President Ford, again with a pistol from within a crowd of onlookers. She managed to fire one shot, but only after a bystander had knocked her arm

aside. In this case, too, it seems almost certain that the later act of aggression was modeled on the first.

It's likely that many other less distinctive acts of aggression—murders, muggings, even arguments—have also resulted from modeling of events reported in the news or portrayed on TV.

GETTING USED TO IT
Observing violence may have still another undesirable effect: the more we see or read about, the less it seems to bother us. Just as we become habituated to loud noises or other sensory stimuli, so that we no longer notice them, we may also become habituated to violence, so that it no longer seems notable or upsetting.

The more we see or read about violence, the less it seems to bother us.

Ronald Drabman and Margaret Hanratty Thomas (1975) demonstrated this habituation process in an experiment with third- and fourth-graders. The children were taken individually into a game room, where half of them watched a violent eight-minute segment of a Western movie and the other half just played without being exposed to violence. Afterward, each child was asked to watch a video monitor in order to keep an eye on two younger children who were playing in another room. Although the younger children's interaction was actually videotaped, the subjects believed that it was live. The experimenter left the room while the subjects observed the younger children, but he instructed them to call him right away if anything seemed to go wrong. About a min-

"The Avengers" is only one of the many television shows that make violence seem commonplace, so much so that it may no longer be particularly upsetting.

particular social roles can lead to violent behavior. They set up a mock prison in the basement of the psychology building at Stanford University and developed a detailed set of prison rules and procedures, modeled after those of real prisons. For example, the "prisoners" were given ID num-

In some situations, people who might otherwise be gentle play violent roles.

bers and were made to wear stocking caps, while the "guards" were given such symbols of power as billy clubs, whistles, handcuffs, and keys. To play the roles of prisoners and guards, 22 normal, well-adjusted college students were recruited to serve in a 14-day simulation of prison life. Neither the prisoners nor the guards were the sorts of people you would expect to be callous or brutal. They were all emotionally stable young men, and they were assigned to the role of "prisoner" or "guard" on the basis of a flip of a coin.

Although the subjects of Zimbardo's simulation were not normally violent people, placing them in the simulated prison roles had unexpected and dramatic effects on their behavior. In particular, students assigned to be guards exhibited brutal and sadistic behavior. A striking example of the way in which one of these students was gradually drawn into his guard role comes from the diary that he kept during the course of the experiment (excerpted from Zimbardo et al., 1974, pages 70–71):

PRIOR TO THE EXPERIMENT: As I am a pacifist and nonaggressive

ute into the observed interaction, a fierce and destructive fight began. The children on the videotape started hitting each other, were soon crying, and even seemed to have smashed the camera. It turned out, as Drabman and Thomas had predicted, that the third- and fourth-graders who had watched the violent movie took longer to call for help than did the children who hadn't seen the movie. The children who had seen the film had apparently become habituated to violence, so that it took longer for them to consider the children's fight significant. If these results can be extended to adolescents and adults (and it seems likely that they can), then the conclusion is clear: the more violence we observe—in movies, on the news, or in the streets—the more we may come to accept it as a natural part of life.

Meanwhile, though, there seems to be as much violence on television as ever. A recent sampling of prime time and weekend shows revealed that criminals made up 17 percent of all television characters, and two-thirds of them are involved in violence (Gerbner and Gross, 1979). And early morning cartoons aimed at young children are still full of bashings, beatings, pushes over cliffs, and other such antics.

INSTITUTIONAL VIOLENCE
Our behavior depends to a large extent on our social *roles*—on how we are expected to behave in particular situations or in particular jobs or social positions. And, unfortunately, in some situations and occupations people who might otherwise be quite gentle and peaceful play violent roles. Violence that is encouraged by people's roles in large organizations or social institutions is called *institutional violence.*

Philip Zimbardo and his coworkers (1974) provided a striking example of how placing people into

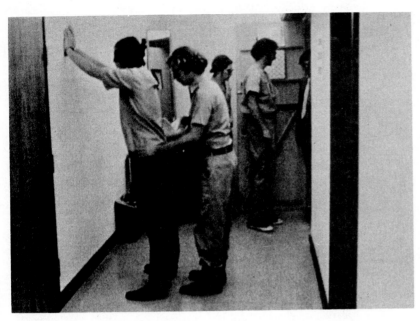
A guard frisks a prisoner in the "prison" set up by Philip Zimbardo in the basement of Stanford University's psychology building.

individual, I cannot see a time when I might guard and/or maltreat other living things.
First day: *Felt sure that the prisoners will make fun of my appearance. . . . At cell 3 I stop and setting my voice hard and low say to 5486, "What are you smiling at?" "Nothing Mr. Correctional Officer." "Well, see that you don't." (As I walk off I feel stupid.)*
Second day: *5704 asked for a cigarette and I ignored him. . . . Meanwhile, since I was feeling empathetic toward 1037, I determined not to talk with him. . . .*
Third day: *I made sure I was one of the guards on the yard, because this was my first chance for the type of manipulative power that I really like. . . . 817 is being obnoxious and bears watching.*
Fourth day: *The psychologist rebukes me for handcuffing and blindfolding a prisoner before leaving the office, and I resentfully reply that it is both necessary security and my business anyway.*
Fifth day: *The real trouble starts at dinner. The new prisoner (416) re-*

fuses to eat his sausage . . . we throw him into the Hole ordering him to hold sausages in each hand. We have a crisis of authority, this rebellious conduct potentially undermines the complete control we have over the others. . . . I decided to force feed him, but he wouldn't eat. I let the food slide down his face. I didn't believe it was me doing it. I hated myself for making him eat, but I hated him more for not eating.
Sixth day: *The experiment is over. I feel elated but am shocked to find some other guards disappointed somewhat because of the loss of money and some because they are enjoying themselves.*

The planned two-week experiment was cancelled after only six days. The prison simulation was becoming too real, and Zimbardo could no longer risk the physical and psychological well-being of his subjects. But real prisons can't be cancelled. Prisoners and guards can't simply stop pretending and go home. These institutions are permanent, and in their present state they give violence a permanent place in American life.

Other institutions, including police forces, armies, and national guards, also place individuals in roles that encourage and even require violence in the name of preserving order. Police officials, soldiers, and guardsmen are not "naturally" aggressive people, nor for that matter are the gang members or terrorists whom they are likely to oppose. In all of these cases, violence is institutionalized; it is part of the set of social roles and obligations that regulate people's behavior.

Institutional violence on the part of forces of law and order often seems justified, since it protects society from criminals, terrorists, or other enemies. As such tragedies as the slaughter of college students during a protest at Kent State University have taught us, however, it is often difficult to determine where justified violence ends and unjustified violence begins.

SUMMARY

1. Some theorists have suggested that violence is a part of human nature. However, this explanation falls short of accounting for actual patterns of aggression and violence.
2. According to the frustration-aggression hypothesis, aggression often results from a frustrating experience.
3. According to the catharsis theory, people can reduce aggressive drives by engaging in or simply observing violent behavior.
4. Many studies have shown that observing violence is likely to increase the incidence of violent behavior in the observer.
5. Observing violence can also lead to habituation—the more you are exposed to violence, the less it bothers you.
6. Violence that is encouraged by people's roles in large organizations or social institutions is called institutional violence.

Chapter 9

From Infancy to Adolescence

A child is born capable of certain basic experiences and responses but certainly not capable of much more. Newborn infants experience a wide range of sensations, and they can cry, turn their heads, suck, and sleep. As we saw at the end of the last chapter, they can even learn from experience in certain ways. But infants cannot move around on their own, remember things, use language, or solve problems. Although infants are unmistakably human, they still lack many of the essential characteristics of intellect and character that we usually associate with being a "person."

But all of this changes, and it does so with remarkable speed. Within the first month after birth, infants develop some control over their heads and necks. Three months or so after birth they are reaching for objects. By the age of 10 months a baby is likely to begin crawling and by about 15 months is walking alone. A relative who visits the baby once every three or four months is likely to be amazed by the changes from one visit to the next. It is almost as if there is a new person to meet on each visit.

While these developments in motor skills are taking place, equally dramatic changes are occurring in the domain of the intellect. A baby may not utter her first words until about the end of the first year, but once the baby does so, language development proceeds rapidly. Within a year the child will have a vocabulary of at least 50 words and by the age of 3 will be chattering away, using the basic grammar of adult speech. And, as we will see, extremely important intellectual changes take place during the first year of life, even before the baby begins to talk.

Like physical growth, psychological changes take place most

quickly and dramatically during the first few years of life, at a somewhat slower pace during childhood and adolescence, and still more slowly during adulthood. It is perhaps for this reason that developmental psychologists, as "professional visiting relatives" to individuals as they progress through life, have traditionally devoted the vast majority of their attention to the years of infancy and childhood, when development is most noticeable. But, in fact, development continues to take place throughout life—through infancy, childhood, adolescence, and adulthood. In this chapter, we will survey the course of development from infancy through adolescence. We will pay special attention to early cognitive development—the ways in which a child discovers the concepts that we as adults take for granted. In discussing cognitive development, we will draw heavily on the work of the renowned Swiss psychologist Jean Piaget. We will also focus on the child's developing social relationships and on the adolescent's development of a sense of identity. In Chapter 10, we will extend our examination of development through the years of adulthood.

THE NATURE OF DEVELOPMENT

Development refers to the relatively enduring changes in people's capacities and behavior that occur as they grow older. We develop both *physically*—in size, biological functions and physical skills—and *psychologically*—in intellectual abilities, personality, and social behavior.

How does development take place? How, for example, do babies come to be able to utter their first words? Why do 1- and 2-year-olds display an increased desire to explore their environment? Why do school-age children often become preoccupied with playing games "according to the rules," and why do adolescents often exhibit a new sort of self-consciousness that they did not have at earlier stages? Progressing further through the life span, what accounts for the fact that certain intellectual capacities, such as short-term memory, typically decline as a person gets older, while other intellectual capacities, such as the ability to generalize from experience, remain stable or even improve?

Learning and Maturation

Each of the above questions is a complex one, because in each case the answer involves a combination of several factors. Throughout this chapter, it will be helpful for you to keep in mind two sets of processes that jointly account for psychological development: *learning* and *maturation*. Learning, as we have already defined it in Chapter 5, refers to relatively enduring changes in behavior that take place as the result of experience. Learning takes place throughout life—in the home, at school, on the job, and in most other places, as well. Maturation, in contrast, refers to changes that take place without any specific experience or practice, as long as environmental conditions stay within a normal range. For example, children will begin to crawl when they are about 10 months old and to walk when they are about 15 months, even if they are not given any special training or reinforcement for these accomplishments. Even when infants are prevented from walking by being wrapped in swaddling clothes during the first year, as is the custom in some cultures (see Figure 9.1), the infants begin walking at the usual age (Orlansky, 1949). Whereas learning reflects the impact of the environment on behavior, maturation reflects the unfolding of inherited biological patterns that are "preprogrammed" into the individual.

Until recently, researchers in psychological development have devoted more attention to the role of learning than to the role of maturation. The impact of maturation is obvious in the areas of physical and motor development. Most people would agree that such behaviors as crawling and walking depend in large measure on the gradual maturing of the infant's muscles and coordination. As Jerome Kagan (1976) notes, however, we tend to underestimate the role of maturation—and to overestimate the role of learning—in cognitive and social development. When a baby starts crying after his mother leaves the room, or when a child starts to play make-believe games, we often assume that these behaviors reflect the child's training and experience, rather than the natural unfolding of the child's innate capacities. Psychologists now believe, however, that these and many other cognitive and social changes are to a large extent dependent on maturation, in quite the same way that physical changes are. Jean Piaget, himself a biologist by training, played a major role in demonstrating the strong impact of maturation on psychological development.

WALKING BEFORE YOUR TIME

Can you teach a child to walk? Few professionals would advise parents to try it. Motor skills such as sitting, crawling, and walking have long been accepted as purely a product of maturation, uninfluenced by experience. But recently researchers have succeeded in speeding up walking in a group of infants by capitalizing on the newborn's stepping reflex (Zelazo, Zelazo, and Colb, 1972). This reflex, which usually disappears by eight weeks, consists of walking movements when the newborn is held above a flat surface. The researchers had parents give their infants extra opportunity to use this reflex during the first eight weeks. These infants began walking at an average age of 10 months, one month earlier than a comparable group who were not given the extra stepping practice. The parents may wonder whether the two months of effort was worth the one month of earlier walking, however. Think of the items that might be knocked off coffee tables—one month sooner.

FIGURE 9.1
Indian babies bound to cradleboards in their first year learn to walk at about the same age as infants in other cultures. This indicates that maturation, rather than experience, plays the greater role in the development of walking.

At present, psychologists emphasize the *interplay* of learning and maturation in human development. Our consideration of language development in Chapter 6 provided one example of this interplay. Babies all over the world start talking at roughly the same age (although there is wide individual variation) and go through some of the same grammatical stages (from the single word to the two-word phrase, and so on). This development probably reflects a biological program that is "prewired" into all human beings. But whether the child begins to speak in French or Chinese, with a New England twang or a Southern drawl, is *not* part of the biological program—these specific features of language must be learned. The biological program provides the readiness to acquire language at a particular age and in particular ways, but the specific words and rules that are used depend on experience. The same interplay between maturation and learning is characteristic of psychological development more generally.

One of the implications of the interplay of learning and maturation is that it may be futile (and, indeed, even harmful) to try to teach a person something before she is maturationally ready for it. Such attempts, whether to teach a 2-year-old to ride a bicycle or a 7-year-old to do geometry, typically bring temporary results at best.

Critical Periods

The interaction between learning and maturation is dramatically illustrated in the case of *critical periods*. That is, in certain animals particular behaviors must be learned at a certain early time in their development or the behaviors will not be learned at all. The classic

Soon after hatching, ducklings will follow the first moving object they see. In this case, they saw ethologist Konrad Lorenz. This is an example of the process of imprinting.

example of a critical period involves the process of *imprinting*, first identified by Konrad Lorenz (1937). Lorenz noticed that soon after ducklings are born they start following the mother duck around, and he wondered why this particular response occurred. By arranging things so that he would be the first moving object seen by a group of newly hatched ducklings, Lorenz found that they would follow him around instead of the mother. These ducklings had "imprinted" on Lorenz during a critical period, in which any object that fit certain characteristics became the mother figure to be followed. Other experimenters have confirmed that ducks are imprintable only at a certain time shortly after hatching.

In a different sort of study, J. P. Scott (1969) raised a newborn female lamb on a bottle and kept it in his house for ten days. The lamb quickly became attached to family members; everywhere the Scotts went, the lamb was sure to go. But when the lamb was introduced to other sheep, it paid them no attention. It had passed the critical period for attachment to other sheep. Three years later, it was still wandering around the field by itself while the rest of the flock stayed together, as sheep normally do.

Are there critical periods in human development? As we saw in Chapter 6, a case for them has been made in the area of language development. Eric Lenneberg (1967) studied the language skills of deaf children and related them to the age at which the children had become deaf. He found that children who did not become deaf until age 3 or 4 had an easier time learning language than did children who had lost their hearing at an earlier age. From such studies Lenneberg has concluded that children have a critical period for learning language skills that begins at about age 2.

Others have suggested that there are also critical periods for the formation of social attachments in humans, just as with ducks and lambs. For example, infants who are confined to institutions during the first six months of life, and who are deprived of parental love, tend to become maladjusted more often than infants institutionalized at a later age (Goldfarb, 1947).

It is undoubtedly true that experiences in the first few years of life—and especially early deprivations—can sometimes have a pro-

WILD CHILDREN

Several cases have been recorded of children who have grown up in the absence of other human beings. One of the most famous was the "wild child of Aveyron." This boy, who seemed to be about 12 years old, was found living in a French forest and was brought to Paris. A doctor took on the job of trying to teach the boy to behave in a civilized manner. Although the boy learned social manners and how to groom himself, he never learned more than a few words, despite persistent efforts to teach him to talk. Although there is some speculation that the boy was mentally retarded, it may also be that he had gone beyond the critical period for learning to use language.

found impact on later development. Programs to provide disadvantaged children with intellectual stimulation in the first years of life are based on the assumption that these years are critical for intellectual development. Nevertheless, there is less evidence for true critical periods among humans than among other animals. Jerome Kagan (1978) has called into question the "doctrine of irreversibility"—the idea that if children are deprived of a particular experience by a certain age they are beyond repair. He cites the case of a 14-year-old girl who had spent most of her first few years of life "in a crib in a small bedroom with no toys and a sister one year older than herself." When she was moved to a foster home at age $2\frac{1}{2}$, she could not speak at all and was severely underdeveloped physically. But 12 years later, as a result of the good care she received in her foster home, she had an IQ in the normal range.

More generally, studies of children who were adopted after the stage of infancy indicate that a good home can overcome severe early disadvantages (Kagan, Kearsley, and Zelazo, 1978). Both continuing maturation and exposure to new experiences can often offset or outweigh the effects of early experience. Instead of viewing early experiences as crucial in determining later development, psychologists are now more likely to view them as links in a chain and to regard a person's capacities as a product of continuing experiences throughout life (Sameroff and Chandler, 1975).

Before commencing our tour through infancy, childhood, and adolescence, we should provide one note of caution. In what follows, we will sometimes note that particular behaviors or capacities typically emerge at a particular age. You should bear in mind, however, that these are *average* ages and that there is a wide range of variation among individuals. Babies may start walking as early as 9 months or as late as 18 months; girls may begin to menstruate as early as age 10 and as late as 17. Whereas the *sequences* of developmental milestones are relatively constant across individuals, the specific ages are not. Moreover, a rapid rate of early cognitive development does not necessarily imply that the person will be an unusually intelligent adult, nor does a slow rate of early development mean that the person will always be at the bottom of the class. To cite just one example, Albert Einstein, who became one of the greatest scientists in the history of the world, was an unusually "slow" child.

INFANCY

The first two years of life are perhaps the most crucial two years for the developing individual. As we have noted, physical and psychological changes take place more rapidly during infancy than during any other period in the span of life. Figure 9.2 gives a brief overview of the infant's development of physical and motor skills. In this section, we will concentrate on some important features of the infant's cognitive and social development.

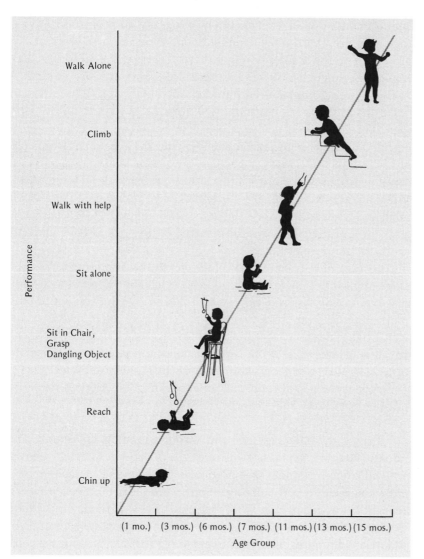

Walk Alone

Climb

Walk with help

Sit alone

Sit in Chair,
Grasp
Dangling Object

Reach

Chin up

Performance

(1 mo.) (3 mos.) (6 mos.) (7 mos.) (11 mos.) (13 mos.) (15 mos.)

Age Group

FIGURE 9.2
Although there are individual differences, children usually develop their motor skills in this sequence. The average age at which each event occurs is indicated.

Cognitive Development

Much of our knowledge of cognitive development comes from the research and writings of Jean Piaget (see Box 1). According to Piaget (1952; Piaget and Inhelder, 1958), a person's cognitive abilities—ways of perceiving and thinking—progress through four qualitatively different stages in infancy and childhood (ages are approximate):

Stage 1. Sensorimotor period (from birth to age 2).
Stage 2. Preoperational period (ages 2 to 7).
Stage 3. Concrete-operational period (ages 7 to 12).
Stage 4. Formal-operational period (ages 12 to 15).

We will discuss each of these stages in the context of the life period in which it falls.

The infant's stage of cognitive development is called the *sensorimotor period,* because the newborn's knowledge of the world is limited to what he perceives through his senses and acts on with motor (muscle) activities. The infant only gradually builds up symbols of objects in his mind; he begins with what he can physically see or do.

— *Box 1* ——————————————————

Jean Piaget

Jean Piaget was born in 1896 and was originally trained as a biologist. He then worked at Alfred Binet's laboratory school in Paris, where the first intelligence tests were being developed (see Chapter

Jean Piaget.

6). It was while doing some routine intelligence testing that Piaget first got the idea of getting behind children's right and wrong answers to the underlying modes of thought involved. This quest occupied Piaget's professional life for more than half a century, extending from intellectual development to social and moral development, as well.

Piaget's techniques have typically been informal ones, involving interviewing and playing games with children at various ages. In fact, the three primary subjects for a good deal of his research were his own three children, Lucienne, Laurent, and Jacqueline. Some psychologists have been critical of the informality of Piaget's methods and, as a result, have raised doubts about some of his conclusions (for example, Bower, 1977). But his status as a major psychological theorist is unquestioned.

Even in his eighties, Piaget and his students in Geneva, Switzerland, continued to advance our understanding of intellectual development. He wrote more than thirty books and hundreds of articles, and his work habits were nothing short of astounding. Writing when Piaget was 71, Elkind (1968) described his summer "working vacations" in the Alps as follows: "During the summer Piaget takes walks, meditates, writes *and* writes. Then, when the leaves begin to turn, he descends from the mountains with the several books and articles he has written on his 'vacation.'"

One of Piaget's last books, published in 1980, is called *Vital Adaptation and Intelligence*. Its title reflects Piaget's continuing interest in links between intellectual development and people's adaptation to their environment. This great observer and thinker died in 1980, at the age of 84.

The first cognitive challenge the infant faces is to coordinate the various impressions of the world that he gains through his senses (especially vision and touch) with motor activities (for example, by sucking, reaching for, and grasping objects). During the first months of life, the baby's sense impressions are uncoordinated. For example, the baby may see a certain pattern of lines and curves, corresponding to a toy hanging over the crib, but he does not know that he can reach for the toy. Or the baby may accidentally touch an object but will not turn around to look for it. After infants are a few months old, however, they begin to put these isolated impressions together, so that they can reach toward an object that they see or turn to look for the source of a sound that they hear. By further integrating sensory and motor information, the infant then begins to discover the various properties of objects, such as that a ball is something that feels smooth, can be rolled, and can be bounced.

During the first year of life, according to Piaget, infants are also discovering the principle of *object permanence*—that a physical object continues to exist even when it is out of sight or out of reach. As adults we take this principle for granted. When we look away from our desk for a moment, we remain certain that the desk and the open book on top of it are still there. But we are not born with this sort of assurance. The infant is like a philosopher who makes absolutely no assumptions about what the world is like when it is not directly perceived. As a result, infants behave as if they can literally destroy and create objects by closing and opening their eyes. This is what makes the game of peek-a-boo so exciting for a baby. Each time that a face reappears in view, it is as if a totally new object has been created out of nothingness.

By the end of the first year of life, infants learn that objects continue to exist even when they are out of sight. Before an infant has developed the notion of object permanence (at about 8 or 9 months), if you take a small toy that the baby is interested in and place it behind a pillow, she will not reach behind the pillow for the toy. As far as she is concerned, out of sight *is* out of mind; it is as if the toy no longer exists. But if you repeat this exercise a few months later, the baby will immediately reach behind the pillow for the toy. By this time the baby knows that the toy continues to exist, and she knows just where to find it. By the time the baby nears the end of the sensorimotor period (about age 2), these concepts are developed to such a point that an adult can move an object around several times without fooling the baby as to its whereabouts. With her new understanding that an object exists even when out of sight, the infant begins to have a mental representation of the object, not tied to her own vision or actions. And with this understanding, the child has advanced from purely sensorimotor experience to *thought*.

This example also shows that as infants develop the notion of object permanence, they also develop basic conceptions of *causality* and *space*. The baby learns that an object can be moved by a person's hand (including the baby's own hand) from one place to another. The idea that the hand's movement leads to the object's movement represents the basic principle of causality, and the notion of physical displacement provides an elementary understanding of space. The baby also develops a basic concept of *time*—that one event can take place

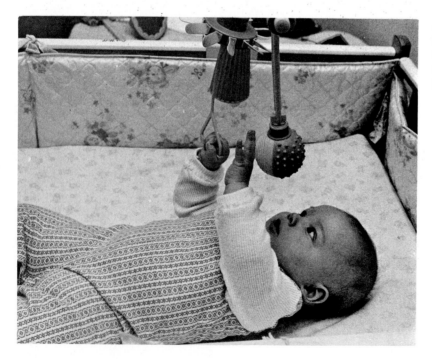

During the sensorimotor period, the infant learns to associate sensory information (such as sights and sounds) with motor experiences (such as reaching and grasping).

before or after another. By this time it can be said that the infant has a basic understanding of the physical workings of the world.

Social Development: Attachment

Infancy is an important period not only in the development of a basic understanding of the physical world, but also in the development of social behavior. During the first two years of life, infants typically develop a strong *attachment* to a small number of people. The baby's attachment is reflected in his selective responding to the mother, father, or other caretaker. The baby is much more likely to approach this person or these persons than anyone else, is more willing to be cared for by them, and is least afraid in their presence.

In the first month of life, infants do not have strong preferences for specific people. The infant does not care very much who picks her up, rocks her, or feeds her. At two or three months, she will smile and babble to all visitors, without showing any special preferences. By the age of 4 or 5 months, however, the baby becomes much more discriminating. She will interact freely and securely with familiar people and will be wary and insecure with strangers. And starting at about the age of 6 months, the baby is likely to protest or withdraw when approached by an unfamiliar person, a phenomenon known as *stranger anxiety*. You can tell the baby, "But she's your grandmother!" or "It's only Harry, my old roommate," but unless the baby has had a great deal of contact with these people, it won't do much good. The baby shows less distress if his mother or father is present, and whether he will cry hysterically or merely stop smiling depends on his individual temperament and on the circumstances. The reaction of stranger anxiety typically reaches its peak at about 8 months and generally disappears by 15 months, when the baby has gotten used to the idea that these other people are humans, too, and are not to be feared (Sroufe, 1977).

What causes the baby to become attached to a particular person or persons and not to others? Psychologists used to believe that it was a matter of learning—specifically, of secondary reinforcement (see Chapter 5). They thought that since the mother provides the infant with food, either by nursing or bottle-feeding, the baby learns to approach the mother whenever he is hungry. As a result, the mother herself was thought to take on more general reward value for the infant. But this view of attachment has changed, partly as a result of pioneering research by Harry Harlow (1959) with infant rhesus monkeys. Harlow separated the infant monkeys from their mothers and raised them instead with wire and terrycloth constructions that he called *surrogate mothers*. In one study, the infants had access to both a "wire mother" fitted with a nipple that the monkey could obtain milk from and a "cloth mother" that did not provide milk but that the baby could cling to much more comfortably (see Figure 9.3). If the infant's attachment were the result of associating a particular object with the receipt of nourishment, we would expect the monkeys to become attached to the wire mother rather than the cloth mother. But Harlow found the opposite to be true. The infants became attached to the cloth mother. Not only would they cling to her, but they

LINUS'S BLANKET

Various theories of attachment agree that during the second year of life there is a period of necessary "separation" between the mother and toddler as they break away from the intimacy and dependency that characterized the first year of their relationship. About two-thirds of the children in this stage have what psychologists call a *transitional object*—a blanket, a teddy bear, or some other toy to which they are intensely attached. With these objects, children are sure they always have something familiar nearby to reassure them if need be. The transitional object is also something that can be controlled, which is not always true of mothers (Busch et al., 1973).

also were less fearful and more venturesome in her presence, just as human infants are in the presence of an attachment figure. When the infant monkeys were hungry, they would go to the wire mother to feed but then returned immediately to the cloth mother.

As a result of his research, Harlow concluded that attachment is *not* a learned response to a food-giving object but rather an innate tendency to love a mother (or a mother surrogate) for the sheer pleasure of contact with her body. *Contact comfort*, as Harlow called it, may play a role in the development of human attachments, as well. More generally, human infants appear to develop attachments toward people they repeatedly interact with in a variety of situations, whether or not they happen to be the ones who supply their food.

Harlow and others view the development of mother-infant attachment (or of attachment to other persons) in infancy as the first stage in the development of the capacity for close relationships in adulthood. In the view of Erik Erikson (1950), the quality of the interaction between infants and their parents during the first years of life plays a major role in determining whether children will grow up with a trustful or mistrustful attitude toward other people. In Erikson's scheme, *trust versus mistrust* is the first of eight central themes or stages of psychological and social development through the life cycle (see Box 4).

Mary Ainsworth and her colleagues (1967) have demonstrated how differences in the quality of the mother-infant relationship affect the infant. Based on observations of infants who were placed in an unfamiliar room, both with and without their mothers, Ainsworth has defined certain infants as being "securely attached." Securely attached infants have developed a concept of their mother as a safe haven. They play contentedly in her presence, protest vigorously at her departure, and greet her happily when she returns. "Insecurely attached" infants, on the other hand, are less confident about their

Infants who are "securely attached" to their parents protest vigorously when separated from their mother or father.

mothers. They may not leave her side to play, fail to protest her leaving because they are not sure such protests will have any effect, and fail to greet her upon her return to the room. Recent studies show that the quality of the infant's attachment to the mother influences the infant's later competence. Securely attached infants perform better on cognitive tasks at age 2 and are more competent with peers at age 3 (Easterbrooks and Lamb, 1979).

Although most research focuses on relationships with the mother, infants become attached to their fathers, as well (Kotelchuck, 1976). Many studies have found that infants seem to be more secure with their mothers than with their fathers when in an unfamiliar situation; however, these findings may simply reflect the fact that in most families fathers spend less time with their babies. In fact, one study found that the infant's attachment to the father was directly related to the number of diapers he changed per week (Ross et al., 1975). Although mother may be more comforting in times of stress, father is more likely to be sought out for playing. Mothers generally do more of the caretaking and talk more to infants than fathers, but fathers engage in more physical play. Thus, fathers can serve as a source of security much as mothers do, and they can also enrich the child's experience by providing a somewhat different kind of experience (Parke, 1978). The question of whether infants who spend their days in day-care centers while their parents work can form healthy attachments to their parents is explored in Box 2.

CHILDHOOD

Although human development is most rapid during the first two years of life, the period between ages 2 and 12 may be even more eventful. During this period children gradually develop modes of reasoning that are essentially identical to those of adults. And during this period, individuals venture from home for the first time and develop a sense of mastery and competence. The psychological developments of childhood are too numerous for us to cover in only one chapter. You will find that developmental issues are discussed in several other chapters, as well. We have already discussed Freud's theory of psychosexual development in Chapter 8 and language development was covered in Chapter 6. We will discuss the development of sex-role identity in Chapter 13. In this section we will continue Piaget's account of cognitive development during childhood, discuss the ways in which patterns of child rearing affect the development of a sense of competence, and consider the importance of children's relationships with their peers.

Cognitive Development

Between the ages of 2 and 7, according to Piaget, children are in the *preoperational period* of cognitive development. Although 2-year-old children have acquired the basic concepts of object permanence, space, time, and causality, they are still unable to perform certain

— Box 2 —

Is day care dangerous?

With the increasing number of working mothers and of single-parent families, more and more infants and young children are spending eight hours a day, five days a week, in day-care centers. This has led to concern on the part of some parents and educators that, without the presence of a primary attachment figure, the children might be emotionally and intellectually harmed. In a recent book stressing the importance of "mothering" in the early years, Selma Fraiberg (1977) argues that the day-care arrangements available to most parents do not provide the love, stability, and individual attention necessary to a child's well-being. "The majority, by far, of the preschool, full-day nurseries that are known to me," Fraiberg writes, "do not have expert teachers or professional staffs attuned to the individual needs of each child and his family; the programs themselves are not educational programs; they offer, at best, custodial care. . . . In the years when a baby and his parents make the first enduring human partnerships, when love, trust, joy, and self-valuation emerge through the nurturing love of human partners, millions of small children in our land may be learning . . . that the world outside of the home is an indifferent or even a hostile world" (pages 87, 111).

Fears such as these have led to extensive research comparing day-care infants with infants raised at home. On the basis of the initial results of such studies, the verdict seems to be that well-managed day care is not harmful.

In one of the most comprehensive studies of the effects of day care, Jerome Kagan and his colleagues set up their own day-care center in Boston and compared

the 35 children enrolled in the center with children from the same background who spent their days at home with their mothers (Kagan, Kearsley, and Zelazo, 1978). After three years in day care, with extensive testing and observation throughout, the two groups of children showed no differences in intellectual or social competence. Nor was there any difference in the day-care and home-reared infants' attachment to their mothers. In fact, there is some evidence that day care can have positive effects. Several studies have suggested that children from less privileged homes show better cognitive development when in day care than at home (Belsky and Steinberg, 1978).

Despite this encouraging evidence, the possibility that day care for infants and toddlers can have adverse effects must still be taken seriously. Most of the recent studies of day care, like Kagan's, have been conducted in high-quality, university-sponsored day-care

centers. We cannot be assured of such positive results in the day-care settings most parents have to choose from. In 1975, only 38 percent of the day-care centers in the United States were rated as being of high quality. Nevertheless, most psychologists feel that Fraiberg has overstated the negative side. The limited evidence available from less-than-model centers does not support Fraiberg's claim that they destroy the capacity for healthy social relationships (Belsky and Steinberg, 1978).

The reservations Fraiberg and others have raised do not necessarily imply that mothers or fathers should stay home, but they do suggest to policy makers that high-quality day care should be available to all who wish or need to work. Perhaps a new trend in day-care research will be not to decide whether it is good or bad but to recognize the need for day care and to define more clearly what makes it work best for children and their families.

basic mental operations that we adults take for granted. Children in this period typically find it difficult to take the perspective of another person. A colleague of ours, knowledgeable in cognitive development, took advantage of his child's lack of perspective-taking ability. When his 3-year-old called out from another room, "Dad, is this the finger a ring goes on?" the father answered, "Yes, that's right," without getting up from his desk, and the child went on playing contentedly. The child could not put himself in his father's place and realize his father had no way of knowing which finger he was talking about.

Piaget called this lack of ability to take another person's point of view *egocentrism.* He did not use this term to connote selfishness but rather to signify the simple fact that young children are capable of viewing the world from only a single point of view—their own. Nevertheless, this limitation of the child's mode of thought may sometimes get him into trouble with adults. As David Elkind (1975) notes, young children "are impervious to whatever activity the adult is engaged in, no matter how delicate or precarious." A child will chatter away to his mother when she is engaged in an important phone conversation, apparently not realizing that she cannot conduct two conversations at the same time, or he will want his father to play a game with him even though Dad is busy shaving. We should bear in mind, however, that it is the child's inability to take another person's point of view that produces these behaviors, not any sort of selfishness or perversity.

By the time they are about 7 years old, children have entered the period of *concrete operations.* The children are still tied to thinking about what is "concrete"—what is immediately present in the situation rather than what can be abstracted or inferred. But now, for the first time, they can mentally manipulate objects. Piaget reports, for example, that if you show preoperational children a row of sticks and ask them to select the same number of sticks from a second pile, they will do so by matching the new sticks to the old, one by one. Concrete-operational children, in contrast, can count the sticks mentally—they do the necessary matching in their heads. With this ability of mental manipulation, concrete-operational children become capable of many new skills, from the use of arithmetic to the ability to place themselves in someone else's shoes.

A central concept acquired in the concrete-operational period is *conservation*—the notion that a substance's weight, mass, or volume will remain the same even if it changes in shape. If you pour water from a short, wide beaker into a tall, thin beaker, a preoperational child will usually conclude that you now have more water than you did before (see Figure 9.4). The child concentrates on only one of the beaker's dimensions, its height, and fails to take into account the other dimensions at the same time. As children acquire concrete operations, however, they come to realize that as long as no water is added or subtracted, it will have the same volume, regardless of the shape of the beaker it is in.

Concrete operations help the child to view the world more accurately. In some cases, however, the child who is acquiring new rules associated with concrete operations may make new *mistakes* in problem solving. For example, suppose a child is presented with two beakers of water, each containing the same concentration of sugar, and the contents of the two beakers are then combined in a larger container. If the child is 4 or 5, she will tell you that the "sweetness" of the water in the new container remains the same, relying on her own experiences with sweet substances. But if the child is 6 to 9 years old, she is likely to indicate that the water in the larger beaker must be "twice as sweet." Such school-age children have learned the rule that adding quantities makes something greater. But they apply the rule incorrectly in the case of sweetness, leading to the error. By the time they are 10 or so, children realize that, because there is both more sugar *and* more water, the overall sweetness will remain the same (Gardner, 1979). This example illustrates the more general point that cognitive growth does not always translate into being "right" more of the time. From the standpoint of cognitive development, whether the answer is right or wrong is less important than the underlying reasoning process.

Since concrete operations are necessary skills in reading and arithmetic, parents and teachers often wonder whether it is possible to hasten the development of this mode of thought. (Americans seem to be particularly concerned with "getting there faster"—so much so that Piaget called the issue of accelerating cognitive development "the American question.") Recent studies suggest that, within limits, such acceleration is possible, by using techniques in which children are confronted with contradictions in their own judgment (Inhelder, Sinclair, and Bovet, 1974). There is no evidence, however, that such acceleration has long-lived effects on intellectual ability—the children will "get there anyway" with or without special programs. As Elkind (1975) suggests, "Children have so much to learn that it seems short-sighted to spend a lot of time on what they can learn on their own rather than on skills that only we can help them acquire" (page 19).

Child Rearing and the Development of Competence

Most parents hope that their children will become competent people, capable of making decisions for themselves, taking initiative, and relating effectively to others. For Robert White (1959), competence is the most central of human motives (see Chapter 7), and for Erik Erikson, the development of autonomy and of initiative (as opposed to doubt and guilt) are the central psychological challenges of childhood. The extent to which children develop such competence depends to a large extent on their parents' approach to child rearing. (In Box 3, we consider the special problems of child rearing that must be faced by parents who have divorced.)

Several different approaches to child rearing have been distinguished. One approach, often associated with the "old school," is the *authoritarian* style. Authoritarian parents deliberately try to shape the behavior of the child according to their own standards of conduct. These parents put a premium on obedience, and they may use punishment to curb rebellion in the child. In an authoritarian family, there is little room for discussion and debate; "do it because I told you to" is sufficient reason for obedience.

Nowadays such an authoritarian approach seems to be out of

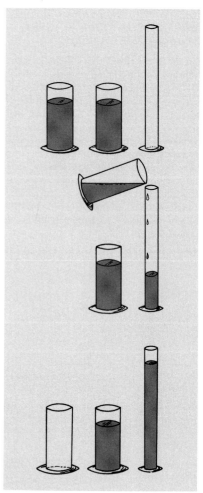

FIGURE 9.4
A problem used to study the development of conservation of volume, one of the concepts acquired in the concrete-operations stage. Children of different ages agree that the amount of water in the two identical beakers (top picture) is the same. But when the water in one of the beakers is poured into a tall, thin beaker, children under about age 7 are likely to say that the taller beaker now has more water, whereas older children recognize the amounts are still equal.

Parents try to help their children develop a sense of competence and self-reliance.

favor, especially among middle-class parents. Instead, a *permissive* style of child rearing has gained favor. Instead of trying to actively shape the child's behavior, permissive parents adopt the policy of keeping hands off and letting children "be themselves." These parents hope that by maximizing the children's freedom, they will also encourage the development of initiative and self-reliance. As Robert White (1976) wisely points out, however, when parents really care about their children's well-being (as most parents do), it is very hard to live up to this permissive ideal. Devoted parents can't help worrying about how far they should go in letting children make their own decisions. "Parents who care about their children," White adds, "inevitably harbor wishes and hopes for their future. They do not want to see this future compromised by shortsighted impulsiveness and youthful impatience" (page 46).

— Box 3 —

Children of divorce

Divorce—increasingly prevalent in the United States—has a psychological impact not only on the divorcing couple but on their children, as well. According to recent predictions, by 1990 one-third of all 18-year-olds will have experienced the divorce of their parents (Glick, 1979). With so many children and adolescents affected, researchers have focused on the short- and long-term effects of divorce on children.

Children involved in the divorce situation often live disrupted lives. First, they must deal with the trauma of their parents' separating and of one parent leaving home. "I remember it was near my birthday when I was going to be 6 that Dad said at lunch he was leaving," one 8-year-old recalled. "I tried to say, 'No, Dad, don't do it,' but I couldn't get my voice out. I was too much shocked" (Francke et al., 1980).

In addition, the child of divorce now has only one parent to turn to on a day-to-day basis, and that parent—usually the mother—may often be too busy with work, housekeeping, or finding a social life to offer sufficient support and guidance to the child. Children of divorce must also often deal with the continuing conflict between warring parents. This conflict is especially traumatic in cases of child custody battles, where the parents vie with each other for custody of the child, while the child awaits the outcome.

Judith Wallerstein and Joan Kelly (1980) interviewed the parents and children in 60 families who had gone through a recent divorce, then interviewed them again 18 months and five years after the divorce. They found a prevailing sense of sadness, loneliness, and anger in children of all ages. Young children, unable to understand the reason for the separation, often blamed themselves for the break-up, thinking that perhaps they were being punished for being bad. Older children were less likely to blame themselves, but were particularly torn by the loyalty dilemma—the feeling that

whenever they sided with one parent they were betraying the other. By the end of the first year, most of the children had learned to cope at least moderately well; yet an alarming number of them were intensely unhappy and dissatisfied with their life in the postdivorce home even after five years.

In another study, E. Mavis Hetherington and her coworkers compared forty-eight 3- and 4-year-olds whose parents had recently divorced with other children attending the same nursery school. Children were observed interacting with their mothers and fathers in laboratory sessions and with their peers in the nursery school. In the laboratory, the divorced parents demonstrated a lack of control over their children. They used less consistent discipline and tended to be less affectionate with their children than parents who had not divorced. Preschoolers from divorced homes showed less creativity and imagination in their play than their counterparts, and they also played less often with other children. These effects were more pronounced and long-lasting

---

As a result, most "permissive" parents put limits on their children. Some parents refrain from directly telling their children what to do but instead point the child in a particular direction by saying that it is "what a sensible person would do" or by praising a neighbor's child for doing it. Other parents are permissive in some areas (for example, they will defend their child's right to choose his own style of dress and haircut) but not in others (they will insist that she do her homework and do well academically). Another version of the permissive pattern is the "low control by default" that occurs when parents are unsure about themselves. "Confused by their own values, the parents do not convey a clear or consistent pattern of expectations; they let the child's inclinations prevail because they have no guidelines of their own" (White, 1976, page 48).

Research suggests that neither an authoritarian pattern nor a pattern of total permissiveness is as effective in the development of competence as is a child-rearing pattern that combines acceptance of the child's behavior within certain limits with relatively firm control. On the basis of extensive observations of parents and their preschool

for boys than for girls (Hetherington, Cox, and Cox, 1978, 1979).

The effects of divorce on children are not necessarily all bad. Studies of long-term psychological effects suggest that children from broken homes may well experience less unhappiness in the long run than children in unbroken homes that are full of conflict and hostility (Bane, 1979). Children of divorced parents sometimes become more self-reliant and responsible, as a result of their increased participation in the household decisions; in some ways, children of divorce "grow up a little faster" (Weiss, 1979).

Moreover, surveys of adult personal adjustment do not point to clear differences between those who did and did not grow up in broken homes (Kulka and Weingarten, 1979). Children of divorce *are* more likely to get divorced themselves, however, perhaps in part because of the model their parents provided—the idea that divorce is a legitimate solution to family conflict (Pope and Mueller, 1979).

Most children of divorce eventually emerge from the experience in good shape. Nevertheless, divorce remains a traumatic experience for the child, one that can lead to many months or years of pain and deprivation, and one that probably no one gets over completely. Psychologists have been working on various intervention programs for helping children—and their parents—cope with this experience. Such programs include role playing and storybooks dealing with divorce for younger children and discussion groups for older ones. The best remedy may be the most difficult to achieve: reducing the high rate of divorce in our society.

children, Diana Baumrind (1971) concludes that the most independent, creative, and cooperative children tend to have parents who have definite standards but also encourage their children's independence and solicit their opinions. Similarly, Stanley Coopersmith (1967) found that 10- to 12-year-old boys were most likely to develop high self-esteem when their parents provided them with clearly defined limits and respected the boys' right to make decisions for themselves within those limits.

Peer Relations

For all of the importance of parent-child relationships, children's relationships with their peers also play a crucial role in their development. Friendships, from as early as age 3 through the course of childhood, provide a context in which children can meaningfully compare themselves to others, as revealed in the following encounter observed by Zick Rubin (1980, page 5) between two 3-year-olds in nursery school:

> (Steven and Claudia stand near the sandbox and hug each
> other affectionately.)
>
> Steven: *You're bigger than me—right, Claudia?*
>
> (They turn and stand back to back, measuring themselves.
> Claudia is in fact taller than Steven.)
>
> Claudia: *We're growing up.*
>
> Steven: *Yeah, I'm almost as big as you, right? I'm gonna grow this
> big, right?* (He stretches his arms far apart.)
>
> Claudia: *Me too.*

Children compare their personal attributes, styles, and interests with those of their peers in order to develop a valid sense of their own identity. Adults are so different from children on most dimensions that they are relatively useless as standards of comparison. Instead, as Katherine H. Read (1976) writes, "We must measure ourselves against others who are like us, finding our strengths and facing our weaknesses, winning some acceptance and facing some rejection. . . . A favorable family situation helps us to feel secure, but experiences with our own age group help to develop an awareness of ourselves and of social reality which family experience alone cannot give" (page 340).

Psychiatrist Harry Stack Sullivan (1953) emphasized that relationships with parents and with peers play distinct roles for children. He suggested, for example, that peer relationships can save "spoiled" children from social maladjustment in adult life. Whereas overly indulgent parents may lead some children to "expect everything," peers may help bring them back to reality. Three-year-old David is the sort of child whom Sullivan had in mind. During his three years of life, David learned from his parents to expect praise for whatever he did. Tony, although he was David's closest friend, did not feel the need to indulge him to such an extent (Rubin, 1980, page 8):

> (David and Tony are sitting together at their nursery school's
> drawing table.)
>
> David: *Do you like my drawing?*
>
> Tony: *No.*
>
> David: *You have to like it.*
>
> Tony: *I don't have to like it if I don't want to.*
>
> David: *Why?*
>
> Tony: *I don't like it, that's why.*

One may hope that from a series of such experiences with his peers, David will obtain a more accurate picture not only of his public appeal as an artist but also of the degree of approval he can expect from others.

Several studies have provided support for Sullivan's view that children's peer relations may affect their long-term development. One group of researchers found that ratings of 8-year-old children by their classmates were related to whether or not these children would have psychiatric difficulties over the next 11 to 13 years. Those children who later developed psychiatric problems were relatively likely to have been scorned and disparaged by their 8-year-old peers (Cowen et al., 1973). A correlational study such as this one does not

Friendships are of central importance to children from as early as age 3 through the course of childhood.

establish conclusively that the children's rejection of their peers actually contributed to the later problems. It is possible, for example, that certain of the 8-year-olds already had psychological problems that led their peers to dislike them. Nevertheless, the available evidence is at least consistent with our intuitions that by providing opportunities for social comparison and for obtaining a realistic self-appraisal, children's friendships are likely to have effects that will extend into later life.

Psychologists have recently been developing ways of helping children who lack the social skills needed to establish satisfactory friendships. For example, training programs have been established in which preschool or school-age children who have been identified as isolates or outcasts are given a series of sessions that may include demonstrations of specific social skills (such as techniques for handling conflict), opportunities to practice these skills, and feedback on their performance (Stocking and Arezzo, 1979). Another useful approach is to pair an older child who has trouble relating to his peers with a younger child to whom he can serve as "big brother." In the process, the older child may learn that he can win the approval of others without being a bully. Such experiences can in some instances pave the way to better relationships with age-mates, as well (Furman, Rahe, and Hartup, 1979).

ADOLESCENCE

Whereas the changes that take place in childhood are relatively slow and gradual, adolescence begins (at about age 12) with changes that are abrupt and dramatic. Along with the rapid physical and sexual development that occurs in early adolescence, cognitive development enters a new stage. The growth of adolescents' bodies and the continuing development of their modes of thinking provide the backdrop for what is probably the adolescent's central psychological challenge: the formation of a stable sense of identity.

Physical Development

The beginnings of adolescence are marked by the physical changes that take place at about this time. For both sexes, these changes include the maturing of the reproductive system and rapid changes in body size and shape. For girls, the budding of the breasts and the onset of menstruation are especially dramatic changes. For boys, the changes include the sprouting of facial hair and the deepening of the voice.

There is a wide range of variation in the age at which these developments take place (Tanner, 1972). Although the average age of menarche (first menstrual period) in American girls is about 13, it can take place anywhere between ages 10 and 17. The height spurt can begin for girls anywhere between $7\frac{1}{2}$ and 11 and for boys anywhere between $10\frac{1}{2}$ and 16. As a result, it is quite possible for three girls or three boys of the same age in early adolescence to look as if their ages are widely different (see Figure 9.5).

Because of these differences, girls and boys are likely to be acutely self-conscious about their size and shape during early adolescence. In one national survey, about half of all boys between 12 and 17 said they wished they were taller than they were, and nearly half of the girls wished they were thinner. Late-maturing boys, in particular, are likely to feel less adequate, less self-assured, and more anxious than boys who mature earlier (Mussen and Jones, 1957; Simmons et al., 1979), and some of these personality differences may persist into adulthood (Jones, 1957). Among girls, in contrast, early maturing may sometimes lead to reduced popularity with one's peers—until the peers catch up (Faust, 1960). To reduce such negative effects, it is important for young people to be informed that wide variations in the age of the height spurt and sexual maturation are perfectly normal. And there is no difference in the average heights of early-maturing and late-maturing boys by the time they stop growing (Tanner, 1972).

Cognitive Development

At approximately age 12, children enter Piaget's stage of *formal operations*. To understand how adolescent thinking differs from that of younger children, consider how children at different ages would react to the following syllogism:

> *All children hate candy.*
> *Boys are children.*
> *Therefore, boys hate candy.*

The preadolescent child, still in the stage of concrete operations, will focus on the content of the statement and, recognizing that most boys like candy, will say that the conclusion is false. But an adoles-

THEY'RE GROWING UP FASTER THAN EVER

When adults comment, "Those kids are growing up faster than ever!" they're right, in more ways than one. Over the past century the age of puberty in the Western world has declined sharply. In 1900, the average age of menarche (first menstruation) for American girls was over 14; it is now under 13. Boys are also undergoing the physical changes of puberty earlier than before. Although several factors may be involved in the declining age of puberty, better nutrition seems to be the most important. Will the decline continue? Probably not to any large extent. The evidence suggests that by now young people in the United States are growing up at something close to the fastest possible speed (Tanner, 1972).

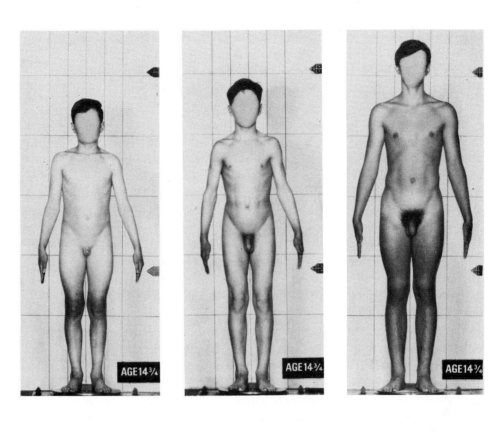

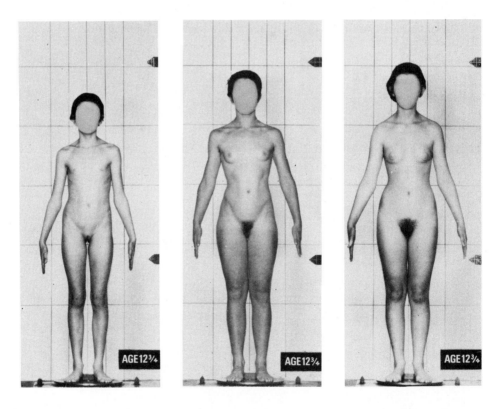

FIGURE 9.5
The rate of physical maturation in adolescence varies widely from individual to individual. The three boys are all 14¾ years old, and the three girls are all 12¾ years old.

cent who has acquired formal operations will focus on the *form* of the argument and will recognize that the conclusion is true. The adolescent can think about not just what is real but also what is possible. Freed from what Piaget called "the primacy of perception," the adolescent can consider all possible solutions to a problem, can generate hypotheses, and can test solutions systematically.

Formal operations allow adolescents to think about thought itself. It is not until early adolescence that most people can play complex word games, learn algebra, and do other tasks that involve the mental manipulation of complex thoughts and concepts. Formal operations are also necessary for a fuller grasp of historical time (what does it mean for something to have occurred "five centuries ago"?) and geographical distance (how far is "a thousand miles"?).

In Piaget's original formulation, formal operations were viewed as the inevitable culmination of the process of cognitive development. More recently, Piaget (1972) and others have speculated that formal thinking, unlike the earlier stages, may not be universal. Regardless of their cultural background and specific experiences, all normal children acquire concrete operations. But the degree to which they acquire formal operations may depend both on education and on day-to-day experiences. Scientific training in such fields as physics, logic, and mathematics has been associated with a greater ability to use formal operations. Nevertheless, even people without any schooling have been found to use formal operations.

The acquisition of formal operations has far-reaching effects on adolescents. Because they can think about thought itself, adolescents

Adolescents often develop a new self-consciousness which may include heightened concern about their appearance.

now think and talk about such abstract notions as beliefs, values, and ideals. In fact, as Elkind (1975) notes, "At least some of the 'storm and stress' associated with adolescence is a consequence of the disaffection between their real and ideal worlds," a comparison that cannot be made before the acquisition of formal operations.

Once they are able to think about their own thought processes, adolescents are also likely to begin thinking about what other people are thinking. And in many cases, they assume that other people are thinking about *them*. This new self-consciousness can lead to insight and sensitivity as the adolescent begins to view himself from other people's points of view. But it can also lead to dissatisfaction and depression, especially if one begins to discover one's lacks and failings (Meissner, 1966).

Identity Formation

Closely related to the adolescent's emerging self-consciousness is the need to develop a clear sense of identity. For Erik Erikson, identity formation is the central developmental task of the adolescent years (see Box 4). From all the separate roles that the adolescent plays—as son or daughter, sibling, boyfriend or girlfriend, athlete, student, and so on—he or she must struggle to emerge with a clearly defined sense of self. The adolescent must answer the question, "Who am I—and where am I heading?" In Erikson's words:

The identity the adolescent seeks to clarify is who he is, what his role in society is to be. Is he a child or is he an adult? Does he have it in him to someday be a husband and father? What is he to be as a worker and an earner of money? Can he feel confident in spite of the fact that his race or religious or national backgrounds make him a person some people look down upon? Overall, will he be a success or a failure? (1951, page 9)

As this quote suggests, Erikson seems to have been more specifically concerned with male than with female identity formation. Elizabeth Douvan and Joseph Adelson (1966) have suggested that because of the lower status of women in American society, girls find it harder than boys to develop a strong sense of identity and that girls often postpone this task until after marriage. At this time their identity may depend in large part on the accomplishments and plans of their husband. One of the concerns of the women's movement is to remove this sort of socially imposed obstacle to women's identity formation.

The formation of a stable sense of identity is not an easy task for anyone, however, regardless of sex. The rapid physical changes and sexual awakening of adolescence may often lead young people to be confused about the continuity between their past and their present. And the rapid changes taking place in today's society only serve to compound the difficulty. It is no wonder, therefore, that many adolescents fail to establish a clear identity and instead suffer what Erikson calls *role confusion*. Many of the social, political, and religious causes that attract adolescents may hold their appeal because they seem to provide solutions to the adolescent identity crisis.

— *Box 4*

Erikson's eight stages of psychosocial development

Erik Erikson was born in Germany in 1902. As a young man he moved to Vienna, where he became an acquaintance and disciple of Sigmund Freud. He later went on to become perhaps the foremost theorist of the development of personality through the life cycle. The initial impetus for Erikson's theory was Freud's theory of psychosexual development, which we discussed in Chapter 10. But whereas Freud's stages covered only the years between birth and puberty, Erikson's stages extended through adulthood and old age. And whereas Freud focused on the relationships between children and their parents, Erikson took into account the impact of the larger society on development.

In *Childhood and Society* (1950), Erikson presented each of eight *psychosocial stages* as a polarity, with a positive pole representing successful development at that stage and a negative pole representing unsuccessful development.

Erik Erikson.

Erikson did not see these stages as fixed or rigid, however. To some degree, we all continue to work on these eight challenges or crises throughout our lives. Erikson's eight stages are as follows:

1. *Trust versus mistrust.* In the first year of life infants depend on others to feed them, dress them, and carry them about. The parents cuddle them, talk to them, and play with them, and these interactions determine the children's attitude later in life. If a child's physical and emotional needs are met, he learns to trust his environment. If not, he will become fearful and mistrust the people and objects around him.
2. *Autonomy versus doubt.* In the second and third years, when children learn to walk, talk, and do things for themselves, parental encouragement and consistency in discipline can help the child to develop autonomy and independence. But if parents are overprotective, are inconsistent in their disciplinary techniques, or show disapproval when the child does things on her own, she will become doubtful and ashamed of herself.
3. *Initiative versus guilt.* By ages 4 and 5, children are ready to roam about, to explore unfamiliar places, and to get to know new people. If the child's inquisitiveness and exploration of his environment are encouraged by his parents, he will find it easier to use his initiative to go out on his own. But if parents inhibit such actions, the child will develop guilt feelings whenever he tries to be independent.
4. *Industry versus inferiority.* From about ages 6 to 11, children learn to manipulate objects and events by themselves. If encouraged, the child will develop a sense of industry, will enjoy solving problems and completing tasks, and will seek intellec-

tual stimulation. If not, she will develop a sense of inferiority and will have to be bribed or cajoled to complete a task.
5. *Identity versus role confusion.* Between the ages of 12 and 18 sexuality emerges and the adolescent faces the task of finding himself. He must integrate all that he has previously experienced in order to develop a sense of ego identity. If he is unable to reconcile his various roles in life into one identity, he is said to be suffering from role confusion.
6. *Intimacy versus isolation.* If the adult has achieved a sense of identity, then she can form close relationships and share with others. Failure at this stage consists of being unable to relate intimately to others. The person may develop a sense of isolation, feeling there is no one but herself she can depend on in the world.
7. *Generativity versus self-absorption.* By middle age the individual must have taken a stance toward the world, the future, and his readiness to contribute to it. Generativity is the ability to look outside oneself and be concerned with other people. The generative individual is productive and happy. The person who fails at this stage becomes self-centered.
8. *Integrity versus despair.* If life has been satisfying and the individual has achieved a sense of unity within herself and with others, old age will be a happy time. But if the old person feels that her life has been full of disappointments and failures and she cannot face life at this age, she will develop a sense of despair.

We will make reference to each of the last three of Erikson's stages in Chapter 10, when we discuss development through the course of adulthood.

The years of childhood slide by swiftly.

As we have seen, the years from infancy to adolescence are years of dramatic change—physical, intellectual, emotional, and social. The changes come swiftly. As this chapter was being completed, Zick Rubin's younger son, Noam, who had been born only 10 weeks earlier, had begun to explore the world with his eyes and hands, to reach for objects, and to smile. Noam's older brother, Elihu, had just finished going over the guestlist for his fourth birthday party, and was sitting across the table from me cutting out the "tickets" that he planned to give each of the other children. As children move through the years of childhood and adolescence, their development is influenced by many forces, including "built-in" processes of maturation, and the learning that takes place both at home and in school. We will consider an additional influence on development, a child's birth order in her family, in the Psychological Issue that follows.

SUMMARY

1. *Development* refers to the relatively enduring changes in people's capacities and behavior as they grow older. People develop both physically and psychologically.

2. *Maturation* refers to the unfolding of inherited biological patterns. Maturation interacts with learning to produce psychological development. Although the role of maturation is most obvious in physical development and language learning, it may also play a significant role in cognitive and social development.

3. Some animals go through *critical periods,* during which certain things must be learned if they are to be learned at all. For example, the time shortly after hatching is a critical period for the duckling to *imprint* on its mother figure. The evidence for critical periods in human development is less clear.

4. The infant (from birth to age 2) is in what Piaget called the *sensorimotor period* of cognitive development. During this stage babies learn to coordinate sensory information with motor activities and discover the principle of *object permanence.* At this early age they also develop basic concepts of causality, space, and time.

5. During the first year of life, the infant develops a strong *attachment* to a small number of people. The presence of the attachment figure helps to reduce the reaction of *stranger anxiety* that typically occurs at this stage.

6. Harlow's studies with infant monkeys imply that attachments develop out of the need for *contact comfort,* rather than from the satisfaction of the need for food.

7. Many psychologists view the development of parent-infant attachment in infancy as fundamental to the development of the capacity for close relationships in adulthood. Infants who are "securely attached" to their parents appear to be more competent than their peers. Mothers are most often the primary attachment figures, because in most families they spend more time with the infant; but infants commonly become attached to their father, as well.

8. Studies of day-care and home-raised infants generally indicate that high-quality day care is not harmful and can be beneficial in some cases. However, concern has been expressed that lower-quality centers may be harmful to infants' emotional and social development.

9. Children between 2 and 7 are in Piaget's *preoperational stage* of cognitive development. Children at this stage are *egocentric*—they cannot see things from another person's point of view.

10. At about age 7 children enter the period of *concrete operations.* They are now able to mentally manipulate objects and to understand the principle of *conservation.*

11. Children of divorced parents must cope both with the disruption caused by the divorce and with the fact that they have only one parent available to them on a day-to-day basis. Chil-

dren of divorce encounter many psychological difficulties, although most of them emerge from the experience successfully.

12. *Authoritarian* parents deliberately try to shape their children's behavior according to their own standards of conduct. *Permissive* parents adopt the policy of "hands off" and let their children "do their own thing." Actually, most parents who call themselves permissive still impose some limits on their children's behavior.

13. When parents set definite standards but also encourage their children's independence and opinions, the children tend to be more independent, creative, cooperative, and helpful than children of authoritarian or overly permissive parents.

14. Children's relationships with their peers allow them to compare themselves to others and help them to appraise themselves realistically. Psychologists have introduced techniques of social-skills training to help children who have difficulty relating to their peers.

15. Adolescence begins with maturation of the reproductive system and rapid body changes. There is wide variation in the age at which major developments occur, and early or late maturation can have significant effects on the individual's self-concept and personality.

16. Most adolescents have reached Piaget's stage of *formal operations*. They are able to mentally manipulate complex thoughts and concepts and to think about thought itself. The stage of formal operations may not be universal. Adolescence leads to a new self-consciousness, as the adolescent begins to think about what others think of her.

17. Erik Erikson has identified eight stages of *psychosocial development*, each characterized by a specific task that must be mastered. In adolescence, for example, the task is to develop a clear sense of *identity*. If the identity problem is not resolved, the individual suffers from what Erikson calls *role confusion*.

BIRTH ORDER

Being the first-born child in your family may be important if you want to increase your chances of becoming an astronaut—twenty-one of the first twenty-three astronauts to fly into outer space were first-borns. If you'd rather be a professional football player, your chances may be better if you are a later-born (Nisbett, 1968).

Twenty-one of the first twenty-three astronauts were first-borns.

In the past 20 years or so, birth-order research has become something of a fad among psychologists, and studies have been published about the links between a person's birth order and almost every imaginable psychological characteristic—everything from pain tolerance (later-borns seem to be able to withstand more pain) to the likelihood of becoming a stripper (first-born women are more likely to enter this profession [Skipper and McCaghy, 1970]).

Some of the findings of these hundreds of studies are probably statistical flukes and should be taken with a grain of salt. But the research taken as a whole confirms what many of us have already suspected—that people's position of birth in their family is likely to have an impact on their childhood experiences and on the sorts of adults they will become.

THE EMINENCE OF FIRST-BORNS

The relation of birth order to achievement has been investigated for at least a hundred years. The first known data appeared in Sir Francis Galton's *English Men of Science,* published in 1874. Galton selected eminent scientists of that time and found a more-than-chance number of them to be first-borns or only sons (Altus, 1966). Thirty years later, Havelock Ellis published *A Study of British Genius,* based on the biographies of 975 eminent men and 55 eminent women. He found that the probability of appearance in the *Dictionary of National Biography* was much greater for a first-born than for a middle child. The youngest was similarly favored over the intermediate child.

A bit closer to home, first-borns are overrepresented (considering their proportion in the general population) in *Who's Who in America* and *American Men and Women of Science,* as well as among Rhodes scholars and university professors. And Stanley Schachter (1963) found that first-borns are overrepresented among graduate students and medical students and that first-borns (on the average) have higher grades in college than later-born children.

Why is it that first-born children are more likely to achieve eminence than their siblings? Even though they are "Number 1," first-borns seem to try harder—especially in the school setting. This academic striving seems to reflect the aspirations and pressures of the parents—after all, their first child is their first entry in the race for success.

First-borns seem to try harder—especially in the school setting.

The tendency for first-borns to achieve eminence has also been explained in terms of Alfred Adler's theory of personality. Adler viewed the first-born child as a

Older siblings often help and nurture younger siblings.

result they are not very reliable. Two findings that have been found in extremely large samples, however, are that people who grow up in small families tend to get higher scores on intelligence tests than people from larger families and that within families first-borns tend to have the highest IQs, second-borns the next highest, and so on, with the last-born child tending to get the lowest scores.

This pattern was shown in an extensive analysis of the IQ scores of almost 400,000 young men—the entire population of 19-year-olds—in Holland (Belmont and Marolla, 1973, see Figure 9.6). The same pattern was found even when the men's social class was held constant. A similar finding was obtained in a study of 800,000 high school seniors who took the Na-

"dethroned-king" who suddenly loses his monopoly on parental attention. According to Adler, this dethronement leads to a lifelong need for recognition, attention, and approval, which the child may try to earn through high achievement. As Richard Zweigenhaft (1975) suggests, politics is a good occupation for people with such needs—which may be why first-borns are overrepresented among American presidents, senators, and representatives.

BIRTH ORDER, FAMILY SIZE, AND INTELLIGENCE

Many of the findings related to birth order are based on relatively small samples of people, and as a

FIGURE 9.6
Average scores on a test of intellectual ability among 400,000 young men in Holland, as a function of birth order and family size.

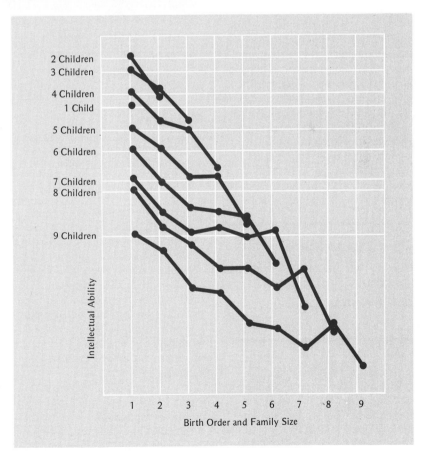

tional Merit Scholarship Qualifying Test: Scores declined as the students' family size and birth order within the family increased (Breland, 1974).

Although these patterns were quite clear, why they occurred remained something of a mystery. The birth-order decline seemed especially mysterious. It is conceivable that some physical factors may be involved—for example, that the uterine environment may become less nourishing for a mother's later-born children—but there is no good evidence that this is the case. Nor is there any reason to suspect that genetic factors are any different for early- and later-borns. Recently, psychologist Robert Zajonc (1976) has come up with a mathematical model that, although quite speculative, accounts for the pattern very nicely (Figure 9.7). Zajonc's model is based on the premise that a child's intellectual development depends on the intellectual environment of his family. For first-born children, this environment consists of the two parents, each of whom has an adult's level of intelligence. A second-born child, in contrast, enters a family in which there are two people with an adult-sized intelligence and one person—the older sibling—with a pint-sized intelligence.

Does the presence of an older sibling dilute the newborn's intellectual environment?

The presence of an older sibling, according to Zajonc's model, dilutes the newborn's intellectual environment and makes it less likely that the newborn will de-

Consider the absolute intellectual levels of the parents to be an arbitrary 30 units each, and that of the newborn child to be 0.

Then the intellectual environment of the first child is:

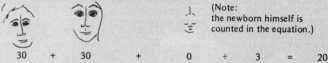

(Note: the newborn himself is counted in the equation.)

$$30 + 30 + 0 \div 3 = 20$$

Suppose the second child is born when the intellectual level of the firstborn reaches 4. The intellectual environment of the secondborn is then:

$$30 + 30 + 4 + 0 \div 4 = 16$$

If a third child is born when the intellectual level of the firstborn has reached, say, 7, and that of the secondborn is 3, the family intellectual environment will then be reduced to 14.

$$30 + 30 + 7 + 3 + 0 \div 5 = 14$$

For twins who are the first offspring, the intellectual environment at birth is:

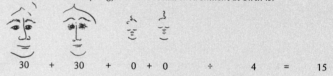

$$30 + 30 + 0 + 0 \div 4 = 15$$

FIGURE 9.7

A pictorial representation of Robert Zajonc's model of the effects of birth order and family size on intelligence.

velop her maximum intellectual potential. Things are even worse for the third-born child, and so on down the line—since the more undeveloped minds there are around, the less intellectual stimulation there will be for the newborn. If the older siblings are *much* older, however, then the younger child's intelligence would not be expected to suffer—and might even be enhanced.

To the extent that Zajonc's model is correct, it has interesting practical implications. One of these is that parents who want to optimize their children's intellectual

growth should have no more than two children. And, if possible, they should wait until the first child is pretty old before having the second. (Just in case you're wondering, Robert Zajonc is an only child.)

THE NEED TO AFFILIATE

The current concern with birth order was spurred on by a 1959 study by Stanley Schachter. By accident, really, he found that female college students who were first-borns or only children regularly chose to wait with other people when they expected to receive a painful electric shock in an experiment. However, those who were later-borns didn't care as much whether they waited alone or with others.

Why might this be the case? It

probably has a lot to do with how parents treat first-born as opposed to later-born children. Inexperienced parents tend to overreact to their first-born children—to make more of a fuss over them, to reward them more, and to rush to their side at the first sign of distress. As a result, first-born children become highly dependent on their parents for dealing with fearful situations and for developing their self-image. And because inexperienced parents tend to be inconsistent in giving out rewards and punishments, first-borns stay dependent. They never know for sure whether what they are doing is right and must always look to their parents for approval. In later life, these first-borns continue to look to others for affirmation and approval, particularly in anxiety-arousing situations. In this way, the first-born's preference for affiliating with others in the Schachter experiment can be explained.

When expecting a shock, first-borns chose to wait with others.

This explanation, mind you, is highly speculative. Furthermore, the evidence that links birth order and affiliation has been much less consistent than that linking birth order and achievement or intelligence (Warren, 1966). On the whole, it does seem to be true, however, that first-borns are more likely than later-borns to seek out others when they are anxious and troubled.

HELPING LITTLE BROTHER
Other effects of birth order stem from the direct interaction between brothers and sisters. Even

though there is usually a great deal of rivalry between siblings, older children are also likely to take responsibility for their younger siblings and to serve as models for them. A 4-year-old big brother or sister will proudly pick up the baby, play gently with him, and offer toys or food when he is crying. As the children grow up together, the older child will help

---

"Helping my younger brothers grow up gave me a sense of accomplishment."

---

the younger one with her schoolwork, coach her in athletics, or advise her about social relations.

These opportunities can enhance the older child's sense of competence. One first-born woman recalls: "Watching my brothers grow up gave me a sense that I was learning and growing. I can remember helping one of my brothers struggle to read a storybook I had long since discarded. He was about six at the time and I was eight. I realized how easy reading had become for me, and I had a real sense of accomplishment." In addition, experience with assisting a younger brother or sister may help the older child to become a more caring person outside the family. Studies in several cultures have found that children who have younger siblings tend to be more helpful and nurturant than children who do not (Staub, 1975).

Younger siblings, for their part, not only receive help from their big brothers and sisters but also must learn to get along with these more powerful and sometimes domineering figures. It may be as a result of this learning that later-

born children have been found to be slightly more socially skilled and better liked than first-borns (Miller and Maruyama, 1976).

THE ONLY CHILD
About 5 percent of Americans are only children and, by at least some accounts, they are a disadvantaged minority. In national surveys of Americans, about four-fifths of those polled say that they think being an only child is a handicap (Blake, 1974). And, when asked, college students described only children as more self-centered, temperamental, unhappy, and unlikeable than children with two siblings (Thompson, 1974). Parents, too, seem to have accepted a negative view of the only child. They often decide to have a second child in order to keep their first child from being lonely.

Are only children a disadvantaged minority?

Is there any reality behind this picture of only children as selfish, lonely, and maladjusted? Psychologist Toni Falbo decided to check it out. After reviewing the available studies that compared only children with those who have siblings and conducting additional studies of her own, Falbo (1979) concluded that there is little basis for the negative stereotype. Only children attending college do say they have fewer friends and belong to fewer clubs, on the average, than those with siblings. But the only children have just as many *close* friends, and in the clubs they do belong to they are likely to be leaders. Only children also seem to be especially independent and autonomous, perhaps because they are more likely

Only children tend to be independent and autonomous and rarely fit the stereotype of being lonely and maladjusted.

to have grown up in "adult-oriented" families.

Although there is no evidence that only children tend to be maladjusted, Falbo points out that the negative stereotype may itself have unfortunate effects. For example, teachers and counselors may be more likely to recommend professional help for a child who displays problem behaviors if he is an only child than if he has siblings. The teacher may reason that the only child runs a greater risk of maladjustment and therefore

needs help more. From Falbo's point of view, such special attention is misguided. Indeed, it may even lead the child to live up to the expectations held for him by becoming maladjusted.

In Falbo's opinion, there is nothing wrong with being an only child; in fact, it may be an advantage. She advises parents to stop thinking that they must have a second child "in order to keep the first from being neurotic, selfish, and lonely."

THE BIRTH ORDER OF BIRTH-ORDER RESEARCHERS
As we have already mentioned, the published research on birth order

has not always been notably consistent. In fact, much of it has been downright contradictory. For example, first-born males placed in threatening situations have been found to be more influenceable, less influenceable, more hostile, and less hostile than later-borns. It all depends on which report you read. Similarly, depending on which study you trust more, first-borns either choose more-popular others as friends and are less popular themselves *or* they choose less-popular others and are more popular themselves.

How can we make sense out of this mass of contradictions? While sitting in the laundromat one day, waiting for his clothes to dry, Zick Rubin pondered this question and came up with what he thought was a brilliant idea. His idea was that the psychologists who conduct research on birth order, being either only children, first-borns, or later-borns themselves, have a stake in the results of the research. Sometimes their results make first-borns look better than later-borns, and sometimes their results make later-borns look better. Rubin, who is not a suspicious sort, certainly did not think that the psychologists faked their data to make their own birth order look good. But he did entertain the notion that a more subtle process might be going on—that the researchers may well have *expected* their own birth position to come out looking better and that they managed to construct their research in such a way that their expectations would be borne out (such experimenter effects are discussed in Chapter 1).

As he took his clothes from the dryer and began rolling his socks into neat little balls, Rubin decided he wouldn't simply let this hypothesis fade into oblivion, as most of his hypotheses do. Instead, he would test it. And he proceeded to do so. He went to the journals and located a sample of 41 articles on birth order. Then he wrote to the psychologists who had written the articles and asked them about their own birth order.

While he was waiting for the postcards to come back, Rubin enlisted two friends (to be fair about it, he chose one first-born and one later-born) and asked them to help him code the articles the birth-order researchers had written. They then coded the articles as to being either more favorable to first-borns, more favorable to later-borns, or equally favorable. For example, some of the reports judged to be more favorable

to first-borns concluded that first-borns are more honest, better adjusted, less hostile, and less likely to be schizophrenic then later-borns. Some of the reports judged to be more favorable to later-borns concluded that later-borns are more popular, less dependent, less anxious, and less conforming than first-borns. Then, as Rubin held his breath, the postcards came back (from all but one of the 41 researchers) and Rubin was able to find out whether his hypothesis was correct. Was there in fact a tendency for researchers to obtain and publish results that were favorable to their own birth position?

Unfortunately, Rubin's brilliant idea fell flat on its face. When the returns were all in, it turned out that there was absolutely no relationship between birth-order researchers' birth order and the results of their research (Rubin, 1970). The inconsistencies that haunt birth-order research, he was forced to conclude, must stem from some other source. And the next time he went back to the laundromat, he resolved to stick to more practical questions, like making sure not to pour too much bleach in with his colored undershorts.

But even if the effects of birth order are difficult to predict on a group level, it is hard to doubt its effects on individual lives. Imagine how different your own experience of growing up would have been if you had older siblings rather than younger ones or if you had grown up in a large rather than a small family. And these experiences are likely to have an enduring influence on your life. "It's hard to shake the feeling of being the baby," a woman who is the youngest of three sisters confides. "I never really had to push to get ahead—others did that for me. And now I look around and see that

others are more independent, more self-reliant."

Another woman reports: "We're all grown up now, and whatever satisfaction or problems I had from being the oldest child are long over. But when we get together now, I am still in some way John's and Michael's 'big sister.' And these two grown men continue to be my 'little brothers.'" Thus, even in adulthood birth order continues to be an important part of our lives.

SUMMARY

1. First-born children tend to achieve eminence more often than later-born children. For example, there are disproportionate numbers of first-borns among astronauts, people listed in *Who's Who*, and American presidents.
2. First-borns tend to score highest on IQ tests, followed by second-borns, third-borns, and so on. Zajonc suggests that this pattern occurs because later-borns receive less intellectual stimulation—they are exposed to more immature minds in their home environment.
3. Schachter found that first-borns have a greater need than later-borns to affiliate with others when they are anxious.
4. Interactions between siblings may account for some differences in children of different birth order. First-borns learn to serve as role models and care for younger siblings; later-borns must learn to get along with dominating older siblings.
5. The stereotypical picture of the only child as lonely, selfish, and maladjusted is not borne out by research.
6. The results of birth-order research tend to be contradictory, but it cannot be disputed that birth order affects individual lives.

Chapter 10

Adulthood and Aging

If you are now in your late teens or early twenties, a vast span of life stretches out before you. In your twenties you may complete your formal education, start your first real job, perhaps get married and start a family. In your thirties, you may be working hard at a career, raising children, reaffirming—or maybe ending—an intimate relationship. In your forties, you may begin to cope with physical changes caused by growing older and with psychological questions about the meaning of your life, now that it is half over. In your fifties you may be a different person in some respects—perhaps more relaxed, more reflective, more mellow than you were earlier in life. In your sixties you may retire, begin to collect Social Security, and establish new relationships with your children and grandchildren. In your seventies and the years beyond, you are likely to experience chronic illnesses, although they may not limit your daily functioning, and you may turn to new interests and endeavors. You are also likely to experience the death of a spouse or other loved ones. Your own death becomes more imminent.

The specific progression of events through the span of life varies greatly from one individual to another. For all of us, though, development continues throughout life. As we noted in Chapter 9, most research on human development has focused on the years of infancy, childhood, and adolescence, when physical and psychological changes are most rapid and dramatic. In recent years, however, psychologists have paid increasing attention to the changes that take place later in the life span, particularly the psychological tasks and challenges that people face as they proceed through the years of adulthood.

SUMMARY

PSYCHOLOGICAL ISSUE:
FACING DEATH

We will begin this chapter by considering the nature of adult development, including the ways in which it is similar to and different from development earlier in life. We will then examine three broad stages or eras of life: early adulthood (roughly from age 18 to age 40), middle adulthood (between 40 and 65), and late adulthood (from age 65 on). The age boundaries between these stages are fuzzy, and indeed some social scientists would prefer not to discuss adulthood in terms of stages at all. Nevertheless, the intellectual skills, self-perceptions, and social circumstances of a 20-year-old are likely to differ from those of a 45-year-old, and these in turn are likely to differ from those of a 70-year-old. We will consider these differences as we examine the course of adult life.

THE NATURE OF ADULT DEVELOPMENT

Just like development during infancy and childhood, development in adulthood involves an interplay between maturation (changes that are biologically preprogrammed) and learning (changes that are caused by experience). For example, when a woman will have her menopause and whether and when a man will bald are changes that are primarily maturational. But development through most of adulthood is influenced to a greater extent by the experiences of life than by maturation.

Paul Baltes (1979) and others have found it useful to distinguish between two sorts of factors that influence adult development: age-graded influences and non-age-graded influences. *Age-graded influ-*

The nature of adult development   **319**

ences are experiences and events that commonly occur at a given stage of life. For example, it is common for people to get married and start a family in their twenties and thirties, to ascend the occupational ladder in their forties, and to retire and experience widowhood in their sixties and seventies. *Non-age-graded influences* are experiences and events that are unique to the individual rather than associated with a particular stage of life. For example, a person may have a serious accident at age 25, inherit a sum of money at 35, get divorced at 45, or move to a new job assignment at 55.

As Baltes points out, age-graded influences seem to be especially common in infancy and childhood. As we saw in Chapter 9, in infancy and childhood physical and cognitive growth and specific life events (such as going through the school grades) are highly correlated with age. After adolescence, however, age-graded influences become less central. Thus, there are no clear stages of physical and intellectual development in adulthood as there are in infancy and childhood. And there is a greater diversity of social paths in adulthood than in childhood. Some adults go to college and some do not; some get married and some remain single; some write poetry and some sell insurance. It is not until the years of late adulthood, when such predictable events as retirement, widowhood, and certain physical declines are common, that age-graded influences once again become relatively strong. Because of the greater importance of non-age-graded influences during adulthood, people tend to become more diverse as they age: two 50-year-olds are likely to be more different from each other in their personalities and outlooks on life than two 10-year-olds or even two 20-year-olds.

Despite the diversity of adult lives, however, certain psychological tasks and challenges do seem to characterize particular stages of life. Erik Erikson (1950) influenced much of the current research on adult development by outlining three major stages of adult development. (These are the last three of Erikson's stages of psychosocial

Some adults maintain relatively stable lives, but others undergo major changes. Jerry Rubin, for example, was an antiestablishment Yippie leader in 1968, but a decade later was a research analyst on Wall Street.

development that we presented in Chapter 9, Box 4). In early adulthood, Erikson believes, the central psychological challenge is to establish *intimacy*—a close bond with another person, usually a husband or wife. In middle adulthood, the central psychological challenge is *generativity*—having an impact on the next generation, whether through guiding one's own children or through one's contribution to society. And in late adulthood or old age, Erikson emphasizes the theme of *integrity*, the ability to look back at one's life with satisfaction. We will return to each of these themes later in this chapter.

A central issue in the study of adult development is the extent to which it is characterized by *stability versus change*. For example, will the artistic and literary woman of 23 remain absorbed in cultural matters as she grows older, or will these interests become overshadowed by the demands of career and family when she reaches 33? Will the ambitious, aggressive man of 35 still be so hard-driving when he is 50, or will he become more inward-looking and mild-mannered? The best way to answer these questions about stability and change in development is through *longitudinal* studies, in which the same people are assessed periodically through their adult years. (It is also valuable to compare the traits and life-styles of members of different generations, as illustrated in Box 1.)

Although the evidence to date is limited, longitudinal studies have provided evidence for both stability and change. Despite the fact that people often turn to different activities as they age—a middle-aged man may give up competitive sports and take up gardening—a person's overall level of activity seems to be quite stable through the life span, with those who are most energetic and active in their youth also being the most energetic and active in late adulthood (Haan and Day, 1974). Similarly, studies have found a great deal of stability in people's personality traits, such as outgoingness, over the adult years (Costa and McCrae, 1980). As Jack Block (1980) concludes, "Amidst change and transformation, there is an essential coherence to personality development" (page 623).

At the same time, recent studies have also emphasized the potential for significant changes in skills, values, and self-concept through the course of adulthood. As people deal with the tasks and challenges of adult life, they may also come to view themselves in new ways and in some respects become "different people." For example, a quiet and deferential housewife who enters law school at 32, after her children are in school, may emerge several years later as a much more forceful, outspoken woman, not only in her professional life as a corporate lawyer but in her family roles, as well. Robert Butler (1963) also suggests that substantial reorganization of personality often takes place in old age, leading to the wisdom and serenity that are characteristic of many old people.

EARLY ADULTHOOD

When is a person an adult? There is no single criterion. Legal definitions of adulthood rely on chronological age. In most states, for example, one can vote at 18 and drink at 20 or 21. But a person's age is

— Box 1 —

Generations

We are often struck by the differences between people of different generations—the old, the middle-aged, and the young. A study conducted by Vern Bengtson (1973) and his colleagues at the University of Southern California, involving more than 2100 family members in three different generations, shed light on such generational differences. Some of these differences are illustrated by three generations of men in the fictional "Johnson" family:

JOHANN JOHNSON (age 73)

Retired against his will from a factory job, he spends much of his time gardening, listening to religious radio programs, and talking with friends. . . . He describes his "most important events in life" as follows: came to America as a five-year-old; lost a good farm during the Depression because of speculation; started making good money in a factory during World War II; lost wife from cancer in 1970. . . . He says he doesn't have any goals any more . . . and that his only concern is to "keep active."

He answers questions in our research questionnaire as follows:

Johann Johnson

Best thing that could happen to you: *"To see our nation return to God."*
Worst thing that could happen to you: *"To lose my health, which is excellent."*
Self-rated liberal to conservative: *"Very conservative."*
Church attendance: *"Every week, when I can get a ride."*

ARCHIE JOHNSON (age 48)

Spends 45 hours per week as an engineer for an aerospace contractor. His salary is good . . . but he works harder than he did a decade ago because in 1970 he was laid off for 18 months before finding a new job. . . . He describes the most important events in his life thus: ran away from home to join

Archie Johnson

the Navy in 1942, fathered two children, got a college degree on the G.I. bill while supporting his family, got a house in the suburbs. . . . He has a carefully ordered list of goals for the next year—economic, social, and self-development—which he and his wife go over every three months.

His questionnaire shows the following answers:

Best thing that could happen to you: *"To see my children grow and make the world a better place."*
Worst thing that could happen to you: *"To lose my job."*
Self-rated liberal to conservative: *"Slightly conservative."*
Church attendance: *"About once a month."*

---

not really a good indicator of her physical and psychological development. One 18-year-old may support herself and feel quite independent, while another may remain her parents' "little girl" until she is well into her twenties. Nevertheless, all of us must at some time, usually in our late teens or early twenties, leave the relatively sheltered world of adolescence and enter the world of adulthood. The period of early adulthood extends from this time until about the age of 40, when people make the transition into the middle years of life.

Physical and cognitive changes take place in early adulthood, just as they do in infancy, childhood, and adolescence. For example, physical strength and heart functions usually peak in the mid-twenties, with a gradual decline from then on (Hershey, 1974). Sensory acuity and reaction time also tend to be at their peaks in the twenties and to decline gradually thereafter (Birren, 1964). But the physical

KIRK JOHNSON (age 23)

Says he spends most of his time during the week "studying with time out for meditating and turning on." He is finishing his degree in sociology at a local state college. He lives with Joan, a sophomore nursing student, and enjoys seeing his parents wince when he asserts that he and his "old lady" have no intention of getting married— ever. . . . He at first does not want to talk about his life goals—"Hanging loose and acting on feelings is very important to me"—but then talks animatedly about his desire to become a social worker, to have a career helping people, to form an urban commune which will really last, and to work for world peace.

Answers to questionnaire:

Best thing that could happen to you in life: *"To have the world free from war and everyone to be my brother."*
Worst thing: *"To have someone tell me I can't do my own thing."*
Self-rated liberal to conservative: *He wrote in "radical."*
Church attendance: *"Never."*

Among the study's findings, which are graphically illustrated in the Johnson family example: (1) people in the grandparent generation assign greater importance to religious participation than do young people; (2) grandparents describe

Kirk Johnson

themselves as much more conservative politically; (3) those in the middle-aged generation rank the value of "achievement" higher than do the other generations.

How do we explain these differences? Some of them are related to the person's stage in the life cycle. Kirk's goals are long-range, humanitarian, intense—he has a long life ahead of him. Archie's goals are more immediate and concern his own situation. Johann looks back on his life with satisfaction and won't talk about goals.

There are also biological differences between people at different ages. Thus Johann discusses his health at great length, Archie mentions a decline in energy—"I have to put more time in to compete

with the younger guys," he says— and Kirk dismisses the subject.

Other differences are best explained in terms of differences in historical time. Johann's conservatism does not reflect his age, but rather the fact that people in his generation have tended to vote for conservatives since he first voted in 1922. (As Cutler and Kaufman [1975] have found, people do *not* generally become more conservative as they grow older.) Similarly, Archie's orientation toward working and saving is less a result of being middle-aged and more a result of having grown up during the Depression. And Kirk's living with his girlfriend without benefit of marriage seems to be more a matter of contemporary views of man-woman relationships than a matter of youth sowing wild oats. Generational differences of this sort, which apply to groups—or cohorts—of people who grow up during particular historical periods, are called *cohort effects.*

Bengtson's research makes clear that any difference between generations may have several possible explanations. We must be concerned with the psychological, the biological, and the historical sources of such differences before we can begin to understand them.

and cognitive changes of early adulthood are much less noticeable than the corresponding changes of childhood or of old age, and they play a comparatively minor role in development. Instead, the most significant aspects of early adult development involve the ways in which individuals deal with several central psychological tasks and decisions: separating from the world of childhood and becoming one's own person, choosing an occupation, establishing an intimate relationship, and starting a family.

The Stages of Early Adulthood

On the basis of an intensive study of the lives of forty men, psychologist Daniel Levinson (1978) has proposed that early adulthood—at least for men—consists of several discrete stages, involving an alter-

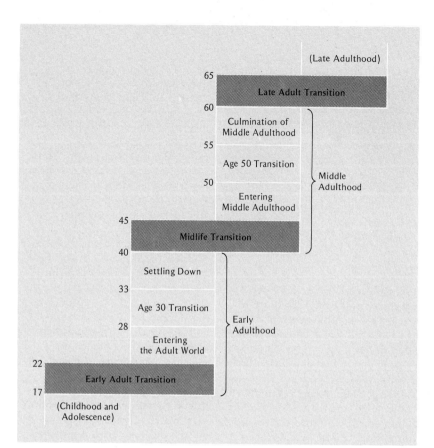

FIGURE 10.1
The stages of adult development postulated by Daniel Levinson.

nating sequence of relatively stable periods and periods of transition. Through all of the stages, each person engages in a continuing struggle to evolve a *life structure:* the basic pattern or design of one's life at a given time. A life structure includes both external features (such as career, marriage, and family) and one's internal view of oneself, or sense of identity. The stages Levinson proposes, extending on through the entire life span, are depicted in Figure 10.1.

The Early Adult Transition (Ages 17–22). During these years, the man must start moving out of the preadult world of his childhood and take his first steps into the adult world. College is one setting in which many men (and women) work on their separation from the family and expand their outlook on life.

Entering the Adult World (Ages 22–28). Now the young man is a "novice adult," with a life of his own. At this stage, he must find the right balance between two opposing tasks. One is to explore the possibilities of adult life, keeping his options open. The other is to create a stable life structure, to begin to "make something" of his life. During this period, most men embark on careers, form intimate relationships, and start families.

The Age 30 Transition (Ages 28–33). As the man approaches 30, he is drawn to examine the initial adult life structure that he has established and in many cases to modify it. Life becomes more serious—now it's "for real." Some men make major life changes during the age 30 transition, such as changing careers or getting married. Whether the transition is smooth or abrupt, the man's life structure is always different at the end of this period than it was at its start.

"DON'T TRUST ANYONE UNDER 30"

Whether young people are politically radical or conservative seems to be less a matter of their age than of the times. Thus, the campus radicalism of the 1960s had given way to a more moderate mood by the late 1970s. Jerry Rubin, the former Yippie leader who used to say, "Never trust anyone over 30" is in his 40s now and says, "Don't trust anyone under 30. You know how conservative young people are today." Rubin has gone pretty straight himself—he's now a stock analyst on Wall Street.

Settling Down (Ages 33–40). Following the age 30 transition, the man invests himself in his "second life structure." He tries to establish a place for himself in society, to solidify his family life, and to make it in the world of work. Toward the end of this stage (during the years between 36 and 40), Levinson speaks of the period of "becoming one's own man," when the man is most concerned with becoming a full-fledged senior member of the adult world.

Settling down and "becoming one's own man" do not conclude the story of adult development, from Levinson's perspective. To the contrary, this stage is typically followed by a new period of self-doubt and questioning, the midlife transition, which we will consider later in this chapter.

Although his study focused on forty American men, Levinson believes that all men go through the same stages at approximately the ages specified, give or take a few years. "Even the most disparate lives," he suggests, "are governed by the same underlying order" (page 64). Other researchers doubt that the stages of men's lives are in fact as clear and unvarying as Levinson suggests. Rather than describing people's lives in terms of distinct stages, they would prefer to view them in terms of continuous movement along different dimensions (see, for example, Costa and McCrae, 1980).

There is also controversy about the extent to which Levinson's stages might be applicable to women's development. Levinson himself conjectures that women go through the same basic adult developmental periods as men, but other researchers believe that there are some fundamental differences between women's and men's development. As Rosalind Barnett and Grace Baruch (1978) note, Levinson's stages reflect in large measure men's preoccupations with careers. For women, however, careers are less taken for granted. As we will see, women's experiences in early and middle adulthood depend to a large extent on the specific decisions they make about work, marriage, and child rearing. In any event, Levinson's proposed stages, as well as the related stages postulated by Roger Gould (1978), provide valuable starting points for further research on the course of adult development.

Choosing an Occupation

Although we think of adulthood and work as going hand in hand, this connection is a relatively recent historical development. Until the early twentieth century, children often worked long hours in factories, on farms, or as apprentices. But today work is usually a central force behind adult identity, life-style, and growth. Try to imagine all the ways in which work can affect your life. Did you include the time you get up in the morning, the clothes you wear, your health, your leisure activities, your friends, the time you spend with your family, and your civic activities? Think about the one question you usually ask when you meet someone: "What do you do?" And think about the feelings the person might have when answering "I'm an architect" or "I'm unemployed."

Initial decisions about an occupation may be made in adolescence or even childhood. These early decisions are often quite unre-

Work and career are a central focus of adult life. Some people choose an occupation and stick with it for a lifetime; others may explore a number of careers over the course of adulthood.

alistic, however. For example, as many as half of all teenagers indicate a preference for professional occupations, whereas only about 14 percent actually become professionals (Cosby, 1974). Observing the work roles of one's parents can have a major impact on career decisions. In particular, having a working mother as a model often plays a crucial role in women's decisions to enter professions (Lopate, 1968). It is not until early adulthood, however, that one must actually crystallize and implement one's career plans, by getting appropriate training and by finding one's first job.

Actually entering the work world can produce "reality shock"—the discovery of the awful gap between idealized images of the job and the skills taught in school, on the one hand, and the actual rewards and demands of the job, on the other. As Judith Stevens-Long (1979) notes, "Typing classes and television comedies don't offer a realistic picture of life as a medical receptionist/secretary, and law school provides at best only meager contact with the realities of the occupation of attorney" (page 168). Such reality shock contributes to the high turnover in certain fields, such as nursing and teaching (Ritzer, 1977). In most cases, however, the young workers get over their initial shock and strive to advance in their chosen field. The years between the late twenties and about 40 are typically ones in which the worker advances in status and seniority and in which job satisfaction increases.

Some approaches to career development postulate an orderly progression through stages of career implementation, establishment, maintenance, deceleration, and retirement (Super, 1969). But how much sense do such models of orderly career development make in the 1980s? What is the "normal career cycle" of the working mother, the disabled veteran, or the executive who decides that he really wants to write novels? Recently many social scientists have been suggesting alternatives to the "one life–one career" model, in which people can be freer to explore many occupations, perhaps interspersed with periods away from work, within a single lifetime (Sarason, 1977). For example, a young woman may plan a short stint as an elementary-school teacher, concentrate on being a homemaker during her childbearing years, then resume her career later on as a candidate for the local school board, hoping to run eventually for the state legislature (Stevens-Long, 1979).

Establishing an Intimate Relationship

For Erik Erikson, the central psychological challenge of early adulthood is to establish an intimate relationship. Such intimacy, usually in the context of a close heterosexual relationship, involves a high degree of sharing and communication between two people. With the achievement of intimacy, the person feels enriched and connected to others; without it, he is lonely and isolated.

"In youth," Erikson (1974) writes, "you find what you *care to do* and where you *care to be*. . . . In young adulthood you learn whom you *care to be with*—at work and in private life, not only exchanging intimacies, but sharing intimacy" (page 124). As this implies, Erikson believes that a clear sense of one's own identity—who one is and what one believes in—is a prerequisite for the establishment of intimacy. A truly intimate relationship requires "a fusing of identities" while at the same time retaining a sense of self. A person with a weak identity will be too fearful of losing her own fragile sense of self to be able to

A central challenge of early adulthood is to establish an intimate relationship with another person without losing one's own identity.

achieve such intimacy. At best, such a person might form unstable or highly dependent relationships.

Recent studies have provided support for Erikson's view. In one study, measures of college students' "identity status" and "intimacy status" were derived from interviews about their life commitments and interpersonal relationships. Men and women who had achieved a clear sense of identity were found to have deeper and more committed relationships than those who had not yet developed a clear identity (Kacerguis and Adams, 1980). The results of this and other correlational studies do not show that identity achievement necessarily precedes intimacy, however. In fact, intimacy has an impact on one's identity, as well. As David Matteson (1975) observes, "In every real sharing experience both persons grow; identities are rediscovered and altered" (page 161).

Erikson believes that true intimacy must take place within a committed relationship, in which two persons pledge themselves to each other for a long period of time. Most specifically, Erikson is thinking of marriage. In recent decades, more and more people have questioned the necessary link between intimacy and commitment or permanence. In particular, many people have questioned the need and value of the institution of marriage. Nevertheless, the vast majority of people do get married in early adulthood. And an increasing number are also getting unmarried either in early adulthood or later in life. We will return to the themes of intimacy and commitment in Chapter 14.

Starting a Family

Early adulthood is the time when most people not only get married but also have children. Nineteen of twenty married couples today have at least one child, and almost all of these children are born during the parents' early adult years. Most of the psychological research on parents and children has focused on the parents' impact on the children. In Chapter 9, for instance, we considered the ways in which different approaches to child rearing may affect children's development. It is important to recognize, however, that having and raising children also has a great impact on the parents' development. Parents typically report that having children makes them feel "more like an adult" and more responsible. Parents also feel that they obtain many satisfactions from their children, including affection, fun, and a sense of purpose (Hoffman and Manis, 1979). But the rearing of children has its negative side, as well. Once they have children, the couple have greater financial difficulties, less time to spend with each other, and greater difficulty balancing work and family demands.

Until relatively recent years, married couples were expected to have children if they were biologically able to do so, and this expectation was one that few couples thought to defy. In the last decade, however, the option of not having children—*voluntary childlessness*—has become more acceptable for young couples. Couples are now considering more carefully the decision of whether to have children, and a significant minority are deciding that the costs would outweigh

THE HAPPINESS QUOTIENT

In 1957, American men and women in their twenties were considerably more likely than people in their sixties to describe their lives as "very happy." In 1978 this difference had disappeared in national surveys. The young adults of 1978 were less ready than the young adults of 1957 to say that they were very happy, while the old people were slightly more ready. Angus Campbell (1980) noted that in 1978 people in their twenties were considerably more likely than their 1957 counterparts to be single, separated, or divorced, and that this situation may have contributed to their lesser happiness. Campbell also suggested that the rapid social changes of the past two decades have created uncertainty and conflict for many young people, which doesn't make them very happy.

the rewards. The decision to remain "childfree" rarely seems to be made explicit early in the marriage. Instead, the pair decide to postpone having children for varying periods of time, until they finally decide to make the postponement permanent (Veevers, 1973).

In addition to deciding whether to have children, couples decide *when* to have them. Whereas in previous generations most couples launched their families when they were in their early twenties, more and more couples today are waiting until their late twenties or early thirties to have their first child. Pamela Daniels and Kathy Weingarten (1982) recently interviewed couples in three different generations who had their children "early" (in their early twenties) or "later" (in their late twenties or early thirties). Their interviews emphasized the major impact that family timing has on people's lives. The couples who had their children later generally believed that the postponement helped give them a chance to solidify their marriage, to advance both the husband's and wife's careers, and in general to do more "growing up" before bringing a child into the world. For example, an artist who became a mother at 32 felt that if she had had children when she was younger, her work "never would have formed itself." As she put it, "The twenties were the years I was putting everything together, without even knowing what I was doing, evolving a style, and getting my work going." But many later mothers also found that the arrival of a baby created new conflicts with their rising careers that they had not anticipated. Moreover, some of the early parents stressed the advantage of having their children grow up sooner. One early mother, now a systems analyst, summarized the tradeoff involved:

I like the fact that my children are as old as they are, and that I'm as young as I am and my career is so open ahead of me. I'd hate to be in my career position, wanting to have children and not knowing when to make the break. On the other hand, I missed that

More and more couples are waiting until their late twenties or early thirties to launch a family.

early period of freedom, of trying my wings and doing things on my own. (Daniels and Weingarten, 1982)

The issue of family timing serves to illustrate the importance of the links between the different tasks of early adulthood: work, intimacy, and the family. Today people are able to make a wide range of decisions about each of these tasks. But the decisions are not independent of one another. It is the interplay of these decisions, including their timing, that affects the person's development through the course of early adulthood.

MIDDLE ADULTHOOD

The years between 40 and 65 often seem to be a stable, even static period of life. People in middle age have "gotten there." They run our country and most of our major institutions. They have reached some stability in their struggles to establish a career, a family, and a life-style. But in fact, middle age is characterized by development and change, as well as by stability. It is a time of adaptation to physical changes, of new demands from one's work and family, and of evaluation of one's past and future.

Physical Changes in Middle Adulthood

The physical changes that begin in early adulthood continue through the middle adult years. In middle age, there are changes in physical appearance, health and energy, sensory acuity, and sexual functioning. For the most part these changes are gradual, continuing the processes of physical and behavioral decline that begin in the early twenties and extend through the course of life. What is most important in many cases is not so much the changes themselves but how the middle-aged person reacts to them. Sometimes the changes are hardly noticed, sometimes they are welcomed, and sometimes they lead to worry and concern.

One sort of change that one can hardly avoid noticing, especially in a society that gives inordinate emphasis to a "youthful" physical appearance, is changes in one's face and body. The middle-aged person looking in the mirror will find an image quite different from her high-school graduation picture. The eyes are deeper set, the lips are thinner, the facial contours are less pronounced. The skin is becoming wrinkled, and the hair is thinning and may be turning gray. Weight gain, especially in the stomach and hips, is common. Although some changes in appearance are inevitable, the amount of change depends on behavior, as well as on biology. "Middle-aged spread," for example, is in part a result of the redistribution of fatty tissues that naturally occurs as we get older, but it also reflects a life-style common to many middle-aged people—eating more, eating richer foods, and getting less exercise.

Changes in health may also be quite important in middle age. Even if one has no immediate health problems, one begins to take seriously the threat of death or disease. For men, in particular, the

Some of the physical changes that take place in adulthood can be seen in the face of John F. Kennedy as he aged from 22 (left), *to 29* (center), *to 46* (right).

concern is not unfounded. The risk of heart diseases, which are the primary cause of death for men in the United States, increases after age 30, and the highest risk is between the ages of 50 and 60. Similarly, the risk of breast cancer for women is greatest in middle age (Owen, 1978). As with changes in appearance, declining health is not a necessary product of getting older. It is related not only to biologically "preprogrammed" processes but also to one's habits throughout life. Stress in the job or family, tobacco or alcohol abuse, overeating, and lack of exercise all increase one's susceptibility to disease.

Even when he is in the best of health, the middle-aged person may notice some changes in what he can do. Heart and lung capacity continue to decline in middle adulthood, leading to a gradually diminishing capacity for strenuous work (see Figure 10.2). Changes in the brain's capacity to initiate and coordinate sets of movements leads to decreasing speed in the performance of many tasks, such as copying sets of numbers. Changes in sexual functioning may also occur in middle adulthood. For men, decreases in the volume of blood in the penis can cause erection and ejaculation to occur more slowly. For women, drops in hormone levels can cause vaginal walls to thin and vaginal secretions to be reduced (Masters and Johnson, 1966). But in the domains of both physical ability and sexuality, the extent of change is largely determined by individual physical condition, attitudes, and habits. Many people remain active in sports throughout middle adulthood, and exercise programs begun even late in life can yield marked improvements in physical capacity (deVries, 1970). Both men and women with positive attitudes toward sexuality usually continue to lead active sex lives throughout middle adulthood. Contrary to some people's assumptions, the woman's menopause, at about age 45 to 50, need not interfere with her sexual functioning (see Box 2).

Although middle-aged adults often ignore gradual changes in their physical and sensory functioning, becoming aware of such changes can be useful. For example, changes in the eye's structures

— *Box 2* ————————————————

Menopause

Sometime during the years of middle adulthood women experience a particular developmental change not shared by men: menopause. Medically, menopause is defined as 12 consecutive months without a menstrual period. Over a span of about two years, at roughly 50 years of age, a woman's hormonal function reorganizes itself. At the end of this reorganization period, estrogen levels are quite low and the ovaries no longer release eggs for fertilization; the woman can no longer bear children. This process is sometimes accompanied by uncomfortable physical symptoms, such as "hot flashes" and headaches.

Because menopause is associated with the loss of reproductive capacity and with aging, many psychologists and physicians have assumed that it is a disturbing, even traumatic event in a woman's life. Such an attitude toward menopause is captured in the writing of Helene Deutsch (1944), a prominent psychoanalytic theorist: "Woman has ended her existence as a bearer of a new future, and has reached her natural end—a partial death—as servant of the species. . . . With the lapse of her reproductive service, her beauty vanishes, and usually the warm vital flow of her feminine emotional life as well" (page 477). Such views betray a pervasive sort of sexism: Since women's roles have traditionally been limited to those of wife and mother, it is assumed that the end of the childbearing years must be a terrible and irreparable loss for a woman.

The narrowness of this view of women's aging experiences is underscored when we look at researchers' approaches to men's middle years. While women's lives have been thought to center around reproduction and family, men's lives have been seen as encompassing a wider range of concerns, including work and achievement. The main sources of concern to middle-aged men have been described as reevaluation of long-standing goals, a desire to make a contribution to the next generation, a recognition of mortality, and a renewed questioning of the meaning of their lives (Brim, 1976). Thus, researchers have approached middle-aged men's lives in a fuller way, while confining themselves to the physical transitions in women's middle years.

As a result, we know very little about how middle-aged women evaluate the worth of their lives and almost as little about the physical aspects of the midlife transition in men. Both men and women go through a *climacteric*, a process of physical and sexual slowing down spread out over 15 or 20 years as the adult moves from middle to late adulthood. Menopause is one aspect of the female climacteric. There is no comparable "male menopause" in the sense that fertility ends, but male sex hormone levels do tend to drop generally throughout the climacteric. Whether this drop directly interferes with sexual function or reproductive capacity is not known.

What role does the uniquely female experience of menopause play in women's development? Does the loss of reproductive ability mean the loss of sexuality and attractiveness? Is the nonfertile woman so grief-stricken by her loss that she considers her life over? The evidence suggests not. Far from mourning the loss of their sexuality, many women, now freed from worry over pregnancy or use of contraceptives, enjoy sex more than ever (Weideger, 1977). In reviewing the research on menopause, Malkah Notman (1979) concludes that other events of the middle years, such as release from child-care responsibilities, return to the work force, and changes in marital relationships, are usually much more important to women than menopause itself. The "partial death" that Deutsch describes seems to have more reality for the psychologists and psychiatrists who write about it than for the women who are supposed to be experiencing it.

result in a gradual loss of visual acuity over the course of adulthood (Fozard et al., 1977). Some losses are correctable with glasses, and in many cases are so slight that they might not be noticed by the individual until about the age of 70 (Birren, 1964). However, it may be important for the person to be aware of such sensory declines to make sure her daily functioning is not impaired. In a study of the effect of lighting conditions on work performance, for example, younger (19- to 27-year-old) and middle-aged (46- to 57-year-old) office workers were given the task of finding certain numbers on several sheets of paper under three different levels of illumination. In-

FIGURE 10.2

Physical changes with age. As we get older, our physical functioning becomes less efficient, as indexed by decrements in the cardiac index (the heart's output of blood to the body), vital capacity (the volume of air that can be exhaled from the lungs after a deep breath), and maximal breathing capacity (the volume of air that can be breathed in 15 seconds).

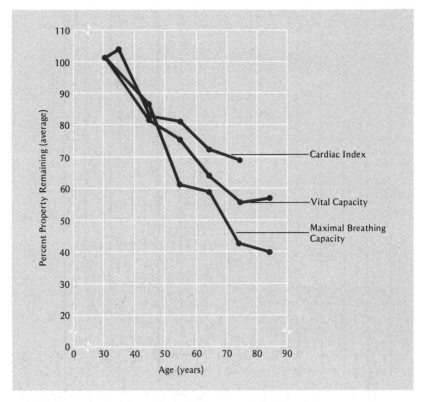

creased lighting improved the performance of both younger and middle-aged workers, but the middle-aged workers benefited more (Hughes, 1977). By optimizing the conditions in which they work, middle-aged adults can keep their functioning at an optimal level.

The Midlife Transition

Sometime around the age of 40, people must make the transition from early to middle adulthood. They must come to a new conception of themselves as middle-aged people, with new tasks, limitations, and opportunities. This shift is called the *midlife transition.*

In his study of men's lives, Daniel Levinson (1978) found that the midlife transition begins at about age 40 and lasts about five years. Levinson also reports that for 80 percent of the men he studied, the midlife transition involved a painful and disruptive struggle. In such cases, the men were seen as having a *midlife crisis:*

Every aspect of their lives comes into question, and they are horrified by much that is revealed. They are full of recriminations against themselves and others. They cannot go on as before, but need time to choose a new path or modify the old one. . . . A profound reappraisal of this kind cannot be a cool, intellectual process. It must involve emotional turmoil, despair, the sense of not knowing where to turn or of being stagnant and unable to move at all. (Levinson, 1978, page 199)

Whether the midlife transition is smooth or abrupt (see examples in Box 3), Levinson believes that it is a normal and necessary developmental stage. As a man reaches the middle of his life, he is drawn to

— Box 3 —

Paths through the midlife transition

In Daniel Levinson's view, there are many possible paths through the midlife transition, ranging from relatively smooth, uneventful movement from early to middle adulthood to painful, tormented struggles with one's life. The cases of two of the blue-collar workers in Levinson's study provide examples:

Perhaps the most stable, yet continually evolving life was that of Ralph Ochs. At 45, he is still working in the plumbing department of the factory where, at 18, he started as an apprentice to his father. A man of great integrity and modest aspirations, he enriched his life over the course of early adulthood by his active involvement in organizing and running a union, becoming a shop steward, and, as he passed 40, serving as an informal adviser to younger workers. His major investment is now in his family. He speaks with unusual

perceptiveness and caring about his three adolescent children. He would like all three to go to college. His eldest son is graduating from high school and has no interest in college. Ochs recognizes that this is a source of tension between them, and he is trying with considerable tact and insight to be helpful but not overly controlling. He takes considerable delight in the talents and projects of his youngest daughter, the brightest and most successful of the children. He enjoys and works at being an active father.

Contrasting sharply with Ralph Ochs's stable midlife transition was the more stressful passage of another worker:

Larry Strode left a black middle-class home in the South following military service in World War II. At 40, after fifteen years in the same factory, he was a skilled worker, shop steward, and occasional foreman. He was oppressed by the realization that he could advance no further in industry and that his life was of little value. During his midlife transition (age 40 to 45) he started his own barber

shop, continued at the factory, completed high school, explored the work world for alternative occupations, and tried desperately to improve his failing marriage. The son of a minister, he had long wanted a career that would more directly benefit human minds and souls. At 45, Strode began to build a new life structure. He left the factory and became a mental health worker at a local factory, while continuing to manage his barber shop. He separated from his wife, and divorced her a few years later. During the late forties he tried to develop a new occupation and family life (including the children of his former marriage, with whom he was strongly involved). At 49, when we last saw him, he was just beginning to succeed in making a life different from that of his early adulthood.

Whether the transition is easy or painful, Levinson believes that it involves important tasks of self-examination and development. In all cases, the individual's life in the late forties will differ in important respects from that in the late thirties.

---

appraise his values and talents and the degree to which he has lived up to them. One man may decide that as a result of his youthful ambition to get to the top he has become an overly aggressive, grasping person. Another man may regret the fact that he gave up his early dream to become a musician and may decide that he must find a way to recapture this side of himself. By the time a man is 40, he must also give up certain illusions that he may have had in early adulthood—for example, "If I can only become president of the company, then I'll be happy." Now the man may have to face up to the fact that he'll never be company president. Or he may *be* president and realize that he is still dissatisfied. Through the course of the midlife transition, the man must come to terms with himself and build a new life structure that is better suited for the years of middle adulthood. Through the remaining stages of middle adulthood (see Figure 10.1), the man proceeds to solidify and further modify this new life structure.

There are additional factors that may bring on such a period of transition or crisis in midlife (Brim, 1976). For example, hormonal changes and the awareness of a physical slowdown may force the man to recognize that he is not "young" anymore. Midlife may also bring on a new time orientation (Neugarten, 1968). The person stops counting "time since birth" and begins to view life in terms of "time left to live." Instead of thinking, "I'm only 41," he might begin to think, "I have maybe 25 good years left." In the view of Elliot Jaques (1965), the primary impetus for the midlife crisis is the recognition of one's own mortality: "Death . . . instead of being a general conception, or an event experienced in terms of the loss of someone else, becomes a personal matter . . ." (page 506). All of these factors may contribute to the inner struggle and despair of a midlife crisis.

Levinson's formulation of the midlife transition is highly controversial. Several researchers have challenged the view that the midlife transition is typically a time of crisis and have maintained that the transition is more often than not a relatively gradual shift from a "younger" to an "older" self-conception (see, for example, Vaillant, 1977). In addition, statistical studies with larger samples than Levinson's have generally failed to support his conclusion that personal turmoil and struggle are at their height during the years between 40 and 45 (Costa and McCrae, 1980). The relevance of Levinson's conclusions to women has also been questioned (Barnett and Baruch, 1978). Further research is needed before conclusive statements about the nature of the midlife transition, for both men and women, will be possible.

Personality in Middle Adulthood

Regardless of the precise timing and nature of the midlife transition, there is no doubt of the importance of the shift from early to middle adulthood in people's lives, from a time when men and women think of themselves as young to a time when they think of themselves as middle-aged. There is evidence that the period of middle adulthood is associated with greater introspection and inward-turning for many people, a process of increasing self-knowledge that often continues

According to Erik Erikson, the challenge of middle age is to achieve generativity—to make a contribution to members of the younger generation either by raising them, teaching them, or serving as an example for them.

into the years of old age (Neugarten, 1968). At the same time, it has been suggested that middle adulthood in many cultures—including our own—is a time of sex-role reversal when many men become more interpersonally sensitive and nurturant, while many women become more outgoing and assertive (Gutmann, 1969). To the extent that such changes take place, middle adulthood may be a time during which both men and women recapture "lost" parts of themselves and become more fully human. (In Chapter 13 we will return to the theme of transcending the limitations of one's sex role.)

In Erik Erikson's view, the major psychological challenge in middle adulthood is achieving *generativity*—to feel that one is making significant contributions to the next generation. Without such generativity, one may feel a sense of worthlessness or stagnation. The middle-aged person may achieve generativity by guiding her children as they make the transition from adolescence into early adulthood. Although such relationships between middle-aged parents and their children almost always involve conflict—sometimes described in terms of the "generation gap"—they can also be sources of considerable satisfaction. As one woman said of her daughter's transition to adulthood, "I haven't lost a daughter—I have gained a friend and confidante" (Hagestad, 1980).

Generativity can also be achieved in the world of work, as middle-aged people strive to make contributions that they feel will have some lasting importance. Increasing numbers of men and women are switching jobs or careers in middle adulthood, in a search for work that will be more satisfying. And many women enter a new career or reenter an old one in their thirties and forties, once their children are in school or have left home. One of the most important career rewards for many middle-aged people is the opportunity to be a *mentor*—someone who can influence and further the development of young adults, such as students or younger coworkers. As Levinson writes, "Good mentoring is one of the special contributions that persons in middle adulthood can make to society" (page 234).

LATE ADULTHOOD

In the 25 years prior to 1978, the age group of people 65 and over grew twice as fast as the U.S. population as a whole. As medical advances extend life expectancies, the elderly are becoming a larger and larger proportion of the total population—4 percent in 1930, 10 percent in 1980, and probably about 13 percent in 2020. A man of 65 can now expect to live to almost age 79, and a woman to age 83. Researchers in both medicine and psychology, aware of the increasing population of the elderly, are addressing the question, "What does it mean to be old?"

Before we examine some of their findings, we should point out that late adulthood may itself encompass several stages of life, from the 70-year-old who continues to lead an active, vigorous life to the 85-year-old whose activities may have greatly slowed down. Because of such differences, Bernice Neugarten (1975) suggests that we distinguish between the "young-old" and the "old-old," rather than talking

THE EMPTY NEST

When the last child leaves home, do parents sit tearfully over faded baby pictures, or do they break out the champagne? More often than not, it's the champagne. Many people have assumed that parents, especially mothers, feel a sense of loss and of purposelessness when the children leave. But studies have found that the majority of men and women actually look forward to the "empty nest" (Lowenthal and Chiriboga, 1972). There may be a feeling of regret, to be sure. But after having had children in the home for some 20 or 25 years, parents may find the prospect of a more private life to be a relief. And parents' relationships with their children tend to *improve* after the children have left home (Sullivan and Sullivan, 1980).

Although beauty is often associated with youth, the age-weathered faces of the elderly can also be seen as beautiful.

about old age as a single category. Some of our prevailing cultural attitudes—and prejudices—about old age are examined in Box 4.

The Biology of Aging

Like every other period of life, late adulthood is marked by its own set of changes and experiences. Many of the physical changes that were barely noticeable in middle age become marked in the late sixties. Visual acuity and hearing may become noticeably impaired. Changes in the spinal column can produce stooped posture. Muscles and joints may become stiff enough to reduce physical activity. Blood vessels lose their elasticity, which can lead to circulatory problems. Changes in the central nervous system produce a general slowing down of behavior. The body's system of immune responses for fighting disease becomes less efficient.

All these changes relate to aging. Why do they occur? Can aging and ultimate death be slowed or even eliminated? No one knows for sure why we age and die. But there are several biological theories of aging, and each may provide part of the answer. One group of theories is based on changes in the individual cells that make up our bodies. Some of our cells, such as those of the heart and brain, do not divide; when they die, they can never be replaced. Theorists have suggested that these cells "wear out" over time, as a result of such influences as exposure to radiation and excessive changes in body temperature. In addition, certain chemical reactions within cells produce waste materials that the cells cannot dispose of and that may ultimately lead to the death of the cell (Timiras, 1978). One such substance is *lipofuscin*, the chemical that causes brown "age spots" to appear on the skin of older persons. Even those body cells that do

HOW LONG CAN WE LIVE?

All forms of life have some upper limit on their life span—from 10 to 20 days for the house fly to about 2000 years for some trees. Human beings live longer than any other mammals, and our maximum life span is probably about 110 years (Medvedev, 1975). Claims that eating yogurt or living in high altitudes produces much longer life spans than 110 have not been substantiated. Although researchers are investigating a variety of ways of prolonging animal life spans—from reducing body temperatures to intestinal surgery—it does not appear that the maximum human life span can be extended much beyond 110 or so. What probably *can* be done is to conquer and control diseases of old age so that more and more people will live into their nineties or even past 100.

— Box 4

Ageism

When one group of college students were asked how they felt about old age, their responses included: "Dread, disgust, I will not get old"; "It's frightening. . . . I wish I didn't have to"; "I hope I die before I get there"; "It will never happen to me" (Barrow, 1976). It seems clear that, at least for this group of students, old age is not something desirable.

Our society places a high value on the attributes of youth, and we tend to demean old age. The resulting bias against old people is a particular form of discrimination called *ageism*. Ageism is most obviously reflected in our stereotypes of elderly women and men. The stereotypical old person is not someone one would care to become: dependent on others, mentally unreliable, uninterested in sex (and unable to perform anyway), cranky, fretful, and rigid ("You can't teach an old dog new tricks"). "Old age is seen as path-

The popularity of cosmetic treatments to make old people "look younger" is one reflection of ageism in our society.

ological," Richard Kalish (1979) writes, "a time of sickness and strangeness and falling-apartness. It is also seen as a static period without much chance for change in a positive direction."

Even young children are likely to latch onto the prevailing negative view of old people. In one recent study, preschool children were shown photographs of young, middle-aged, and old people and asked to indicate which pictures "went with" each of a list of adjectives. The children linked negative adjectives (such as sad, bad, ugly, poor, and dirty) much more often with photographs of old people than with photographs of the young or middle-aged (Chitwood and Bigner, 1980).

Some aspects of the ageist stereotype may have a grain of truth. Older people are more prone to disease than younger people. The mental processes of the elderly tend to be slower (though not necessarily less powerful) than they were in youth. And there is some evidence that older people tend to be more cautious and less flexible than younger people (Riley, Foner et al., 1968). But most of the research on the personalities of old people reveals what we should have known in the first place: that the personalities of old people are quite as diverse as the personalities of people at any other stage of life (Maddox and Douglas, 1974). The stereotype fools us into viewing a 70-year-old or an 80-year-old as an "old person" rather than as a distinctive individual with unique strengths and weaknesses.

Ageism is also reflected in the feeling of discomfort that many younger people have with older adults, perhaps because of our mental link between old age and sickness and death. Even health professionals—doctors, nurses, social workers, and students in these fields—have tended to avoid working with the elderly, prefer-

ring to work instead with children or younger adults (Palmore, 1977). In hospital emergency rooms, old people are less likely to get a thorough examination than young people, are less likely to elicit the fullest efforts of the medical staff, and are more likely to be declared "dead on arrival" (Sudnow, 1967).

In addition to the stereotype of old persons, there is another, more subtle form of ageism. Because advanced age is so little valued in our society, there is only one way to age successfully, and that is not to age at all. Older people are seen as aging "successfully" to the extent that they continue to behave the way they did when they were younger—that is, like middle-aged people. As Kalish (1975) points out, this definition of "successful aging" is an example of ageism at its worst, because it presumes that one age group's pattern of behavior is inherently superior to that of another age group. Nevertheless, such a definition is often held, at least implicitly, even by many professionals who work with the aged. "She looks like a woman twenty years younger" or "He still plays a set of tennis every day" is often taken as the highest compliment one can pay to an older person.

With the increasing proportion of old people in our society, negative attitudes toward the old may decline. There are already signs of such change: Large numbers of college students now take courses on aging, and increasing numbers of younger adults are becoming interested in careers that involve service to older people. But such change requires us to learn what to respect and admire in the elderly, and that means shifting from a youth-biased set of values that emphasize aggressive competition, glamour, and power and that underemphasize wisdom, freedom from competitiveness, and self-knowledge.

divide eventually stop reproducing themselves, for reasons that are not yet well understood (Hayflick, 1980).

Over the course of time there may also be damage to the genetic information stored in cells. The genetic code used to construct the proteins required by the cell for its survival is stored in DNA molecules in the cell's nucleus. The information is copied and carried to other parts of the cell by another complex molecule, RNA. Damage to the DNA itself, or errors in copying the information in it, could lead to cell death. A single copying error would not necessarily kill the cell, but because cells are constantly renewing themselves, the error would repeat and accumulate over time until the cell eventually died (Timiras, 1978).

Other theories of aging examine whole systems of the body rather than single cells. The immune system normally protects the body from foreign and mutant cells, such as cancer cells. Late in life this system appears to be less efficient in detecting mutant cells and in fighting them off (Makinodan, 1977). This may be one cause of the higher cancer rates in old people. Further, in old age the immune system may become disorganized and start attacking normal cells, producing an *autoimmune reaction* (Walford, 1969).

Still other theories suggest that the endocrine system (see Chapter 2) is primarily responsible for aging. Age-related changes occur in the endocrine glands, leading either to lowered or less efficient endocrine function. Just as the brain controls the hormonal activity that directs physical growth and development, it may induce hormonal changes that lead to aging and death, as well. As Paola Timiras (1978) notes, it is as if there is a "biological master plan" to prevent us from living forever.

In some cases, especially in extreme old age, damage to the brain's cells leads to *senile dementia,* or senility, which can include such symptoms as memory loss, disorientation in time and place, impaired attention, and the loss of the ability to acquire new information. Contrary to many people's assumptions, senility is not a "normal" or usual aspect of old age, but rather a disease that afflicts a minority of very old people. Most forms of senile dementia are incurable. But its symptoms are sometimes mistaken for those of other diseases that can be reversed or cured. One recent study found a treatable medical or psychiatric condition in 35 percent of a group of patients who were originally diagnosed as having irreversible senile dementia (Altman, 1980).

Intellectual Changes in Late Adulthood

Until recently, psychologists believed that people's intellectual capacity leveled off in their twenties and thirties and then started to decline rapidly in middle age and more rapidly in old age. Those people now in their thirties and forties should therefore be gratified to learn of recent research suggesting that in fact intelligence does not generally decline with advancing years. According to these studies, intelligence may actually increase on some measures well into the seventies (Baltes and Schaie, 1974).

These findings rest in part on new forms of intelligence testing. Intelligence in adulthood is not best understood by a single IQ score (see Chapter 6). Rather, intelligence consists of many different abilities that can be grouped into two main categories: fluid intelligence and crystallized intelligence (Horn and Cattell, 1967). *Fluid intelligence* refers to the kind of mental agility, especially nonverbal, that allows people to see old problems in new ways. Such skills as finding the pattern in a string of letters, visualizing an object in space, and piecing together a jigsaw puzzle rely on fluid intelligence. *Crystallized intelligence* includes verbal skills, the ability to define words, and other information accumulated through the course of living in society. Most formal education is concerned with crystallized intelligence.

Fluid intelligence is thought to be more sensitive to changes in the central nervous system. Because aging is accompanied by such changes, it might be expected that fluid intelligence declines over time. Crystallized intelligence on the other hand, relies more on ongoing experience, so it might be expected to improve with age. In fact, these predictions have been supported by research findings. Fluid intelligence seems to begin a gradual decline in middle age and may drop more sharply for many people in late adulthood (Botwinick, 1978). Crystallized intelligence appears to remain the same or to improve at least until the early eighties (Nesselroade, Schaie, and Baltes, 1972). These patterns are summarized in Figure 10.3.

One reason that earlier studies indicated more serious declines in intelligence with greater age is that they tended to compare old people's performances with younger people's at a single point in time. Using this *cross-sectional* approach, the younger people tested higher on the average than the older ones. But the younger people were also born in a time of greater educational opportunities, and this situation almost certainly contributed to their higher scores on some measures of intelligence (Labouvie-Vief, 1979). (This is a cohort

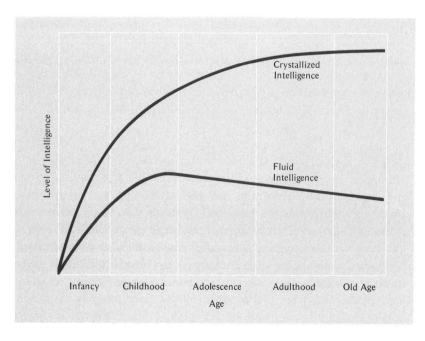

FIGURE 10.3
Changes in two types of intelligence with age. While crystallized intelligence (use of accumulated information and verbal skills) continues to increase through most of the life span, fluid intelligence (mental agility) typically reaches its peak in early adulthood and then gradually declines.

Donald Hebb in his seventies.

effect similar to those we discussed in Box 1.) *Longitudinal* studies, in which the same people are followed over many years, tend to show less decline, and the declines come later in life (Botwinick, 1978). In the very last years of an old person's life, some loss of mental ability is common—a phenomenon known as the "terminal drop" (Botwinick, West, and Storandt, 1978). Aging itself does not necessarily cause cognitive deterioration, but certain diseases, of the sort that can lead to death, often do.

Although fluid intelligence or mental agility does seem to decline with advancing age, there is a great deal of variation between individuals in the patterns of change for different specific abilities. At the age of 74 the prominent psychologist Donald O. Hebb (1978) reflected on some of the changes he had noticed in himself, including a decreasing ability to remember the word he was seeking and a reduced facility with certain sorts of problem solving.

It's embarrassing when you have trouble finding the word you want, particularly when you are lecturing to an undergraduate class and must ask them to tell you the word you can't remember. It is also puzzling as an effect of age, since it's new learning that's supposed to be fragile and easily lost, not old learning. I never used a thesaurus in my writing until eight or nine years ago, in my mid-60s. . . . I have gradually lost interest in Martin Gardner's entertaining mathematical posers in the Scientific American—*and that's likely because I am getting less able to deal with them effectively. On the other hand, I am still addicted to the tough crosswords in the London* Observer; *they're not easier, but they do not require the same ability to juggle ideas. (pages 21-23).*

At the same time, Hebb's ability to reflect on the intellectual changes of late adulthood—and to speculate about the reasons for them—indicates that many of his intellectual abilities remained quite intact.

Social Changes in Late Adulthood

As people enter and move through the years of late adulthood, they inevitably experience changes in the social fabric of their lives—how they spend their time and whom they spend it with. Among the most important social changes of late adulthood are retirement, widowhood, and changing relationships with family and friends. In still later years, a number of old people experience institutionalization.

Retirement. If we have any recognized marker of the onset of late adulthood, it is retirememt. Unlike other life-markers, such as college graduation, marriage, or having a first child, retirement seems to signal an ending more than a new beginning; it isn't clear what is coming next. The average worker can expect to spend the last fourteen years of life in retirement (Butler, 1977).

Most studies show that as long as individuals maintain their health and have an adequate income, they find retirement a satisfying stage of life. Richard Barfield and James Morgan (1978) questioned a number of retired men and their wives on their feelings about retirement. Some of the most positive responses were: "Enjoy every minute of it! Have the time at last to do just what I want or not do anything if I want that." "I like it! We enjoy life a lot more if we're out of the rat race." The negative responses were usually related to poor health: "Not much to think about—you got the black lung; you just sit and wait." "He feels helpless and lost. It gives him a sad feeling seeing the land lying vacant and not being able to plant something" (page 20).

Achieving satisfaction with retirement often requires considerable adjustment. Our society places its highest value on the work-oriented life, and it takes time to switch to a leisure-oriented life and still feel important. Judith Stevens-Long (1979) suggests that three conditions must be met before the retired can be completely comfortable with a leisure-centered life. First, they must have enough money to spend on leisure activities. Second, they must develop a new ethic, based on the belief that leisure is as important and valuable as work. Third, many people may have to learn to use their time in a new way. Just as vocational counseling provides people with information about the work they are best suited for, "leisure education" might help people determine where to redirect their energy and how to restructure their time. Some people prefer "true" leisure activities such as reading and golf; others pursue "work" leisure in civic activities and volunteer work.

Widowhood. Most married women can expect to outlive their husbands, so there are many more widows than widowers. More than half of married women in the United States are widowed by their early sixties, and 80 percent are widowed by their early seventies. Among people over 65, widows outnumber widowers four to one (Hendricks and Hendricks, 1977).

No matter when it occurs in the life span, widowhood can impose serious financial strains on the woman. Just as important, widowhood—for both men and women—can shatter a person's social world. Most of our society's social activities are built around couples; there is no obvious social position for the single adult. This social isolation may be underscored by physical isolation, as well; three-fourths of widowed adults live alone. In at least one recent study, people who were single throughout their lives felt more satisfied in late adulthood than did widows and widowers of the same age; this may be because the single people had chosen a single life-style for themselves and had become adjusted to it (Gubrium, 1974).

Although widowers tend to be better off financially than widows, they have their own particular problems. In one study of 403 persons 62 and over, Carol Barrett (1978) found that widowers felt lonelier, had a harder time with routine household tasks, and were generally less happy with their lives than widows. Many men have become highly dependent on their wives for emotional support, as well as for their housekeeping, and they may also be less likely than women to have close friendships and family ties to fall back on. Perhaps in part for these reasons, widowers are considerably more likely to remarry—and to do so sooner—than widows.

Family and Friends. Another area of change for the aging adult is in relationships with children. After their children have established their own independent lives, older people find that the old bases of their parent-child relationship have been removed and new ones must be formed. Although 80 percent of older people in the United States have living children, only 12 percent of them live with a grown child. One reason for living apart is a mutual wish for independence and privacy. Neither children nor parents want to be viewed as dependent on the other.

Relationships between elderly parents and their adult children can be stressful. Parents may impose demands for time and assistance that the children have difficulty meeting. Children may make too many demands themselves or may disappoint their parents by seeming aloof. But there are important rewards, as well. Half of the older persons studied by Ethel Shanas (1979) lived within 10 minutes of a grown child and saw the child frequently. Grown children can often help their parents with household repairs, care in illness, and finances. Elderly parents can provide their children with similar sorts of help and often assist in child care, as well. Relationships with grandchildren are often particularly rewarding for older people, who now have the opportunity to love and nurture a child without having

to deal with all the day-to-day hassles of child rearing (Robertson, 1977).

Friendships, too, are likely to change in late adulthood. People who have previously lived relatively private lives typically continue to do so in late adulthood, while people who have always had many friends continue their sociable pattern (Lowenthal and Robinson, 1977). On the whole, however, our social contacts are reduced as we grow older (Fischer and Phillips, 1981). Nevertheless, several studies show that relationships with friends remain very important to elderly people and that friends play a larger role than relatives in preventing loneliness (Perlman, Gerson, and Spinner, 1978). Because old people, just like younger people, generally prefer friends of their own age, many elderly people enjoy living in retirement communities or housing for the elderly, where many social contacts are available on a daily basis.

Institutionalization. Despite the prevalent image of the aged person spending his last days in an old-age home, only 4 to 5 percent of the aged population are currently institutionalized. But for very old adults, institutionalization becomes an increasingly likely possibility. Women face a higher probability of institutionalization than men because they live longer, and people who never married or had children are more likely than others to be institutionalized because of the limited number of people in their lives available to take care of them (Palmore, 1976).

Institutions for the aged range widely, from posh old-age homes that resemble hotels, to skilled nursing facilities for the ill and handi-

A small percentage of older adults live in old-age homes. The care received by the elderly in institutions varies widely.

capped, to mental hospitals. While some of the residents of these facilities are truly unable to care for themselves, many have only limited disabilities. They are not helpless—only poor and alone. Some psychologists suspect that institutionalization contributes to a decline in intellectual skills among old people, because the institutional environment does little to encourage people to keep thinking for themselves. Programs that encourage and reward cognitive activity by institutionalized old people may be able to halt or reverse the decline in such skills as short-term memory (Langer et al., 1979). Partly because of the prevalent negative view of old-age facilities, there is a growing movement to provide these persons with the services they need within the community, rather than through an institution. Day centers and retirement communities extend to elderly persons the daily services they need while allowing them to live in their own homes, doing as much for themselves as possible.

Successful Aging

Which person does a more "successful" job of growing old—the person who spends most of his time in a rocking chair reflecting on his past life, or the person who keeps up an active practice of law or dentistry and continues an active life of social activities?

Social scientists have debated this question. One suggested answer comes from *disengagement* theory. According to the disengagement approach, the mutual withdrawal of society from the individual (mandatory retirement, children reaching independence, deaths of friends and of spouse) and of the individual from society (reduced social activities and a somewhat solitary life out of the mainstream) is the most appropriate way to age (Cumming and Henry, 1961). However, some studies have indicated that elderly persons who are socially active and involved with their families and communities are the most satisfied (Neugarten and Havighurst, 1969).

More recent research has pointed to a more common-sense answer to the question of successful aging. The findings of Bernice

Neugarten (1972) and her colleagues lead to the view that an individual will select a style of aging best suited to her personality. Thus, the book editor who has been active in political groups throughout her life, has kept a large circle of friends, and has enjoyed traveling will probably maintain many of these pursuits after retirement and would be unhappy without them. But the accountant who has spent most of his recreational time working on his vegetable garden and who has always avoided social gatherings will probably spend his later years in quiet withdrawal and be just as satisfied with his life as the retired editor is with hers. Neugarten stresses that there is no single way to age successfully; different types of people will find different ways of adapting to old age and enjoying it.

Erik Erikson (1950) believes that the developmental task of the old is to establish *integrity*—the sense that one has lived a whole and fulfilling life. In Erikson's framework, the achievement of integrity represents successful aging. Robert Butler (1963) suggests that much of the reminiscing that is common late in life may be a valuable way of "sorting out" the past and the present. As one 76-year-old man wrote, "My life is in the background of my mind much of the time; it cannot be any other way. Thoughts of the past play upon me; sometimes I play with them, encourage and savor them; at other times I dismiss them" (Butler, 1963, page 68).

Prompted by the recognition of impending death, the elderly reexamine old conflicts, consider how they've treated others, and come to some conclusions about themselves and their lives. This *life review,* as Butler calls it, may lead to a new sense of accomplishment, satisfaction, and peace—in Erikson's terms, integrity. In one study, old people who reminisced frequently were found to be better adjusted (on a measure based on Erikson's theory) than people of the same age who did less reminiscing (Boylin, Gordon, and Nehrke, 1976). But the life review can also lead to self-hate and despair if the person concludes that her life was not well lived.

Some individuals review their lives privately and internally; others share their memories and reflections with those around them. For this latter group, the life review serves a double purpose: It organizes a final perspective on their lives for themselves, and it leaves a record that will live on with others. Butler (1963) describes a 78-year-old man who had become increasingly hostile to his wife, children, and grandchildren. The hostility mysteriously disappeared after he bought a tape recorder. It was discovered that the man was reciting his history into the recorder, and his increased well-being seemed to come from reexamining his life and from the belief that he was leaving a record of himself that would survive his death. One very old woman described her feelings about participating in a "living history" class where elderly people shared their pasts: "The memories came up in me like lava. So I felt I enriched myself. And I am hoping maybe I enriched somebody else. All this, it's not only for us. It's for the generations" (Myerhoff, 1978, page 39).

The last stage of life, of course, is not old age but death. We will discuss the challenge of facing death in the Psychological Issue that follows this chapter. One task of life, and especially of late adulthood, is to prepare for death. And the most important part of this prepara-

FAMOUS LAST WORDS

Throughout history, people have said good-bye to the world in ways that reveal their distinctive personalities and interests. For example, the waspish Oscar Wilde glared at the curtains near his deathbed and said, "Either they go or I do!" (He did.) And Dominique Bonhours, a nineteenth-century grammarian, is said to have gasped in his last breaths, "I am about to, or I am going to die. Either expression is used" (Ramsay and Toye, 1979).

tion may be the feeling that one has lived a satisfying and meaningful life. "In such final consolidation," Erikson writes, "death loses its sting."

SUMMARY

1. Development in adulthood continues to involve an interplay between maturation and learning. *Age-graded influences* are experiences and events that commonly occur at a given stage of life. *Non-age-graded influences* are experiences and events that are unique to the individual. Whereas age-graded influences are central in child development, non-age-graded influences take on greater importance in adult development.

2. Longitudinal studies have shown that adult development is characterized by both stability and change over time.

3. Differences between generations have psychological, biological, and historical sources. The differences that are based on the historical period in which people grow up are called *cohort effects*.

4. According to Levinson, early adulthood consists of several discrete stages: the early adult transition (ages 17–22), entering the adult world (ages 22–28), the age 30 transition (ages 28–33), and settling down (ages 33–40). Throughout all the stages an individual engages in a continuing struggle to evolve a *life structure*.

5. One of the tasks of early adulthood is to choose, prepare for, and enter an occupation. Entering the work world can produce "reality shock"—discovery of the gap between idealized images of a job and the actual job itself.

6. According to Erikson, the central psychological challenge of early adulthood is to establish an intimate relationship. Most people get married in early adulthood, and a majority have children at this time, although a significant number are choosing *voluntary childlessness*. Many couples are also waiting until their late twenties or early thirties to have children.

7. Middle adulthood (ages 40 to 65) is a time of adaptation to physical changes, including changes in appearance, health and energy, sensory acuity, and sexual functioning. One of the most noticeable changes is the *menopause*, or cessation of menstruation, in women. Rather than being a "partial death," menopause is usually a comparatively minor event in the life of a middle-aged woman.

8. Around the age of 40 people make the *midlife transition*, in which they must come to see themselves as "middle-aged," with new tasks, limitations, and opportunities. Some individuals experience a *midlife crisis*, a painful and disruptive struggle in which they reevaluate their lives.

9. Erikson sees the major psychological challenge of middle adulthood as the need to achieve *generativity*—to feel that one is making a significant contribution to the next generation. Generativity can be achieved by guiding children into adult-

hood, by achieving in the world of work, and by serving as a *mentor* for young adults.

10. Although late adulthood (ages 65 and over) is often discussed as a single period, it might be thought of as encompassing both the "young-old" and the "old-old."

11. *Ageism* refers to discrimination against old people. The stereotype of old people as all being alike is far from the truth, because individual differences are as marked in old age as at any other time of life. Ageism is also reflected in our society's praise of those people who don't "show" their age.

12. Late adulthood is marked by numerous physical changes. According to one theory of aging, cells wear out over time and die. Another theory suggests that damage to DNA or RNA over time leads to cell death. Or perhaps the immune system becomes less efficient or disorganized. It may even be that the endocrine system undergoes changes that are preprogrammed to lead to aging and death.

13. *Senile dementia* (senility) is a disorder that affects a small minority of the elderly. It is characterized by memory loss, disorientation in time and place, impaired attention, and loss of the ability to acquire new information.

14. Contrary to popular opinion, intelligence does not generally decline with advancing years. *Fluid intelligence*, or mental agility in solving problems, is likely to decline with age. But *crystallized intelligence*, or acquired knowledge and verbal skills, is likely to remain the same or even improve at least until one's eighties.

15. Among the most important social changes of late adulthood are retirement, widowhood, and changing relationships with family and friends.

16. Only a small percentage of old people are institutionalized, some because of illnesses and handicaps and others simply because they are poor and alone.

17. According to *disengagement* theory, the mutual withdrawal of society from the individual and of the individual from society is the most appropriate way to age. However, Neugarten stresses that different types of people will find different ways of adapting to old age.

18. Erikson sees the primary task of old age as the establishment of integrity—the sense that one has lived a whole and fulfilling life. Old people engage in a *life review*, a process of sorting out one's previous life. An additional task of old age is preparing to face death.

FACING DEATH

Death can occur at any time in the life span. A sudden accident or fatal disease can cut short even the youngest life, but the fact is that most people in today's America die when they are old. The fact that people are living longer than they used to is reflected in changing causes of death. In 1900, influenza, pneumonia, and tuberculosis were the three leading causes of death in the United States. But once such infectious diseases were conquered with antibiotics and immunizations, they were replaced as the leading causes of death by heart disease, cancer, and strokes. These degenerative diseases are more likely to affect older people; their increased frequency is in large measure the result of people living long enough to develop them. At present, the most common cause of death for people between 25 and 34 is accidents, for people between 35 and 44 it is cancer, and for people 45 and over it is heart disease (U.S. Department of Health, Education, and Welfare, 1978).

Regardless of when we die and what we die from, there is nothing in life more certain than death. People through the ages have fantasized about immortality, but no one has ever escaped death permanently. Death is a reality that each of us must face. But our society, as we will see, encourages us to avoid the issue.

THE DENIAL OF DEATH

If you are under 40 and in good health, your own death probably has little reality for you. You probably have not considered where you would like to die, how your body should be disposed of, and whether you are willing to have an autopsy performed on your body. These issues don't seem compelling to healthy young people, because they consider death to be something that happens to old people. As Robert Kastenbaum (1979) writes, "One of our society's odd customs is to 'save' death for the elderly." Meanwhile, younger people avoid thoughts of death. Try asking people at a party, "Do you prefer burial or cremation?" As Georgia Barrow and Patricia Smith (1979) suggest, the stunned reactions you would receive would probably convince you that death is an improper subject for open discussion—it's "too morbid" or "in bad taste." Instead, people push death out of their minds, engaging in what some social scientists call an "illusion of immortality."

Children are curious about death, but adults are generally reluctant to discuss the issue with them. One mother first realized how much she had been influenced by a death-denying society when she read a children's book about death to her 4-year-old son.

One of our society's odd customs is to "save" death for the elderly.

She had borrowed a book called *The Dead Bird* (Brown and Charlip, 1965) from the library without examining its contents. She felt a sense of panic and a desire to protect her son as she began reading the words:

The bird was dead when the children found it. . . . it was still warm and its eyes were closed . . . but there was no heart beating. That was how they knew it was dead. . . . It began to get cold. . . . The children were very sorry the bird was dead and could never fly again.

The mother had an urge to hide the book and not read the story. But her son treated the material matter-of-factly and learned about both life and death from the book (Barrow and Smith, 1979).

The mother had an urge to hide **The Dead Bird** *and not read her son the story.*

The denial of death extends even to medical personnel. Although doctors generally agree that patients should be told of terminal conditions, and most patients themselves want to be told, doctors tend to avoid informing patients that they are dying. Doctors may also avoid contact with dying patients. One professional, who leads seminars to help hospital personnel come to grips with their own anxieties about death, noted that physicians and nurses feel an involuntary anger toward the dying patient, whom they associate with their own failure and help-lessness: "When you've exhausted everything you can do for a patient medically, it becomes difficult to walk into the room every day and talk to that patient" (Barrow and Smith, 1979).

Our society tends to try to "protect" children from death. But it is better for children to learn about death as a fact of life than to be taught that death is a topic to be avoided.

THE DYING PATIENT

What of people who know they are dying? How do they face impending death? In an influential book called *On Death and Dying* (1969), Elisabeth Kübler-Ross outlined five stages that dying persons pass through. She based her stages on interviews with terminally ill adults, both young and old. Not all people experience all five stages, and individuals can experience more than one stage at a time.

In the first stage, *denial*, the individual refuses to believe the news that she is terminally ill. She might insist that the test results are inaccurate, or may change doctors. She may refuse to discuss her illness with anyone, or may treat it lightly. A few people may maintain this attitude right up to death.

The second stage is *anger*. The enraged patient asks, "Why me?" Medical staff and family may be subjected to angry demands and tantrums as the patient works through her resentment of her illness and envy of others' health.

In the third stage, *bargaining*, the person tries to postpone death. He may offer his body to science if the doctors can extend his life, or he may promise to devote himself to God if his life can last a little longer. A common theme in this stage is that there is one more place to be visited, one final task to be completed, one important wrong that must be righted before the patient can give in to death.

The fourth stage is *depression*; it often accompanies advancing symptoms of disease. The overwhelming sense is one of loss—loss of one's memories, loss of close relationships, and loss of a future.

The final stage is *acceptance*. Acceptance can be achieved with the support and help of surrounding family, friends, and medical personnel. Having worked through anger and grief, the dying patient can come to her end quietly and peacefully. Although the generality of these stages has been questioned (Schulz and Aderman, 1974),

Having worked through anger and grief, the dying patient can come to her end quietly and peacefully.

they can help us understand some of the emotions experienced by those facing death.

DEATH AND THE LIFE SPAN

Attitudes toward death appear to change as we age. Richard Kalish and David Reynolds (1976) questioned 434 Los Angeles residents in three age groups: 20–39, 40–59, and over 60. They probed such issues as where individuals would prefer to die, what respondents would do if they knew they had only six months to live, how often they thought about death, and how frightening death was to them. Kalish and Reynolds found that the oldest group both thought more about death and were less frightened by it than the other two groups. Considering the increasing likelihood of death as one gets older and the increasing frequency of death of spouses, siblings, and friends, the fact that older people think more about death is not surprising. The lessened fear of death in old age may result from many factors. In old age one's own death may take on an appropriateness it lacked in earlier years. And some of the increased thinking about death, as well as the achievement of a sense of integrity, may help the person to accept death (Kalish, 1976).

But even among old people, attitudes toward death are as individual as the people who hold them. Robert Kastenbaum and Avery Weisman (1972) describe two very different responses to impending

death. Some people are "acceptors"; they view their coming death as timely and appropriate. "One 90-year-old woman was a very alert, independent person. . . . As her health began to decline she initiated arrangements for her funeral. She also expressed a readiness for death in the most straightforward manner. She declared that she had lived her life and was now ready to see it come to an end" (page 215). Other elderly patients are more annoyed than anything else by the prospect of dying. "One 82-year-old woman . . . became quite involved in the social and recreational life of the institution. [Three years later] she faced death as though it were a regrettable interruption of her participation in activities and relationships" (page 215).

HUMANIZING DEATH

Facing death at any time of life is a complex and painful experience. But there are other ways that the terminally ill patient of any age can be helped and supported through the process. Richard Schulz (1978) lists three major needs of dying persons: relief from and control of physical pain; a sense of dignity and self-worth; and love and affection.

Like anyone else, a dying person needs to feel effective, competent, and in control of his life.

The terminally ill patient often faces severe physical pain. Standard medical practice is to treat the pain with heavy doses of narcotics, which can leave the patient "fuzzy-headed" or unconscious

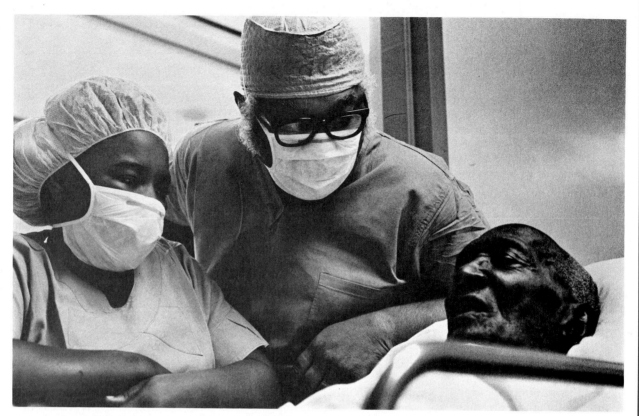

The needs of dying patients are not easily met in hospital settings, although medical personnel are becoming more aware of people's need to die with dignity.

much of the time. Experimentation with nonnarcotic substances, including LSD and marijuana, has suggested that patients can be freed from pain while staying alert. Involving the patient himself in determining the dosages and timing of medication can also help to anticipate and prevent pain, rather than simply to reduce it when it occurs.

Like anyone else, a dying person needs to feel effective, competent, and in control of his life; these are basic components of dignity. By participating in his own treatment, a dying patient can maintain a sense of competence and self-worth. The love and recognition of the people around the dying person can relieve the loneliness of

her situation and provide reasons for enjoying whatever time is left to her.

These needs are not easily met in the institutions, such as hospitals and nursing homes, where over 60 percent of us die. Such institutions are frequently more concerned with efficient control of patients than with cooperative responses to them. One alternative to such institutions are *hospices.* "Hospice" is a medieval term for a traveler's rest station; in the 1800s the name was applied to places where nuns cared for the dying. Modern hospices are facilities designed for the care of the dying. They are committed to helping the terminally ill die without pain, in peace and dignity, surrounded by

their loved ones. Patients' families are involved in their care and can themselves receive counseling and support from the hospice staff. Family involvement can range from daily visits and meal preparation to actually moving into the hospice for closer contact with the patient. Hospice staff members also provide services to individuals who prefer to live their final weeks at home. One of the major goals of the hospice movement is to break down the isolation that usually surrounds a dying individual (Kastenbaum, 1978).

LIFE AFTER DEATH
Is there a life after death? This is a religious question, not a medical

or psychological one. And yet recent medical advances and psychological research have given a new focus to this ultimate mystery.

Until recently, anyone who stopped breathing or whose heart stopped pumping simply died—and took his experiences with him. But advanced medical technology has altered this age-old reality. Because it is now possible to maintain basic vital functions mechanically, people can survive physical traumas that temporarily halt cardiac and respiratory function. This situation has raised complex questions about when a person has actually died. In 1968 the Harvard Ad Hoc Committee to Examine the Definition of Brain Death suggested the criteria for death that are now used in most of the United States: unreceptivity and unresponsivity, no movements or breathing for at least one hour, no reflexes, a continued absence of brain-wave activity for at least 24 hours, and no change in these conditions for 24 hours.

Beyond the question of defining death, a few people believe that this technology has produced something entirely new in human history, a group of individuals who have "come back"—people whose hearts had stopped beating as a result of an illness or accident and who were then "restored to life." Such people sometimes report ex-

Some people have reported experiences "from the other side"— glimpses of the afterlife.

periences "from the other side," raising the possibility that they had had a glimpse of the afterlife (Moody, 1975).

Most scientists remain skeptical of such an interpretation of the patients' reports. Nevertheless, research is being carried on to investigate the meaning of the "near-death" experience. When psychologist Kenneth Ring (1980) interviewed over 100 hospital patients who had come close to death, he found that 48 percent of them had some conscious recollection of the event. Among those reporting such recollections, Ring found that the reported "near-death" experience included five stages that occur in a particular order. People seem to pass from an initial stage of great peace and contentment to a second stage in which they feel detached from their bodies. The third stage involves some experience of darkness that gives way to the fourth stage, in which people see a brilliant light. In the fifth and final stage people report a variety of spiritual experiences, including reunions with departed relatives. The whole experience is accompanied by feelings of comfort and serenity. The descriptions are not explicitly religious but they share much of the imagery that many religious groups, particularly Christians, associate with death. Ring found, however, that religious persons were no more likely to have such experiences than people who were not religious.

What is the meaning of these experiences? Most researchers believe that these are not glimpses of the afterlife, but rather hallucinations brought on either by the patient's physical condition or by the deep emotion aroused by the crisis of facing death. While most researchers don't take these reports very seriously, some consider them potentially dangerous. Robert Kastenbaum (1978) believes that the positive picture of death presented in such reports could encourage suicide attempts, particularly among the terminally ill.

Kastenbaum is also concerned that a belief in death as an uplifting experience could reduce the quality of care given to terminally ill and elderly patients, in a misguided effort to "release" these people to a "better place."

"I don't believe in an afterlife, although I am bringing along a change of underwear."

But then, of course, there is always that lingering—if unlikely—possibility that the reports really reflect a glimpse of the world beyond. As Woody Allen (1971) put it, "I don't believe in an afterlife, although I am bringing along a change of underwear."

SUMMARY
1. Our society tends to deny the idea of death and to reserve it for the elderly.
2. Kübler-Ross suggested that the dying person goes through five stages in dealing with impending death: denial, anger, bargaining, depression, and acceptance.
3. Older people tend to be less fearful of death than younger people, although attitudes toward death vary widely.
4. Hospices are facilities that are committed to helping terminally ill people die without pain and in dignity, surrounded by their loved ones.
5. People who have had near-death experiences sometimes report having felt a detachment from their bodies and a spiritual encounter of some kind. Such experiences have been interpreted both as glimpses of an "afterlife" and as hallucinations.

PSYCHOBIOGRAPHY
William McKinley Runyan

William McKinley Runyan

As we learn more about the workings of personality and the course of development through life, we may be tempted to apply our knowledge to the lives of famous people—to painters and poets, party leaders and presidents. These endeavors in psychobiography have often been viewed skeptically, as exercises in the "armchair psychoanalysis" of people whom the psychobiographer has typically never even met. But recent work in psychobiography has become more sophisticated and cannot be dismissed so easily. In this Update, Dr. William McKinley Runyan of the University of California at Berkeley—the author of Life Histories and Psychobiography—*surveys the developing field of psychobiography. He concludes that psychobiography has its pitfalls but also has the potential to deepen our understanding of the lives of great (and not-so-great) men and women.*

Can we develop a psychological understanding of the creativity of Leonardo da Vinci, the deceitfulness of Richard Nixon, the virulent anti-Semitism of Adolf Hitler, or the sensitivity and seclusiveness of Emily Dickinson? Is it possible to do valid psychological analyses of the personalities, the unconscious motives and conflicts, and the critical influences in the lives of public or historical figures?

Psychologists and historians have been increasingly active in attempting such analyses. For example, a recent psychobiography of Richard Nixon (Brodie, 1981)

Psychobiographer Fawn Brodie contends that Richard Nixon had a lifelong pattern of lying. His involvement in the Watergate affair led to his resignation from the presidency in 1974.

contends that Nixon lied persistently throughout his life—as a boy in dealing with his parents, in his first campaign for Congress in 1946 when he falsely accused his opponent of having ties with the Communist party, in his "Checkers" speech of 1952 when he defended himself against charges of financial wrongdoing, through his lies and coverups in the Watergate affair. How is such a pattern of lifelong lying to be explained? Fawn Brodie (1981) suggests that Nixon learned to lie convincingly in order to avoid punishment by a harsh father, and subsequently used lies effectively in almost all of his later political victories. She states that President Nixon lied to gain love, to bolster a wavering sense of identity, and to gain political ends. Brodie also reports that Nixon lied most forcefully to deny that he had lied in the past, and reinforced these denials by accusing others of lying. Perhaps Nixon even came to believe his own denials. Brodie interprets this pattern in psychoanalytic terms. Nixon would project upon others what he felt guilty about in himself, and then freely attack them for lying.

As a second example, how is one to explain the consuming force of Hitler's anti-Semitism? There were anti-Semitic currents in early twentieth century Ger-

many, but Rudolph Binion (1976) argues that the intensity of Hitler's anti-Jewish feelings was partly caused by rage at what he believed to be the poisoning of his mother by a Jewish doctor in the course of her treatment for breast cancer.

These questions about Nixon and Hitler illustrate the concerns of the field of *psychobiography,* or the explicit use of psychology in interpreting the lives of biographical subjects. Initially, the field was defined as the use of psychoanalysis in biography. But more recently it has been recognized that, in addition to psychoanalysis, psychobiography can draw on other theories of personality, as well as on social and developmental psychology.

Work in psychobiography was launched with Freud's own *Leonardo da Vinci and a Memory of His Childhood*, published in 1910. Since then, psychobiographical studies have been made of a fascinating range of individuals from all walks of life. Two of the best known studies are those of Martin Luther and Mahatma Gandhi by Erik Erikson (1958, 1969). Psychobiographies have also been written of Dostoevsky, Tolstoy, Abraham Lincoln, Napoleon, Lenin, Stalin, Charles Darwin, Isaac Newton, Henry James, Emily Dickinson, Beethoven, Jimmy Carter, and dozens of other writers, artists, musicians, politicians, religious leaders, scientists, and criminals.

As the practice of psychobiography has become more widespread, it has also become more controversial. Advocates of psychobiography (e.g., Erikson, 1958, 1969; Waite, 1977) see the use of systematic psychology as a significant advance over the informal psychology traditionally used in biography. Biographers inevitably make use of psychological ideas and assumptions when they describe and interpret people's lives. Thus, the question is not whether to use psychology or not, but whether the biographer should draw upon the discipline of psychology, as well as upon common sense and intuition.

On the other hand, critics (Stannard, 1980; Stone, 1981) claim that the whole enterprise of psychobiography has failed because of the flimsiness of evidence about childhood experience, the uncertainty of connections between childhood experience and adult behavior, and because of a tendency to overemphasize psychological factors while neglecting the importance of social, cultural, and historical influences on behavior. Before evaluating these criticisms, let us examine in greater detail the kinds of interpretations which have generated such conflicting assessments, with examples drawn from studies of Woodrow Wilson and Emily Dickinson.

In three major executive positions—as president of Princeton University, as governor of New Jersey, and as president of the United States—Woodrow Wilson displayed a pattern of impressive early accomplishments, followed by a period of controversy, ending in serious setbacks or defeats. As president of Princeton, Wilson instituted an important series of reforms, but then became embroiled in a battle over the formation of a new graduate school, in which he alienated both faculty and trustees in his rigid refusal to compromise with competing interests. As gov-

President Woodrow Wilson, shown here on his sixty-fifth birthday in 1921, was often rigid and uncompromising.

ernor of New Jersey, Wilson attacked the Democratic machine which had supported his election, and this eventually led to his loss of control of the New Jersey legislature. The last and most serious of Wilson's defeats was his failure as president, at the conclusion of World War I, to persuade the Senate to ratify the Versailles Treaty, which would have led to America's participation in the League of Nations. This failure, which had damaging personal consequences for Wilson, is seen by some as one of the causes of World War II.

When Wilson was seeking power, he could be flexible and adaptive. But in conflicts that developed in the exercise of power, he often became rigid and uncompromising. In the Senate battle over the Versailles Treaty, for example, Wilson alienated the moderate elements who would have supported him, and drove them into the arms of his opponents. In their psychobiography of Wilson, Alexander and Juliette George (1964) observe that once he was committed to a position, Wilson seemed to experience opposition to his will as an unbearable threat to his self-esteem. The Georges argue that such opposition brought forth buried anxieties and aggressive feelings which Wilson initially experienced in his childhood relationship to his father.

His father was a perfectionistic Presbyterian minister, who used ridicule and harsh criticism to force his son to meet his unbending standards. Wilson's resentment of this treatment was repressed during childhood, and covered over by an extraordinary degree of conscious affection for his father. The Georges maintain that this unconscious anger was never directly expressed toward his father, but remained to influence Wilson's inflexible behavior in situations of conflict throughout his adult life.

Emily Dickinson was eventually recognized as one of the finest poets in the English language, but during her lifetime in the nineteenth century, she was better known in her home town of Amherst, Massachusetts, for her seclusiveness than for her poetry. As early as age 22, Dickinson was going out of her way to avoid people. By 28, she would run upstairs if the doorbell rang, and several years later, would retreat to her room when friends visited and listen to their voices from upstairs. She began dressing exclusively in white, and for the last 15 years of her life, was not seen outside. "On the rare occasions when she consented to visit with old friends," writes psychobiographer John Cody, "she and the visitor conversed from opposite sides of a door left slightly ajar. She would not allow a physician to examine her during an illness, and he was expected to arrive at his diagnosis from a glimpse of her, fully clothed, as she walked past a doorway" (Cody, 1971, p. 20). Cody argues that Emily Dickinson's disturbance was caused in part by what she experienced as a cruel rejection by her mother. Even though there is no direct evidence of the mother's rejection, Cody holds that this experience can be reconstructed on the basis of psychoanalysts' work with patients having similar characteristics, inferences from psychoanalytic theory, and interpretations of Dickinson's poetry and correspondence.

Emily Dickinson, a great poet, tried to avoid all contact with other people.

In the debate over psychobiographical interpretations, such as those of Woodrow Wilson and Emily Dickinson, one of the most frequent criticisms is that interpretations are based on inadequate evidence. In regard to psychoanalytic psychobiography, this is sometimes expressed as, "You can't put the person on the couch." In other words, the psychobiographer does not have access to the kinds of material that are available to the psychoanalyst, such as the patient's free associations, dreams to interpret, or the transference relationship with the analyst (see Chapter 12).

What are the implications of these problems of evidence for the psychobiographical enterprise? They do not mean that psychobiography is impossible, as is sometimes suggested, but rather that attention is best devoted to historical figures about whom there is sufficient evidence to develop and test psychological explanations.

Furthermore, the psychobiographer is likely to have access to some pieces of evidence that the psychotherapist does not have. For one thing, the psychobiographer often has information about a person who has lived his or her entire life, while the average patient in therapy is relatively young and may not yet have lived through important life experiences, such as the rearing of children, the peak of his or her career, or the death of parents, all of which may reveal significant aspects of personality. Second, the psychobiographer is not limited to information coming from the subject alone, but may draw heavily on outside sources in order to learn how a variety of other people perceived the situation the subject was in, and their reactions to the individual's personality. Third, if the subject is a literary or creative person, the psychobiographer has a wealth of material such as poems, paintings, letters, or novels which may, with caution, be drawn upon in interpreting the subject's personality. Cody (1971), for example, uses Emily Dickinson's correspondence and poetry as evidence that she experienced a starvation for affection and love so pervasive that it must have originated in childhood. As she once remarked, "Affection is like bread, unnoticed till we starve, and then we dream of it, and sing of it, and paint of it."

Another criticism is that psychobiographical interpretations are overly speculative, or are put forward without critically evaluating them or comparing their plausibility to that of alternative explanations. Consider, for example, the question of why the nineteenth century painter Vincent van Gogh, when he was 35 years old, cut off the lower half of his left ear and took it to a brothel where he gave it to a prostitute he had known and asked her to keep the ear carefully.

Many explanations of van Gogh's self-mutilation have been put forth by psychoanalytically oriented psychobiographers. One interpretation of van Gogh's behavior is in terms of Oedipal themes. The painter Paul Gauguin, with whom van Gogh was sharing a house, later reported that the day before the ear mutilation van Gogh had threatened him with a razor, but, under Gauguin's powerful gaze, had then run away. It has been suggested that Gauguin represented van Gogh's hated father, and that after failing in his initial threat, van Gogh deflected the resentment and hate onto himself. Then, "in giving the ear to a prostitute, Vincent fulfilled an unconscious wish to possess his mother following the fantasized assault upon a father-substitute, Gauguin" (Lubin, 1972, pp. 157–158). A second interpretation is that the self-mutilation resulted from a conflict over homosexual impulses aroused by the presence of Gauguin. According to this account, the ear was a phallic symbol, and the act was a symbolic self-castration. A third explanation rests on the fact that van Gogh was emotionally and financially dependent on his brother Theo, and usually spent the Christmas holidays with him. This year, however, Vincent learned that Theo would spend the holiday with his new fiancée and her family. This interpretation suggests that van Gogh's self-mutilation was an unconscious strategy for holding on to his brother's attention, and a way of getting Theo to come and care for him rather than to spend the holidays with his fiancée.

Other explanations are that van Gogh identified himself with Jack the Ripper, who had been mutilating the bodies of prostitutes, or with Jesus Christ, or with the matador in a bullfight who cuts off the ears of the bull and presents them to a lady of his choice. More than a dozen different psychoanalytic explanations of van Gogh's self-mutilation have been proposed, and it is necessary to evaluate such proposed explanations in terms of such criteria as their logical soundness, their comprehensiveness in accounting for a number of puzzling aspects of the event in question, their consistency with the full range of available evidence, and their credibility relative to other possible explanations (Runyan, 1981). By applying these criteria, we can rule out a number of the proposed explanations and accumulate evidence in favor of others. In this case, one of the most important factors in

There have been many attempts to explain why Vincent van Gogh cut off the lower half of his left ear. Van Gogh painted this self-portrait in 1889.

Vincent's breakdown seems to be the perceived loss of his brother's care. Specifically, the ear-cutting incident and two later mental breakdowns coincided with learning of Theo's engagement, his marriage, and the birth of his first child. In each case, Vincent was threatened by the prospect of losing his main source of emotional and financial support, as it seemed that Theo might direct his love and money toward his new family. When faced with a puzzling biographical event, there is sometimes a temptation to accept the first psychological interpretation that makes previously mysterious events appear comprehensible. It is essential, however, that psychobiographical explanations be evaluated critically and compared in plausibility with alternative explanations of the same events.

Psychobiographical interpretations are also accused of being "reductionistic" or oversimplified. One form of the reductionist critique is that internal psychological factors are overemphasized at the expense of external social and historical factors. A second criticism is that psychobiography focuses excessively on psychological disorder and gives insufficient attention to normality and creativity. A third type of reduction-

ism is to explain adult character and behavior exclusively in terms of early childhood experience, while neglecting important later influences. It must be acknowledged that too many psychobiographies *have* suffered from these flaws. A number of contemporary psychobiographers (such as Bate, 1977; Erikson, 1969; and Mack, 1976) are aware of such dangers, however, and are avoiding them by integrating the psychological with the social and historical, by analyzing not just pathology but also strengths and adaptive capacities, and by studying formative influences not just in childhood but throughout the life span.

Because of the importance of childhood experience within psychoanalytic theory, psychobiographers have, when direct evidence was unavailable, sometimes used psychoanalytic theory to reconstruct or "postdict" what *must have* happened in childhood. Cody (1971) has argued that interpreting the life of an historical figure is in some respects like the reassembling of a fossil skeleton, where the laws of anatomy allow one to estimate roughly the shape of a missing bone in a skeleton and to replace it with a plaster bone. Cody suggests that one such "plaster bone" is his assumption that early in life Emily Dickinson "experienced what she interpreted as a cruel rejection by her mother. Many of her statements, her choice of certain recurring metaphors and symbols, and the entire course of her life, viewed psychoanalytically, argue for the truth of this assumption" (Cody, 1971, p. 2).

This practice of reconstruction has been severely criticized by many historians and psychologists. In light of the uncertainties of psychoanalytic theory and the variety of possible processes that can lead to a given outcome, the case for avoiding reconstruction in psychobiography is a fairly strong one. The practice of making inferences about what must have happened in the past is particularly troubling when an earlier event is

first reconstructed, and then later assumed to be firmly established.

In these pages we have briefly examined several of the central issues involved in the current debate over the merits and limitations of psychobiography. (The issues are discussed in greater detail in Anderson, 1981; Runyan, 1981; and Runyan, 1982). There are unquestionably too many cases of reductionistic and unconvincing psychobiographical interpretation, but these examples of poor practice are counterbalanced by an increasing number of sophisticated psychobiographical studies which take into account social and historical as well as psychological factors, and which study adaptive as well as pathological processes throughout the life course. Several of the best examples are recent studies of Lawrence of Arabia (Mack, 1976), Beethoven (Solomon, 1977), and Joseph Stalin (Tucker, 1973).

The psychobiographical study of lives can provide insights into the motives, experiences, and ways of coping of eminent figures in all walks of life. Such analyses can be of value to those with similar career interests or faced with similar situations. It may be helpful, for example, for young artists to learn about the psychological struggles of van Gogh or Picasso, for aspiring scientists to learn about the lives of Isaac Newton or Albert Einstein, and for writers to read about the experiences of Emily Dickinson or Virginia Woolf. Psychobiographical analyses can also be of value in public affairs. Indeed, studies of the motives and personalities of presidential candidates may aid citizens in deciding whom to vote for. After all, when we choose the person who will guide the nation's economy, shape its social programs, and make decisions about the use of nuclear weapons, can we afford *not* to take into account insights that psychology may provide about this individual's personality and likely responses under stress?

Part Four

Disorder and Therapy

The study of psychological disorders is often referred to as abnormal psychology. *As we will see, it is by no means easy to determine which patterns of thought, feeling, and behavior are "normal" and which are "abnormal." Nevertheless, we cannot deny that millions of people suffer painfully from mental and emotional problems. Among the central challenges of psychology are the attempts to understand the causes of these problems and the efforts to develop ways of treating them.*

In Chapter 11, Psychological Disorder, *we will first consider the elusive concept of "abnormality" and then explore the range of psychological disorders. The Psychological Issue focuses on what is perhaps the most frightening manifestation of disorder:* Suicide.

Chapter 12 examines the major forms of Therapy *used to treat psychological problems and disorders. We will find that theory and research in different areas of psychology—including research on personality, learning, and brain mechanisms—have given rise to specific approaches to therapy. The Psychological Issue on* The Therapy Marketplace *surveys some of the new therapies that have arrived on the scene—from primal screams to* est—*and provides some perspective on what to make of them all.*

In the Update on "Veterans and the Legacy of Vietnam," *Arthur Egendorf discusses the psychological problems experienced by many Vietnam veterans after they returned home and how they are trying to deal with these problems.*

Psychological Disorder

On any given day, hundreds of thousands of people are under psychiatric care in hospitals in the United States. At any given time, roughly 1 million people are being treated for schizophrenia, an extremely serious psychological disorder (Kramer, 1976). In one recent year, about 25,000 deaths in the United States were attributed to suicide, 1,000 to drug dependence, and 19,000 to alcoholism—and these are only the cases that actually came to the attention of health authorities (National Center for Health Statistics, 1974). On a much milder level, the President's Commission on Mental Health estimated in 1978 that as many as one-fourth of all Americans have at least some degree of depression, anxiety, or other indications of emotional disorder. It is clear that psychological disorders often place large burdens not only on the people who have them, but also on their families and on society at large.

Psychological disorder is typically considered to be "abnormal"—and, indeed, the study of psychological disorder is often called *abnormal psychology*. In this chapter, we will explore a wide range of psychological disorders, their symptoms, and what is known about their causes. Before we do so, however, we need to examine the controversial concept of abnormality.

DEFINING ABNORMALITY

There are many ways to approach abnormality, and the definition can easily change from era to era and from culture to culture. Here we will look at four major approaches that can be used to define who

is normal and who is abnormal: the statistical approach, the adequacy approach, the medical model, and the cultural model.

The Statistical Approach

If *abnormal* were used in a strictly literal sense, statistical norms would be sufficient to define it. Any deviation from the majority would be abnormal: geniuses, the mentally retarded, members of the radical left and right would all be considered abnormal.

This definition of the word *abnormal* would be accurate but useless if we wanted to distinguish between desirable and undesirable deviations. Indeed, a statistical definition suggests equating mental health with conformity. Most people have average intelligence because the majority of IQ scores fall into the middle section of a distribution of all scores. Only a few people have high intelligence; fewer yet have *very* high intelligence; and geniuses are rare indeed. On the other hand, there are certain types of psychological disorders, such as states of anxiety or depression, that are so common that from a statistical viewpoint they are not abnormal at all. Yet they cause an individual considerable distress. The upshot is that a purely statistical approach to abnormality is of little value as an approach to psychological disorder.

The Adequacy Approach

Several approaches to abnormality have focused on psychological *adequacy*—that is, on how well people adjust to and cope with their environment. If a man is willing and able to feed and dress himself, to hold a job, to support himself, and to communicate rationally with others, he would be regarded as functioning more adequately than a man who cannot or will not do these things. Furthermore, adequacy can be judged in terms of the amount of discomfort an individual feels in the course of everyday experiences.

These elements of an adequacy approach to abnormality are reflected in the definition of mental disorder put forth in the third edition of the American Psychiatric Association's *Diagnostic and Statistical Manual of Mental Disorders* (*DSM-III*), published in 1980:

[A] mental disorder is conceptualized as a clinically significant behavioral or psychologic syndrome or pattern that occurs in an individual that is typically associated with either a painful symptom [distress] or impairment in one or more important areas of functioning [disability].

This definition makes explicit that the "mentally disordered" person must either experience personal distress or be incapable of functioning adequately in an important area.

The task force that developed *DSM-III* readily concedes that there are problems with this definition. It is often difficult to tell how "distressed" a person is, and it is not clear what constitutes an "impairment in an important area of functioning." It all depends on who is doing the judging and on what their values are. As the developers of *DSM-III* note, their definition is intended only to point to the basic concepts relevant to defining psychological disorder: "It does not pretend to offer precise boundaries between 'disorder' and 'normality'" (Spitzer, Williams, and Skodol, 1980).

The Medical Model

The notion that abnormal behavior is a result of mental illness became popular around the middle of the nineteenth century. Great advances in the field of medicine convinced many physicians that some form of physical or organic disorder was responsible not only for physical ailments but for emotional difficulties, as well. This view that individuals exhibiting deviant behavior were "sick" was a great reform for the mental health movement. Up until that time, "insane" persons had been sent to prisons or chained and forgotten in asylums. With the acceptance of the medical view of psychopathology, these individuals were instead sent to hospitals for treatment.

Although it soon became apparent that many persons who deviated from socially acceptable behavior did not actually have any organic impairment of their brains, the medical model continued to exert its influence, creating a framework that influences our view of abnormal behavior even today. Behaviors are classified into diagnostic categories much as we diagnose a runny nose, fever, and chills as a cold. As Brendan Maher (1966) observes, the vocabulary that we use in referring to psychological disorder is borrowed from medical terminology: "[Deviant] behavior is termed *pathological* and is classified on the basis of *symptoms*, classification being called *diagnosis*.

Processes designed to change behavior are called *therapies* and are applied in *mental hospitals*. If the deviant behavior ceases, the patient is described as *cured*" (page 22).

The continuing influence of the medical model is reflected in the "official" definition of mental disorder quoted earlier. According to this definition, a mental disorder always stems from "a clinically significant behavioral or psychologic syndrome." *Syndrome* is another term borrowed from medicine—it refers to an underlying disease.

Can psychological disorders really be viewed as "illnesses," as the medical model suggests? This question is the focus of great controversy among mental health professionals. Those who favor the medical model believe that it provides an appropriate way of approaching psychological disorder, because it first diagnoses the problem as belonging to a particular category of disorders before a treatment is chosen, just as a doctor would do with a physical illness. They also argue that physical causes for psychological disturbances will ultimately be found, even though they have not yet been discovered for most disorders. Finally, proponents of the medical model believe that it is more socially acceptable for a disturbed person to be regarded as "ill" than to be stigmatized for having some basic moral defect (Blaney, 1975).

In recent years, however, many mental health professionals have become dissatisfied with the medical model. Among these opponents is psychiatrist Thomas Szasz (1970), who claims that mental illness is a "myth." Szasz argues that the individual is not actually sick; rather, she is having difficulty coping with the stresses of everyday life. By assigning the causes of problems to an illness rather than to the individual's own inappropriate behaviors, mental health professionals may encourage the individual not to take any responsibility for her actions. This implication of the label "mental illness" is most dramatic in criminal cases, in which a person judged to be "mentally ill" is usually relieved of all responsibility for a criminal act (see Box 1).

Critics of the medical model argue that most people who are having problems in adjustment are not suffering from "disease," as that word is usually defined. Such people usually do not show any signs of physical damage or dysfunctions in their brains or nervous systems. And the critics argue that rather than removing the stigma from psychological disorder, the medical model leads many people who are coping with the normal pains and frustrations of life to view themselves as "sick" (Gross, 1978).

Psychiatrists tend to be more favorable to the medical model of abnormality than psychologists. In one recent study, about half of the psychiatrists surveyed agreed with the statement, "I believe that mental illness is an illness like any other," while two-thirds of the clinical psychologists surveyed disagreed with the statement (Morrison and Hanson, 1978). This is not surprising, because psychiatrists are themselves M.D.'s who view their work as a branch of medicine, whereas psychologists typically view their field as being distinct from medicine. But there is a good deal of disagreement *within* each profession, as well.

— *Box 1* —

Insanity and the law

In 1968 Sirhan B. Sirhan shot and killed Robert Kennedy in front of a group of witnesses. At his trial the defense admitted that Sirhan had assassinated Kennedy, but argued that he was "in a dissociated . . . twilight state" at the time of the crime and therefore not guilty. The prosecution insisted

that Sirhan was sane at the time of the shooting. Each side brought in its own psychiatrists as expert witnesses. The jury agreed with the prosecution, and Sirhan was convicted of first-degree murder. He received a death sentence, which was later commuted to life imprisonment.

In 1979 city council member Dan White entered San Francisco City Hall and shot and killed the

mayor and a fellow council member. His lawyers claimed that White was operating under "diminished capacity." The murder charges were dropped and were replaced by charges of manslaughter, for which White received two four-year sentences.

Was Sirhan "sane" at the time of his crime? Was White "insane" when he committed his crimes? There is increasing feeling that the courts, even with the benefit of expert testimony from psychologists and psychiatrists, are not equipped to judge these matters.

Legal definitions of insanity have been a problem in the courts for hundreds of years. The ruling that provided the cornerstone for the legal position on criminal responsibility in the United States was made in England in 1843. Daniel M'Naghten fatally shot the secretary of Britain's prime minister. He said he had intended to kill the prime minister, on instructions from the "voice of God." The judges ruled him innocent by reason of insanity. Following the trial, the British Parliament issued the M'Naghten rule stating that a defendant is legally insane if he

Sirhan Sirhan

Dan White

The Cultural Model

However you choose to define it, abnormality depends to a large extent on the society and culture you live in. If most people in a particular culture have a common type of dance, manner of speech, or way of dressing, these behaviors are declared normal. If you behave in a way that does not follow the norms of your society, your actions will be labeled abnormal. Because abnormality is culturally defined, abnormal behavior in one society may be normal in another. For example, women in one tribe of Melanesian islanders never leave their cooking pots unguarded because they are afraid of being poisoned (Arieti and Meth, 1959). In our culture such behavior would be considered paranoid. Furthermore, when a society's norms change, what was once said to be abnormal behavior might come to be considered normal.

The example of homosexuality shows how the dividing line between normal and abnormal is continually shifting. The Bible says,

doesn't know what he is doing at the time of the crime or cannot distinguish right from wrong.

In 1954 legal insanity received a much broader definition in the United States. The Durham decision, handed down in a federal appellate court, stated that a person is not criminally responsible for any act "if his unlawful act was the product of either a mental disease or a mental defect." The court thus endorsed a medical view of insanity, in contrast to the moral view of the M'Naghten rule. The Durham decision had the effect of leaving the determination of insanity in the hands of mental health professionals.

With so broad a definition of insanity, it is easy to imagine the problems that arise in trying to establish it in court. It is notoriously difficult to get two experts to agree on a psychiatric diagnosis. As a result, the court can usually count on hearing expert testimony from both sides, with firm conclusions that the defendant is sane from one side and equally firm statements that he is insane from the other side. A deputy district attorney says, "I get the im-

pression that some of the expert witnesses write their reports on the basis of who's paying for it—the prosecution or the defense" (Gross, 1978).

The diagnostic process itself may be practically impossible. The law requires only that it be demonstrated that a person was insane *at the time of the crime.* (If a person is judged insane at the time of arrest, she is considered "not competent to stand trial" and is hospitalized rather than tried.) This means that psychiatrists and psychologists must make judgments about a person's state of mind as it was at some point in the past, not in the present. This may be one reason why it is so difficult to get a psychiatric consensus.

Legislators and mental health experts alike complain that the vagueness of legal definitions of insanity encourages abuses of this plea. Hundreds of insanity pleas are filed each year in both criminal and civil cases, including child custody cases, settlements of wills, and other lawsuits. Many law enforcement officials believe most of these pleas are baseless. In 1966,

for example, a man was indicted for income tax evasion. A court-appointed psychiatrist testified to the man's "temporary insanity," caused by "psychotic reactive depression." The defendant lost his first trial, but the conviction was reversed when appealed to a higher court (Gross, 1978). Such decisions reinforce criticisms that the insanity laws are no longer humane protection for the disabled but legal loopholes for the irresponsible. After all, lots of people get depressed at income tax time.

Few people argue that the concept of insanity should be abandoned in the law. It is generally felt that the truly psychotic person who cannot control his behavior or understand its consequences should not be held legally responsible for what he does. But such persons may be extremely rare. The great majority of persons in society are aware and in control of their behavior, even if they are diagnosed as "mentally ill." Many critics of the current legal definitions of insanity believe that these people should be held responsible for their conduct.

"If a man also lieth down with a man as he lieth with a woman, both of them have committed an abomination. They shall verily be put to death." Yet, in ancient Greece, homosexuality was tolerated and even encouraged. Until recently homosexuality was considered abnormal in American society, but now it is becoming more acceptable. For 23 years homosexuality was listed as a mental disorder in the American Psychiatric Association's official diagnostic manual. In 1974, however, the association voted to remove that label. "For a mental condition to be considered a psychiatric disorder," the board explained, "it should either regularly cause emotional distress or regularly be associated with generalized impairment of social functioning; homosexuality does not meet these criteria."

The cultural aspect of abnormality is emphasized by the fact that the *same* behavior may be viewed as normal or abnormal depending on the situation. For example, as Michael Mahoney (1980) writes: "Killing a person is not essentially abnormal (e.g., in war, self-defense, and law enforcement). It is labeled 'abnormal' when it occurs in certain culturally prohibited circumstances." Other examples

What is considered normal in one context may be considered abnormal in another.

of situations in which a behavior can be normal or abnormal depending on its context are provided in Table 11.1

THE PROBLEM OF CLASSIFICATION

Later in this chapter, we will refer to the diagnostic categories employed by psychiatrists and psychologists to talk about psychological disorders. These categories of "mental disorder" reflect to a large extent the medical model of abnormality, with each disorder having its own list of symptoms. It is important to remember, however, that diagnosing a particular type of behavior is merely a way of classifying it and not necessarily a way of explaining it. The diagnostic categories are useful because they allow mental health professionals to communicate in an agreed-upon fashion about abnormal behavior. But psychologists and psychiatrists readily admit the many problems and limitations of such classification.

TABLE 11.1
SITUATIONS AND NORMALITY

Behavior	Situation in which it is "normal"	Situation in which it is "abnormal"
Crying	At sad movies, weddings, etc.	At a restaurant, laundromat, grocery store, etc.
Sexual intercourse	In private	In public
Talking aloud	In a social situation	When alone
Laughing	After hearing a joke	At a funeral
Eating	When the material consumed is food	When the material consumed is not considered "food"
Killing	In war, self-defense, law enforcement, etc.	In the process of committing burglary
Attempting suicide	In espionage, as a patriotic act to protect government secrets	After loss of job or loved one
Extreme anxiety	Prior to surgery	Prior to toothbrushing

Source: M. J. Mahoney, *Abnormal Psychology* (New York: Harper & Row, 1980), page 11.

In fact, people with psychological problems do not fall neatly into the diagnostic categories. A person classified as "schizophrenic," for example, does not necessarily display all the symptoms of schizophrenia that we will discuss. Such a person would also be quite likely to display symptoms that could be classified in other diagnostic categories. For example, Edward Zigler and Leslie Phillips (1961) examined case records of 793 patients with a variety of diagnoses to determine how frequently each of 35 symptoms occurred. They found that the same symptoms appeared in many of the categories and that the relationship between individual symptoms and a particular category was actually quite small.

Many other researchers have investigated the *reliability* of diagnostic judgments—that is, the extent to which experts agree about the particular diagnostic category a person should be placed in—or, indeed, whether she should be placed in any category at all. These studies indicate that although reliability has tended to be better than chance for the major categories, it has been disturbingly low for decisions that have so great an impact on people's lives (Ullman and Krasner, 1975).

Diagnoses have been unreliable primarily because the system has lacked clear criteria (Kendell, 1975). The new edition of the American Psychiatric Association's diagnostic manual, *DSM–III*, instituted in 1980, has addressed itself in large part to the problem of unclear criteria. This new manual covers a broader range of disorders, gives more specific categories, and uses more precise language than the previous versions did. In addition, diagnoses are now based more on observable symptoms of behavior than on interpretations of those symptoms. A patient must display a certain number of symptoms on a checklist in order to be diagnosed as having a particular disorder. For example, in order to be diagnosed as having depression, the patient must have a symptom pattern that includes at least some of the following: poor appetite, difficulties in sleeping,

THE INSANITY OF POWER

Throughout history, some national and political leaders have been mentally disturbed, sometimes quite seriously. Josef Stalin is believed to have been insane, at least during the last years of his life. And Adolf Hitler was certainly insane by most definitions. While the idea that Stalin and Hitler were mad may be easy for most of us to accept, it may be more difficult to believe that an American president has been emotionally disturbed. Yet some historians have suggested that Abraham Lincoln suffered from a manic-depressive psychosis, even as he honored the office of president (Gaylin, 1973).

fatigue, excessive guilt, and suicidal thoughts. Recent tests run on the new diagnostic system have indicated that the clearer criteria lead to much higher levels of reliability than did previous diagnostic categories (Spitzer, Forman, and Nee, 1979).

The fact that a group of professionals can agree about whether a patient suffers from "disorder X" or "disorder Y" does not necessarily mean that they have an accurate understanding of the causes of these disorders or that they can predict the future course of the disorders. These sorts of understandings relate to the *validity* of diagnoses. But without greater agreement on what constitutes a particular disorder, little progress can be made in understanding the disorder's causes or predicting its course. In other words, without reliability, there cannot be much validity. It is hoped that *DSM–III*, by increasing the reliability of diagnoses of mental disorder, will lead to increased validity—our understanding of the causes and nature of these disorders. Such understanding is needed, in turn, in order to develop more effective ways of treating psychological disorder.

Related to these problems of classification is the fact that a diagnosis (or label) can then have major effects on how the patient is viewed. Even if the diagnosis is incorrect, it can come to take on a reality all its own (Scheff, 1975). In Chapter 6 we saw that the labels people use affect the way they perceive their environment. Labels can also affect the way we see other people, such as those who are labeled "insane" or are placed in a specific diagnostic category. As a result, once individuals are labeled "sick," it may be very difficult for them to get "well" again, because people continue to view them as sick and to treat them that way (see Box 2).

THE RANGE OF DISORDERS

Mary T., a wife and mother of five children, has spent almost all of the past three years inside her house. On the two occasions that she went out, she was filled with anxiety and dread.
Mary T. is suffering from an *anxiety disorder*.
John F. has not smiled for months, does his job poorly and with little ambition, feels worthless, and can't seem to enjoy anything anymore. John F. is suffering from *depression*.
Cathy P. rocks on the floor in the corner all day, mumbling to herself, occasionally telling passers-by that she is the president's wife, and screaming answers to voices only she seems to be able to hear. Cathy P. has been diagnosed as having *schizophrenia*.

Despite the difficulties involved in defining and categorizing psychological disorder, *DSM-III*, the newly instituted diagnostic system that we have discussed, does the best job currently available of classifying psychological problems—or, in *DSM-III's* own terms, "mental disorders." We will employ this classification system as a convenient framework for examining the entire range of psychological disorders.

DSM-III includes about fifteen major categories of psychological disorders, with many specific disorders included in each category (see Table 11.2). In this chapter we will devote most of our attention

THE STIGMA OF
MENTAL ILLNESS

In 1972, George McGovern, then the Democratic nominee for the presidency, selected as his vice-presidential running mate a well-regarded senator from Missouri, Thomas Eagleton. But Eagleton was dropped from the ticket after it was revealed that he had suffered from a severe depression some time previously and had received electroshock therapy as part of his treatment. Eagleton's removal from the ticket—which was greeted with a sense of relief by many Americans—dramatized the fear that people have of the spectre of "mental illness," even long after it has been treated and cured.

— Box 2 —

On being sane in insane places

Can psychiatrists and psychologists tell a sane person from a crazy one? David Rosenhan (1973) suggests that they can't. Rosenhan conducted a study in which eight "normal" people succeeded in getting themselves admitted to twelve different mental hospitals by pretending to hear voices. (The voices were saying "empty," "hollow," and "thud.") These "pseudopatients" were instructed to abandon their pretended symptoms once they became patients and from then on to behave "normally." Their task was to get discharged from the hospital by convincing the staff that they were really sane.

The eight patients were three women and five men of different ages—a psychology graduate student, three psychologists, a psychiatrist, a painter, and a housewife. Rosenhan himself was one of the pseudopatients. They entered a wide variety of hospitals in five different states.

At the time of admission, the patients altered their names and occupations, but they presented the other details of their life histories accurately. The patients were always cooperative, except that they never actually swallowed the medicines they were given. When asked how he was feeling, the person always replied "fine" and reported that his symptoms had disappeared.

Despite their sanity, the psuedopatients were never detected. Admitted with a diagnosis of schizophrenia, a serious mental disorder, each was ultimately discharged (after a period ranging from 7 to 52 days) with a diagnosis of "schizophrenia in remission," meaning that the condition might return at any time. At no time during hospitalization was any question raised about possible pretense. Interestingly, it was quite common for the other patients in these hospitals to detect that a pseudopatient was not really one of them—a suspicion that was never entertained by the hospital staff.

Rosenhan presented his results as an indication of the shortcomings of psychiatric diagnoses. But his report quickly aroused the anger of many mental health professionals, who protested that sending people to fake symptoms was not a fair test of their ability to diagnose mental disorder. Psychiatrist Seymour Kety (1974) drew an apt medical analogy:

If I were to drink a quart of blood, and, concealing what I had done, came to the emergency room of any hospital vomiting blood, the behavior of the staff would be quite predictable. If they labeled and treated me as having a peptic ulcer, I doubt that I could argue convincingly that medical science does not know how to diagnose that condition. (page 959)

Given the pseudopatients' actual behavior—including their report of hearing voice

ever to admit that they had faked their symptoms—the behavior of the hospital staff seems quite reasonable.

Despite this persuasive criticism of Rosenhan's conclusion, his study did emerge with some important observations. It helped to document the ways in which a label of "mental illness," once applied, can be difficult for a person to shake. Rosenhan reports that once the patients were labeled "schizophrenic," their history and behavior came to be viewed in schizophrenic or "sick" terms. The pseudopatients took copious notes and, in fact, were worried that the hospital personnel would catch on that they were observers and not really schizophrenic patients. Instead, the personnel viewed the note taking as "writing behavior" and interpreted it as another aspect of their illness! As Rosenhan put it, "Given that the patient is in the hospital, he must be psychologically disturbed. And given that he is disturbed, continual writing must be a behavioral manifestation of that

Which of these patients in a mental hospital cooking class might be perfectly normal?

TABLE 11.2
Major Categories of Psychological Disorder in *DSM-III*

Category	General description	Examples of specific disorders
Anxiety disorders	Disorders in which anxiety is the main symptom, or in which the symptom seems to be an attempt to defend against anxiety.	* Anxiety attacks * Phobias * Obsessive-compulsive disorders
Affective disorders	Disturbances of mood that color one's entire life.	* Depression * Bipolar disorder (alternating mania and depression)
Schizophrenic disorders	Disorders involving serious alterations of thought and behavior that represent a split from reality.	* Disorganized, catatonic, paranoid, and undifferentiated types of schizophrenia
Disorders arising in childhood or adolescence	Disorders that are usually first evident in infancy, childhood, or adolescence.	Hyperactivity (attention deficit disorder) Infantile autism Mental retardation (see Chapter 6)
Dissociative disorders	Sudden alteration in the normally integrated functions of consciousness or identity.	Amnesia (when not caused by an organic mental disorder) Multiple personality
Personality disorders	Deeply ingrained, inflexible, and maladaptive patterns of thought and behavior.	* Antisocial personality disorder (Box 3)
Organic mental disorders	Psychological or behavioral abnormalities associated with a temporary or permanent dysfunction of the brain.	Senile dementia (see Chapter 10) Korsakoff's syndrome
Substance use disorders	Undesirable behavioral changes associated with drugs that affect the central nervous system.	Alcohol abuse or dependence Amphetamine abuse or dependence Cannabis (marijuana) abuse or dependence
Somatoform disorders	Disorders marked by physical symptoms for which no physical causes can be found, and which are linked to psychological stresses or conflicts.	Conversion disorder (physical symptoms that cannot be explained by known physical causes) Psychogenic pain disorder (severe pain that cannot be explained by known physical causes)
Psychosexual disorders	Disorders of sexual functioning or sexual identity that are caused by psychological factors.	Sexual dysfunctions, e. g., impotence; inhibited orgasm (see Chapter 13) Transsexualism (see Chapter 13)
Adjustment disorder	Impairment of functioning due to identifiable life stresses, such as family or economic crises.	Adjustment disorder with depressed mood Adjustment disorder with anxious mood
Factitious disorders	Physical or psychological symptoms that are voluntarily produced by the patient, often involving deliberate deceit.	Factitious disorder with psychological symptoms Factitious disorder with physical symptoms

* Asterisks denote specific disorders that are discussed in this chapter.

Based on the *Diagnostic and Statistical Manual of Mental Disorders* (American Psychiatric Association, 1980).

to three of the most common categories of disorder: anxiety disorders, depression, and schizophrenia. In addition, Box 3 discusses antisocial personality disorder, which is classified in the category of personality disorders.

Traditionally, the various types of psychological disorders have been divided into two main groupings, neuroses and psychoses. *Neuroses* are typically characterized by anxiety, an inability to cope effectively with life's challenges, and difficulty in social relationships. Although neuroses are sometimes quite painful and debilitating, they do not involve any loss of contact with reality. A neurotic is not the sort of person one would ordinarily identify as "crazy." *Psychoses*, in contrast, are disorders that do involve a loss of contact with reality. Psychotics may experience *delusions* (false beliefs about themselves or the world), *hallucinations* (seeing or hearing things that aren't there), disturbed thought processes, and loss of control over feelings and actions.

Because "neuroses" encompass a wide variety of symptoms, the developers of *DSM–III* chose to abandon this term in favor of more precise terminology based on specific observable symptoms. Most disorders that used to be called neuroses now come under the heading of anxiety disorders. The term *psychosis* is still used to describe states that are divorced from reality. Schizophrenia is the best known type of psychosis, and certain depressive disorders can also include psychotic symptoms.

ANXIETY DISORDERS

Anxiety is that vague, unpleasant feeling that suggests something bad is about to happen. It is so closely related to fear that there is no sharp dividing line between the two. Physiologically, anxiety and fear are quite similar; they include the same physical symptoms, such as sweating, difficulty in sleeping, and increased heart rate (see Chapter 7). In general, however, fear is a reaction to something specific, whereas anxiety remains vague and has no immediate apparent cause. Freud believed that anxiety is caused by one's unconscious fear that repressed sexual and aggressive impulses will come to the surface. Because this fear remains unconscious, one doesn't know what one is afraid of; hence, one experiences anxiety.

Anxiety Attacks

Anxiety sometimes expresses itself in sudden overwhelming episodes called *anxiety attacks.* One person described such an attack as "a knot in my stomach, a feeling of hot flashes and warmth through my entire body, tightening of the muscles, a lump in my throat, and a constant feeling that I am going to throw up." Another person said, "I noticed that my hands began to sweat, my legs crumpled under me, I saw white spots floating before my eyes. I felt like getting up and running" (Sarnoff, 1957).

Richard Lazarus (1974) describes the case of a college student who suffered periodic anxiety attacks. The student complained that

Anxiety is a vague feeling that something bad is about to happen. It is closely related to fear, and it upsets us both physically and psychologically.

he was extremely jittery and uneasy, that he couldn't sleep, that he couldn't concentrate on his studies, and that his stomach hurt. The campus psychologist noted that these anxiety attacks occurred just before a long holiday when the student would have to return home to his family. According to the student, he looked forward to these times at home. Yet when the end of the semester approached, and with it the prospect of another trip home, the student once again experienced waves of anxiety. It finally came out in sessions with the psychologist that the student's home environment was filled with conflict—a fact the student was able to deny as long as he was away at school. Because the student was unable to acknowledge to himself his repressed negative feelings toward his parents, he tried to hide them. But whenever the prospect of experiencing the reality of his family situation came close, anxiety over these buried feelings gave him away.

Whereas in anxiety attacks the person experiences anxiety directly, psychoanalytic theorists view other anxiety disorders as resulting from the defense mechanisms that people use to avoid experiencing anxiety. As we noted in Chapter 8, all of us occasionally make use of defenses to deal with anxiety and conflict, and this can be perfectly healthy. But defense mechanisms can have their psychic costs, as well, producing (according to the psychoanalytic view) the phobias and obsessive-compulsive disorders to be discussed in the following sections.

Phobias

Anxiety disorders are frequently marked by *phobias*—intense fears of particular objects or activities that seem out of proportion to the real dangers involved. Some fears are quite normal—everyone is frightened by what he only partly comprehends. For example, a school-age child may express a dislike for dogs and be uneasy around them. But

People with an extreme fear of heights (or acrophobia) may not even want to look at the adjacent photograph.

— *Box 3* —

The antisocial personality

It has been more than ten years since Charles Manson was sentenced to jail, but many people still actively fear his release. Manson, along with a group of young people who followed him as their leader and called themselves his "family," was convicted of murdering three men and two women, including actress Sharon Tate, in 1969. The mass murder took place in an expensive home in Hollywood. The killers left the word *pig* scrawled in blood on the front door.

Almost as alarming as the mass murder itself was the reaction of the murderer. "I have no guilt," Manson stated at his trial. Throughout his past, he had delighted in escaping from reformatories, getting away with criminal acts, and emerging from prisons totally unrepentant, having learned only to be more careful

Charles Manson would probably be diagnosed as having an antisocial personality disorder.

and more determined. He had always been described as charming, charismatic, and captivating, able to adapt himself easily to different roles in accordance with the needs and expectations of those around him. He would become "what each person wanted him to be—without ever really being what anyone thought he was" (Nathan and Harris, 1980, page 358). He seemed to be a man without any real emotion.

It is difficult and a bit dangerous to diagnose people on the basis of newspaper stories about them. Yet it seems very likely, as Peter Nathan and Sandra Harris (1980) suggest, that Charles Manson would be diagnosed as having an *antisocial personality disorder*. (More familiar terms for the antisocial personality are *psychopath* and *sociopath*.) The antisocial personality is one of a larger category of *personality disorders*. A person with a personality disorder has a

---

if the child becomes preoccupied with the possibility of encountering a dog and lives in a constant state of anticipatory anxiety, his feeling goes beyond a normal fear and becomes a *phobia*.

Phobias are relatively common in childhood. As children grow up they tend to leave these irrational fears behind. Nevertheless, many adults suffer from phobias. Among the most common adult phobias are *agoraphobia* (fear of open places), *claustrophobia* (fear of closed, cramped places), and *acrophobia* (fear of heights). Such phobias can be quite debilitating—a person with agoraphobia, for example, might refuse to go out of the house. It is easy to see how each of these phobias might lead to additional problems. Since people with such phobias cannot feel comfortable in many places, they are likely to feel inadequate and tense and to have problems with interpersonal relations.

According to the psychoanalytic view, phobias are symptoms of the repression of unacceptable basic urges. When repression is effective, phobic symptoms need not exist. But when repression fails, the anxiety may become attached to an undeserving object, person, or situation. That is, instead of fearing one's unacceptable impulses, one fears a symbolic substitute for these impulses and thereby avoids having to deal with them. As a result, harmless objects such as snakes or heights or open spaces come to produce enormous fear and are

WATCH OUT FOR THE PEANUT BUTTER!

It is possible, at least in theory, to develop an extreme fear or phobia of practically anything. And when you do, rest assured the psychological wordsmiths already have a word for it. Here are some of the more esoteric phobias (Wallechinsky and Wallace, 1975):

anthophobia: fear of flowers
belonophobia: fear of pins and needles
decidophobia: fear of making decisions
ergophobia: fear of work
gephyrophobia: fear of crossing bridges
iatrophobia: fear of doctors
ombrophobia: fear of rain
taphophobia: fear of being buried alive
trichophobia: fear of hair

and would you believe—

arachibutyrophobia: fear of peanut butter sticking to the roof of your mouth

rigid and narrow range of responses that significantly restrict his way of relating to the environment. The paranoid personality disorder, for example, is characterized by extreme suspiciousness. People with a schizoid personality disorder are withdrawn and reclusive. However, personality disorders do not bring a break of contact with reality, as do schizophrenia and other psychoses. Because the disorder is so deeply ingrained a part of personality, the person is typically not made anxious or troubled by his behaviors, even though they disturb other people.

The antisocial personality is characterized by superficial charm and intelligence, insincerity, lack of remorse or guilt, failure to learn from experience, self-centeredness, inability to love, and failure to follow any life plan. An individual with this disorder cannot tolerate frustration. If he wants something *now*, he will do anything to get it, unconcerned about the harm he may do to others along the way.

There is some evidence that the antisocial personality disorder has a biological basis. People with this disorder do not show the same physiological responses that other people do when they are put into a stressful situation—for example, when they are told they are about to receive a strong electric shock (Hare, 1978). As a result, these people may have trouble learning behaviors that most people learn out of fear, and they may not become anxious about the outcome of their behaviors. The many jail sentences that Charles Manson served never taught him to avoid those actions that put him in jail.

In addition to any biological predisposition that may exist to develop an antisocial personality disorder, such people are quite likely to come from broken homes or from homes with sociopathic or alcoholic fathers (Robins, 1966), and they are also likely to have lost a parent at an early age (Greer, 1964). These findings suggest that antisocial personality disorder may be caused in part by inadequate love and discipline in childhood, especially on the part of one's father. Charles Manson never knew his real father and spent his childhood being shunted between an alcoholic mother, other relatives, boarding schools, and juvenile institutions.

Most research on the antisocial personality disorder has been confined to males. It may be that our society does not breed this type of personality as readily in women as it does in men. With changing sex roles, this situation, too, may change. In fact, recent cases of repeating crimes by female criminals have been linked to diagnoses of antisocial personality disorder (Martin, Cloninger, and Guze, 1978).

COUNTERPHOBIA

One way to deal with phobic feelings is to take defensive (counterphobic) measures rather than avoid the feared object. Thus some adults indulge vigorously in precisely those behaviors they dread most, even though they may be unaware of the source of their fascination with such actions. Cameron (1963) describes this as a form of "reactive courage." Those who fear heights may climb mountains. Those who fear speed may drive racing cars. And those who suffer from claustrophobia may devote their lives to spelunking—the exploration of caves.

anxiously avoided. In this way the phobia protects the individual from recognizing the true nature of the emotional problem.

The classic example of phobia was the case of "Little Hans," a 5-year-old boy who lived in terror of horses. Hans's phobia, according to Freud, was not so much fear of horses as fear of his own frightening impulses. First, Hans repressed his wish to attack his father. Then, fearing the father might somehow learn of this wish and punish him horribly, Hans "solved" the problem by fearing horses instead of his father. Now Hans could hate horses while loving his father.

In contrast to psychoanalytic theory, the behavioral view contends that phobias are learned—the person learns to connect intense fear responses with otherwise neutral objects or situations. Wolpe and Rachman (1960) note, for example, that Little Hans experienced a series of traumatic exposures to horses during the time his phobia developed and suggest that these experiences provide a more reasonable explanation of Hans's phobia than the explanation provided by Freud.

The behaviorists' version of Little Hans is Watson and Rayner's (1920) "Little Albert." As we noted in Chapter 7, the 11-month-old Albert acquired a phobia as a result of classical conditioning. The experimenters struck a steel bar near Albert's head, producing a terrifying noise, whenever the baby reached to touch a rat. As a result, Albert came to fear the rat and, through a process of stimulus generalization, to fear other furry objects as well.

One limitation of the behavioral approach to phobia is that many phobias seem to develop without any specific frightening experience. Many people with severe fears of snakes, germs, airplanes, or heights report that they have had no particular unpleasant experiences with these objects or situations. And many people who have had a bad automobile accident or fall do not become phobic about these situations.

Why do particular experiences lead some people, but not others, to develop phobias? At least part of the answer may be biological. There is evidence that certain people are more likely to develop phobias than others. There are "jumpy" people whose autonomic nervous systems are easily aroused by a wide range of stimuli. Such a biological tendency to be susceptible to phobia is likely to be hereditary to some extent.

Obsessive-Compulsive Disorders

Obsessive-compulsive disorders reflect another pattern of defenses against anxiety. Instead of avoiding particular objects that symbolize the anxiety, the obsessive-compulsive person attempts to master the threat by repeatedly engaging in behavior unconsciously connected with it. Obsessive-compulsive reactions involve two sets of related patterns. First, the person keeps thinking certain thoughts over and over and is unable to put those thoughts out of her head (the obsession). Second, seemingly against her will, the individual engages in ritualistic acts, such as stepping over cracks, knocking on wood, or repeatedly washing her hands (the compulsion).

Gerald Davison and John Neale (1978) report the case of a woman who washed her hands over 500 times a day in spite of the painful sores that resulted. She reported that she had a strong fear of being contaminated by germs and that she could temporarily alleviate this concern only by washing her hands. Psychoanalytic theorists speculate that this sort of repetitious handwashing represents an unconscious attempt to make penance for one's forbidden thoughts or impulses. Behaviorists, for their part, believe that compulsive behaviors persist because they have been repeatedly reinforced by their consequences (Meyer and Chesser, 1970). Each time that the woman washed her hands, for example, she was rewarded by the knowledge that her hands were clean.

Another obsessive-compulsive pattern is that of extreme neatness. Neatness can of course be a normal and healthy pattern, but it may be a symptom of disorder if taken to an extreme, so that, for example, the person gets terribly upset whenever he sees a speck of dust or when a piece of furniture is moved an inch. This kind of behavior may be seen as a defense mechanism Freud called *reaction formation*—doing the opposite of the repressed wish or impulse. Thus, for some persons excessive cleanliness may mask the urge to express opposing patterns of behavior—to soil, to be slovenly, to be disorganized.

KNOCK ON WOOD
KNOCK ON WOOD

A business manager, Harold Parker, developed an intricate system of rituals that he used to ward off bad luck, bad thoughts, or bad feelings. When his plant manager, Edgar, first told him that his company was failing, Parker started chanting to himself, "Edgar will have his health, Harold will have his wealth," and he would touch something solid twice, once with his right foot and once with his left. Over the years he developed more and more such magical rituals, to the point where he spent most of his time thinking about the rituals and little time thinking about his real problems. His would be considered an obsessive-compulsive disorder (Viscott, 1972).

DEPRESSION

Depression has been described as the common cold of mental illness. That is because it is by far the most common psychological problem, and in its milder forms almost all of us are familiar with it. You can probably remember times when you felt discouraged and dejected, when nothing that you did seemed to go right, and when you felt there was little chance things would turn for the better. Thoughts like "I'm a hopeless case" or "I'll never amount to anything" may have gone through your mind. Such depressions are perfectly normal. They are particularly likely to occur after a loss or a disappointment, whether in love, at school, or at work. In most cases, such depressions blow over after a couple of days or weeks. In other cases, however, depressions involve more severe symptoms, and they last for months or years. It has been estimated that there are from 5 to 10 million seriously depressed people in the United States (Schmeck, 1975). About 15 percent of American adults have at some time had a major depression, and about one in twenty have been depressed seriously enough to require hospitalization. Serious depression is about twice as common among women as among men (American Psychiatric Association, 1980). College students are among the groups of people who are highly prone to depression.

Like the common cold, depression is extremely widespread. But whereas colds rarely kill anyone, depressions often do. As many as half of the suicides in the United States occur among persons suffering from depression (see the Psychological Issue at the end of this chapter). Far too many serious cases go unrecognized and untreated. This is especially unfortunate because, of all psychological disorders, depression is probably the most susceptible to effective treatment, whether through traditional psychotherapy or drug treatment.

The Range of Depression

It is quite normal to feel some degree of depression during certain periods of life. We all encounter experiences, such as deaths of loved ones and personal failures, that can lead to depression. However, sometimes depression is unusually deep and long-lasting and can even reach psychotic proportions, involving delusions or hallucinations with themes of disease, death, or deserved punishment. The following case of depression, reported by Martin Seligman (1975), is somewhere near the middle of the range and also illustrates some typical features of the disorder:

Recently a middle-aged woman presented herself to me for psychotherapy. Every day, she says, is a struggle just to keep going. On her bad days she cannot even bring herself to get out of bed, and her husband comes home at night to find her still in her pajamas, with dinner unprepared. She cries a great deal; even her lighter moods are continually interrupted with thoughts of failure and worthlessness. Small chores such as shopping or dressing seem very difficult and every minor obstacle seems like an impassable barrier. . . .

Her gait and speech are slow and her face looks very sad. Up until last fall she had been vivacious and active, the president of

CHURCHILL, LINCOLN, AND VAN GOGH

Many famous people through history have suffered from depression. Winston Churchill wrote about the "black dog" that followed him throughout his life and finally immobilized him in his old age. Abraham Lincoln had bouts of depression and often dreamed of his own coffin. And artist Vincent Van Gogh cut off his own ear in a fit of despair.

her suburban PTA, a charming social hostess, a tennis player, and a spare-time poet. Then two things happened: her twin boys went away to college for the first time, and her husband was promoted to a position of much greater responsibility in his company, a position that took him away from home more often. She now broods about whether her life is worth living, and has toyed with the idea of taking the whole bottle of her antidepressant pills at once. (pages 1–2)

This woman's feelings of worthlessness and hopelessness and her slow and lethargic behavior are common characteristics of depression. In more severe cases, depressed people may remain motionless for hours on end, with their faces frozen in expressions of grief. They may lose their appetite, and in some cases they lose a tremendous amount of weight. They may also have a great deal of difficulty sleeping and may experience uncontrollable outbursts of crying.

This woman's depression was apparently triggered by specific incidents in her life—her children's leaving home and her husband's promotion. Many depressions can be traced at least in part to such difficult life events. But there are also cases of depression that do not have any apparent external cause. These cases are often chronic conditions, sometimes lasting an entire lifetime. In some cases, moreover, the state of depression alternates with an opposite state of extreme elation, known as *mania*. The alternation between mania and depression is known as *bipolar disorder*. One lawyer spent most of his life alternating between the highs and lows of bipolar disorder. "I literally enjoyed the manic phases," he reported. "I was a big shot, on

Almost all of us have experienced depression at some time in our lives. But some people have unusually long-lasting or deep depressions that interfere with their ability to function in their daily lives.

top of the world. I spent not only my own money, but everybody else's I could get my hands on—I bought six suits at a time, a lot of stupid unnecessary things." Some people in manic states also become loud and aggressive and show little concern about what other people will think of them. After being in such a phase for a while, however, the manic individual comes crashing down into the low phase. In this phase, the lawyer reported, "I feared getting out of bed, and was anxious to get into bed at night because I could block out the horror of my daily life" (*Newsweek*, 1973). One explanation of this pattern is that the manic is running away from depression by plunging into so much activity. But clearly it is a strategy that doesn't work very well. It is now believed that bipolar disorders are caused by biochemical imbalances in the brain and nervous system, as will be discussed shortly.

What Causes Depression?

Almost all people experience losses or disappointments at some point in their lives, yet only some people become seriously depressed. What accounts for this difference? Several explanations have been proposed.

Psychoanalytic Theory. Freud emphasized the importance of early life events in accounting for later psychological disorder, and his theory of depression (1917) was no exception. He suggested that some people become excessively dependent on others for the maintenance of their self-esteem, as a result of either too much or too little gratification of their needs during the oral period of psychosexual development (see Chapter 8). When these people experience a loss during adulthood, such as the death of a loved one, they feel unconscious anger toward this person for leaving them. This anger, however, is not directly expressed but is instead turned inward against the self, leading to the self-blame and self-hatred characteristic of depression. The loss that triggers such reactions is not necessarily someone's death. It may also be a symbolic loss, such as rejection, which the person experiences as a total withdrawal of love. Although many psychologists and psychiatrists agree with aspects of Freud's theory, there is little firm evidence for it.

Learned Helplessness. Learning theorists agree that the predisposition to become seriously depressed may have roots in childhood experiences. Rather than talking about oral deprivation, however, they focus on the person's history of reinforcement. Martin Seligman (1975) has suggested that depression may be the result of *learned helplessness*—that is, of experiences in which the person learns that her efforts have little to do with the outcome of the situation.

As we noted in Chapter 7, studies with both humans and other animals have shown that lack of control over one's own outcomes can cause an individual to give up on trying to effect changes. Seligman points out that the symptoms of depressed patients, including passivity, loss of appetite, and a lack of outward aggression, are similar to those of animals in learned-helplessness experiments. Seligman believes that people become depressed when they find that their actions bear no relation to the rewards and punishments they receive.

WHEN TASKS BECOME ORDEALS

Although depressed patients often do poorly on various tasks, they tend to believe that they are even worse than they really are—that their actions don't have any chance of succeeding (Seligman, 1975). For example, Seligman was giving patients a graded-task assignment as therapy for depression. He brought one of the patients, a middle-aged woman, into the testing room, chatted with her, and then said, "I have some tasks here I should like you to perform." When he said the word "tasks," the woman burst into tears and could not continue. As Seligman put it, "A mere task is seen by a depressive as a labor of Hercules" (page 85).

Seligman's theory suggests that the best way to help depressed patients is to demonstrate to them that their actions *do* make a difference. Moreover, the theory suggests that individuals could be better protected against depression in adulthood if they had childhood experiences of active striving and mastery, in which they learned that positive and negative reinforcements were contingent on their own actions.

Some researchers believe that the phenomenon of learned helplessness may help to explain why women are twice as susceptible to depression as men. Women have traditionally been trained to act and feel helpless, and society often keeps them that way. If women learn to be dependent on others—fathers, boyfriends, husbands, bosses—for their reinforcements, they may ultimately come to feel ineffective and, as a result, prone to depression.

Physiological Factors. Various explanations of the physiological basis of depression have been offered. One likely possibility is that depression involves a depletion of norepinephrine and serotonin, two of the chemical transmitter substances conveying impulses from one neuron to another in the brain and nervous system (see Chapter 2). This may cause an inhibition or slowing down of neural transmission, which in turn gives rise to periods of depression. As we will see in Chapter 12, drugs that have been effective in treating depression have, as one of their effects, the ability to increase the level of norepinephrine and serotonin in parts of the nervous system.

The role of brain chemistry is especially clear in cases of bipolar disorder, in which depression appears to be associated with low levels of the transmitter substance dopamine, as well as norepinephrine and serotonin, in certain areas of the brain. Furthermore, the manic phase is associated with excessively high levels of these chemicals (Iversen, 1979). The biochemical imbalances that lead to bipolar disorder appear to be highly heritable. Studies have shown, for example, that bipolar disorders tend to run in biological families but not in adoptive families (Kety, 1979). Although these biochemical imbalances are not yet well understood, bipolar disorder can often be treated effectively by drugs such as lithium carbonate. The lawyer with bipolar disorder whom we mentioned earlier in this chapter found that this drug brought his condition under control after 40 years of suffering.

SCHIZOPHRENIA

Although most of us can understand very well what it is like to be depressed, schizophrenia remains a strange, unfathomable disorder to most people. But it is a condition that afflicts approximately 1 percent of the American population and accounts for half the patients confined to mental institutions. Many other schizophrenics live outside the hospital, in many cases returning periodically for treatment. Regardless of where they may live physically, schizophrenics seem to live in a mental world that is different from the one the rest of us experience.

The term *schizophrenia* was coined by a Swiss psychiatrist,

Eugen Bleuler, in 1911. The word literally means "split personality" or "split mind." But schizophrenia should not be confused with the rare cases of multiple personality that we sometimes hear about. Rather, the "splitting" refers to the patient's departure from social reality. The hallmarks of schizophrenia are serious alterations of perception, activity, emotion, and thought. Sometimes schizophrenics are extremely withdrawn and unresponsive and seem oblivious to things going on around them. They may display extremely unusual motor behavior, ranging from frenzied excitement to complete immobility. They sometimes react with emotions that seem totally inappropriate, and they may entertain thoughts about themselves and others that are far out of touch with reality. And there are many schizophrenics who at times seem perfectly normal, so much so that, as Roger Brown puts it, "The hospital volunteer who converses informally with [schizophrenic] patients usually finds it difficult to tell some of the patients from some of the doctors" (Brown and Herrnstein, 1975, page 627).

Not all schizophrenics have all these symptoms and, depending on which symptoms are most prevalent, a schizophrenic may be diagnosed as belonging to one of four subtypes. The person with the *disorganized* type of schizophrenia exhibits bizarre behavior, including strange facial expressions and speech and inappropriate or silly emotional reactions. *Catatonic* schizophrenics display severe motor disturbances; such persons may show either extreme immobility or agitation. *Paranoid* schizophrenics may sometimes seem fairly normal; their thinking often seems clear and logical in its own terms, but they are plagued by unrealistic fears and suspicions. Finally, many schizophrenics are diagnosed as having *undifferentiated* schizophrenia, which means they have so many overlapping symptoms that it isn't clear what subtype to classify them as. Now let us take a closer look at the delusions and thought disorders displayed by schizophrenics.

Delusions

Many schizophrenics, particularly those diagnosed as paranoid, experience delusions—thoughts about themselves or the world that seem (to the rest of us, at least) to be totally divorced from reality. Often these are *delusions of persecution*—the idea that other people are conspiring against you. Roger Brown reports an encounter with a high-school friend of his who looked him up eight years later:

We had half an hour or so of pleasant chatter about old friends, and then I noticed that my guest was looking at me in a rather curious "knowing" way that seemed to suggest that he did not mind playing this game of reunion after a long separation if I had a taste for it, but the guest was not "taken in" by this pretense. Then he came out with the remark: "I saw you in Cleveland last week, you know." That rocked me a bit as I had not been in Cleveland. And then it all came out. My guest believed that his entire circle of high school friends—who had, in fact, gone their separate ways for years—had had him under surveillance since high school. (Brown and Herrnstein, 1975, page 631)

When Brown tried to convince his friend that his suspicions were unfounded, the man told of "darting shadows" he had seen following him in various cities, of overhearing whispered conversations, and so on. This man had interpreted all sorts of ordinary insignificant events as centered directly on himself. He had what are called *ideas of reference*—the assumption that all things other people are doing and saying refer to oneself.

In addition to such delusions of persecution, schizophrenics may also have *delusions of grandeur*, believing themselves to be saviors or famous people—such as Napoleon, God, or Jesus Christ.

Thought Disorders

Whether or not they have delusions, almost all schizophrenics have thought disorders of one sort or another. Sometimes these are revealed in incoherent, rambling conversations, as illustrated by the following conversation between a doctor and patient:

Doctor: What would you like, Mr. Kelly?
Patient: The power of the ancients. The Asunder. I want the Asunder.
Doctor: Did you ever have the power before? Was it something you lost?
Patient: Holy, Holy, Holy, Adonai Echod. Te Deum Laudamus. Ex Post Christo, Ex Post Facto, Ex Rel Post Office. There you have it. (Viscott, 1972, page 224)

In addition, some schizophrenic patients make up new words to use in their conversations, as in the following excerpt:

Patient: I was sent by the government to the United States to Washington to some star, and they had a pretty nice country there. Now you have a body like a young man who says he is of the prestigitis.
Doctor: Who was this prestigitis?
Patient: Why, you are yourself. You can be prestigitis. They make you say bad things; they can read you; they bring back Negroes from the dead. (White, 1932, page 228)

Such manufactured words, meaningful only to the speaker and no one else, are called *neologisms*.

Schizophrenic thought is also likely to be characterized by *loose associations*. The person may be talking about one thing and then drift off on a train of thought that listeners find hard to follow. A schizophrenic patient himself reported, "My thoughts get all jumbled up. I start thinking or talking about something but I never get there" (McGhie and Chapman, 1961, page 108). Schizophrenics may also make *clang associations*, in which the words seem to follow because they rhyme or sound similar rather than because they make sense. For example: "How are you today by the bay as a gay, Doctor?" (Davison and Neale, 1978).

Experimental studies in which patients are given problems to solve have suggested that schizophrenics find it especially difficult to differentiate between relevant and irrelevant information and are easily distracted. This difficulty may be at the heart of schizophrenic thought disorders.

DELUSION OR REALITY?

It's not always easy to decide what is delusion and what is reality. One woman told a psychologist that she was constantly being followed—obviously a delusion of persecution. Upon careful checking, however, it was found that her husband had hired a private detective to watch her (Davison and Neale, 1974).

What Causes Schizophrenia?

Schizophrenia sometimes strikes suddenly, in reaction to a stressful event; this is called *reactive* schizophrenia. In other cases, schizophrenia develops slowly and gradually; this is called *process* schizophrenia. The reactive schizophrenic sometimes seems more disturbed than the process schizophrenic does, but the reactive schizophrenic is also more likely to recover. The underlying causes of both of these forms remain a mystery, however. It is likely that there is no single cause but rather a number of contributing factors operating at different levels—biochemical, psychological, and social. The following are several of the factors that are currently believed to be important.

Genetic and Biochemical Factors. Schizophrenia is highly heritable. People with schizophrenic close relatives are much more likely to be schizophrenic themselves than people who do not have schizophrenic relatives. And if one identical twin has the disorder, there is about a 50 percent chance that the other twin (who shares all the same genes) has it as well. This relationship is much lower—there is only about a 10 percent chance—in the case of fraternal twins, who are less similar genetically (Kety, 1979). These data indicate that schizophrenia has a large genetic component. There is almost certainly a biochemical factor, predisposing people to schizophrenia, that is passed on through the genes. Scientists are hard at work trying to pin down this biochemical factor. The latest evidence suggests that schizophrenia is associated with an overproduction of the transmitter substance dopamine or an overresponsiveness to dopamine in certain brain regions. As we noted in Chapter 2, dopamine transmits

Schizophrenics seem to live in their own worlds, separate from the reality that the rest of us experience.

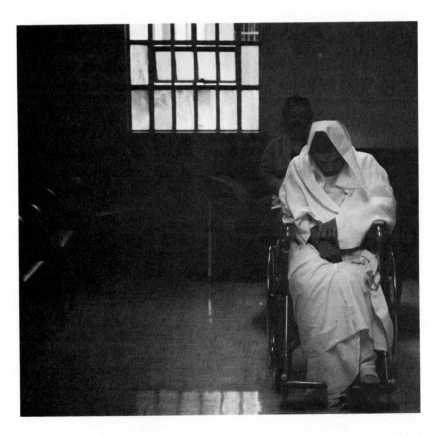

messages to portions of the limbic system that regulate emotional responses. An excess of dopamine in these areas may give rise to the hallucinations and other disruptions of thought and emotion that characterize schizophrenia. The most direct support for this hypothesis comes from recent studies that have found high levels of dopamine in the brains (especially in the limbic system) of deceased schizophrenics (Iversen, 1979).

Family Patterns. Schizophrenics often seem to come from families in which there is disturbed communication between husband and wife and between parents and children. One well-known theory holds that the preschizophrenic child is exposed to *double-bind* communications, in which the parent says one thing but apparently means another. What the parent says is characteristically contradicted by her actions, tone of voice, or facial expressions. For example:

A young man who had fairly well recovered from an acute schizophrenic episode was visited in the hospital by his mother. He was glad to see her and impulsively put his arm around her shoulders whereupon she stiffened. He withdrew his arm and she asked, "Don't you love me any more?" He then blushed and she said, "Dear, you must not be so easily embarrassed and afraid of your feelings." The patient was able to stay with her only a few minutes more and following her departure he assaulted an aide. (Bateson et al., 1956, page 258)

It is possible that the mother's inconsistent communications contributed to putting this patient into the hospital in the first place. Such contradictory messages may put a great deal of pressure on the child and ultimately lead him to withdraw from reality into a more "consistent" inner world (Bateson et al., 1956). But despite the popularity of the double-bind hypothesis there is little solid evidence that such contradictory messages in fact contribute to schizophrenia.

Psychological Stress. As mentioned earlier, psychologically stressful events can trigger a schizophrenic episode. In 1971 Mark Vonnegut, the son of writer Kurt Vonnegut, became severely schizophrenic. He later wrote, "Just prior to my crackup, my parents were splitting up, the woman I had been virtually married to took off with another man, my father was becoming more and more outlandishly famous" (1975). All of these stresses may have had a role in precipitating his psychosis. Vonnegut subsequently recovered from his schizophrenia and entered medical school.

It should be emphasized that these explanations are not mutually exclusive. To explain schizophrenia, researchers will eventually have to explain how a variety of factors interact with one another. As Vonnegut points out, many other young people experience events as traumatic as those in his life without becoming schizophrenic. It seems likely, therefore, that such traumatic events lead to schizophrenia only among people who are predisposed to it for other reasons—most likely related to inherited abnormalities of brain chemistry.

We have sampled only a relatively small number of the psychological disorders that afflict people. Despite the difficulties of defining

MENTAL ILLNESS AND THE ECONOMY

People may be predisposed to psychological disorders for a variety of reasons, including genetic factors and early childhood experiences. But current events in the person's life can trigger the disorder. Economic conditions may be crucial in this regard. In an extensive study of economic change and mental hospitalization in the United States, M. Harvey Brenner (1973) documented that economic recessions lead to increased mental disorder. Men between 35 and 54 and women between 25 and 34 were most likely to be affected by economic downturns, presumably because these people are in their peak years of employment and are thus most affected by the unemployment that accompanies recession. As one psychiatrist put it, "A lot of people's identity is wrapped up in their job. Take the jobs away and you've taken away their security and self-esteem" (Rice, 1975).

and categorizing disorder, it is evident that psychological disorders can, quite as much as physical diseases, cause great suffering in people's lives. Psychological disorders can even take people's lives, as we will see in the Psychological Issue that follows. And then, in Chapter 12, we will move to a more hopeful topic—the ways in which such disorders can be treated.

SUMMARY

1. Four major approaches are currently used to define abnormal behavior. The *statistical* approach defines normality in terms of what the majority of the members of a society are like. The *adequacy* approach focuses on people's ability to adjust to or cope with their environment without feeling undue distress.

2. According to the highly influential *medical model*, mental disorders should be seen as illnesses, with diagnoses, symptoms, and treatments. Szasz and other critics of the medical model say that it absolves the disturbed person from responsibility for her condition.

3. Finally, the *cultural* approach suggests that abnormality is defined in terms of the norms of the society or cultural group in which the behavior occurs—what is normal in one culture, time period, or situation may be abnormal in another.

4. Legal definitions of insanity have been a problem in the courts for hundreds of years. The M'Naghten rule equated insanity with the inability to tell right from wrong. The Durham decision took a medical view of insanity, defining it as a mental disease or defect.

5. The diagnostic categories that are used to classify psychological disorders provide a means for mental health professionals to communicate about abnormal behavior. However, such categories have tended to be unreliable. *DSM-III* has been designed to improve their reliability.

6. The labels given to patients can affect the way the patients view themselves and are viewed by others, even if the labels are incorrect. Rosenhan's study with "pseudopatients" showed, for example, that once people are labeled with a mental illness their "normal" behaviors may be considered symptoms.

7. Traditionally, the various types of psychological disorders have been divided into two main groupings, *neuroses* (disorders characterized by anxiety and inability to cope with life's challenges) and *psychoses* (disorders characterized by loss of contact with reality and sometimes involving *delusions* and *hallucinations*). *DSM-III* no longer refers to neuroses, most of which are now categorized as *anxiety disorders*.

8. *Anxiety* is a vague, unpleasant feeling that something bad is about to happen. Freud believed that anxiety is caused by an unconscious fear that repressed impulses will rise to the sur-

face. Anxiety is sometimes expressed in the form of *anxiety attacks*.

9. A *phobia* is an intense fear of something that is out of proportion to the real danger involved. According to psychoanalytic theory, phobias displace fears from one's unacceptable impulses onto harmless objects. According to the behavioral view, phobias are learned responses.

10. In *obsessive-compulsive disorders*, the person, seemingly against his will, keeps thinking certain thoughts (obsession) and engaging in repetitive acts (compulsion). One sort of obsessive-compulsive pattern is that of extreme neatness.

11. *Antisocial personality disorder* is characterized by superficial charm and intelligence, insincerity, lack of remorse or guilt, inability to learn from experience, self-centeredness, and a lack of concern for other people.

12. The most common psychological problem is *depression*. Depression ranges in severity. It is characterized by feelings of worthlessness, hopelessness, and lethargy. Depressions may be triggered by external events or may appear as the result of forces within the individual.

13. In *bipolar disorder*, the individual alternates between states of deep depression and extreme elation. Such disorders appear to be caused by imbalances in transmitter substances in the brain.

14. What causes depression? Freud believed that the depressed person turns inward her anger toward a person who has rejected or abandoned her, leading to self-hatred. Seligman has suggested that depression is the result of *learned helplessness*—the person has found that her actions have little effect on the world. Depression may also have a biochemical basis, involving the depletion of the transmitter substances norepinephrine and serotonin.

15. The primary characteristics of *schizophrenia* include serious alterations of perception, activity, emotion, and thought. The person with *disorganized* schizophrenia exhibits bizarre behavior. *Catatonic* schizophrenics may show either extreme immobility or agitation. *Paranoid* schizophrenics are plagued by delusional fears and suspicions. And *undifferentiated* schizophrenics have overlapping symptoms of the other types.

16. Schizophrenics may experience *delusions of persecution* and believe that other people are conspiring against them. Such people often have *ideas of reference*—they believe that everything other people say and do somehow refers to them. Schizophrenics may also have *delusions of grandeur*, believing themselves to be famous persons or religious figures.

17. Schizophrenia is also characterized by thought disorders, and schizophrenics' conversation is often incoherent and rambling. They sometimes invent words—*neologisms*—and make *loose associations* or *clang associations* in building sentences.

18. Schizophrenia may strike suddenly (*reactive* schizophrenia) or it may develop slowly and gradually (*process* schizophrenia).

Among the possible causes of schizophrenia are genetic and biochemical factors, family patterns characterized by *double-bind* situations, and psychological stress. These factors may all interact to produce a particular case.

SUICIDE

In ancient times suicide was considered a heroic way of dealing with an impossible life situation. The Japanese hero confronted with an intolerable "loss of face" committed hara-kiri, just as the Greek or Roman warrior fell on his own sword to save his honor. For centuries the suicide of religious martyrs was glorified as an example of dedication to the highest principles.

Today suicide is rarely seen as heroic (although there may be occasional exceptions, as in time of war), and it is frowned upon by virtually all religions. Indeed, some religious groups will still not give religious burial to someone who has taken his life. Yet suicide remains a major cause of death in America today. According to official figures, someone in the United States commits suicide about

According to official figures, someone in the U.S. commits suicide about every 20 minutes.

every 20 minutes—a total of almost 30,000 a year (U.S. Department of Commerce, 1979). And these "official" suicides are actually a vast underestimate of the number of people who take their own lives.

THE MEASURE OF SUICIDE
Who commits suicide? It's sometimes difficult to know for sure. Suicide statistics are notoriously unreliable. Many suicides are never reported as such because of the shame attached to the act by family members. Furthermore, what looks like an accident may actually be a deliberate suicide. About 50,000 people die each year in automobile accidents, but no one knows how many of these

drivers consciously or unconsciously set up the conditions for a fatal crash.

Even if we confine ourselves to the officially recorded suicides, we find that suicide is a personal and social tragedy of tremendous magnitude. Suicide has ranked tenth among causes of death for adults and it is the third leading cause of death for teenagers, after accidents and homicides (Holinger, 1979). And suicide rates have been on the

Some suicidal people can be talked out of taking their lives. This man threatened to jump from the upper structure of the Charlestown Bridge in Boston but police finally talked him down.

increase. Between 1960 and 1977, the suicide rate in the United States rose by about 25 percent (U.S. Department of Commerce, 1979).

Suicides are three times as common among men as among women. However, women are three times as likely as men to attempt suicide unsuccessfully. Some think that most of these unsuccessful attempts are probably pleas for help rather than real attempts to take one's life. Men are more likely to use guns to commit suicide, whereas women tend to use sleeping pills.

Men are more likely to use guns, while women tend to use sleeping pills.

The older a man is, the more likely he is to commit suicide—the rate for men 65 and over is almost twice as great as that for men between 15 and 24. Among women, the rate increases until the 45–54 age range and declines after that. But suicides among young people have shown the most striking increases in recent years: from 1961 to 1975 the suicide rate for adolescents more than doubled (Holinger, 1978). Suicide is a problem among college students, although the rate appears to be lower than among nonstudents of the same age (Schwartz and Reifler, 1980).

The suicide rate of married persons is lower than that of single, widowed, or divorced persons, suggesting that marriage may provide protection against some of the stresses that lead people to take their lives.

Suicide among blacks is significantly lower than among whites. This lower rate may be related to the generally lower socioeconomic status of blacks in our society; if you are already at the bottom of the social class structure, there is less shame attached to not rising in the world. It is often assumed, particularly by black persons, that suicide represents a white solution to white problems. As Dick Gregory once cracked, "You can't kill yourself by jumping out of the basement" (Seiden, 1970).

Times are changing, though, and although the white suicide rate is still about twice that of blacks, the rate among blacks has increased much more sharply than the rate for whites in the last 20 years (U.S. Department of Commerce, 1979).

Finally, suicide rates vary predictably with economic conditions. In general, the number of people

---

Dear Folks :

I know this won't seem the right thing to do but from where I stand, it seems like the best solution, considering what is inevitably in store for the future.

You know I am in debt. Probably not deeply compared to a lot of people but at least they have certain abilities, a skill or trade, or talents with which to make financial recovery. Yes, I am still working but only "by the grace of the gods". You know how I feel about working where there are a lot of girls I never could stand their cattiness and I couldn't hope to be lucky enough again to find work where I had my own office and still have someone to rely on like Betty...

Some girls can talk about their work to their girl friends and make it sound humorous. But I guess it sounds like complaining the way I talk...

But just what is there to talk about when you get tired of the same old questions and comments on the weather "how are you," "Working hard or hardly working?" and you know better than to say very much about things they are interested in or concerned about... Due to these, and many, many more frustrations... and other causes I have become much more nervous than I was...

How I wish I could make "small talk" or "party chatter" like some girls do. But I can't compete with most of them for many reasons and after trying to enter social activities with kids in my age range, especially the past year, I find I can't compete with most of them. Can if I had all the clothes to look the part I still wouldn't be able to act the part. Sorry I am such a disappointment to you folks.

I am saying these things so you'd understand why it's so futile for me to even hope for a better job. As long as I go on living there will be "working conditions" when there are so many other better places for the money.

One reason for doing this now is that Bill will be back and may want his .22. But the primary reason is one I think you already know— Mike. I love him more than anyone knows and it may sound silly to you but I can't go on without him. What is there that's worth living for without him ?

Partial contents of a suicide note left by a 23-year-old woman who shot herself to death.

taking their lives seems to increase during times of recession and depression, to stabilize in times of prosperity, and to decrease during war years.

THE MOTIVES FOR SUICIDE

Why do people take their lives? Many possible reasons have been suggested. They include turning aggression inward, retaliating against others by making them feel guilty, trying to make amends for perceived past wrongs, trying to rid oneself of unacceptable feelings (such as homosexual attraction), desiring to rejoin a dead loved one, and escaping from pain, stress, or emotional problems (Mintz, 1968).

Gerald Davison and John Neale (1978) suggest that at a fundamental level a person chooses suicide as the best means available for withdrawing from a seemingly unsolvable problem in living. But they are quick to point out that this explanation does not account for the fact that not all people faced with the same sorts of problems commit suicide.

Suicide is known to be related to psychological disorder, especially depression. But not everyone who attempts or commits suicide is depressed. In one study, psychiatric patients rated as seriously suicidal were more likely to have a feeling of being out of control and to experience physical disequilibrium than to be depressed (Leonard, 1974). It seems that these individuals were more troubled with problems of channeling their energy than with feelings of hopelessness and despondency. It has also been found that people are especially susceptible to suicide when they are coming up out of depression. Severely depressed individuals are prone to commit suicide just after their spirits begin to rise.

In a study of suicides among college students, Robert Seiden (1966) concluded that the suicidal act is really a final dramatic gesture summing up a lifetime pattern of inadequate adjustment. To fellow students, the suicidal individual seems to be doing well, yet he usually believes that his achievements don't measure up to his or others' expectations. The suicidal student tends to be shy, withdrawn, and virtually friendless. To make up for his lack of social activities, he often becomes totally absorbed in studying or other solitary pursuits.

Severely depressed people may commit suicide just after their spirits begin to rise.

THE RIGHT TO DIE?

Despite the general condemnation of suicide, there are some who contend that society has no right to force individuals to live and who even advocate suicide in certain situations. In particular, there are those who view suicide as an ethically acceptable alternative when life would be too painful to enjoy, as in the case of terminally ill people who would rather die with dignity than subject themselves and their families to a long, perhaps expensive, and dehumanizing death.

In 1979, for example, a 62-year-old artist and social worker, Jo Roman, took her life in her New York apartment after long and deliberate preparations. She had informed her family and friends of her plans and consulted a lawyer to be sure that those she informed would not be held legally responsible to stop her. Finally, after an elaborate farewell toast, she took an overdose of pills and died. Jo Roman had been diagnosed as having breast cancer and was told that she could expect to live only five more years, provided she underwent painful treatments. Her

Jo Roman, who believed she had the right to die on her own terms.

suicide was not a rash decision but a deliberate and rational one. She even made a videotape about her suicide that was later broadcast on public television, fulfilling her desire to publicize an act that she believed deserved respect.

One woman videotaped her own suicide, an act she believed deserved respect.

In another case, Dr. Henry Van Dusen, the former president of Union Theological Seminary, and his wife carried out a suicide pact by swallowing overdoses of sleeping pills together. He was 77 and she was 80. They were both advocates of a person's right to terminate her own life, and they had entered into the pact to avoid the prospect of debilitating old age. In cases like these, argue advocates of the right to die, who are we to say that these people should not take their own lives?

Recently the "right to die" has taken on the trappings of a social movement. Exit, a British society advocating the right to die with dignity, has even prepared a pamphlet titled "A Guide to Self-Deliverance," listing (among other methods) lethal doses of common prescription and nonprescription drugs. "We won't recommend any particular pill," Exit's general secretary says. "Each one will have a summary of its advantages and disadvantages. We're saying, 'Choose from this range of pills'" (Leo, 1980).

Although the right to die may have an increasing number of advocates, it has at least as many opponents. Even if we grant that some terminally ill patients might be better off if they could end their pain, legitimizing suicide of any sort may encourage people to take their lives even when their prospects are not nearly so dim.

PREVENTING SUICIDE
Despite the controversy surrounding people's right to die in some instances, in the large majority of cases society has a clear obligation to do whatever it can to prevent the tragedy of suicide. One way in which society is trying to meet this obligation is through community suicide prevention centers, which offer 24-hour services to people who are feeling suicidal. When such people call the center, staff members try to determine how serious their threats are and to establish personal contact. Workers on such suicide "hotlines" have specific goals in talking to callers. These goals include communicating empathy to the caller, conveying understanding of the problem, providing information on where to go for professional help, convinc-

ing the caller to agree to measures that will take her a step away from the suicide, and providing hope that the caller's crisis will end (Speer, 1972).

Such crisis centers and hotlines are based on the fact that about three-fourths of suicides are preceded by warnings that can usually be interpreted as cries for help. These warnings are usually directed toward friends and relatives, but especially if people lack such important others, hotlines can save lives.

Why are we so concerned about preventing suicide? Why not let individuals decide for themselves when they have had enough of living? One reason we try to prevent suicide is that these people, when prevented, often go on to lead happy, productive lives. In addition, suicide does not involve a single life; it affects the lives of all those connected with the victim.

Three-fourths of suicides are preceded by warnings—cries for help.

The family suffers not only sorrow but usually guilt; they blame themselves for not preventing the tragedy. Children, too, suffer from the social stigma attached to the suicide of a parent; frequently, they become fearful that they are destined to follow the parent's example. Considering that ten attempts are made for every successful suicide, we must believe that most people really don't want to die and would not kill themselves if they could find any other solution to life's problems.

Another good reason for doing everything we can to prevent suicide is offered by Martin Seligman (1975): "Suicide usually has its roots in depression, and depression

dissipates in time. When a person is depressed, his view of the future is bleak; he sees himself as helpless and hopeless. But, in many cases, if he waited a few weeks,

---

Most people who commit suicide don't really want to die.

---

this cognitive set would be changed, and by reason of time alone the future would seem less hopeless" (page 89). Often the best gift we can give to someone contemplating suicide is the gift of time, the great healer.

SUMMARY
1. Suicide statistics are notoriously unreliable. Nevertheless, we do know that suicide rates are on the increase, that men are more likely to commit suicide than women (although women are more likely to make unsuccessful attempts), that married persons are less likely than single persons to commit suicide, and that whites are more likely than blacks to take their lives.
2. There are many possible reasons for suicide, but the fundamental reason is the inability to cope with a seemingly unsolvable problem. Suicide is related to depression and to feelings of being out of control.
3. The right to die is a controversial idea. Some say that anyone who wants to commit suicide should have the right to, whereas others feel society has a responsibility to prevent suicide.
4. Suicide centers and hotlines are designed to help potential suicides change their minds and seek professional help with their problems. Prevention programs view suicide threats as cries for help.

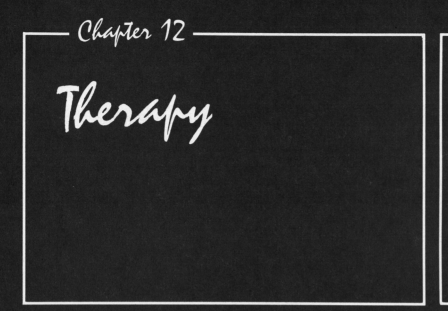

Chapter 12

Therapy

We have seen that psychological disorders take many forms and can cause individuals and their families considerable distress. What can psychology and psychiatry do to help people who suffer from these disorders? This question brings us to the domain of *therapy,* the professional application of techniques intended to treat psychological disorders and reduce distress. It is estimated that some 6 million Americans receive therapy each year—1.5 million in therapists' offices, 2.4 million in outpatient psychiatric clinics, 1.5 million in community mental health centers, and several hundred thousand in mental hospitals (Gross, 1978).

The field of therapy is so diverse that it might be more appropriate to speak of *therapies.* There are more than 130 different schools of therapy, from the well-established and traditional approaches (such as psychoanalysis) to the avant-garde and "pop" approaches, some of which will be discussed in the Psychological Issue that follows this chapter. Additional therapies are continually being developed, almost always with high claims and expectations. As Morris Parloff (1976) notes, "No school has ever been withdrawn for failure to live up to its claims, and as a consequence all continue to coexist" (page 14).

Therapy may be conducted individually or in groups, in settings that range from hospital rooms to private offices to auditoriums. It may be administered by psychiatrists, clinical psychologists, social workers, and sometimes by members of other professions, such as the clergy. It may take years of several sessions per week to be considered successful, or it may consist of a single treatment. The tech-

niques for therapy range from listening quietly as the client talks to administering powerful drugs.

Therapy addresses itself to a wide spectrum of problems, from serious disorders such as major depression and schizophrenia to mild problems of adjustment that are not really "psychological disorders" at all. Particularly because of these latter kinds of problems, it is often difficult to distinguish between therapy and counseling. For the most part, however, *counseling* focuses on specific decisions or adjustments that a person needs to make (such as with respect to schoolwork, occupation, or marriage), whereas therapy is concerned with more generalized or deeper-rooted psychological problems.

Despite the wide variations in forms taken by therapy, all approaches seem to share certain goals: giving the client relief from anxiety, symptoms, and conflict; establishing personal maturity, feelings of adequacy, and integration of the different parts of the self; improving interpersonal relationships; and helping the client to adjust to his culture and society (Watkins, 1965). Different therapies may emphasize one or more of these goals to the exclusion of others, and they may differ in what they consider to be "maturity" or "adjustment."

In this chapter, we will focus on three major types of therapies. First we will examine the major "insight therapies," which emphasize the patient's talking through her problems. Then we will discuss the behavior therapies, which are based on principles of experimental psychology, especially principles of learning. Third, we will consider the somatic therapies, which involve direct physiological intervention, including the use of drugs. After our tour of this variety of therapies, we will consider some general issues regarding their effectiveness and ethics.

INSIGHT THERAPIES

The basic idea of the "insight therapies" is that open discussion of a problem can bring insights into its causes and possible solutions. This type of therapy emphasizes getting one's feelings out into the open—bringing out the concealed thoughts and emotions that are often the cause of psychological problems.

Two major varieties of insight therapy are psychoanalysis and client-centered therapy. Although both types emphasize expression of inner feelings by the client, they differ greatly in their theoretical basis and in their approach to the client-therapist relationship. Another variety of insight therapy, Gestalt therapy, is discussed in Box 1.

Psychoanalytic Therapy

Psychoanalysis is the system of therapy developed by Sigmund Freud, and it is part and parcel of his general theory of personality (see Chapter 8). Psychoanalysis was born with the case of "Anna O." In the early 1880s physician Josef Breuer told Freud of a patient he was treating, a woman who was suffering from hysteria—the presence of physiological symptoms with no organic basis. Breuer found that when he hypnotized the patient (whom he called "Anna O.") she could remember painful events from her past—events she could not recall when awake. During hypnosis Breuer helped his patient to reexperience the painful events and to express the feelings that accompanied them. Upon being awakened, Anna expressed a great relief—both physical and emotional. After several sessions of the "talking cure," as Anna referred to it, her condition showed significant improvement.

This case illustrates the basic hypothesis of the theory Freud subsequently developed: that painful thoughts and emotions are often hidden in the unconscious mind. The goal of psychoanalysis is to open the doors to the unconscious and release these pent-up emotions, as Breuer did with Anna. Freud developed several techniques designed to help the patient achieve *catharsis*, this ultimate emotional release. Perhaps the most important of these techniques is *free association*, in which patients are asked to let their thoughts flow freely and to say whatever comes to mind. Freud would say to his patients:

You will notice that as you relate things various thoughts will occur to you which you would like to put aside on the ground of certain criticisms and objections. You will be tempted to say to yourself that this or that is irrelevant here, or is quite unimportant, or nonsensical, so that there is no need to say it. You must never give in to these criticisms, but must say it precisely because *you feel an aversion to doing so. (Freud, 1913, page 135)*

Freud believed that even the most "irrelevant" thoughts can have meaning and that pauses or breaks in a train of thought indicate a *resistance* to touch on sensitive topics. The psychoanalyst is trained to notice points of resistance and to try to help the patient overcome them. In the process of *interpretation,* the analyst points out resistances and offers some reasons for them.

Some patients find themselves becoming furious at their psychotherapists or at other times forming strong attachments to them. Freud believed that these emotions had less to do with the patients' actual relationship with the therapists than with residues from the patients' relationships to people from the past, usually their parents, which are then shifted to the therapists. Freud called this process of shifting emotions *transference,* and he believed it to be a central ingredient of successful psychoanalysis. By permitting patients to reexperience and express conflicts from their earlier life, the transference relationship allows them to gain awareness of the unconscious forces and conflicts underlying their behavior.

The process of transference can be seen in the following excerpt from a psychoanalytic session:

Patient (a 50-year-old male business executive): I really don't feel like talking today.
Analyst (remains silent for several minutes, then): Perhaps you'd like to talk about why you don't feel like talking.
Patient: There you go again, making demands on me, insisting I do what I just don't feel up to doing. (Pause) Do I always have to talk here, when I don't feel like it? (Voice becomes angry and petulant) Can't you just get off my back? You don't really give a damn how I feel, do you?
Analyst: I wonder why you feel I don't care.
Patient: Because you're always pressuring me to do what I feel I can't do. (Davison and Neale, 1978, page 472)

The patient in this excerpt had been in therapy for about a year. In previous sessions the analyst had learned enough about the patient to suspect that, although he was a successful businessman, he had feelings of weakness and incompetence that seemed to stem from childhood experiences with his father. The father had been highly critical and never seemed satisfied with his son's efforts. The analyst interpreted the above comments by the patient as an expression of resentment against the father, not against the analyst. "The patient's tone of voice (petulant), as well as his overreaction to the analyst's suggestion that he talk about his feelings of not wanting to talk, indicated that the patient was angry not at his analyst but at his father" (Davison and Neale, page 472). The therapist used this transference as the basis for subsequent sessions.

Freud believed that therapists should remain somewhat aloof and provide a neutral screen on which patients can project whatever image (such as father, mother, or spouse) they require for working out basic conflicts. In Freud's words, the therapist should be "impenetrable to the patient, and, like a mirror, reflect nothing but what is shown him" (1956, page 331). This is one of the reasons why the patient traditionally lies on a couch, while the psychoanalyst sits behind the patient where she cannot be seen.

In a traditional psychoanalytic session, the analyst sits behind the patient, who lies on a couch.

From the psychoanalytic viewpoint, the patient's need to discover and reexperience deeply buried psychological forces is a time-consuming process. Traditional psychoanalysis involves hour-long sessions three to five times a week, often extending over several years. In recent years, however, traditional psychoanalysis has become less prevalent, at least in part because of the high costs involved. At $60 an hour, four days a week, it can cost well over $10,000 a year. Now psychoanalytic therapy is more likely to be conducted in once- or twice-weekly sessions. There is also a trend toward limiting the length of such therapy, often to 20 or 30 sessions. The therapist and patient typically sit facing each other, and the therapist plays a more active role than in traditional psychoanalysis, providing guidance in exploring current, as well as past, problems. Contemporary psychoanalytic therapists also tend to be eclectic, borrowing techniques from other schools when appropriate rather than relying solely on free association, transference, and other Freudian techniques. Nevertheless, the emphasis remains on the individual gaining insight into the unconscious forces governing her behavior.

How effective is psychoanalytic therapy? As with all of the therapies we will consider, this is a matter of considerable dispute, especially in the absence of many well-controlled studies. It is known that psychoanalytic therapy, as Freud himself acknowledged, is *not* effective with schizophrenic or other psychotic patients. Rather, it is best directed at patients with anxiety disorders or relatively mild depressions—what Freud called neuroses. Psychoanalytic therapy seems to work better with highly educated and verbal people who already have some skill in exploring their own emotions. Certainly many people feel better over the course of this type of extended therapy. We will return to the question of the effectiveness of various forms of therapy later in this chapter.

Client-centered Therapy

According to Carl Rogers, the humanistic psychologist who developed *client-centered therapy*, the aim of therapy is to help clients realize and become their true selves by allowing them to test out the feelings that they have previously refused to admit are part of their life. As we saw in Chapter 8, Rogers believes that maladjustment is a result of denying those feelings and behaviors that do not conform to one's image of oneself, even when that image is false. Rather than correcting that self-image, the individual continues to evade the contradictory experiences. When these attempts fail, the inconsistency brings intense anxiety.

Client-centered therapists help individuals express and experience their true feelings by providing *unconditional positive regard.* That is, the therapist continues to respect the client no matter what he says or does. With such unconditional positive regard, the client worries less about how he will be evaluated by others and instead concentrates on the primary goal of evaluating his behavior for himself and considering how it will contribute to his personal growth.

Unlike the psychoanalyst, the client-centered therapist does not probe or make interpretations of the client's hidden thoughts and feelings. Instead, the therapist's main task is to create conditions that will help the client to change *by herself.* These conditions include acceptance, unconditional positive regard, and clarification of feelings, in the context of a warm relationship.

During the therapy session, the therapist will often rephrase clients' statements in such a way as to highlight the things the client seems to be suggesting but will not admit to in so many words. The following example from a client-centered therapy session shows how this technique is used:

Client (an 18-year-old female college student): My parents really bug me. First it was Arthur they didn't like, now it's Peter. I'm just fed up with all their meddling.
Therapist: You really are angry at your folks.
Client: Well, how do you expect me to feel? Here I am with a 3.5 GPA, and providing all sorts of other goodies, and they claim the right to pass on how appropriate my boyfriend is. (Begins to sob)
Therapist: It strikes me that you're not just angry with them. (Pause) Maybe you're worried about disappointing them.
Client (Crying even more): I've tried all my life to please them. Sure their approval is important to me. They're really pleased when I get the A's, but why do they have to pass judgment on my social life as well? (Davison and Neale, 1978, page 479)

In this example, the therapist had learned from previous sessions that the client's efforts to do well academically were motivated by a

---

TELEPHONE THERAPY

The value of the telephone in treating psychological disorder has only recently been recognized. Psychiatrist Gerald Grummet (1979) suggests that the phone may be the ideal form of communication for certain clients who are too anxious to tolerate face-to-face therapy sessions. Grummet describes one woman who was prone to extreme anxiety and occasional fits of rage during treatment sessions. After several crisis-type phone calls, the therapist realized that the client communicated better on the telephone. The client herself eventually eliminated visits, but therapy proceeded in nightly phone calls for ten years.

— *Box 1* —

Gestalt therapy

While Freud sought to cure patients' problems by helping them to understand their complicated pasts, Fritz Perls (1894–1970) emphasized becoming whole through awareness and appreciation of the here and now. His approach to achieving such wholeness is called *Gestalt therapy,* from the German "gestalt," meaning "configuration" or "arrangement of parts in a whole."

Fritz Perls received his medical degree in Germany in 1921 and originally became a psychoanalyst, but he rejected parts of Freudian theory. He left Germany in the 1930s to escape the Nazis, ultimately coming to the United States to live. The concepts and techniques he developed here have attained great popularity.

The aim of Gestalt therapy is to put individuals in touch with their entire selves and with their surroundings. According to Perls (1969), people tend to block out awareness of aspects of themselves and their experience and look at only a part of who they

Fritz Perls, founder of Gestalt therapy.

are or what they are doing. The therapist's job is to make such individuals "whole" again by helping them recognize all facets of their personalities and experiences. The client is made aware of his feelings, thoughts, and actions as they occur together. The goal of Gestalt therapy is for the individual to accept, take responsibility for, and appreciate those feelings, thoughts, and actions.

Gestalt therapy stresses feeling rather than thinking. "Intellect is the whore of intelligence," Perls (1969) wrote. "It's a drag on your life." Perls frowned on asking the question "why?" and said that the question to be asked is "how?" "Why" implies a search for intellectual understanding of what went wrong in the past; "how" implies a search for an understanding of what *is*. What *is* needs to be accepted, not criticized. Three of Perls's main rules for living are:

Be concerned with the present rather than with your past or future.
Do not use the word "should."
Surrender to being the kind of person you are.

Gestalt therapy shares with psychoanalytic and client-centered therapy the emphasis on increasing clients' insights into their own feelings and behavior. To accomplish this goal, the Gestalt therapist makes use of nonverbal, as well as verbal, clues to the client's feelings—her tone of voice, posture, walk, eye contact—every expression and movement she makes. By becoming aware of what her body is doing, Gestalt therapy says, the client can become more aware of what she is feeling. Gestalt therapy also makes use of *psychodrama,* in which one acts out scenes in order to bring out their emotional significance. In this technique, the person might "talk to his father," trying to picture his father on the

empty chair across from him. The client might then switch chairs and be his father, talking to him. Gestalt therapy is typically done in groups, although the focus remains on the distinctive experiences of individual group members.

Physical communication is an important part of Gestalt therapy. Laura Perls, Fritz's wife and a Gestalt therapist herself, says she will do almost anything physical with her clients if she feels it will increase their awareness: "I will light a cigarette, feed someone with a spoon, fix a girl's hair, hold hands, or hold a patient on my lap. I also touch them and let them touch me." When a female group member once asked Fritz Perls, "Could you explain the difference between words and experiences?" Perls kissed her, then proudly exclaimed, "O.K. That'll do it!" (Gross, 1978).

Gestalt therapy takes the view that people are responsible for their own lives and can make their own choices. Perls made this philosophy explicit in a memorable credo:

I do my thing and you do your thing. I am not in this world to live up to your expectations. And you are not in this world to live up to mine. You are you and I am I. And if by chance we find each other, it's beautiful. If not, then not. (Perls, 1969)

Gestalt therapy has been criticized by some for being antiintellectual and unscientific. Like other "growth-oriented" therapies, its lack of clear criteria for measuring personal growth makes it difficult to evaluate. But Gestalt therapy's emphasis on emotional experience has had a major impact on the human potential movement of recent decades, and some of its specific techniques have been adopted by therapists from a wide variety of theoretical persuasions.

need to please her parents and avoid their criticism. Even though at first the client is expressing anger at her parents, the therapist is helping her to realize that she really is afraid of their disapproval.

According to Rogers, warmth and empathy from the therapist are the most important factors in the success of therapy. Rather than emphasizing specific techniques, he stresses the personal qualities and emotional style of the therapist (Rogers, 1951). Studies of the effectiveness of various therapies seem to bear this idea out. They suggest that therapists who are genuine, warm, and empathic (having an accurate understanding of the client) obtain the best outcomes (Truax and Mitchell, 1971). These qualities are likely to be helpful to therapists of any orientation, not just client-centered therapists. As one client of a warm, helpful therapist put it, "Right from the start, I felt she really cared about me. She seemed to be upset by my problems and to be happy when I made progress. I felt so relaxed with her that it was easy to talk about very personal things" (Derlega and Chaikin, 1975, page 104).

BEHAVIOR THERAPIES

The *behavior therapies* are based on the principles of experimental psychology, especially of learning theory (see Chapter 5). Behavior therapists do not focus on deep underlying causes for psychological problems, nor do they see therapy as a process of drawing out buried emotions or hidden thoughts. Rather, they concentrate on the factors that are currently maintaining the person's inappropriate or self-defeating behaviors. The tasks of behavior therapy are to help the client "unlearn" inappropriate or unsatisfying behaviors and to replace them with appropriate ones, and to help the client acquire skills needed to cope effectively with life's challenges.

There are a number of techniques available to the behavior therapist; these techniques may be used alone or in combination, depending on the client's problem. The techniques to be examined here are desensitization, operant conditioning, modeling, and role playing.

Desensitization

We noted in Chapter 7 that fears can be acquired through a process of classical conditioning. For example, we recounted the case of Little Albert, who was conditioned to fear rats by having a loud noise sounded near his head whenever he reached toward a rat. The fear response was generalized from the initial object of fear (the noise) to the objects that were associated with it. *Desensitization therapy* is an attempt to reverse this process by linking feared objects or situations with new responses that replace the fear. That is, the fear object becomes linked to something pleasant, and the client is "desensitized" to the object.

What later came to be called desensitization therapy was first introduced by Mary Cover Jones (1925), a colleague of John Watson, the psychologist who had conditioned Little Albert. She was able to eliminate a fear of rabbits in a 3-year-old named Peter by giving him

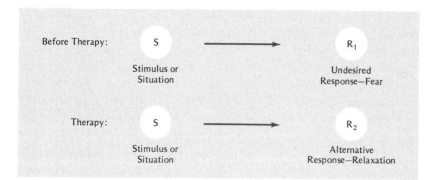

FIGURE 12.1

In desensitization therapy, a stimulus or situation (S) that elicits an undesirable response (R_1), such as fear or anxiety, is now associated with relaxation (R_2). Because the new response of relaxation is incompatible with the old response of fear, the old response disappears.

candy and other foods he liked while he was in the presence of a rabbit. At first the animal was kept at the far end of the room, then it was brought closer and closer on successive occasions. Jones proceeded to study seventy other children using variations of this strategy. The underlying idea of this approach is *counterconditioning:* the fearful stimulus (in Peter's case, the rabbit) is repeatedly paired with an object that produces positive, nonfearful responses (candy and food). This new conditioned association "crowds out" the previous association between the object and fear (see Figure 12.1).

Several decades after Jones's pioneering work, Joseph Wolpe (1958), a psychiatrist from South Africa, developed the technique of *systematic desensitization* to treat a wide range of fears and anxieties. Because most of the fears that therapists are called upon to treat are not as concrete as the fear of rabbits, Wolpe had subjects *imagine* the anxiety-evoking event or situations, whether it was fear of taking tests, of asserting oneself, or of speaking in public. And instead of giving patients candy, he taught subjects techniques of deep muscle relaxation. In systematic desensitization, the client is asked to arrange scenes in an *anxiety hierarchy,* from the least arousing to the most arousing. The patient then relaxes while imagining the least fearful scene and progressively moves on to more and more anxiety-arousing scenes, analogous to the way Jones brought the rabbit closer and closer to Peter. The ability to imagine more and more fearful scenes while relaxing has been found to reduce anxiety in the real-life situations, as well. The client learns to associate relaxation, not fear, with these situations.

In one experimental study of systematic desensitization, researchers were concerned with reducing test anxiety, a common problem among students (Freeling and Shemberg, 1970). A group of students rated high in test anxiety met once a week for six weeks. At the first meeting they were asked to develop an anxiety hierarchy of fifteen items, ranging from "You are sitting in a classroom of 100 students listening to a lecture" to "The test papers are being passed out and you are sitting in your seat waiting to receive your paper." The students were then taught techniques for deep muscular relaxation and were told to practice them for 15 to 30 minutes a day.

At the following sessions the group first relaxed. Then the experimenter presented items from the anxiety hierarchy, starting with the least anxiety-arousing scene. The students were asked to imagine the scene, and when all could do so without feeling anxious, the next

THERAPY IS GOING TO THE DOGS

Psychologists have adapted certain psychotherapeutic techniques for use with household pets. One team of psychologists (Tuber, Hothersall, and Voith, 1974) recently reported success in using desensitization to cure Higgins (an Old English sheep dog) of his intense fear of thunderstorms. They began by playing a recording of a thunderstorm very softly. If Higgins remained calm, he was rewarded with chocolate bars. As long as Higgins remained calm, the intensity of the artificial thunderstorm was gradually increased. When a real thunderstorm came along, Higgins was able to keep his anxiety under control.

In one type of desensitization, the client learns to relax while viewing films of the feared object (in this case, dogs). The next step is to learn to relax while being within sight of a live dog, and progressively work toward being close to a dog without feeling fearful.

higher item was presented. No more than four items were introduced at each meeting. In between items, the subjects were repeatedly told to relax, to feel calm and heavy. The whole process went slowly, step by step, until the entire hierarchy was covered.

At the end of the six weeks, the students were less anxious, as measured both by anxiety questionnaires and performance in an actual test situation. Similar desensitization techniques have been used to help treat a variety of problems, including claustrophobia, fear of heights, and sexual impotence.

Operant Therapy

Whereas desensitization was suggested by the principles of classical conditioning, *operant therapy* relies heavily on the operant conditioning procedures developed by B. F. Skinner and his followers. Positive reinforcement is the main tool in operant therapy. By rewarding desired behaviors—for example, self-care behaviors by a retarded person or homework completion by a child in school—one can add these behaviors to the person's repertoire or increase their frequency. To be successful, the reward administered must be something geared to motivate the specific client, it must be given only after performance of the desired behavior, and there must be a method for gradually molding existing behavior into more complex behaviors not yet in the person's repertoire (Bandura, 1967).

We have already discussed some examples of operant therapy in the Psychological Issue for Chapter 5, where we considered such behavior modification techniques as the token economy, in which residents of institutions (such as mental hospitals and juvenile detention homes) receive tokens for desired behaviors. The tokens can in turn be exchanged for rewards. Operant therapy techniques are used widely—and often successfully—with children. Behavior therapists teach parents or teachers how to administer rewards more effectively at home and in school. For example, teachers at one nursery school

A NEW USE FOR THE RUBBER BAND

A 15-year-old girl compulsively pulled her hair while reading and speaking on the phone, and during other such activities. This behavior sometimes resulted in bald spots. She was instructed to wear a rubber band on her wrist and to snap it after each instance of hair pulling or whenever she felt like hair pulling. The snaps served not only as punishment but, perhaps more important, as a systematic reminder to the girl of her habit and her own desire to conquer it. After three days of following these instructions, the hair pulling stopped (Mastellone, 1974).

Operant therapy has been used with some success with autistic children. Here an autistic child is receiving a pretzel from a therapist as reinforcement for desired behavior.

were concerned about the socially withdrawn behavior of one little boy who spent about 80 percent of his time playing alone (Harris, Wolf, and Baer; cited by Bandura, 1967). Because the teacher's attention seemed to serve as a reward for this behavior, the procedure was for the teacher to ignore the boy's solitary activities but to give her full attention whenever the boy played with other children. Before long he was spending 60 percent of his time with others. Eventually the enjoyment of playing in the group came to be a reward in itself and the teacher was able to reduce her role in providing reinforcement.

A major goal of operant therapy is to insure that the behavior change will persist even after the reinforcement ceases. After all, we don't want to teach people to behave in new and better ways only when other people keep giving them candy or patting them on the back. One approach to this challenge is to move from total reinforcement to a partial reinforcement schedule, in which the desired behavior is rewarded only some of the time. As we saw in Chapter 5, behavior rewarded on such a partial reinforcement schedule is likely to become more autonomous and more resistant to extinction. In addition, behavior therapists often attempt to teach clients to evaluate their own behavior and then to reward themselves when appropriate, rather than relying on reinforcement from external sources. Finally, as in the case of the little boy who was rewarded for playing with others, once a desired behavior is established, it is often rewarded by the natural environment of the person so that special efforts to reward the behavior are no longer necessary.

Modeling and Role Playing

One of the best ways to acquire a new response or skill is to watch another person demonstrate it. For example, we can sometimes re-

duce our fears of certain situations—say, flying in airplanes—by observing other people take the situation in stride. Behavior therapists
have put the potential of such *modeling* to good use. One experiment
demonstrated, for example, that people could reduce their fear of
snakes by watching other people, both in person and on videotape,
move gradually closer to snakes without any dire consequences
(Bandura, Blanchard, and Ritter, 1969). Other studies have used
modeling to help children overcome their fear of dogs (Hill, Liebert,
and Mott, 1968), and even of dentists (Adelson et al., 1972).

Another use of modeling is to show people how to handle social
situations more effectively. Thus, the therapist may demonstrate how
to join others in conversation or may show problem drinkers how to
refuse a drink gracefully. Videotaped models are also commonly
used in such social-skills instruction.

Modeling is often augmented by *role playing*, in which the client
practices the desired behavior and gets feedback on his performance. By practicing in a protective setting, such as a therapy session,
clients need not become anxious about the initial mistakes they
make. It is not unlike practicing a new dance step alone before trying
it out in public. In one application of role playing, college men and
women volunteered for a program to improve their dating skills
(Christensen and Arkowitz, 1974). Each participant went on as many
as six "practice dates" with participants of the opposite sex. After
each date the students exchanged feedback forms on which they had
listed four positive aspects of the other person and one behavior that
the other should change. At the end of the program the participants
reported that they felt more confident and skillful in dating situations
and they began to have more interaction with people of the opposite
sex. Both modeling and role playing are often used as part of programs of *assertiveness training*, which are designed to help previously
timid people stand up for themselves.

Modeling and role playing are techniques that reflect the current

*Assertiveness training makes use of
role playing in helping people to be
less timid and to stand up for
themselves.*

— Box 2 —

Rational-emotive therapy

Albert Ellis, founder of RET.

Rational-emotive therapy (RET) is an approach to therapy that assumes that emotional difficulties are caused by irrational thinking. Albert Ellis (1962), the founder of rational-emotive therapy, believes that events themselves do not cause emotional reactions. Rather, it is a person's belief system that leads her to interpret events in particular ways, which in turn causes her emotional reactions. A person's belief system is like a set of internal sentences that the person continually repeats to herself. A disturbed patient's belief system may include unrealistic expecta- tions, such as "It is necessary for me to succeed in everything I do," or illogical reasoning, such as "If he doesn't love me, then I am a worthless person." Thus, when the patient inevitably confronts situa- tions in which she is unsuccessful or feels unloved, she comes to the distorted—and crushing—conclu- sion: "I am a failure."

According to Ellis, the bases of psychoanalytic therapy and most of the humanistic therapies are "just nonsense" (Gross, 1978). What Ellis criticizes most in these therapies is their focus on emo- tion. He particularly scorns Ge- stalt therapy (see Box 1) for its tendency to overemphasize feel- ings at the expense of rational thinking and to encourage all feel- ings, regardless of whether or not they are appropriate. Ellis argues that letting out one's emotions rarely cures anyone. Instead he advocates *cognitive restructuring*— getting the patient to substitute more rational beliefs for irrational

emphasis on integrating cognitive learning (as discussed in Chapter 5) into behavior therapy. The prevailing view is that people's under- standings and expectations of themselves are central determinants of their behavior. Following this line of reasoning, some approaches to behavior therapy stress *cognitive restructuring*, or modification of the client's thoughts. One such approach that has gained great popularity is Albert Ellis's rational-emotive therapy, described in Box 2.

Although we have described several behavior therapy tech- niques, in practice the behavior therapist rarely uses a single tech- nique in isolation. Rather, the typical procedure is to use several techniques, either simultaneously or in succession, to provide the most effective program for changing the client's behavior in desired ways. The behavior therapist often takes a stance of experimentation, trying out different approaches to see which work best for the prob- lems of a particular client.

SOMATIC THERAPIES

Somatic therapies make use of drugs, brain surgery, electric shocks, or other direct physiological means to treat the symptoms of a psy- chological disorder (the term *somatic* comes from the Greek *soma*, or "body"). Somatic methods can be used only by medical doctors, al- though they are often used in conjunction with other therapies, such as those already described in this chapter.

ones. The patient is made to recognize the faulty reasoning on which his distorted conclusions are based. Thus, for example, he is made to see that it is unrealistic to expect to succeed in everything and is led from his distorted "I am a failure" to the rational "I have failed in this situation."

It is the therapist's job to point out the irrational thinking, how that thinking has led to the emotional stress, and what would be a more rational way of viewing things. The therapist attempts to change the patient's thinking through logic, persuasion, occasional lecturing, and even prescribing specific activities. Whereas psychoanalytic and cli-

ent-centered therapists are relatively nondirective, with the emphasis on helping the patient find his own way, the rational-emotive therapist is highly directive—she *tells* the patient what to think and do if he wants to get better.

A common complaint is that rational-emotive therapists do not try to build a warm, caring relationship with their patients. This complaint is based on the assumption that it is important to build such a relationship before moving on to the patient's specific problems. But rational-emotive therapists have a different view of the matter. "If you give clients a lot of warmth, support, attention, and caring," they contend, "you

may be reinforcing their dire needs for love, which frequently and even usually are the central core of their disturbances. You also run the risk of making the client dependent on you and therapy instead of helping him or her cope with life's difficulties directly" (Saltzberg and Elkins, 1980, page 326).

Like the founders of many other therapeutic schools, Albert Ellis believes that his approach is the single right way. Although most therapists would not go so far as Ellis in his belief in RET to the exclusion of all other approaches, RET has influenced many of them to give more emphasis to their patients' belief systems.

Psychopharmacology

Sigmund Freud himself predicted that drugs would ultimately be used in the treatment of psychological disorder. "The future may teach us how to exercise a direct influence by particular chemical substances," he wrote. The future that Freud foresaw is now. Perhaps the most promising frontier in the treatment of psychological disorder is *psychopharmacology*, the use of drugs that affect the patient's mood and behaviors. Drugs have been used to treat mental illness since ancient times. But only in the past quarter of a century have several classes of drugs been developed that seem truly effective in relieving the symptoms of certain disorders, even if they can't actually cure them. And in the past decade advances in our understanding of brain chemistry (see Chapter 2) have begun to explain how these drugs work and have offered a promise that more effective drugs will be developed in the 1980s.

Three major classes of drugs are now in widespread use in the treatment of psychological disorders: antianxiety drugs, antidepressants, and antipsychotics.

The *antianxiety drugs* (also known as "minor tranquilizers") are prescribed to millions of Americans to take the edge off their anxiety and tension and to help them function more effectively. Before the 1950s the most widely used antianxiety drugs were barbiturates—strong sedatives that cause drowsiness and sometimes depression and that have the potential for addiction and lethal overdose. The antianxiety drugs that are most widely prescribed today belong to a chemical family called the *benzodiazepines*, including diazepam (better known by the trade name Valium) and chlordiazepoxide (Librium). These drugs have the valuable ability of relieving anxiety without having a sedative effect, and they are less susceptible to abuse. As a result, they have become the most widely used prescription drugs in America. It is not clear just how the antianxiety drugs work, but specific receptors in the brain where they exert their influence have been identified. Although antianxiety drugs have been a great boon to many people, they can also be habit-forming, and health authorities have recently voiced great concern about the possibility that they are being overprescribed and used too freely.

The *antidepressant drugs* are able to lift the spirits of many depressed patients. The most widely used group of antidepressants, first used for this purpose in the 1950s, are the *tricyclics*, which include imipramine (Tofranil) and amitriptyline (Elavil). As we noted in Chapter 11, one cause of depression seems to be a deficiency of the transmitter substances norepinephrine and serotonin in certain areas of the brain. Recent research has suggested that the antidepressant drugs work by blocking the breakdown of these chemical transmitters, thus increasing their levels in the brain. Interestingly, the chemical action (but not the effects) of these drugs seems to resemble that of cocaine (Iversen, 1979). Antidepressants are not effective with all depressed patients, but they are effective in a large number of cases.

In addition to the tricyclics, another drug, *lithium carbonate*, has been used during the past decade for treatment of bipolar disorder—the disorder that involves extreme mood swings between agitated

Drugs rarely cure psychological disorders but they often relieve many of the most disturbing symptoms.

highs (mania) and depressed lows. Although researchers do not yet know how it works, lithium is often extremely successful in bringing people down from their highs and in preventing them from plunging to the depths of their lows. In many cases, these patients will continue to take lithium for the rest of their lives. In addition, many of these patients, like other patients treated with various drugs, undergo other forms of psychotherapy, often of the insight-oriented variety.

The most controversial of the psychopharmacological agents are the *antipsychotic drugs* (or "major tranquilizers"). Among the several chemical families of antipsychotic drugs, the most widely used are the *phenothiazines*, including chlorpromazine (or Thorazine) and trifluoperazine (Stelazine). These drugs act to relieve the agitation, delusions, and thought disorders of schizophrenia. Although the drugs do not cure the underlying disorder, they relieve its symptoms to a point that allows a majority of patients taking them to live outside the hospital, in the general community. For example:

Phillip G., 44, is a New Yorker who spent a dozen years in mental hospitals. He takes one antipsychotic drug to overcome lethargy and a tendency to withdraw, another to prevent his becoming overly irritable and agitated, and a third to control his paranoid delusions. In the twelve years he has been following this regimen, he has been sent back to the hospital only once. Like most schizophrenics, Phillip will never lead a completely normal life. But he is able to work and to live at home. "It's a pretty dull life," his mother says, "but he has an identity, a feeling of being useful." (Clark, 1979, page 99)

As Phillip G.'s case suggests, the antipsychotic drugs have had a large impact on mental hospitals themselves. Some of the controversial issues involved are discussed in Box 3.

Researchers' best guess about the primary cause of schizophrenia is an excess of the chemical transmitter dopamine in certain brain areas, in both the limbic system and the cerebral cortex. The antipsychotic drugs seem to work by attaching themselves to dopamine receptors in the brain, thereby preventing dopamine from reaching them (Iversen, 1979) (see Figure 12.2).

The phenothiazines were first used to treat schizophrenics in the United States in 1954; by 1970 over 85 percent of all patients in state mental hospitals were receiving these drugs (Davison and Neale, 1978). The widespread use of the antipsychotic drugs is a hotly debated issue. Proponents of these drugs argue that they not only help schizophrenics return to socially acceptable behavior but also make it easier for professionals to treat them with other therapies. But critics contend that the drugs are no more than chemical constraints, used to keep patients under control. Some charge that the drugs are overused and that they turn patients into placid, unthinking "zombies." The antipsychotic drugs also have adverse side effects, including a dry mouth, blurred vision, and constipation—reasons why patients are not always eager to take them. Prolonged use can bring on *tardive dyskinesia*, a neurological condition that involves uncontrollable facial twitches and grimaces.

Most psychiatrists and psychologists who work with schizophrenic patients are convinced of the value of antipsychotic drugs for their patients. But there is currently a heightened awareness of their possible overuse and of the rights of patients themselves to decide whether or not to accept such medication. In particular, many professionals feel that the drugs have too often been used to replace talking to people and making them feel cared about (Sobel, 1980).

Electroshock Therapy

Electroshock therapy (or electroconvulsive therapy) is the application of brief electrical currents to the brain, producing convulsions. First an anesthetic is given to the patient to put him to sleep; then a muscle relaxant is injected into the patient so there will be no bodily convulsion. Electrodes are then placed at one or both sides of the head, and from 70 to 150 volts are applied for less than a second. The patient experiences a brain convulsion, lasting about a minute, that is identical to an epileptic seizure. Treatment usually consists of five or six sessions, spaced over a period of about two weeks. Maggie Scarf (1979) recently observed the application of electroshock at a Boston hospital and described it as follows:

> (The patient was already lying asleep, and the relaxant drug had been injected. The drug was prevented from going into the right arm, to provide a means of monitoring the seizure.)
>
> Dr. Mandel placed one electrode toward the top of the patient's head, and on the right side; Nurse Cahill took the other electrode and held it on the right side of the face, midway between Mrs. Garvey's eye and her ear. Dr. Mandel pressed the button to deliver the current. Almost instantaneously, the patient's right arm shot up, the fingers clenched . . . in an odd, clawlike fashion. . . . [Then] . . . the muscles unclenched, in short bursts of movement. Slowly, guided gently downward by the nurse, Mrs. Garvey's arm underwent a series of spastic-seeming, fluttery motions. Within a few seconds it lay quietly at her side. Both the brain seizure and the convulsion were over . . . It had lasted 40 seconds . . . A few minutes later she was sitting up in bed.

"Perhaps more than any other form of medical treatment," Scarf notes, "electroshock therapy arouses fantasies and fears of the Frankenstein-style physician who is tinkering with matters that ought to be beyond human intervention." But electroshock treatment, first introduced in 1938, continues to be widely used because of its success in alleviating the symptoms of severe depression, often within one or two weeks. As many as 100,000 Americans a year receive shock treatment. Nobody knows just how electroshock works, although it is assumed that the convulsion somehow restores balance to the imbalanced brain chemistry that underlies many severe depressions. Especially for severely depressed patients who do not respond well to antidepressant drugs and for the patients who are suicidal, electroshock therapy appears to be the best available treatment (Scovern and Kilmann, 1980).

It is clear that electroshock therapy has been overused. In the 1940s and 1950s it was used for a large variety of hospitalized pa-

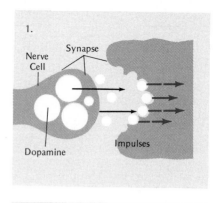

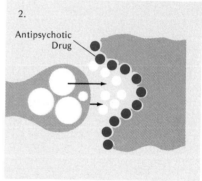

FIGURE 12.2
How antipsychotic drugs are thought to work. Dopamine, a transmitter substance that affects movement, thought, and mood, crosses the synapse and activates other neurons. It is suspected that in schizophrenia, dopamine levels are excessively high. The antipsychotic drugs block the receptor sites on neurons, preventing them from accepting the dopamine at the synapse.

— Box 3 —————————————————————————————

In and out of the mental hospital

At any one time, several hundred thousand Americans are patients in mental hospitals. Some of these patients need short-term hospitalization for acute (brief and intense) psychological disorders or episodes. However, the majority of hospitalized mental patients suffer from long-term disorders, such as chronic schizophrenia, and are likely to require special care for the rest of their lives.

The kinds of hospitals available to mental patients span a wide range, from attractive facilities with excellent care to decrepit institutions with inadequate staff and treatment. Until the 1950s, many of the patients admitted to mental hospitals could expect to remain there for years—often for the rest of their lives. Only about 5 percent of all patients hospitalized for longer than two years were eventually discharged (Paul, 1969). In the last few decades, however, there has been a movement to reduce the number of chronic patients in mental hospitals and to allow chronically disturbed people who are not dangerous to themselves or to others to return to community life. This shift is now embroiled in a great deal of controversy.

The process of returning chronically disturbed patients to community life is referred to as *deinstitutionalization*. The movement for deinstitutionalization was initially welcomed because it would reduce the drain on the taxpayer dollars spent on state mental hospitals and because, at least in the ideal, it would allow patients to lead more normal lives. Two factors came together in the 1950s and early 1960s to bring about this movement: (1) the introduction of antipsychotic drugs, which could reduce or eliminate the more severe symptoms of schizophrenics, and (2) the community mental health movement (see Box 4), which included plans for treatment and rehabilitation of chronic mental patients within the community.

One of the goals of the deinstitutionalization movement was a 50 percent reduction in the patient population of state hospitals in America within two decades. In keeping with this goal, between 1955 and 1975 that population was reduced from 559,000 to 193,000—a 65 percent decrease. The average number of days spent in the hospital also decreased by more than two-thirds (Bassuk and Garson, 1978).

These statistics sound impressive, but many mental health professionals now have serious questions about the value of deinstitutionalization. In most cases, chronic mental patients leave the hospital with their most troubling symptoms relieved, but they are by no means "cured." They need extensive support from the community if they are to live successfully outside the hospital. Most ex-patients need supervised living units, such as halfway houses, and almost all of them need special job training and continued treatment programs.

Unfortunately, many of these services are not being run very well. Staffed housing for discharged patients has ranged from excellent to awful to nonexistent. Too many ex-patients live in poorly supervised rundown housing, and thousands live on their own, with no money and no work. They wander the streets, and their appearance and sometimes bizarre behavior is often frightening to their neighbors. People living in neighborhoods in which large numbers of ex-patients have come to live have actively protested the deinstitutionalization process. One mayor recalls being bombarded with calls, letters, and petitions from every side: "We had neighborhood groups telling us, 'Get 'em [the patients] out of here! They're urinating on our lawns, they look depressing . . .'" (Williams, 1977, page 127).

A final blow to deinstitutionalization is the fact that, although the number of patients in state hospitals at any one time has decreased significantly, the number of admissions has increased— about half of the discharged patients are readmitted within a year of leaving. What exists, in many cases, is a revolving door policy, with patients going in and out of the hospital.

While some consider deinstitutionalization a failure, others believe that well-run programs can eliminate many of the problems and have estimated that more than half of the revolving-door readmissions could have been avoided if the necessary community facilities had existed. In San Jose, California, for example, an organization run by the state university provided a large corps of volunteers to work with the former mental patients housed in the nearby community (Williams, 1977). According to their survey, 75 percent of the patients felt they had benefitted from community living, and only 5 percent wanted to return to the hospital.

Providing adequate community resources for former mental patients could in the long run save the taxpayers money because ex-patients who receive the support they need are probably less likely to return to the hospital. More than that, it could give ex-patients, who in prior years would have spent their lives in the impersonal environments of state hospitals, their best chance of leading relatively normal lives.

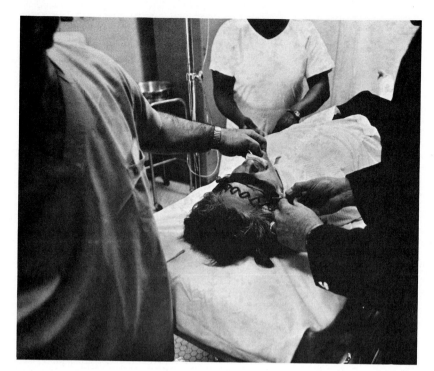

In electroshock therapy, brief electrical currents are applied to the brain, inducing convulsions. It has been highly successful in the treatment of severe depression, but many also feel that it has been overused.

tients, and there are reports—the best known, perhaps, in Ken Kesey's 1962 novel (and the 1974 movie) *One Flew Over the Cuckoo's Nest*—that it was used to punish or sedate troublemakers. Before the introduction of anesthesia and muscle relaxants, it also used to be a rather violent procedure. Electroshock therapy still has such side effects as headaches, nausea, and—perhaps most troublesome— memory loss that can last for days or months. Some critics claim that there is permanent memory loss, but this has never been proven. Current research with new forms of electroshock—using less powerful currents, using shorter intervals of administration, and applying currents to only one brain hemisphere—give promise of reducing the side effects. Thus, despite the heightened awareness of potential for its abuse, and despite some critics' views that it remains dangerous to use at all (for example, Friedberg, 1976), electroshock therapy is now generally regarded as a useful form of therapy, whose benefits outweigh its drawbacks (American Psychiatric Association, 1978).

Psychosurgery

Psychosurgery refers to the surgical destruction or disconnection of portions of the brain in an attempt to regulate disordered behavior. It was introduced in the 1930s by Antonio de Egas Moniz, a Portuguese neurologist, who surgically severed the frontal lobes from the rest of the brain in some agitated patients. Thousands of such operations, called *prefrontal lobotomies*, were performed in the United States in the 1940s and 1950s. But the overall results of the operations were not encouraging. The surgery calmed down some agitated patients, but it also made vegetables of others—they walked, they talked, they looked like human beings, but they were without ambition, imagination, or self-awareness (Greenblatt, 1967). With the introduction of the antipsychotic drugs in the mid-1950s, the number of lobotomies decreased dramatically.

There continue to be some 400 psychosurgical operations performed in the United States each year. Surgical procedures have been greatly improved, so that it is possible to separate the frontal cortex from lower brain areas that regulate emotional response, with minimal destruction of brain tissue (Shevitz, 1976). And there is evidence that such operations do help a small minority of patients who are totally incapacitated by obsessions or depression and for whom no other techniques are helpful (Goodwin, 1980). For the most part, however, the current view of psychosurgery is one of extreme caution.

DOES THERAPY WORK?

There has been a great deal of debate over whether psychotherapy—especially the nonsomatic therapies, which do not involve direct physiological manipulation of the brain—works at all. In 1952 Hans Eysenck created a storm when he reviewed the existing literature on therapy (mainly psychoanalytic) and concluded that it had no favorable effect at all. He claimed that as many patients "improved" as would have improved anyway with the passage of time. Others disputed Eysenck's interpretation, and by now, with many more studies having been conducted, it is fair to conclude that although therapy does not help everybody (and in some cases it may even have negative effects), on the whole it has modest positive effects (Bergin and Suinn, 1975).

In one study (Sloane et al., 1975), ninety outpatients at the Temple University outpatient clinic were randomly assigned to one of three groups: one that received behavior therapy, one that received short-term psychoanalytic therapy, and a "waiting list" group that was given only minimal treatment. The clients were generally anxious, depressed, or otherwise troubled—not severely disturbed or psychotic. The therapists were experienced. After four months of treatment (or waiting), the clients were assessed by an independent rater who did not know to which groups the clients were assigned. On the average, clients in all three groups improved, even those on the waiting list, which shows that time itself can sometimes heal psychic wounds. But clients in the two treatment groups improved more than the waiting-list clients. Neither psychoanalytic therapy nor behavior therapy was superior overall.

As this study helps illustrate, one method of therapy is not necessarily better than another. This is the general consensus of recent research. A review by Lester Luborsky and associates (1971) concluded that the best predictions of whether a particular client will improve are the client's own characteristics: Clients who are relatively healthy, intelligent, and highly motivated are most likely to make effective use of therapy. Of secondary importance are characteristics of the therapist—her experience, attitudes, and empathy. Of least importance is the particular technique or "school" of therapy.

A recent study by Hans Strupp and Suzanne Hadley (1979)

— Box 4 —

Community mental health

A recently widowed father feels lonely and goes to a single-parents group to meet and talk with other parents who are alone.

A single mother on welfare frequently feels depressed and goes to a local mental health center for weekly therapy.

A high-school student worries about his growing dependence on drugs and calls a hotline when he feels tempted to get high.

The community mental health movement was founded on the idea of preventing psychological disorder by helping people deal with their problems in their own community, rather than waiting until their problems are serious enough to land them in a mental hospital.

Perhaps the best known community mental health programs in the United States are the some 650 federally funded Community Mental Health Centers. Through legislation passed in 1963, funds were made available to establish centers and staffs in local communities. Staff members get to know the people and their needs, give educational presentations to community groups (on problems of child rearing, for example), and work closely with schools and health clinics, in order to help detect problems early enough to prevent them from becoming more serious.

Community mental health centers also offer treatment for existing problems to people for whom services have not been available in the past. People can obtain help without making an appointment or paying a high fee. Mental health centers are most likely to offer brief or short-term therapy, rather than the unhurried, detailed exploration of the person provided in expensive traditional therapies. In these centers, only a specific problem is typically addressed, and therapy characteristically lasts four to six weeks.

In cases of *crisis intervention*, both prevention and treatment are emphasized. Help provided following a particularly stressful event in a person's life, such as rape or the death of a family member, can often ward off more serious difficulties later. A mental health center might offer one session and a follow-up call to help the person restore equilibrium and make necessary decisions.

Other forms of crisis interven-

---

helped to demonstrate that therapists personal characteristics are likely to be more important than the specific techniques they use. Male students seeking therapy were treated either by highly experienced psychotherapists (both psychiatrists and psychologists) or by college professors chosen for their ability to form understanding relationships; they included professors of English, history, mathematics, and philosophy. The patients treated by the professors were found to show just as much improvement, on the average, as the patients treated by the professional therapists.

It is likely, of course, that particular techniques may be more effective for particular problems; for example, specific behavioral techniques, such as systematic desensitization, seem especially useful in treating certain phobias and anxieties. But the superiority of one therapy over another, even for specific problems, is not yet well established.

In light of these results, many therapists are eclectic, drawing on psychoanalytic, client-centered, behavioral, or other techniques as they seem appropriate, rather than maintaining an unyielding allegiance to a single school. Jerome Frank (1973) does not find this conclusion surprising, as he believes that the common features of different therapies, rather than their unique characteristics, are what account for most of their effectiveness. These key common features include the close relationship between therapist and client, the special setting, and the existence of a theory or rationale.

tion are available from both mental health centers and other concerned organizations. Hotlines provide trained, sympathetic listeners to help people with such problems as child abuse, suicidal tendencies, and drug abuse. Another approach to crisis intervention is the *self-help group*. One such group, "Seminars for the Separated," was developed at Harvard Medical School's Laboratory of Community Psychiatry. People who were in the process of separation or divorce came to a series of lectures and group meetings, where they learned about what to expect with regard to relations with children and in-laws, finances, housework, and sex. They were able to share feelings with others going through the same experience (Weiss, 1975). Analogous groups have been formed for alcoholics, single parents, gam-

blers, widows, cancer victims, and many others facing a particular stress or transition.

Community mental health programs often rely on the use of *paraprofessionals*—community residents who are trained by professionals to provide therapy or support. In some cases *peer counseling*—for example, mothers on welfare working with other mothers on welfare—helps to bridge gaps and bring services to those who may not have access to professionals. In other cases, parents or teachers are trained to work with troubled children or volunteers are trained to work with a particular group in need of help. For example, adult community residents in Hawaii were trained by psychologists to act as "buddies" for 11- to 17-year-old youths referred by the family court for behavior and academic

problems. The buddies were taught to use various operant therapy methods, such as making attention or material rewards (going to the movies) contingent on improved school attendance and behavior. This approach was successful in reducing some of the youths' problem behaviors (Fo and O'Donnell, 1974).

Community mental health has its critics. They say that community centers still reach only a small proportion of community members who need help and that nonprofessional groups or individuals often do not deliver adequate therapy. But despite such criticisms, community mental health efforts have made support and guidance available to many people who badly needed it—and, as a result, such efforts have furthered the vital goal of preventing psychological disorder.

In addition to their attempts to make therapy more effective, psychologists and other mental health professionals are increasingly concerned with ways of *preventing* the emergence of psychological disorder. This is the primary focus of the community mental health movement, described in Box 4.

THERAPY AND RESPONSIBILITY

The enterprise of therapy places important responsibilities on the therapist—and on the client, as well. By virtue of his role as an "expert" to whom one turns in times of personal trouble, the therapist is likely to have great impact on his clients. Many schools of therapy emphasize the therapist's neutrality—she is there to help the client achieve the goals that the client himself wants, not to impose her own. But, as Seymour Halleck (1971) argues, the notion of a "neutral" therapist may to a large extent be a myth: "In the very process of defining his needs in the presence of a figure who is viewed as authoritarian, the patient is profoundly influenced. He ends up wanting some of the things the [therapist] thinks he should want." Clients often adopt not only the ideals but even the mannerisms of the therapist. Having this sort of impact is a responsibility that the therapist must come to terms with. He must always keep aware of the primary need to work in the client's best interests, even if that means the client will live a life different from what the therapist values most.

Particular techniques of therapy are sometimes singled out as ethically questionable, such as the physical assaults of electroshock therapy and psychosurgery and the occasional use of physical punishment in certain forms of behavior therapy. Any instance in which physical damage or pain is inflicted in the process of therapy must, of course, be examined carefully. As Gerald Davison and John Neale (1978) point out, however, pain can be psychological, as well as physical: "Shall we permit a Gestalt therapist to make a patient cry by confronting him with feelings he has turned away from for years? Shall we forbid a psychoanalyst from guiding a patient to an insight that will likely cause great anguish, all the more so for the conflicts having been repressed for years?" (page 599). What Davison and Neale are implying, quite appropriately, is that in *all* forms of therapy the therapist must consider whether the pain being inflicted is justified by the expected gains.

In the 1980s, therapy is more popular than ever. "The demand for psychotherapy is nonending," one psychologist says in mild amazement. "In prior times, people would take care of ordinary life crises by themselves, or with the help of their families. Now they all want psychotherapy" (quoted by Gross, 1978, page 7). But the very popularity of therapy itself brings up ethical questions about its impact on mental health. As Jerome Frank (1973) has observed, the more treatment facilities are available and the more widely they are known, the more people will seek their services. As a result, mental health professionals, by focusing attention on people's disappointments and dissatisfactions, may in fact stimulate personal insecurity. Frank puts the proposition most baldly: "Psychotherapy is the only form of treatment which, at least to some extent, appears to create the illness it treats" (page 8). This possibility adds to the ethical dilemma of the therapist, who is dedicated to the reduction of distress, not its creation.

At the same time, the client, or prospective client, must share the responsibility for therapy. It is up to her to decide what sort of help she needs, to choose a therapist or treatment facility, to participate actively in her own treatment, and to discontinue the therapy if she feels it is not helping. There are, of course, some patients, such as children or people with serious disorders, who cannot exercise this responsibility fully; in such cases therapists, family members, and the legal system have to take on added responsibility for the patient's welfare. In most cases, however, people must assume major responsibility for their own treatment.

The choice of a therapist is a particularly important one. As Morris Parloff (1976) points out, even within any single school of therapy, treatment is by no means standardized. It depends on the characteristics of the particular therapist and her interaction with the specific patient. "When the patient is 'therapist-shopping,'" Parloff advises, "it is wise for him to select carefully from among an array of qualified therapists the one whose style of relating is acceptable to him—and preferably from a school whose philosophy, values, and goals are most congenial to his own." When in the market for therapy, don't be afraid to shop around and don't be afraid to ask a prospective therapist specific questions about his orientation and approach. Such

In recent years, therapy and counseling have become widespread media events. Psychologist Toni Grant has a daily call-in radio show in Los Angeles that is heard by an estimated 115,000 people, and similar radio and television shows across the country reach millions. Some programmers believe that radio call-in shows are replacing soap operas. Listeners can tune into calls from wife beaters, rapists, child abusers, and victims of incest. Some of Dr. Grant's calls are less dramatic: a mother concerned about her 16-year-old son dating a 20-year-old woman, and a young man who wonders why he just quit a good job (*Time*, May 26, 1980). Some psychologists believe that dispensing advice to unknown and undiagnosed people can be dangerous. Media therapists counter, however, that they routinely refer people with serious problems to other forms of therapy, and that they provide support and hope to others (Foltz, 1980).

careful shopping becomes especially important with the wide range of new therapies and quasi-therapies on the market, as we will see in the Psychological Issue that follows.

SUMMARY

1. *Therapy* is the professional application of techniques intended to treat psychological disorders and reduce distress. There are many kinds of therapy, and they differ in setting, time frame, professionals involved, and techniques used. All types share similar goals, however, such as relieving symptoms and increasing feelings of adequacy.

2. *Insight therapies*, such as psychoanalysis and client-centered therapy, emphasize expression of inner feelings by the patient or client.

3. Freud's system of *psychoanalysis* is based on the idea that psychological distress is caused by painful thoughts and emotions buried in the unconscious mind. Freud developed the techniques of *free association* and *interpretation* to help the patient achieve *catharsis*—release of buried emotions. Freud also believed that the therapist should remain neutral so that the process of *transference* could occur.

4. Modern-day psychoanalytic therapy uses many of Freud's techniques but is usually less time consuming. The therapist generally faces the patient and plays a more active role than in classical psychoanalysis.

5. In Carl Rogers's *client-centered therapy*, the therapist provides *unconditional positive regard*, encouraging the client to express his true feelings and desires. The client, not the therapist, does the analyzing. The warmth and acceptance of the therapist are emphasized in this approach.

6. The aim of *Gestalt therapy*, developed by Fritz Perls, is to put individuals in touch with all facets of their personalities and experiences. It emphasizes nonverbal, as well as verbal, techniques.

7. *Behavior therapies* see the client as someone who has learned inappropriate ways of behaving, rather than one who has deep underlying psychological problems. Behavior therapists use such techniques as desensitization, operant conditioning, modeling, and role playing to eliminate the inappropriate behavior and create a desired behavior.

8. In *desensitization therapy*, the client learns to substitute a new response (such as relaxation) for an old response (fear or anxiety) associated with a particular stimulus. *Systematic desensitization* involves arranging fear-causing stimuli in an *anxiety hierarchy* and learning to relax in the presence of the least anxiety-arousing items first.

9. In *operant therapy*, the client is rewarded for performing a desired behavior or for refraining from performing an undesired behavior.

10. In *modeling*, the client observes someone else perform the

desired behavior before trying it herself. In *role playing* the client tries out the desired behavior in an unthreatening setting.

11. The idea that irrational thinking is the basis of emotional problems forms the foundation for Albert Ellis's *rational-emotive therapy*. In RET, the therapist attempts to convince the patient to change his belief system.

12. *Somatic therapies* make use of drugs, electric shocks, brain surgery, or other physiological means to treat the symptoms of psychological disorder.

13. *Psychopharmacology* is the use of drugs to affect a patient's mood or behavior. The most widely used drugs for this purpose are the *antianxiety drugs* (minor tranquilizers), *antidepressants*, and *antipsychotic drugs* (major tranquilizers).

14. The last few decades have seen a movement toward *deinstitutionalization*—returning mental patients to the community. This movement has been the focus of a great deal of controversy.

15. *Electroshock therapy* is the application of brief electrical currents to the brain, producing convulsions. This treatment is widely used with severely depressed patients.

16. *Psychosurgery* is the surgical destruction or disconnection of portions of the brain in an attempt to regulate disordered behavior. Such procedures are rarely used today.

17. Although psychotherapy does not help everyone, on the whole it seems to have a positive effect. No one type of therapy seems to be superior, and many people improve without professional help. Among the most important factors in the success of therapy are the therapist's personal characteristics.

18. In an effort to help people with their problems in their own communities, *community mental health centers* have been established throughout America. Among services available are counseling, educational programs, crisis intervention, and hotlines.

19. The enterprise of therapy places important responsibilities on the therapist, including not imposing his own values on the client, and assessing the potential pain inflicted by certain therapeutic techniques. It is also important that the client share the responsibility for therapy.

THE THERAPY MARKETPLACE

Over the past 15 years many new forms of psychological assistance have been offered to the public—forms that go far beyond the relatively traditional types of psychotherapy we have discussed thus far. In the 1980s, no one is limited to therapists' offices or counseling centers in their search for ways to ease emotional distress. Help for the depressed, the anxious, and the desperate is offered in urban basements, hotel ballrooms, bathtubs, over the radio, on television, and in the great outdoors. Help is even offered to those who don't really feel distressed at all but would still like to move toward greater self-fulfillment. Nor are clients limited to talking their way to inner peace. They can scream, chant mantras, float in warm water, or subject themselves to verbal abuse from strangers. Various therapy programs use such props as snorkels and nose clips, hot tubs, baby bottles, mattresses, and punching bags.

There are now at least 130 different forms of therapy available to the troubled person, including the traditional forms already described. Primal therapy, *est*, cocounseling, rebirthing, Arica, transcendental meditation, biofeedback, psychosynthesis, bioenergetics,

encounter groups, and Rolfing are just a few of the offerings in the therapy marketplace. Some people doubt whether many of these

---

Clients can scream, float in warm water, or subject themselves to verbal abuse.

"therapies" are really therapies at all, suggesting that they are fads, crazes, or social movements. Furthermore, some of these approaches state clearly to their clients that they are not "cures" for anything. But they all have in common the stated goals of their founders to reduce psychological problems and to increase individual happiness and self-fulfillment. The therapy marketplace also includes hundreds of psychological self-help books that profess to contain the answers to your problems within their covers.

With so many forms of therapy—or therapylike programs—available, it is important to be a

discriminating consumer in the therapy marketplace. Although each of the therapies may have something to offer some people, many of them are commercially packaged operations that offer overly "easy" solutions for problems and in some cases may even be dangerous. In this Psychological Issue we will introduce some of the most popular therapies in the marketplace.

A THERAPY SAMPLER

The following is just a small sampling of some of the new therapies on the market.

Primal therapy. Primal therapy was introduced in the late 1960s by Arthur Janov, a psychologist who established the Primal Institute in Los Angeles. Janov's approach centers on the idea of pain. Each time a child is not held when he cries, not fed when hungry, or ignored when he needs attention, it contributes to a "primal pool of pain," which, when deep enough, can produce neurosis as a way of life. The goal of primal therapy is to achieve the primal state, an emotional return to infancy in which the client screams, weeps, thrashes, writhes, and (for extra psychological credit) babbles baby

A primal therapy session.

talk. This state is achieved by talking to a therapist trained at Janov's Institute, by acting out scenes of childhood, or by introspection. It may take several months of primalling to expel all the pain, but Janov claims the effort is worth it. "Primal man," he

man" is also free of excessive modesty.

Scream therapy. Scream therapy sounds a lot like primal therapy, but its originator, Daniel Casriel, contends that it is not. He created scream therapy after observing encounter groups at Synanon, the

drug addiction halfway house. Scream therapy is practiced in groups, where individuals one by one share their problems with the others. Then all hold hands and are instructed to scream. Sessions include a variety of assertiveness training exercises and supportive measures from the group and its leader. Individuals are encouraged to scream whenever they feel especially overwhelmed, which, what with one thing or another, is pretty often. Casriel disdains Janov's primal therapy, claiming that its theory is oversimplified and that most of Janov's clients fake their primals. But, like Janov, Casriel believes he has wrought a psychological revolution: "I believe I've found what professionals are looking for, a quick way to get to feelings, the science of emotions" (Gross, 1978, page 284).

Rebirthing. The opportunity to reexperience one's own birth is offered by an organization, Theta, developed by Leonard Orr. Rebirthing is designed to eliminate The Big Feeling—the panic we all experienced at birth when the umbilical cord was cut and we

> **"Primal man," Janov writes, "is a new kind of human being."**

writes, "is indeed a new kind of human being with a different kind of brain functioning and a new physiology" (Janov, 1973). Brushing aside Freud and Jung, from whom primal therapy derives, Janov states, "this renders all other psychological theories obsolete and invalid" (Gross, 1978, page 278). Although Janov doesn't say so, we can assume that "primal

An encounter group session.

had to breathe by ourself. Orr claims that The Big Feeling has blighted all our lives and is most clearly evidenced in improper breathing habits. His therapy involves learning new breathing patterns and reexperiencing the trauma of birth in order to exorcise the pain. After a few dry runs, the client strips, dons a snorkel and nose clips, and enters a tub of warm water. Nude assistants suspend the client in water and murmur reassuring words. The client eventually experiences a kind of primitive panic, which Orr calls "the creeping crud," and is removed from the tub, towelled off, and congratulated on being reborn. It often takes several dunks to become completely free of "the creeping crud."

Encounter groups. One of the longest established routes to "consciousness raising" is the encounter group. The aim of encounter groups is to bring people together to increase trust, openness, and sensitivity. Encounter groups have been around since the 1940s but were developed into therapeutic tools in the 1950s by such prominent psychologists as Abraham Maslow and Carl Rogers. Most contemporary encounter groups stress emotional experience and include a great deal of kissing, weeping, hugging, yelling, and professions of love. Many people report that encounter groups have helped them greatly in experiencing and expressing their feelings.

Variations on encounter groups include the marathon encounter and the nude encounter. In marathon encounters, the emotions run on for 24 hours or more without rest. In nude encounters members are divested of their protective "disguises" (clothing) to facilitate honesty and to release inhibitions.

Some critics of encounter groups say that the "instant emotion"

demanded of participants actually undercuts real intimacy. One veteran of these groups says, "Going around hugging people in the encounter groups I went to didn't

---

"Going around hugging people in encounter groups didn't make me feel any less lonely."

---

make me feel any less lonely. I suppose there are some people who can't hug anyone and it's good for them to go around getting practice hugging people, but that isn't my problem. I can hug people, but I like to hug selectively. In encounter groups, I've been told, you're supposed to enjoy hugging anyone, people for whom you have no feeling. It's just unselective hugging, and it doesn't make me feel very good" (Gordon, 1976, page 277).

Ten years ago Carl Rogers (1970) expressed his own doubts about the turns some encounter groups seemed to be taking: "The faddists, the cultists, the nudists, the manipulators, those whose needs are for power or recognition, may come to dominate the encounter group horizon. In this case, I feel it is headed for disaster."

est. Erhard Seminars Training (*est*) was established in 1971 by Werner Erhard. It is estimated that more than 100,000 people have participated in Erhard's program, which consists of seminars held in hotels or other public facilities for a 60-hour period stretching over two weekends. The program uses a variety of techniques, from aggressive confrontation of participants

to relaxation and "trust" exercises borrowed from Gestalt therapy and renamed "processes." Here is how one participant described a process: "We were asked to lie down on the floor and imagine that we were afraid of the people next to us. Then . . . people began to moan and cry. . . . I'm not the kind of person to be afraid of other people. But as the process went on and on I began to be afraid of people in the room—they were people who were so incredibly suggestible they had become a mob" (Gordon, 1976, page 296).

est offers no specific changes. Basically, it tries to persuade people to accept themselves. Once participants have done so, they have, in the parlance of *est*, "gotten It." *It* remains undefined. A participant described the conclusion of an *est* seminar as follows: "At the end of the training the trainer asks if people 'got it.'" One group of people say they got it; they are applauded. Then another group says they weren't sure they

Werner Erhard, who developed est.

got it; the trainer talks to them and they all say they got it. One group says they definitely didn't get it. He talks to all but one, and

Getting It and not getting It are considered equally successful and cost the same—about $350.

finally this last person says he didn't get it, and the trainer says, 'Well, you got it, 'cause there's nothing to get' and they turn the whole thing into a joke" (Gordon, 1976, pages 298–299). Getting It and not getting It are considered equally successful and cost the same—about $350.

Transpersonal therapies. In 1968 Abraham Maslow termed humanistic psychology, which focuses on people's inner potential for growth, the "Third Force" in psychology, following psychoanalytic theory and behaviorism. He predicted that the Third Force would give way to a "still higher Fourth Psychology which would be transpersonal, transhuman, centered on the cosmos, rather than human needs and interest" (Maslow, 1968). Transpersonal psychology appears to have arrived, as more and more organizations concern themselves not with psychological problems but with the individual's state of consciousness and relationship with the universe.

One such approach, transcendental meditation, was discussed in the Psychological Issue following Chapter 3. Another route to enlightened consciousness is Arica, developed by Oscar Ichazo. Arica includes selected elements of a variety of mystic disciplines such as yoga, Zen, Sufism (the mystical branch of Islam), and the Oriental martial arts. The Arica Institute has plush headquarters in New York City and branches across the United States and in Europe. Its followers are trained in dietary rules, certain forms of meditation, breathing patterns, sensory awareness, and "energy generation." The results of Arica training are said to be primarily mystical alterations in consciousness, but presumably these alterations have some positive effects on day-to-day living, as well.

EVALUATING ALTERNATIVE THERAPIES

Most of the creators of alternative therapies claim high rates of success for their programs, but little research has been done to substantiate their claims. One of the problems with investigating such claims is that it is difficult to define "success."

In a major study of encounter groups conducted at Stanford University, more than 200 students were randomly assigned to seventeen groups representing ten major styles of encounter. Control subjects did not participate in any group. Participants were assessed six months and one year after taking part in the study. In general, the results were not encouraging: about one-third of the students showed positive effects, about one-third showed negative effects (including some who experienced psychological damage), and the remaining third showed no effects. Generally, the encounter subjects showed no more change for better or worse than the control subjects (Lieberman, Yalom, and Miles, 1973).

For a few individuals, some of these alternative therapies may actually be dangerous. The confrontation aspects of *est*, for exam-ple, may be more than some people can handle. There have been several reports of psychotic breakdowns in persons without previous psychiatric histories after completing *est* training (Glass, Kirsch, and Parris, 1977). One 39-year-old man developed a sudden increase in self-esteem and energy after the second day of training. His feelings rapidly expanded until he felt he had godlike powers. At home he jumped into the swimming pool and tried to breathe under water. After two days of manic activity, he was finally hospitalized. He was released six days later, and after four months of treatment he returned to his pre-*est* level of functioning. This and other such episodes cannot be attributed exclusively to the impact of *est*; nevertheless, *est* may be threatening to people with certain types of personalities. Unfortunately, few alternative therapies screen their applicants carefully, to warn off those who might be adversely affected.

Some social commentators have decried the explosion of alternative therapies, saying that they are merely exploitations of our society's increasing narcissism. Martin Gross (1978) describes "the appar-

Many psychologists see a dangerous antiintellectualism in the alternative therapies.

ently rotating clientele that has been analyzed by Freudians, screamed for Casriel . . . and confronted one another in Encounter" (page 311). In a similar vein, R. D. Rosen (1975) comments, "The problem is not that so many people are constantly looking for enlightenment these days, but that so many are constantly finding it" (page 245). Both of these authors, along with many psychologists, see a dangerous antiintellectualism in the alternative therapies, in that most of the organizations condemn the "thinking" person in favor of the "feeling" person. But whether the alternative therapies are creating a false need or meeting a real one, they are a considerable presence in today's society.

A BETTER YOU THROUGH READING

For those unwilling or unable to undertake a course in primal therapy, *est*, or any of the other alternative therapies, there are other opportunities for psychological self-improvement. These other approaches are outlined in self-help books, which tell you how to get along with other people, how to assert yourself, how to improve your sex life, how to overcome depression, how to like yourself

It is hard to come up with a human problem that isn't addressed in a self-help book.

more or worry less, how to take risks, and how to start or end a marriage. It is hard to come up with a human problem that isn't addressed in a self-help book.

Even a small paperback bookstore is likely to have at least a hundred psychological how-to books in stock. And they move fast. Wayne Dyer's *Your Erroneous*

Zones (1976) sold 150,000 hardbound copies in its first six months of publication and millions of copies in paperback. Other best-selling psychological how-to books in recent years have had such titles as *How to Be Your Own Best Friend*, *How to Take Charge of Your Life*, *Looking Out for Number 1*, *How to Live with Another Person*, *How to Make Winning Your Lifestyle*, *How to Say No When You Want to Say Yes*, *Help Yourself to Happiness*, and even *The Do-It-Yourself Psychotherapy Book*. Best-seller lists almost always contain a few self-help books.

Like the leaders of the new therapies, some of the authors of these books are well-trained psychologists and psychiatrists, while other authors have no professional credentials. Many mental health professionals are skeptical of the value of self-help books. They charge that many of the books mislead potential buyers with excessive claims. Who could resist a book that claims to "give you ways to create a new life for yourself, whoever you are, whatever you are now"? Another book claims to be "an admission ticket to a happier life," and still another describes itself as "the proven new method for coping successfully with other people every day of your life."

Raphael Bevcar (1978) adds that self-help books may give rise to new problems. The routine stresses of everyday life can produce perfectly normal anxiety, depression, and anger. By suggesting that negative emotions are neurotic or unnecessary, self-help books may create "pseudoproblems" for people who are actually coping quite well. On the other hand, seriously troubled people may delay or avoid seeing a professional therapist, confident that these books can solve their problems.

While acknowledging the need for caution, other professionals believe that the self-help literature can be valuable. Josiah Dilley (1978) suggests that particularly in the areas of reducing tension, increasing self-esteem, and improving personal relationships, self-help books can provide useful insights. "There is a gold mine of exciting possibilities in the self-help literature," Dilley advises fellow professionals, "techniques, suggestions, ideas and success stories not to be found elsewhere. Don't knock it 'til you try it" (page 295).

There is no doubt that some self-help books have helped their readers sort out particularly trying problems. But there are also drawbacks to relying on them as psychological counselors. In the final analysis, we shouldn't rule out self-help books or the new therapies in the marketplace, but we should caution the buyer to beware.

SUMMARY

1. In recent years there has been a proliferation of "alternative" therapies that are often oriented toward personal growth rather than toward solving specific psychological problems.

2. Among the alternative therapies in the marketplace are primal therapy, scream therapy, rebirthing, various types of encounter groups, *est*, and transpersonal therapies such as Arica.

3. Alternative therapies have been criticized as antiintellectual fads that are possibly dangerous to some people.

4. Hundreds of self-help books offer solutions to psychological problems and insights into personal growth. Some books may be helpful to readers with specific problems, but they may also be misleading.

VETERANS AND THE LEGACY OF VIETNAM
Arthur Egendorf

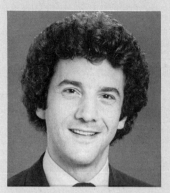

Arthur Egendorf

It has been 10 years since the last Americans returned from Vietnam in 1973. But many Vietnam veterans think about their war experiences every day, and some still experience great emotional distress. More generally, as Dr. Arthur Egendorf writes, Vietnam has left a painful legacy for all Americans. Himself a Vietnam veteran, Dr. Egendorf is a clinical psychologist who coordinated the first rap groups formed by Vietnam veterans. Together with his coworkers at the Center for Policy Research, he conducted the Vietnam Era Research Project, an important nationwide study of the psychological effects of Vietnam on its veterans.

The day I left Vietnam, April 14, 1969, I was very sick. It wasn't anything I ate. Coming back scared me—even more than going over there. Not knowing what the fear was made it worse. It took several weeks after I arrived home to realize what was happening. I saw and spoke with a man who was an old friend, but I couldn't remember how I knew him. It took days to recall: I had had lunch with him in Saigon right before leaving for home.

I realized that something in me wanted to erase the year I spent there. I also understood that giving into the urge to block it out would weaken me. But it wasn't going to be as simple as saying, "OK. So I won't do it anymore." The blocking happened without my being aware of it. I began to notice the front I put up with people, pretending all the time, even with myself. If somebody started to get close—asking me about the war, for example—I'd play cool, pretending that I wasn't pretending, just to keep my defenses up.

Soon I realized that the hiding was to keep from feeling things. I was sadder than I wanted to admit about the soldiers who were being shot and killed. But I was also glad I wasn't one of them. In fact I was proud. I had known how to get the army to treat me better than most—living in a hotel room and having a car and an expense allowance in Saigon. I had managed to avoid the dirty work. But I couldn't admit that either.

It was also pain I didn't want—the kind that came just with thinking about the Vietnamese. I didn't want to know what was happening. But in 1969, the height of the longest war in U.S. history, it was on page one. Hundreds were being killed every day. Government officials in Washington and Saigon kept trying to explain

Almost 3 million Americans served in Vietnam, the longest war in U.S. history.

and justify it all with words I couldn't believe. We were supposedly fighting for our image in the world and for democratic purposes. But I had been there. The picture in my mind of a half million unruly American soldiers with billions of dollars of war machinery rampaging through a country of peasants was horrifying. And, in the middle of a war that was gruesome and brutal on both sides, all principle was gone.

Some days the feelings would flood me: I'd pick up a newspaper, see a picture of a Vietnamese woman mourning her dead husband, and I'd burst into tears. But most of the time I held back, believing I couldn't take too much.

The day I left the Army, a year after returning from Vietnam, I no longer had to worry about being a good enough soldier to stay out of jail. My attitude changed. I realized that the block on my feelings had been a way to play it safe. To feel things would mean to let myself be touched—by my own judgments of what was called for. If I faced those squarely, it wouldn't be enough to have opinions about the war. I'd have to do something about it.

Several months after I left the Army in 1970 I became the coordinator of the first rap groups formed by Vietnam veterans. We'd talk about the war and about our difficulties and challenges. Sometimes one of us would cry, belatedly, for a friend who died in his arms in a green jungle hell that had no room for tears. Sometimes we simply listened as one of us told of killing, of bloody horror, of rape or torn limbs—things that needed to be said when someone is really listening but that few people in everyday life are prepared to hear.

In the groups veterans told of going to war in search of accomplishment and purpose, willing to throw themselves into virtually anything that promised to rescue them from domestic life. Some went for thrills, some with a fear of staying still, while others were reluctant to move too far ahead and clutched at the reassurances of a rigidly orchestrated life in a disciplined army. Many wanted to "earn their spurs"—to command respect among men, to win admiration among women, to be recognized and celebrated. Many simply wanted to have sex, get drunk, and get by—doing what they were supposed to do because they saw no choice. A few went because they worshipped the flag.

For those of us who studied ourselves closely it wasn't what happened that was the problem. It was the difficulty we had in living with it all later on. It didn't make sense when we were over there. Seeing how many Americans were against the war made it seem even more senseless when we came back. When the government we had been fighting to support in South Vietnam toppled, in 1975, it was the last straw for many vets. What was the sense of all the death and horror? Where do we go from here?

The rap groups were a safe haven, to be with others like ourselves, to hear reassurances that "I'm not the only one feeling this way," to say what couldn't be uttered elsewhere, and to make a statement. We were announcing our dedication to the possibilities of building new lives, no matter

An antiwar demonstration. "Seeing how many Americans were against the war made it seem even more senseless when we came back."

how bad it looked sometimes. Journalists sometimes wrote about our groups. But we wanted to reach out further. We wanted the Congress, the Veterans Administration, and the mental health professions to play a role. To carry our message to these circles and to the American public, some of us decided to make use of one of the most potent tools for persuasion in our society: survey research.

Several activist colleagues and I formed the Vietnam Era Research Project. We wanted to address the question: what's going on among Vietnam veterans? We launched an in-depth study of an unbiased sample of the men of the entire generation, as a basis for comparing veterans with their peers. After several years of groundwork—1973 to 1976—we sent interviewers in the major regions of the country to talk for three to five hours with each of 1400 randomly selected American men in their twenties and thirties, the generation that had become eligible for military service during the peak years of the war (Egendorf, Kadushin, Laufer, Rothbart, and Sloan, 1981).

Some background information may be useful here. With the exception of the higher ranking enlisted men and officers, the men who served in Vietnam were drawn from the 20 million males born in this country during the years from 1940 to 1953. Nine million served in the American military from 1964 to 1973, the years designated as the Vietnam Era. These are the Vietnam *Era* veterans. Those who have received most attention are the 2.8 million men (and 6500 women) who actually served in the war zone, the Vietnam veterans.

During the war years, government officials repeatedly noted that the Vietnam Era army was the best educated military force in U.S. history. While true, that assertion needs to be balanced with another: the men sent to Vietnam were significantly less educated than those who served elsewhere or who managed not to enter the military at all. These differences resulted from Selective Service regulations that made it possible for college students to be exempted from the draft. (This exemption was eliminated in 1969, when a lottery was established.) In addition, young men from privileged backgrounds were more aware of alternatives to military service—medical and occupational deferments, political influence, and conscientious objection. Once in the military, those with more education were likely to be assigned to technical positions other than combat duty. Self-selection was also at work: by the time Vietnam came around, the traditional notions of manhood, "blood and guts and John Wayne and the flag," were more likely to bring working-class adolescents to volunteer for infantry duty. College-educated men tended to treat such notions with more skepticism. As a result, Vietnam veterans were mostly children of lower-middle-class and working-class families.

In our research, we used various statistical procedures to take account of racial, educational, and other social-class differences between veterans and non-veterans. To summarize the results, we found that Vietnam veterans, on the average, had more psychological difficulties than either Vietnam Era veterans who did not serve in Vietnam or non-veterans of comparable background. The Vietnam veterans also had less education and lower status jobs at the time they were interviewed than did other men of their generation.

It is important to emphasize what this does *not* mean. We did not find that all veterans have serious problems. About one-fifth of all those who went to Vietnam—about the same proportion as among non-veterans—may suffer from a diagnosable disorder. About one-third of those who served in combat have such a disorder. When we applied a looser criterion of "unresolved war experiences," about one-half of all Vietnam veterans seemed troubled. This does not mean, however, that "Vietnam did it." As in most studies of the social distribution of psychological difficulties, we found that class background and present economic circumstances play a more prominent role than any single experience. Clearly, *many* factors are involved, the war being only one of them. And yet, the conclusion still stands: involvement in the war, particularly intense involvement of the kind that combat veterans engaged in, is significantly related to later difficulties.

Many observers view these difficulties as a consequence of stress—the many strains of going to war and coming home. Spurred by clinical reports about veterans whose symptoms may not appear until years after coming home—the so-called "delayed stress response"—the American Psychiatric Association included in its recent edition of the Diagnostic and Statistical Manual (DSM-III; see Chapter 11) a new entry called "Post-traumatic Stress Disorder." Veterans who are diagnosed as suffering from this disorder may

After they came home from Vietnam, veterans had difficult adjustments to make.

be haunted by recurrent thoughts, memories, dreams, or tendencies to act impulsively as if they were still in the war. They may also be withdrawn emotionally, "numbed" in their responses to other people, oftentimes complaining of not being able to love. There may also be one or more "nervous" symptoms, such as sleep disturbance, guilt, trouble concentrating, or psychosomatic complaints.

Vietnam veterans exhibit the same variety of personality types and psychological disorders that appears in the general population. The difference is that veterans are more likely to be preoccupied by war experiences, even years later. The more combat that the veterans saw, the more likely it is that their preoccupations include the stressful recollection of brutal encounters with death and destruction. It is the sudden eruption of this underlying preoccupation, as in unpredictable emotional outbursts, that is called a "delayed stress response."

Healing is still a possibility, of course. For veterans, therapeutic change always involves a crucial shift, from seeing ourselves as helpless victims of what the war did to us, to recognizing the latitude for choice and action regarding the way we now relate to and draw on our past.

Our data help to document the importance of this shift in perspective. In studying differences in

postwar interpersonal experiences, several of my colleagues found that exsoldiers who have built supportive marriages and who maintain friendships with a close-knit set of friends are significantly less likely to exhibit symptoms of stress. Our interviews also allowed us to observe differences in the extent to which veterans were willing and able to probe and make sense of their war experiences. We found that those who show a greater readiness to "work through" their past, as Freud termed it, are more likely to see their current lives as going well.

What does "working through" war experiences consist of? Veterans who have not moved very far with it are the ones locked into various forms of avoidance, wanting not to deal with issues they find troubling. Some are aware of this tendency in themselves, and will say outright, "I want to forget the whole thing." But many simply present themselves as untroubled, leaving it to a trained observer to notice the inconsistencies and vague complaints that indicate some unacknowledged difficulty. A sizeable minority has moved beyond total avoidance, but only "letting in" as much conflict regarding the war as they can attribute to acts committed by others: "the government blew it" or "the protestors screwed things up," for example. Their implicit goal is to minimize their own responsibility for the difficulties that bother them. Those who constantly blame others for their pain often seem incapable of correcting difficulties in their own lives, and complain of a lack of direction.

Another tendency, often overlapping with avoidance and blame, is for veterans to open themselves, only to feel more conflict and pain than they think they can handle. Frequently, these veterans show signs of having resigned themselves to suffering, as if they believe that once they "let in" or acknowledge what troubles them no option is left but to pity or punish themselves.

About a third of the men we studied seem able to stretch beyond avoidance, blame, self-pity, and self-punishment by actively engaging whatever has happened in their lives. It's as if they've said, "These are the cards I got dealt—now how am I going to play them?" Rather than talk about what "it" or "others" did to them, they speak of "our" war and of what "we" did or might have done differently. These men seem not only to have given thought to their war experience but also to have talked considerably about it with others who support their explorations. We find that those who have gone furthest in this process have usually done so in the context of a fulfilling intimate relationship. The fact that more men have not gone this far may say as much about the people around them and *their* tendencies to avoid the issue as it does about the veterans themselves.

What is the relevance of this research? Veterans' problems, while serious in their own right, are symptomatic of a historic dilemma that faces the country as a whole. Years after the war has ceased to be an everyday preoccupation, questions about it still evoke confusion, pain, resentment, and mistrust among an overwhelming majority of the men who came of age during that time. It is still hard for most Americans to talk openly with each other about the events of the war years. Many men who served in the military think that others neither know nor want to understand what it was like. Nonveterans are often constrained by a mix of sympathy and envy for exsoldiers, along with a sense of relief tinged with guilt that they themselves were spared.

Americans need to recognize that along with the dead and wounded, our sense of common purpose was a major casualty of the war. The strain on exsoldiers, who risked their lives for that purpose, is only a part of the damage. Decreasing trust in public

The Vietnam war caused a rift between different groups of Americans. "It is still hard for most Americans to talk openly with each other about the events of the war years."

institutions, dwindling voter participation, and lagging productivity are others.

The fundamental problem raised by the Vietnam war is not just that it was long, controversial, and bloody. Nor even that we lost. It's that war itself is in question now. *Any* war raises doubts in our minds about our species' capacity to survive. We have the weapons now to make life on this planet extinct.

The healing that needs to take place, therefore, is far-reaching. It's not just that we have to forgive ourselves for Vietnam, forgive the people of Indochina, and have them forgive us. All this must, of course, take place before the traumas of the past will fade. But we need to extend ourselves beyond any healing from this war, in particular, to address the roots of war itself. It is this deeper rift that haunts us—the ancient tradition of dividing ourselves into opposing camps to commit mass murder over issues that soon after disappear.

After I returned from Vietnam, I heard that one of my high-school classmates had been there. I looked forward to seeing him at our tenth reunion in 1972, expecting us to share the intense feeling of brotherhood common among my fellow veteran activists. He sur-

prised me though. After I told him what I was doing, he laughed: "I knew you would take it too seriously." I was furious and wouldn't talk to him after that.

Several years later I called to thank him. During the interim I had kept on searching for what it was, deep within myself, that had allowed me to support the effort to persuade people by killing them. I discovered it in the realm my high-school chum had pointed to. Righteousness, sanctimony, the conviction that "I'm right and the other guy is wrong, no question about it," when untempered by irony or humor, is the root of war. War is serious business. Mass murder, the holocausts of our century aren't to be taken lightly. But how about ourselves? It's clear that we won't build a culture that makes war outmoded until *we*, preaching and moralizing with our favorite ideas, "lighten up" about ourselves.

On the phone I conveyed some of this to my high-school buddy. He then said, "Thanks. I'm glad you called. You made me think, too. I realize I had blocked it all out by playing it cool. I guess I didn't want to deal with it before we talked back then."

That made *me* laugh. Turns out we had something to say to each other after all.

Part Five

Relating to One Another

A fundamental aspect of being human is the way we affect—and, in turn, are affected by—our fellow human beings. In this part we will focus on the ways in which people relate to one another, drawing from the field of social psychology.

Chapter 13, Female and Male, is concerned with relations between the two sexes. We will examine the differences and similarities between men and women, and we will explore the domain of sexuality. In the Psychological Issue, we will discuss the controversial issue of Changing Sex Roles and the possibility of moving toward a society in which people's traits and opportunities are not affected by their sex.

Chapter 14 deals with some of the central themes that run through our Social Relationships—needing others, perceiving others, liking others, loving others, and leaving others. Several of these themes relate closely to psychological processes that we discussed in previous chapters—"needing others" relates to the social aspects of motivation, "perceiving others" to the social aspects of perception, and "loving others" to the social aspects of emotion. The Psychological Issue concerns Prejudice and Racism, dangerous sets of attitudes that influence our relationships with entire groups of people.

In the Update on "The Social Psychology of Appearance," S. Michael Kalick discusses the influence of our physical appearance on our social relationships—an influence that has only recently been studied systematically.

Chapter 13

Female and Male

There are many things about you that are central to your identity as a distinctive human being—your talents, your habits, your appearance, your occupational aspirations, your political views, your ideals. Yet of all the elements of individual identity, the one that is quite regularly singled out for special attention is your sex. When we hear another person described, it is often in a sentence like "He's the guy who . . ." or "She's the woman who . . ." Even before we hear the end of the sentence, we already know the person's sex. And for each of us, our sexual identity becomes one of the most central elements of our self-definition. Ask a child as young as 5 or 6 the question, "Who are you?" The chances are that the child will not give such answers as "I'm a first-grader" or "I'm an American," even though these answers would be perfectly logical. Instead, the child is most likely to answer, "I'm a boy" or "I'm a girl."

Adults, too, typically regard their identity as female or male, or *sexual identity*, as perhaps the most important fact about themselves. The importance of one's sex is reflected in the fact that men and women often behave differently from each other. Are there, in fact, basic psychological differences between women and men? If so, how important are they? These are the questions we will address at the beginning of this chapter. We will discover that there are some real sex differences in personality and behavior, although these differences are smaller than many people believe them to be. Then we will consider some explanations for the differences that do exist, including the possibility of biological predispositions and the force of cultural dictates about how males and females *should* behave. Next, we will turn to one of the central aspects of the interactions between

428

men and women, sexual behavior, and discuss some of the important changes in sexual attitudes and behavior that have occurred in the past two decades. Finally, in the Psychological Issue for this chapter, we will focus on the ways that sex roles have been changing in our society, as well as on the continuing obstacles to such change.

PSYCHOLOGICAL DIFFERENCES BETWEEN MEN AND WOMEN

Some of the differences between men and women are obvious: the two sexes differ in genital organs, internal reproductive systems, and secondary sex characteristics, such as breasts and facial hair. There are other physical differences, as well. Although there is considerable overlap between the two sexes, on the average men are taller, heavier, and more muscular than women. Men are also more likely to be bald, to be color-blind, and to live shorter lives. In and of themselves, however, these physical differences do not have much to do with men's and women's personalities or with their social and occupational roles. Only a few occupations, such as playing professional basketball, place much emphasis on a person's height. Physical strength was once important in human affairs, but in today's age of machines and push-buttons, it is no longer a crucial quality.

In fact, the disparities between the roles that men and women play—the likelihood that the man is the wage-earner and the woman is the child rearer, that he is the boss and she the secretary—are not based on physical differences at all. Rather, they are often based on assumptions about *psychological* differences between men and women—differences in their intellectual capacities, temperaments, and styles of relating to others. For example, it might be reasoned that men become political leaders because they are by nature more dominant than women, or that women excel at taking care of children because they are more loving and nurturant than men. The existence of such psychological differences between the sexes is often taken for granted. As we will see, however, many of these assumptions may be unfounded.

Stereotypes About Sex Differences

When Shakespeare wrote, "Men have marble, women waxen, minds" he was expressing (most poetically, to be sure) one sort of stereotype about sex differences. He was suggesting that men are decisive and independent, whereas women are uncertain and compliant. As we noted in Chapter 6, such beliefs are called *stereotypes*—concepts about entire groups of people. "Blacks are musical," "Italians are emotional," and "football players are unintelligent" are other examples of stereotypes.

What are the stereotypes of men and women held in America today? In a study done by Inge Broverman and her colleagues (1972), subjects were given a list of over a hundred traits and were asked to rate "an adult male" or "an adult female" according to these characteristics. The researchers found that men were consistently described as being more aggressive, independent, dominant, active, competitive, and self-confident than women. Women were consistently described as being more tactful, gentle, sensitive, emotional, expressive,

In American culture, girls are expected to be neat, quiet, gentle, and nurturant.

neat, and quiet than men. Such stereotypes can be dangerous. Even if we assume for the moment that, *on the average,* men and women differ in these ways, the stereotypes are misleading, because they encourage us to overgeneralize, to assume that the stereotype accurately describes *all* (or, at least, the large majority of) members of the group. In reality, stereotypes are never accurate in this blanket sense, as evidenced by the existence of large numbers of tone-deaf blacks, calm Italians, and intellectual football players, not to mention submissive men and insensitive women.

Yet we are all likely to make errors of overgeneralization in which we react to individuals as if they had all the stereotypical characteristics of their group. Recently Zick Rubin showed his wife, Carol, the work of two different editors who had worked on material for a book. He had told Carol that one of the editors was a man and the other was a woman. In discussing the material, Carol began referring to one of the editors as "he" and the other as "she." It turned out that she had assumed that the editor whose work was tighter and more compact was a man and that the one whose work was more expansive and expressive was a woman. Needless to say, her assumptions were wrong; in fact, "he" was a she, and "she" was a he.

As this example suggests, stereotypes about men and women can lead to bias in the way we evaluate people's work. This point was demonstrated in an experiment conducted by Kay Deaux and Tim Emswiler (1974). Students were told that either a man or a woman had done very well on a task involving identification of mechanical objects. When the person was identified as a man, the subjects indicated that they thought he was quite skillful. When the person who turned in an identical performance was a woman, the subjects gave her lower skill ratings and instead gave her high ratings on "luck." The stereotype that men are more mechanical than women apparently led the subjects to assume that the man's performance reflected greater ability than the woman's identical performance. Even psychologists are not immune from stereotypes about sex differences— and these stereotypes may have the effect of biasing their research (see Box 1).

Facts About Sex Differences

We can all probably agree that stereotypes about men and women are often exaggerations or overgeneralizations. Regardless of what the stereotype might be, we know that many women are more aggressive and more dominant than most men and that many men are warmer and more sensitive than most women. We may still suspect, however, that the stereotypes reflect some real differences between the two sexes. Such suspicions cannot substitute for direct evidence, however, and the evidence for psychological sex differences is slim.

In a review of the extensive research literature on psychological sex differences, especially in infants and children, Eleanor Maccoby and Carol Nagy Jacklin (1974) concluded that many of the differences that are commonly believed to exist between males and females are in fact myths. For example, there is no good evidence that boys are more independent, ambitious, or achievement-oriented

— Box 1 —

Psychology's sex bias

Psychology is supposed to be the science of human behavior. But is it really? In fact, a great deal of psychological research makes use of subjects of only one sex, and that sex is usually male. According to one count of studies in personality and social psychology, males are used as subjects twice as often as females (Holmes and Jorgensen, 1971).

What lies behind this preference for male subjects? One possible explanation is that psychological researchers, who are themselves predominantly male, feel they can understand men better than women. In addition, psychologists may share society's implicit assumption that the male sex is somehow more important than the female sex and therefore more worthy of study.

Whatever the reasons for the preference for male subjects, it can clearly have the effect of biasing our research. Even though psychologists often focus their research on men, they still discuss the results as if they pertain to everyone. As a result, researchers run the risk of enshrining men's typical patterns of behavior as the "normal" patterns for all people. "We have a psychology of men," writes Joanna Bunker Rohrbaugh (1979), "but it is called simply 'psychology.'"

In addition to the overall preference for male subjects, men and women are typically used in different sorts of studies. Wendy McKenna and Suzanne Kessler (1977) surveyed hundreds of recent experiments and found that there were five times as many all-male as all-female studies of the "manly" phenomenon of aggression. In the "gentler" area of interpersonal attraction, female subjects were relatively more likely to be employed.

Even within a particular field of research the specific measures used with men and women tend to be different. For example, men's aggression has frequently been measured by making them think they are giving electric shocks to another person and seeing how much they administer. In contrast, women's aggression has usually been measured in a less brutal and more passive way, such as by simply asking the subjects to indicate how angry they feel.

These differences suggest that psychologists allow their own stereotypes about men and women to influence their selection of subjects and the way they treat them. "I manipulated anxiety," one researcher explained, "and I frankly couldn't bring myself to do this with college girls" (Prescott, 1978).

As long as researchers' stereotypes affect their procedures in such ways, it is likely that the results of research will simply perpetuate the stereotypes. Men will appear to be more active and aggressive than women, because they are studied in more active and aggressive ways; for similar reasons, women will appear to be more passive and gentle. A better approach, of course, is for researchers to use subjects of both sexes in more of their studies.

---

than girls or that girls are more nurturant or sociable than boys. A recent review by Alice Eagly (1978) also puts to rest the myth that women are more easily influenced than men. She found that the major factor affecting whether or not people are likely to be influenced is how unsure they feel in a particular sphere and that this factor is equally important for both sexes.

There are a few psychological sex differences that have been reliably established, however. On the average, males are more aggressive than females, both in childhood and in later life. Boys tend to fight more than girls, to engage in more verbal aggression (such as taunting or insulting others), and to fantasize more about aggressive themes. We will consider the possible reasons for this difference in the next section. In addition, girls tend to have greater verbal ability than boys, while boys tend to have greater spatial and mathematical ability.

There is also evidence that females are more concerned about other people's feelings than males. Girls and women have consistently been found to be better than boys and men at accurately "reading" people's nonverbal behavior (Hall, 1978). Females also tend to

THE SWORDTAIL AND THE BRISTLEWORM

With the rare exception of people who undergo sex-change surgery, the sex of a human being is unambiguous and unchangeable. But this is not so for all of the earth's creatures. Among species of tropical fish called swordtails, the males are identified by their extended swordlike tails. When there is a shortage of males, some of the females will grow extended tails and turn into males. There is also a species of bristleworm that grows by adding new segments. Once the worm develops twenty segments, it is a female and produces eggs. If the worm is then cut back to five or ten segments, it is converted into a male. If two female bristleworms are kept together in isolation, one will become a male and fertilize the other's eggs (Wickler, 1973).

be more empathic than males—that is, they seem to be more predisposed to put themselves in another person's place and experience that person's joy or pain (Hoffman, 1977). Indeed, even newborn girls are more likely than newborn boys to cry "sympathetically" when they hear another baby's cry, as if they were more prone to "feel for" the other baby (Sagi and Hoffman, 1976). Martin Hoffman speculates that this may be a first sign of later sex differences in empathy.

Research on psychological sex differences continues actively, and it is likely that further research will lead to the refinement and, perhaps, the revision of some of Maccoby and Jacklin's conclusions (see Block, 1976). It remains safe to say, however, that the basic psychological differences between the two sexes are fewer and of lesser magnitude than has generally been assumed. On the whole, as Maccoby and Jacklin conclude, males and females are much more similar to one another than they are different, and they share the same fundamental needs, emotions, and abilities.

If many of the stereotypical differences between the sexes are myths, then why are they perpetuated? If, for example, men are not really more ambitious than women, why does everyone persist in thinking that they are? What's more, doesn't the fact that almost all of the world's political leaders are men provide ample proof of men's greater ambition, not to mention their greater dominance and competence?

There are two good answers to these questions. The first is that, as we saw in Chapter 4, our perception of other people is selective. When someone behaves in an expected way (a boy running and shouting, a girl sitting and playing quietly), we take note of the behavior and assume that it reflects the person's underlying temperament. The boy is "rambunctious" and the girl is "dainty," just as boys and girls are supposed to be. When, on the other hand, someone behaves in an unexpected way, the behavior may go unnoticed or may be passed off as a fluke. An active, shouting little girl may be viewed as simply imitating her brother, while a quiet little boy may be seen as being tired. "As a result," Maccoby and Jacklin write, "myths live on that would otherwise die out under the impact of negative evidence."

The second reason for the perpetuation of the myths concerns the different opportunities that society provides for men and women. In fact, as children grow up, boys undoubtedly do become more politically and professionally ambitious than girls, and girls become more interested in taking care of children. When we view these "ambitious" men and "nurturant" women, we might assume that we are viewing the reflections of basic differences between men's and women's temperaments. But this conclusion would probably be mistaken. Many of the differences that we observe result from social values and opportunities, rather than from basic psychological differences. Boys have traditionally had more opportunities to become politicians, doctors, and lawyers, so there has been more for them to be ambitious about. And their ambition has been encouraged by parents and teachers, while that of girls has been suppressed or redirected in more "feminine" directions. Similarly, women may become more nuturant than men because society encourages them to display such nurturance as mothers, while it discourages men from doing so.

EXPLAINING THE DIFFERENCES: BIOLOGY AND CULTURE

Do any of the sex differences that show up in childhood have a biological basis? Or are they entirely the product of social and cultural conditioning, reflecting the fact that men and women are likely to become the sort of people they are expected to be? We will consider this issue with respect to one of the psychological sex differences that has been consistently found—the tendency for males to be more aggressive than females. As we will see, it does not turn out to be a simple question of biology *or* culture. In fact, both biology *and* culture are involved in determining a person's level of aggressive behavior, and both forces interact to produce the sex differences that have been observed.

Biological Influences

If sex differences in aggression are based in part on biology, we would expect to see the same sex differences in societies throughout the world. After all, even though cultures may differ, the basic biological nature of all people is the same. In fact, the male's greater aggressiveness is not peculiar to American society. Men are the hunters, the warriors, and the aggressors in virtually every society that has been studied (D'Andrade, 1966). Boys roughhouse more and exchange insults more than girls in societies throughout the world (Whiting and Edwards, 1973).

A second sort of evidence that points to the role of biological predisposition comes from observations of our animal relatives. Because culture, as we know it, does not play a large role in shaping the

Human males are more likely than human females to behave aggressively.

behavior of other animals, any consistent sex differences in other animals must almost certainly have a biological basis. And, in fact, males are more aggressive than females in almost all species of monkeys and apes, our closest relatives in the animal kingdom, as well as in most other mammals.

Neither the cross-cultural generalities nor the biological sex differences in other animals proves beyond doubt that sex differences in humans have a biological basis. Nevertheless, both sorts of evidence are consistent with the idea that a predisposition toward greater male aggressiveness is part of our evolutionary heritage.

If there is a biological predisposition for males to be more aggressive than females, how is it brought about? In other animals—and probably in humans, as well—the predisposition toward greater male aggressiveness seems to result from the action of the male hormones on the brain and, through the brain, on behavior. Most of this hormonal influence takes place before birth. At the time of conception and shortly thereafter, "male" and "female" embryos are essentially identical. The only difference is that the female has two X chromosomes while the male has an X and a Y. Sexual differentiation begins when the XY chromosomes send a biochemical signal that leads to the production of the male hormone testosterone. The hormone causes certain embryonic tissues to develop into male sex organs. If no male hormone is produced, these tissues develop instead into female organs (see Figure 13.1). Were it not for this hormonal influence, all of us would develop as females (Money and Ehrhardt, 1972).

In addition to its effects on the genitals and reproductive system, the male hormone causes certain changes in brain pathways, which in turn has an impact on the individual's temperament and behavior. In one study, testosterone was administered to pregnant monkeys (Young, Goy, and Phoenix, 1964). The female offspring of these monkeys were born with masculinized genitals, attesting to the physical effect of the hormone. What's more, these female monkeys showed elevated levels of rough-and-tumble play, behaving in this respect more like male than female monkeys. The prenatal hormones had affected not only anatomy but behavior, as well.

For obvious ethical reasons, experiments like this have never been done with humans. There are rare cases, however, in which a similar sort of androgenization (addition of male hormone) takes place naturally in humans as a result of a glandular defect or the use of certain drugs. In these cases, a genetic female becomes exposed to an excess of male hormone before birth. Such an infant may have masculinized genitals, but this condition can be corrected surgically; with proper medical treatment, the infant can grow into a normal woman. There is some evidence, however, that prenatal androgenization can have an effect on such a woman's behavioral predispositions. Anke Ehrhardt and Susan Baker (1973) studied seventeen girls who had been prenatally androgenized and compared them with their normal sisters. Even though the androgenized girls did not look any different from normal girls, they did tend to act in more "tomboyish" ways. Compared to their sisters, they liked outdoor sports more, liked dolls less, and were somewhat more likely to start fights. Although these data are not conclusive, they suggest that the male hor-

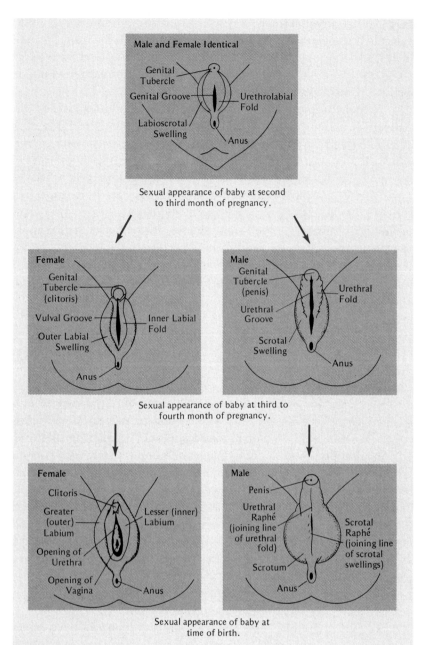

Male and Female Identical

Genital Tubercle
Genital Groove
Urethrolabial Fold
Labioscrotal Swelling
Anus

Sexual appearance of baby at second to third month of pregnancy.

Female

Genital Tubercle (clitoris)
Vulval Groove
Inner Labial Fold
Outer Labial Swelling
Anus

Male

Genital Tubercle (penis)
Urethral Fold
Urethral Groove
Scrotal Swelling
Anus

Sexual appearance of baby at third to fourth month of pregnancy.

Female

Clitoris
Greater (outer) Labium
Lesser (inner) Labium
Opening of Urethra
Opening of Vagina
Anus

Male

Penis
Urethral Raphé (joining line of urethral fold)
Scrotal Raphé (joining line of scrotal swellings)
Scrotum
Anus

Sexual appearance of baby at time of birth.

FIGURE 13.1
Sexual differentiation before birth in the male and female embryos.

mones may have predisposed these girls to behave more aggressively. These cases also provide indirect evidence for the hypothesis that the average difference in aggressiveness between normal males and normal females may be due in part to the effects of male hormones.

One important caution is necessary here. Most instances of girls who like sports, climb trees, start fights, and so on have absolutely nothing to do with prenatal androgenization. Such behavior is perfectly normal for girls, as well as for boys, and in the overwhelming majority of cases has no relation to unusual hormone levels. Prenatal androgenization is an extremely rare occurrence, and it is only in these rare cases that a causal link between male hormones and "tomboyish" behavior has been suggested.

SEX DIFFERENCES IN THE BRAIN

Yes, there *are* sex differences in the brain—and there is a lot of controversy about their importance. Recent studies of animals such as rats and songbirds have shown that certain clusters of brain cells, including areas involved in sexual behavior, are larger in males than in females (Schmeck, 1980a). In humans, brain-wave studies suggest that men have a greater degree of hemispheric specialization than women. When performing spatial tasks, men tend to activate their right hemispheres, while women are more likely to activate both hemispheres, suggesting that a larger portion of the female brain is involved in spatial ability (Restak, 1979). Some observers are convinced that such differences contribute importantly to sex differences in skills and behavior. Others are just as convinced that they don't.

Dane Archer and his coworkers (1978) have discovered a subtle way in which the mass media reflect—and may help perpetuate—traditional sex roles. By carefully measuring photographs of men and women in newspapers and magazines, they found that photographs of men tend to emphasize their faces whereas photos of women emphasize their bodies. In the average photo of a man, almost two-thirds of the photo was devoted to the man's face; in contrast, less than half of the average photo of a woman was devoted to the face. Always ready to turn a phrase, Archer dubbed this phenomenon *face-ism*. He suggests that it may be related to the tendency to view men as more intellectual (the head) and women both as more emotional and as sexual objects (the body). You might want to check for yourself whether the photographs in this textbook also display face-ism.

Cultural Influences

Having said all this about biological influences on aggressive behavior, it is now time to look at the other side of the coin. We have been using the word *predisposition* quite regularly in this chapter. A *predisposition* is a readiness to behave or to develop in a particular way. On the average, men apparently have more of a readiness to be aggressive than women, for reasons that seem to be partly biological. But human behavior rarely if ever reflects such predispositions in a simple or direct way. As we noted in the Psychological Issue following Chapter 8, whether or not someone will in fact behave aggressively in a particular situation depends to a large extent on what the person has learned about the appropriate situations in which to express aggression. In our culture men are permitted or encouraged to be aggressive to a much greater degree than women are. Boys are given toy guns and toy soldiers to play with and are expected to make loud noises with them, while girls are given dolls and tea sets and are expected to play more quietly. On television children are more likely to see aggressive men, whether they are cowboys, cops, or robbers, than aggressive women. This sort of cultural shaping probably has considerably more impact on patterns of aggressive behavior than does biological predisposition.

One example of the role of culture in shaping aggressive behavior comes from a study done among the Luo people of Kenya (Ember, 1973). Among the Luo, boys and girls are typically assigned to different sorts of household tasks, such as heavy work for boys and child care for girls. However, when there is no older girl in the family to take care of the "female" tasks, a boy will be assigned to do this work. Ember found that boys who were assigned to do female work tended to be less aggressive, less dominant, and more dependent than other boys; in these respects their behavior was more like that of girls. These boys were of course no different from other boys biologically. Rather, the fact that they were placed in a traditionally female role had a direct effect on their temperament and behavior.

Further evidence for the cultural shaping of sex differences in aggression comes from studies that show that under some conditions women are *not* less aggressive than men. These include situations in which there is a clear justification for the aggression, such as when the subjects were first provoked by another person and were then given the opportunity to retaliate. Under such conditions, women have sometimes been found to be just as aggressive as men are (Frodi, Macaulay, and Thome, 1977).

In the last analysis, our own conclusion (and that of most psychologists) is that psychological differences between men and women are shaped to a much larger extent by culture than by biology. Biology does set certain of the boundaries of male and female behavior, and its role should not be overlooked. But the biological boundaries are extremely broad. The actual development of traits, skills, and aspirations depends in large measure on society's values about what men and women can and should do with their lives. In the next section, we will look more closely at how these values help to shape the characteristics of men and women.

Learning Sex Roles

Our expectations about what men and women should do and what they should be like are called *sex roles*. Whereas stereotypes are widely held assumptions of what men and women *are like*, sex roles are widely held notions about the way men and women *ought to be*. Each of us learns about these expectations as we grow up, and the expectations in turn are likely to have a major impact on our personalities and behavior.

Even before a child is born, the expectant parents have notions of what they would like their sons and daughters to be like, and they proceed to communicate these expectations to their children, beginning in infancy. Boys are taught to "get ahead" and "stay cool" (Pleck and Sawyer, 1974). They are encouraged to be ambitious and assertive and are discouraged from expressing their weaknesses or their tender feelings. Girls, on the other hand, learn to play a more submissive and dependent role. They are taught to be well-behaved and cooperative and to act as if they had no aggressive impulses at all. Girls are also expected to be tender and nurturant, whether with their dolls or with baby sisters and brothers.

Sex-role learning goes along with learning the "proper" occupations for men and women. This learning comes early: by the time they are in kindergarten children usually know what sorts of work are "for men" and what sorts are "for women." Sandra and Daryl

Girls are taught very early in life about the characteristics they need to be a "woman."

Women's occupational opportunities have traditionally been more limited than men's.

Bem (1970) provide examples of how boys' and girls' occupational interests are shaped by their parents, both by direct reinforcement and by the models provided by same-sex parents:

Boys are encouraged to take more of an interest in mathematics and science. Boys, not girls, are given chemistry sets and microscopes for Christmas. Moreover, all children quickly learn that mommy is proud to be a moron when it comes to mathematics and science, whereas daddy knows all about these things. When a young boy returns from school all excited over a biology class, he is almost certain to be encouraged to think of becoming a physician. A girl with similar enthusiasm is told that she might want to consider nurse's training. . . . (page 91)

Sex roles are also taught in school, sometimes in subtle but nevertheless effective ways. In nursery school, teachers are likely to scold boys more harshly than girls for aggressive behavior—which may, as Lisa Serbin and K. Daniel O'Leary (1975) note, have the paradoxical effect of providing the boys with attention and thus encouraging the very behavior that it is intended to discourage: "For John [but not Nancy], being disruptive is an effective way of getting a far larger dose of attention than good behavior can bring."

Explaining the differences: biology and culture   **439**

Children model themselves on same-sex adults as part of the process of sex-role learning.

The process of sex-role learning is not a passive one on the part of the child. To the contrary, as Lawrence Kohlberg (1966) has emphasized, once the child learns his or her sex—which virtually all children do by age 3—the child invariably wants to demonstrate that he or she can behave like a member in good standing of that sex. This reflects every child's motivation to be a competent and consistent human being. As a result, the child actively seeks clues as to how a "boy" or a "girl" should behave, not only from direct rewards from parents and teachers but from imitating their same-sex parent and other models, such as on television. This desire to behave consistently with one's sex helps to explain why sex roles often seem so difficult to change. Even in "nonsexist" nursery schools that make every effort to treat boys and girls alike, one is still likely to see boys and girls playing separately, at different sorts of activities (Rubin, 1980). In the process, they confirm their own identity as "boy" or "girl." (In Box 2, we consider a fascinating exception to the normal tendency of children—and adults—to identify themselves with their biological sex. This is the case of *transsexuals,* who believe that they actually should belong to the opposite sex.)

A great deal of sex-role learning takes place through the mass media, especially television. Even though there have been some changes recently, men are still portrayed as strong, competent, resourceful people who occupy such exalted roles as physician, lawyer, or police detective. These male role models are sometimes permitted to show warmth and sensitivity, but only when coupled with great achievement and self-reliance. It is still rare to see a man cry on television. Women, on the other hand, are depicted as gentler, more sensitive beings who frequently reveal their weaknesses and their emotions. Even when women have achieved high-status occupations (policewoman, news reporter, lawyer), they typically remain subordinate to their bosses and dependent on their husbands and boyfriends. These sex-role stereotypes can also be seen in Saturday morning children's shows. One study found that male characters on these shows are portrayed as being more active, independent, and capable of solving problems than female characters (McArthur and Eisen, 1976). Such television images are likely to have an influence on children's own aspirations and styles of behavior.

With all these opportunities to learn sex roles—in the family, in school, on television—coupled with the child's own desire to behave consistently with his or her sex, it's no wonder that by the time they finish elementary school boys and girls behave in quite different ways.

HUMAN SEXUALITY

Our "maleness" and "femaleness" is most obviously reflected in the area of sexuality—our sexual responses, experiences, and relationships. As we will see, there have long been basic differences between men and women in the experience and expression of sexuality. Although some of these differences may have a basis in biology, recent research has shown that the physiology of sex in men and women is much more similar than had previously been suspected. But cultural attitudes have perpetuated differences between men's and women's orientations toward sexuality.

Human Sexual Response

Much of what we know about our body's sexual responses comes from the research of William Masters and Virginia Johnson (1966). These investigators were the first to scientifically examine physical responses to sexual stimulation in the laboratory.

One of Masters and Johnson's most important findings was that patterns of sexual response are very similar in women and men. For both sexes there are four stages of sexual arousal (see Figure 13.2). The first stage, the *excitement phase*, can be initiated by physical factors (such as genital stimulation), or by psychological factors (such as fantasy). In this phase, heart rate and respiration increase and blood flows into the genitals, making the penis erect and causing the clitoris to swell. Moisture forms on the vaginal walls. Both women's and men's nipples may become erect. In the second, or *plateau phase*, the genitals reach their maximum engorgement. The clitoris retracts into the clitoral hood and the uterus raises slightly, expanding the vagina. The glans of the penis enlarges and darkens in color, while the testes swell, pulling up into the scrotum. At the end of the plateau phase both sexes may have a sense that orgasm is inevitable. In the *orgasmic phase*, muscular contractions push the blood in the genitals back

— Box 2 —

Transsexuals

In 1974, Dr. Richard Raskind was a successful physician with a large practice. He also played amateur tennis and ranked thirteenth nationally in the men's division for players 35 and over. In 1977, Dr. Renée Richards had discontinued her active medical practice in order to concentrate on professional tennis. She ranked tenth among women players in America, an unprecedented accomplishment for a 42-year-old who had never before played professionally. Richard Raskind had undergone sex-change surgery to become Renée Richards after years of feeling that he was a woman locked inside a man's body.

Similarly, James Morris, a noted British journalist, withdrew from circulation for a brief period and emerged as Jan Morris. She went on to write *Conundrum* (1974), a moving account of her life as a *transsexual*—a person who felt that his anatomy conflicted with her true sexual identity—and of her decision to have this "mistake of nature" corrected surgically.

Between 10,000 and 20,000 men and women in the United States, by one rough estimate, are transsexuals (Restak, 1979). These people share the feeling that they are trapped in a body of the wrong

James Morris (left) *was a foreign correspondent and father of four children before he had a sex-change operation and became Jan Morris* (right).

sex, and they have an intense desire to transform their bodies to those of the opposite sex. About four out of five transsexuals seen by doctors have been males, although the number of females has recently been increasing.

The transsexual's feeling that his body is "the wrong sex" usually begins early in life. Transsexuals commonly report that as children they preferred activities characteristic of the opposite sex and that they enjoyed cross-dressing (wearing clothes made for members of the opposite sex). They also report that they were upset by the development of their bodies at puberty, since these

changes heightened the conflict between their sexual anatomy and their personal sense of sexual identity.

No one knows what causes transsexualism. Transsexuals show no abnormalities in their sex organs or hormone levels, and no biological explanation for their desire to change their sex has been found. Psychological theories, such as an unusually intense identification with the opposite-sex parent, have been put forth. But so far, there is no conclusive evidence in support of any such theories.

Regardless of what its underlying causes might be, transsexual-

into the bloodstream. The vaginal walls move in and out and the uterus pulsates. Muscles in and around the penis pulse to cause ejaculation, the discharge of semen. Some people experience muscular contractions in other parts of the body, such as in the face, arms, or legs. In the *resolution phase* the body returns to its preexcitement state.

Although men and women share these basic stages of sexual response, there are a few differences in their physiological reactions. Women, of course, do not ejaculate. And Masters and Johnson's findings indicate that men undergo a *refractory period* in the resolution

ism is a condition that places a person in a state of extreme conflict—between the state of his body, on the one hand, and the state of his mind, on the other. This conflict, particularly before the advent of the sex-change operation in the mid-1960's, led some transsexuals to desperate measures, including self-castration. Before undertaking surgery, one male-to-female transsexual went so far as to eat large quantities of women's face cream containing estrogens (female hormones), in the hope of bringing about desired physical changes (Hyde, 1979).

Attempts to change transsexuals' sexual identities through psychotherapy have generally been unsuccessful. But if psychotherapists could not change transsexuals' minds to match their bodies, surgeons decided that they could change transsexuals' bodies to match their minds. The sex-change operation was first performed in the United States at the Johns Hopkins Hospital in 1966, and later began to be performed at other hospitals as well.

Sexual reassignment through surgery is no simple procedure. In the male-to-female operation, the patient's testicles are cut away and his penis is cored out, leaving the skin, which is used to line an artificially formed vagina. In the female-to-male operation, the breasts, uterus, and ovaries are removed, the vagina is sealed, and an artificial penis is created. All patients are treated with opposite-sex hormones prior to the surgery, and many obtain additional cosmetic surgery to make their facial features, hair growth, and skin texture seem more appropriate to the sex they want to be. After the operation, transsexuals are incapable of reproduction, but they can experience some degree of sexual stimulation.

The sex-change operation was initially greeted with great enthusiasm. Where psychiatrists and psychologists had failed, surgeons had succeeded. In recent years, however, professionals' views about sexual reassignment have become much more guarded. Although some transsexuals, such as Renée Richards and Jan Morris, apparently made good adjustments after the operation, many others still had serious psychological problems. Some became seriously depressed, suicidal, or psychotic after the surgery. Their family lives were often ruined, and the surgery often left patients with physical complications as well, such as infections and the need for further surgery.

In 1979 Jon Meyer, a psychiatrist at Johns Hopkins, and a coworker published a followup study on two groups of transsexuals—one group who had received sex-change surgery and another group who had been denied the surgery (Meyer and Reter, 1979). The researchers found no difference between the adjustment of the two groups. "[Surgery] does not cure what is essentially a psychiatric disturbance," Meyer concluded, "and it does not demonstrably rehabilitate the patient." In the wake of Meyer's study, Johns Hopkins, the hospital that had pioneered the surgery in this country, refused to continue performing it.

Meyer's report remains controversial, and many other hospitals continue to carry out sex-change surgery. At Stanford University, for example, it is believed that an extensive psychological screening of applicants for surgery increases the chance of the operation's success. Stanford also requires patients to live as a member of the opposite sex for a minimum of two years before surgery, thus providing further evidence that they will be able to adjust successfully to their new sexual identities.

On the whole, however, sex-change surgery is no longer regarded with the same enthusiasm that it was initially. At the same time, renewed efforts are being made to change people's sexual identity through behavior modification procedures (Barlow, Abel, and Blanchard, 1979). Today most professionals would probably agree with Richard Restak's (1979) conclusion that if sex-change surgery is carried out at all, it should be defined as "experimental" surgery, and subjected to the closest possible scrutiny.

stage, during which further excitement to orgasm is impossible. Women, however, may skip the refractory period and can be stimulated to orgasm again. This is a finding that contradicts prevalent social attitudes. Rather than being less sensual than men, it appears that women have a greater sexual capacity than men do. There is more recent evidence, however, that at least some men, too, can have multiple orgasms in a short period of time (Tavris, 1976).

Masters and Johnson also found that the same kinds of orgasms can be achieved through masturbation, intercourse, or even fantasy for both men and women. The fact that mere fantasy can prompt the

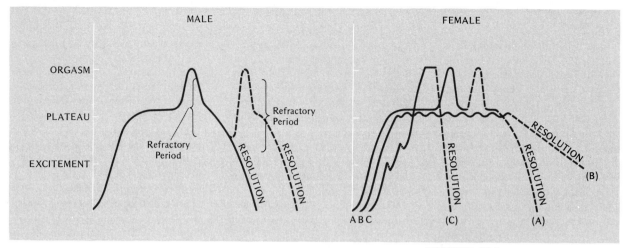

FIGURE 13.2

Typical sexual response patterns in the human male and female (after Masters and Johnson, 1966). In both sexes, sexual excitement increases until it reaches a plateau. The orgasm is a sudden surge of arousal beyond this plateau. After orgasm, men have a refractory period during which further excitement to orgasm is impossible. For women, several different patterns are typical. The woman may remain at the plateau stage without proceeding to orgasm (line B); she may have an orgasm followed by resolution (return to the preexcitement stage) (line C); or she may have two or more orgasms in succession before resolution (line A).

same sexual response as actual intercourse suggests a fundamental fact about human sexuality: for humans, sex is as much cognitive and psychological as it is genital.

The importance of cognitive activity in sexual arousal is apparent in the ease with which humans become aroused—an erotic novel or picture can be as effective as direct genital stimulation. It has traditionally been thought that men are more easily aroused by explicit pornographic materials than women, while women have been thought to be more responsive to romantic or sentimental stimuli. But the results of a study done by Julia Heiman (1975) suggest otherwise. Heiman studied male and female college students' sexual responses to a variety of tape-recorded stories. Some subjects heard erotic or explicit sexual material, some heard romantic but nonsexual material, and some heard combined erotic-romantic material. Sexual arousal was measured by devices placed on the penis (to record the size of erections) or in the vagina (to record increased blood flow during arousal). Heiman found that those subjects who listened to the romantic tapes or to neutral tapes showed low levels of sexual arousal, while those who listened to the erotic or erotic-romantic tapes showed high levels of arousal. Furthermore, females who listened to the erotic material were as aroused as males, while the romantic tapes had no more effect on women than on men. These findings indicate that sexual response occurs as a result of *mental* stimulation and in the presence of the same stimuli for men and women.

The findings of James Geer and Robert Fuhr (1976) further demonstrate the cognitive aspect of sexual arousal. They showed that distracting males from erotic material by asking them to perform mental arithmetic dramatically reduced sexual arousal. Their results indicate that people have to pay attention to get turned on—it's not a completely automatic response.

The idea that sexuality is to a large extent in the mind becomes particularly apparent in cases of sexual dysfunction. Sexual dysfunction takes a number of forms, including problems with performing intercourse, enjoying sex, or reaching orgasm. All of these problems are very common. Couples who are distressed by such problems can now seek *sex therapy*, which utilizes techniques pioneered by Masters and Johnson (1970). As it turns out, very few sexual dysfunctions are caused by physical problems (Kaplan, 1974). A major contributor to sexual dysfunction is worrying: worry about becoming pregnant, worry about having orgasms, worry about how one's body looks and smells, worry about rejection. Sex therapists try to combat these worries by encouraging people with sexual problems to focus on sensual pleasure rather than on sexual expertise (Heiman, 1979).

All through history human beings have searched for effective aphrodisiacs: substances that will insure sexual potency. Oysters, ginseng root, and antelope antlers are just a few of the items that have been touted as means to becoming the perfect lover. But as Donn Byrne (1976) concludes, "Though much time, effort, money, and wishful thinking have been directed toward the search for an effective aphrodisiac, many individuals have learned that they are carrying one of the most powerful instruments for stimulation right in their own heads." In other words, our true sex organs are our brains.

Changing Sexual Attitudes

If you had grown up on the Polynesian island of Mangaia, you would probably be having sexual intercourse every night, with two or three orgasms each time. You would have been taught the value of mutual pleasure in sex. Sex is of such importance in Mangaia that the people have many different words for intercourse, just as the Eskimos have many different words for snow in all its various forms (Marshall, 1971). On the other hand, if you had grown up on the Irish island of Inis Beag, you would find sex to be a rushed, secretive matter, with no knowledge or expectation of female orgasm. The main thing you would have learned about sex is that it depletes your energy and should be kept to a minimum (Messenger, 1971). The natives of Mangaia and of Inis Beag are not different from each other biologically, but their culture shapes their sexuality in profoundly different ways.

Our own sexual attitudes and values are just as much affected by the time and place we live in as the attitudes and values of the people of these two diverse cultures. Our most recent and influential cultural legacy concerning sexuality stems from the Victorian era, which spanned approximately the last two-thirds of the nineteenth century, when Queen Victoria ruled England. For the Victorians, sex was considered a necessary evil for men and as something basically foreign to the nature of women. A "good" husband would impose sex on his wife as seldom as possible, and a "good" wife would tolerate sex as one of her marital duties. The idea that a woman could derive pleasure from sex was regarded as an insult. According to an old English joke, when a Victorian girl asked her mother what to do on her wedding night, the mother advised, "Lie still and close your eyes, dear, and think of England" (Tavris and Offir, 1977, page 61). It is doubtful that all Victorian men and women lived up to these cultural standards, yet the era unmistakably created a legacy of sexual restraint

---

IS MASTURBATION DANGEROUS?

In the Victorian era, masturbation was considered evil and disgusting. Victorian physicians warned that stimulating yourself sexually could lead to acne, blindness, impotence, warts, coughing spells, and even insanity. To protect little girls from themselves, some doctors went so far as to apply a hot iron to the clitoris or to sew the vaginal lips together. In the 1940s and 1950s Kinsey stunned the American public when he announced that 92 percent of the men in his sample and (even more shocking) 62 percent of the women had masturbated. More recent surveys have shown that women are beginning to masturbate earlier and with greater frequency than in previous decades (Hunt, 1974). Sex therapists have found that masturbation is one of the most useful techniques for treating women who have never experienced orgasm. Women learn to masturbate and find out what arouses them, and then transfer the lesson to intercourse (Tavris and Offir, 1977).

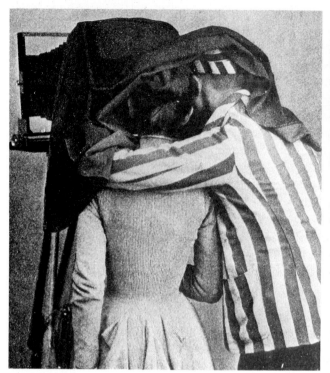

In the Victorian era, sexual behavior was highly restrained. Even though we have undergone a "sexual revolution" and sexual behavior has become more open, Victorian attitudes still underlie many of our sexual patterns.

and repression in both Europe and America that has been difficult to shake. A central part of this legacy is the sexual *double standard*, which allows for very different patterns of sexual behavior for men than for women.

During the first half of the twentieth century, significant changes in sexual attitudes and behavior took place. In his widely influential theory of personality (see Chapter 8), Sigmund Freud viewed sex as a central motivational force and thus helped establish the normality of sexual desire for both sexes. But Freud believed that women's sexual motivation derived mainly from the wish to have children, while men experienced sexual desire as an end in itself. In Freud's view, it was "normal" for men to play the active role in sex and for women to play a passive role. Thus, although Freud's influence led people to be more open and accepting about sex, it left the sexual double standard as strong as ever. Freud also emphasized that heterosexual intercourse was the only psychologically mature form of sex. He viewed other practices, such as oral sex, masturbation, and homosexuality, as tending toward the perverse (Heiman, 1979).

Changes in sexual behavior in the first half of this century were documented by the pioneering surveys conducted by Alfred Kinsey and his colleagues (1948, 1953), who were the first to actually ask large numbers of people—more than 11,000 men and women—about their sexual behavior. One area that Kinsey explored was premarital sex. He found that while six out of seven women born before 1900 had been virgins on their wedding nights, more than half of the married women in 1950—and over two-thirds of the men—had had premarital intercourse. Perhaps even more significantly, Kinsey documented the wide range of sexual activities that were commonly practiced in America, including masturbation, arousal by porno-

SEXUAL ATTITUDES AND BIRTH CONTROL

Despite the widespread availability of contraceptives, many adolescents and young adults—including many college students—fail to use them. At Indiana University, for example, the student health service provides lectures about birth control and makes pills, diaphragms, and IUDs freely available. But of ninety-one sexually active undergraduate women who responded to a survey, fewer than a third said they always used contraceptives and more than a third said they never did. Donn Byrne (1977) believes that the failure to use contraceptives regularly reflects negative or ambivalent feelings about sex. After all, using a contraceptive means admitting to yourself that you may have sex, and it involves dealing with doctors or druggists, discussing birth control plans with your partner, and actually taking a pill daily or using a device. Byrne finds that people who are anxious about sex tend to avoid these sexually oriented behaviors. As a result, these sexually anxious people also run the greatest risk of unwanted pregnancy.

graphic materials, and homosexual activity. By "normalizing" practices that were previously considered to be perverse or sinful, Kinsey's reports had a great impact on American sexual standards. As Julia Heiman (1979) notes, we can imagine the great sigh of relief that came from the millions of people who had until then felt that they were the "only ones" engaged in one activity or another.

In the past two decades, sexual attitudes and behaviors in America have continued to undergo massive change—so much so that many people refer to the changes since 1960 as a "sexual revolution." The revolution can be measured only in part by determining the numbers of people who engaged in particular sexual activities. It is clear, for example, that many more college students have premarital intercourse in the 1980s than students did in the 1950s. Just as important have been changes in many people's feelings about sex, from viewing it as something to be engaged in with guilt or anxiety to something that can be a normal and natural source of pleasure. But the "sexual revolution" notwithstanding, and despite increasing similarities in the sexual behavior of men and women, the sexual double standard lives on (see Box 3).

The Impact of the Sexual Revolution

Masters and Johnson's research was one of the forces that led to a further move away from the sexual repression of the Victorian era toward a new emphasis on sexual enjoyment and openness in the 1970s and 1980s. The values of humanistic psychology (see Chapter 8) and the human potential movement also contributed to this shift,

William Masters and Virginia Johnson conducted pioneering studies of the human sexual response and developed techniques employed in sex therapy.

— Box 3 —

Sex on campus: the persisting double standard

In the early 1960s a female student at a college in Massachusetts became sick at her boyfriend's apartment and stayed there overnight instead of returning to her dormitory. She was subject to disciplinary action for this behavior, even though she had slept in a separate bed. At about the same time there was national publicity about a Barnard College student who shared an apartment with her boyfriend while officially occupying a dormitory room. She, too, was punished for her offense. Throughout the country the penalties for sexual improprieties on college campuses were severe, including expulsion. Elaborate security measures were devised to keep the sexes divided. Men's and women's dormitories were often built far apart to emphasize the separation of the sexes (Katz and Cronin, 1980).

In the mid-1960s, college students began to protest these re-strictions on their personal lives and gradually persuaded college administrations to relax the rules. When Stanford opened its first coresidential dormitory in 1966, it was a controversial experiment. But the idea caught on and soon over half of American campuses offered coresidential living.

Along with these official relaxations of the rules came striking changes in sexual attitudes and behavior. In the 1950s an estimated 25 percent of unmarried college women and 55 percent of unmarried college men had had sexual intercourse (Hopkins, 1977). By the late 1970s, the estimated figures had been upped to two-thirds of women and three-fourths of men. Noting that today nearly as many college women as men are nonvirgins, Joseph Katz and Denise Cronin go so far as to conclude that "the double standard has clearly become a thing of the past" (page 45).

But this judgment is premature. Even though more women are having sex than before, there remain fundamental differences between the orientations of the two sexes toward sexual behavior. Men are still expected to be the initiators of sexual activity, while women are still expected to play a more passive role and to be the ones to set the limits on sexual activity. In a study of college dating couples in the Boston area, Letitia Anne Peplau, Zick Rubin, and Charles Hill (1977) found that among couples who were having sex, three times as many students said that the boyfriend was more interested in sex than the girl-friend. And among couples who were not having sex, the women's background and attitudes were usually the major restraining force.

Other recent studies in Los Angeles and New York State echo the conclusion that men are expected to push for sex and women are expected to make sure that it doesn't happen too soon (McCormick, 1979; LaPlante, McCormick, and Brannigan, 1980). In addition, the link between sex and love may be more important for women than for men. As Peplau

by stressing that people can move toward self-actualization by doing the things they personally find enjoyable and fulfilling.

As a result of these new attitudes, sex became more pleasurable for many people during the 1970s than it had been in previous decades. Not only was there more premarital sex than there used to be, but there was more enjoyment of sex in marriage. According to one national survey, the average duration of sexual intercourse for married couples increased from two minutes to ten minutes, as couples began to think of sex less as an obligation and more as a pleasurable experience (Hunt, 1974). People also report using more variations in sexual foreplay, engaging in oral sex more often, and experimenting more with different positions for intercourse. Homosexuality, though not necessarily on the increase, has clearly come out of the closet (see Box 4).

Many aspects of the sexual revolution have been seen as welcome changes, but it has created new problems, as well. Although people's values about premarital sex range widely, one obviously negative aspect of the increase in premarital sex has been an increase in unwanted adolescent pregnancies. More than half of the 21 million

Coresidential dormitories were a controversial experiment in the mid-1960s. Now they are commonplace.

and her colleagues conclude, "Permissive sex attitudes and increased frequency of premarital intercourse have apparently not changed the basic script for sexual intercourse in dating couples" (page 108).

These continuing expectations can put strong pressures on both men and women. Women may fear that if they are sexually active and assertive they will seem to be "bad girls" or scare men off. And they are sometimes right, as illustrated by the report of one of the men in the Boston study: "I dated a girl once and—talk about the best way to damage a guy's ego—she pulls me into bed with her the first night, something you just can't imagine doing on a first date. . . . It was a really distasteful experience" (Peplau, Rubin, and Hill, 1977, page 106).

On the other hand, men may feel they are inadequate if they don't play a sexually active and assertive role. In a study of senior men at an Ivy League college, Mirra Komarovsky (1976) reported that for most of those who were still virgins, "chastity was a more or less disturbing personal problem." Mark, one of the men in the Boston study, was a virgin, but he implied to his male friends that he was sexually experienced in order to avoid their ridicule. "You tell somebody you're a virgin at 22," he commented, "and they don't believe you" (page 107).

Pressures like these to conform to the social expectations for one's sex make it clear that the "sexual revolution"—on campus or elsewhere—has not yet been fully liberating.

15- to 19-year-olds in the United States have sexual intercourse at least on occasion (Zelnik and Kantner, 1977) and no more than 20 percent use contraceptives regularly. The result is almost 700,000 unwanted teenage pregnancies a year. Of these, about 300,000 are ended by abortion and 100,000 by miscarriages, while 200,000 lead to out-of-wedlock births and 100,000 end in quick and often short-lived marriages (Byrne, 1977). One in six of the sexually active college women surveyed by Katz and Cronin (1980) reported having undergone an abortion at some time.

The sexual revolution has also created a need in many people to keep up with what they perceive as the new sexual standards. People are prone to believe that other people's sex lives are better than their own, and as a result they feel dissatisfied. In a 1976 survey, for example, 22 percent of the unmarried men and 21 percent of the unmarried women had never had sexual intercourse, yet only 1 percent and 2 percent respectively thought their peers were virgins (Shaver and Freedman, 1976). Nowadays many people think they're missing something sexually, even when they're really not. Sex therapists report that couples are beginning to come to them even though they

— Box 4 —

Homosexuality and homophobia

The prevalent attitude toward homosexuals in America has been strongly negative. As recently as 1970, two-thirds of Americans surveyed indicated that they regarded homosexuality as "very obscene and vulgar." In 1975, after *Time* magazine had run a cover story on homosexuality, the magazine received a flood of letters such as the following: "Disgusting, repulsive, lowbrow, nauseating. I'm no Victorian, but these individuals should crawl into a hole—and take *Time* with them" (Hyde, 1979). Many people believe that homosexuality is a sickness, and many others believe that it is immoral or perverse.

In fact, current research suggests that homosexuals are no "sicker" than heterosexuals and that gay people are not a dangerous or corrupting influence on society (Bell and Weinberg, 1978). Gay people are as diverse as straight people are, and they differ from heterosexuals only in their preference for sexual partners of the same sex rather than of the opposite sex. But the strongly negative attitudes toward homosexuals persist. These attitudes can

best be explained as a reflection of *homophobia*, an irrational fear or intolerance of gay people (Morin and Garfinkle, 1978).

Homophobia can be demonstrated in laboratory situations. In one study, college students were interviewed by a male or female experimenter about their attitudes toward homosexuality and other issues (Morin, Taylor, and Kielman, 1975). In one experimental condition, the experimenter wore a "Gay and Proud" button and was introduced as working for the Association of Gay Psychologists. In a second condition, the experimenter wore no button and was simply introduced as a grad student. It was found that subjects placed their chairs significantly further away from the experimenter identified as a homosexual than from the experimenter who was not so identified.

Many studies have suggested that heterosexual men tend to be more threatened by homosexuality than heterosexual women are. In the experiment just described, for example, male subjects showed much more aversion to a "homosexual" man than female students showed to a "homosexual" woman. Stephen Morin and Ellen Garfinkle (1978) suggest that heterosexual men fear homosexual men

because of their own need to preserve traditional sex roles. Heterosexual men often view gay men as being effeminate—as more delicate, passive, small, and yielding than heterosexual men (Karr, 1975). Men who are strongly homophobic also tend to suspect any man who exhibits "feminine" characteristics of being homosexual (Dunbar, Brown, and Amoroso, 1973). The heterosexual man's aversion to homosexuals—and his fear of being labeled homosexual himself—serves as a powerful force for him to remain in a traditionally masculine role—unemotional, tough, and assertive.

In the past decade, social attitudes toward homosexuality have begun to become more tolerant. Gay men and lesbians (homosexual women) themselves have been more likely to come "out of the closet" and acknowledge their sexual orientation openly, and gay people have banded together to fight for their civil rights. As a result of these efforts, many states and cities have passed laws that forbid discrimination against homosexuals in jobs and housing, and many large corporations have announced nondiscrimination policies. In addition, both the American Psychological Association and the American Psychiatric Associa-

don't have any sexual problems; they just want their sex lives to be "better." Thus, a couple may be dissatisfied because the woman is having "only" one orgasm during intercourse or because the man wants to have sex "only" three times a week (Tavris and Offir, 1977).

There is the danger, then, that the sexual revolution can give people new anxieties and insecurities, rather than reducing them. As Irene Frieze (1980) has put it: "Each sexual experience does not have to be record-breaking. The sexual revolution can free people sexually only when they see it for what it is—an expansion of the number of options for expressing themselves sexually—and not a mandate" (page 98).

As we saw in Box 3, the sexual revolution has not affected the two sexes in quite the same way. Men are still asked to play the role of sexual initiators, while women are expected to play a more passive

In recent years, increasing numbers of gay people have openly and proudly acknowledged their sexual orientation.

tion have explicitly recognized that homosexuality is not a sickness.

The increasing number of gay people who have "come out" has made it easier for other gay men and lesbians to acknowledge their sexual orientation to themselves and others, without shame or guilt. As one psychologist points out, "Ten or 15 years ago, homosexuality was just not discussed, and many people suffered because they simply did not know that there have always been people like themselves. Everything that has happened in the past few years has reduced the potential for that isolation" (*Time*, 1979, page 76).

The changes come slowly, and homophobia remains deeply ingrained in many people. In the long run, however, we can expect the increasing openness and self-acceptance of a vanguard of gay people to increase the level of tolerance in society as a whole. "Ten years ago, few people knew that they knew a gay person," one gay teacher points out. "Today, most kids grow up knowing that they know someone who is gay" (*Time*, 1979, page 76). Such contact between straight and gay people on a person-to-person level may be the best way to overcome the oppressive effects of homophobia.

role and to be sexual limit-setters. Thus, in the domain of sexuality, as in so many other spheres of life, differences between the roles of the two sexes persist. Over the past two decades, concerted efforts have been made to change these sex roles in order to achieve greater equality between women and men. These attempts are the focus of the Psychological Issue that follows this chapter.

SUMMARY

1. Social *stereotypes*—concepts about entire groups of people—characterize men as basically more aggressive, independent, dominant, active, competitive, and self-confident and women as more tactful, gentle, sensitive, emotional, neat, and quiet.

2. There is no good evidence that boys are more independent, ambitious, or achievement-oriented than girls or that girls are more nurturant, sociable, or suggestible than boys. It does appear to be true, however, that on the average boys are more aggressive than girls and that girls have greater verbal ability than boys and are more concerned about other people's feelings.

3. Psychological research tends to be biased toward men: male subjects are used twice as often as female subjects. In addition, men and women are typically used in different sorts of studies.

4. Although the basic psychological differences between the sexes are fewer and of lesser magnitude than has generally been assumed, sexual stereotypes continue to exist. One reason is that people tend to see what they expect to see (appropriate sex-role behavior). Another reason is that society offers different opportunities for men and women, channeling men into competitive occupations and women into nurturant roles.

5. Sex differences in aggression do seem to reflect a biological *predisposition* for males to behave more aggressively. This predisposition apparently results from the action of male hormones on the brain. Most psychologists agree, however, that culture plays a greater role than biological predispositions in shaping psychological differences between men and women.

6. *Transsexuals* are people who believe that they are trapped in a body of the wrong sex. Although sex-change surgery for transsexuals was initially greeted enthusiastically, it is now regarded with greater caution.

7. Our expectations about what men and women should do and what they should be like are called *sex roles*. Sex-role learning occurs through imitation of adults, parental rewarding and punishing of behaviors, and the child's motivation to be a member in good standing of his or her sex. Sex-role learning also occurs in schools and through the mass media, especially television.

8. The patterns of sexual response in men and women are remarkably similar. Masters and Johnson identified four stages of sexual response: the *excitement phase*, the *plateau phase*, the *orgasmic phase*, and the *resolution phase*.

9. Human sexual response depends greatly on psychological factors. This is apparent from the fact that fantasy can produce sexual arousal in both men and women and that few sexual dysfunctions can be traced to physical disorders.

10. In recent times sexual attitudes and behaviors have undergone massive changes. Freud helped establish the fact that sexual desires are natural, and Kinsey helped people realize that a wide variety of sexual behaviors are "normal." Nevertheless, there continues to be a double standard in sexuality, with men expected to be the initiators of sexual activity and women expected to play a more passive role.

11. Although the "sexual revolution" has brought benefits to many people, it has also brought an increase in teenage pregnancies and new kinds of anxieties about sexual performance.

12. The prevalent attitude of heterosexuals toward homosexuals has been strongly negative, reflecting an attitude of *homophobia*. During the past decade, however, social attitudes toward homosexuals have begun to become more tolerant, as more gay people themselves have openly acknowledged and accepted their sexual orientation.

CHANGING SEX ROLES

In the past decade there have been dramatic changes in men's and women's roles in the spheres of work and family. More and more women are entering traditionally male professions, such as medicine, law, and politics, while men are beginning to enter some traditionally female jobs, becoming airline attendants, telephone operators, and nurses. Furthermore, men are playing a larger role in caring for young children.

These changes reflect the accomplishments of the women's movement—and, to a lesser extent, the men's movement—that became active in the 1960s and 1970s. The ultimate goal of these movements is to bring about basic changes in society's sex roles—the views that are held of what women and men should be like and what behaviors each sex should engage in.

THE LEGACY OF SEXISM
Changing sex roles is not easy. The attempt to change people's views about men and women flies in the face of a long history of *sexism*, in which the sexes were viewed not only as different but also as inherently unequal. Male supremacy

has been a dominant theme of societies throughout the world. Men have had a virtual monopoly on power and prestige, holding most positions of political and religious leadership and enjoying the respect that goes with these positions. Within the family, the father is usually considered the "boss," despite the fact that the mother takes care of the house and the children.

The attempt to change sex roles flies in the face of a long history of sexism.

The notion that men are superior to women is part of the ideology of the world's major religions. Consider the following passage, for example, from the New Testament:

For a man . . . is the image and glory of God; but the woman is the glory of the man. For the man is not of the woman, but the woman of the man. Neither was the man created for the woman, but the woman for the man. . . . Let your

women keep silence in the churches; for it is not permitted unto them to speak, but they are commanded to be under obedience, as also saith the law. And if they will learn anything, let them ask their husbands at home; for it is a shame for women to speak in the church. (1 Cor. 11:14)

Nowadays, most people reject such blatant statements of male supremacy and see them as reflecting the traditions of another age. Nevertheless, there are still signs of this implicit belief in our culture. Even at the start of the 1980s the official code of Georgia stated, "The husband is the head of the family, and the wife is subject to him; her legal civil existence is merged in the husband." The idea of male supremacy is also revealed in humor. A survey of the jokes in *Reader's Digest* in the 1940s, 1950s, and 1960s found six times as many antifemale jokes as antimale ones (Zimbardo and Meadow, 1976). Most typically, women were depicted as stupid or foolish. For example: "Sweet young thing to husband: 'Of course I know what's going on in the world. I just don't understand any of it, that's all.' "

The assumption of male supremacy was revealed in a study conducted by Philip Goldberg (1968). He asked college students to read a number of professional articles from six different fields. The articles were assembled in two sets of booklets, so that the same article was attributed to a male author ("John T. McKay") in some booklets and to a female author ("Joan T. McKay") in others. The students were then asked to rate the articles for value, competence, and writing style. Goldberg found that the same article was given significantly lower ratings when it was supposedly written by a woman than when it was supposedly written by a man. The subjects downgraded "female-authored" articles not only in such traditionally male-dominated fields as law and city planning, but even in such female-dominated fields as dietetics and elementary education.

Male superiority is a "nonconscious ideology."

Sandra and Daryl Bem (1970) suggest that male superiority has become a "nonconscious ideology"—a set of assumptions that we do not specifically acknowledge, even to ourselves, but that nevertheless has a great impact on our behavior. One of the goals of the women's and men's movements has been to make this "nonconscious ideology" more conscious. Such consciousness-raising is an important prerequisite for change.

THE WOMEN'S MOVEMENT

The women's movement surfaced in the 1960s as a resurgence of earlier feminist movements in America. The resurgence was spurred by the increasing numbers of women in the work force who realized they were being discriminated against. In addition, many women in the civil rights movement came to the recognition that they themselves were being treated in discriminatory ways. An important event in the birth of the movement was the publication of Betty Friedan's book *The Feminine Mystique* in 1963. She tried to explain why American housewives, despite being well housed and well fed, were distressed and unhappy.

Since the 1960s the goals of the women's movement have included equal pay for equal work, an end to job discrimination by sex, adequate child-care programs, an equal sharing of family responsibilities, the right to abortion, an end to all forms of sexual exploitation, and most fundamentally, restructuring of women's roles. Much of the social and legal history of the 1970s is a history of the gains of the women's movement. For example (from a chronology assembled by Sweet, 1979):

1971: The University of Michigan becomes the first university to incorporate an affirmative action plan for the hiring and promotion of women.
1973: The Supreme Court outlaws sex-segregated classified advertisements for employment.
1974: The national Little League agrees to admit girls to teams.
1977: The American Telephone and Telegraph Company announces that it is ready to allow dual listings of married couples (both the husband's and wife's names) in phone directories.
1978: More women than men enter college for the first time in United States history.
1979: More than 290 women hold seats on the boards of major corporations, almost double the number in 1975. And the National Weather Service starts naming storms for men as well as for women.

Perhaps the most significant gains for women have come in the area of employment. Between 1970 and 1978 the number of female medical students almost tripled, from about 9 percent of those enrolled in 1970 to 24 percent of those enrolled in 1978. The number of women law students also tripled—to 30 percent of the total—in only six years, from 1972 to 1978.

For every dollar that men make, women make only 57 cents.

Women received 27 percent of all doctoral degrees in 1978, up 50 percent in only five years. The number of women holding elective offices doubled between 1969 and 1975 and then almost doubled again between 1975 and 1979. All told, about 50 percent of all women worked outside the home in 1980, up from about 20 percent at the turn of the century and 43 percent in 1970. In the late 1970s, women were for the first time trained as pilots by the Air Force, assigned as permanent shipboard crew members by the Navy, and selected to be astronauts. And the U.S. Labor Department issued regulations to increase the number of women in construction jobs.

Despite all this progress, the world of work has by no means become sex blind. Men continue to hold high-status jobs in much greater numbers than women and continue to be paid much more—for every dollar that men make, women make only 57 cents.

In recent years, many women have entered previously "male" occupations.

A major part of the problem is that jobs that are held predominantly by women are relegated to lower status—and lower pay—because society downgrades women's work. When significant numbers of men enter a formerly "female" occupation, salaries are likely to rise. Gloria Steinem (1979), long a leader of the women's movement, concludes:

We might describe the '70s as the decade in which we advanced half the battle. We've learned that women can and should do "men's jobs," for instance, and we've won the principle (if not the fact) of getting equal pay. But we haven't yet established the principle (much less the fact) that men can and should do "women's jobs": that homemaking and child rearing are as much a man's responsibility, too, and that those jobs in which women are concentrated outside the home would probably be better paid if more men became secretaries, file clerks, and nurses, too. (Page 71)

In the first edition of this text, the word man was used to refer to all human beings.

While women are still striving to make further gains in the area of employment, the women's movement has had an impact on other aspects of American society, such as the media and education. School textbooks, for example, have been scrutinized for their presentation of sex-role stereotyping and have been revised to reduce their sexist bias. In the first edition of this text, published in 1974, the major sections had such titles as "Of Mind and Man," "Thinking Man," and "Relating Man." We now recognize, however,

that it is misleading to use the word "man" to refer to all human beings. This usage makes it seem as though males are really psychology's central concern. In the subsequent editions we have switched to nonsexist titles and we have avoided using only the personal noun "he" to refer to people in general.

Not all women or men are in favor of the changes that have been brought about by the drive for women's equality. The strong opposition to the Equal Rights Amendment to the U.S. Constitution in the late 1970s and early 1980s reflects the feeling of many Americans that the attempt to change sex roles may be going too far and, in the process, may be jeopardizing aspects of traditional sex differences that are positively valued. Nevertheless, by the end of the 1970s a majority of the American public had come to favor greater equality for the sexes in most spheres of life (Klemesrud, 1980).

MEN'S LIBERATION

If women are to take on an equal role in the world of work, it is clear that men will have to take on an equal role in homemaking and child rearing. But there is great resistance to such changes in the male role. No country in the world has ever been fully successful in getting men and women to share domestic work equally (Tavris and Offir, 1977). Taking care of young children—and, more generally, being tender and nurturant—have not been regarded as manly.

Within the past decade, however, more and more men have decided that they themselves want to change their roles—not primarily in order to give more power to women, but because they believe that the male role has been as limiting and stifling, in its own way, as the female role has been. As part of their dominant role, men

have learned to place tremendous emphasis on achievement and competition. Men are taught to put women in weak, dependent roles, while remaining tough and independent themselves. Men are taught that a "real" man never shows weakness, never cries, never lets his emotions show. One group of men's liberationists, the Berkeley Men's Group, has expressed their situation and goals as follows:

"We, as men, want to take back our full humanity."

We, as men, want to take back our full humanity. We no longer want to strain and compete to live up to an impossible oppressive masculine image—strong, silent, cool, handsome, unemotional, successful, master of women, leader of men, wealthy, brilliant, athletic, and 'heavy'. . . . We are oppressed by conditioning which makes us only half-human. This conditioning serves to create a mutual dependence of male (abstract, aggressive, strong, unemotional) and female (nurturing, passive, weak, emotional) roles. We are oppressed by this dependence on women for support, nurturing, love, and warm feelings. We want to love, nurture, and support ourselves and other men, as well as women. (Berkeley Men's Center, 1974)

The men's liberation movement is especially concerned with helping men to relate to one another in a less competitive way. Competition is a central theme in "learning to be a man." Boys are taught to play to win on the sports field. As the famous football coach Vince Lombardi is supposed to have said, "Winning isn't the main thing—it's the only thing." This ethic can place tremendous pressure on boys, especially those who are not athletically inclined. One man vividly recalled, years later, a father-and-son softball game that took place when he was a freshman in high school:

I was the only person on both teams, the fathers and the sons, not to get a hit. I struck out every time. I don't think I have ever felt so ashamed of myself as I felt then, or felt that anyone else was so ashamed of me as my father was then. In the picnic that followed my father and I avoided each other completely. Driving home with him was excruciating. . . . I had failed the test. No matter how else we related to each other, my father and I had to go through a male sex role ordeal that would leave us feeling horrible about each other and ourselves. Why? (Pleck, 1974)

Men's liberationists believe that competitive relationships between men are something that is "laid on" by the masculine mystique in our society and are something that must be overcome.

In recent years more and more men have become concerned about their role as parents and have taken on greater responsibility in child rearing. In spite of myths about the "maternal instinct," there is no evidence that women are by nature more nurturant than men or that they have the capacity to form stronger bonds with infants. Indeed, when they are given the opportunity to do so, fathers relate just as closely to their newborn infants as mothers do (Parke and O'Leary, 1975).

One sign of the growing recognition that fathers have needs and rights to participate in the care of their children is that more and more employers are granting paternity leave to fathers who wish to care for new infants and are altering work schedules to enable fathers to play a greater role in child rearing (Fein, 1978).

Fatherhood has also been getting increased recognition in the less happy domain of divorce proceedings. In the past, child custody was almost always granted to the mother, often on the assumption that she is "naturally" better suited to be a parent. Recently, however, increasing numbers of men have challenged this assumption and have successfully peti-

Fathers are becoming more willing to take on major responsibilities in child rearing. In the process, men are learning that they can be nurturant, warm, and gentle without suffering a loss of "masculinity."

tioned for custody. In the District of Columbia, for example, a judge gave one couple's children to the father, a geographer, and ordered the mother, a chemist, to pay $200 a month in child support. The judge said the father had a

The judge ruled that the father would better fulfill "the mothering function."

"warm, affectionate, caring kind of relationship" with the children, and concluded that he would better fulfill "the mothering function" (Edmiston, 1975).

TOWARD ANDROGYNY?

Some psychologists believe that the best way to change sex roles is to change the basic personality traits of women and men. Although some people are worried that such personality changes would produce confusion about sexual identity, researchers point out that virtually all girls and boys learn without much trouble which sex they belong to, and the extensive sex-role training that they receive is not necessary to develop a stable sexual identity (Pleck, 1975). Psychologists also point out that considerable changes in sex roles could be accomplished by changing our values and expectations without doing violence to our biological nature (Maccoby and Jacklin, 1974).

Studies have found that the healthiest people are not those who are highly "masculine" males or highly "feminine" females but rather individuals who tend to incorporate some of the traits traditionally associated with the opposite sex—that is, men who can be warm and expressive and women

who can be strong and assertive (Bem, 1972, 1975). Sandra Bem has called the ability to combine "masculine" and "feminine" traits *psychological androgyny*. (The word *androgyny* is derived by combining the Greek words for "man" and "woman.") Bem measured androgyny by asking students how often various adjectives were descriptive of themselves. Some of the adjectives were traditionally masculine ("ambitious," "self-reliant," "independent") and some were traditionally feminine ("affectionate," "gentle," "sensitive"). Subjects were categorized as androgynous if they indicated that they were about equally well described by masculine and feminine traits. Bem found that androgynous students of both sexes behaved more effectively in a variety of laboratory situations than students who were highly masculine or highly feminine.

The healthiest people tend to incorporate traits associated with the opposite sex.

Highly masculine men lacked the ability to express warmth and playfulness. They were not responsive to a kitten, to a baby, or to another student who was emotionally troubled. Highly feminine women showed concern for others, but they were not independent or assertive. They conformed more to people's opinions and found it difficult to turn down an unreasonable request. "In contrast," Bem writes, "the androgynous men and women . . . could be independent and assertive when they needed to be, and warm and responsive in appropriate situations" (1975, page 62). Instead of having to defend

against behavior that might seem inappropriate or inconsistent for their sex, they were able to behave in a more flexible and more fully human manner.

Is androgyny the wave of the future? There is evidence that American parents are treating their sons and daughters more alike than they used to in certain areas; for example, they are encouraging girls more to participate in competitive sports and are having boys do more domestic tasks (Klemesrud, 1980). Should we encourage our children to develop both masculine and feminine traits and interests and look forward to a time when we transcend sex roles and "masculine" and "feminine" become outmoded notions? Many people believe that this is the way to go. Others are not so sure. If we do away with all the traditional differences between men and women, might we lose something in the process? These are questions that all of us are now being called upon to answer.

SUMMARY

1. The idea of male supremacy has been a dominant theme of societies throughout the world. There are still many signs of this sexist belief in our culture.
2. The women's movement has met with many successes in restructuring women's roles in the past two decades, especially in the sphere of employment.
3. More and more men are deciding that the traditional male role is limiting. They are trying to reduce their competitiveness and to devote more time to fathering.
4. People who combine both masculine and feminine characteristics in their personalities are termed androgynous. There is evidence that such people may behave more flexibly and effectively in a variety of situations.

Chapter 14
Social Relationships

Unless you've made a firm decision to spend the rest of your days sitting on top of a flagpole, your relationships with other people will undoubtedly remain among the most important parts of your life. From our earliest attachments to our parents to our later relationships with playmates, work associates, friends, and lovers, social relationships provide the most central satisfactions, as well as the most difficult challenges, of being human. In this chapter, we will focus on several facets of the psychology of social relationships. First we will examine the human need to form relationships with others. Then we will explore the ways in which we form impressions of other people, and the factors that lead us to like or dislike others. After that, we will turn to the thorny topic of human love relationships, including the links between love and sex. And finally, we will consider how and why relationships end.

NEEDING OTHERS

According to the popular song, "People who need people are the luckiest people in the world." If that's the case, then we can all consider ourselves to be lucky, because we all have a strong need for the companionship and support of other people.

The Need for Social Comparison

One of the main reasons that we seek the company of others is to be able to compare our own emotions and attitudes with those of other

460

WHEN YOU WANT TO BE ALONE

People who are fearful or anxious often seek others' company. But intense feelings often lead to the opposite reaction—a desire to be alone. Several days after President Kennedy's assassination in 1963, a nationwide survey of Americans' reactions to the tragedy was conducted (Sheatsley and Feldman, 1964). A majority of those surveyed reported that immediately after hearing that the President had been shot, they had felt a desire to talk to others. But 40 percent of the sample said that they had wanted to be alone at this time. Significantly, the desire for privacy was greatest among those groups of people who admired President Kennedy the most. The feelings that these Americans experienced may have been so strong and personal that they did not wish to share them with others.

people. In Chapter 9 we discussed the importance of such social comparison for children. It is also clear that people's political and social attitudes are strongly influenced by other people; no one acquires his attitudes in a social vacuum. More generally, Leon Festinger (1954) has pointed out that many of our life experiences would be thoroughly confusing and meaningless unless we had an opportunity to compare our own reactions with those of other people. Which situations should we fear and which should we feel comfortable in? When should we laugh, when should we cry, and when should we remain impassive? What are our own strengths and weaknesses? What standards of behavior should we teach our children? None of these questions can be answered by a person living in isolation. To answer them, we need to compare our own experiences and reactions with those of other people.

This need for *social comparison* often leads us to seek the company of others when we are afraid or upset. This tendency was demonstrated by Stanley Schachter (1959) in an experiment with college women. Half of the subjects (the high-fear group) were told that as part of an important scientific study, they would receive a series of extremely painful electric shocks. The other half of the subjects (the low-fear group) were told that they would experience mere "tingles" and that they would enjoy the experiment. Then the experimenter told the subjects that while he was setting up the equipment, they could choose to wait either in a room by themselves or in a room together with other subjects. Fully two-thirds of the high-fear subjects chose to wait with others, compared to only one-third of the low-fear subjects. Thus, the fearful subjects tended to seek company,

We often need to compare our situations and experiences with others who are similar to us.

just as people are likely to huddle together during power failures or other potentially frightening events. In a follow-up study, Schachter demonstrated that fearful subjects did not want to wait with just anybody, but only with other subjects who were in the same situation that they were in. "Misery doesn't love just any kind of company," Schachter observed, "only miserable company." And the reasons subjects gave for this preference reflected the need for social comparison. In fact, the subjects were probably not sure just how they should react and behave in this strange set of circumstances. Should they feel fear for their safety? Anger at the diabolical experimenter? Gratitude for being allowed to suffer for the sake of science? Should they submit bravely to their fate or mount a protest? The subjects wanted to affiliate with others in the same situation in order to find out.

What Relationships Provide

We are motivated not only to seek the company of others in general but to form close and enduring relationships with specific other people. Robert Weiss (1974) believes that each of us needs to form two different kinds of social relationships—*emotional attachments* to one other person (usually a lover or a spouse) and *social ties* to a network of friends. Each type of relationship provides its own special set of provisions. Emotional attachments provide a sense of comfort and security, and social ties provide a sense of group identity and integration. The adult need for an emotional attachment seems to develop from the infant's attachment to its parents. The infant feels secure and comfortable only when in the parent's presence and terrified

We need two kinds of social relationships: emotional attachments to one other person, and social ties to a network of friends.

when the parent leaves (see Chapter 9). As adults, we no longer require the constant physical presence of an attachment figure, but we still retain a strong need for an emotional attachment in order to feel secure. Social ties, usually to a group of friends of one's own age, become important in childhood and even more so in adolescence. Adolescents achieve a sense of belonging and of identity by affiliating with and comparing themselves to other members of their peer group. And this need for a network of friends with whom we can share activities and concerns persists into adulthood.

Being Lonely

When people lack either an emotional attachment or a social network, the outcome is likely to be the condition called *loneliness*—an experience of longing and of emptiness that one noted psychiatrist, Harry Stack Sullivan, has described as "so terrible that it practically baffles clear recall" (Sullivan, 1953, page 261). One does not have to be physically isolated in order to be lonely. Rather, loneliness stems from the lack of social relationships and of their provisions.

Robert Weiss (1973) has identified two kinds of loneliness. The loneliness of *emotional isolation* results from the loss or absence of an emotional attachment, and the loneliness of *social isolation* results from the loss or absence of social ties. Each of these conditions is likely to be extremely painful, including symptoms of restlessness and depression. Weiss has found, moreover, that one sort of relationship cannot readily substitute for another in alleviating loneliness. Thus a person suffering from the loss of a love relationship is likely to feel painfully lonely, even though she may have children at home or friends to spend time with. One divorced mother described her experience in the following terms:

OLD AND LONELY?

The popular conception that old people, as a group, are especially prone to loneliness is apparently a myth. In fact, surveys find that people in their sixties, seventies, and eighties report that they are less lonely than younger adults do. In particular, older widows and widowers seem to be better protected from loneliness than younger ones. It is possible that emotional attachments become less important in old age, as a result of a process of "disengagement" from society. Or, as Joseph Hartog speculates, "Maybe there are fewer lonely old people because they're dead." If a tendency to be lonely were in fact associated with a shorter life expectancy, as some researchers suspect, then old people who make it into the survey results are those "survivors" who are less likely to be lonely (Rubin, 1979b).

Your house is so noisy all day long, phones, people, kids, all kinds of action going on and come eight o'clock everybody's in bed, and there's this dead silence. Like the whole world has just come to an end. All of a sudden you get this feeling that you're completely alone, that there is no one else in the world. You look out the window, you walk back and forth from room to room, you watch television, and you're dead. (Weiss, 1973, page 136)

And people who have close emotional attachments may still feel great loneliness if they lack a network of friends. Weiss recounts the case of one woman who had a close marriage but who felt devastated when the couple moved to a new region where they had no friends: "Isolated in the new community, she listened hungrily to her husband's stories of meeting people during his work day and then was furious with envy. She was bored and miserable. Finally she and her husband moved into a suburb in which there were people they felt to be like themselves, where she could take a place for herself. Almost instantly her symptoms vanished" (Weiss, 1973, pages 152–153).

Being lonely is not the same thing as being alone. Although it is painful to be lonely, most people value periods of solitude. Especially in big cities, people are often overloaded with stimuli—including other people—to a point that can be physically and emotionally stressful. "The antidote," says Peter Suedfeld, "is solitude and stillness and time-out. Loneliness can hurt, but we have to admit that

Loneliness comes from a lack of emotional attachments and social ties.

aloneness can heal" (quoted by Rubin, 1979b). Unfortunately, Suedfeld points out, we have been conditioned to dread solitude. If we want to be alone, people may think there is something wrong with us. Such negative views of being alone can have the effect of poisoning the experience of solitude. That is, if we expect aloneness to be painful, it probably will be (Suedfeld, 1981). But in fact, surveys show that people who live alone by choice are no more likely to be lonely than people who live with others (Rubenstein and Shaver, 1981).

As Robert Weiss points out, to prevent loneliness it is less important to be in the physical presence of a spouse, sweetheart, or friend than to know that he will be there when needed. Loneliness seems to be especially prevalent among unmarried, widowed, and divorced people, but none of us is entirely immune to it. In one national survey of Americans, 26 percent of those interviewed reported that they had felt "very lonely or remote from other people" within the previous few weeks (Bradburn, 1969). Far from being a sign of weakness, loneliness is a manifestation of the basic need for social relationships—a need we all share. Although various activities can help us to cope with our loneliness, the only real cure seems to be the establishment of relationships that will provide the resources that we so badly need. Our need for social relationships can also be a factor in promoting conformity, as discussed in Box 1.

PERCEIVING OTHERS

You arrive in biology class on the first day of the term, and a bearded man wearing a rumpled suit stands up in front of the class and begins telling jokes about the sex life of planaria. On the cafeteria line at lunchtime you find yourself standing behind a petite woman with

We often make inferences about people's personalities from their appearance. For example, people who wear glasses may be assumed studious or intellectual.

— Box 1 —

Conformity

To most of us, *conformity* is a dirty word suggesting robotlike acceptance of the attitudes and actions of others. Buckling under to group pressure suggests that we are too weak to think for ourselves. Our heroes are likely to be the nonconformists of the world who march to the sound of a different drummer.

At the same time, however, we recognize that conformity to the norms of our groups and culture is the price of living in social groups without anarchy and chaos. We conform to common standards of expression, behavior, and belief because they make our day-to-day interaction smoother and more predictable. In our culture, for example, a nod means "yes" and a shake of the head means "no"; in India, the expressions are reversed. Within either culture, a "nonconformist" who chose to ignore these conventions would not be much of a hero at all. And we conform to certain beliefs—from the notion that the earth is round to the tenet that all people should have equal rights—because they provide a common basis for life in society. The issue, then, is not *whether* to conform or to remain independent, but *when* to conform and when to hold out for an unpopular position.

Solomon Asch (1951) conducted an experiment that dramatically illustrated the dilemma of whether or not to conform to group pressures. Asch assembled groups of eight subjects to participate in a study of visual judgment. The subjects sat around a table and judged the length of various lines. But only one member of each group was a genuine subject. All the others were Asch's confederates, and on prearranged trials they reported ridiculously incorrect judgments. In a case such as that in Figure 14.1, the confederates each reported confidently that Line 1 was most similar in length to the comparison line on the left.

These events put the real subject, who was one of the last to call out his decision, in a difficult situation. Should he report his real judgment, even though it would make him look silly in the eyes of other group members, or

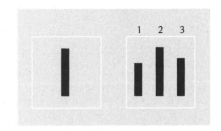

FIGURE 14.1
Example of stimulus used in Asch's experiment. Which of the three lines matches the line on the left?

should he go along with the crowd? The situation was an extremely uncomfortable one for many of Asch's subjects, and different subjects resolved the dilemma in different ways: some of the subjects never conformed, while others conformed almost all of the time. Overall, subjects conformed to the false group consensus on 32 percent of the trials.

In some cases, subjects' confidence was genuinely shaken by the reports of the unanimous majority. One subject who went along with the group on almost every trial explained afterward, "If they had been doubtful I probably would have changed, but they an-

long dark hair who keeps looking around the room furtively as if she were a foreign spy. In the afternoon you go to the library and see someone whom you recognize from the newspaper as the star tackle on the football team and are surprised to discover that he is immersed in a book of Emily Dickinson's poetry. In each of these cases, you inevitably begin to ask yourself questions: What sort of a person is this? Why is this person behaving in these particular ways? Is this the sort of person I would like to get to know better? We are constantly forming impressions of other people, both out of sheer curiosity and because such impressions have a large impact on the way we relate to others. This process of forming inferences about other people is analogous to the way we come to perceive the physical environment (Chapter 4), and as a result it is called *person perception*.

Physical Appearance

A person's size, shape, color, and manner of dress are all likely to affect the inferences we make about the person's personality. These

"I DON'T LIKE THE WAY HE TALKS"

We form impressions about people not only from the way they look but also from the way they talk. Former baseball pitcher Jim Bouton (1971) made the following observation in his diary of a major league season: "I'm not sure I'm going to like Don Mincher. It's prejudice, I know, but everytime I hear a Southern accent I think: Stupid. . . . It's like Lenny Bruce saying he could never associate a nuclear scientist with a Southern accent" (page 52). Each of us brings our own prejudices to our encounters with other people, but we're not always as ready as Bouton to admit them.

swered with such confidence." Most of the subjects who went along with the majority admitted later that they really didn't believe that the majority was correct, but they were afraid of seeming foolish in the eyes of their fellow students. Similar effects can take place outside the laboratory. In jury deliberations, for example, a juror who finds herself to be a lone dissenter on the initial ballot will find it extremely difficult to hold out for her point of view. On the other hand, if there is at least one additional dissenter to provide support for one's minority opinion, conformity is drastically reduced. Asch found that when just one of the confederates in his groups was instructed to give the right answers instead of going along with the majority, the amount of conformity declined sharply from 32 percent to 5 percent.

Social psychologist Irving Janis (1972) has identified a particularly dangerous form of conformity that he calls *groupthink*. Groupthink refers to the tendency for members of a policy-making group to suppress all individual doubts and

In Asch's experiment, several subjects were asked by the experimenter (right) *to compare the length of lines* (as in Figure 14.1). *Six of the subjects have been instructed ahead of time to give unanimously wrong answers. The seventh* (sixth from the left) *has merely been told that it is an experiment in perception.*

dissent, creating an illusion of unanimity. Both in President Kennedy's inner circle of advisers who gave the go-ahead to the ill-fated Bay of Pigs invasion of Cuba and in the council who advised President Johnson to escalate the Vietnam war, critical judgment seems to have been suspended in favor of shared illusions. More recently, Janis (1980) has speculated that groupthink may have contributed to the decision by President Carter and his

advisers to attempt a poorly conceived rescue mission of U.S. hostages in Iran.

Especially in a group that has high morale, no individual wants to be the one to bust the balloon by raising doubts or reservations. And the group as a whole acts to suppress such expression of doubts. Having suppressed all dissent, the group feels invulnerable, that nothing can go wrong—and, as a result, it is likely to make dangerous, ill-considered decisions.

impressions often reflect the operation of physical stereotypes, similar to the racial stereotypes that we will examine in the Psychological Issue that follows this chapter. We mentally place a person in the category of those who have a particular physical characteristic, and we then infer that the person resembles other members of that category in other respects, as well. Redheads may be assumed to be hot-tempered, people who wear glasses to be studious, fat people to be jolly. We also have preconceived notions about what physically attractive and unattractive people are apt to be like (see the Update on "The Social Psychology of Appearance"). Whether or not these stereotypes have any basis to them, they often organize our initial impressions of a person.

Reputations

We often begin to form impressions of people even before we meet them. This is because people are likely to be preceded by their reputations. Students learn what to expect from their professor by talking to students who took the same course the previous year. And before going out on a blind date, we are usually given a good deal of information about what our date will be like. In each case, the person's reputation is likely to have an impact on the way she is later perceived.

Harold Kelley (1950) conducted an experiment that demonstrated how a person's reputation can affect the way he is perceived. Kelley arranged to have students told that their class would be taken over by a new instructor, whom they would be asked to evaluate at the end of the period. Before the instructor arrived, the students were given a brief description of him to read. Half of the students were told that the instructor was a 26-year-old graduate student who was considered to be "a rather warm person, industrious, critical, practical, and determined." The other half of the students received precisely the same information, except that the adjective "warm" was replaced with "cold." This difference of a single word proved to have a large impact on the students' reactions to the instructor. After the instructor had led the class in a 20-minute discussion, the students who had been told that he was "warm" rated him as more considerate, sociable, good-natured, and humorous than did the students who had been told that he was "cold." The instructor's reputation also affected students' willingness to interact with him: 56 percent of the "warm" subjects took part in the class discussion, compared to only 32 percent of the "cold" subjects.

It seems that people's reputations, just like stereotypes based on physical appearance or group membership, provide a context within which we then interpret their behavior. For example, if a woman is told in advance that her blind date is extremely witty, she will be primed to categorize his remarks as witty ones. If the same date were billed as solemn and humorless, the same "witty" remarks might well fall flat. This is the secret of many comedians. Since they have the reputation of being uproariously funny, people are predisposed to laugh at practically everything they say.

Attribution Processes

In forming impressions of people, our primary goal is to make inferences about a person's underlying traits or dispositions on the basis of his observable actions. Such inferences are important because they allow us to predict how the person is likely to behave in the future. This inference process is not always an easy one, however. Suppose that you observe a person donating blood as part of the annual Red Cross drive. Do you infer that she is an unusually altruistic person who decided to give blood because of her commitment to helping others? And, as a result, can we expect her to behave altruistically in the future? Perhaps. But what if you also knew that intense pressure had been put on all of the residents of her dormitory to give blood, and that the names of all those who refused to do so were to be posted publicly? In that case, it would be more difficult to infer anything about the woman's altruism from her behavior. Instead, her behavior might simply reflect conformity to group pressure. We are constantly confronted with dilemmas of this sort as we form impres-

A PLEASANT SCENT

The way we smell can have a powerful effect on the impressions that others form about us, a fact that is capitalized on by both deodorant manufacturers (who urge us to cover up "bad" smells) and perfume merchandisers (who encourage us to create "good" smells). But the effects of a pleasant scent on impressions can be complicated. In one recent experiment, male undergraduates met and chatted with a young woman who either wore perfume or did not and who was dressed either informally (in jeans and sweatshirt) or more formally (in a blouse, skirt, and hose). The pleasant scent led the men to view the woman more positively when she was dressed informally but more negatively when she was dressed formally. They apparently saw her as aloof and conceited when she was both dressed up *and* wearing perfume (Baron, 1981).

sions of people. In particular, we must try to determine whether a person's behavior reflects an underlying disposition of that person or whether it is primarily a consequence of the situation in which the person was placed. The ways in which we try to sort out the causes of people's behavior are called *attribution processes*.

In recent years, attribution processes have been the topic of a large outpouring of social-psychological research (Schneider, Hastorf, and Ellsworth, 1979). One of the central conclusions of this research is that people have a tendency to overestimate the degree to which other people's behavior is caused by their individual traits or dispositions and to underestimate the extent to which it is caused by situational factors. Even when we *know* that there are strong situational pressures affecting a person's behavior, we are still likely to overestimate the role of personal dispositions. In one study (Jones and Harris, 1967), students read statements that they were told had been written by a college debater who had to argue in favor of an assigned position. Even though the students knew that the debater had no choice in deciding which position to argue, they still tended to conclude that he privately supported the position that he was arguing for.

This tendency to overestimate the role of personal dispositions and to underestimate the role of situational constraints affecting people's behavior is so pervasive that it has been called the *fundamental attributional error* (Ross, 1977). Another example of this tendency was provided by Gustav Ichheiser:

> We are passing by the army barracks and see how a sergeant is handling his subordinates. He barks his commands, snaps at any attempted questions on the part of his men, listens to no excuses or explanations, and is downright rude. Now, confronted with this type of behavior, we are not, as a rule, inclined to say . . ., "This man is performing certain functions defined by the context of military regulations and standards. . . ." Rather, we tend to [say] . . . something like this: "The man is rude," or "The man has such-and-such personality characteristics which make him behave in this way." (Ichheiser, 1949, page 27)

One of the reasons for this fundamental attributional error is that behaviors themselves, such as the debater's speech or the sergeant's commands, tend to grab more of our attention than do the contexts of the behaviors, such as the fact that the debater was assigned his position or that the sergeant was playing an expected role. As a result, the behavior itself is weighted more heavily in our attributions. (Recall, in this regard, our discussion in Chapter 4 of the role of attention in our perception of our physical environment.) In addition, we typically observe people's behavior in only a limited range of situations. If we had the chance to observe the sergeant at home, playing gently with his children, we would be more likely to appreciate the impact of situational constraints on his behavior.

In forming impressions of people, finally, we rely not only on their overt actions and statements but also on subtler nonverbal clues, as discussed in Box 2.

— *Box 2* —

Reading nonverbal clues

In forming impressions of people—what they are like, what they are feeling, and what their behavior really means—we must take into account not only their overt actions and statements but also subtler nonverbal messages.

Take the case of sarcasm. If someone says to us, "That's wonderful!" how do we decide whether the remark is sincere or sarcastic? As Dane Archer (1979) points out, there is a specific nonverbal "script" for sarcasm, just as there is a script for other messages. When Americans and Canadians perform the sarcasm script, they usually employ one or more nonverbal devices, such as raising both eyebrows in an exaggerated way, saying the sentence very slowly, or changing the tone of voice and placing unusual emphasis on the word "wonderful."

All of us learn to read nonverbal messages such as these. But some people seem to be better readers of nonverbal clues than others. To assess people's ability in this domain, Archer and Robin Akert (1977) have developed a measure called the Social Interpretation Task (SIT), in which subjects are presented with videotaped scenes of people interacting and then asked to make certain inferences about the actors. Two examples of these situations are presented in Figure 14.2.

What were your answers? Although the still photos provide

FIGURE 14.2
Scene 1 Which one of these two women is the mother of the baby?
a. The woman on the left.
b. The woman on the right.
c. Neither woman.

Scene 2 Are these two people:
a. Friends who have known each other for at least six months?
b. Acquaintances who have had several conversations?

much less information than the 30-second videotaped scenes that Archer and Akert use, they still provide an opportunity to exercise our nonverbal reading abilities. Interested in the correct answers? In Scene 1, the woman on the

right is the mother of the baby. In Scene 2, the two people are strangers. After watching the entire videotape, 64 percent of the subjects Archer and Akert studied got the right answer for Scene 1, and 62 percent were correct for Scene 2.

In many cases the videotape provides types of information that words could not. In Scene 1, for example, one videotape viewer explained that the woman on the left was holding the baby gingerly, "as if he were made of porcelain." The viewer correctly interpreted this as indicating unfamiliarity with the baby. Another viewer correctly concluded that the people in Scene 2 were strangers because "there was no eye contact on the part of the woman, while the man has an appraising gaze, watching her and the impression he's making." These clues suggested that while the two people were trying to hold a relaxed conversation, they were not succeeding.

Researchers have found that on the whole, women are better at reading nonverbal clues than men are (Hall, 1978). In addition, parents of small children have been found to be better readers of nonverbal cues than people without small children, perhaps because of the practice they get in reading the unspoken messages of their prelinguistic children (Rosenthal et al., 1979). Archer (1980) also believes that we can all train ourselves to be better readers of nonverbal clues by recognizing their importance and consciously paying greater attention to them.

LIKING OTHERS

Liking, perhaps even more than love, is what makes the world go round. On one series of surveys, the most common problem or wish listed by American high-school students was "[I] want people to like me more" (Remmers and Radler, 1958). And our patterns of liking and disliking determine in large measure which people we will spend time with and which people we will avoid. Psychologists have explored many factors that lead us to like particular other people. In this section we will explore two such factors—proximity and similarity. In both cases, as we will see, liking can be explained by a basic economic principle: We like people who can provide us with the greatest possible rewards at the least possible cost. Of course, these rewards and costs are not usually financial ones. Rather, they are the social rewards that we gain from interacting with particular others and the social costs of interactions that are difficult or unpleasant.

The Nearness of You

If you live in California and I live in Michigan, it is not very likely that we will become fast friends, or even get to know each other. But even at much closer range, the physical *proximity* of any two people has a direct impact on their likelihood of becoming friends. One study in a college dormitory found a striking tendency for students to like the person next door more than the person two doors away, to like that person more than the person three doors away, and so on (Priest and Sawyer, 1967). Another study found that people assigned to be roommates become friends far more often than one would expect simply on the basis of their other characteristics (Newcomb, 1961).

As you may already be thinking, physical proximity doesn't *always* foster liking. It is certainly common enough for people who are assigned to be roommates to end the year, if they stick it out for that long, as mortal enemies. Close and frequent contact can breed hostility, as well as attraction. Nevertheless, researchers have found that such contact more often leads to liking than to disliking. Contact with all sorts of people is likely to bring us certain social rewards, such as the opportunity to engage in joint activities or to compare our reactions and experiences. But with a roommate or someone else who lives close by, we can obtain these rewards without having to take the trouble of going far out of our way. Thus, physical proximity is likely

The closer people live to each other, the more likely they are to be friends.

to bring us rewards at low cost. And this interpersonal "profit" is translated into liking. It may sound crass, but that is the way liking often works—we like those who can bring us the biggest profit on the "interpersonal marketplace" (Rubin, 1973).

The same principle of proximity also applies to love and marriage. Studies by sociologists have documented that the closer a man and a woman live within a city, the more likely they are to marry one another (Katz and Hill, 1958). The tendency to be attracted to people who are close at hand makes perfect sense in terms of the profit motive of the interpersonal marketplace. If a suitable mate lives next door, there is no need for a man in search of a partner to scour the entire block. If she lives in the neighborhood, there is no need for him to spend time and money on the cross-town bus. "When I'm not near the girl I love," as the song goes, "I love the girl I'm near."

Birds of a Feather

Once we have had an opportunity to meet another person, the single factor that plays the largest role in determining whether we will like each other is how *similar* we are. The principle that "Birds of a feather flock together" is not a new discovery of social psychologists. They were beaten to the punch by Aristotle many centuries ago:

And they are friends who have come to regard the same things as good and the same things as evil, they who are friends of the same people, and they who are enemies of the same people. . . . We like those who resemble us, and who are engaged in the same pursuits.

As Aristotle's statement suggests, we tend to choose friends who are similar to us in many different respects, including age, occupational status, educational level, and political preferences (Laumann, 1969). Similarities are important in our choice of husbands and

Similarity in age, background, and interests is a basic foundation for friendship.

wives, as well. Hundreds of statistical studies have found husbands and wives to be much more similar to each other than one would expect by chance, on characteristics ranging from height to intelligence (Rubin, 1973).

The most critical similarities, however, are similarities of people's beliefs and attitudes. In a famous study conducted at Bennington College in the 1930s, Theodore Newcomb (1943) found that many students adopted a liberal set of attitudes in order to gain the liking and acceptance of their classmates. In a later study, Newcomb provided a more direct demonstration of the influence of attitude similarity on liking. Newcomb (1961) rented a boarding house at the University of Michigan and provided one term's free room and board to students transferring to the university in exchange for their participation in his study of friendship formation. He discovered that as the term progressed, friendship patterns among the students were determined primarily by similarities of attitudes and values. For example, one group of friends consisted of five men who were all enrolled in the liberal arts college and who had liberal political views and strong intellectual and artistic interests. Another clique consisted of three veterans, all in the college of engineering, politically conservative, and with interests that were more "practical" than "theoretical."

Our tendency to like other people with similar attitudes has also been demonstrated in many experiments in which subjects are shown a questionnaire that was supposedly filled out by another person. The "other person's" responses are fabricated in such a way as to indicate a specific degree of agreement with the subjects' own attitudes about a variety of topics. Subsequently the subjects are asked to indicate how much they think they would like the person who filled out the questionnaire. The consistent result of such studies: The larger the proportion of items on which the "other person" agrees with the subject, the more the subject likes the other person (Byrne, 1971).

Why does similarity of attitudes have such a large impact on our likes and dislikes? Psychologists have suggested that it is rewarding to be agreed with for several reasons (Rubin, 1973):

Agreement may provide a basis for engaging in joint activities, whether it be attending a prayer meeting or taking over a university hall.

A person who agrees with you helps increase your confidence in your own opinion—and this, in turn, will bolster your self-esteem.

Most people are vain enough to believe that anyone who shares their views must be a sensible and praiseworthy individual, while anyone who does not must have his head on backward.

People who agree about things that matter to them generally find it easier to communicate with each other.

We often assume that people whose attitudes are similar to ours will like us—and, therefore, we tend to like them in turn.

TO ERR IS HUMAN

We usually like people who are intelligent, able, and competent. But most of us have misgivings about people who are *perfect*. In 1961, President John F. Kennedy made one of the worst blunders of his career when he approved the ill-fated Bay of Pigs invasion in Cuba. But strangely enough, a Gallup Poll taken right after the fiasco showed that Kennedy's popularity had increased rather than decreased. As Elliot Aronson (1969) suggests, once we know that a person has high ability, evidence of that person's fallibility is likely to make him seem more attractive. The failure of the Bay of Pigs invasion apparently proved to many Americans that their President wasn't perfect—and, as a result, they liked him more.

There are, to be sure, exceptions to the "birds of a feather" principle. We are sometimes attracted to people who are quite different from ourselves, especially if those people provide a fresh perspective that we would like to learn more about. Robert White provides an example of such a "friendship of opposites" between two teenage boys:

Ben, whose school experience had been so unstimulating that he never read a book beyond those assigned, discovered in Jamie a lively spirit of intellectual inquiry and an exciting knowledge of politics and history. Here was a whole world to which his friend opened the door and provided guidance. Jamie discovered in Ben a world previously closed to him, that of confident interaction with other people. Each admired the other, each copied the other, each used the other for practice. (White, 1976, page 337)

On balance, however, the principle of similarity plays a much larger role in attracting people to one another than does the lure of diversity. Diversity is valuable and enriching, and under certain conditions people actively seek it. But we also need to recognize without embarrassment that people with fundamentally different approaches to life are unlikely to become fast friends. For a human being to adapt to a rapidly changing world, he needs the companionship and support of others with whom he may sometimes disagree, but nevertheless feels a fundamental bond of likemindedness.

— Box 3

Should we study love?

As psychologists begin to investigate love, shouts of criticism are being voiced by those who believe that love is not a proper object of study. Perhaps the most vocal of these critics has been United States Senator William Proxmire of Wisconsin. In his role as chairman of the Senate committee that oversees appropriations to the National Science Foundation, Proxmire has habitually kept a sharp eye out for federally-funded projects that seem impractical or frivolous. When he discovered in 1975 that the National Science Foundation had awarded a grant to social psychologist Ellen Berscheid to study aspects of romantic love, Proxmire was en-

raged. He fired off a press release in which he called the project "the biggest waste of the taxpayer's money for the month of March." He went on to say that "I believe that 200 million Americans want to leave some things in life a mystery, and right at the top of the things we don't want to know about is why a man falls in love with a woman and vice versa."

Soon afterward Proxmire expanded his attack to include other programs of research on social relationships. "I think it is time the National Science Foundation put a stop to the Federal version of 'The Love Machine,'" Proxmire declared, "and rearrange its research priorities to address our scientific, not our erotic curiosity."

Many psychologists and other scientists felt that Senator

Senator William Proxmire believes that love should be left a mystery.

Proxmire's criticisms were cheap shots, phrased in such a way as to

LOVING OTHERS

Although psychologists have been studying liking for some time, they have been slower to grapple with the more delicate and complicated topic of love. In a presidential address to the American Psychological Association in the late 1950s, Harry Harlow described the situation as he saw it:

Love is a wondrous state, deep, tender, and reassuring. Because of its intimate and personal nature it is regarded by some as an improper topic for experimental research. But, whatever our personal feelings may be, our assigned mission as psychologists is to analyze all facets of human and animal behavior into their component variables. So far as love or affection is concerned, psychologists have failed in their mission. The little we know about love does not transcend simple observation and the little we write about it has been written better by poets and novelists. (Harlow, 1958, page 673).

Some people *still* view love as an improper topic for research, including at least one United States senator (see Box 3). But in the decades since Harlow made his statement, and especially in the past ten years, many psychologists have begun to study love systematically. One psychological approach is that taken by Harlow himself, who investigated mother-infant attachments (or "love") in monkeys (see Chapter 9). There is, of course, quite a jump from mother-infant

gain publicity rather than to shed light on the underlying issues. Nevertheless, Proxmire's complaint did focus attention on serious issues about research on social relationships. Is the senator right when he claims that love is one of those phenomena that should be left shrouded in mystery, rather than poked at by inquisitive psychologists? And should taxpayers' money be invested in such efforts?

Many people agree wholeheartedly with Senator Proxmire's indictment of research on love. One psychologist went so far as to declare that "The scientist in even attempting to interject love into a laboratory situation is by the very nature of the proposition dehumanizing the state we call love" (Karmel, 1970). Many newspaper

columnists and editorialists jumped on Proxmire's bandwagon, echoing his conclusion that trying to understand love is a ridiculous and money-wasting enterprise.

But many other people disagree vehemently with Proxmire's point of view, and the authors of this book are among them. Social relationships are extremely complicated phenomena, and psychologists have no illusions that they will ever unlock all of love's mysteries. But social relationships are also the source of great confusion and distress for many people. As we will see in the Psychological Issue that follows, for example, divorce rates in America have been skyrocketing, leaving a tremendous amount of human suffering in their wake. If further research of the sort that is reported

in this chapter can make even a small contribution to people's understanding of their relationships with others, then the relatively small amount of money expended for such research will be more than justified.

Each of you will have to draw your own conclusion about this controversy. But speaking for ourselves, we agree wholeheartedly with a response to Senator Proxmire that was offered by *New York Times* columnist James Reston (1975): "If the sociologists and psychologists can get even a suggestion of the answer to our patterns of romantic love, marriage, disillusion, divorce—and the children left behind—it could be the best investment of Federal money since Mr. Jefferson made the Louisiana Purchase."

love in monkeys to adult love relationships in human beings. But Harlow's research helped to demonstrate that one aspect of love is the need for close contact with another member of one's species, similar to what Robert Weiss calls an emotional attachment.

In Chapter 7 we discussed another approach to love, in the context of Stanley Schachter's labeling theory of emotion. From this perspective, love can be viewed as a label that people learn to place on their own physiological arousal. Most of the time, however, love does not involve intense physical symptoms. Instead, love can be viewed as a particular sort of attitude that one person has toward another person.

Measuring Love

Through the course of history love has been defined in countless ways, as everything from "a spirit all compact of fire" (by Shakespeare) to "a state of perceptual anesthesia" (by H. L. Mencken) to "not ever having to say you're sorry" (by Erich Segal). Not wishing to be outdone by these people of letters, Zick Rubin (1970) made an initial attempt to define and measure this attitude. On the basis of a questionnaire administered to several hundred dating couples at the University of Michigan, Rubin developed an attitude measure that he called a love scale. On this scale, respondents are asked to indicate how much they agree or disagree with a series of statements about their feelings toward another person, usually their boyfriend or girlfriend (see Figure 14.3). As defined by Rubin's scale, love consists of three components, *attachment, caring,* and *intimacy:*

> *Attachment* refers to a person's need for the physical presence and emotional support of the other person. It corresponds to the sort of love studied by Harlow in infant monkeys and to the emotional attachment discussed by Weiss.
> *Caring* refers to a person's feelings of concern and responsibility for another person. Caring corresponds to Erich

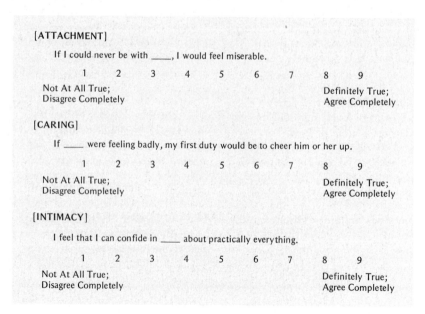

[ATTACHMENT]

If I could never be with _____, I would feel miserable.

    1   2   3   4   5   6   7   8   9

Not At All True;   Definitely True;
Disagree Completely   Agree Completely

[CARING]

If _____ were feeling badly, my first duty would be to cheer him or her up.

    1   2   3   4   5   6   7   8   9

Not At All True;   Definitely True;
Disagree Completely   Agree Completely

[INTIMACY]

I feel that I can confide in _____ about practically everything.

    1   2   3   4   5   6   7   8   9

Not At All True;   Definitely True;
Disagree Completely   Agree Completely

FIGURE 14.3
Sample items from Rubin's love scale.

Fromm's (1956) definition of love as "the active concern for the life and growth of that which we love."

Intimacy refers to a person's desire for close and confidential communication with another person. When we love someone, we want to share certain of our thoughts and feelings with that person more fully than with anyone else.

Rubin views love as an attitude held by one person toward another that includes all three of these components. Skeptics may point out, of course, that a paper-and-pencil love scale does not really measure how much people love each other but simply how much they *say* they love each other. But Rubin (1970) also obtained behavioral evidence for the love scale's validity. In one study, boyfriends' and girlfriends' scores on the love scale were checked out against the well-known folk wisdom that lovers spend a great deal of time staring into each other's eyes. Couples were observed through a one-way mirror in the psychological laboratory while they were waiting for an experiment to begin. These surreptitious observations confirmed that "strong lovers" (couples whose members received above-average scores on the love scale) made significantly more eye contact than "weak lovers" (couples whose scores on the love scale were below average). Or, as the popular song has it, "I only have eyes for you."

At the same time that Rubin developed his love scale, he also developed a parallel liking scale, to help pinpoint the distinctions between these two sentiments. The items on the liking scale did not refer to attachment, caring, or intimacy but rather to having a favor-

Love includes components of attachment, caring, and intimacy.

able evaluation of the other person (for example, "Most people would react favorably to _____ after a brief acquaintance"), and respect for her (for example, "I have great confidence in _____'s good judgment"). As one might expect, partners' love scores were highly correlated with their estimates of the likelihood that they would get married. The correlation between liking scores and marriage estimates were much lower. This pattern of correlations seems quite reasonable. After all, the link between love and marriage in our society is taken almost as a matter of faith, while the link between liking and marriage is too often a well-kept secret.

Rubin's love scale can be applied to friendships, as well as to romantic or sexual relationships. Rubin (1970) found that when students filled out the love scale in terms of their feelings toward their closest same-sex friends, women reported that they loved their friends more than men did. There were no such differences in liking scores. This result is hardly surprising, in light of what we know about the roles of the two sexes. As we noted in the Psychological Issue for Chapter 13, men in our society learn to "stay cool" and to suppress emotions, especially when they are with other men. As a result, surveys have shown that women's friendships tend to be more intimate than men's, involving more spontaneous joint activities and more exchanging of confidences (Caldwell and Peplau, 1982). Loving for men may often be channeled into a single opposite-sex relationship, while women may be more able to experience attachment, caring, and intimacy in other relationships, as well.

Love and Sex

Within opposite-sex, romantic relationships, what are the links between love and sex? One view, suggested by Sigmund Freud (1905), is that sex can diminish love. Love, for Freud, was "aim-inhibited sex"—that is, a channeling of sexual impulses into the less overt form of tender and affectionate feelings. As a result, when lovers express their sexual needs directly, their love for each other is likely to become less intense. Most other observers would take exception to this idea, however, maintaining that sexual communication between two people can often heighten their love for each other.

In one recent experiment, Marshall Dermer and Thomas Pyszczynski (1978) found that sexual arousal tended to increase male college students' love for their girlfriends. These men were aroused sexually by reading an explicit account of the sexual behaviors and fantasies of a college woman. Afterward, the men were asked to complete Rubin's love and liking scales in terms of their feelings toward their own girlfriends. The love scores—but not the liking scores—of these men increased. Although Rubin's love scale itself does not include items referring to sexual attraction, it seems that sexual feelings can also lead to increases in the feelings of attachment, caring, and intimacy that are measured by the love scale.

In actual relationships, the link between love and sex is likely to depend in large measure on the sexual values of the people involved. Whereas many men and women in dating couples believe that their sexual relationship helps to strengthen their love and commitment,

The link between love and sex depends greatly on the sexual values of the couple.

many others believe that their love will remain just as strong or stronger without sex (see Box 4). In their study of student dating couples, Letitia Anne Peplau, Zick Rubin, and Charles Hill (1977) found that whether or not a couple had sexual intercourse had no clear effect on the future of their relationship. Couples who had had intercourse were no more nor less likely to stay together over a two-year period than couples who had not had intercourse.

LEAVING OTHERS

The "romantic ideal," celebrated in song and story, holds that love strikes at first sight, overcomes all obstacles, and lasts forever. The ending of most love stories, whether in fairy tales like "Sleeping Beauty" or comic books like *Young Romance,* is "and they lived happily ever after." But this ideal does not quite match up with reality. Love rarely strikes at first sight; it usually needs time to grow and develop. Love does not overcome all obstacles, such as those of race, religion, or social status; the large majority of love relationships and marriages are between people who come from highly similar social

— *Box 4* —————————————————

Three couples

Couples on today's college campuses show a wide range of orientations toward love and sex. In their study of 231 student dating couples, Letitia Anne Peplau, Zick Rubin, and Charles Hill (1977) identified three types of couples. For *sexually traditional couples*, love alone is not a sufficient justification for sexual intercourse—the more permanent commitment of marriage is a necessary prerequisite. For *sexually moderate couples*, sex is considered permissible if a man and woman love each other; in this view, sex is an expression of love and caring. For *sexually liberal couples*, sex is acceptable even without love; sex is considered an enjoyable activity to be valued for its own sake.

The following are examples of each of the three types of couples (from Peplau, Rubin, and Hill, 1977):

A SEXUALLY TRADITIONAL COUPLE: PAUL AND PEGGY

Peggy believes that intercourse before marriage is wrong. She explained that "even if I were engaged, I wouldn't feel right about having sex." Many of Peggy's girlfriends are having sexual affairs, which Peggy accepts "for them." It's not right for Peggy, however, and she believes that Paul respects her views. For his part, Paul indicated that he would like to have intercourse with Peggy . . . . but added that intercourse "just isn't all that important for me."* (*Page 97*)

A SEXUALLY MODERATE COUPLE: TOM AND SANDY

Three weeks after their first date, Tom told Sandy that he loved her. She was in love, too, and their relationship grew quickly. In a few months they were spending weekends together at one of their dorms. They slept in the same bed but did not have intercourse. Although Tom was very attracted to Sandy, he was slow to initiate intercourse. "I didn't want to push it on her," he said. "I felt that we shouldn't have sex until our relationship reached a certain point. [Sex] is something I just can't imagine on a first date." Tom and Sandy first had intercourse with each other just before becoming engaged. For Tom, "Sex added another dimension to our relationship; it's a landmark of sorts." (*Page 98*)

A SEXUALLY LIBERAL COUPLE: DIANE AND ALAN

About two weeks after they started dating, Alan asked if Diane would like to make love. She declined, saying she wasn't ready yet, but implying that she would be soon. Since they were alone in Alan's apartment, she jokingly suggested that he go "exhibit himself" across the room so she could get used to his body. They spent the weekend together, and by Sunday Diane felt ready for intercourse. Diane told us that she and Alan were not in love when they first had intercourse. Nonetheless, she enjoyed the sex and felt it was "part of our getting to know each other. It led to an obvious closeness."* (*Pages 98–99*)

The central distinction between these three orientations concerns the links between sexual intimacy and emotional intimacy. For traditionalists, sexual intimacy develops in the context of limited sexual activity; sexual intercourse is tied not only to love but to a permanent commitment, as well. For moderates, emotional intimacy sets the pace for sexual intimacy. As feelings of closeness and love increase, greater sexual exploration is possible. For liberals, sexual intimacy and emotional intimacy need not be related. Sex can be enjoyed in its own right, or sexual intimacy can be a route to developing emotional intimacy.

As you may have noticed, in all three of the couples the man was the one who took the lead in increasing sexual intimacy, while the woman played a more passive or limit-setting role. In all types of couples—traditional, moderate, and liberal—aspects of the sexual double standard that we described in Chapter 13 live on.

---

backgrounds (Rubin, 1973). And love does not necessarily last forever. Although love often leads to long-term relationships or to marriage, in many other cases true love runs its course and ends.

Why Do Relationships End?

Relationships end for many different reasons, ranging from simple boredom to conflicts about life-styles. In their study of student dating couples, Zick Rubin and his co-workers investigated some of the factors that lead people to leave one another (Hill, Rubin, and Peplau, 1976). Over a two-year period, about half of the couples in their sample stayed together and the other half broke up. The researchers found that the people who stayed together tended to be more similar to each other in age, intelligence, career plans, and physical attractiveness than the people who broke up. In addition, when people who had broken up were asked to explain why the relationship had ended, they frequently mentioned differences in interests, backgrounds, sexual attitudes, and ideas about marriage. It seems that similarities between people not only lead to attraction in the first place but also encourage the continuation of relationships. Partners who have serious differences or disagreements are likely to end up going their separate ways.

Rubin and his co-workers also found that relationships were most likely to end if one of the partners was considerably more involved in the relationship than the other. Of the couples in which both members initially reported that they were equally involved in the relationship, only 23 percent broke up during the subsequent two-year period. But among those couples in which one partner was more involved than the other, 54 percent broke up. There seems to be an inherent lack of stability in relationships in which one partner is more invested than the other. In such a relationship, the more involved partner may feel overly dependent and exploited, while the less involved partner may feel restless and guilty. As a result, as sociologist Peter Blau (1964) writes, "Commitments must stay abreast for a love relationship to develop into a lasting mutual attachment. . . . Only when two lovers' affection for and commitment to one another expand at roughly the same pace do they tend mutually to support their love" (page 84).

When Do Relationships End?

Hill, Rubin, and Peplau (1976) found that the breakups of the college student couples in their sample were most likely to take place at specific points during the school year—in the months of May–June, September, and December–January (see Figure 14.4). At such times, when the school year is beginning or ending or during vacations, people may be more likely to be separated from one another or to meet new partners. In addition, if one has already been thinking about ending a relationship, such events as the end of the school year may make it easier to actually call the relationship off. For example, it is probably easier to say, "While we're apart we ought to date others" than it is to say, "I've grown tired of you and would rather not date any more." By attributing the impending breakup to external circumstances, such as unavoidable physical separation, it may be possible to reduce some of the guilt and embarrassment that is otherwise likely to be associated with ending a close relationship.

The Aftermath of Breaking Up

The ending of a close relationship often leads to feelings of pain and distress, similar to the symptoms of loneliness that we discussed earlier. These feelings are likely to be most acute for the partner who was broken up with (assuming that the ending was not completely mutual), but they affect the partner who wanted to break up, as well.

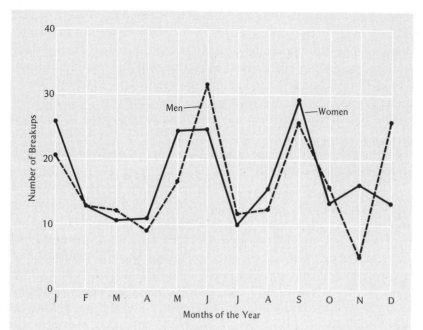

FIGURE 14.4
Charles Hill, Zick Rubin, and Letitia Anne Peplau (1976) found that most breakups of student dating couples took place at turning points in the school year—in June, when school ended for the summer; in September, when the new school term began; and in December–January, when students left campus for winter vacation.

But in spite of the pain involved, the ending of close relationships can teach us valuable lessons. By experiencing first-hand the difficulties of close relationships, we are likely to learn more about our own interpersonal needs, preferences, strengths, and weaknesses. These lessons can be of value to us as we enter new relationships. After the ending of her relationship with David, for example, Ruth told the researchers that "I don't regret having the experience at all. But after being in the supportive role, *I* want a little support now. That's the main thing I look for" (Hill, Rubin, and Peplau, 1976, page 156). And after his breakup with Kathy, Joe indicated that he would exercise greater caution in future relationships. "If I fall in love again," he said, "it might be with the reservation that I'm going to keep awake this time" (page 155). Breakups are most valuable if they take place before marriage. For marital breakups are likely to be considerably more painful and stressful than breakups that take place before marriage. As an anonymous wise man once said, "The best divorce is the one you get before you get married."

SUMMARY

1. People often seek the company of others because of the need for *social comparison*—the need to compare one's experiences and reactions with those of other people. This is especially true when people are afraid or upset.

2. According to Weiss, people have a need for two kinds of social relationships: *emotional attachments* to one other person, and *social ties* to a network of friends. When people lack either type of relationship they are likely to experience *loneliness*. Lack of emotional attachment brings the loneliness of

emotional isolation, while lack of social ties produces the loneliness of *social isolation*.

3. The way we form impressions of people is called *person perception*. Our perceptions of others are highly influenced by their physical appearance and by their reputations.

4. Group pressure can give rise to *conformity*, even when the conforming individuals know the group is wrong. Asch found that people may distort their judgments to avoid being a lone dissenter. When group members are afraid to challenge a decision for the sake of keeping group solidarity, they are victims of *groupthink*.

5. A person's actions often lead us to form ideas about her underlying traits. The ways in which we try to infer the causes of people's behavior are called *attribution processes*. There is a pervasive tendency, known as the *fundamental attributional error*, to overestimate the role of personal dispositions and to underestimate the role of situational constraints affecting people's behavior.

6. In forming impressions of people, we also try to interpret their nonverbal messages, such as facial expressions and tones of voice. On measures such as the Social Interpretation Task, women have been found to be better at reading nonverbal clues than men are.

7. The physical *proximity* of any two people has a direct impact on their likelihood of becoming friends. For example, studies have shown that people who live next door to each other are more likely to become friends than people who live two doors away.

8. A major factor in whether two people will become friends is their *similarity* to each other. Friends and married couples tend to be similar in age, occupational status, educational level, and even height. However, the most important area of similarity is beliefs and attitudes—people who agree with us provide us with many kinds of rewards.

9. How does one measure love? Rubin developed a scale that assumes love to be made up of three components: *attachment*, *caring*, and *intimacy*. He distinguished love, as measured by this scale, from liking. Some people believe, however, that love is not a proper object of scientific study.

10. The link between love and sex is likely to depend on the sexual values of the people involved. Some people believe that sexual intercourse is acceptable without love, some believe that love should precede sex, and some believe that the permanent commitment of marriage is a necessary prerequisite for sex.

11. Love does not necessarily last forever. Many factors can contribute to the ending of a relationship, including differences in interests, background, sexual attitudes, and ideas about marriage. Also, relationships are more likely to end if one partner is considerably more involved in the relationship than the other.

PREJUDICE AND RACISM

Racism runs deep in American culture. Thomas Jefferson believed in the innate inferiority of black people. Although he personally opposed slavery, he agreed to compromise with Southern slavery

---

Thomas Jefferson believed in the innate inferiority of black people.

---

interests and to delete an antislavery statement from the Declaration of Independence. Abraham Lincoln was also convinced that black people were inferior to whites and felt that equality was not attainable as long as blacks and whites lived in the same society. And these are two of the presidents who were *most* sympathetic to the plight of black people in America (Jones, 1972). Although overt racism has declined in recent decades, more subtle forms of racism,

as we will see, remain strong in America.

Racism is, of course, just one type of prejudice. We have already met up with several other varieties of prejudice in this book—for example, prejudice against old people (ageism), against women, and against gay people. In this Psychological Issue, we will focus on *racism*, differential attitudes toward and treatment of individuals on the basis of their racial group membership, grounded in a belief (whether conscious or nonconscious) that one race is inherently superior to another. But our discussion will illustrate the more general process of *prejudice*, the prejudgment of people in negative ways on the basis of their group membership. Whether it is the prejudice of whites against blacks, Anglos against Chicanos, or men against women, it is an attitude that we need to understand as well as we can if we are ever to succeed in eliminating it.

Prejudice is not the same as *discrimination*. Whereas prejudice refers to unfairly negative *attitudes*

toward members of a particular group, discrimination refers to unfairly negative *actions* toward such groups. Attitudes and actions are usually closely intertwined, and so are prejudice and discrimination.

RACIAL ATTITUDES IN AMERICA

Ever since 1942, researchers at the National Opinion Research Center have been asking questions about racial attitudes to representative national samples of white Americans. Through the years, whites have been asked such questions as, "Do you think white students and black students should go to the same schools or to separate schools?" and whether they agree or disagree that "White people have a right to keep blacks out of their neighborhoods if they want to." These surveys have indicated that racial attitudes have steadily become more positive and tolerant. Whereas some observers believed that there was a "white backlash" against racial integration in the early 1970s, the surveys taken between 1970 and 1976 indicated increasing support for integration of schools and housing (Taylor, Sheatsley, and Greeley, 1978).

In at least some respects, then, racial prejudice in America seems to be on the wane. But the increasing support for racial integration does not tell the whole story about American racial attitudes. Many studies of whites' behavior toward blacks in the 1970s, including many studies using college students as subjects, have shown that antiblack sentiments remain much stronger than the survey data might lead one to expect (Crosby, Bromley, and Saxe, 1980).

These studies have involved the measurement of prejudice through people's actual behavior. In one study, for example, a completed application to graduate school was "planted" in an airport telephone booth. Half of the time the applicant (shown in a photograph) was white, and the other half he or she was black. In all cases, a stamped, addressed envelope and a note asking "Dad" to mail the form were attached. The context made it clear that "Dad" had lost the letter in the airport. The researchers found that more of the white subjects who found the application bothered to mail it when the applicant was white than when the applicant was black (Benson, Karabenick, and Lerner, 1976).

In another experiment, white college students attending Princeton met and interviewed either a black or a white high school student. The interviewees were actually confederates of the experimenters who had been trained to behave in a standard fashion. It was found that although the subjects did not discriminate against the black interviewees in any overt fashion, they sat further away from the black students than the white students, made more speech errors in talking to them, and terminated the interviews more quickly (Word, Zanna, and Cooper, 1974).

These and many other studies suggest that among white Ameri-

cans there has been a shift from blatant forms of discrimination to

---

There has been a shift among whites to more subtle forms of discrimination against blacks.

---

more subtle forms. Whereas many whites will deny that they are prejudiced against blacks if you ask them directly—indeed, they may truly believe they are unprejudiced—their prejudice may reveal itself in their differential treatment of whites and blacks at times when they do not know that they are being observed and when the social pressure to behave in an "appropriate" way is not strong. Whites have been found to be less likely to help stranded motorists when they were black, less likely to make an emergency phone call for a black, and more likely to report shoplifters when they were black (Crosby, Bromley, and Saxe, 1980). In addition, whites may feel

uneasy or anxious when dealing with blacks, which leads to the sort of differential treatment shown in the Princeton study (Poskocil, 1977). Even at an overt level, racism is far from dead in America, as recent demonstrations against forced busing of schoolchildren in Northern cities such as Boston readily attest.

What perpetuates such prejudice and discrimination? There are many factors to be considered, each of which may provide one piece of the answer. Here we will consider three such factors: the workings of stereotypes, personality predispositions, and the impact of social norms.

STEREOTYPES
The literal meaning of *prejudice* is "prejudgment." We prejudge members of other groups when we view them in terms of *stereotypes* that are applied to entire groups of people, like the physical stereotypes discussed in Chapter 14. If we were capable of responding to every person as an individual—if we didn't categorize people at all—we would be free of prejudices about blacks, gay people, or old people. But freeing ourselves of such categorizations completely is an unattainable ideal. We depend on categories in order to handle the tremendous amount of information that constantly confronts us.

However, most of the racial and national stereotypes that we hold—happy-go-lucky blacks, shrewd Jews, inscrutable Orientals—have little if any basis in reality. And by relying on such stereotypes, we are blinded to the immense diversity among individuals. We expect people to behave like our stereotypes of those who happen to have the same skin color, speak with the same accent, or have the same background, rather than to behave like themselves.

If our stereotypes have little

Although such blatant signs of racism are now rare, it still manifests itself in more subtle forms.

basis in reality, why do they persist as strongly as they do? A large part of the answer lies in the phenomenon of *selective perception*. We tend to focus on information that is consistent with our stereotypes and to screen out or reinterpret information that is inconsistent with these preconceived notions (Hamilton, 1979). For instance, once you have reached the conclusion that all Cubans are "lazy," you will be more likely to notice examples of lazy Cubans. If you see a lazy Anglo, you will pay little attention or else you will interpret his behavior quite differently—"He must be resting after doing some hard work."

An experiment by Birt Duncan (1976) illustrates such selective perception. White college students viewed a videotaped interaction between two other students who were supposedly taking part in a discussion. After some initial conversation, the students got into an argument that became more and more heated until finally Student B shoved Student A. The subjects were later asked for their impressions of the two students. When the shover was black and the person he shoved was white, 70 percent of the subjects classified the shove as an instance of "violent behavior." But when the shover

Black shovers were viewed as "violent," white shovers as "playing around."

was white and the person he shoved was black, only 17 percent of the subjects considered this "violent behavior," while 42 percent described it as either "playing around" or "dramatizing." Blacks

are often viewed by whites as being prone to violence. As Duncan's study demonstrates, selective perception can serve to maintain this stereotype.

Without being fully aware of it, we all become skilled at perceiving only those events that are consistent with our prejudices. After a while, we amass a pile of evidence that assures us that our prejudices are justified. In addition, movies and television often portray members of various groups in ways that conform to popular stereotypes and, as a result, help to perpetuate them.

THE PREJUDICED PERSONALITY
There is evidence that some people tend to be generally prejudiced—not just toward blacks or toward Mexican-Americans or toward Jews, but toward practically *all* "outgroups." Eugene Hartley (1946) helped to make this point when he obtained measures of people's attitudes toward various minority groups, including three minorities that Hartley made up: Walonians, Pirenians, and Danerieans. People who were prejudiced toward blacks and other outgroups expressed prejudice toward the made-up groups as well. "I don't know anything about them," one prejudiced respondent replied. "Therefore, I would exclude them from my country."

In the 1940s a group of psychologists at the University of California at Berkeley, influenced by Freud's psychoanalytic theory of personality (see Chapter 8), looked intensively into the origins of a prejudiced personality. The researchers (Adorno et al., 1950) concluded that highly prejudiced people are likely to have *authoritarian personalities*. These people tend to see the world as divided sharply into two categories—the weak and the strong. They tend to be power oriented in their personal relationships. They are most

Authoritarian personalities divide people into two categories—the weak and the strong.

comfortable when they are either taking orders from a superior or dishing it out to a subordinate. The Berkeley researchers believed that these were the sorts of people who would have been likely to be drawn to the Fascist ideology of Nazi Germany.

As the centerpiece of their research, the Berkeley researchers developed a personality scale, known as the *F* scale (the *F* stands for fascism), to measure the extent to which a person has an authoritarian personality. "High *F*s," or authoritarians, tend to agree with statements such as "Obedience and respect for authority are the most important virtues children should learn" and "No weakness or difficulty can hold us back if we have enough will power."

By means of detailed studies of individuals with this ideology, Adorno and his colleagues concluded that they tend to come from families that stress harsh discipline and obedience and in which there is anxiety about family status. People from such backgrounds may often find it difficult to accept personal weakness or to acknowledge their own sexual or aggressive motives. Instead, they are likely to make use of the Freudian defense mechanism of *projection*, seeing themselves and their own groups as being without weakness and, instead, seeing the undesirable traits that they are afraid of in members of outgroups. In this way the authoritarian personality arrives at his racial and religious prejudice.

Although research on the authoritarian personality has been valuable, individual bigotry can explain only a small proportion of the racial discrimination that is found in America. For example, even though overt discrimination against blacks has traditionally been greater in the South than in the North, white Southerners have not scored higher than white Northerners on measures of authoritarianism. Rather, the discrimination patterns against blacks in the South have been mainly a result of conformity to *social norms* that developed through the course of history.

The fact that social norms bear most of the responsibility for prejudice and discrimination helps to explain certain apparent inconsistencies in interracial behavior. R. D. Minard (1952) reported, for example, that black and white coal miners in West Virginia followed a pattern of almost complete integration below the ground and almost complete segregation above the ground. This pattern makes sense only when viewed in terms of people's conformity to changing norms of acceptable and unacceptable conduct (Pettigrew, 1971). We

To reduce prejudice, massive psychotherapy is not the answer.

must recognize that prejudice, like our other attitudes, has a strong social foundation. We learn to be prejudiced not as a general way of life, but in the form of specific attitudes and behaviors illustrated to us by our parents, our peers, and the mass media.

To reduce prejudice, therefore, massive psychotherapy is not the answer. Instead, we need to develop ways of changing the social norms that perpetuate discriminatory behavior.

REDUCING PREJUDICE
The best way to reduce prejudice is to take seriously the principle that attitudes often follow, rather than precede, actions. Instead of preaching lofty ideals of equality, we need to *create* greater equality, by law or by individual action.

Each of the long series of moves toward greater racial integration and equality in America has been met by resistance. Whites, and sometimes blacks as well, have argued that by integrating the buses, or the lunch counters, or the schools, we will only cause tension and discomfort, and as a result we will only make matters worse.

Of course, these critics have been right about the tension and discomfort. It is impossible to change long-standing and deeply

When whites and blacks work together on the job, they may be friendly. However, the same people may be unlikely to visit each other's homes because of social norms that permit interracial interaction in some contexts but not in others.

As this 1980 letter to the **Boston Globe**
*suggests, children are likely to learn
prejudiced attitudes from their parents.*

ingrained behavior patterns without generating a great deal of tension. Nevertheless, the general experience has been that once such
changes are instituted, people
gradually come to accept them
and even to like them. Surveys
reveal, for example, that attitudes
toward integration on the part of
both black and white Americans
are more favorable among those
who have experienced it and least
favorable among those who have
had no interracial contacts (Pettigrew, 1971).

As Daryl Bem (1970) concludes,
"Legislation and court decisions
can change the 'hearts and minds
of men.' . . . They do so, in part,
by effecting a change in behavior;
then, when behavior has been
changed, attitudes often follow"
(page 69).

MAKING DESEGREGATION WORK

Despite the general tendency to
accept moves toward integration,
it would be a mistake to conclude
that the desegregation of American
schools has been a resounding success. In its famous school desegregation decision of 1954, the U.S.
Supreme Court ruled that separate
schools for blacks and whites are
inherently unequal. Chief Justice
Earl Warren declared that when
black children are separated from
white children on the basis of race
alone, it "generates a feeling of
inferiority as to their status in the
community that may affect their
hearts and minds in a way unlikely ever to be undone."

In its decision, the Court cited
psychological research that at-
tested to the low self-esteem of
black children in a segregated society. For example, black children
as young as 3 years old had been
found to reject black dolls as inferior to white dolls (Clark and
Clark, 1947). A committee of social
scientists, including psychologists,
also submitted a brief to the Court
which predicted that desegregation, if brought about in the right
way, would lead to decreasing racial prejudice and discrimination.

Unfortunately, school desegregation has not achieved many of its
goals. Many studies have shown
that minority children's self-esteem

**Black children as young
as 3 years old had been
found to reject black dolls
as inferior to white dolls.**

rarely increases—and sometimes
decreases—when they enter deseg-
regated schools. And in eighteen
studies reviewed by Walter Ste-

phan (1978), desegregation increased the prejudice of whites
toward blacks at least as often as
it decreased it.

What went wrong? Did the social scientists, as Stuart Cook (1979)
asks, mislead the Supreme Court?
It now seems clear that school
desegregation in the United States
has not been carried out in the
way that social scientists stipulated
was necessary for it to be successful. Simply increasing the amount
of contact between members of
different racial groups is not going
to make them like each other
more or to increase the minority
group's sense of pride. As Elliot
Aronson (1980) points out, many
whites have always had a great
deal of contact with blacks—for
example, as dishwashers, wash-
room attendants, and domestics.
Such contact may simply fortify
the stereotypes of blacks as inferior and fan the flames of prejudice.

**To be effective in reducing
prejudice, interracial
contact must be between
people of equal status.**

To be effective in reducing prejudice, interracial contact must be
between people who have *equal
status* in the situation, who can
then, as Gordon Allport wrote in
1954, come to recognize their
"common interests and common
humanity." The problem is that
the contact between white and
minority children is not usually
equal status. The whites have already had greater advantages than
the black or Hispanic children,
have acquired better academic
skills, and are likely to look down

For integrated classrooms to be successful, they must foster cooperation and equal status contact among the children.

on minority children. Especially in competitive classroom atmospheres, where children vie with one another to impress the teacher, the minority children may feel worse about themselves than ever.

For desegregation to succeed in breaking down prejudices, then, it must be instituted in a way that leads both to equal-status contact and to a cooperative classroom atmosphere. Educators are now more aware of these needs than they used to be, and various programs of fostering cooperative and equal-status interaction in the classroom show great promise of success (Cook, 1979).

One such program, developed by Elliot Aronson and his coworkers (1978) is called the *jigsaw technique* because it works much like a jigsaw puzzle, whose pieces must be fitted together. In this technique, children are assigned to small interracial learning groups. Each child in the group gets material that represents one piece of the lesson to be learned. For example, in a lesson for fifth graders on the life of the publisher Joseph Pulitzer, one child received a para-

graph about Pulitzer's ancestors, another on his childhood, another on his early adulthood, and so on. Each child had to learn her part and then communicate it to the others in the group. At the end of the period, the entire group was to be tested on the lesson.

With this technique, the majority and minority children are forced—sometimes for the first time—to pay attention to each other, to teach and learn from each other, and to respect each other's contributions. Aronson and his coworkers have found that children in jigsaw classrooms grow to like each other better, and the minority children come to achieve more academically and to develop higher self-esteem. Aronson adds that the technique works best with young children, before prejudicial attitudes have a chance to become deeply ingrained.

The jigsaw technique and other methods of fostering cooperative interdependence in the classroom are not, to be sure, cure-alls for prejudice and racism. Prejudice must be battled on many fronts, including more equitable exposure

of minorities in the mass media, greater educational and job opportunities for minorities, and programs with young children, when they make the most difference. Although racism is far from dead in America, efforts are now being made to combat it on all these fronts. These efforts must continue if the United States is to become a truly just and tolerant society.

SUMMARY

1. *Prejudice* is prejudgment of people on the basis of their membership in a particular group. *Discrimination* is acting differentially toward people on the basis of their membership in a particular group. *Racism* is holding negative attitudes toward and discriminating against people on the basis of a belief that one race is inherently superior to another.

2. Although racial attitudes of whites about blacks seem to have become less prejudiced in recent years, whites still show subtle behavioral discrimination toward blacks.

3. Although racial *stereotypes* have little basis in reality, they tend to be perpetuated by *selective perception*, in which people notice only those aspects of others that coincide with their stereotypes.

4. People who appear prejudiced toward all outgroups are likely to have *authoritarian personalities*.

5. Prejudice and discrimination in America are perpetuated by *social norms* that dictate appropriate and inappropriate conduct.

6. Studies have shown that it takes contact with the outgroup people for ingroup people to break down their prejudices. However, this contact must be on an equal-status basis and should be of the sort that encourages cooperation if it is to produce the desired effect.

THE SOCIAL PSYCHOLOGY OF APPEARANCE
S. Michael Kalick

S. Michael Kalick

In past decades, social psychologists devoted little attention to the impact of people's physical appearance on their social interactions and relationships—perhaps they took too seriously the maxim that "beauty is skin deep." But recent research demonstrates that our appearance has profound effects both on our relations with others and on our views of ourselves. Dr. S. Michael Kalick of the University of Massachusetts at Boston is a leading reseacher in this area. He has conducted groundbreaking studies of the impact of plastic surgery and other cosmetic medical treatments on social reactions and self-conceptions. In this Update, he discusses this research and reflects on its implications.

It is a crisp morning in the spring of 1980. Andrew W. and his wife are visiting relatives and have just spent the night in the guest bedroom. Andrew is shaving in the guest bathroom, examining his face in the large, well-lit mirror. Something about the lighting or the unfamiliar setting has prompted him to take an unusually close look at himself. He becomes aware of more wrinkles and more sagging skin on his 64-year-old face than he has ever noticed before. This puts him into a melancholy mood. For years he has had heart trouble, and he has had two heart bypass operations, but he has always thought of himself as youthful. This chance reflection in an unaccustomed mirror has made him, for the first time, lament that he is getting old. Within weeks he will be in a plastic surgeon's office, finding out how many years surgery can erase from the image of an aging face.

At about the same time, Karen T., a high-school student, has also found her way to a plastic surgeon's office. She is upset by what she has seen in a different kind of "mirror": the behavior of some of her classmates toward her. They

have hit upon her rather large, humped nose as an object of ridicule, pelting her with wisecracks such as, "Why don't you finish eating the banana?" She now feels she doesn't want to live with her nose as it is, so she decides to undergo corrective surgery.

These chains of events would perhaps not have surprised Charles Horton Cooley, a sociologist who some eighty years ago originated the notion of the "looking glass self" (1902). According to this notion, the image we form of ourselves is based on our perception of how others see us. The behavior of others is the looking glass within which we come to know ourselves. Traditionally, character traits have been regarded as the stuff of the social looking glass. The more our fellows convey their impression of us as kind and considerate, for example, the more firmly these traits become established in our *self-concept*, our view of ourselves.

But actual physical characteristics have also been recognized as important determinants of treatment by others, as well as building blocks of self-concept. During the past two decades, researchers

have found that physically attractive individuals enjoy an impressive variety of advantages in their social interactions. Coincidentally, during this same time period the public has discovered plastic surgery in a large way, and many people have sought it to enhance their appearance or correct observable flaws. This trend has brought to light a sharp difference of opinion regarding plastic surgery: it has been deplored or disdained by some, while others have seen it as potentially a rational, constructive response to life.

My own research on the social impact of physical appearance has led me to gather information from a number of plastic surgery patients over a period of years. Andrew W. and Karen T. are two members of my interview sample. The reports of such patients can help us understand what plastic surgery has meant to people who seek it, as well as shedding light on the links between physical appearance, social experience, and self-concept. But first, an overview of research on the social consequences of physical attractiveness is in order.

Until the mid-1960s, researchers

Our assessment of the way we look is likely to have a major impact on the way we feel about ourselves.

paid scant attention to beauty as a social-psychological variable. Perhaps the notions that beauty is "skin deep" or "in the eye of the beholder" gave rise to the assumption that physical appearance cannot play an important role in determining our attitudes and behavior toward one another. About fifteen years ago this assumption was finally put to the test, as investigators designed studies which could objectively examine the social influence of physical attractiveness.

In the first of these studies (Walster, Aronson, Abrahams, and Rottman, 1966), several hundred male and female college students were more-or-less randomly paired for a supposedly computer-matched dance. The researchers had obtained ratings of each participant's intelligence, scholastic achievement, and personality. Also, when the students had bought tickets to the dance, four raters had secretly assessed each student's appearance. In this study, as in others, there was considerable agreement between different raters' assessments of the participants' physical attractiveness, reflecting a shared cultural

definition of "good looks." At the end of the dance, the participants were asked how much they liked their partner and how much they would like to see him or her again. The only significant finding was that the better-looking men and women were better liked and more desired for a future date. Intellect and personality were not found to have any effect at all on these evaluations. Subsequent "computer-dance" studies came up with similar findings.

That people prefer physically attractive dates may not be startling. However, as researchers dug deeper, they themselves were surprised by the strong and far-ranging effects beauty was found to have in influencing the opinions we form of others. For example, Karen Dion, Ellen Berscheid, and Elaine Walster (1972) asked subjects to give their impressions of male and female college students shown in photographs. The researchers found that the more attractive students were rated as more sensitive, kind, interesting, poised, and sociable than the less attractive students. The subjects also predicted that the better-looking students would have more successful careers, better marriages, and happier lives. Thus, there seems to be a "physical attractiveness stereotype," with beautiful people being evaluated favorably on a variety of traits that are not obviously related to physical beauty.

Many other studies using photos have shown that beauty wins points with others in a variety of ways. Fifth-grade teachers, for example, were found to rate better-looking children as more capable (Clifford and Walster, 1973). Prospective jury members were more lenient with better-looking criminal defendants in a hypothetical trial (Efran, 1974), and job interviewers were more likely to hire better-looking applicants (Dipboye, Fromkin, and Wiback, 1975). Taken as a whole, these studies have strongly confirmed the initial suggestion that the bet-

ter-looking, both male and female, are stereotyped as more "valuable," vital human beings and are given preferential treatment.

At this point we are justified in asking whether the physical attractiveness stereotype influences not only our impressions of others but even our impression of ourselves. Are the more physically attractive likely to develop a more favorable overall self-concept? This question has not yet been investigated extensively, but evidence is available which does allow the beginnings of a picture to be constructed. The general shape of this picture follows from the assumption that others can strongly influence our "looking glass self" by conveying their impressions of us in the way they treat us.

Research by Mark Snyder, Elizabeth Tanke, and Ellen Berscheid (1977) indicates that others' behavior toward us based on our appearance can quickly influence our own behavior, either enhancing or diminishing our sociability. The researchers arranged to have unacquainted male-female student pairs converse for ten minutes by intercom. Fifty-one such pairs took part, and their conversations were tape-recorded. Prior to each conversation, half the men were given a photo of an attractive woman and half were given a photo of a relatively unattractive woman. The photos were distributed at random, but the men were falsely told that the photo was of the woman with whom they were about to converse. After the conversations took place, each tape recording was edited so that only the woman's utterances could be heard. The tapes were then reviewed by a panel of raters. It turned out that the women whose partners believed them to be attractive conversed in a manner which the raters found significantly more friendly, likable, and sociable than the women whose partners believed them to be unattractive. Somehow the men, based on how they thought the women

When someone else thinks we are physically attractive, we are likely to respond in a way that fits their expectations—we become more outgoing and likable. This process was demonstrated in an experiment by Mark Snyder, Elizabeth Tanke, and Ellen Berscheid, as described in this Update.

looked, had in a 10-minute conversation treated them in a way that had a substantial impact on the way the women themselves behaved. There seemed to be a "self-fulfilling prophecy" at work: women who were *expected* (on the basis of their presumed appearance) to be likable and outgoing actually turned out to behave in a likable and outgoing way.

Showing that people's appearance (or presumed appearance) can cause their behavior to be influenced in a specific setting is still several steps short of demonstrating that appearance can affect one's relatively enduring self-concept. Some of these steps can be filled in with the help of the reports of people who have sought plastic surgery. In one case, a young woman seeking to have her large nose made smaller was asked her reasons for requesting surgery. "It's not just my nose," she replied, "it's my disposition. I'm so nasty to people and I want to change that" (Meyer, Jacobson, Edgerton, and Canter, 1960, p. 198). The woman had equated her "masculine" large nose with her pugnacious character, and she

seemed to assume that a change in one would go along with a change in the other.

So direct an equation of appearance and self-perceived character seems to be rare among plastic surgery patients. But these pa-

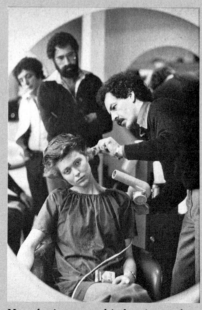

Many businesses and industries, such as hair-styling salons and cosmetics, have grown up around people's desire to enhance their appearance.

tients will frequently comment that their flaw of appearance gives them a general feeling of social vulnerability. After interviewing 58 prospective patients, Linn and Goldman (1949) noted, "They go through special maneuvers to avoid presenting to others what they regard as the unfavorable view of their face . . ." (p. 307). While interacting with other people, these patients felt compelled to try to manage the other people's view of their appearance. This preoccupation can make normal social interaction unusually taxing and anxiety-producing. Such anxiety may even affect one's health: One recent set of studies found that relatively unattractive female high-school and college students had higher blood pressure than their more attractive female classmates (Hansell, Sparacino, and Ronchi, 1982).

Vulnerability is exactly the feeling that Karen T.—the high-school student described earlier—reported to me during our conversations. The prospect of being taunted by some of her classmates, and of having her appearance viewed in an unfavorable light, took on highly alarming overtones in her mind. In her earlier years, Karen had managed to develop the self-concept of an attractive, "o.k." person—not the sort who is likely to be ridiculed by peers. But this positive self-concept was being threatened in her current experiences, and she sought plastic surgery in order to remove the threat.

The question of what motivates people to undergo plastic surgery has, in fact, been the subject of considerable controversy. For many years, a dominant point of view was that plastic surgery applicants were probably focusing on their appearance as a "scapegoat" for their personal failings. In an influential article written 30 years ago, the authors flatly claimed that the desire to undergo plastic surgery is "a symptom of neurosis" (Hill and Silver, 1950). This viewpoint has been voiced more recently as well, although

These photographs are of the same woman, taken before and after cosmetic facial surgery. While some people have deplored such plastic surgery, others believe that it is often a constructive response by people who are dissatisfied with their appearance.

generally in milder terms (Gifford, 1972).

If people tend to focus on flaws of appearance as an excuse for deeper personal problems, then corrective surgery would be unlikely to be of much value. After all, the "real" source of the patient's discontent would not have been treated. In line with this logic, it has long been part of the "common knowledge" among plastic surgeons that some patients are delighted after receiving technically flawed surgery while other patients express disappointment or even bitterness after getting technically outstanding results. These reactions seem to confirm the notion of plastic surgery patients acting out a troubled psychology rather than reacting to true changes in appearance. But this "common knowledge" about reactions to plastic surgery was never given a systematic test to see whether it really applies to many patients.

Such a dim view of the value of plastic surgery was perhaps inspired by our traditional assumption, as discussed earlier, that beauty can't really be an important factor in people's lives. Our

democratic ideals make us want to believe that everyone has an equal chance in life regardless of how he or she looks. But this belief has been challenged by the recent research findings on physical attractiveness that I have described. If looks have more social importance than we would like to believe, then traditional assumptions about plastic surgery may also be mistaken. One of my own studies suggests that plastic surgery may have real and important effects on the way in which patients are viewed by others (Kalick, 1977, 1979). College students were asked for their impressions of photos which, unknown to the students, were actually presurgery or postsurgery photos of a group of plastic surgery patients. The patients had undergone corrections of the nose, the chin, or both. I found that the postsurgery patients were rated as having more desirable personalities, better marriage prospects, and happier lives in store for them. Also, the students expressed a far greater interest in meeting the people shown in the postsurgery than in the presurgery photos.

This finding may help us to in-

terpret the fact, now widely accepted, that the great majority of plastic surgery patients later report that they are happy they had the surgery (Edgerton, Jacobson, and Meyer, 1961; Reich, 1975). If the surgery removes a social bias against the patients and increases their chances of receiving more favorable treatment, then patients should indeed be satisfied with the surgery. This line of explanation is complemented by a recent study I conducted of patients being treated by a plastic surgeon for a red-to-purple skin discoloration known as "port wine stain" (Kalick, 1982). I found that these patients' long-term satisfaction with their treatment was strongly related to the degree of actual physical improvement, and relatively unrelated to quirks of personality within each patient. The conclusion which emerges from these bits of evidence is that, for many people, the decision to seek surgery is a rational response to their life circumstances. Their reaction to treatment may follow closely from their accurate assessment of the self-improvement, as well as from the more favorable reactions their "new look" elicits from others.

With her nasal correction completed, Karen T. told me she felt much stronger, much less vulnerable to insults from some of her classmates. I mentioned that many people would probably find her more attractive than they would have before, but she was reluctant to discuss this aspect of her surgery. Perhaps it is easier to talk with others about wanting to be rid of a troublesome flaw than about wanting to be prettier, which smacks of vanity and self-absorption. Karen did talk of how she now looked forward to starting college the next year, and to meeting new and interesting people. These new people's reactions to her remained to be tested, but at least for the time being, in Karen's "looking glass," her reflection had become decidedly brighter.

Glossary

abnormality See *adequacy approach; cultural model; medical model; statistical approach.*

acetylcholine A transmitter substance in the brain that seems to be involved in memory, sleep disturbances, and motor coordination.

achievement motive The striving to maintain or increase one's competence in activities in which a standard of excellence is thought to apply.

activation-synthesis model The idea that dreams begin with the firing of giant cells in the brain stem, leading to activation of certain areas of the brain. The dreams then synthesized depend on which areas of the brain are stimulated.

acupuncture A medical practice, developed by the Chinese, in which the insertion of needles into various sites on the body surface relieves pain in either the surrounding area or distant body parts.

adequacy approach In abnormal psychology, defining normality in terms of the efficiency with which

a person is able to carry out the tasks of everyday life.

afferent neurons The neurons that collect messages from inside and outside the body and transmit them to the central nervous system; sensory neurons. See also *efferent neurons.*

affiliation motive The need of human beings to associate with one another.

ageism The high value placed on youth in our society, resulting in a negative view of old people and discrimination against them.

age-graded influences Experiences and events that commonly occur at a given stage of life. See also *non-age-graded influences.*

alarm reaction According to Selye, the first stage in an animal's response to stress; it involves general physiological arousal. See also *exhaustion stage; resistance stage.*

all-or-none principle The idea that a stimulus must be of a minimum strength to stimulate an axon to fire and that once this threshold is reached the axon will fire completely.

alpha wave A rhythmic electrical impulse of the brain, occurring during wakefulness and relaxation.

amnesia A dissociative disorder characterized by loss of memory of one's identity.

amphetamine psychosis A psychosislike state produced by long-term or excessive use of amphetamines. It is characterized by paranoid delusions, compulsions, and stereotyped behaviors.

amphetamines A group of drugs that act to stimulate the central nervous system.

amygdala A structure in the limbic system that appears to be involved in rage and violent behavior.

anal stage According to Freud, the second stage of psychosexual development (ages 2 to 3), during which bowel control is achieved and gratification centers on the anal area.

androgenization Excess exposure to male hormone by a genetic female before birth, often resulting in masculinized genitals and possibly affecting the brain and behavior.

495

androgyny See *psychological androgyny.*

antianxiety drugs The minor tranquilizers, such as Valium and Librium, which are commonly prescribed to relieve tension and anxiety.

antidepressant drugs Drugs prescribed to lift the spirits of depressed patients.

antipsychotic drugs The major tranquilizers, used primarily to treat the symptoms of schizophrenia.

antisocial personality A type of personality disorder characterized by superficial charm, insincerity, lack of remorse or guilt, failure to learn from experience, and inability to tolerate frustration.

anxiety A vague, unpleasant feeling that something bad is about to happen.

anxiety attacks Overwhelming attacks of dread, uneasiness, and apprehension, accompanied by various physical symptoms.

anxiety disorders Mental disorders characterized by excessive anxiety, such as phobias and obsessive-compulsive disorder.

aphasia Loss of language ability because of brain damage.

applied research Research designed to help solve a practical problem.

assertiveness training A program designed to help timid people stand up for themselves.

association neurons Neurons found primarily in the central nervous system that make the connection between incoming and outgoing messages.

attachment An infant's bond or affectional tie to her parent or a parent figure.

attention The process of selectively responding to certain stimuli while ignoring others.

attitudes The ways in which we think and feel about people, objects, and issues.

attribution processes People's methods of trying to infer the underlying causes of other people's behavior.

auditory nerve The nerve that carries messages from the ear to the hearing portion of the brain.

authoritarian child rearing A child-rearing style in which the parent attempts to shape and control the behavior of the child according to specific standards of conduct. See also *permissive child rearing.*

authoritarian personality A personality type characterized by admiration of strength, hatred of weakness, and a strong belief in obedience to authority.

autoimmune reaction A situation in which the immune system begins to attack the body's own cells.

autonomic nervous system The part of the peripheral nervous system that controls glands and involuntary movements. See also *somatic nervous system.*

avoidance A defense mechanism characterized by refusal to put oneself in situations that will produce anxiety.

axon A long fiber extending from a neuron and transmitting messages to other neurons, to muscles, or to glands.

axonal transmission The movement of electrical impulses along the surface of a neuron.

barbiturate A type of sedative drug that acts to depress the functioning of the central nervous system.

basic research Research conducted to advance knowledge, without any immediate concern for the practical uses of that knowledge.

behavior control See *behavior modification.*

behavior modification Alteration or control of behavior through systematic application of principles of learning.

behavior therapy Applications of the principles of experimental psychology, especially principles of learning to treat psychological problems. See also *desensitization; operant therapy; role playing; token economy.*

behaviorism A school of psychology that emphasizes observable behavior as opposed to unobservable conscious processes.

benzodiazepines Tranquilizers such as Valium and Librium that relieve anxiety without having a sedative effect.

binocular vision The cooperation of the two eyes in giving solidity and distance to viewed objects.

biofeedback A technique for monitoring bodily processes (such as brain waves and blood pressure) so that a person can identify fluctuations in these processes and try to control them.

biological rhythms Daily, monthly, annual, and other quicker rhythms or cycles that characterize behavior and experience. See also *circadian rhythm, infradian rhythm, ultradian rhythm.*

biorhythms The idea, now discredited, that people are influenced by three biological rhythms initiated at the time of birth: a 23-day physical rhythm, a 28-day emotional rhythm, and a 33-day intellectual rhythm.

bipolar disorder A psychological disorder characterized by alteration between states of deep depression and extreme elation.

blind spot The area of the retina where the optic nerve leaves the eye.

blood flow measurement Monitoring of the amount of blood flowing to different parts of the brain in order to determine what parts of the brain are involved in various activities.

brain stem The central core of the brain; its functions are connected to the fundamental processes of survival and the emotions.

brain waves Rhythmic electrical impulses given off by the neurons in the cerebral cortex.

brightness constancy The tendency for objects to appear to be the same brightness no matter what the lighting conditions.

Broca's area An area of the left frontal lobe of the brain that is involved with language.

Cannon-Bard theory The idea that both the subjective experience and the physiological arousal associated with an emotion occur simultaneously, rather than one causing the other.

case study Research based on long-term examination of an individual subject.

castration anxiety According to Freud, a boy's fear that his father will discover the boy's attraction to his mother and will punish him by castration.

catatonia A type of schizophrenia

characterized by alternation between long periods of extreme immobility and bursts of aggressive or violent behavior.

catharsis The release of emotional tension thought to occur when a person engages in or observes violent activity; in psychoanalysis, the release of pent-up emotions as the result of bringing buried thoughts to the surface of consciousness.

central nervous system The brain and spinal cord.

cerebellum A structure at the back of the brain concerned primarily with the control of body position and movement.

cerebral cortex The largest area of the human brain, covering the rest of the brain parts; it is responsible for sensory and perceptual processes and is the site of thought, consciousness, and memory.

cerebral hemispheres The two halves of the cerebral cortex; each controls one side of the body and is somewhat specialized in its functions.

circadian rhythm A biological rhythm that occurs about every 24 hours, such as the sleep-waking cycle.

clairvoyance The ability to know about an object or event without employing the usual senses; a form of extrasensory perception.

clang associations In schizophrenics, creation of sentences by associating words with similar sounds.

classical conditioning A type of learning in which a neutral stimulus, as the result of being paired with an unconditioned stimulus, comes to elicit a response originally elicited by the unconditioned stimulus.

client-centered therapy A humanistic approach to therapy, developed by Carl Rogers, in which the client is encouraged to express her true feelings and become her true self.

clinical psychology The subfield of psychology that focuses on diagnosing psychological problems and providing psychotherapy.

clinical retardation Moderate to profound mental retardation, usually diagnosed at birth. It usually has a specific neurological, metabolic, or genetic cause that can be determined. See also *sociocultural retardation.*

closure The tendency to perceptually fill in the gaps in an incomplete figure.

cochlea The spiral-shaped part of the inner ear that contains the receptor cells for hearing.

cognitive labeling theory Schachter's idea that an emotion is the result of mental appraisal of physiological sensations that arise in a particular context.

cognitive learning The acquisition of information and of ways of dealing with information.

cognitive map A mental representation of the relationships between locations.

cognitive motives Motives based in people's higher mental processes rather than in their physical needs.

cognitive restructuring In rational-emotive therapy, getting the patient to substitute more rational beliefs for irrational ones.

cohort effects Differences between people who grow up during different historical periods.

collective unconscious According to Jung, a part of the human mind that is filled with archetypes of universal human experience and that is shared by all human beings. See also *personal unconscious.*

color blindness See *dichromatic color blindness; monochromatic color blindness.*

color constancy The tendency for objects to appear to be the same color despite changes in lighting conditions or proximity to other colors.

community psychology The subfield of psychology that focuses on preventing and treating psychological problems at a community level.

competence motive The need to confirm one's ability to interact effectively with one's environment.

compulsion An irrational desire to engage in ritualistic acts.

concept A word or idea that represents a category of things with related characteristics.

concrete operational period According to Piaget, the third stage of cognitive development (ages 7 to 12), during which the child learns to mentally manipulate objects and to understand concepts such as conservation.

condensation According to Freud,
the fact that symbols in a dream can have multiple meanings.

conditioned response A response that has come to be elicited by a stimulus that does not naturally elicit that response.

conditioned stimulus A previously neutral stimulus that, through repeated pairing with an unconditioned stimulus, comes to elicit a response.

cones Light-sensitive cells in the retina that are responsible for color vision.

conformity Acceptance of the norms of a group or society.

consciousness A level of thought that integrates and regulates experience; it is sometimes necessary for normal activities but often is not.

conservation The fact that a substance's weight, mass, or volume remains the same even when the substance changes shape.

constancy The tendency to perceive objects in a constant way, despite changes in lighting or distance.

consumer psychology The subfield of psychology that is concerned with the application of psychological principles to the purchase and consumption of goods and services.

contact comfort The infant's innate tendency to derive pleasure from contact with another body, especially that of his mother.

continuous reinforcement Reinforcement of a response every time it is emitted.

control group In an experiment, a group of subjects against which the experimental group is compared.

cornea The transparent protective coating on the front part of the eye.

corpus callosum A mass of nerve fibers connecting the two hemispheres of the cerebral cortex.

correlation The degree to which two sets of measures are associated with each other.

correlation coefficient A statistic that describes the degree to which one set of scores is related to a second set of scores.

correlational studies Research in which psychologists try to discover a relationship between two factors by measuring each separately and then comparing results.

counseling psychology The subfield of psychology that focuses on helping people with such issues as career decisions, marital problems, and readjustment to life after an illness or injury.

countertransference In psychoanalysis, the phenomenon that occurs when a patient begins to react to the therapist on the basis of the therapist's problems and not her own.

critical period A point early in an animal's life during which a relatively small amount of learning can produce a major and lasting effect; if the behavior is not learned at this time, it may never be learned at all.

cross-sectional study A research study based on subjects of different ages all measured at a single point in time. See also *longitudinal study*.

cross-situational consistency The assumption that people have the same personality at all times and in all situations.

crystallized intelligence The kind of mental ability that includes verbal skills, the ability to define words, and accumulated knowledge. See also *fluid intelligence*.

cultural model In abnormal psychology, defining normality in terms of the accepted standards of a particular culture.

cumulative deficit The finding that as disadvantaged children grow older their IQ scores tend to fall farther behind the scores of more advantaged children.

decibel Unit for measuring the loudness of a sound.

defense mechanism A method used by the ego to deny, change, or channel unacceptable impulses or ideas so that they need not be dealt with consciously.

deinstitutionalization The process of returning chronically disturbed mental patients to community life.

delayed reinforcement Reward administered long after the response was emitted.

delta sleep The stage of sleep in which the sleeper is hardest to waken; deep sleep.

delusion A false belief about oneself or one's environment.

delusion of grandeur The irra-tional belief that one is a famous person or religious figure.

delusion of persecution The irrational belief that other people are conspiring against one.

dendrites Short fibers projecting from a neuron that receive messages from other neurons.

dependent variable In an experiment, the behavior that is being measured—that may be affected by changes in the independent variable.

depression Feelings of worthlessness, hopelessness, lethargy, and helplessness; a psychological disorder marked by such feelings.

depth perception The ability to perceive that objects are three-dimensional and at a certain distance just by looking at them.

descriptive studies Research in which the scientist is primarily concerned with setting forth a clear account of the subject's behavior or self-reports.

desensitization A method of behavior therapy in which the client is taught to relax in anxiety-producing situations.

developmental psychology The subfield of psychology concerned with human development through the life cycle.

dichromatic color blindness The inability to distinguish between red and green or between yellow and blue.

discrimination In learning, the ability to distinguish between stimuli; responding to one stimulus while not responding to a similar stimulus. In social psychology, behaving differently toward members of a specific group on the basis of prejudice toward that group.

discriminative stimulus A stimulus that becomes associated with the delivery of reinforcement because reinforcement occurs in its presence.

disengagement theory The idea that the most appropriate way to age is mutual withdrawal of the individual from society and of society from the individual.

disorganized schizophrenia Schizophrenia characterized by bizarre behavior, including strange facial expressions, speech, and emotional reactions.

displacement Redirecting unconscious urges toward a more accessible or more socially acceptable object.

dissociation A separation between different aspects of consciousness.

dopamine A chemical transmitter substance in the brain.

double bind A situation in which an individual cannot win, because he is given contradictory directions.

double standard The idea that the rules governing male sexual behavior are different from the rules governing female sexual behavior.

Down's syndrome A disorder caused by incorrect distribution of genetic material in the zygote; it is characterized by mental retardation and various physical abnormalities.

drive The psychological experiencing of a biological need.

drive reduction theory The idea that motivation involves a basic physiological need that is experienced as a psychological drive; this drive is reduced when the physiological need is satisfied.

dualism The idea that the mind (consciousness) is separate from the brain (body).

ectomorph The slender physical type of person, with long bones, poor musculature, and delicate constitution. See also *endomorph; mesomorph*.

educational psychology The subfield of psychology involved with the design of educational settings and teaching techniques and with the training of teachers.

EEG See *electroencephalograph*.

efferent neurons Neurons that carry messages from the central nervous system to the muscles and glands; motor neurons. See also *afferent neurons*.

ego According to Freud, the part of the personality that directs and controls basic biological urges by seeking to gratify them within socially acceptable bounds.

egocentrism The inability to see things from perspectives other than one's own.

eidetic imagery The ability to retain sharp visual images of things no longer in one's field of vision.

electrical stimulation of the brain (ESB) The application of an electrical current to specific areas of the brain in order to discover the functions of the areas and to alter behavior.

electroencephalograph (EEG) A machine used to record brain waves. The printed-out record of the brain waves is called an electroencephalogram.

electroshock therapy Application of electrical current to the brain in order to relieve symptoms of depression.

Electra complex According to Freud, a young girl's attraction to her father and envy of her mother that occurs during the phallic stage of psychosexual development.

emotion The physiological changes, subjective experience, and expression of reactions involved in such phenomena as joy, fear, grief, and anger.

emotional isolation See *loneliness.*

encoding Linking information to concepts and categories that one has already learned in order to store it in long-term memory.

encounter groups Therapy groups in which people can meet for the purpose of increasing their openness and sensitivity to one another.

endocrine system A group of glands that secrete chemicals directly into the bloodstream.

endomorph The heavy, fat physical type of person. See also *ectomorph; mesomorph.*

endorphins Morphinelike chemicals in the brain that seem to be involved in mood and pain control.

engineering psychology The subfield of psychology that focuses on appropriate design of equipment to be used by human beings.

enkaphalins Morphinelike chemicals in the brain that seem to be involved in mood and pain control.

epilepsy A convulsive brain disorder characterized by mental blackouts and sometimes seizures.

epinephrine A hormone secreted by the adrenal glands that is involved in physiological arousal.

equilibrium The sense of balance.

erogenous zones Pleasure-giving areas of the body.

ESB See *electrical stimulation of the brain.*

ESP See *extrasensory perception.*

est A seminar program in which participants go through a series of exercises designed to help them accept themselves.

estrogen A female sex hormone.

evoked potential A computer-derived average of the brain waves produced in response to a particular stimulus.

exhaustion stage According to Selye, the final stage in an animal's physiological response to long-term stress. See also *alarm reaction; resistance stage.*

exorcism A ritual used to cast out evil spirits from the body.

experiment A study in which the researcher places subjects in different conditions and compares their effects.

experimental group In an experiment, the group of subjects being studied. See also *control group.*

experimental psychology The subfield of psychology that focuses on research on such fundamental psychological processes as perception, learning, memory, motivation, and emotion.

experimenter expectancy effects Cases in which the results of research are unintentionally affected by what the researcher expects to find.

extinction The weakening of a learned response. In classical conditioning, it results from repeated presentation of the conditioned stimulus without the unconditioned stimulus; in operant conditioning, it results from withdrawal of reinforcement.

extrasensory perception (ESP) Perception of objects, events, or thoughts by other than normal sensory means.

extravert According to Jung, an extreme personality type characterized by sociability and an outgoing manner. See also *introvert.*

extrinsic motivation Doing something for an external reward. See also *intrinsic motivation.*

F scale A personality scale used to measure the extent to which a person has an authoritarian personality.

farsightedness Poor visual acuity for close objects, caused by the image falling behind the retina. See also *nearsightedness.*

figure-ground perception The tendency to differentiate between an object and the background against which the object stands.

fissures Two grooves that divide the cerebral cortex into lobes.

fixation According to Freud, a focusing of sexual energy at an early stage of psychosexual development because of unresolved conflicts at that stage.

fixed-interval schedule Administering reinforcement after a set period of time. See also *variable-interval schedule.*

fixed-ratio schedule Administering reinforcement after a fixed number of responses. See also *variable-ratio schedule.*

flashbulb memories Sharp, vivid memories of the setting and manner in which one heard of a major event that has had an impact on one's life.

fluid intelligence The kind of mental ability, especially nonverbal, that allows people to see old problems in new ways and to solve puzzles and visual problems. See also *crystallized intelligence.*

formal operational period According to Piaget, the adolescent stage of cognitive development, during which the individual learns to deal with complex concepts and with abstract notions.

free association A method used in psychoanalysis in which the client is asked to say whatever comes to mind.

frequency distribution A summary of the number of subjects who receive each score.

frontal lobe The section of the cerebral cortex believed to be the site of personality and to be concerned with some aspects of speech.

frustration The blocking of one's efforts to achieve a desired goal.

frustration-aggression hypothesis The idea that most aggressive behavior results from frustration.

functional fixedness The inability to see a new use for a familiar object.

functionalism An early school of psychology that emphasized practical applications of the study of conscious processes.

fundamental attribution error The tendency to overestimate the role of personal dispositions in causing people's behavior and to underestimate the role of situational constraints.

g According to Spearman, a single general-intelligence factor on which individuals can vary.

galvanic skin response (GSR) A change in the electrical conductivity of the skin caused by the activity of the sweat glands.

gate control theory The idea that the transmission of pain signals in the body depends on "gates" in the central nervous system that allow or prevent passage of pain signals. See also *specificity theory*.

generalization Making the same response to separate but similar stimuli.

genital stage According to Freud, the final period of psychosexual development. Beginning with puberty, sexual energies are again focused on the genitals, and the individual seeks adult heterosexual relationships.

Gestalt psychology A school of psychology that identified the basic principles of perceptual organization.

gestalt therapy A humanistic approach to therapy in which the client attempts to pull together all aspects of her personality into a unified whole.

glia Cells in the brain that surround, cushion, and nourish nerve cells.

graphology Handwriting analysis.

groupthink The tendency for members of a policy-making group to suppress all individual doubts and dissent, creating the illusion of unanimity.

GSR See *galvanic skin response.*

habituation Becoming used to a novel stimulus so that it no longer seems notable or upsetting.

hallucination Seeing or hearing things that aren't there.

heritability An estimate of how much of the variation between individuals on a particular trait is due to genetic factors.

hippocampus A structure in the brain's limbic system that appears to play a role in short-term memory.

homophobia An irrational fear or intolerance of homosexuals.

hormones Chemicals secreted by glands of the endocrine system.

hospices Facilities designed for terminally ill people to die in peace and dignity.

humanistic psychology An approach to psychology that emphasizes the uniqueness, self-esteem, and dignity of the individual.

hyperphagic Pertaining to animals whose hypothalamus has been lesioned, resulting in compulsive overeating and excessive weight gain.

hypnosis A state of increased suggestibility, or willingness to comply with another person's directions, that is brought about through use of relaxation-producing techniques.

hypnotic amnesia Forgetting that is induced by hypnotic suggestion.

hypothalamus A structure in the brain stem that monitors body activities such as eating and sleeping and that plays a major role in controlling emotional behavior.

hypothesis An educated guess as to why something occurs as it does.

id According to Freud, the reservoir of basic biological urges that motivate the individual.

ideas of reference The belief that everything other people say and do somehow refers to oneself.

identification The process of taking on the values and behaviors of another person or a group.

identity crisis According to Erikson, the adolescent's struggle to establish a stable sense of self.

ideology A system of beliefs to which people can have a strong commitment.

idiographic approach An approach to personality in which researchers focus on the detailed study of specific individuals. See also *nomothetic approach.*

imitative aggression Aggressive acts that duplicate those observed in another person. See also *nonimitative aggression.*

imprinting A form of learning in which certain stimuli very early in life produce behavior patterns that are not generally reversible.

incongruence According to Rogers, a discrepancy between a person's self-concept and his experience, or between his real self and ideal self.

incus One of the three small bones of the middle ear.

independent variable In an experiment, a factor manipulated by the experimenter in order to see what effect it has on the dependent variable.

inferiority complex According to Adler, the real or imagined feelings of inferiority that motivate people to achieve goals.

infradian rhythm A biological cycle that occurs over a period longer than a day, such as the menstrual cycle.

insight A sudden understanding of a problem—seeing it in a new light, thereby finding a solution.

insomnia Difficulty in falling or staying asleep.

instincts Inborn, unlearned, biologically purposeful responses.

institutional violence Violence that is encouraged by people's roles in organizations or social institutions, such as prisons and armies.

intellectualization Reducing anxiety by analyzing threatening issues intellectually, thereby detaching them from the self.

intelligence The capacity to acquire and apply knowledge.

intelligence quotient (IQ) A measure of mental ability obtained by dividing a child's mental age by his chronological age and multiplying by 100. In adults, IQ is determined by comparing test scores to those of a standardized sample.

interpretation In psychoanalysis, pointing out aspects of the patient's narrative that are important and explaining their significance.

interval schedule See *fixed-interval schedule; variable-interval schedule.*

intrinsic motivation Doing something for the pleasure of the activity itself. See also *extrinsic motivation.*

introspection The careful examination of one's own conscious experience.

introvert According to Jung, an extreme personality type characterized by shyness and a desire to be alone. See also *extravert.*

IQ See *intelligence quotient.*

iris The colored portion of the eye that contains muscles that control the widening and narrowing of the pupil.

James-Lange theory The idea that an event or stimulus causes bodily changes, which then produce the subjectively experienced emotion.

jigsaw technique A teaching method designed to foster cooperative interdependence among learners.

kinesthesis The sensation of the body's position, movement, and tension.

language A rule-governed system of symbols used for communicating information, thoughts, or feelings.

latency period According to Freud, the period of psychosexual development (about ages 6 to 12) during which sexual urges are dormant.

latent dream content According to Freud, the hidden meaning of a dream.

latent learning Learning that occurs without any direct reinforcement or intent to learn.

learned helplessness The discovery that one's actions are ineffective, leading to passivity and depression.

learning A relatively permanent change in behavior as the result of experience or practice.

learning by observation See *modeling*.

lens The portion of the eye that captures light and focuses it on the retina.

levels of generality A concept's grouping of objects in broader or narrower categories (for example a "fruit" vs. an "apple").

life review A self-examination that many old people undergo when they realize they are approaching death.

life structure The basic pattern or design of one's life at a given time.

limbic system A set of structures attached to the bottom of the cerebral cortex that appear to be involved in emotional expression.

lipofuscin The chemical that causes brown "age spots" to appear on the skin of older persons.

lithium carbonate An antidepressant drug used to treat bipolar disorders.

locus of control The perceived site of factors that influence what happens to a person. Persons with an *internal* locus of control believe their own behaviors generally determine their outcomes, whereas those with an *external* locus of control believe that external forces control their lives.

loneliness A feeling of longing and emptiness caused by a lack of emotional attachments (*emotional isolation*) or of social ties (*social isolation*).

longitudinal study A research study in which subjects are followed over a long period of time. See also *cross-sectional study*.

long-term memory Mental storage of information for an indefinite period of time.

LSD (lysergic acid diethylamide) A drug chemically derived from ergotic alkaloids that is capable of producing vivid imagery, hallucinations, and mental disorganization.

malleus One of the three small bones of the middle ear.

mania A state of intense excitement that may be so extreme that the individual becomes disoriented, incoherent, unresponsive to others, and potentially violent.

manic-depressive disorder See *bipolar disorder*.

manifest dream content According to Freud, the surface meaning of a dream, hiding its latent content.

mantra A word or series of words on which to meditate.

marijuana A psychoactive drug made from the hemp plant, *Cannabis sativa*.

maturation The unfolding of inherited biological patterns that are preprogrammed into each individual.

mean A measure of central tendency that is determined by adding individual scores and dividing by the total number of scores in order to arrive at an average. See also *median; mode*.

median A measure of central tendency represented by the score that falls in the exact middle of the distribution; half the scores fall above this number and half fall below. See also *mean; mode*.

medical model In abnormal psychology, defining normality in terms of health and disease and treating mental illness as a disease to be cured.

meditation A state of consciousness achieved by relaxing the body and focusing the mind on one thought or object.

medulla A structure in the brain stem that controls such basic rhythms as heartbeat and breathing and that contains reflex centers for vomiting, sneezing, coughing, and swallowing.

menarche The first menstrual period.

menopause The cessation of menstruation.

mental age A measure of intellectual ability obtained from tests that have been standardized using average scores of children at each age level.

mental retardation Intellectual deficits marked by IQ scores lower than 70. Retardation ranges from mild (IQ of 55–69) to profound (IQ lower than 25). See also *clinical retardation; sociocultural retardation*.

mesomorph The muscular or athletic physical type. See also *ectomorph; endomorph*.

midlife crisis The sudden recognition, at around age 40, that one's life is half over, accompanied by a questioning of the meaning of one's life and a reassessment of one's goals.

midlife transition The shift, at around age 40, from early to middle adulthood, involving changes in tasks, limitations, and opportunities.

Minnesota Multiphasic Personality Inventory (MMPI) A personality test, consisting of 550 items, originally designed to assess psychological disorders.

mode The score that occurs most often in a frequency distribution—the most "popular" score. See also *mean; median*.

modeling Observing the behavior of others and emulating their behavior.

monocular cues Clues to an object's distance that can be perceived with only one eye.

motivated forgetting Forgetting things because remembering them would be embarrassing or painful.

motivation A tendency to act to achieve a particular goal or state.

motives The internal factors that arouse and direct behavior.

motor neurons See *efferent neurons*.

Müller-Lyer illusion An optical illusion demonstrating that lines of equal length will appear unequal if arrow shapes pointing inward are placed on one line and arrow shapes pointing outward are placed on the other.

myelin sheath A white, fatty substance encasing certain nerve fibers.

narcolepsy A disorder characterized by brief attacks of deep sleep.

nearsightedness Poor visual acuity for distant objects, caused by the image falling in front of the retina. See also *farsightedness*.

Necker cube An ambiguous graphic presentation of a cube.

need A biological condition of deprivation that stimulates activity toward correcting the condition.

need to achieve See *achievement motive*.

negative reinforcement The strengthening of a response by removing an unpleasant stimulus.

neo-Freudians Psychoanalytic theorists who were strongly influenced by Freud's theory but gave less priority to the role of instinctual drives and fixed stages of development.

neologisms Invented words that have meaning only to the inventor.

nervous system See *central nervous system; peripheral nervous system*.

neurons The basic cells of the nervous system.

neuropeptides A recently discovered family of chemicals in the brain that have major effects on experience and behavior.

neuroses Relatively mild psychological disorders characterized by anxiety, inability to cope effectively with challenges, and difficulty in interpersonal relationships.

neutral stimulus A stimulus that does not produce a specific unconditioned response.

nomothetic approach An approach to personality in which researchers examine large numbers of people in order to discover similarities, differences, and general patterns of personality. See also *idiographic approach*.

non-age-graded influences Experiences and events that are unique to the individual rather than associated with a particular stage of life. See also *age-graded influences*.

nonimitative aggression Aggressive acts engaged in by children who have observed an aggressive model but whose aggression does not duplicate that of the model. See also *imitative aggression*.

non-REM sleep That period of sleep during which the person passes through four sleep stages, each characterized by specific EEG patterns, but does not dream. See also *REM sleep*.

norepinephrine A hormone secreted by the adrenal glands that is involved in physiological arousal; also, a transmitter substance in the brain.

normal distribution Distribution of scores on a test in which the majority of the test-takers achieve scores in the middle range, while increasingly fewer achieve scores toward the higher and lower ends of the range.

norms See *social norms*.

object permanence The recognition that a physical object continues to exist even when it is out of sight or out of reach.

observation A method of research in which the researcher observes behavior as it occurs in a particular situation.

obsession A persistent unwanted thought.

obsessive-compulsive disorder An anxiety disorder characterized by persistent unwanted thoughts and repeated, ritualistic behavior.

occipital lobe The section of the cerebral cortex primarily involved in seeing and perhaps in memory.

Oedipus complex According to Freud, the young boy's feeling of sexual attraction toward his mother and hostility toward his father.

operant conditioning A type of learning in which behaviors increase or decrease in frequency as the result of application or withdrawal of rewards.

operant response A response that operates on the environment to produce some effect.

operant therapy A method of behavior therapy in which rewards are used to motivate a client to perform a desired behavior or to refrain from performing an undesired behavior.

optic nerve The nerve tract that carries messages from the eye to the visual portion of the brain.

oral stage According to Freud, the first stage in psychosexual development (from birth to age 2), during which the mouth is the primary focus of pleasure.

organizational psychology The subfield of psychology that focuses on devising methods for businesses and other organizations to function more effectively.

overregularization In language learning, a child's tendency to apply a grammatical rule in all instances—even when it is incorrect.

paranoid schizophrenia A type of psychosis characterized by intense delusions and hallucinations.

parapsychology The study of phenomena, such as ESP, that are beyond the usual bounds of psychology.

parascience Ways of looking at the world that do not employ the traditional methods of science.

parasympathetic nervous system A subdivision of the autonomic nervous system; it acts to slow down bodily functions, especially after a stress reaction. See also *sympathetic nervous system*.

parietal lobe The section of the cerebral cortex concerned with the skin senses and the sense of bodily position.

partial reinforcement Rewarding a particular response some but not all of the time.

peak experience According to Maslow, a feeling of total appreciation of a moment in time or of intense fulfillment.

peer counseling An approach to

therapy in which people with problems and backgrounds similar to those of clients are used as counselors.

perception The processes by which people come to experience the stimuli in their environment.

perceptual constancy See *constancy*.

perceptual illusions Instances in which perception and reality do not agree.

perceptual set The tendency to perceive what one expects to.

peripheral nervous system Nerve fibers and tissues lying outside the brain and spinal cord.

permissive child rearing A child-rearing style in which the parent avoids attempts to actively control the child's behavior. See also *authoritarian child rearing*.

person perception Forming inferences about other people on the basis of their physical appearance, reputation, or observable behavior.

personal unconscious According to Jung, repressed or forgotten material. See also *collective unconscious*.

personality The distinctive patterns of behavior, thought, and emotions that characterize an individual's adaptation to the situations of his or her life.

personality disorder A psychological disorder characterized by a rigid and narrow range of responses that significantly restrict the person's way of relating to his or her environment.

personality inventory A collection of statements or questions to be answered along such dimensions as agree-disagree and like-dislike; such tests are used to assess people's interests, attitudes, social relations, values, and adjustment.

personnel psychology The subfield of psychology concerned with selecting workers for particular jobs and with issues of morale and job satisfaction.

peyote The Mexican name for the mescale cactus, from which mescaline is derived. Used as a drug, peyote produces intense sensory experiences and hallucinations.

phallic stage According to Freud, the stage of psychosexual development (ages 4 to 5) during which

the sex organs become the focus of pleasure and the Oedipal and Electra conflicts must be resolved.

phenothiazines Antipsychotic drugs used in the treatment of schizophrenia.

phobia An intense irrational fear of a particular object or activity.

phrenology A discredited approach to the study of personality based on the idea that the bumps and hollows of the skull represent specific personality traits.

pitch The high or low quality of a sound.

Ponzo illusion An optical illusion in which equal horizontal lines placed over converging vertical lines appear to be unequal in length.

positive reinforcement Rewarding a behavior in order to increase its frequency.

posthypnotic suggestion An instruction given during hypnosis to perform some behavior once the trance is over.

precognition Foreknowledge of future events; a form of extrasensory perception.

predisposition A readiness to behave or develop in a particular way.

prefrontal lobotomy An operation in which the frontal lobes are separated from the rest of the brain.

prejudice An unfavorable attitude held about a particular group of people.

preoperational period According to Piaget, the second stage of cognitive development (ages 2 through 7), during which the child has not yet mastered such basic mental operations as conservation.

primal therapy Arthur Janov's method of therapy, in which the client is encouraged to reexperience childhood pain and to release emotions built up over a lifetime.

primary reinforcers Stimuli that naturally increase a response, such as food, water, and affection. See also *secondary reinforcers*.

process schizophrenia Schizophrenia that develops gradually and slowly; it is more resistant to treatment than reactive schizophrenia.

projection The unconscious attribution of one's own unacceptable

thoughts and feelings to other people.

projective tests Personality tests in which the individual is asked to provide her own interpretation of materials such as pictures or inkblots.

prosopagnosia An inability to identify people from their faces.

prototypical concepts Instances of a concept that are most representative of that concept.

proximity In social psychology, the physical distance between people. In perception, the tendency to link objects that are close to one another.

psilocybin A psychedelic drug derived from mushrooms.

psychedelic drugs Drugs that cause extreme alterations in perception and thought processes, often producing delusions, hallucinations, and intensified sensory awareness.

psychiatrist A medical doctor who specializes in the diagnosis and treatment of mental disorders.

psychoactive drugs Drugs that have a noticeable impact on consciousness and behavior.

psychoanalysis The method of psychotherapy based on Freud's psychoanalytic theory of personality; its basic premise is that the unconscious mind contains buried impulses and desires that must be brought to the surface if anxiety is to disappear.

psychoanalytic theory Freud's theory that all human behavior is dominated by instinctual biological urges that must be controlled; it is the conflict between the urges and the efforts to control them that leads to emotional problems.

psychodrama A method of therapy in which one acts out scenes in order to bring out their emotional significance.

psychological androgyny The ability to integrate both "masculine" and "feminine" traits into one's personality.

psychological reactance The motive to restore or reassert a threatened freedom, sometimes by doing the opposite of whatever we feel others are trying to make us do.

psychology The science of behavior and mental processes.

psychopharmacology The use of drugs to affect patients' moods and behaviors.

psychoses Major psychological disorders characterized by loss of contact with reality, loss of control over feelings and actions, and such symptoms as delusions and hallucinations.

psychosexual stages According to Freud, stages that children go through in which their sexual energy is focused on different areas of the body. See also *anal stage; genital stage; latency period; oral stage; phallic stage.*

psychosocial stages Eight stages of personality development through the life cycle, as proposed by Erikson. At each stage the individual must resolve a different crisis.

psychosomatic disease Physical disorder caused at least in part by stress or other psychological factors.

psychosurgery Brain surgery designed to relieve psychological symptoms.

punishment An unpleasant event or outcome following a response.

pupil The opening in the eye that allows light rays to enter.

racism The differential attitudes toward and treatment of individuals on the basis of their racial group membership, grounded in a belief (whether conscious or unconscious) that one race is inherently superior to another.

random sample In statistics, a sample in which each member of the population being studied has an equal chance of being chosen.

range The variability of a set of scores as indicated by the lowest and highest scores in the distribution.

ratio schedule See *fixed-ratio schedule; variable-ratio schedule.*

rational-emotive therapy Albert Ellis's approach to therapy, which assumes that emotional difficulties are caused by irrational thinking.

rationalization Justifying one's actions by substituting an acceptable explanation for the real, unacceptable reason.

reaction formation Developing behavior patterns the opposite of those that would create anxiety.

reactive schizophrenia Schizophrenia that strikes suddenly, in reaction to a stressful life event. See also *process schizophrenia.*

rebirthing A therapy designed to help the individual reexperience the trauma of birth in order to exorcise the pain.

receptors Sensitive cells in sense organs.

reflex An automatic action involving sensory nerves, motor nerves, and the spinal cord, with no intervention from higher brain centers.

rehearsal Repeating of information to oneself in order to store it in long-term memory.

reinforcement Any event following a response that strengthens that response or that increases the probability of the response occurring again. See also *delayed reinforcement; negative reinforcement; partial reinforcement; positive reinforcement; schedules of reinforcement.*

reliability In abnormal psychology, the extent to which experts agree on the particular diagnostic category to place a patient in. See also *validity.*

REM sleep A period of sleep during which rapid eye movements and a specific EEG pattern occur and the individual appears to be dreaming. See also *Non-REM sleep.*

replication Repetition of an experiment to see whether the same results will be obtained.

repression The exclusion of unpleasant or painful memories or impulses from conscious awareness.

research See *applied research; basic research.*

resistance In psychoanalysis, the reluctance to bring important ideas into consciousness.

resistance stage According to Selye, the second stage in an animal's physiological response to stress; it involves mobilizing the body to deal with the stressful situation. See also *alarm reaction; exhaustion stage.*

reticular activating system Nerve tissue in the brain stem that serves to screen incoming messages and alert higher brain centers to important information.

retina An inner lining at the back of the eye that contains the light-sensitive rods and cones.

rhodopsin (visual purple) A chemical in the rods of the retina that changes when exposed to light.

rods Light-sensitive cells in the retina that are insensitive to color.

role playing In behavior therapy, practicing a set of desired behaviors in a protective setting in which clients need not worry about the consequences of their behavior.

rooting response The newborn baby's tendency to turn its head in the direction of a touch on its cheek.

Rorschach test A personality test in which individuals are asked to respond to a series of ambiguous inkblots.

sample A group of subjects representing a larger population.

schedules of reinforcement Administration of reinforcement according to a fixed or varying number of responses or time interval.

schizophrenia A type of psychosis characterized by serious alterations of perception, activity, emotion, thought, and personality. See also *catatonia; disorganized schizophrenia; paranoid schizophrenia; process schizophrenia; undifferentiated schizophrenia.*

scream therapy A type of group therapy in which individuals are encouraged to scream whenever they feel especially overwhelmed.

secondary reinforcers Stimuli that become reinforcers as a result of association with primary reinforcers.

self-actualization According to Maslow, full realization of one's potential as a human being.

self-esteem One's positive regard for oneself.

self-fulfilling prophecy The idea that one's expectations can influence or bring about that which one expects to happen.

self-help groups Groups of individuals with similar problems who meet to exchange information and feelings.

self-reports People's own assessments of their thoughts and feelings, as reported to researchers.

semicircular canals The sense organs for equilibrium located in the inner ear.

senile dementia A disease caused by damage to brain cells in old age, producing such symptoms as memory loss, disorientation in time and place, and impaired attention.

senses The organs and neural pathways through which information about the environment is received, including vision, hearing, the skin senses, smell, and taste.

sensorimotor period According to Piaget, the first stage of cognitive development (from birth to age 2), during which the child learns to coordinate sensory information and motor (muscle) activities.

sensory deprivation Placing a person in a specially designed environment devoid of sensory stimulation, producing alterations in perception and consciousness.

sensory neurons See *afferent neurons.*

sensory storage The momentary retention of sensory information after it has been received.

serotonin A transmitter substance in the brain that apparently plays a role in temperature regulation and sensory perception.

sex roles Social expectations about what men and women should do and should be like.

sex therapy Various techniques used to treat sexual dysfunction.

sexism The idea that one sex is inherently superior to the other.

sexual identity One's perception of oneself as male or female.

shaping Producing a desired behavior by rewarding responses that come closer and closer to the behavior until the desired response is finally achieved.

short-term memory Information that has just been learned and that may be retained for up to 20 seconds before being forgotten or transferred to long-term memory.

similarity The tendency to perceive as a unit elements that are similar to one another.

size constancy The process by which we take into account changing distances and other cues in order to perceive objects as remaining the same size.

skin senses The receptors in the skin for pressure, temperature, and pain.

Skinner box An apparatus, developed by B. F. Skinner, used for studying operant conditioning of animals.

sleep apnea A disorder characterized by stoppage of breathing several times during a night's sleep.

social comparison The idea that people have a need to compare themselves with others in a similar situation in order to clarify their own feelings and experiences.

social isolation See *loneliness.*

social learning theory An approach to personality that focuses on the role of imitation and social rewards in the learning of patterns of behavior.

social motives Motives that involve our orientation toward other people, such as the need to affiliate.

social norms Rules that dictate appropriate and inappropriate behavior in a society.

social psychology The subfield of psychology that focuses on the ways in which people's behavior is affected by other people and by the social environment.

sociocultural retardation Mild mental retardation that is not usually diagnosed until a child enters school and that has multiple causes related to economic and social disadvantages. See also *clinical retardation.*

somatic nervous system The part of the peripheral nervous system that controls voluntary muscles and hence most body movements. See also *autonomic nervous system.*

somatic therapy The use of drugs, electroshock, or psychosurgery to treat the symptoms of psychological disorder.

somatotypes The three basic body types identified by Sheldon. See also *ectomorph; endomorph; mesomorph.*

specificity theory The idea that there are specific pain receptors throughout the body that relay signals of pain directly to the brain. See also *gate control theory.*

spinal cord A cylindrical structure of nerve tissue stretching from the base of the spine down through the center of the backbone; it provides basic connections between motor and sensory neurons and serves as a pathway for messages traveling to and from the brain.

split-brain surgery Severing of the corpus callosum, thereby greatly reducing communication between the two cerebral hemispheres.

spontaneous recovery The later reappearance of an extinguished response.

standard deviation A statistic that indicates the amount of variability in a set of scores. It is computed on the basis of the distance of each score from the mean.

standardization Administration of a test to a large sampling of subjects to determine the usual distribution of scores on the test.

Stanford-Binet An intelligence test emphasizing verbal and mathematical skills.

stapes One of the three small bones of the middle ear.

statistical approach In abnormal psychology, defining normality in terms of what is true of the average person in a population.

statistical significance The extent to which an observed difference between samples reflects real differences and not chance.

statistics Numbers used to describe and interpret data and observations.

stereotypes Notions of what entire groups of people are like based on their race, sex, occupation, or other group membership.

stimulus control A situation in which a response occurs only in the presence of a specific discriminative stimulus.

stranger anxiety The tendency of an infant to protest or withdraw when approached by an unfamiliar person.

stress Pressure from the environment that makes physical and emotional demands on a person.

stroke Blockage of a blood vessel in the brain, depriving the brain of oxygen.

structuralism An early school of psychology that emphasized the structure of conscious processes.

superego According to Freud, the part of the personality that acquires the values and ideals of the parents and society and imposes constraints on the id and ego; the conscience.

surrogate mother An artificial or substitute mother, such as those used by Harlow in his experiments with infant monkeys. Also, a woman who carries and gives birth to a child for a woman physically unable to do so.

survival motives Motives that must be satisfied if an organism is to survive.

syllogism A logical statement comprising a major premise, a minor premise, and a conclusion.

sympathetic nervous system A subdivision of the autonomic nervous system; it acts to accelerate certain bodily processes in response to stress. See also *parasympathetic nervous system*.

synapse The microscopic gap that separates the end of each axon from the dendrite or cell body of another neuron and across which transmitter substances travel.

synaptic transmission The movement of nerve impulses across a synapse from one neuron to another.

synesthesia The blending of senses, such as hearing color or seeing tastes.

tardive dyskinesia A neurological condition caused by prolonged use of antipsychotic drugs.

TAT See *Thematic Apperception Test*.

telepathy The awareness of another person's thoughts without benefit of normal sensory channels; a form of extrasensory perception.

temporal lobe The section of the cerebral cortex that contains centers for hearing and speech and possibly sites for memory and learning.

testosterone The male sex hormone.

Thematic Apperception Test (TAT) A personality test in which the person is asked to react to a series of drawings.

theory A set of ideas and principles that fit together to provide a perspective on some aspect of the world.

therapy The professional application of techniques intended to treat psychological problems and reduce stress.

thought The mental manipulation of ideas and concepts.

threshold The smallest amount of stimulation that can be detected by a particular sense organ.

timbre The richness or quality of a sound that comes from a particular sound source.

tip of the tongue (TOT) phenomenon The feeling of almost, but not quite, being able to recall a word or name.

token economy A form of behavior therapy in which the individual is given a token for each task accomplished; the tokens can later be traded for items that are rewarding to the individual.

trait theory The idea that people can be described in terms of the pattern of personality characteristics (traits) that they possess. *Common traits* are found to some degree in all individuals, whereas *individual traits* are unique to specific persons.

transcendental meditation (TM) A system of meditation developed by Maharishi Mahesh Yogi.

transference In psychoanalysis, the patient's tendency to treat the analyst in the same way he would treat an important authority figure in his life.

transmitter substances A group of chemicals in the nervous system that carry messages across synapses.

transsexual A person who believes that he or she is trapped in a body of the wrong sex.

trial and error Trying many solutions to a problem, one after another, in hopes that one will finally work.

tricyclics Widely used antidepressant drugs.

twins See *fraternal twins; identical twins*.

tympanic membrane The eardrum.

type theory The idea that people can be classified on the basis of overall personality types.

ultradian rhythm A biological rhythm or cycle that occurs more often than once a day, such as the heartbeat.

unconditional positive regard In client-centered therapy, the idea that the therapist should accept and respect the client and anything she has to say.

unconditioned response A response that naturally occurs for a given stimulus, before any conditioning takes place.

unconditioned stimulus A stimulus that produces an unconditioned response.

unconscious Ideas or impulses that a person has but is not aware of. See also *collective unconscious; personal unconscious*.

undifferentiated schizophrenia Schizophrenia characterized by a wide variety of symptoms.

validity In abnormal psychology, the extent to which a diagnostic category provides an accurate understanding of the causes and future course of the disorder. See also *reliability*.

variable See *dependent variable; independent variable*.

variable-interval schedule Administering reinforcement after a time period has passed, with the interval varying around some average. See also *fixed-interval schedule*.

variable-ratio schedule Administering reinforcement after a number of responses, with the number varying around some average. See also *fixed-ratio schedule*.

visual acuity The ability to discriminate details in the field of vision.

visual cliff An experimental apparatus designed to test depth perception in infants.

visual purple See *rhodopsin*.

visual threshold The smallest amount of stimulation the rods and cones will respond to.

Wechsler Adult Intelligence Scale (WAIS) A test of adult mental ability assessing both verbal abilities and performance skills.

Wernicke's area An area of the left temporal lobe of the brain that is involved in language.

Bibliography

Aarons, L. Sleep-assisted instruction. *Psychological Bulletin*, 1976, *83*, 1–40.

Adams, B., and Cromwell, R. Morning and night people in the family: A preliminary statement. *Family Coordinator*, 1978, *27*, 5–13.

Adams, V. Behavioral scientists argue guilt's role. *New York Times*, July 24, 1979.

Adelson, R., et al. A modeling film to reduce children's fear of dental treatment. *International Association of Dental Research Abstracts*, March 1972.

Adolph, E. F. The internal environment and behavior: Water content. *American Journal of Psychiatry*, 1941, *97*, 1365–1372.

Adorno, T. W., et al. *The authoritarian personality*. New York: Harper & Row, 1950.

Ainsworth, M.; Salter, D.; and Wittig, B. A. Attachment and exploratory behavior of one-year-olds in a strange situation. In B. M. Foss (Ed.), *Determinants of infant behavior*, vol. 4. New York: Wiley, 1967.

Allen, W. *Getting even*. New York: Random House, 1971.

Allport, G. W. *The nature of prejudice*. Reading, Mass.: Addison-Wesley, 1954.

Allport, G. W. *Personality: A psychological interpretation*. (2nd ed.) New York: Holt, Rinehart and Winston, 1961.

Allport G. W. The general and the unique in psychological science. *Journal of Personality*, 1962, *30*, 405–422.

Altman, L. K. Perceptions hinder treatment of senility. *New York Times*, June 24, 1980.

Altus, W. D. Birth order and its sequelae. *Science*, 1966, *151*, 44–49.

Amabile, T. M. Effects of external evaluations on artistic creativity. *Journal of Personality and Social Psychology*, 1979, *37*, 221–233.

American Psychiatric Association. *Electroconvulsive therapy: Task force report 14*. Washington, D.C.: APA, 1978.

American Psychiatric Association, *Diagnostic and statistical manual of mental disorders*. (3rd ed.) Washington, D.C.: APA, 1980.

Amoore, J. Stereochemical theory of olfaction. In H. Schultz et al. (Eds.), *Chemistry and physiology of flavors*. Westport, Conn.: Avi Publishers, 1967.

Anderson, J. W. The methodology of psychological biography. *Journal of Interdisciplinary History*, 1981, *11*, 455–475.

Andersson, B. Thirst—and brain control of water balance. *American Scientist*, July–August 1971.

Anthony, D. S. Is graphology valid? *Psychology Today*, August 1967.

Archer, D. Reading nonverbal clues. In Z. Rubin and E. B. McNeil, *The psychology of being human*. (Brief update ed.) New York: Harper & Row, 1979.

Archer, D. *How to expand your S.I.Q. (social intelligence quotient)*. New York: M. Evans, 1980.

Archer, D., and Akert, R. Words and everything else: Verbal and nonverbal cues in social interpretation. *Journal of Personality and Social Psychology*, 1977, *35*, 443–449.

Archer, D.; Kimes, D. D.; and Barrios, M. Face-ism. *Psychology Today*, September 1978.

Arehart-Treichel, J. The great pain plan. *Science News*, October 14, 1978.

Arieti, S., and Meth, J. M. Rare, unclassifiable, collective, and exotic psychotic syndromes. In S. Arieti (Ed.), *American handbook of psychiatry*, vol. 1. New York: Basic Books, 1959.

Aronson, E. Some antecedents of interpersonal attraction. In W. J. Arnold and D. Levine (Eds.), *Nebraska symposium on motivation, 1969*. Lincoln: University of Nebraska Press, 1969.

Aronson, E. *The social animal*. (3rd ed.) San Francisco: W. H. Freeman, 1980.

Aronson, E., et al. *The jigsaw classroom*. Beverly Hills, Calif.: Sage Publications, 1978.

Asch, S. E. Effects of group pressure upon the modification and distortion of judgments. In H. Guetzkow (Ed.), *Groups, leadership, and men*. Pittsburgh: Carnegie Press, 1951.

Asimov, I. *Is anyone there?* Garden City, N.Y.: Doubleday, 1967.

Atkinson, K.; MacWhinney, B.; and Stoel, C. An experiment on recognition of babbling. *Papers and reports on child language development*. Stanford, Calif.: Stanford University Press, 1970.

Atkinson, R. C., and Shiffrin, R. M. Human memory: A proposed system and its controlled processes. In K. W. Spence and J. T. Spence (Eds.), *The psychology of learning and motivation*, vol. 2. New York: Academic Press, 1968.

Ax, A. F. The physiological differentiation of emotional states. *Psychosomatic Medicine*, 1953, *15*, 433–442.

Ayllon, T., and Azrin, N. *The token economy: A motivational system for therapy and rehabilitation*. New York: Appleton-Century-Crofts, 1968.

Baltes, P. B. Life-span developmental psychology: Some converging observations on history and theory. In P. B. Baltes and O. G. Brim (Eds.), *Life-span development and behavior*, vol. 2. New York: Academic Press, 1979.

Baltes, P. B., and Schaie, K. W. Aging IQ: The myth of the twilight years. *Psychology Today*, March 1974.

Bandura, A. Behavioral psychotherapy. *Scientific American*, March 1967.

Bandura, A. *Aggression: A social learning analysis*. Englewood Cliffs, N.J.: Prentice-Hall, 1973.

Bandura, A. Behavior theory and the models of man. *American Psychologist*, 1974, *12*, 859–869.

Bandura, A.; Blanchard, E. B.; and Ritter, B. Relative efficacy of desensitization and modeling approaches for inducing behavioral, affective, and attitudinal changes. *Journal of Personality and Social Psychology*, 1969, *13*, 173–199.

Bandura, A.; Ross, D.; and Ross, S. Imitation of film-mediated aggressive models. *Journal of Abnormal and Social Psychology*, 1963, *67*, 601–607.

Bane, M. J. Marital disruption and the lives of children. In G. Levinger and O. C. Moles (Eds.), *Divorce and separation: Context, causes, and consequences*. New York: Basic Books, 1979.

Barber, T. X. *LSD, marihuana, yoga, and hypnosis*. Chicago: Aldine, 1970.

Bard, B., and Sachs, J. Language acquisition patterns in two normal children of deaf parents. Paper presented at Second Annual Boston University Conference of Language Acquisition, 1977.

Bardwick, J. *The psychology of women*. New York: Harper & Row, 1971.

Barfield, R. E., and Morgan, J. N. Trends in satisfaction with retirement. *The Gerontologist*, 1978, *18*, 19–23.

Barnett, R. C., and Baruch, G. K. Women in the middle years: A critique of research and theory. *Psychology of Women Quarterly*, 1978, *3*, 187–197.

Baron, R. A. Olfaction and human social behavior: Effects of a pleasant scent on attraction and social perception. *Personality and Social Psychology Bulletin*, 1981, *7*, 611–616.

Baron, R. A., and Byrne, D. *Social psychology*. (2nd ed.) Boston: Allyn and Bacon, 1977.

Barrett, C. J. Effectiveness of widows' groups in facilitating change. *Journal of Consulting and Clinical Psychology*, 1978, *46*, 20–31.

Barron, F. The creative personality: Akin to madness. *Psychology Today*, July 1972.

Barrow, G. Personal reactions to growing old. Unpublished study, Santa Rosa Junior College, 1976.

Barrow, G. M., and Smith, P. A. *Aging, ageism, and society*. St. Paul, Minn.: West, 1979.

Bartrop, R. W.; Luckhurst, E.; Lazarus, L.; et al. Depressed lymphocyte function after bereavement. *Lancet*, 1977, *1*, 834–836.

Bassuk, E. L., and Gerson, S. Deinstitutionalization and mental health services. *Scientific American*, February 1978.

Bate, W. J. *Samuel Johnson*. New York: Harcourt Brace Jovanovich, 1977.

Bateson, G., et al. Toward a theory of schizophrenia. *Behavioral Science*, 1956, *1*, 251–264.

Battle, E., and Rotter, J. B. Children's feelings of personal control as related to social class and ethnic groups. *Journal of Personality*, 1963, *31*, 482–490.

Baumrind, D. Current patterns of parental authority. *Developmental Monographs*, 1971, *4*, 1–103.

Becker, L. J.; Seligman, C.; and Darley, J. M. *Psychological strategies to reduce energy consumption: Project summary report*. Princeton, N.J.: Center for Energy and Environmental Studies, Princeton University, 1979.

Begley, S. How smart can computers get? *Newsweek*, June 30, 1980.

Bell, A. P., and Weinberg, M. *Homosexualities: A study of human diversity*. New York: Simon & Schuster, 1978.

Belmont, L., and Marolla, F. A. Birth order, family size, and intelligence. *Science*, 1973, *182*, 1096–1101.

Belsky, J., and Steinberg, L. D. The effects of day care: A critical review. *Child Development*, 1978, *49*, 929–949.

Bem, D. J. *Beliefs, attitudes, and human affairs*. Belmont, Calif.: Brooks/Cole, 1970.

Bem, D. J., and Allen, A. On predicting some of the people some of the time: The search for cross-situational consistencies in behavior. *Psychological Review*, 1974, *81*, 506–520.

Bem, S. L. Psychology looks at sex roles: Where have all the androgynous people gone? Paper presented at UCLA Symposium on Women, May 1972.

Bem, S. L. Androgyny vs. the tight little lives of fluffy women and chesty men. *Psychology Today*, September 1975.

Bem, S. L., and Bem, D. J. Case study of a nonconscious ideology: Training the woman to know her place. In D. J. Bem, *Beliefs, attitudes, and human affairs*. Belmont, Calif.: Brooks/Cole, 1970.

Bem, S. L., and Bem, D. J. Does sex-biased job advertising "aid and abet" sex discrimination? *Journal of Applied Social Psychology*, 1973, *3*, 6–18.

Bengtson, V. L. *The social psychology of aging*. Indianapolis: Bobbs-Merrill, 1973.

Benson, H. *The relaxation response*. New York: William Morrow, 1975.

Benson, H., and Wallace, R. K. Decreased drug abuse with transcendental meditation—a study of 1,862 subjects. In C. J. Zafronetis (Ed.), *Drug abuse: Proceedings of the International Conference*. New York: Lea and Febiger, 1972.

Benson, P. L.; Karabenick, S. A.; and Lerner, R. M. Pretty pleases: The effects of physical attractiveness, race, and sex on receiving help. *Journal of Experimental Social Psychology*, 1976, *12*, 409–415.

Bergin, A. E., and Suinn, R. M. Individual psychotherapy and behavior therapy. In M. R. Rosenzweig and L. W. Porter (Eds.), *Annual review of psychology*, vol. 26. Palo Alto, Calif.: Annual Reviews, 1975.

Berkeley Men's Center Manifesto. In J. H. Pleck and J. Sawyer (Eds.), *Men and masculinity*. Englewood Cliffs, N.J.: Prentice-Hall, 1974

Berkowitz, L. The case for bottling up rage. *Psychology Today*, July 1973.

Berlyne, D. E. Arousal and reinforcement. In D. Levine (Ed.), *Nebraska Symposium on Motivation*. Lincoln: University of Nebraska Press, 1967.

Berlyne, D. E. Attention as a problem in behavior theory. In D. I. Mostofsky (Ed.), *Attention: Contemporary theory and analysis*. New York: Appleton-Century-Crofts, 1970.

Berscheid, E., and Walster, E. A little bit about love. In T. L. Huston (Ed.), *Foundations of interpersonal attraction*. New York: Academic Press, 1974.

Bevcar, R. J. Self-help books: Some ethical questions. *Personnel and Guidance Journal*, 1978, *56*, 160–162.

Binion, R. *Hitler among the Germans*. New York: Elsevier, 1976.

Birren, J. E. *The psychology of aging*. Englewood Cliffs, N.J.: Prentice-Hall, 1964.

Bisiach, E., and Luzzatti, C. Unilateral visual neglect of representational space. *Cortex*, 1970, *14*, 129–133.

Bixler, E. O., et al. Prevalence of sleep disorders in the Los Angeles metropolitan area. *American Journal of Psychiatry*, 1979, *136*, 1257–1262.

Blake, J. Can we believe recent data on birth expectations in the United States? *Demography*, 1974, *11*, 25–44.

Blaney, P. H. Implications of the medical model and its alternatives. *American Journal of Psychiatry*, 1975, *132*, 911–914.

Blau, P. M. *Exchange and power in social life*. New York: Wiley, 1964.

Block, J. From infancy to adulthood: A clarification. *Child Development*, 1980, *51*, 622–623.

Block, J. H. Issues, problems, and pitfalls in assessing sex differences: A critical review of *The psychology of sex differences*. *Merrill-Palmer Quarterly*, 1976, *22*, 283–308.

Boneau, C. A., and Cuca, J. M. An overview of psychology's human resources: Characteristics and salaries from the 1972 APA survey. *American Psychologist*, 1974, *29*, 821–840.

Botwinick, J. *Aging and behavior*. (2nd ed.) New York: Springer, 1978.

Botwinick, J.; West, R.; and Storandt, M. Predicting death from behavioral test performance. *Journal of Gerontology*, 1978, *33*, 755–762.

Bouton, J. *Ball four*. New York: Dell, 1971.

Bower, G. H. Stimulus sampling theory of encoding variability. In A. W. Melton and E. Martin (Eds.), *Coding processes in human memory*. Washington, D.C.: Winston, 1972.

Bower, T. G. R. *A primer of infant development*. San Francisco: W. H. Freeman, 1977.

Bowers, K. Situationism in psychology: An analysis and a critique. *Psychological Review*, 1973, *80*, 307–336.

Boylin, W.; Gordon, S. K.; and Nehrke, M. F. Reminiscing and ego integrity in institutionalized elderly males. *The Gerontologist*, 1976, *16*, 118–124.

Bradburn, N. *The structure of psychological well-being*. Chicago: Aldine, 1969.

Brady, J. V. Ulcers in "executive monkeys." *Scientific American*, October 1958.

Brehm, J. W. *A theory of psychological reactance*. New York: Academic Press, 1966.

Breland, H. M. Birth order, family configuration, and verbal achievement. *Child Development*, 1974, *43*, 1011–1019.

Brenner, M. H. *Mental illness and the economy*. Cambridge, Mass.: Harvard University Press, 1973.

Bridges, K. M. B. Emotional development in early infancy. *Child Development*, 1932, *3*, 324–341.

Brim, O. G., Jr. Theories of the male mid-life crisis. *Counseling Psychologist*, 1976, *6*, 2–9.

Broad, W. J. Identical twins reared apart. *Science*, 1980, *207*, 1323–1327.

Broadbent, D. E. *Perception and communication*. London: Pergamon Press, 1958.

Brodie, F. *Richard Nixon: The shaping of his character*. New York: Norton, 1981.

Bronfenbrenner, U. Is early intervention effective? In J. Hellmuth (Ed.), *Exceptional infants*, vol. 3. New York: Brunner/Mazel, 1975.

Brooks, L. Spatial and verbal components of the act of recall. *Canadian Journal of Psychology*, 1968, *22*, 349–368.

Broverman, I. K., et al. Sex-role stereotypes: A current appraisal. *Journal of Social Issues*, 1972, *28* (2), 59–78.

Brown, B. B. Recognition of aspects of consciousness through association with EEG alpha activity represented by a light signal. *Psychophysiology*, 1970, *6*, 442–452.

Brown, F. A., Jr.; Hasting, J. W.; and Palmer, J. D. *The biological clock: Two views*. New York: Academic Press, 1970.

Brown, M. W., and Charlip, R. *The dead bird*. Reading, Mass.:Addison–Wesley, 1965.

Brown, R. *Words and things*. New York: Free Press, 1958.

Brown, R. *Social psychology*. New York: Free Press, 1965.

Brown, R. *A first language: The early stages*. Cambridge, Mass.: Harvard University Press, 1973.

Brown, R. Introduction. In C. E. Snow and C. A. Ferguson (Eds.), *Talking to children: Language input and acquisition*. Cambridge: Cambridge University Press, 1977.

Brown, R., and Herrnstein, R. J. *Psychology*. Boston: Little, Brown, 1975.

Brown, R., and Kulik, J. Flashbulb memories. *Cognition*, 1977, *5*, 73–99.

Brown, R. W., and McNeill, D. The "tip of the tongue" phenomenon. *Journal of Verbal Learning and Verbal Behavior*, 1966, *5*, 325–327.

Bruner, J. S. On perceptual readiness. *Psychological Review*, 1957, *64*, 123–152.

Bruner, J. S., and Goodman, C. C. Value and need as organizing factors in perception. *Journal of Abnormal and Social Psychology*, 1947, *42*, 33–44.

Burgess, R. L.; Clark, R. N.; and Hendee, J. C. An experimental analysis of anti-litter procedures. *Journal of Applied Behavioral Analysis*, 1971, *4*, 71–75.

Busch, F., et al. Primary transitional objects. *Journal of the American Academy of Child Psychiatry*, 1973, *12*, 193–214.

Butler, R. A. Curiosity in monkeys. *Scientific American*, February 1954.

Butler, R. N. The life review: An interpretation of reminiscence in the aged. *Psychiatry*, 1963, *26*, 65–76.

Butler, R. N. Alternatives to retirement. Testimony before the Subcommittee on Retirement Income and Employment, House Subcommittee on Aging. Department of Health, Education, and Welfare No. (NIH) 78-243. Washington, D.C.: U.S. Government Printing Office, 1977.

Butterfield, E. C., and Siperstein, G. N. Influence of contingent auditory stimulation upon non-nutritional suckle. In *Proceedings of the third symposium on oral sensation and perception: The mouth of the infant.* Springfield, Ill.: Charles C Thomas, 1974.

Byck, R., and Ritchie, J. M. Nine-tetrahydro-cannabinol: Effects on mammalian nonmyelinated nerve fibers. *Science*, 1973, *180*, 84–85.

Byrne, D. *The attraction paradigm.* New York: Academic Press, 1971.

Byrne, D. Sexual imagery. In J. Money and H. Musaph (Eds.), *Handbook of sexology.* Amsterdam: Exerpta Medica, 1976.

Byrne, D. A pregnant pause in the sexual revolution. *Psychology Today*, July 1977.

Caldwell, M., and Peplau, L. A. Sex differences in same-sex friendship. *Sex Roles*, 1982, *8*, 721–732.

Cameron, N. *Personality development and psychopathology.* Boston: Houghton Mifflin, 1963.

Campbell, A. Growing up: The happiness quotient. *Change*, April 1980.

Campbell, D., and Beets, J. Lunacy and the moon. *Psychological Bulletin*, 1978, *85*, 1123–1129.

Cannon, W. B. *The mechanical factors of digestion.* London: Arnold, 1911.

Cannon, W. B. *Bodily changes in pain, hunger, fear, and rage.* New York: Appleton, 1929.

Carmichael, L.; Hogan, H. P.; and Walter, A. A. An experimental study of the effect of language on the reproduction of visually perceived form. *Journal of Experimental Psychology*, 1932, *15*, 73–86.

Carroll, J. B. *Language and thought.* Englewood Cliffs, N.J.: Prentice-Hall, 1964.

Cartwright, R. D. Happy endings for our dreams. *Psychology Today*, December 1978.

Casler, L. Hypnotic maximization of ESP motivation. *Journal of Parapsychology*, 1976, *104*, 187–193.

Cassel, J. The contribution of the social environment to host resistance. *American Journal of Epidemiology*, 1976, *104*, 107–123.

Chase, M. Every 90 minutes a brainstorm. *Psychology Today*, November 1979.

Chilman, C. S. *Adolescent sexuality in a changing American society: Social and psychological perspectives.* Washington, D.C.: U.S. Government Printing Office, 1979.

Chitwood, D., and Bigner, J. *Home Economics Research Journal*, 1980, *8*.

Chomsky, N. Language and the mind. *Psychology Today*, February 1968.

Christensen, A., and Arkowitz, H. Preliminary report on practice dating and feedback as treatment for college dating problems. *Journal of Counseling Psychology*, 1974, *21*, 92–95.

Churchill, J. A. The relationship between intelligence and birth weight in twins. *Neurology*, 1965, *15*, 341–347.

Clark, K. B., and Clark, M. P. Racial identification and preference in Negro children. In

T. M. Newcomb and E. L. Hartley (Eds.), *Readings in social psychology.* New York: Holt, 1947.

Clark, M. Drugs and psychiatry: A new era. *Newsweek*, November 12, 1979.

Clark, M.; Hager, M.; and Shapiro, D. How safe is pot? *Newsweek*, January 7, 1980.

Clarke, A., and Ruble, D. Young adolescents' belief concerning menstruation. *Child Development*, 1978, *49*, 321–324.

Clifford, M. M., and Walster, E. The effect of physical attractiveness on teacher expectation. *Sociology of Education*, 1973, *46*, 248–258.

Cody, J. *After great pain: The inner life of Emily Dickinson.* Cambridge, Mass.: Harvard University Press, 1971.

Cohen, S. Marijuana as medicine. *Psychology Today*, April 1978.

Cohen, S.; Glass, D. C.; and Singer, J. E. Apartment noise, auditory discrimination, and reading ability in children. *Journal of Experimental Social Psychology*, 1973, *9*, 407–422.

Cohen, S., et al. Psychological, motivational, and cognitive effects of aircraft noise on children: Moving from the laboratory to the field. *American Psychologist*, 1980, *35*, 231–243.

Coleman, J., et al. *Equality of educational opportunity.* Washington, D.C.: U.S. Government Printing Office, 1966.

Cook, S. W. Social science and school desegregation: Did we mislead the Supreme Court? *Personality and Social Psychology Bulletin*, 1979, *5*, 420–437.

Cooley, C. H. *Human nature and the social order.* New York: Scribner, 1902.

Coopersmith, S. *Antecedents of self-esteem.* San Francisco: W. H. Freeman, 1967.

Coopersmith, S. Studies in self-esteem. *Scientific American*, February 1968.

Cosby, A. Occupational expectations and the hypothesis of increasing realism of choice. *Journal of Vocational Behavior*, 1974, *5*, 53–65.

Costa, P. T., Jr., and McCrae, R. R. Still stable after all these years: Personality as a key to some issues in aging. In P. B. Baltes and O. G. Brim (Eds.), *Life-span development and behavior*, vol. 3. New York: Academic Press, 1980.

Cowen, E. L., et al. Long-term follow-up of early detected vulnerable children. *Journal of Consulting and Clinical Psychology*, 1973, *41*, 438–446.

Cox, C. M. *The early mental traits of three hundred geniuses.* (Vol. 2 of *Genetic studies of genius.*) Stanford, Calif.: Stanford University Press, 1926.

Craik, F. I., and Lockhart, R. S. Levels of processing: A framework for memory research. *Journal of Verbal Learning and Verbal Behavior*, 1972, *11*, 671–684.

Crick, F. H. C. Thinking about the brain. *Scientific American*, September 1979.

Cronbach, L. J. *Essentials of psychological testing.* (2nd ed.) New York: Harper & Row, 1960.

Cronbach, L. J. Five decades of public controversy over mental testing. *American Psychologist*, 1975, *30*, 1–14.

Crosby, F.; Bromley, S.; and Saxe, L. Recent unobtrusive studies of black and white discrimination and prejudice: A literature review. *Psychological Bulletin*, 1980, *87*, 546–563.

Crumbaugh, J. C. A scientific critique of parapsychology. In G. Schmeidler (Ed.), *Extrasensory perception.* New York: Atherton, 1969.

Cumming, E., and Henry, W. E. *Growing old.* New York: Basic Books, 1961.

Cunningham, M. R. Weather, mood, and helping behavior: Quasi-experiments with the

sunshine Samaritan. *Journal of Personality and Social Psychology*, 1979, *37*, 1947–1956.

Cutler, S., and Kaufman, R. Cohort change in political attitude. *Public Opinion Quarterly*, 1975, *39*, 69–81.

Dalton, D. *The premenstrual syndrome.* Springfield, Ill.: Charles C Thomas, 1964.

D'Andrade, R. G. Sex differences and cultural institutions. In E. E. Maccoby (Ed.), *The development of sex differences.* Stanford, Calif.: Stanford University Press, 1966.

Daniels, P., and Weingarten, K. *Sooner or later: The timing of parenthood in adult lives.* New York: W. W. Norton, 1982.

Darley, J. M., and Batson, C. D. From Jerusalem to Jericho: A study of situational and dispositional variables in helping behavior. *Journal of Personality and Social Psychology*, 1973, *27*, 100–108.

Davison, G. C., and Neale, J. M. *Abnormal psychology.* New York: Wiley, 1974.

Davison, G. C., and Neale, J. M. *Abnormal psychology.* (2nd ed.) New York: Wiley, 1978.

Deaux, K., and Emswiler, T. Explanation of successful performance on sex-linked tasks: What is skill for the male is luck for the female. *Journal of Personality and Social Psychology*, 1974, *29*, 80–85.

Deci, E. *Intrinsic motivation.* New York: Plenum, 1975.

Delgado, J. M. R., et al. Two-way transdermal communication with the brain. *American Psychologist*, 1975, *30*, 265–272.

Dember, W. N. Motivation and the cognitive revolution. *American Psychologist*, 1974, *29*, 161–168.

Dement, W. *Some must watch while some must sleep.* San Francisco: W. H. Freeman, 1972.

Dement, W. C. The effect of dream deprivation. *Science*, 1960, *131*, 1705–1707.

Dement, W. C. An essay on dreams: The role of physiology in understanding their nature. In *New directions in psychology*, vol. 2. New York: Holt, Rinehart and Winston, 1965.

Dempsey, D. Noise. *New York Times Magazine*, November 23, 1975.

Derlaga, V. J., and Chaikin, A. L. *Sharing intimacy: What we reveal to others and why.* Englewood Cliffs, N.J.: Prentice-Hall, 1975.

Dermer, M., and Pyszczynski, T. A. Effects of erotica upon men's loving and liking responses for women they love. *Journal of Personality and Social Psychology*, 1978, *36*, 1302–1309.

Derogatis, L.; Abeloff, M.; and Melisgratos, N. Psychological coping mechanisms and survival time in metastatic breast cancer. *Journal of the American Medical Association*, 1979, *242*, 1504–1508.

Deutsch, H. *The psychology of women*, vol. 2. New York: Grune & Stratton, 1944.

deVilliers, P. A., and deVilliers, J. G. *Early language.* Cambridge, Mass.: Harvard University Press, 1979.

deVries, H. A. Physiological effects of an exercise training regimen upon men aged 52 to 88. *Journal of Gerontology*, 1970, *25*, 325–336.

Dewhirst, J. R. Biological rhythms and behavior. In Z. Rubin and E. B. McNeil, *The psychology of being human.* (Brief update ed.) New York: Harper & Row, 1979.

Dichter, E. *Handbook of consumer motivations.* New York: McGraw-Hill, 1964.

Dilley, J. Self-help literature: Don't knock it till you try it. *Personnel and Guidance Journal*, 1978, *57*, 293–295.

Dion, K. K.; Berscheid, E.; and Walster, E. What is beautiful is good. *Journal of Personality and Social Psychology*, 1972, *24*, 285–290.

Dipboye, R. L.; Fromkin, H. L.; and Wiback, H. Relative importance of applicant sex, attractiveness, and scholastic standing in evaluation of job applicant resumés. *Journal of Applied Psychology*, 1975, *60*, 39–43.

Doering, C., et al. A cycle of plasma testosterone in the human male. *Journal of Clinical Endocrinology and Metabolism*, 1975, *40*, 492–500.

Dollard, J., et al. *Frustration and aggression.* New Haven, Conn.: Yale University Press, 1939.

Douvan, E., and Adelson, J. *The adolescent experience.* New York: Wiley, 1966.

Doyle, A. C. A study in scarlet. In *The complete Sherlock Holmes.* Garden City, N.Y.: Doubleday, 1927.

Drabman, R. S., and Thomas, M. H. Does TV violence breed indifference? *Journal of Communication*, Autumn 1975.

Duncan, B. L. Differential social perception and attribution of intergroup violence: Testing the lower limits of stereotyping of blacks. *Journal of Personality and Social Psychology*, 1976, *34*, 590–598.

Duncan, S. The great ape debate. *New York*, December 3, 1979.

Dutton, D. G., and Aron, A. P. Some evidence for heightened sexual attraction under conditions of high anxiety. *Journal of Personality and Social Psychology*, 1974, *30*, 510–517.

Dunbar, J.; Brown, M.; and Amoroso, D. Some correlates of attitudes toward homosexuality. *Journal of Social Psychology*, 1973, *89*, 271–279.

Dworkin, R. H., et al. A longitudinal study of the genetics of personality. *Journal of Personality and Social Psychology*, 1976, *34*, 510–518.

Dyer, W. W. *Your erroneous zones.* New York: Thomas Y. Crowell, 1976.

Eagly, A. H. Sex differences in influenceability. *Psychological Bulletin*, 1978, *85*, 86–116.

Easterbrooks, M., and Lamb, M. The relationship between quality of infant-mother attachment and infant competence in initial encounters with peers. *Child Development*, 1979, *50*, 380–387.

Ebon, M. Iron curtain ESP. *Human Behavior*, November 1978.

Edgerton, M. T.; Jacobson. W. E.; and Meyer, E. Surgical-psychiatric study of patients seeking plastic (cosmetic) surgery: Ninety-eight consecutive patients with minimal deformity. *British Journal of Plastic Surgery*, 1961, *13*, 136–145.

Edgerton, R. B. *Mental retardation.* Cambridge, Mass.: Harvard University Press, 1979.

Edmiston, S. Out from under! A major report on women today. *Redbook*, May 1975.

Edson, L. Superbrain. *Across the Board*, August 1978.

Efran, M. G. The effect of physical appearance on the judgment of guilt, interpersonal attraction, and severity of recommended punishment in a simulated jury task. *Journal of Research on Personality*, 1974, *8*, 45–54.

Egendorf, A.; Kadushin, C.; Laufer, R. S.; Rothbart, G. and Sloan, L. *Legacies of Vietnam: Comparative adjustment of veterans and their peers.* Washington, D.C.: U.S. Government Printing Office, 1981.

Ehrhardt, A. A., and Baker, S. W. Fetal androgens, human central nervous system differentiation, and behavior sex differences. In R. C. Friedman, R. M. Richart, and R. L. Vande Wiele (Eds.), *Sex differences in behavior.* New York: Wiley, 1973.

Elkind, D. Giant in the nursery: Jean Piaget. *New York Times Magazine*, May 26, 1969.

Elkind, D. *Cognitive development.* Homewood, Ill.: Learning Systems Company, 1975.

Ellis, A. *Reason and emotion in psychotherapy.* Secancus, N.J.: Lyle Stuart, 1962.

Ellis, H. *A study of British genius.* (New rev. ed.) Boston: Houghton Mifflin, 1926. (Originally published in 1904.)

Ember, C. R. Feminine task assignment and the social behavior of boys. *Ethos*, 1973, *1*, 424–439.

Engel, G. Sudden and rapid death during psychological stress. *Annals of Internal Medicine*, 1971, *74*, 771–782.

Englander-Golden, P.; Whitmore, M.; and Dienstbier, R. Menstrual cycle as a focus of study and self-reports of moods and behaviors. *Motivation and Emotion*, 1978, *2*, 75–86.

Erikson, E. *Childhood and society.* New York: Norton, 1950.

Erikson, E. H. *A healthy personality for every child. A fact finding report: A digest.* (Midcentury White House Conference on Children and Youth.) Raleigh, N.C.: Health Publications Institute, 1951.

Erikson, E. H. *Young man Luther: A study in psychoanalysis and history.* New York: Norton, 1958.

Erikson, E. H. *Gandhi's truth.* New York: Norton, 1969.

Erikson, E. H. *Dimensions of a new identity.* New York: Norton, 1974.

Everett, P. B.; Hayward, S. C.; and Meyers, A. W. The effects of a token reinforcement procedure on bus ridership. *Journal of Applied Behavior Analysis*, 1974, *7*, 1–9.

Eysenck, H. J. The effects of psychotherapy: An evaluation. *Journal of Consulting Psychology*, 1952, *16*, 319–324.

Falbo, T. Does the only child grow up miserable? *Psychology Today*, May 1976.

Falbo, T. Only children, stereotypes, and research. In M. Lewis and L. A. Rosenblum (Eds.), *The child and its family.* New York: Plenum, 1979.

Farson, R. E. Emotional barriers to education. *Psychology Today*, October 1967.

Faust, M. S. Developmental maturity as a determinant in prestige of adolescent girls. *Child Development*, 1960, *31*, 173–184.

Fein, R. A. Research on fathering: Social policy and an emergent perspective. *Journal of Social Issues*, 1978, *34* (1), 122–135.

Fenz, W. D., and Epstein, S. Gradients of physiological arousal in parachutists as a function of an approaching jump. *Psychosomatic Medicine*, 1967, *29*, 33–51.

Fernstrom, J. D., and Wurtman, R. J. Nutrition and the brain. *Scientific American*, February 1974.

Festinger, L. A. A theory of social comparison processes. *Human Relations*, 1954, *7*, 117–140.

Fields, H. L. Secrets of the placebo. *Psychology Today*, November 1978.

Fischer, C. S., and Phillips, S. L. Who is alone? Social characteristics of people with small networks. In L. A. Peplau and D. Perlman (Eds.), *Loneliness: A Sourcebook of current theory, research, and therapy.* New York: Wiley-Interscience, 1982.

Fitzgerald, H., and Bundy, R. S. *Rhythm, time, and human behavior.* Homewood, Ill.: Learning Systems Company, 1975.

Flanagan, J. C. The definition and measurement of ingenuity. In C. W. Taylor and F. Barron (Eds.), *Scientific creativity: Its recognition and development.* New York: Wiley, 1963.

Fo, W. S. O., and O'Donnell, C. R. The buddy system: Relationship and contingency conditions in a community intervention program for youth with nonprofessionals as behavior change agents. *Journal of Consulting and Clinical Psychology*, 1974, *42*, 163–169.

Foltz, D. Psychologists in the media. *APA Monitor*, May 1980.

Fozard, J. L., et al. Visual perception and communication. In J. E. Birren and K. W. Schaie (Eds.), *Handbook of the psychology of aging.* New York: Van Nostrand Reinhold, 1977.

Fraiberg, S. *Every child's birthright: In defense of mothering.* New York: Basic Books, 1977.

Francke, L. B., et al. The children of divorce. *Newsweek*, February 11, 1980.

Frank, J. D. *Persuasion and healing: A comparative study of psychotherapy.* (2nd ed.) Baltimore: Johns Hopkins University Press, 1973.

Freeling, N. R., and Shemberg, K. M. The alleviation of test anxiety by systematic desensitization. *Behavior Research and Therapy*, 1970, *8*, 293–299.

Freud, S. *The psychopathology of everyday life.* New York: Macmillan, 1915.

Freud, S. *Civilization and its discontents.* London: Hogarth Press, 1961. (First German ed., 1930.)

Freud, S. The psychogenesis of a case of homosexuality in a woman. In *Collected papers*, vol. 2. London: Hogarth Press, 1933.

Freud, S. Mourning and melancholia (1917). In *Collected papers*, vol. 4. London: Hogarth Press, 1950.

Freud, S. The interpretation of dreams (1900). In J. Strachey (Ed. and tr.), *The standard edition of the complete psychological works of Sigmund Freud*, vols. 4 and 5. London: Hogarth Press, 1953.

Freud, S. Three essays on sexuality (1905). In J. Strachey (Ed. and tr.), *The standard edition of the complete psychological works of Sigmund Freud*, vol. 7. London: Hogarth Press, 1954.

Freud, S. Recommendations for physicians on the psychoanalytic method. In *Collected papers*, vol. 2. London: Hogarth Press, 1956.

Freud, S. *Leonardo da Vinci and a memory of his childhood* (1910). In *Standard Edition*, vol. 12. London: Hogarth Press, 1957.

Freud, S. Further recommendations on the technique of psychoanalysis. I: On beginning the treatment (1913). In J. Strachey (Ed. and tr.), *The standard edition of the complete psychological works of Sigmund Freud*, vol. 12. London: Hogarth Press, 1958.

Freud, S. Analysis terminable and interminable. In J. Strachey (Ed. and tr.), *The standard edition of the complete psychological works of Sigmund Freud*, vol. 23. London: Hogarth Press, 1964.

Friedan, B. *The feminine mystique.* New York: Norton, 1963.

Friedberg, J. *Shock treatment is not good for your brain.* San Francisco: Glide Publications, 1976.

Friedman, M., and Rosenman, R. H. *Type A behavior and your heart.* New York: Knopf, 1974.

Frieze, I. Being male or female. In P. N. Middlebrook, *Social psychology and modern life.* (2nd ed.) New York: Knopf, 1980.

Frodi, A,: Macaulay; J.; and Thome, P. R. Are women always less aggressive than men? A review of the experimental literature. *Psychological Bulletin*, 1977, *84*, 634–660.

Fromm, E. *Escape from freedom.* New York: Holt, Rinehart and Winston, 1941.

Fromm, E. *The art of loving.* New York: Harper & Row, 1956.

Furman, W.; Rahe, D. F.; and Hartup, W. W. Rehabilitation of socially withdrawn preschool children through mixed-age and same-age socialization. *Child Development*, 1979, *50*, 915–922.

Galanter, E. Contemporary psychophysics. In R. Brown et al., *New directions in psychology*, vol. 1. New York: Holt, Rinehart and Winston, 1962.

Galton, F. *Inquiries in human faculty and its development.* London: Macmillan, 1883.

Galvin, R. M. Probing the mysteries of sleep. *Atlantic Monthly*, February 1979.

Garcia, J. IQ: The conspiracy. *Psychology Today*, September 1972.

Garcia, J., and Koelling, R. A. Relation of cue to consequence in avoidance learning. *Psychonomic Science*, 1966, *4*, 123–124.

Gardner, H. *The shattered mind*. New York: Knopf, 1975.

Gardner, H. "U-shaped" behavior challenges basic concept of development. *New York Times*, September 25, 1979.

Gardner, R. A., and Gardner, B. T. Teaching sign language to a chimpanzee. *Science*, 1969, *165*, 664–672.

Garfield, P. *Creative dreaming*. New York: Simon & Schuster, 1974.

Gauquelin, M. *The scientific basis of astrology*. (Translated from the French.) New York: Stein and Day, 1969.

Gauquelin, M.; Gauquelin, F.; and Eysenck, S. B. G. Personality and position of the planets at birth: An empirical study. *British Journal of Social and Clinical Psychology*, 1979, *18*, 71–75.

Gaylin, W. What is normal? *New York Times Magazine*, April 1, 1973.

Gazzaniga, M. S. The split brain in man. *Scientific American*, August 1967.

Geer, J. H., and Fuhr, R. Cognitive factors in sexual arousal: The role of distraction. *Journal of Consulting and Clinical Psychology*, 1976, *44*, 238–243.

Geis, G., and Huston, T. California's Good Samaritan law: An analysis of its social impact. *Crime Prevention Review*, 1976.

Gelman, D., et al. New look at marijuana. *Newsweek*, January 7, 1980.

George, A. L. Some uses of dynamic psychology in political biography: Case materials on Woodrow Wilson. In F. Greenstein and M. Lerner (Eds.). *A source book for the study of personality and politics*. Chicago: Markham, 1971.

George, A. L., and George, J. L. *Woodrow Wilson and Colonel House: A personality study*. New York: Dover, 1964.

Gerbner, G., and Gross, L. *Violence profile*. 10th Annual Report, Annenberg School of Communication, University of Pennsylvania, 1979.

Gersick, K. E. Fathers by choice: Characteristics of men who do and do not seek custody of their children following divorce. Doctoral dissertation, Harvard University, 1975.

Geschwind, N. Specializations of the human brain. *Scientific American*, September 1979.

Getzels, J. W., and Jackson, P. W. *Creativity and intelligence*. New York: Wiley, 1962.

Giambra, L. Daydreaming across the life span: Late adolescent to senior citizen. *Aging and Human Development*, 1974, *5*, 116–135.

Gibson, E. J., and Walk, R. D. The visual cliff. *Scientific American*, April 1960.

Gifford, S. Cosmetic surgery and personality change: A review and some clinical observations. In R. M. Goldwyn (Ed.), *The unfavorable result in plastic surgery: Avoidance and treatment*. Boston: Little, Brown, 1972.

Glass, D. C., and Singer, J. E. Experimental studies of uncontrollable and unpredictable noise. *Representative Research in Social Psychology*, 1973, *4*, 165–183.

Glass, L. L.; Kirsch, M. A.; and Parris, J. N. Psychiatric disturbances associated with Erhard Seminars Training: I. Report of cases. *American Journal of Psychiatry*, 1977, *134*, 245–247.

Glick, P. C. Children of divorced parents in demographic perspective. *Journal of Social Issues*, 1979, *35* (4), 170–182.

Glucksberg, S. The influence of strength of drive on functional fixedness and perceptual set. *Journal of Experimental Psychology*, 1962, *63*, 36–51.

Goldberg, L. R., and Werts, C. E. The reliability of clinicians' judgments: A multitrait-multimethod approach. *Journal of Consulting Psychology*, 1966, *30*, 199–206.

Goldberg, P. Are women prejudiced against women? *Trans-action*, April 1968.

Goldberg, S., and Lewis, M. Play behavior in the year-old infant: Early sex differences. *Child Development*, 1969, *40*, 21–31.

Goldberg, V. What can we do about jet lag? *Psychology Today*, August 1977.

Goldfarb, W. Variations in adolescent adjustment of institutionally reared children. *American Journal of Orthopsychiatry*, 1947, *17*, 449–457.

Goleman, D. Hypnosis comes of age. *Psychology Today*, July 1977.

Goleman, D. Braintapping on Madison Ave. *Psychology Today*, April 1979.

Goleman, D. 1,528 little geniuses and how they grew. *Psychology Today*, February 1980.

Goodall, K. Shapers at work. *Psychology Today*, November 1972.

Goodwin, D. W. Biological psychiatry. In A. E. Kazdin, A. S. Bellack, and M. Hersen (Eds.), *New perspectives in abnormal psychology*. New York: Oxford University Press, 1980.

Gordon, S. *Lonely in America*. New York: Simon & Schuster, 1976.

Gore, P. M., and Rotter, J. B. A personality correlate of social action. *Journal of Personality*, 1963, *31*, 58–64.

Gould, R. L. *Transformations: Growth and change in adult life*. New York: Simon & Schuster, 1978.

Gray, R.; Graubard, P. S.; and Rosenberg, H. Little brother is changing you. *Psychology Today*, March 1974.

Greenberg, J. Shaping behavior contest for minds. *Miami Herald*, October 3, 1976.

Greenberg, R. P., and Fisher, S. *The scientific credibility of Freud's theories and therapy*. New York: Basic Books, 1977.

Greenberg, R. P., and Fisher, S. Testing Dr. Freud. *Human Behavior*, September 1978.

Greenblatt, M. Psychosurgery. In A. M. Freedman and H. I. Kaplan (Eds.), *Psychiatry*. Baltimore: Williams & Wilkins, 1967.

Greer, S. Study of parental loss in neurotics and sociopaths. *Archives of General Psychiatry*, 1964, *11*, 177–180.

Greer, S.; Morris, T.; and Pettingale, K. W. Psychological response to breast cancer: Effect on outcome. *Lancet*, 1979, *13*, 785–787.

Gregory, R. L. Visual illusions. *Scientific American*, May 1968.

Grinspoon, L., and Bakalar, J. Cocaine: A social history. *Psychology Today*, March 1977.

Grinspoon, L., and Bakalar, J. A kick from cocaine. *Psychology Today*, March 1977.

Gross, M. L. *The psychological society*. New York: Random House, 1978.

Groves, P. M., and Rebec, G. V. Biochemistry and behavior: Some central actions of amphetamine and antipsychotic drugs. In M. R. Rosenzweig and L. W. Porter (Eds.), *Annual Review of Psychology*, vol. 27. Palo Alto, Calif.: Annual Reviews, 1976.

Grummet, G. W. Telephone therapy: A review and case report. *American Journal of Orthopsychiatry*, 1979, *49*, 574–584.

Gubrium, J. F. Marital desolation and the evaluation of everyday life in old age. *Journal of Marriage and the Family*, 1974, *36*, 107–113.

Guilford, J. P. A factor analytic study across the domains of reasoning, creativity, and evaluation: Hypothesis and description of tests. *Reports from the psychology laboratory*. Los Angeles: University of Southern California, 1954.

Gutmann, D. L. The country of old men: Cross-cultural studies in the psychology of later life. In W. Donahue (Ed.), *Occasional papers in gerontology*, Ann Arbor: University of Michigan, 1969.

Haan, N., and Day, D. A longitudinal study of change and sameness in personality development: Adolescence to later adulthood. *International Journal of Aging and Human Development*, 1974, *5*, 11–39.

Haber, R. N. How we remember what we see. *Scientific American*, May 1970.

Hagestad, G. O. Role change and specialization in adulthood: The transition to the empty nest. *Human Development*, 1980.

Halacy, D. S. *Man and memory*. New York: Harper & Row, 1970.

Hall, C. S. *A primer of Freudian psychology*. New York: World, 1954.

Hall, C. S. *The meaning of dreams*. New York: McGraw-Hill, 1966.

Hall, J. A. Gender effects in decoding nonverbal cues. *Psychological Bulletin*, 1978, *85*, 845–857.

Halleck, S. L. *The politics of therapy*. New York: Science House, 1971.

Hamilton, D. L. A cognitive-attributional analysis of stereotyping. In L. Berkowitz (Ed.), *Advances in experimental social psychology*, vol. 12. New York: Academic Press, 1979.

Hansell, S; Sparacino, J.; and Ronchi, D. Physical attractiveness and blood pressure: Sex and age differences. *Personality and Social Psychology Bulletin*, 1982, *8*, 113–121.

Hare, R. D. Psychophysiological studies of psychopathy. In D. C. Forles (Ed.), *Clinical applications of psychophysiology*. New York: Columbia University Press, 1978.

Harlow, H. F. The nature of love. *American Psychologist*, 1958, *13*, 673–685.

Harlow, H. F. Love in infant monkeys. *Scientific American*, March 1959.

Harlow, H. F., and Suomi, S. J. Generalization of behavior from monkey to man. In G. Lindzey, C. Hall, and R. F. Thompson, *Psychology*. New York: Worth, 1975.

Harris, B. Whatever happened to Little Albert? *American Psychologist*, 1979, *34*, 151–160.

Harrower, M. Were Hitler's henchmen mad? *Psychology Today*, July 1976.

Hartley, E. L. *Problems in prejudice*. New York: Kings Crown, 1946.

Hartmann, E. L. *The functions of sleep*. New Haven, Conn.: Yale University Press, 1973.

Hartshorne, H., and May, M. A. *Studies in the nature of character*. vols. 1–3. New York: Macmillan, 1928–1930.

Hauserman, N.; Waylen, S. R.; and Behling, M. Reinforced racial integration in the first grade: A study in generalization. *Journal of Applied Behavior Analysis*, 1973, *6*, 193–200.

Hayflick, L. The cell biology of human aging. *Scientific American*, January 1980.

Hebb, D. O. The role of neurological ideas in psychology. *Journal of Personality*, 1951, *20*, 39–55.

Hebb, D. O. On watching myself get old. *Psychology Today*, November 1978.

Heiman, J. R. A psychophysiological exploration of sexual arousal patterns in females and males. *Psychophysiology*, 1977, *14*, 266–274.

Heiman, J. R. Continuing revolutions in sex research. In Z. Rubin and E. B. McNeil, *The psychology of being human*. (Brief update ed.) New York: Harper & Row, 1979.

Hendricks, J. H., and Hendricks, C. D. *Aging in mass society: Myths and realities*. Cambridge, Mass.: Winthrop, 1977.

Heron, W. The pathology of boredom. *Scientific American*, January 1957.

Hershey, D. *Life span and factors affecting it*. Springfield, Ill.: Charles C Thomas, 1974.

Hetherington, E. M.; Cox, M.; and Cox, R. The aftermath of divorce. In J. H. Stevens, Jr. and M. Mathews (Eds.), *Mother/child father/child relationships*. Washington, D.C.: National Association for the Education of Young Children, 1978.

Hetherington, E. M.; Cox, M.; and Cox, R. Play and social interaction in children following divorce. *Journal of Social Issues*, 1979, *35* (4), 26–46.

Hiatt, J., and Kripke, D. Ultradian rhythms in waking gastric activity. *Psychosomatic Medicine,* 1975, *37,* 320–355.

Hilgard, E. R. *Hypnotic susceptibility.* New York: Harcourt, 1965.

Hilgard, E. R. *Divided consciousness: Multiple controls in human thought and action.* New York: Wiley Interscience, 1977.

Hilgard, E. R., and Hilgard, J. R. *Hypnosis in the relief of pain.* Los Altos, Calif.: William Kaufman, 1975.

Hilgard, J. R. *Personality and hypnosis: A study of imaginative involvement.* Chicago: University of Chicago Press, 1970.

Hill, C. T.; Rubin, Z.; and Peplau, L. A. Breakups before marriage: The end of 103 affairs. *Journal of Social Issues,* 1976, *32* (1), 147–168.

Hill, G., and Silver, A. G. Psychodynamic and esthetic motivations for plastic surgery. *Psychosomatic Medicine,* 1950, *12,* 345–355.

Hill, J. H.; Liebert, R. M.; and Mott, D. E. W. Vicarious extinction of avoidance behavior through films: An initial test. *Psychological Reports,* 1968, *12,* 192.

Hobson, J. A., and McCarley, R. W. The brain as a dream state generator: An activation-synthesis hypothesis of the dream process. *American Journal of Psychiatry,* 1977, *134,* 1335–1348.

Hochberg, J. E. *Perception.* (2nd ed.) Englewood Cliffs, N.J.: Prentice-Hall, 1978.

Hochschild, A. R. Attending to, codifying, and managing feelings: Sex differences in love. Paper presented at meeting of the American Sociological Association, San Francisco, August 1975.

Hoffman, L. W. Fear of success in 1965 and 1974: A follow-up study. *Journal of Consulting and Clinical Psychology,* 1977, *45,* 310–321.

Hoffman, L. W., and Manis, J. D. The value of children in the United States: A new approach to the study of fertility. *Journal of Marriage and the Family,* 1979, *41,* 583–596.

Hoffman, M. L. Sex differences in empathy. *Psychological Bulletin,* 1977, *84,* 712–722.

Hokanson, J. E. Psychophysiological evaluation of the catharsis hypothesis. In E. I. Megargee and J. E. Hokanson (Eds.), *The dynamics of aggression.* New York: Harper & Row, 1970

Holinger, P. C. Violent deaths among the young: Recent trends in suicide, homicide, and accidents. *American Journal of Psychiatry,* 1979, *136,* 1144–1147.

Holmes, D. S., and Jorgensen, B. W. Do personality and social psychologists study men more than women? *Representative Research in Social Psychology,* 1971, *2,* 71–76.

Holmes, D. S., et al. Biorhythms: Their utility for predicting postoperative recuperative time, death, and athletic performance. *Journal of Applied Psychology,* 1980, *65,* 233–236.

Holmes, T. H., and Rahe, R. H. The social readjustment rating scale. *Journal of Psychosomatic Research,* 1967, *11,* 213–218.

Hopkins, J. R. Sexual behavior in adolescence. *Journal of Social Issues,* 1977, *33* (2), 67–85.

Horn, J. Organization of data on lifespan development. In L. R. Goulet and P. B. Baltes (Eds.), *Life-span development psychology.* New York: Academic Press, 1970.

Horn, J. L., and Cattell, R. B. Age differences in fluid and crystallized intelligence. *Acta Psychologica,* 1967, *26,* 107–129.

Horner, M. S. Sex differences in achievement motivation in competitive and noncompetitive situations. Doctoral dissertation, University of Michigan, 1968.

Horner, M. S. Toward an understanding of achievement-related conflicts in women. *Journal of Social Issues,* 1972, *28* (2), 157–175.

House, J. S. The effects of occupational stress on physical health. In J. O'Toole (Ed.), *Work and the quality of life.* Cambridge, Mass.: MIT Press, 1974.

House, J. S., and Wells, J. J. Occupational stress, social support and health. In *Reducing occupational stress: Proceedings of a conference.* Washington, D.C.: National Institute for Occupational Safety and Health, 1978.

House, J. S., et al. Occupational stress and health among factory workers. *Journal of Health and Social Behavior,* 1979, *20,* 139–160.

Howard, J. W., and Dawes, R. M. Linear prediction of marital happiness. *Personality and Social Psychology Bulletin,* 1976, *2,* 478–480.

Hubel, D. H. The brain. *Scientific American,* September 1979.

Hubel, D. H., and Wiesel, T. N. Brain mechanisms of vision. *Scientific American,* September 1979.

Hughes, P. C. The contribution of lighting to productivity and quality of work life. Paper presented at meeting of the Institute of Electrical and Electronics Engineers, Industry Applications Society, Los Angeles, 1977.

Hunt, M. *Sexual behavior in the 1970s.* Chicago: Playboy Press, 1974.

Hyde, J. S. *Understanding human sexuality.* New York: McGraw-Hill, 1979.

Hyde, T. S., and Jenkins, J. J. The differential effects of incidental tasks on the organization of recall of a list of highly associated words. *Journal of Experimental Psychology,* 1969, *82,* 472–481.

Ichheiser, G. Misunderstandings in human relations: A study of false social perception. *American Journal of Sociology,* 1949, *55,* part 2.

Inhelder, B.; Sinclair, M.; and Bovet, M. *Apprentissage et structures de la connaissance.* Paris: Presses Universitaires de France, 1974.

Isen, A. M., and Levin, P. F. The effect of feeling good on helping: Cookies and kindness. *Journal of Personality and Social Psychology,* 1972, *21,* 384–388.

Iversen, L. I. The chemistry of the brain. *Scientific American,* September 1979.

Izard, C. E. *Human emotions.* New York: Plenum, 1977.

Izard, C. E. On the development of emotions and emotion-cognition relationships in infancy. In M. Lewis and L. Rosenblum (Eds.), *The development of affect.* New York: Plenum, 1978.

Izard, C. E., et al. The young infant's ability to produce discrete emotion expressions. *Developmental Psychology,* 1980, *16,* 132–140.

James, W. *The principles of psychology.* New York: Holt, 1890.

James, W. H.; Woodruff, A. B.; and Werner, W. Effects of internal and external control upon changes in smoking behavior. *Journal of Consulting Psychology,* 1965, *29,* 184–186.

Janis, I. L. *Victims of groupthink.* Boston: Houghton Mifflin, 1972.

Janis, I. L. In rescue planning, how did Carter handle stress? *New York Times,* May 18, 1980.

Janov, A. (Ed.) *The Journal of Primal Therapy,* 1973, *1.*

Jaques, E. Death and the mid-life crisis. *International Journal of Psychoanalysis,* 1965, *46,* 502–514.

Jason, L. A. Preventive community interventions: Reducing school children's smoking and decreasing smoke exposure. *Professional Psychology,* 1979, *10,* 744–752.

Jemmott, J.; Borysenko, M.; Borysenko, J.; Chapman, R.; Meyer, D.; and Benson, H. Stress, power motivation and immunity. Presented at annual meeting of the American Psychological Association, Los Angeles, August 1981.

Jensen, A. R. How much can we boost IQ and scholastic achievement? *Harvard Educational Review,* 1969, *39,* 1–123.

Jensen, A. R. Cumulative deficit in IQ of blacks in the rural South. *Developmental Psychology,* 1977, *13,* 184–191.

Jones, E. E., and Harris, V. A. The attribution of attitudes. *Journal of Experimental Social Psychology,* 1967, *3,* 1–24.

Jones, J. M. *Prejudice and racism.* Reading, Mass.: Addison-Wesley, 1972.

Jones, M. C. A laboratory study of fear: The case of Peter. *Pedagogical Seminary,* 1925, *31,* 308–315.

Jones, M. C. The later careers of boys who were early or late maturing. *Child Development,* 1957, *28,* 113–128.

Jung, C. *Man and his symbols.* Garden City, N.Y.: Doubleday, 1964.

Kacerguis, M. A., and Adams, G. R. Erikson stage and resolution: The relationship between identity and intimacy. *Journal of Youth and Adolescence,* 1980, *9,* 117–126.

Kagan, J. Emergent themes in human development. *American Scientist,* March–April 1976.

Kagan, J. *The growth of the child.* New York: Norton, 1978.

Kagan, J.; Kearsley, R. B.; and Zelazo, P. R. *Infancy: Its place in human development.* Cambridge, Mass.: Harvard University Press, 1978.

Kahn, M.; Baker, B. L.; and Weiss, J. M. Treatment of insomnia by relaxation training. *Journal of Abnormal Psychology,* 1968, *73,* 556–558.

Kahneman, D. *Attention and effort.* Englewood Cliffs, N.J.: Prentice-Hall, 1973.

Kalick, S. M. *Plastic surgery, physical appearance, and person perception.* Doctoral dissertation, Harvard University, 1977.

Kalick, S. M. Aesthetic surgery: How it affects the way patients are perceived by others. *Annals of Plastic Surgery,* 1979, *2,* 128–133.

Kalick, S. M. Laser treatment of port wine stains: Observations concerning psychological outcome. In K. A. Arndt, J. M. Noe, and S. Rosen (Eds.), *Lasers and the skin.* New York: Wiley, 1982.

Kalish, R. A. *Late adulthood: Perspectives on human development.* Monterey, Calif: Brooks/Cole, 1975.

Kalish, R. A. Death and dying in a social context. In R. H. Binstock and E. Shanas (Eds.), *Handbook of aging and the social sciences.* New York: Van Nostrand Reinhold, 1976.

Kalish, R. A. The new ageism and the failure models: A polemic. *The Gerontologist,* 1979, *19,* 398–402.

Kalish, R. A., and Reynolds, D. K. *Death and ethnicity: A psycho-cultural study.* Los Angeles: University of Southern California Press, 1976.

Kaplan, H. S. *The new sex therapy.* New York: Brunner/Mazel, 1974.

Karmel, L. The case for love. Paper presented at meeting of the American Psychological Association, Miami Beach, 1970.

Karr, R. *Homosexual labeling: An experimental analysis.* Doctoral dissertation, University of Washington, 1975.

Kassarjian, H. H. Voting intentions and political perception. *Journal of Psychology,* 1963, *56,* 85–88.

Kastenbaum, R. Death, dying, and bereavement in old age. *Aged Care and Services Review,* May–June, 1978.

Kastenbaum, R. *Humans developing: A lifespan perspective.* Boston: Allyn & Bacon, 1979.

Kastenbaum, R., and Weisman, A. D. The psychological autopsy as a research procedure in gerontology. In D. P. Kent, R. Kastenbaum, and S. Sherwood (Eds.), *Research planning and action for the elderly.* New York: Behavioral Publications, 1972.

Katchadourian, H. A., and Lunde, D. T. *Fundamentals of human sexuality.* (2nd ed.) New York: Holt, Rinehart and Winston, 1975.

Katkin, E. S.; Fitzgerald, C. R.; and Shapiro, D. Clinical applications of biofeedback: Current status and future prospects. In H. L. Pick et al. (Eds.), *Psychology: From research to practice.* New York: Plenum, 1978.

Katz, A. M., and Hill, R. Residential propinquity and marital selection: A review of theory, method, and fact. *Marriage and Family Living,* 1958, *20,* 27–34.

Katz, J., and Cronin, D. M. Sexuality and college life. *Change,* February–March, 1980.

Kazdin, A. E. *Behavior modification.* Homewood, Ill.: Learning Systems Company, 1975.

Kearsley, R. B. The newborn's response to auditory stimulation: A demonstration of orienting and defense behavior. *Child Development,* 1973, *44,* 582–590.

Kelley, H. H. The warm-cold variable in first impressions of persons. *Journal of Personality,* 1950, *18,* 431–439.

Kendell, R. E. *The role of diagnosis in psychiatry.* Oxford: Blackwell, 1975.

Kesey, K. *One flew over the cuckoo's nest.* New York: Viking, 1962.

Kety, S. S. From rationalization to reason. *American Journal of Psychiatry,* 1974, *131,* 957–963.

Kety, S. S. Disorders of the human brain. *Scientific American,* September 1979.

Kevan, S. M. Season of life–season of death. *Social Science and Medicine,* 1979, *12* (D), 227–232.

Kinsey, A. C.; Pomeroy, W. B.; and Martin, C. E. *Sexual behavior in the human male.* Philadelphia: Saunders, 1948.

Kinsey, A. C.; Pomeroy, W. B.; Martin, C. E.; and Gebhard, P. H. *Sexual behavior in the human female.* Philadelphia: Saunders, 1953.

Kleitman, N. The basic rest-activity cycle. In N. Wuhlfson and A. Sances (Eds.), *The nervous system and electric currents.* New York: Plenum, 1970.

Klemesrud, J. Survey finds major shifts in attitudes of women. *New York Times,* March 13, 1980.

Kobasa, S. Stressful life events, personality, and health: An inquiry into hardiness. *Journal of Personality and Social Psychology,* 1979, *37,* 1–11.

Kohlberg, L. A. Cognitive-developmental analysis of children's sex-role concepts and attitudes. In E. E. Maccoby (Ed.), *The development of sex differences.* Stanford, Calif.: Stanford University Press, 1966.

Köhler, W. *The mentality of apes.* New York: Harcourt, Brace, 1925.

Komarovsky, M. *Dilemmas of masculinity: A study of college youth.* New York: Norton, 1976.

Kosslyn, S. M.; Ball, T. M.; and Reiser, B. J. Visual images preserve metric spatial information: Evidence from studies of image scanning. *Journal of Experimental Psychology: Human Perception and Performance,* 1978, *4,* 47–60.

Kosslyn, S. M. *Image and mind.* Cambridge, Mass.: Harvard University Press, 1980.

Kotelchuck, M. The infant's relationship to the father: Experimental evidence. In M. E. Lamb (Ed.), *The role of the father in child development.* New York: Wiley, 1976.

Kramer, M. Population changes and schizophrenia: 1970–1975. Paper presented at the Second Rochester International Conference on Schizophrenia, Rochester, N.Y., May 1976.

Kraus, A. S., and Lilienfeld, A. M. Some epidemiological aspects of the high mortality rate in the young widowed group. *Journal of*

Chronic Diseases, 1959, *10,* 207–217.

Kripke, D., and Sonneschein, D. A 90 minute daydream cycle. *Proceedings of the Association for the Psychophysiological Study of Sleep,* 1973, *2,* 177.

Krippner, S., and Hughes, W. Genius at work. *Psychology Today,* June 1970.

Krueger, A. P., and Reed, E. J. Biological impact of small air ions. *Science,* 1976, *193,* 1209–1213.

Kübler-Ross, E. *On death and dying.* New York: Macmillan, 1969.

Kulka, R. A., and Weingarten, H. The long-term effects of parental divorce in childhood on adult adjustment. *Journal of Social Issues,* 1979, *35,* (4), 50–76.

Labourie-Vief, G. *Does intelligence decline with age?* National Institute on Aging, Science Writer Seminar Series. Bethesda, Md.: National Institutes of Health, 1979.

Lackner, J. R. Psychology and the exploration of space. In Z. Rubin and E. B. McNeil, *The psychology of being human.* (Brief update ed.) New York: Harper & Row, 1979.

Langer, E. J., et al. Environmental determinants of memory improvement in late adulthood. *Journal of Personality and Social Psychology,* 1979, *37,* 2003–2013.

La Plante, M. N.; McCormick, N. B.; and Brannigan, G. G. Living the sexual script: College students' view of influence in sexual encounters. *Journal of Sex Research,* November 1980.

Lassen, N. A.; Ingvar, D. H; and Skinhøj, E. Brain function and blood flow. *Scientific American,* October 1978.

Laumann, E. O. Friends of urban men: An assessment of accuracy in reporting their socioeconomic attributes, mutual choice, and attitude agreement. *Sociometry,* 1969, *32,* 54–69.

Layton, B. D., and Turnbull, B. Belief, evaluation, and performance in an ESP task. *Journal of Experimental and Social Psychology,* 1975, *11,* 166–179.

Lazarus, A. A. *Behavior therapy and beyond.* New York: McGraw-Hill, 1971.

Lazarus, R. S. *The riddle of man.* Englewood Cliffs, N.J.: Prentice-Hall, 1974.

Leeper, R. The role of motivation in learning: A study of the phenomenon of differential motivation control on the utilization of habits. *Journal of Genetic Psychology,* 1935, *46,* 3–40.

Leff, D. N. Brain chemistry may influence feelings, behavior. *Smithsonian Magazine,* June 1978.

Lenneberg, E. *The biological foundations of language.* New York: Wiley, 1967.

Lenneberg, E. H. On explaining language. *Science,* 1969, *164,* 635–643.

Leo, J. How to commit suicide. *Time,* July 7, 1980.

Leon, G. Current directions in the treatment of obesity. *Psychological Bulletin,* 1976, *83,* 557–578.

Leonard, C. V. Depression and suicidality. *Journal of Consulting and Clinical Psychology,* 1974, *42,* 98–104.

Lepper, M. R., and Greene, D. Turning play into work: Effects of adult surveillance and extrinsic rewards on children's intrinsic motivation. *Journal of Personality and Social Psychology,* 1975, *31,* 479–486.

Levin, P. F., and Isen, A. M. Further studies on the effect of feeling good on helping. *Sociometry,* 1975, *38,* 141–147.

Levinson, D. J., et al. *The seasons of a man's life.* New York: Knopf, 1978.

Lewin, R. Starved brains. *Psychology Today,* September 1975.

Lewis, J. L. Semantic processing of unattended messages using dichotic listening. *Jour-*

nal of Experimental Psychology, 1970, *85,* 225–228.

Lewis, M. Culture and gender roles: There's no unisex in the nursery. *Psychology Today,* May 1972.

Lieber, A., and Sherin, C. Homicides and the lunar cycle: Toward a theory of lunar influence on human emotional disturbance. *American Journal of Psychiatry,* 1972, *129,* 69–74.

Lieberman, M. A.; Yalom, I. D.; and Miles, M. *Encounter groups: First facts.* New York: Basic Books, 1973.

Linn, L., and Goldman, I. B. Psychiatric observations concerning rhinoplasty. *Psychosomatic Medicine,* 1949, *11,* 307–314.

Lipinski, E., and Lipinski, B. G. Motivational factors in psychedelic drug use by male college students. In R. E. Hormon and A. M. Fox (Eds.), *Drug awareness.* New York: Avon, 1970.

Lipsey, M. W., and Brayfield, A. H. *The profession of psychology.* Homewood, Ill.: Learning Systems Company, 1975.

Livingston, R. B. Reinforcement. In G. C. Quarton, T. Melnechuck, and F. O. Schmitt (Eds.), *The neurosciences: A study program.* New York: Rockefeller University Press, 1967.

Locke, S. E. Stress, adaptation and immunity: Studies in humans. *General Hospital Psychiatry,* 1982, *4,* 49–58.

Loehlin, J. C.; Lindzey, G.; and Spuhler, J. N. *Race differences in intelligence.* San Francisco: W. H. Freeman, 1975.

Longstreth, L. Revisiting Skeels' final study: A critique. *Developmental Psychology,* 1981, *17,* 620–625.

Lopate, C. *Women in medicine.* Baltimore: Johns Hopkins University Press, 1968.

Lorayne, H., and Lucas, J. *The memory book.* New York: Ballantine, 1974.

Lorenz, K. The companion in the bird's world. *Auk,* 1937, *54,* 245–273.

Lorenz, K. *On aggression.* New York: Harcourt, Brace, and World, 1966.

Louis, A. M. Should you buy biorhythms? *Psychology Today,* April 1978.

Lowenthal, M. F., and Chiriboga, D. Transition to the empty nest. *Archives of General Psychiatry,* 1972, *26,* 8–14.

Lowenthal, M. F., and Robinson, B. Social networks and isolation. In R. H. Binstock and E. Shanas (Eds.), *Handbook of Aging and the Social Sciences.* New York: Van Nostrand Reinhold, 1977.

Lubin, A. J. *Stranger on the earth: A psychological biography of Vincent van Gogh.* New York: Holt, Rinehart and Winston, 1972.

Luborsky, L., et al. Factors influencing the outcome of psychotherapy: A review of quantitative research. *Psychological Bulletin,* 1971, *75,* 145–185.

Luce, G. G. *Body time.* New York: Pantheon, 1971.

Luce, G. G., and Peper, E. Mind over body, mind over mind. *New York Times Magazine,* September 12, 1971.

Maccoby, E. E., and Jacklin, C. N. *The psychology of sex differences.* Stanford, Calif: Stanford University Press, 1974.

Mack, J. E. *A prince of our disorder: The life of T. E. Lawrence.* Boston: Little, Brown, 1976.

Maddox, G., and Douglas, E. Aging and individual differences. *Journal of Gerontology,* 1974, *29,* 555–563.

Maher, B. A. *Principles of psychopathology: An experimental approach.* New York: McGraw-Hill, 1966.

Mahoney, M. J. *Abnormal psychology.* San Francisco: Harper & Row, 1980.

Makinodan, T. Immunity and aging. In C. G. Finch and L. Hayflick (Eds.), *Handbook of* *the biology of aging.* New York: Van Nostrand Reinhold, 1977.

Mandell, A. J. Pro football fumbles the drug scandal. *Psychology Today,* June 1975.

Mandler, G. Emotions. In R. Brown et al., *New directions in psychology,* vol. 1. New York: Holt, Rinehart and Winston, 1962.

Mark, V. H., and Ervin, F. R. *Violence and the brain.* New York: Harper & Row, 1970.

Marks, L. E. Synesthesia: The lucky people with mixed-up senses. *Psychology Today,* June 1975.

Marshall, D. S. Too much in Mangaia. *Psychology Today,* February 1971.

Marshall, G. D., and Zimbardo, P. G. Affective consequences of inadequately explained physiological arousal. *Journal of Personality and Social Psychology,* 1979, *37,* 970–988.

Martin, R. L.; Cloninger, C. R.; and Guze, S. B. Female criminality and the prediction of recidivism. *Archives of General Psychiatry,* 1978, *35,* 207–214.

Maslach, C. Negative emotional biasing of unexplained arousal. *Journal of Personality and Social Psychology,* 1979, *37,* 953–969.

Maslow, A. H. A theory of human motivation. *Psychological Review,* 1943, *50,* 370–396.

Maslow, A. H. *Motivation and personality.* New York: Harper & Row, 1954.

Maslow, A. H. *Toward a psychology of being.* New York: Van Nostrand Reinhold, 1962.

Maslow, A. *Motivation and personality.* (2nd ed.) New York: Harper & Row, 1970.

Mastellone, M. Aversion therapy: Another use for the old rubber band. *Journal of Behavior Therapy and Experimental Psychiatry,* 1974, *5,* 311.

Masters, W. H., and Johnson, V. E. *Human sexual response.* Boston: Little, Brown, 1966.

Masters, W. H., and Johnson, V. E. *Human sexual inadequacy.* Boston: Little, Brown, 1970.

Matteson, D. R. *Adolescence today: Sex roles and the search for identity.* Homewood, Ill.: Dorsey, 1975.

Maugh, T. H. Marijuana: Does it damage the brain? *Science,* August 30, 1974.

Maupin, E. W. Individual differences in response to a Zen meditation exercise. *Journal of Consulting Psychology,* 1965, *29,* 139–145.

Maurer, H. *Not working: An oral history of the unemployed.* New York: Holt, Rinehart and Winston, 1979.

McArthur, L. Z., and Eisen, S. V. Television and sex-role stereotyping. *Journal of Applied Social Psychology,* 1976, *6,* 329–351.

McBain, W. N., et al. Quasi-sensory communication: An investigation using semantic matching and accentuated effect. *Journal of Personality and Social Psychology,* 1970, *14,* 281–291.

McCall, R. B. *Intelligence and heredity.* Homewood, Ill.: Learning Systems Company, 1975.

McClelland, D. C. *The achieving society.* Princeton, N.J.: Van Nostrand Reinhold, 1961.

McClelland, D. C. *Motivational trends in society.* New York: General Learning Press, 1971.

McClelland, D. C. Testing for competence rather than for "intelligence." *American Psychologist,* 1973, *28,* 1–14.

McClelland, D. C. Managing motivation to expand human freedom. *American psychologist,* 1978, *33,* 201–210.

McClelland, D. C., and Winter, D. G. *Motivating economic achievement.* New York: Free Press, 1969.

McClelland, D. C., et al. *The achievement motive.* New York: Appleton-Century-Crofts, 1953.

McCormick, N. B. Come-ons and put-offs: Unmarried students' strategies for having and avoiding sexual intercourse. *Psychology of Women Quarterly,* 1979, *4,* 194–211.

McGhie, A., and Chapman, J. S. Disorders of attention and perception in early schizophrenia. *British Journal of Medical Psychiatry,* 1961, *34,* 103–116.

McKellar, P. The investigation of mental images. In S. A. Barnett and A. McLaren (Eds.), *Penguin science survey.* Harmondsworth, England: Penguin Books, 1965.

McKenna, W., and Kessler, S. J. Experimental design as a source of sex bias in social psychology. *Sex Roles,* 1977, *3,* 117–128.

Mednick, S. A. The associative basis of the creative process. *Psychological Review,* 1962, *69,* 220–232.

Medvedev, Z. A. Aging and longevity: New approaches and new perspectives. *The Gerontologist,* 1975, *15,* 196–201.

Meissner, W. W. Family dynamics and psychosomatic process. *Family Process,* 1966, *5,* 142–161.

Melzack, R. *The puzzle of pain.* New York: Basic Books, 1973.

Messenger, J. C. The lack of the Irish. *Psychology Today,* February 1971.

Meyer, J.; Jacobson, M. E.; Edgerton, M. T.; and Canter, A. Motivational patterns in patients seeking elective surgery (I. Women who seek rhinoplasty). *Psychosomatic Medicine,* 1960, *22,* 193–203.

Meyer, V., and Chesser, E. S. *Behavior therapy in clinical psychiatry.* Baltimore: Penguin, 1970.

Milgram, S. The experience of living in cities. *Science,* 1970, *167,* 1461–1468.

Miller, G. A. The magical number seven, plus or minus two: Some limits on our capacity for processing information. *Psychological Review,* 1956, *63,* 81–97.

Miller, G. A. On turning psychology over to the unwashed. *Psychology Today,* December 1969.

Miller, M. M., et al. Sleeplessness, sleep attacks, and things that go wrong in the night. *Psychology Today,* December 1975.

Miller, N., and Maruyama, G. Ordinal position and peer popularity. *Journal of Personality and Social Psychology,* 1976, *33,* 123–131.

Miller, N. E. Biofeedback and visceral learning. *Annual Review of Psychology,* 1978, *28,* 373–404.

Minard, R. D. Race relations in the Pocahontas coal field. *Journal of Social Issues,* 1952, *8* (1), 29–44.

Mintz, R. S. Psychotherapy of the suicidal patient. In H. L. P. Resnik (Ed.), *Suicidal behaviors.* Boston: Little, Brown, 1968.

Mischel, W. *Personality and assessment.* New York: Holt, Rinehart and Winston, 1968

Mischel, W. *Introduction to personality.* (2nd ed.) New York: Holt, Rinehart and Winston, 1976.

Money, J., and Ehrhardt, A. A. *Man & woman, boy & girl.* Baltimore: Johns Hopkins University Press, 1972.

Moody, R. A. *Life after life.* Atlanta: Mockingbird Books, 1975.

Morgan, A. H., and Hilgard, E. R. Age differences in susceptibility to hypnosis. *International Journal of Clinical and Experimental Hypnosis,* 1973, *21,* 78–95.

Morin, S. F., and Garfinkle, E. M. Male homophobia. *Journal of Social Issues,* 1978, *34* (1), 29–47.

Morin, S. F.; Taylor, K.; and Kielman, S. Gay is beautiful at a distance. Paper presented at meeting of the American Psychological Association, Chicago, August 1975.

Morishima, A. His spirit raises the ante for retardates. *Psychology Today,* June 1975.

Morrison, J. K., and Hanson, G. D. Clinical psychologists in the vanguard: Current attitudes toward mental illness. *Professional Psychology,* 1978, *9,* 240–248.

Morse, W. C., and Weiss, R. S. The function and meaning of work and the job. In D. G. Zytowski (Ed.), *Vocational behavior.* New York: Holt, Rinehart and Winston, 1968.

Mowrer, O. H. Hearing and speaking: An analysis of language learning. *Journal of Speech and Hearing Disorders,* 1958, *23,* 143–151.

Murray, H. A. *Explorations in personality.* New York: Oxford University Press, 1938.

Muson, H. Teenage violence and the telly. *Psychology Today,* March 1978.

Mussen, P. H., and Jones, M. C. Self-conceptions, motivations, and interpersonal attitudes of late and early maturing boys. *Child Development,* 1957, *28,* 243–256.

Myerhoff, B. *Number our days.* New York: Simon & Schuster, 1978.

Nabokov, P. The peyote road. *New York Times Magazine,* March 9, 1969.

Naranjo, C., and Ornstein, R. E. *On the psychology of meditation.* New York: Viking, 1971.

Nathan, P. E., and Harris, S. L. *Psychopathology and society.* (2nd ed.) New York: McGraw-Hill, 1980.

Nesselroade, J. R.; Schaie, K. W.; and Baltes, P. B. Autogenic and generational components of structural and quantitative change in adult behavior. *Journal of Gerontology,* 1972, *27,* 222–228.

Neugarten, B. L. Adult personality: Toward a psychology of the life cycle. In B. L. Neugarten (Ed.), *Middle age and aging.* Chicago: University of Chicago Press, 1968.

Neugarten, B. L. Personality and the aging process. *The Gerontologist,* 1972, *12,* 9–15.

Neugarten, B. L. The future and the youngold. *The Gerontologist,* 1975, *15,* no. 1, part 2, 4–9.

Neugarten, B. L., interviewed by E. Hall. Acting one's age: New rules for old. *Psychology Today,* April 1980.

Neugarten, B. L., and Datan, N. Sociological perspectives on the life cycle. In P. B. Baltes and K. W. Schaie (Eds.), *Life-span developmental psychology: personality and socialization.* New York: Academic Press, 1973.

Neugarten, B. L., and Havighurst, R. J. Disengagement reconsidered in a cross-national context. In R. J. Havighurst, et al. (Eds.), *Adjustment to retirement,* Assess, Netherlands: Van Gorcum, 1969.

Newcomb, T. M. *Personality and social change.* New York: Dryden Press, 1943.

Newcomb, T. M. *The acquaintance process.* New York: Holt, Rinehart and Winston, 1961.

Newsweek. Coping with depression. January 8, 1973.

Nisbet, B. C. An ostensible case of auditory ESP. *Journal of the Society for Psychical Research,* 1977, *49,* 440–445.

Nisbett, R. E. Birth order and participation in dangerous sports. *Journal of Personality and Social Psychology,* 1968, *8,* 351–353.

Nisbett, R. E. Hunger, obesity, and the ventromedial hypothalamus. *Psychological Review,* 1972, *79,* 433–453.

Norman, D. A., and Bobrow, D. G. On data-limited and resource-limited processes. *Cognitive Psychology,* 1975, *7,* 44–64.

Notman, M. Midlife concerns of women: Implications of the menopause. *American Journal of Psychiatry,* 1979, *136,* 1270–1274.

Olds, J. Self-stimulation of the brain. *Science,* 1958, *127,* 315–324.

Orlansky, H. Infant care and personality. *Psychological Bulletin,* 1949, *46,* 1–48.

Orne, M. T. On the simulating subject as a quasi-control group in hypnosis research: What, why, and how. In E. Fromm and R. E. Shor (Eds.), *Hypnosis: Research development and perspectives.* Chicago: Aldine-Atherton, 1972.

Orne, M. T., and Wilson, S. K. On the nature of alpha feedback training. In G. E. Schwartz and D. Shapiro (Eds.), *Consciousness and self-regulation: Advances in research.* New York: Plenum, 1978.

Ornstein, R. E. *The psychology of consciousness.* San Francisco: W. H. Freeman, 1972.

Paige, K. Women learn to sing the menstrual blues. *Psychology Today,* September 1973.

Palmore, E. Total chance of institutionalization among the aged. *The Gerontologist,* 1976, *16,* 504–507.

Palmore, E. Facts on aging. *The Gerontologist,* 1977, *17,* 315–320.

Parke, R. D. Perspectives on father-infant interaction. In J. D. Osofsky (Ed.), *Handbook of infant development.* New York: Wiley, 1978.

Parke, R. D., and O'Leary, S. Father-mother-infant interaction in the newborn period: Some findings, some observations, some unresolved issues. In K. Riegel and J. Meacham (Eds.), *The developing individual in a changing world,* vol. 2. The Hague: Mouton, 1975.

Parke, R. D., et al. Film violence and aggression: A field experimental analysis. In L. Berkowitz (Ed.), *Advances in experimental social psychology,* vol. 10, New York: Academic Press, 1975.

Parlee, M. The premenstrual syndrome. *Psychological Bulletin,* 1973, *80,* 454–465.

Parlee, M. The rhythms in men's lives. *Psychology Today,* April 1978.

Parloff, M. B. Shopping for the right therapy. *Saturday Review,* February 21, 1976.

Paul, G. L. Chronic mental patients: Current status–future directions. *Psychological Bulletin,* 1969, *71,* 81–94.

Penfield, W. The interpretive cortex. *Science,* 1959, *129,* 1719–1725.

Peplau, L. A.; Rubin, Z.; and Hill, C. T. Sexual intimacy in dating relationships. *Journal of Social Issues,* 1977, *33* (2) 86–109.

Perlman, D.; Gerson, A. C.; and Spinner, B. Loneliness among senior citizens: An empirical report. *Essence,* 1978, *2,* 239–248.

Perls, F. S. *Gestalt therapy verbatim.* Moab, Utah: Real People Press, 1969.

Peterson, L. R., and Peterson, M. J. Short-term retention of individual verbal items. *Journal of Experimental Psychology,* 1959, *58,* 193–198.

Pettigrew, T. F. Regional differences in anti-Negro prejudice. *Journal of Abnormal and Social Psychology,* 1959, *59,* 28–36.

Pettigrew, T. F. *Racially separate or together?* New York: McGraw-Hill, 1971.

Phillips, J. Syntax and vocabulary of mothers' speech to young children: Age and sex comparisons. *Child Development,* 1973, *44,* 182–185.

Piaget, J. *The origins of intelligence in children.* New York: International Universities Press, 1952.

Piaget, J. Intellectual evolution from adolescence to adulthood. *Human Development,* 1972, *15,* 1–12.

Piaget, J., and Inhelder, B. *The growth of logical thinking from childhood to adolescence.* New York: Basic Books, 1958.

Pierrel, R., and Sherman, J. G. Train your pet the Barnabus way. *Brown Alumni Monthly,* February 1963.

Pines, M. How children learn to talk. *Redbook,* November 1979.

Pleck, J. H. My sex role–and ours. *Win,* April 11, 1974.

Pleck, J. H. The psychology of sex roles: Current data and some implications. Paper presented at Aspen Workshop on Women and Men, August 1975.

Pleck, J. H., and Sawyer, J. (Eds.). *Men and masculinity.* Englewood Cliffs, N.J.: Prentice-Hall, 1974.

Pope, H., and Mueller, C. W. The intergenerational transmission of marital instability: Comparison by race and sex. In G. Levinger and O. C. Moles (Eds.), *Divorce and separation: Context, causes, and consequences.* New York: Basic Books, 1979.

Poskocil, A. Encounters between blacks and white liberals: The collision of stereotypes. *Social Forces,* 1977, *55,* 715–727.

Premack, A. J., and Premack, D. Teaching language to an ape. *Scientific American,* November 1972.

Prescott, S. Why researchers don't study women: The responses of 62 researchers. *Sex Roles,* 1978, *4,* 899–905.

Pressey, S. L. Concerning the nature and nurture of genius. *Scientific Monthly,* September 1955.

Priest, R. F., and Sawyer, J. Proximity and peership: Bases of balance in interpersonal attraction. *American Journal of Sociology,* 1967, *72,* 633–649.

Ramsey, R., and Toye, K. *The goodbye book.* New York: Van Nostrand Reinhold, 1979.

Raudsepp, E. More creative gamesmanship. *Psychology Today,* July 1980.

Read, K. H. *The nursery school.* (6th ed.) Philadelphia: Saunders, 1976.

Reich, J. Factors influencing patient satisfaction with the results of esthetic plastic surgery. *Plastic and Reconstructive Surgery,* 1975, *55,* 5–13.

Reinhold, R. Tranquilizer prescriptions drop sharply; so does reported incidence of abuse. *New York Times,* September 9, 1980.

Remmers, H. H., and Radler, D. H. Teenage attitudes. *Scientific American,* June 1958.

Restak, R. *The brain: The last frontier.* New York: Doubleday, 1979.

Reston, J. Proxmire on love. *New York Times,* March 14, 1975.

Rheingold, H. L.; Gerwitz, J. L.; and Ross, H. W. Social conditioning of vocalizations in the infant. *Journal of Comparative and Physiological Psychology,* 1959, *52,* 68–73.

Rhine, J. B. *Extra-sensory perception.* Boston: Boston Society for Psychic Research, 1934.

Rice, B. Mental stress in the economic crunch: The worry epidemic. *Psychology Today,* August 1975.

Rice, B. Going for the gifted gold. *Psychology Today,* February 1980.

Riley, M. W.: Foner, A.; and Associates. *Aging and society,* vol. 1: An inventory of research findings. New York: Russell Sage Foundation, 1968.

Riley, V. Neuroendocrine influences on immunity and neoplasia. *Science,* 1981, *211,* 1100–1109.

Riley, V. Mouse mammary tumors: Alteration of incidence as apparent function of stress. *Science,* 1975, *189,* 465–467.

Ring, K. *Life at death: A scientific investigation of the near death experience.* New York: Coward, McCann, & Geoghegan, 1980.

Ritzer, G. *Working: Conflict and change.* (2nd ed.) Englewood Cliffs, N.J.: Prentice-Hall, 1977.

Robertson, J. F. Grandmotherhood: A study of role conceptions. *Journal of Marraige and the Family,* 1977, *39,* 165–174.

Robins, L. N. *Deviant children grow up.* Baltimore: Williams & Wilkins, 1966.

Rock, I., and Kaufman, L. The moon illusion. *Science,* 1962, *136,* 1023–1031.

Rogers, C. R. *Client-centered therapy.* Boston: Houghton Mifflin, 1951.

Rogers, C. *On becoming a person.* Boston: Houghton Mifflin, 1961.

Rogers, C. *On encounter groups.* New York: Harper & Row, 1970.

Rohrbaugh, J. B. *Women: Psychology's puzzle.* New York: Basic Books, 1979.

Rorschach, H. *Psychodiagnostics: A diagnostic test based on perception.* New York: Grune & Stratton, 1942.

Rosch, E. H. On the internal structure of perceptual and semantic categories. In T. E. Moore (Ed.), *Cognitive development and the acquisition of language.* New York: Academic Press, 1973.

Rosch, E. H.; Simpson, C.; and Miller, R. S. Structural bases of typicality effects. *Journal of Experimental Psychology: Human Perception and Performance,* 1976, *2,* 491–502.

Rosen, R. D. *Psychobabble.* New York: Atheneum, 1975.

Rosenblatt, P. Communication in the practice of love magic. *Social Forces,* 1971, *49,* 482–487.

Rosenhan, D. L. On being sane in insane places. *Science,* 1973, *179,* 250–258.

Rosenthal, A. M. *Thirty-eight witnesses.* New York: McGraw-Hill, 1964.

Rosenthal, R. *Experimenter effects in behavioral research.* New York: Appleton-Century-Crofts, 1966.

Rosenthal, R., et al. *Sensitivity to nonverbal communication: The PONS test.* Baltimore: Johns Hopkins University Press, 1979.

Rosenzweig, M. R.; Bennett, E. L.; and Diamond, M. C. Brain changes in response to experience. *Scientific American,* February 1972.

Ross, G., et al. Separation protest in infants in home and laboratory. *Developmental Psychology,* 1975, *11,* 256–257.

Ross, L. The intuitive psychologist and his shortcomings: Distortions in the attribution process. In L. Berkowitz (Ed.), *Advances in experimental social psychology,* vol. 10. New York: Academic Press, 1977.

Roth, S., and Kubal, L. Effects of noncontingent reinforcement on tasks of differing importance: Facilitation and learned helplessness. *Journal of Personality and Social Psychology,* 1975, *32,* 680–691.

Rotter, J. B. Generalized expectancies for internal and external control of reinforcements. *Psychological Monographs,* 1966, vol. 80, no. 1, whole no. 609.

Routtenberg, A. The reward system of the brain. *Scientific American,* November 1978.

Rubenstein, C., and Shaver, P. The experience of loneliness. In L. A. Peplau and D. Perlman (Eds.), *Loneliness: A sourcebook of current theory, research, and therapy.* New York: Wiley-Interscience, 1982.

Rubin, Z. Measurement of romantic love. *Journal of Personality and Social Psychology,* 1970, *16,* 265–273.

Rubin, Z. The birth order of birth-order researchers. *Developmental Psychology,* 1970, *3,* 269–270.

Rubin, Z. *Liking and loving: An invitation to social psychology.* New York: Holt, Rinehart and Winston, 1973.

Rubin, Z. Seasonal rhythms in behavior. *Psychology Today,* December 1979. (a)

Rubin, Z. Seeking a cure for loneliness. *Psychology Today,* October 1979. (b)

Rubin, Z. *Children's friendships.* Cambridge, Mass.: Harvard University Press, 1980.

Ruble, D. N., and Brooks-Gunn, J. Menstrual symptoms: A social cognition analysis. *Journal of Behavioral Medicine,* 1979, *2,* 171–194.

Runyan, W. M. *Life histories and psychobiography: Explorations in theory and method.* New York: Oxford University Press, in press.

Runyan, W. M. Why did van Gogh cut off his ear? The problem of alternative explanations in psychobiography. *Journal of Personality and Social Psychology,* 1981, *40,* 1070–1077.

Saarni, C. Children's understanding of display rules for expressive behavior. *Developmental Psychology,* 1979, *15,* 424–429.

Sachs, B. D., and Marsan, R. Male rats prefer sex to food after 6 days of food deprivation. *Psychonomic Science*, 1972, *28*, 47–49.

Sagi, A., and Hoffman, M. L. Empathic distress in newborns. *Developmental Psychology*, 1976, *12*, 175–176.

Saltzberg, L., and Elkins, G. R. An examination of common concerns about rational-emotive therapy. *Professional Psychology*, 1980, *11*, 324–330.

Samelson, F. J. B. Watson's Little Albert, Cyril Burt's twins, and the need for a critical science. *American Psychologist*, 1980, *35*, 619–625.

Sanford, F. H. *Psychology.* (2nd ed.) Belmont, Calif.: Wadsworth, 1965.

Sarason, S. B. *Work, aging, and social change.* New York: Free Press, 1977.

Sarnoff, C. A. *Medical aspects of flying motivation.* Randolph Air Force Base, Texas: Air University School of Aviation Motivation, 1957.

Scarf, M. The anatomy of fear. *New York Times Magazine*, June 12, 1974.

Scarf, M. Shocking the depressed back to life. *New York Times Magazine*, June 17, 1979.

Scarr, S., and Weinberg, R. A. IQ test performance of black children adopted by white families. *American Psychologist*, 1976, *31*, 726–739.

Schachter, S. *The psychology of affiliation.* Stanford, Calif.: Stanford University Press, 1959.

Schachter, S. Birth order, eminence, and higher education. *American Sociological Review*, 1963, *28*, 757–767.

Schachter, S. The interaction of cognitive and physiological determinants of emotional state. In L. Berkowitz (Ed.), *Advances in experimental social psychology*, vol. 1. New York: Academic Press, 1964.

Schachter, S. Some extraordinary facts about obese humans and rats. *American Psychologist*, 1971, *26*, 129–144.

Schachter, S., and Singer, J. E. Cognitive, social, and physiological determinants of emotional state. *Psychological Review*, 1962, *69*, 379–399.

Scheff, T. J. (Ed.) *Labeling madness.* Englewood Cliffs, N.J.: Prentice-Hall, 1975.

Schleifer, S. J.; Keller, S. E.; McKegney, F. P.; et al. Bereavement and lymphocyte function. Paper presented at annual meeting of the American Psychiatric Association, San Francisco, May 1980.

Schmeck, H. M. Depression is called more common in women. *New York Times*, October 24, 1975.

Schmeck, H. M. Research on marijuana finds many risks, some benefits. *New York Times*, October 9, 1979.

Schmeck, H. M. Brains may differ in women and men. *New York Times*, March 25, 1980. (a)

Schmeck, H. M. "Two brains" of man: Complex teamwork. *New York Times*, January 8, 1980. (b)

Schmeidler, G. R., and McConnell, R. A. *ESP and personality patterns.* New Haven, Conn.: Yale University Press, 1958.

Schneider, D. J.; Hastorf, A. H.; and Ellsworth, P. C. *Person perception.* (2nd ed.) Reading, Mass.: Addison-Wesley, 1979.

Schultz, D. P. The human subject in psychological research. *Psychological Bulletin*, 1969, *72*, 214–228.

Schultz, R. *The psychology of death, dying and bereavement.* Reading Mass.: Addison-Wesley, 1978.

Schultz, R., and Aderman, D. Clinical research and the stages of dying. *Omega*, 1974, *5*, 137–143.

Schwartz, G. E. Biofeedback, self-regulation, and the patterning of physiological processes. *American Scientist*, 1975, *63*, 314–324.

Schwartz, A., and Reifler, C. *Journal of the American College Health Association*, 1980, *28* (4).

Scott, J. P. A time to learn. *Psychology Today*, March 1969.

Scovern, A. W., and Kilmann, P. R. Status of electroconvulsive therapy: Review of the outcome literature. *Psychological Bulletin*, 1980, *87*, 260–303.

Seeman, M. Alienation, membership and political knowledge: A comparative study. *Public Opinion Quarterly*, 1966, *30*, 359–367.

Seeman, M., and Evans, J. W. Alienation and learning in a hospital setting. *American Sociological Review*, 1962, *27*, 772–783.

Segal, M. W. Alphabet and attraction: An unobtrusive measure of the effect of propinquity in a field setting. *Journal of Personality and Social Psychology*, 1974, *30*, 654–657.

Seiden, R. H. Campus tragedy: A study of student suicide. *Journal of Abnormal Psychology*, 1966, *71*, 389–399.

Seiden, R. H. We're driving young blacks to suicide. *Psychology Today*, August 1970.

Seligman, C., and Darley, J. M. Feedback as a means of decreasing residential energy consumption. *Journal of Applied Psychology*, 1977, *62*, 363–368.

Seligman, M. E. P. *Helplessness: On depression, development, and death.* San Francisco: Freeman, 1975.

Selye, H. *The stress of life.* New York: McGraw-Hill, 1956.

Serbin, L., and O'Leary, K. D. How nursery schools teach girls to shut up. *Psychology Today*, December 1975.

Serbin, L. A.; Tonick, I. J.; and Sternglanz, S. H. Shaping cooperative cross-sex play. *Child Development*, 1977, *48*, 924–929.

Shanas, E. Social myth as hypothesis: The case of family relations of old people. *The Gerontologist*, 1979, *19*, 3–9.

Shatz, M., and Gelman, R. The development of communication skills: Modifications in the speech of young children as a function of listener. *Monographs of the Society for Research in Child Development*, 1973, *38* (5).

Shaver, P., and Freedman, J. Your pursuit of happiness. *Psychology Today*, August 1976.

Sheatsley, P. B., and Feldman, J. J. The assassination of President Kennedy: A preliminary report on public attitudes and behavior. *Public Opinion Quarterly*, 1964, *28*, 189–215.

Shekelle, R. B.; Raynor, W. J.; Ostfeld, A. M.; et al. Psychological depression and 17-year risk of death from cancer. *Psychosomatic Medicine*, 1981, *43*, 117–125.

Sheils, D. A cross-cultural study of beliefs in out-of-the-body experiences, waking and sleeping. *Journal of the Society for Psychical Research*, 1978, *49*, 697–741.

Sheldon, W. H. *Varieties of human physique.* New York: Harper & Row, 1940.

Sheldon, W. H. *Atlas of man: A guide for somatotyping the adult male of all ages.* New York: Harper & Row, 1954.

Shepard, R. W., and Metzler, J. Mental rotation of three-dimensional objects. *Science*, 1971, *171*, 701–703.

Shevitz, S. A. Psychosurgery: Some current observations. *American Journal of Psychiatry*, 1976, *133*, 266–270.

Shirley, M. M. *The first two years: A study of twenty-five babies.* Minneapolis: University of Minnesota Press, 1933.

Shock, N. W. The physiology of aging. *Scientific American*, January 1962.

Seigel, A. W.; Kirasic, K. C.; and Kail, R. W. Stalking the elusive cognitive map. In I. Altman and J. F. Wohlwill (eds.), *Children and the environment.* New York: Plenum, 1978.

Siegel, R. K., and Jarvik, M. E. Drug-induced hallucinations in animals and man. In R. K.

Siegel and L. J. West (Eds.), *Hallucinations: Behavior, experience, and theory.* New York: Wiley, 1975.

Sieveking, N. A., and Chappell, J. E. Reactions to the names "Counseling Center" and "Psychological Center." *Journal of Consulting and Clinical Psychology*, 1970, *34*, 124–127.

Siipola, E. M. A study of some effects of preparatory set. *Psychological Monographs*, 1935, *46*, 210.

Simernitskaya, E. G. On two forms of writing defect following focal brain lesions. In S. J. Dimond and J. G. Beaumont (Eds.), *Hemisphere function in the human brain.* New York: Halstead, 1974.

Simmons, R. G., et al. Entry into early adolescence: The impact of school structure, puberty, and early dating on self-esteem. *American Sociological Review*, 1979, *44*, 948–967.

Simonton, D. K. Creative productivity, age and stress: A biographical timeseries analysis of ten classical composers. *Journal of Personality and Social Psychology*, 1977, *35*, 791–804.

Singer, J. L. Daydreaming and the stream of thought. *American Scientist*, July–August 1974.

Singer, J. L. Navigating the stream of consciousness: Research in daydreaming and related inner experience. *American Psychologist*, 1975, *30*, 727–738.

Singer, J. L. Fantasy: The foundation of serenity. *Psychology Today*, July 1976.

Singer, J. L., and Antrobus, J. Eye movements during fantasies. *A.M.A. Archives of General Psychiatry*, 1965, *12*, 71–76.

Sipes, R. G. War, sports, and aggression: An empirical test of two rival theories. *American Anthropologist*, 1973, *75*, 64–86.

Skeels, H. M. Adult status of children with contrasting early life experiences: A follow-up study. *Monographs of the Society for Research in Child Development*, 1966, *31* (3).

Skinner, B. F. *Walden two.* New York: Macmillan, 1948.

Skinner, B. F. *Verbal behavior.* New York: Appleton-Century-Crofts, 1957.

Skinner, B. F. *Beyond freedom and dignity.* New York: Knopf, 1971.

Skipper, J. K., Jr., and McCaghy, C. H. Strip-teasers: The anatomy and career contingencies of a deviant occupation. *Social Problems*, 1970, *17*, 391–405.

Sklar, L. S., and Anisman, H. Stress and coping factors influence tumor growth. *Science*, 1979, *205*, 513–515.

Sloane, R. B., et al. *Psychotherapy versus behavior therapy.* Cambridge, Mass.: Harvard University Press, 1975.

Smart, R. G., and Fejer, D. Drug use among adolescents and their parents: Closing the generation gap in mood modification. *Journal of Abnormal Psychology*, 1972, *79*, 153–160.

Smith, J. C. Meditation as psychotherapy: A review of the literature. *Psychological Bulletin*, 1975, *82*, 558–564.

Smith, T. W. Happiness: Time trends, seasonal variations, inter-survey differences, and other mysteries. *Social Psychology Quarterly*, 1979, *47*, 18–30.

Snow, C. E. Mothers' speech to children learning language. *Child Development*, 1972, *43*, 549–564.

Snyder, S. H. The true speed trip: Schizophrenia. *Psychology Today*, January 1972.

Snyder, S. H. (Interviewed by D. Goleman.) Mind over matter: The big issues raised by newly discovered brain chemicals. *Psychology Today*, June 1980.

Snyder, M.; Tanke, E. D.; and Berscheid, E. Social perception and interpersonal behavior: On the self-fulfilling nature of social stereotypes. *Journal of Personality and Social Psychology*, 1977, *35*, 656–666.

Sobel, D. For stage fright, a remedy proposed. *New York Times*, November 20, 1979.

Sobel, D. Psychiatric drugs widely misused, critics charge. *New York Times*, June 3, 1980.

Solomon, M. *Beethoven*. New York: Schirmer, 1977.

Spearman, C. "General intelligence," objectively determined and measured. *American Journal of Psychology*, 1904, *15*, 201–293.

Speer, D. C. An evaluation of a telephone crisis service. Paper presented at meeting of the Midwestern Psychological Association, Cleveland, 1972.

Spence, J. T. Achievement and achievement motives. Paper presented at meeting of the American Psychological Association, New York, 1979.

Sperling, H. The information available in brief visual presentations. *Psychological Monographs*, 1960, vol. 74, whole no. 498.

Spitzer, R. L.; Forman, J. B. W.; and Nee, J. DSM-III field trials: I. Initial interrater diagnostic reliability. *American Journal of Psychiatry*, 1979, *136*, 815–817.

Spitzer, R. L.; Williams, J. B. W.; and Skodol, A. E. *DSM-III:* The major achievements and an overview. *American Journal of Psychiatry*, 1980, *137*, 151–164.

Stroufe, L. A. Wariness of strangers and the study of infant development. *Child Development*, 1977, *48*, 731–746.

Stannard, D. E. *Shrinking history: On Freud and the failure of psychohistory.* New York: Oxford University Press, 1980.

Starker, S. Daydreaming styles and nocturnal dreaming *Journal of Abnormal Psychology*, 1974, *83*, 52–55.

Staub, E. *The development of prosocial behavior in children.* Morristown, N.J.: General Learning Press, 1975.

Steinem, G. The way we were—and will be. *Ms.*, December 1979.

Stephan, W. G. School desegregation: An evaluation of predictions made in *Brown* v. *Board of Education*. *Psychological Bulletin*, 1978, *85*, 217–238.

Sterman, M. B. Biofeedback and epilepsy. *Human Nature*, May 1978.

Sternberg, R. J. The nature of mental abilities. *American Psychologist*, 1979, *34*, 214–230.

Stevens, C. F. The neuron. *Scientific American*, September 1979.

Stevens-Long, J. *Adult life: Developmental processes.* Palo Alto, Calif.: Mayfield, 1979.

Stocking, S. H., and Arezzo, D. *Helping friendless children: A guide for teachers and parents.* Boys Town, Neb.: The Boys Town Center for the Study of Youth Development, 1979.

Stone, L. *The past and the present.* Boston: Routledge & Kegan Paul, 1981.

Strupp, H. H., and Hadley, S. W. Specific vs. nonspecific factors in psychotherapy: A controlled study of outcome. *Archives of General Psychiatry*, 1979, *36*, 1125–1136.

Sudnow, D. Dead on arrival. *Transaction*, November 1967.

Suedfeld, P. The benefits of boredom: Sensory deprivation reconsidered. *American Scientist*, January–February 1975.

Suedfeld, P. Aloneness as a healing experience. In L. A. Peplau and D. Perlman (Eds.), *Loneliness: A Sourcebook of current theory, research, and therapy.* New York: Wiley-Interscience, 1982.

Sulin, R. A., and Dooling, D. J. Intrusion of a thematic idea in retention of prose. *Journal of Experimental Psychology*, 1974, *103*, 255–262.

Sullivan, H. S. *The interpersonal theory of psychiatry.* New York: Norton, 1953.

Sullivan, K., and Sullivan, A. Adolescent-parent separation. *Developmental Psychology*, 1980, *16*, 93–99.

Super, D. E. Vocational development theory: Persons, positions, and processes. *The Counseling Psychologist*, 1969, *1*, 2–8.

Sweet, E. A '70s chronology. *Ms.*, December 1979.

Szasz, T. S. *Ideology and insanity.* Garden City, N.Y.: Anchor, 1970.

Tanner, J. M. Sequence, tempo, and individual variation in growth and development of boys and girls aged twelve to sixteen. In J. Kagan and R. Coles (Eds.), *Twelve to sixteen: Early adolescence.* New York: Norton, 1972.

Tavris, C. Good news about sex. *New York*, December 6, 1976.

Tavris, C., and Offir, C. *The longest war: Sex differences in perspective.* New York: Harcourt Brace Jovanovich, 1977.

Taylor, D. G.; Sheatsley, P. B.; and Greeley, A. M. Attitudes toward racial integration. *Scientific American*, June 1978.

Teitelbaum, P. Sensory control of hypothalamic hyperphagia. *Journal of Comparative and Physiological Psychology*, 1955, *48*, 156–163.

Teitelbaum, P. Motivation and control of food intake. In C. F. Code (Ed.), *Handbook of physiology: Alimentary canal*, vol. 1. Washington, D.C.: American Physiological Society, 1967.

Terman, L. M. The discovery and encouragement of exceptional talent. *American Psychologist*, 1954, *9*, 221–230.

Terman, L. M., and Merrill, M. A. *Measuring intelligence: A guide to the administration of the new revised Stanford-Binet tests for intelligence.* Boston: Houghton Mifflin, 1937.

Terrace, H. *Nim.* New York: Knopf, 1979.

Thomas, A.; Chess, S.; and Birch, H. G. The origin of personality. *Scientific American*, August 1970.

Thompson, V. D. Family size: Implicit policies and assumed psychological outcomes. *Journal of Social Issues*, 1974, *30* (4), 93–124.

Thurstone, L. L. Primary mental abilities. *Psychometric Monographs*, no. 1. Chicago: University of Chicago Press, 1938.

Time. How gay is gay? April 23, 1979.

Time. Dial Dr. Toni for therapy. May 26, 1980.

Timiras, P. Biological perspectives on aging. *American Scientist*, September–October 1978.

Timson, J. Is coffee safe to drink? *Human Nature*, December 1978.

Totenberg, N. Obiter dicta from the Watergate press table. *New York*, January 20, 1975.

Trefil, J. S. A consumer's guide to pseudoscience. *Saturday Review*, April 29, 1978.

Treisman, A. M. Verbal cues, language and meaning in selective attention. *American Journal of Psychology*, 1964, *77*, 206–219.

Truax, C. B., and Mitchell, K. M. Research on certain therapist interpersonal skills in relation to process and outcome. In A. E. Bergin and S. L. Garfield (Eds.), *Handbook of psychotherapy and behavior change.* New York: Wiley, 1971.

Tuber, D. S.; Hothersall, D.; and Voith, V. L. Animal clinical psychology: A modest proposal. *American Psychologist*, 1974, *29*, 762–766.

Tucker, J. B. New drugs offer help for severe pain. *New York Times*, October 16, 1979.

Tucker, R. *Stalin as revolutionary, 1879–1929: A study in history and personality.* New York: Norton, 1973.

Tulving, E. Cue-dependent forgetting. *American Scientist*, January–February 1974.

Turnbull, C. M. Some observations regarding the experiences and behavior of the Ba Mbuti pygmies. *American Journal of Psychology*, 1961, *74*, 304–308.

Twentyman, C. T., and Zimring, R. T. Behav-

ioral training of social skills: A critical review. In M. Hersen, R. M. Eisler, and P. M. Miller (Eds.), *Progress in behavior modification*, vol. 7. New York: Academic Press, 1979.

Ullmann, L. P., and Krasner, L. *A psychological approach to abnormal behavior.* (2nd ed.) Englewood Cliffs, N.J.: Prentice-Hall, 1975.

Ungerleider, J. T., and Fisher, D. The problems of LSD-25 and emotional disorder. In R. E. Hormon and A. M. Fox (Eds.), *Drug awareness.* New York: Avon, 1970.

U.S. Department of Commerce. *Statistical Abstracts.* (10th ed.) Washington, D.C.: U.S Government Printing Office, 1979.

U.S. Department of Health, Education, and Welfare. *Monthly vital statistics report, final mortality statistics, 1976.* Washington, D.C.: U.S. Government Printing Office, 1978.

Vaillant, G. *Adaptation to life.* Boston: Little, Brown, 1977.

Valenstein, E. *Brain control.* New York: Wiley, 1973.

Valenstein, E. S. Science-fiction fantasy and the brain. *Psychology Today*, July 1978.

Valins, S. Cognitive effects of false heart-rate feedback. *Journal of Personality and Social Psychology*, 1966, *4*, 400–408.

Veevers, J. E. Voluntarily childless wives: An exploratory study. *Sociology and Social Research*, 1973, *57*, 356–366.

Viscott, D. S. *The making of a psychiatrist.* New York: Arbor House, 1972.

Vonnegut, M. *The Eden express: A personal account of schizophrenia.* New York: Praeger, 1975.

Wagner, M. W., and Monnet, M. Attitudes of college professors toward extra-sensory perception. *Zetetic Scholar*, 1979, *5*, 7–16.

Waite, R. G. L. *The psychopathic god: Adolf Hitler.* New York: Basic Books, 1977.

Walford, R. L. *The immunologic theory of aging.* Copenhagen: Munksgard, 1969.

Wallace, R. K., and Benson, H. The physiology of meditation. *Scientific American*, May 1972.

Wallach, M. A., and Kogan, N. Creativity and intelligence in children's thinking. *Transaction*, January–February 1967.

Wallechinsky, D., and Wallace, I. *The people's almanac.* Garden City, N.Y.: Doubleday, 1975.

Wallerstein, J. S., and Kelly, J. B. *Surviving the break-up: How children and parents cope with divorce.* New York: Basic Books, 1980.

Walster, E.; Aronson, V.; Abrahams, D.; and Rottman, L. Importance of physical attractiveness in dating behavior. *Journal of Personality and Social Psychology*, 1966, *4*, 508–516.

Wang, J. Breaking out of the pain trap. *Psychology Today*, July 1977.

Warren, J. R. Birth order and social behavior. *Psychological Bulletin*, 1966, *65*, 38–49.

The Watergate hearings: New York: Viking, 1973.

Watkins, J. G. Psychotherapeutic methods. In B. B. Wolman (Ed.), *Handbook of clinical psychology.* New York: McGraw-Hill, 1965.

Watson, J. B. Psychology as the behaviorist views it. *Psychological Review*, 1913, *20*, 158–177.

Watson, J. B. *The ways of behaviorism.* New York: Harper & Row, 1928.

Watson, J. B., and Rayner, R. Conditioned emotional reactions. *Journal of Experimental Psychology*, 1920, *3*, 1–14.

Watson, J. D. *The double helix.* New York: Atheneum, 1968.

Webb, E. J., et al. *Unobtrusive measures: Nonreactive research in the social sciences.* Chicago: Rand McNally, 1966.

Webb, W. B., and Friel, J. Sleep stage and dreams. In M. E. Meyer (Ed.), *Foundations of contemporary psychology.* New York: Oxford University Press, 1979.

Webb, W. B., and Friel, J. Sleep stage and personality characteristics of "natural" long and short sleepers. *Science,* 1971, *171,* 587–588.

Webb, W. B., and Kersey, J. Recall of dreams and the probability of stage 1-REM sleep. *Perceptual and Motor Skills,* 1967, *24,* 627–630.

Weideger, P. *Menstruation and menopause: The physiology, the psychology, the myth and the reality.* New York: Knopf, 1976.

Weiss, J. M. Psychological factors in stress and disease. *Scientific American,* June 1972.

Weiss, R. S. *Loneliness: The experience of emotional and social isolation.* Cambridge, Mass.: M.I.T. Press, 1973.

Weiss, R. S. The provisions of social relationships. In Z. Rubin (Ed.), *Doing unto others: Joining, molding, conforming, helping, loving.* Englewood Cliffs, N.J.: Prentice-Hall, 1974.

Weiss, R. S. Growing up a little faster: The experience of growing up in a single-parent household. *Journal of Social Issues,* 1979, *35* (4), 97–111.

Weitzman, L. J., et al. Sex role socialization in picture books for preschool children. *American Journal of Sociology,* 1972, *77,* 1125–1150.

White, R. W. Motivation reconsidered: The concept of competence. *Psychological Review,* 1959, *66,* 297–333.

White, R. W. *The enterprise of living: A view of personal growth.* (2nd ed.) New York: Holt, Rinehart and Winston, 1976.

White, W. A. *Outlines of psychiatry.* (13th ed.) New York: Nervous and Mental Disease Publishing Company, 1932.

Whiting, B., and Edwards, C. P. A cross-cultural analysis of sex differences in the behavior of children aged three through 11. *Journal of Social Psychology,* 1973, *91,* 171–188.

Whiting, J. W. M. *Becoming a Kwoma.* New Haven, Conn.: Yale University Press, 1941.

Whorf, B. L. *Language, thought, and reality.* New York: MIT Press-Wiley, 1956.

Whybrow, P. C. Where there's mud, there's momentum. *Yankee Magazine,* April 1979.

Wickler, W. *The sexual code.* Garden City, N.Y.: Anchor, 1973.

Williams, R. M. From bedlam to chaos: Are they closing the mental hospitals too soon? *Psychology Today,* May 1977.

Winograd, T. Artificial intelligence: When will computers understand people? *Psychology Today,* May 1974.

Winter, D. G. *The power motive.* New York: Free Press, 1973.

Winterbottom, M. R. The relation of childhood training in independence to achievement motivation. Doctoral dissertation, University of Michigan, 1953.

Wolcott, J. H., et al. Correlation of general aviation accidents with the biorhythm theory. *Human Factors,* 1977, *19,* 283–293.

Wolfe, J. B. Effectiveness of token rewards for chimpanzees. *Comparative Psychological Monographs,* 1936, *12,* 50.

Wolpe, J. *Psychotherapy by reciprocal inhibition.* Stanford, Calif.: Stanford University Press, 1958.

Wolpe, J., and Rachman, S. Psychoanalytic "evidence": A critique based on Freud's case of Little Hans. *Journal of Nervous and Mental Disease,* 1960, *131,* 135–147.

Wood, P. S. Sex differences in sports. *New York Times Magazine,* May 18, 1980.

Worchel, S., and Arnold, S. E. The effects of censorship and attractiveness of the censor in attitude change. *Journal of Experimental Social Psychology,* 1973, *9,* 365–377.

Word, C. O.; Zanna, M. P.; and Cooper, J. The nonverbal mediation of self-fulfilling prophecies in interracial interaction. *Journal of Experimental Social Psychology,* 1974, *10,* 109–120.

Wortman, C. B., and Brehm, J. W. Responses to uncontrollable outcomes: An integration of reactance theory and the learned helplessness model. In L. Berkowitz (Ed.), *Advances in experimental social psychology,* vol. 8. New York: Academic Press, 1975.

Wurtman, R. Brain muffins. *Psychology Today,* October 1978.

Yates, A. J. *Behavior therapy.* New York: Wiley, 1970.

Young, W. C.; Goy, R. W.; and Phoenix, C. H. Hormones and sexual behavior. *Science,* 1964, *143,* 212–218.

Zajonc, R. B. *Animal social behavior.* Morristown, N.J.: General Learning Press, 1972.

Zajonc, R. B. Family configurations and intelligence. *Science,* 1976, *192,* 227–236.

Zeigarnik, B. Über das Behalten von erledigten und unerledigten Handlungen. *Psychologische Forschung,* 1927, *9,* 1–85.

Zelazo, P. R.; Zelazo, N. A.; and Kolb, S. "Walking" in the newborn. *Science,* 1972, *176,* 314–315.

Zelnik, M., and Kantner, J. F. Sexual and contraceptive experience of young unmarried women in the United States, 1976 and 1971. *Family Planning Perspectives,* 1977, *9,* 55–71.

Zigler, E., and Phillips, L. Psychiatric diagnosis and symptomatology. *Journal of Abnormal and Social Psychology,* 1961, *63,* 69–75.

Zimbardo, P. G., and Meadow, W. Sexism springs eternal—in the *Reader's Digest. Women's Studies Abstracts,* 1976, *5,* 61.

Zimbardo, P. G., et al. The psychology of imprisonment: Privation, power, and pathology. In Z. Rubin (Ed.), *Doing unto others: Joining, molding, conforming, helping, loving.* Englewood Cliffs, N.J.: Prentice-Hall, 1974.

Zinberg, N. The war over marijuana. *Psychology Today,* December 1976.

Zung, W. W., and Wilson, W. P. Time estimation during sleep. *Biological Psychiatry,* 1971, *3,* 159–164.

Zweigenhaft, R. L. Birth order, approval-seeking, and membership in Congress. *Journal of Individual Psychology,* 1975, *31,* 205–210.

Zweigenhaft, R. L. The empirical study of signature size. *Social Behavior and Personality,* 1977, *5,* 177–185.

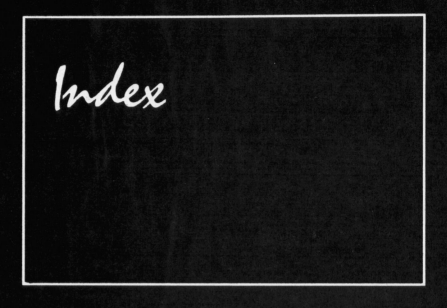

Index

519

Skinner box, 144–145, 148, 151
Skin senses, 116–120
Skydiving, 229
Sleep, 73–85, 157
Sleep apnea, 81
Sleep disorders, 80–81
Sleepwalking, 81
Smell, sense of, 121–122
Social-class differences in intelligence, 193–194
Social comparison, need for, 460–462
Social development
    in adulthood, 327–330, 341–345
    in childhood, 301–303
    in infancy, 293–295
Social Interpretation Task (SIT), 470
Social isolation, 463
Social learning theory, 16, 268–270
Social motives, 212–213
Social norms, 466–467, 487
Social psychology, 29
Social reinforcement, 16
Social relationships, 460–483
Social roles, 282–283
Social support, 236, 424
Sociocultural retardation, 195, 196
Sociopath, 374
Somatic nervous system, 40
Somatic therapies, 404–411
Somatoform disorders, 370
Somatotype, 261
Sound waves, 114
Space, infant's conception of, 292
Spacing of study periods, 164
Specificity theory of pain, 120
Spectrum of color, 111–112
Spinal cord, 39, 40, 41, 118–119
Split–brain patient, 58
Spontaneous recovery, 143
Stability vs. change in adulthood, 321
Stage fright, 222
Stanford-Binet IQ test, 187, 189
Stanford Hypnotic Susceptibility Scale, 93–94
Stapes, 115
Statistical approach to defining abnormality, 361
Stelazine, 407
Stereotypes, 184
    elderly and, 338
    physical appearance and, 467, 491
    racial and national, 485–486
    sex differences and, 430–431

Stimulus, 140–141, 146
Stimulus control, 146, 171
Stranger anxiety, 293
Stress, 232–238, 384
Stroke, 55, 57
Structuralists, 7
Study strategies, 164–165
Subjects of research, 17–19
Substance use disorders, 370
Success, fear of, 246–247
Successive approximation, 145
Suicide, 388–391
Sullivan, Harry Stack, 260, 302, 463
Superego, 252, 256
Surrogate mothers, 293–294
Surveys, 19–20
Survival motives, 212–217
Symbolism, in dreams, 82
Sympathetic system, 40–42, 222
Synapse, 43, 408
Synaptic transmission, 43
Synesthesia, 115
Systematic desensitization, 400

Tardive dyskinesia, 407
Taste, sense of, 122
Teaching psychology, 30
Telepathy, 135
Telephone therapy, 397
Television
    sex-role learning and, 440–441
    violence on, 280–281
Temporal lobes, 52, 53
Testosterone, 216
Thematic Apperception Test (TAT), 265
Theories, 16
Therapy, 392–421
Thirst, 215–216
Thorazine, 407
Thought, 180–186
Thought disorders, 382
Timbre, 115
Time, infant's concept of, 292–293
Tip-of-the-tongue (TOT) phenomenon, 160–161
Token economy, 168, 401
Touch, sense of, 116–117
Trait theories, 263–265
Tranquilizers, 92, 405–408
Transcendental meditation, 100–101, 420
Transference, 395
Transitional object, 293

Transmitter substance, 43, 55, 61, 85, 87, 88, 406
Transpersonal therapies, 420
Transsexuals, 440, 442–443
Trial and error, 184
Tricyclics, 406
Trifluoperazine, 407
Tympanic membrane, 114–115
Type theories, 260–262

Ulcers, 233–235
Ultradian rhythms, 67
Unconditional positive regard, 272, 397
Unconditioned response, 140
Unconditioned stimulus, 140
Unconscious, 72
Unconscious motives, 221–222
Undifferentiated schizophrenia, 381
Unobtrusive measures, 20

Validity of diagnoses, 368
Valium, 405, 406
Van Gogh, Vincent, 356–357, 377
Variables, 22–24
Variable schedule of reinforcement, 150–151
Veterans of Vietnam War, 422–425
Vietnam War, and veterans, 422–425
Violence, 278–283
Vision, 109–114, 206–207
Visual acuity, 111, 331–333
Visual cliff, 113–114
Visual imagery, 204–207
Visual threshold, 111

Watson, John B., 7, 204–205, 230–231
Wechsler Adult Intelligence Scale (WAIS), 189, 191
Wechsler Intelligence Scale for Children (WISC), 189
Wernicke's area, 53–54
White, Dan, 364
Widowhood, 343
Wish-fulfillment, in dreams, 84–85
Women's movement, 455–457
Work, 242–247, 325–327
Work orientation, 246
Work overload, 236
Wundt, Wilhelm, 6–7, 204

Yellow-blue color blindness, 112

Zeigarnik effect, 162